INSIDERS' GUIDE® TO CAPE COD AND THE ISLANDS

HELP US KEEP THIS GUIDE UP TO DATE

Every effort has been made by the author and editors to make this guide as accurate and useful as possible. However, many things can change after a guide is published—phone numbers change, facilities come under new management, etc.

We would love to hear from you concerning your experiences with this guide and how you feel it could be improved and be kept up to date. While we may not be able to respond to all comments and suggestions, we'll take them to heart and we'll also make certain to share them with the author. Please send your comments and suggestions to the following address:

> The Globe Pequot Press
> Reader Response/Editorial Department
> P.O. Box 480
> Guilford, CT 06437

Or you may e-mail us at:

> editorial@GlobePequot.com

Thanks for your input, and happy travels!

INSIDERS'GUIDE®

INSIDERS' GUIDE® SERIES

INSIDERS' GUIDE® TO
CAPE COD
AND THE ISLANDS

SIXTH EDITION

ERICA BOLLERUD

INSIDERS'GUIDE®

GUILFORD, CONNECTICUT
AN IMPRINT OF THE GLOBE PEQUOT PRESS

Publications from the Insiders' Guide® series are available at special discounts for bulk purchases for sales promotions, premiums, or fund-raisings. Special editions, including personalized covers, can be created in large quantities for special needs. For more information, please contact The Globe Pequot Press at (800) 962-0973.

INSIDERS'GUIDE®

Copyright © 2004 by The Globe Pequot Press
Previous editions of this book were published by Falcon Publishing, Inc. in 1999 and 2000.

Text design by LeAnna Weller Smith
Maps created by XNR Productions Inc. © The Globe Pequot Press

ISSN: 1532-6462
ISBN: 0-7627-2999-6

Manufactured in the United States of America
Sixth Edition/First Printing

CONTENTS

CONTENTS

Directory of Maps

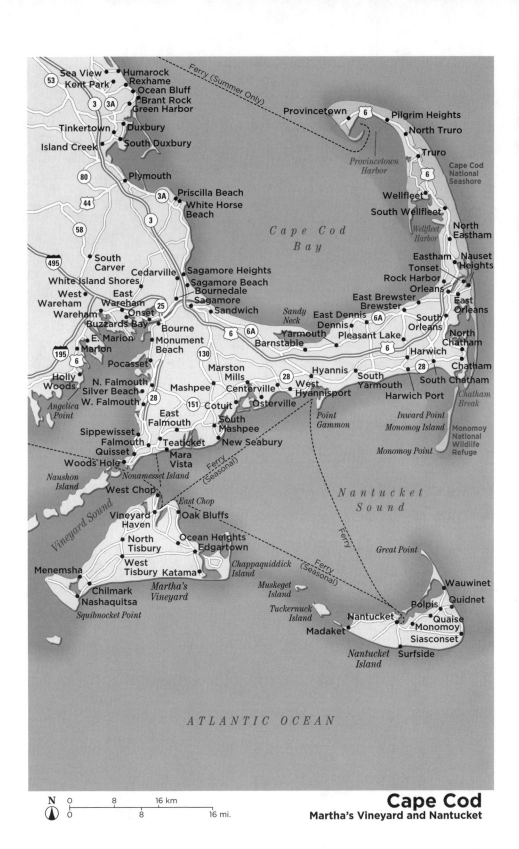

Cape Cod
Martha's Vineyard and Nantucket

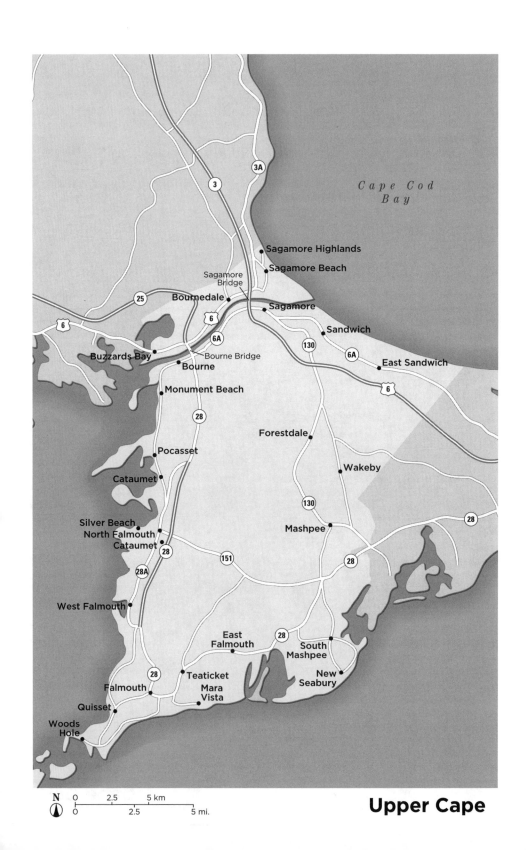

Upper Cape

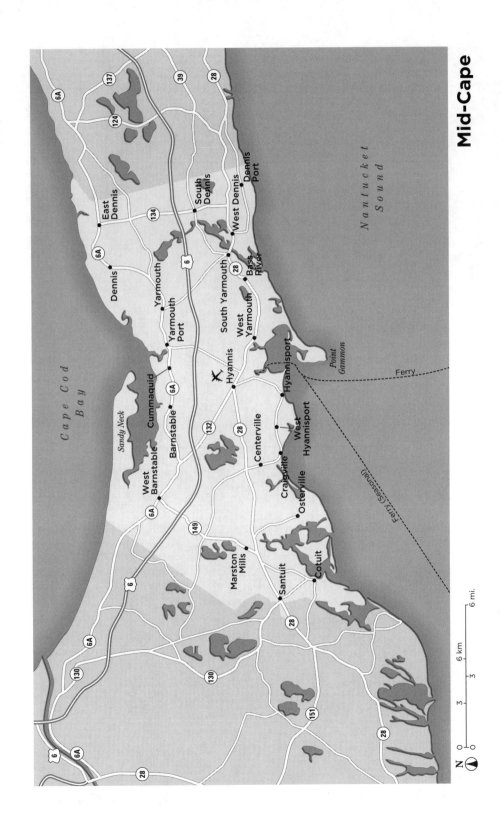

Mid-Cape

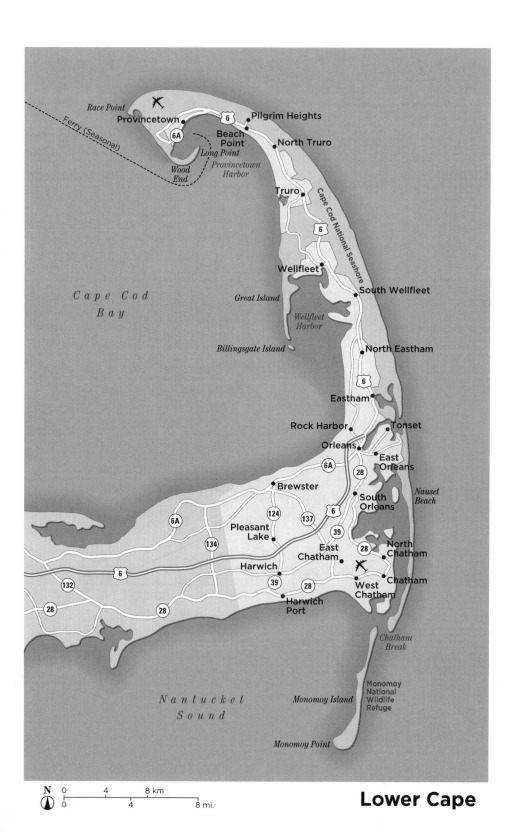

Race Point

Ferry (Seasonal)

Provincetown
6A
Beach Point
Long Point
Wood End
Provincetown Harbor

6
Pilgrim Heights

North Truro

Truro

6

Cape Cod National Seashore

Cape Cod Bay

Great Island

Wellfleet

Wellfleet Harbor

South Wellfleet

Billingsgate Island

North Eastham

6

Eastham

Rock Harbor

Tonset

Orleans

6A
28
East Orleans

Brewster

Nauset Beach

South Orleans

124
137
6

Pleasant Lake
39

134
East Chatham
28
North Chatham

Harwich
Chatham

39
28
West Chatham

132
Harwich Port

28
28

Chatham Break

Nantucket Sound

Monomoy Island

Monomoy National Wildlife Refuge

Monomoy Point

N

0   4   8 km
0   4   8 mi.

Lower Cape

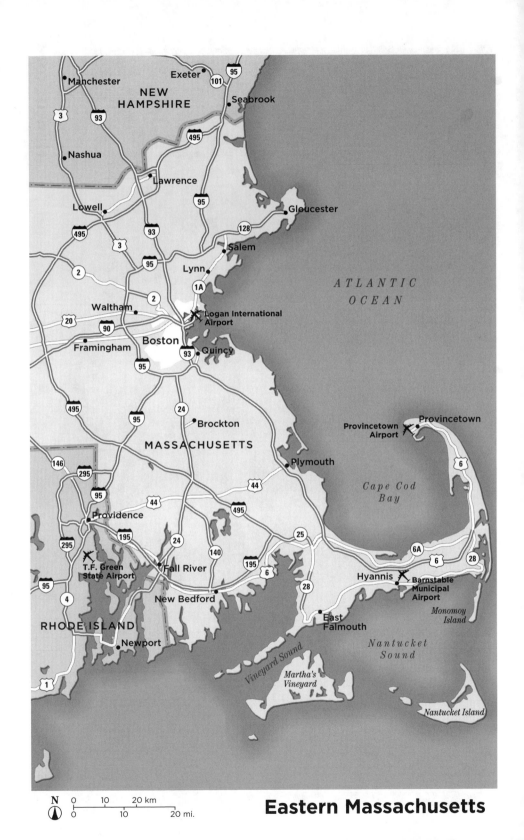

Eastern Massachusetts

Nantucket

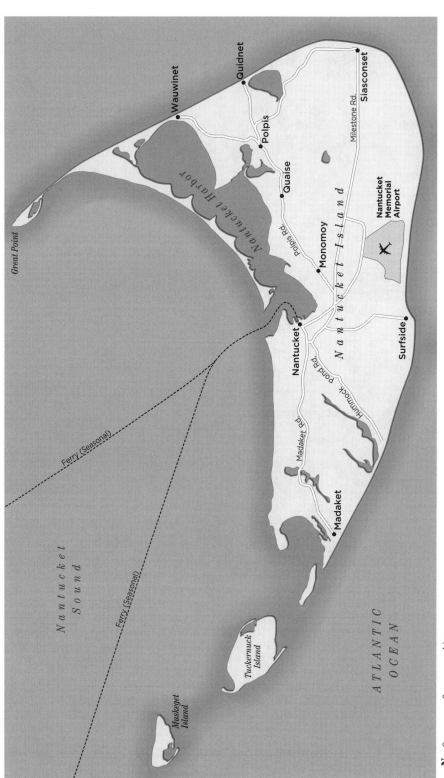

Nantucket Sound

Great Point

Ferry (Seasonal)

Ferry (Seasonal)

Nantucket Harbor

Wauwinet

Quidnet

Polpis

Quaise

Polpis Rd.

Monomoy

Nantucket

N a n t u c k e t   I s l a n d

Nantucket
Memorial
Airport

Milestone Rd.

Siasconset

Surfside

Hummock Pond Rd.

Madaket Rd.

Madaket

Muskeget
Island

Tuckernuck
Island

*A T L A N T I C
O C E A N*

N

0   2   4 km
0   2   4 mi.

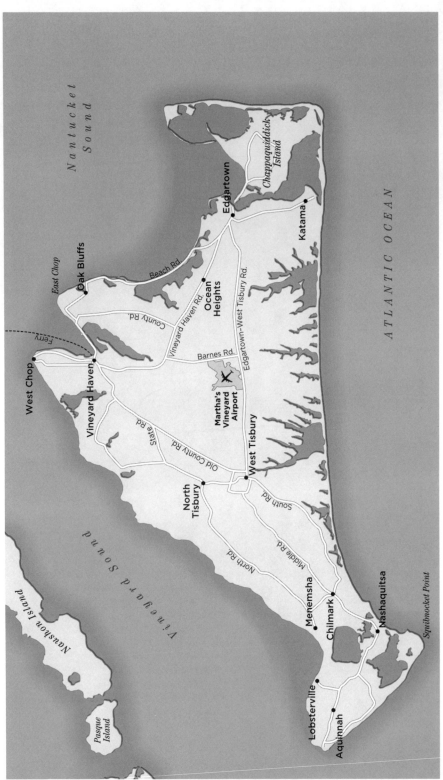

Martha's Vineyard

PREFACE

For as long as anyone can recall, the words "Cape Cod" have conjured up evocative images of sandy beaches, lighthouses, sea captains' homes, picturesque fishing villages, clams, and lobsters. It was many years ago that Patti Page sang these familiar words:

> If you're fond of sand dunes and
> salty air,
> Quaint little villages here and there
> You're sure to fall in love with Old
> Cape Cod.

And it's still true today—people *still* fall in love with Cape Cod, even if they've never heard of Patti Page. So what makes the Cape so special? Maybe it's the quality of light on the dunes on a summer morning, the call of the seagull, the briny scent of sea air at dusk, the sun setting in a splash of color over the bay, the vast expanses of beach and sand flats, and the sense of anticipation at exploring this narrow spit of land.

Today Cape Cod is virtually a year-round resort. No matter what time of year, Cape Cod beaches can always be walked, the bike and walking trails enjoyed, and golf courses played. And Cape Cod's 15 towns keep adding new attractions, which we describe in this latest, sixth edition. Look for new listings for health clubs; minigolf and amusement parks; boutiques; fine restaurants; golf courses; tennis courts; biking, running, and inline skating trails; and conservation areas and opportunities for enjoying the outdoors. Of course we cover the tried and true as well, with in-depth, updated descriptions of the Cape and islands' countless facilities and activities, from Heritage Week events to resort accommodations, from free concerts on village greens to the Pops by the Sea, plus information about restaurants and inns, beaches and antiques shops, museums, parks, and tours.

If you're a lover of the arts, you'll find that Cape Cod's art scene is thriving. Painters have been drawn to this magical region for more than 100 years, since Charles Hawthorne set his easel in the sand in Provincetown in 1899 and started the Cape Cod School of Art. Edward Hopper spent more than 30 summers painting in Truro, and legendary figures of the New York School, such as Jackson Pollack, Mark Rothko, and Robert Motherwell, all lived in Provincetown at one time.

Drama thrives here too. Eugene O'Neill wrote many of his earliest plays in Provincetown, and James Stewart got his first acting break at the Falmouth Playhouse. Bette Davis worked as an usher—and later, as an actress—at the Cape Playhouse in Dennis.

Writers as well have made Cape Cod their home. Pulitzer Prize–winning author Norman Mailer and acclaimed mystery writer Mary Higgins Clark are Cape residents.

Moreover, the Cape has been an especially attractive home to nature writers, ever since Henry Thoreau spent time here walking around the Lower and Outer Cape and chronicling his perambulations in *Cape Cod,* which was published in 1964. In 1928 the writer Henry Beston lived on Coast Guard Beach in Eastham and reflected on his year of solitude in a dune shack on a barrier beach in his classic book, *The Outermost House.* More recently noted nature writer John Hay was the winner of the John Burroughs Award for Best Nature Writing for his book *The Great Beach,* published in 1963. He was also heralded for numerous other books about Cape Cod, including *The Run* (1959) and *In the Company of Light* (1966). These people recognized that

Cape Cod is a unique area for nature lovers, as well as being therapeutic for those craving rest and relaxation. They inspired many latter-day explorers to follow in their footsteps, and so Cape Cod began to attract more nature lovers and bird-watchers, hikers and whale watchers, sailors and surf casters.

Visualize a kayak moving gracefully downstream, heading toward a paradise of dunes and ocean beach, through tidal flats and salt marsh, populated by terns, black-backed gulls and piping plovers. The musical soundtrack of Patti Page has been replaced with the sound of laughing gulls, the cackling call of the kingfisher in flight, and the swoosh of a paddle as it cuts through the water.

This natural Cape Cod is as much our reality as those quaint villages of Patti Page's song. Nowadays visiting Cape Cod for many is as much about nature walks around kettle ponds and understanding migratory paths of birds and marine mammals as it is about eating fried clams and lying on the beach to get a good tan. The people of Cape Cod have embraced the intricate relationship between human interaction and the fragility of their natural resources and have discovered that responsible recreation coupled with managing local resources is essential if they want to retain the traditional images of Cape Cod and still move forward into the 21st century.

If you're a visitor, this book can help make your Cape Cod experience a memorable one. If you've come to stay, we help inform your choices on major decisions, like those on housing and schools. Or maybe you already live here and want to try a new dining spot or check out a new attraction. The *Insiders' Guide to Cape Cod and the Islands* was written with all of you in mind. We hope you will benefit from the in-depth, inside information we provide.

So whether you're choosing a new home or a bed-and-breakfast to spend the night, whether you're picking a restaurant on the water for a sunset dinner, or trying to find the best walking path in town, this book will steer you in the right direction. Once you decide where you're headed, don't forget to check out our maps. Then enjoy your journey. This edition of the *Insiders' Guide to Cape Cod and the Islands* is for the explorer in all of us.

Refer to it when looking for nature trails, scribble in its margins after eating out, use it as a lap desk when you're on the beach writing postcards. We know you will enjoy this book and hope you'll let us know what you think—you may come up with some Insiders' tips of your own to share!

HOW TO USE THIS BOOK

First, we want to thank you for selecting the *Insiders' Guide to Cape Cod and the Islands.* You have made a good choice. This book will help you to get the most out of your time here on the Cape and islands.

No doubt you have already flipped back and forth through the book, thumbing your way from Hotels, Motels, and Resorts to Restaurants to Vacation Rentals, maybe settling briefly on chapters such as Shopping or The Arts or some other chapter whose subject captured your interest. Or perhaps you're thinking of planning that perfect Cape Cod vacation and are suddenly indecisive when confronted with a 500-plus-page book chock-full of information. Where should you start?

This chapter is a good beginning—consider it an instruction manual for this book.

We put this guide together in a way that will allow you easy access to all types of valuable information pertinent to Cape Cod and the islands of Martha's Vineyard and Nantucket. It's not necessary to read the chapters in order, as each chapter stands on its own. It would be helpful to read the Preface, Area Overview, and Getting Here, Getting Around chapters first if you are unfamiliar with the area. Depending on what you're looking for from your visit, other chapters such as Historic Cape Cod, Worship, or Retirement might be considered necessary reading as you make your plans.

If you plan to visit Martha's Vineyard or Nantucket, for a day or for an extended period, it would be helpful to read the introduction to those chapters to get a "lay of the land." An island day trip can be a highly successful one with just a little planning.

With a book this size and an area as diverse as Cape Cod and the islands, you'll find the Contents and the maps at the front of the book to be of great help. If you plan to do a lot of traveling around the Cape, consider picking up a more detailed map—map books are available at most newsstands and bookstores.

Once you get into the individual chapters of your *Insiders' Guide* you'll be happy to know that we've used a consistent geographical order throughout. Whether you're looking for a good place to eat in the Restaurants chapter, that perfect sea captain's house in the Bed-and-Breakfasts, Inns, and Cottages chapter, or a place to take the children on a rainy afternoon in Kidstuff, all entries are listed by town from west to east (from Bourne to Chatham) and then from south to north along the forearm of the Cape to its fist (from Chatham to Provincetown). Within each town we've also used a consistent order for the individual villages. As you grow accustomed to the order, you'll find that locating places within chapters becomes rather easy.

To help even further within each chapter we've divided the Cape into three regions: Upper Cape, Mid-Cape, and Lower Cape. Upper Cape is the westernmost portion of Cape Cod and includes Bourne, Sandwich, Falmouth, and Mashpee. Mid-Cape—located, as you've probably already guessed, in just about the middle of Cape Cod—consists of the towns of Barnstable, Yarmouth, and Dennis. The remaining towns of Brewster, Harwich, Chatham, Orleans, Eastham, Wellfleet, Truro, and Provincetown make up the Lower Cape. You may also have heard another designation: the Outer Cape, which is the Lower Cape towns along the Atlantic, or back side, of the Cape. They include Chatham,

Orleans, Eastham, Wellfleet, Truro, and Provincetown.

All information concerning the islands (history, accommodations, restaurants, annual events, etc.) is in the individual island chapters toward the end of the book. Although the island of Nantucket is one town, Martha's Vineyard consists of six individual towns, so all establishments on that island are listed within the chapter in the following geographic order by town: Vineyard Haven (Tisbury) first, then Oak Bluffs, Edgartown, West Tisbury, Chilmark, and Aquinnah (formerly called Gay Head).

Though most chapters are arranged in the town-by-town format described above, a couple of chapters vary somewhat from this treatment. Annual Events, for example, is arranged first by month, and then within each month by the usual geographic order.

Each entry in the chapters includes the establishment's address, phone number, and Web site, if available. It is important to note that because each town has a number of villages—which over the centuries have acquired and maintained their own individual identities—there exist many cases in which towns contain more than one Main Street or other streets with the same name. For instance the town of Dennis has a Main Street in both South Dennis and Dennisport. Barnstable has Main Streets in eight villages! Yarmouth contains four streets that answer to the name of Pine. In some towns Route 6A along the north side is also known as Main Street, as is Route 28 running along the south side of other towns. In Yarmouth both Route 6A and Route 28 are known as Main Street. We have used route numbers wherever applicable to avoid confusion; you'll find it easier to follow maps that way. Some roads magically change names. Willow Street in Yarmouth, for example, becomes Yarmouth Road once it enters the town of Barnstable. Even within a town streets have been known to change names—take Union Street in Yarmouthport, for example, which becomes Station Avenue in South Yarmouth. Other streets

just change their spelling slightly, such as Setucket Road of Dennis, which becomes Satucket Road in Brewster.

As for phone numbers, all of Cape Cod, Nantucket, and Martha's Vineyard lie within the 508 area code. Now the fun begins—determining which towns constitute a toll call. It all depends on where you're calling from and which towns abut your town. Ordinarily you do not need to dial 1–508 if you are calling a town that abuts the town from which you are calling. Yet this isn't true in all cases. Your best bet is to consult the Local Calling Areas section at the front of your Cape phone book to determine the specifics. By the way, there are three Cape telephone books: Falmouth Area (Upper Cape), Hyannis Area (Mid-Cape), and Orleans Area (Lower Cape). Although all three books contain the same white pages, each has its own Yellow Pages.

We have endeavored to be as accurate as possible. Of course there will be a mistake from time to time or information will change. Unfortunately businesses, organizations, and municipalities sometimes make decisions to change rates, hours, or policies in the spring, right before the busy season—and after our press time! We have used the most up-to-date information available to us. If you find any inaccuracies we would appreciate hearing from you so we can make the necessary changes for future editions. Please write to us at the *Insiders' Guide to Cape Cod and the Islands,* c/o The Globe Pequot Press, P.O. Box 480, Guilford, CT 06437-0480.

We have two final points to make. If, say, an inn in the Bed-and-Breakfasts, Inns and Cottages chapter has a restaurant on-site that is written up in the Restaurants chapter, we'll reference it so you can flip to it for further information (and vice versa). Other types of entries that appear elsewhere in the book will be referenced in a similar fashion. Finally, there is an index at the back of the book to make looking up a particular entry very easy.

Good luck and have fun!

AREA OVERVIEW

WELCOME TO CAPE COD

Cape Cod is a spit of land thrust into the Atlantic Ocean like a sandy arm, with Provincetown at the "fist," Chatham at the "elbow," and Sandwich at the "shoulder." The Cape lies just south of Boston on the East Coast of the United States and is the premier vacation resort in New England. The name Cape Cod conjures up images of sea captains' homes, shipwrecks, whaling ports, pirates, rumrunners, lighthouses, sand dunes, and sunsets. It is these images that even today create the backdrop for a Cape Cod vacation.

As you drive in and approach the Sagamore Bridge, you'll see an arrangement of ornamental shrubs and flowers that spell out WELCOME TO CAPE COD. This living greeting, planted nearly two decades ago, expresses a truth. No matter how many times you visit Cape Cod, you'll sense the welcome, not only from those of us who live here, but from the land itself, which seems to extend an invitation to explore this place that for centuries has attracted people from all parts of the world.

A LAND SURROUNDED BY SEA

The sea has shaped the land. Year by year, tide by tide, storm by storm, unseen currents, waves, and fierce winds driven by the sea have carved channels through barrier beaches and resulted in an ever-changing Cape Cod.

The sea has also shaped the way of life of the people who live here. It was an important economic resource for earlier inhabitants, helping to put food on the table and providing a living for those harvesting the fruits of the sea and engaged in boat building and chandlering. Many a

headstone in our local cemeteries bears the simple words LOST AT SEA, which attests to a darker bond between the Cape's people and the sea that surrounds them. Today Cape Cod's population of nearly 250,000 year-round residents swells in the summer as visitors are drawn to the area's natural beauty, which in great measure comes from its proximity to the sea. So in a sense the sea is still our greatest economic resource. Tourism is our main industry now, with restaurants and lodgings the major employers of our year-round and seasonal workforce.

HOW THE CAPE WAS FORMED

Cape Cod's shape is the gift of ice age glaciers and modern-day coastal erosion. About 22,000 years ago mile-high glaciers made their farthest southerly advance into the lower New England area, and as the front sections, or lobes, encountered warm temperatures, they began to melt. Over the next 4,000 years the glacier would recede, stop, advance, and then recede again with changing temperatures. Each time the glacier stopped, it deposited rocky debris gathered in its long journey from the north. The hills along the northern coast of the Cape are made up of this debris. The coastline was gradually smoothed out by pebbles, stones, and rocks, and sand bars were formed around the Cape by drifting sand. The glaciers also left behind hundreds of ponds and lakes, called "kettle ponds," formed where huge chunks of glacial ice left depressions in the earth. There are approximately 360 of these kettle ponds on Cape Cod. In fact it is an environmentally sensitive area as a result of the uniqueness of its formation.

Vital Statistics

Governor: Mitt Romney

Congressional delegation: Senator Edward Kennedy, Senator John Kerry, and Congressman William Delahunt

Capital: Boston

State motto: *Ense petit placidam sub libertate quietem* (By the sword we seek peace, but peace only under liberty).

Nickname: The Bay State

Major cities (in Eastern Massachusetts): Boston, Worcester, New Bedford

Counties of the Cape and islands: Barnstable, Nantucket, and Dukes (Martha's Vineyard)

Permanent population: According to the 2000 U.S. Census, roughly 247,000 people: 222,230 in Barnstable County, 14,987 in Dukes County, and 9,520 in Nantucket County.

Area: 396 square miles (Barnstable County), 104 square miles (Dukes County), and 48 square miles (Nantucket County)

Average Cape temperatures: July (high/low): 78/63; January (high/low): 40/25

Colleges: Massachusetts Maritime Academy, Cape Cod Community College

Major employment sectors: Retail, services, and local government

Major airports: Logan International Airport (Boston), Barnstable County Municipal Airport (Hyannis)

Military bases: Massachusetts Military Reservation

Daily newspaper: *Cape Cod Times*

State sales tax: 5%

State rooms tax: 5.7%

Municipal hotel/motel surtax: 4%

State meals tax: 5%

A BRIEF HISTORY

Physical evidence suggests that the Cape's earliest inhabitants arrived by 10,000 B.P.—"before present," as local archaeologist at the Cape Cod Museum of Natural History, Fred Dumford, says. During the warmer months they lived along the Cape's major waterways and estuaries and moved inland during the winter. In 1524 explorer Giovanni di Verrazzano spent several weeks exploring the area around Buzzards Bay and described an Algonquin-speaking people as being handsome, well dressed, and friendly.

In 1620 the Pilgrims arrived from England, making landfall at Provincetown, where they remained for about five weeks, exploring the area, before finally sailing on to Plymouth. While on the Cape they encountered native people who hunted, fished, and farmed, raising crops of corn, squash, beans, and tobacco. Within decades after the Pilgrims' arrival, the first handful of Cape towns were settled: Sandwich in 1637, Yarmouth in 1639, and Barnstable in 1640. By the end of the 18th century, all of the Cape towns with the exception of Brewster, Mashpee, and Bourne, were incorporated. These three towns would all see incorporation during the 19th century.

Approximately two-thirds of the Cape's towns are named for English seaports, and all but two have English names (Orleans is named after a French city, and Mashpee is Wampanoag Indian). The Cape itself was named by English explorer Bartholomew Gosnold, who in 1602 arrived in the vicinity of the Elizabeth Islands off Woods Hole in Falmouth. He was impressed, among other things, with the great number of codfish he saw in Cape waters. See our Historic Cape Cod chapter for more on the history of the Cape as well as histories of the individual towns, which we describe here.

THE CAPE TOWNS

Upper Cape

Bourne, the town closest to the mainland, actually straddles the Cape Cod Canal. Bourne consists of nine small villages, as well as the Massachusetts Military Reservation, totaling an area of 40 square miles and containing a population of about 19,000. The village of Gray Gables in Bourne has the distinction of being home to the first summer White House where President Grover Cleveland summered in the 1890s. Monument Beach, Cataumet, and Pocasset are residential seaside villages that are quaint and off the beaten path; Bournedale, nestled between the two bridges on the mainland portion of the town, has a country store and one of the Cape's productive herring ponds; Buzzards Bay is a commercial center, home to the Massachusetts Maritime Academy and pretty views of Buttermilk Bay.

Glaciers once extended down over the Northeast but didn't cover Cape Cod. The pressure of the ice and snow to the west of the Cape, however, displaced the crust below the Cape upward. Now that the glaciers have retreated, the Cape is slowly but surely sinking.

Lying just east of Bourne is historic and charming Sandwich, which has a population of about 21,000 and is the oldest town on the Cape. Famous for the glass industry that thrived there in the 1800s, Sandwich is still home to a few glassmaking studios and the Sandwich Glass Museum. The village of Sandwich, with its shady lanes dotted with antique shops, historic inns, and a working Grist Mill, is the perfect town for a casual stroll.

Falmouth, situated south of Bourne and Sandwich, is the second-largest town on the Cape and has more shore and coastline than any other, with 14 harbors and numerous saltwater inlets reaching up like fingers from Vineyard Sound. With a total year-round population of about 33,000, Falmouth is made up of eight villages. Falmouth Village, the center of the town, has a wonderful village green, a fascinating array of specialty shops, and includes Falmouth Heights, popular among summer visitors. East Falmouth, Hatchville, Teaticket, and Waquoit are residential areas. Quaint North and West Falmouth are known as the keepers of old Cape Cod. Their village centers were placed on the National Register of Historic Places because so many of their 18th- and 19th-century buildings remain.

The village of Woods Hole is home to three important scientific institutions: Woods Hole Oceanographic Institute (WHOI, or "hooey" to locals), the Marine Biological Laboratory, and the National Maritime Fisheries Service. This seaside village is also a terminus for ferries bound for Martha's Vineyard.

East of Falmouth is Mashpee, the town with the strongest ties to the Cape's Native American heritage. It's seen tremendous growth in the last decade; in fact it's become one of the fastest-growing areas of the state. It now has a year-round population of about 13,000 and this increases to 25,000 during the summer.

Mid-Cape

Moving east to the Mid-Cape, Barnstable is the Cape's largest and most populated town with an estimated 48,000 residents in 60 square miles. It serves as the county seat with a complex containing a courthouse and jail. Surrounding quiet, historic Route 6A, Barnstable Village is known for its lovely old houses and its harbor. Also on Route 6A is West Barnstable, which enjoys beautiful views of the salt marshes and barrier beach on Sandy Neck Conservation Area. Barnstable also contains Hyannis, which is the closest thing to a city on Cape Cod. Many residents of other Cape towns, including the far-flung Lower Cape towns, travel regularly to Hyannis for shopping, medical services, or employment. Hyannis Harbor has two docks from which ferries depart for Nantucket and Martha's Vineyard. Hyannisport is famous for the Kennedy Compound, where President John F. Kennedy came to sail and enjoy the relaxed atmosphere of Cape Cod with his family in the "Camelot" days. Other villages in Barnstable are Cotuit, Osterville, Centerville, and Marstons Mills.

Stretching between Nantucket Sound and Cape Cod Bay is Yarmouth. On the north side of the Cape is historic, tranquil Yarmouthport along scenic Route 6A, and on the south side is Bass River and the bustling Route 28. If you're looking for a game of minigolf, a quick lunch, or a little nightlife, head for Route 28. If you're into antiquing and visiting historic sites, mean-der along Route 6A. Yarmouth's year-round population of about 25,000 grows to more than 50,000 in the summer months.

Dennis enjoys a great location and also stretches from the sound to Cape Cod Bay. Historic Route 6A wends through the quiet north side, and, to the south, Dennisport is very much a family-oriented summer resort with a breezy shoreline dotted with cottages and motels. Dennis spans 20 square miles and has a year-round population of about 16,000.

Lower Cape

Just east of Dennis is Brewster, often called the sea captains' town, because it was once home to many wealthy sea captains who built magnificent homes. Today many of those stately sea captains' homes have been converted into bed-and-breakfast inns. With a year-round population of about 10,000, Brewster is a family town, as evidenced by the high number of young children that required the town to construct a second elementary school. Another sign of the town's growth—and its priorities—is the impressive remodeling of the Brewster Ladies' Library. Once the north parish of Harwich, Brewster has eight beautiful beaches and numerous freshwater ponds. It is also home to the Cape Cod Museum of Natural History, with its magnificent nature trails, and the Nickerson State Park.

South of Brewster is Harwich, which boasts 16 saltwater beaches on Nantucket Sound, along with a number of freshwater ponds. Home to about 12,000 year-round residents, Harwich comprises seven villages, including bustling Harwichport, quiet Pleasant Lake, historic North Harwich, and charming Harwich Center, which is home to an old-fashioned hardware

[Facing page] *The Higgins Farm Windmill in Brewster's Drummer Boy Park.*
ERICA BOLLERUD

CLOSE-UP

Autumn on the Cape

Wish you could enjoy the Cape without the crowds? Consider scheduling your visit during September or October. As autumn falls over New England, you'll find that the summer crowds have left, traffic is flowing more normally, and year-rounders are breathing more easily. It's a great time of year for bargains: Prices for rooms and a round of golf have dropped, and stores are having end-of-season sales. Most seasonal attractions stay open until Columbus Day Weekend, and the water is still relatively warm. You may even find that—wonder of wonders—you have the beach all to yourself. Whales continue to call the Cape's waters home until late October, and whale-watch trips are definitely less crowded (see our Whale Watching chapter for more information).

An autumn visit also means you get to enjoy a whole new set of seasonal pleasures on the Cape and islands. New England's famed autumn color reaches the Cape in mid-October. Call the Massa-chusetts Foliage Hotline at (800) 227-6277 for more information on how the color is progressing. The Cape Cod Railroad offers a leaf-peeper luncheon train when color is at its peak. Call (888) 797-RAIL, or visit www.capetrain.com for more information. For a closer view of the changing colors, consider hitting one of the many trails that crisscross the natural beauty of the Cape. Cape Cod's Walking Weekend, held in mid-October, is a great time to start. Guided walks and hikes are scheduled from Falmouth to Truro. Options may range from a beach walk in Eastham with a Cape Cod National Seashore ranger to a sunset stroll in Brewster with a Cape Cod Natural History Museum naturalist. Call for a schedule at (508) 362-3828.

Besides the leaves and sea grass changing hues, the Cape also offers the spectacle of acres and acres of cranberry bogs ripening from a deep green to a bright red. Cranberries are harvested from mid-September through mid-October using the wet method: Bogs are flooded so that the ripe berries float to the surface. Part of life on the Cape since the early 1800s, they are still celebrated as part of the region's heritage every year. More than 100,000 people attend the Harwich Cranberry Festival, held in mid-September at the Harwich High School Fairgrounds, to enjoy arts and crafts, entertainment, a parade, carnival rides, fireworks, and more. Visit www.harwich cranberryfestival.com for more information, and see our Annual Events chapter for more autumn events.

store and a small coffee shop where locals gather each morning to trade news. Har-wich's Wychmere Harbor is perhaps one of the most picturesque harbors on the Cape but development has affected its natural beauty.

Tucked away down on the "elbow" of Cape Cod is Chatham, almost a world unto itself. One thing that sets it apart is its geography; it's not on the way to any other town. With a picturesque Main Street of upscale shops along brick-lined sidewalks, Chatham exudes gentility and sophistication. It is also home to an active fishing fleet, which balances its affluent side. Chatham, with just 7,000 residents, has a high percentage of senior citizens and consistently votes Republican in presidential elections.

One of the most scenic drives on the Cape is Route 28, which runs between Chatham and Orleans, a winding stretch of road filled with beautiful vistas of Pleasant Bay, inlets, and cranberry bogs. If you enter Orleans this way, you'll get a glimpse of woodsy, residential South Orleans and will pass the South Orleans General Store, which uniquely provides most of the necessary conveniences of a pleasant day trip. When you reach Orleans, which has a year-round population of more than 6,000, you won't at first understand why this is called the hub of the Lower Cape—it's just a nice little downtown, you think, but then you'll realize it's got everything you could need. The town has many attractions, including the famed Nauset Beach on the ocean side and quaint Rock Harbor on Cape Cod Bay, home to a fleet of charter fishing boats. South Orleans is home to more senior citizens than any other community in the state.

The gateway to the Cape Cod National Seashore, Eastham is a town with a rural nature and both bay and ocean beaches. With about 5,500 residents, Eastham is predominantly a family town and has numerous summer cottages clustered along the bay side for summer rentals. Roughly one-third of it's 14 square miles are taken up by the Cape Cod National Seashore, established in 1961, and comprising Eastham's entire ocean coastline (see our Cape Cod National Seashore chapter).

Wellfleet is an art lovers' haven and a fishing community, a free-spirited individualistic community of about 2,700 year-round residents. The Cape Cod National Seashore extends the entire length of Wellfleet's ocean coastline, as well as its width as far as Great Island, a narrow strip of land that juts 8 miles into Cape Cod

Don't be confused when you drive along scenic Route 28 between Chatham and Orleans. This route is marked "south" when you will actually be traveling north to Orleans. Likewise, returning from Orleans to Chatham, the signs are marked "north," when in fact you are traveling south. The confusion lies in the fact that Route 28 South takes a turn at Chatham and heads north to Orleans Center.

Bay and shelters Wellfleet Harbor. The harbor is home to an active fishing fleet, and the fishing community coexists amicably with the art world.

Laid-back and woodsy, with dramatic 80-foot beach cliffs overlooking the Atlantic Ocean and Cape Cod Bay, Truro is a summertime haven for those who crave privacy but want proximity to someplace lively—and neighboring Provincetown fills that requirement perfectly. The least populated of all the towns with just 2,000 residents, Truro is currently going through a building development boom as more and more people want to "get away from it all."

Provincetown explodes on the senses with its fun-loving, artsy, carnival-like flavor that is counterbalanced by a fishing community and incredible natural beauty. Well-known for its gay community, Provincetown is both colorful and sophisticated with lots of great restaurants, terrific shops, and fine art galleries. Many of the town's summer residents are from Manhattan—which perhaps explains the undeniable Greenwich Village flair. Some 3,400 people life here year-round, though the population swells to more than 25,000 in the summer months. The Cape Cod National Seashore extends to the tip of Cape Cod at Long Point in Provincetown and encompasses the historic Province Lands, reserved as fishing grounds by the Pilgrim Fathers. The Province Lands are laced with thrilling bicycle trails and the Beach Forest walking trail. There's a visitor center set on a hill with magnificent views of the Atlantic Ocean and across the bay to Plymouth. Once a major whaling port, Provincetown is now home to the largest whale-watching fleet on the East Coast.

The Atlantic Ocean's coastal currents are constantly moving sand from the beaches along the Lower Cape and redepositing sand at the tip of the Cape at Provincetown and to the south at Monomoy Island. In fact a fishing village existed on South Monomoy Island until the shifting sands filled the harbor and blocked off access to the sea, virtually eliminating the village.

THE CAPE'S COMFORTABLE CLIMATE

One of the most interesting things about the Cape is its weather. On Cape Cod you never know what you're going to get. You could be standing on Commercial Street in Provincetown checking out the shops under sunny skies while a little more than a half hour's ride away in Chatham the clouds have rolled in, and the people are packing up their beach gear to head for happy hour at the local watering hole.

It's not uncommon to see a 10-degree or more temperature difference between the north side of a town and the south side. A downright sultry summer's day in Marstons Mills can see lifeguards at Craigville beach donning their windbreakers against cool ocean breezes.

During winter the atmospheric differences are even more pronounced. One winter's day may see the Lower Cape receiving 6 inches of snow, whereas the Mid- and Upper Cape receive only a dusting. Come the next storm the tables are turned, and Falmouth residents are digging out while in Orleans there is but a light frosting to brush off the windshield in the morning.

Isolation from the land mass of New England and enclosure by ocean waters influences the weather on Cape Cod. The peninsula benefits from the warming effects of the ocean in winter and its cooling influences in summer. On the whole the temperature on the Cape is moderate in all seasons. Consider the average monthly temperature range during summer months—June: high 71, low 56; July: 78 and 63; August: 76 and 61. In winter the temperature range is fairly constant: January has an average high of 40 and low of 25; for February, the averages are 41 and 26; March's highs and lows are 42 and 28. The temperatures during the shoulder seasons of spring and fall are comfortable—April: high 58, low 40; May: high 62, low 48; September: high 70, low 56; October: high 59, low 47. The average annual rainfall is about 48 inches, with roughly 3 inches per month falling during the summer and about 4 inches of precipitation per month in the winter.

The temperature of marine waters is delightful along the Cape's southern shores, from Bourne along Buzzards Bay to Chatham on Nantucket Sound. The bracing waters of the Atlantic Ocean beaches are colder than the water along the south shore and in Cape Cod Bay—the perfect remedy for a hot summer's day!

GOVERNMENT BY THE PEOPLE

Most towns are run with the town-meeting style of government, with the exception of Barnstable, which switched to a town council–based government several years ago. The other towns are run by boards of selectmen and town managers or town administrators. Each spring open town meetings are convened to decide budgets, capital expenditures, zoning change, and other significant matters—and most towns have fall meetings as well, along with special meetings to decide pressing

Town Halls

Barnstable
367 Main Street, Hyannis
(508) 790-6200

Bourne
24 Perry Avenue, Bourne
(508) 759-0600, (508) 759-0613

Brewster
2198 Route 6A, Brewster
(508) 896-3701

Chatham
549 Main Street, Chatham
(508) 945-5100

Dennis
485 Main Street, South Dennis
(508) 394-8300

Eastham
2500 U.S. Route 6, Eastham
(508) 240-5900

Falmouth
Town Hall Square, Falmouth
(508) 548-7611

Harwich
732 Main Street (Route 39), Harwich
(508) 430-7513

Mashpee
16 Great Neck Road North, Mashpee
(508) 539-1400

Orleans
19 School Road, Orleans
(508) 240-3700

Provincetown
260 Commercial Street, Provincetown
(508) 487-7000

Sandwich
130 Main Street, Sandwich
(508) 888-5144

Truro
Town Hall Road, Truro
(508) 487-2702

Wellfleet
300 Main Street, Wellfleet
(508) 349-0300

Yarmouth
1146 Main Street (Route 28), South Yarmouth
(508) 398-2231

issues. Often called the purest form of democracy, town meetings guarantee that all voting residents have a say in town affairs. There is a high level of citizen involvement in the towns, with reliance on countless volunteers who serve on a variety of town boards, such as finance committees and conservation commissions.

THE CAPE'S ECONOMY

Tourism is undeniably the number-one force in the area's economy. Many Cape Codders work in the area's health-care system or as professionals in the fields of law and education. Agriculture and commercial fishing, which used to play a major

Chambers of Commerce

Brewster Chamber of Commerce
P.O. Box 1241, 2198 Main Street, Brewster,
MA 02631
(508) 896-3500
www.brewstercapecod.org

Cape Cod Canal Region Chamber of
Commerce (covering Bourne and Sandwich)
70 Main Street, Buzzards Bay, MA 02532
(508) 759-6000
www.capecodcanalchamber.org

Cape Cod Chamber of Commerce
Routes 6 and 132, Hyannis, MA 02601
(508) 862-0700, (888) 33-CAPE-COD
www.capecodchamber.org

Chatham Chamber of Commerce
Main Street, Chatham, MA 02633
(508) 945-5199, (800) 715-5567
www.chathamcapecod.org

Dennis Chamber of Commerce
Routes 134 and 28, South Dennis,
MA 02660
(508) 398-3568, (800) 243-9920
www.dennischamber.org

Eastham Chamber of Commerce
U.S. Route 6 at Fort Hill Road, Eastham,
MA 02651
(508) 240-7211
www.easthamchamber.com

Falmouth Chamber of Commerce
Academy Lane, Falmouth, MA 02540
(508) 548-8500, (800) 526-8532
www.falmouth-capecod.com

Harwich Chamber of Commerce
Main Street, Harwichport, MA 02645
(508) 432-1600, (800) 442-7942
www.harwichcc.com

role in our economic base, have declined in prominence. Technology, on the other hand, is up and coming on Cape Cod. This latter development should greatly increase economic opportunity here.

PROTECTING AND PRESERVING THE CAPE

Operating at the county level is the Cape Cod Commission, a regional land-use and planning agency located in Barnstable Village. Created in 1990, it has one representative from each of the Cape's 15 towns and, under the Cape Cod Commis-

sion Act, has the power to regulate developments of regional impact. It also provides planning assistance to the towns, designates areas of critical concern, and maintains a database of demographic information.

The Cape Cod Commission sprang from a general concern among residents that growth on the Cape needed to be controlled, because the peninsula is a sensitive environment and has limited land. Land conservation is an important issue on the Cape, and conservation trusts have flourished in every town. With large tracts of shoreline, ponds, and wetlands on Cape Cod, conservation com-

Hyannis Chamber of Commerce
1481 Route 132, Hyannis, MA 02601
(508) 362-5230, (877) 492-6647
www.hyannischamber.com

Mashpee Chamber of Commerce
Route 151, Mashpee Commons, Mashpee,
MA 02649
(508) 477-0792
www.mashpeechamber.com

Orleans Chamber of Commerce
44 Main Street, Orleans, MA 02653
(508) 255-1386, (800) 865-1386
www.capecod-orleans.com

Provincetown Chamber of Commerce
307 Commercial Street, Provincetown,
MA 02657
(508) 487-3424
www.ptownchamber.com

Truro Chamber of Commerce
2 Head of the Meadow Beach Road,
North Truro, MA 02652
(508) 487-1288
www.trurocapecod.com

Wellfleet Chamber of Commerce
off U.S. Route 6, South Wellfleet, MA
02663
(508) 349-2510
www.wellfleetchamber.com

Yarmouth Chamber of Commerce
424 Route 28, West Yarmouth, MA 02673
(508) 778-1008, (800) 732-1008
www.yarmouthcapecod.com

For more information on vacationing on
the Cape:
Massachusetts Office of Travel and Tourism
100 Cambridge Street, Boston, MA 02202
(617) 727-3201, (800) 447-6277

missions in every town have authority under state and local laws to oversee developments that take place near the shoreline and wetlands.

Most residents recognize the need to balance environmental concerns with economic ones, and although the two often appear to be in conflict, the trend is toward finding a middle ground. In 1998 voters approved creation of a land bank to fund town purchases of open space. Although the funding mechanism was hotly debated (the approved version uses a 3 percent increase in property taxes, after an earlier version that would have added to the tax on property transfers

was defeated), just about everyone agreed on the need for a land bank.

One of the strongest proponents of the land-bank bill, and for years a champion of the Cape's environment, is the Association for the Preservation of Cape Cod, which is involved in a variety of environmental and preservation issues. With a membership of more than 5,000, the APCC marked its 35th anniversary in 2003.

Historic preservation is as much of an issue as land preservation, and nowhere is that more evident than on quiet Route 6A, which has maintained its historic charm largely thanks to the jurisdiction of the Old Kings Highway Historic District, which

Most of the villages in each town have names that simply repeat the town's name and add a compass direction, such as South Yarmouth and East Harwich. Some village names, though, may leave you scratching your head as to what town it's in. Here is a listing of some of those names and their corresponding towns: Buzzards Bay, Pocasset, Cataumet, Bournedale, Gray Gables,

Monument Beach, and Sagamore are in Bourne; Forestdale is in Sandwich; Woods Hole, Hatchville, and Waquoit are in Falmouth; New Seabury and Popponesset are in Mashpee; Cotuit, Marstons Mills, Osterville, Wianno, Centerville, Craigville, Hyannis, Hyannisport, Cummaquid, and Barnstable Village are in Barnstable; and Bass River is in Yarmouth.

stretches from Sandwich to Orleans. Although some residents may grumble that they can't even paint their house without approval from the Historic District Committee, it's hard to argue with the apparent results: Route 6A is a lovely stretch of road and tasteful to a fault.

RESOURCES FOR MORE INFORMATION ON THE CAPE

Planning a visit to the Cape? Write or call chambers of commerce and other organizations for free brochures, travel packs,

maps, and money-saving coupons. Once you're here stop by chamber-sponsored information booths set up in many towns and villages for last-minute updates and ideas for things to do and see.

See also the listing of the addresses and telephone numbers of the Cape's town halls on page 11. Beach parking stickers are issued by the town hall in each town (see our Beaches chapter for details). The offices can also provide information about the laws and regulations that are in effect in the town, such as fishing regulations, zoning laws, smoking regulations, etc.

[Facing page] *The Pilgrim Monument, which commemorates the first landing of the* Mayflower *Pilgrims, stands out from the Provincetown skyline.*
MASSACHUSETTS OFFICE OF TRAVEL AND TOURISM

GETTING HERE, GETTING AROUND

People flock to the Cape not only because of its beauty but also because it's easy to get to from many places. New York, New Jersey, Pennsylvania, Washington, D.C., even Ohio and Canada are all within a day's drive. From New York City it's about a five-hour drive, from Boston it takes one hour to reach the canal, and from there it's a further one hour and twenty minutes to reach Provincetown at the tip of the Cape.

By land, whether you arrive from the north or from the west, you will cross the Cape Cod Canal at either Bourne or Sagamore over one of two imposing bridges, allowing for a spectacular view of the canal below and Buzzards Bay or Cape Cod Bay stretching off into the distance.

Arriving by air in either Hyannis or Provincetown, a traveler by day will see the entire outline of the Cape and islands surrounded by the bluest sea and fringed with sand dunes; at night the Cape sparkles with thousands of lights and the beams of the many lighthouses that mark the harbor entrances and the treacherous coastline. The short flight from Boston—about 20 minutes—is truly spectacular.

By sea, whether arriving at Martha's Vineyard or Nantucket, or Provincetown via Boston, the Cape emerges from a lush green horizon into a coastline of harbors and gray-shingled buildings, accented by the widow's walks of sea captains' homes and the soaring spires of old churches. These spires provided mariners of centuries past with visible landmarks as they made their way along the coast.

Below we've listed your various transportation options.

BY CAR

From Boston and points north: Take I-93 to Route 3 South. Go straight ahead at the Sagamore rotary, and cross over the Sagamore Bridge, taking U.S. Route 6 (also called the Mid-Cape Highway), which extends the entire length of the Cape to Provincetown. Follow Route 6 until you see the name of the town you wish to visit. Exits are well marked. If you wish to visit Falmouth or Woods Hole, you do not have to go over the Sagamore Bridge, but instead take the first right at the Sagamore rotary and take this road just a few miles to the Bourne Bridge. Cross over the Bourne Bridge, and continue south on Route 28.

From Springfield, Massachusetts, and points west: Take the Mass Pike, I-90 East and follow it to exit 11A; take I-495 South. I-495 merges into Route 25. Follow this road over the Bourne Bridge. If you are going to Falmouth or Woods Hole, go halfway around the rotary where Route 28 leads you on your way. If you are heading to any other town, go three-quarters around the Bourne rotary, where you will see a sign for U.S. Route 6 East, a road that winds along the Cape Cod Canal. Follow this road to the first set of traffic lights, just before the Sagamore Bridge. Take a right at the lights to U.S. Route 6 (Mid-Cape Highway), and follow this road until you reach your exit.

From New York, Connecticut, Rhode Island, and points south: Take I-95 to Providence, Rhode Island. Take exit 20 to I-195 East. Follow this to Route 25 South, which leads to the Bourne Bridge. If you are going to Falmouth or Woods Hole, go halfway around the rotary, where Route 28 leads you to your destination. Otherwise, if you are heading to any other town, go three-quarters around the Bourne rotary, and pick up U.S. Route 6 East. Follow this to the first set of lights, and go right onto Route 6. Exit U.S. Route 6 at the appropriate turning for the town you wish to visit.

Most people do, in fact, come to the Cape by automobile—more than 95,000 vehicles arrive per day during the popular summer months. Major routes can be busy. The Friday evening and Saturday morning approach to the Cape toward both Sagamore and Bourne Bridges is usually quite busy, and often traffic will be brought to a crawl for several miles before the bridge. This is because vacation rentals turn over on Saturday mornings, occasionally resulting in a Saturday afternoon backup going off-Cape, but most folks find a way to stay on the Cape one more day, meaning that the Sunday afternoon traffic usually backs up 2 or 3 miles going off-Cape.

Most of the radio stations have "travel reports" airing frequently Friday through Sunday in the summer for your convenience (try WQRC, 99.9 FM). Another great way to avoid traffic before you leave the house or motel is to call SmarTraveler at (617) 374-1234 (*1 on your cell phone, or www.smartraveler.com) for up-to-the-minute information on traffic. This service employs cameras and airplanes to determine current traffic problems.

U.S. Route 6: The Mid-Cape Highway

The Mid-Cape Highway, technically U.S. Route 6, is the main traffic artery, running down the middle of the Cape as far as Orleans. It then continues as U.S. Route 6 to Provincetown. From the canal to Dennis, the Mid-Cape Highway is a two-lane divided highway; the speed limit is 55

mph. After Dennis (exit 9) the road becomes, for a 13-mile stretch to Orleans, a two-lane highway (one lane going west, one going east), dubbed Suicide Alley by locals. As the highway narrows into this stretch, there's bound to be a bit of congestion, especially in the summer on a busy Saturday morning, so watch out for this area if you're traveling at that time. Posted signs suggest that you use your headlights as you travel this 50-mph stretch, even during the daylight hours, to increase visibility. At the Orleans rotary U.S. Route 6 once again widens to two lanes through Eastham and then narrows again from time to time during the stretch from Wellfleet to Provincetown. Because U.S. Route 6 is the only major thoroughfare on Cape Cod, state police patrol these routes routinely. Also, U.S. Route 6 from Wellfleet to Provincetown is narrow and prone to accidents, so please be careful, especially when making left-hand turns, and do not speed—especially from the Orleans rotary to Provincetown—as the police will not be lenient.

Route 28 handles traffic south of U.S. Route 6 and Route 6A handles it to the north. Both these routes are more scenic and slower than U.S. Route 6. Route 28 connects most of the Cape business districts along the south coast. Route 6A is more of a country road, leading to many of the Cape's cozy inns and antique shops along the north shore. It has been rated one of the top scenic drives in the country (see our Tours and Excursions chapter). These three roads—U.S. Route 6, Route 28, and Route 6A—originate at the canal bridges, spread out over the Upper and Mid-Cape, and then converge at the Orleans-Eastham rotary on the Lower Cape, with U.S. Route 6 alone carrying you northward from Eastham to Provincetown.

In many towns Route 6A is also known as Main Street, as is Route 28 in some towns. But some towns have other Main Streets. To avoid confusion we have decided to use route numbers throughout this book wherever possible.

Cape Routes

Many side roads intercept U.S. Route 6 and Routes 6A and 28; consult a good map to find shortcuts. Locals use several principal north-south state highways (below designated per local usage as routes) to travel between east-west routes of these highways. Below we give a few.

Route 151, which runs from Route 28 in Mashpee (at the Mashpee rotary) to Route 28 in North Falmouth

Route 130 from Route 6A in Sandwich to Route 28 in Mashpee (Route 130 connects with U.S. Route 6 at exit 2)

Route 149 from Route 6A in West Barnstable to Route 28 in Cotuit (Route 149 connects with U.S. Route 6 at exit 5)

Route 132 from Route 6A in Barnstable to Route 28 in Hyannis (Route 132 connects with U.S. Route 6 at exit 6)

Route 134 from Route 6A in Dennis to Route 28 in Hyannis (Route 134 connects with U.S. Route 6 at exit 9)

Route 124 from Route 6A in Brewster to Route 39 in Harwich (Route 124 connects with U.S. Route 6 at exit 10)

Route 137 from Route 6A in Brewster to Route 39 in East Harwich and continuing to Route 28 in Chatham (Route 137 connects with U.S. Route 6 at exit 11)

Route 39 from Harwichport to Route 28 in Orleans

Rotaries

The Cape has some notable traffic circles called rotaries—approximately 19 of them. For those not familiar with rotaries, also called roundabouts, here's an explanation: Their purpose is to provide you with an opportunity to continue on your way without having to stop at major intersections. The traffic in a rotary travels counterclockwise. In other words, you can only turn right into or off a rotary. The law dictates that you *yield to a car already in the rotary,* rather like merging onto the highway—wait for a gap in traffic, and then ease into that spot. Be patient when entering and driving around a rotary. Usually the signs are pretty good, and you can read each one quickly as you enter

the rotary so you'll know which road you need to take. If you do get confused and miss your turnoff, don't panic! Instead of slamming on your brakes (the last thing you want to do in a rotary!), simply drive around again in a circle.

Just where will you find some of these rotaries? The Sagamore rotary is on the mainland side of the bridge and connects Route 3 with U.S. Route 6, the main highway on the Cape, which travels from the Bourne Bridge up to the Sagamore rotary and then over the bridge through to Provincetown. The Bourne rotary lies on the Cape side of the Bourne Bridge (look for the topiary that spells out CAPE COD). At this rotary you can connect with Route 28, which hugs Buzzards Bay and the southern coast of the Cape and temporarily joins with Route 28A before branching out to

Orleans. You can also go three-quarters around the rotary and pick up Route 6A, which runs from Bourne, along the canal, past U.S. Route 6, and then turns sharply to hug the northern coast of the Cape. Route 6A ends at the Eastham-Orleans rotary, though it resurfaces for a 10.5-mile stretch from Truro to Provincetown.

BY PLANE

Perhaps the best way to get a real feel for the Cape is to approach it by air. On a clear day you can see it all. You'll notice the relationships between the Cape peninsula and the two islands to the south, Martha's Vineyard and Nantucket, and you may even be able to see Monomoy Island off Chatham and the Elizabeth Islands off Falmouth. Even Cape residents are surprised by just how narrow this land looks from the sky.

Barnstable Municipal Airport in Hyannis is the Cape's main airport. It should also be noted that this airport has no fancy boutiques and no food courts—just friendly local people willing and able to assist you with your travel questions. The Cape also has a few other smaller airports, sometimes just a runway or two, which, with the exception of the Provincetown Airport, only serve private planes. Once you arrive at Barnstable, there are plenty of car-rental options right at the airport.

Cape Air is the carrier that offers the most daily flights into Hyannis and Provincetown. It is an employee-owned company with top-quality service and loads of experience. Always call two hours ahead of your flight departure time to guarantee that your flight is taking off. Even with the most sophisticated of flight equipment, the fog can sock you in for a couple hours.

Fly to Barnstable Municipal Airport in Hyannis on Cape Air from Boston and Providence, or on US Airways Express from Boston and New York.

Fly to Nantucket on Cape Air from Boston, New Bedford, Providence, Hyannis, Provincetown, and Martha's Vineyard; or on US Airways Express from New York, Boston, Hyannis, and Martha's Vineyard. To fly to Nantucket from Hyannis, you can take Nantucket Airlines and Island Airlines.

Fly to Martha's Vineyard on Cape Air from Boston, New Bedford, Providence, Hyannis, and Nantucket.

Fly to Provincetown on Cape Air from Boston. Most of the 18-minute flight is over Cape Cod Bay, and the views of the dune-studded Cape as the plane sweeps over its tip are—there's no other word for it—breathtaking.

Barnstable Municipal Airport
Hyannis Rotary, Hyannis
(508) 775-2020

Barnstable Municipal Airport, the Cape's major airport, is right in the middle of the peninsula in Hyannis (town of Barnstable). With two 1-mile runways, it is certainly not the largest airport you'll ever land at, but it is far from the smallest. President Kennedy's plane would land here when he was arriving for a Hyannisport vacation. For celebrity watchers, when the rich and famous fly to the Cape, more often than not, they'll come through Barnstable.

Four airlines service the airport, three on a full-time basis and one seasonally. Also, two local airlines, Island Airlines and Nantucket Airlines, provide service from Hyannis to Nantucket (see our Nantucket chapter for more details).

Cape Air (800–352-0714, www.flycape air.com), offers the most daily flights into Hyannis from Boston and to the Cape and islands in the summer. On average there are about seven flights a day year-round between Boston's Logan International Airport and Barnstable Municipal Airport. These flights take about 20 minutes; it seems once the plane reaches its cruising height it's time to prepare for landing. The airline has many flights each day to Nantucket and to Martha's Vineyard. Call ahead for your reservations. Cape Air and Nantucket Airlines also offer off-season specials in addition to discounted commuter tickets.

Colgan Air for US Airways Express (800-428-4322, or www.usairways.com) offers flights from Boston and New York's La Guardia Airport, Philadelphia, and Washington, D.C., to Hyannis, Nantucket, and seasonally to Martha's Vineyard. Pan Am Clipper Connections, (800-FLY-PANAM, www.flypanam.com) offers flights from smaller airports, like Baltimore; Manchester and Portsmouth, New Hampshire; and Westchester County, New York, to Hyannis and the islands.

Outside the main terminal there are normally a number of taxis waiting. If you plan on leaving your car at the airport overnight, there is a daily parking fee.

If you need to rent a car, you're in luck; there are four car rental companies located in the main terminal: Avis, (800) 331-1212; Budget, (800) 527-0700; Hertz, (800) 654-3131; and Enterprise, (800) 736-8222.

Provincetown Airport
Race Point Road, Provincetown
(508) 487-0241

Located at the Province Lands, Provincetown Airport has one 3,500-foot paved runway just down the road from Race Point Beach, a short taxi ride from the town center. Cape Air flies into Provincetown from Boston on a daily basis. During the summer there are sightseeing flights. You can rent a car at Provincetown Airport through Budget, (508) 487-4557; Enterprise, (508) 487-0009; or Thrifty, (508) 487-9418.

Other airports on Cape Cod offer landing for private planes:

Ocean Wings Air Charter
Memorial Airport, Nantucket
(800) 253-5039
www.capecodweb.com/wings

Ocean Wings Air Charter offers 24-hour year-round charter service to and from airports throughout the Northeast. If it is necessary to travel quickly and on the spur of the moment in and out of Nantucket, Martha's Vineyard, or Cape Cod,

Ocean Wings may fit in with your personal demands. This company has a private hangar and offers flight instruction.

Falmouth Airpark
Fresh Pond Road, East Falmouth
(508) 548-9617
www.falmouthairpark.com

This one-runway airport is owned by the people who live around it in fact all the homes have hangars for their planes the way the rest of us have garages for our cars. The 2,400-foot paved airstrip is open to the public and charters. There is a wash-down station available.

Chatham Municipal Airport
George Ryder Road, West Chatham
(508) 945-9000

Chatham Municipal Airport has a 3,000-foot-long, 100-foot-wide paved runway with a grass strip running alongside. The airport is open to the public and offers sightseeing and biplane rides. There's a restaurant on-site as well as a full maintenance facility.

BY BUS

There are buses running nearly every hour to Cape Cod and around our peninsula. Buses are also a convenient way to take a day trip to Boston from Cape Cod if going in that direction interests you. The rates are quite affordable.

Plymouth & Brockton Bus Company and the Bonanza Bus Line provide hourly, scheduled motorcoach service between Logan Airport, downtown Boston, Providence, New York, Plymouth, and throughout Cape Cod.

To get to Hyannis from Boston, take the Plymouth & Brockton bus from Logan Airport or downtown Boston to Hyannis.

To get to Falmouth from Boston, take the Bonanza Bus Line from Logan Airport and downtown Boston to the Falmouth Bus Depot.

From points south to Cape Cod, take Bonanza Bus from New York, T. F. Green

International Airport (Rhode Island), downtown Providence, Fall River, and New Bedford to Hyannis.

The brand-new Hyannis Transportation Center (www.capecodtransit.org), located right off Main Street on Iyannough Road, had its first full season of operation in 2003. It is the home of the Breeze buses and shuttles of the Cape Cod Regional Transportation Authority (see descriptions below), the Plymouth & Brockton Buses, and Bonanza Buses. National and Alamo have rental cars available on-site, and you can book bicycles and taxis as well, or catch a shuttle to the ferry docks. The center also has a park-and-ride lot if you would like to ditch your automobile for a while.

The Cape is making a concerted effort to improve the practicality of their public transportation, which already offers low fares and friendly service. Various beach shuttles are especially useful for tourists who would rather not have to battle traffic every time they go to the beach on a sunny day. Routes are described in more detail below, or you may consult www.smartguide.com, a Web site that will give you the up-to-date skinny on all you need to know about car-free travel on the Cape.

Bonanza
1 Bonanza Way, Providence, Rhode Island (888) 751–8800
www.bonanzabus.com

Bonanza offers many daily trips from Boston to Bourne, Falmouth, and Woods Hole (you can hop a ferry from here to the islands). Connecting service to other points on the Cape is provided via the Plymouth & Brockton line, known locally as the P&B (see below). Bonanza runs seven days a week, 365 days a year, with some seven trips a day from Boston's Logan International Airport and another three a day from South Station (downtown Boston). Tickets from Logan Airport to Bourne run about $19 one-way and $34 round-trip. Bonanza has local terminals at the following locations: Tedeschi Food

Shop, 105 Trowbridge Road, Bourne, (888) 751–8800; Otis Air Base, Pocasset, Otis Traffic Circle, Route 28, (888) 751–8800; Steamship Authority, Woods Hole Wharf, Woods Hole, (508) 548–5011; Bonanza Terminal, 59 Depot Avenue, Falmouth, (508) 548–7588; Plymouth & Brockton Terminal, Hyannis Transportation Center, Hyannis, (800) 751–8800; and Town Wharf, Commercial Street, Provincetown.

Plymouth & Brockton Street Railway Company, Inc.
Plymouth & Brockton Bus Terminal, Hyannis Transportation Center, Hyannis (508) 746–0378
www.p-b.com

Plymouth & Brockton probably handles the most Cape travelers and commuters, as they service the entire U.S. Route 6

Don't be fooled when you see a bumper sticker that reads CAPE COD TUNNEL— RESIDENT'S PERMIT. *There is no such tunnel. It's a local joke first developed in 1994 to cash in on naïve tourists. Today there are three tunnel permit stickers in circulation that are almost identical and seen on vehicles throughout the Cape.*

---

stretch from Provincetown into Boston's South Station and on to Logan International Airport. From Logan Airport to Hyannis, a one-way ticket runs $18 and round-trip fare is $34; from South Station the prices are $14 and $27, respectively. Traveling all the way to Provincetown from Logan Airport costs $27; a round-trip ticket is $52. At Logan Airport your tickets may be purchased from the driver when boarding the bus. Reservations are not necessary. Ask about senior discounts. P&B also offers commuter books at about half the price of a normal fare. There are 12 bus stops on Cape Cod: Sagamore, Barnstable, Hyannis, Harwich, Orleans, Eastham, North Eastham, South Wellfleet, Wellfleet, Truro, North Truro, and Provincetown.

B-Bus
Hyannis Transportation Center, Hyannis
(508) 385-8326, (800) 352-7155
Unique to the Cape is the B-Bus, a fleet of 30 minivans that will transport you door to door between any towns on the Cape Monday through Friday (and on weekends in some towns). Call in advance, between 11:00 A.M. and 5:00 P.M., to schedule a ride. Fees will be discussed when you schedule, but they are generally quite low.

BY SHUTTLE

In the summertime, when the roads are busiest, several Cape towns offer shuttle rides to certain attractions, town centers, shopping centers, and area beaches. Passengers use them for plain old transportation and for sightseeing. You can flag one down at any point during a route, and you don't have to worry about getting tickets ahead of time because you can pay when you get on. All the shuttles we list below are run by the Cape Cod Regional Transit Authority, where you can also pick up a bus schedule. These are available at local chambers of commerce too. See our Tours and Excursions chapter for more details.

Cape Cod Regional Transit Authority
Hyannis Transportation Center,
Iyannough Road, Hyannis
(800) 352-7155
www.capecodtransit.org
The CCRTA operates a number of shuttles in various towns, including Falmouth, Hyannis, Yarmouth, and Provincetown. Fares start at $1.00 for adults, 50 cents for senior citizens and the disabled, and go up according to distance, with the highest fare only about $3.00. Most of the shuttles are seasonal, but two are year-round: the SeaLine between Hyannis and Falmouth, and the Villager in Hyannis, which goes to Barnstable Village and the Barnstable County Complex, and in the off-season makes stops at shopping areas on Route 132. Below we describe the shuttles run by the CCRTA.

Falmouth's Whoosh Trolley
(800) 352-7155
thebreeze.info
This ride takes in Main Street from the Falmouth Mall on Route 28 and goes right into Woods Hole, including the Woods Hole Steamship Authority, the aquarium, and the Shining Sea Bike Path. The service runs from Memorial Day weekend through the end of September, with two trolleys running seven days a week from June through Labor Day and limited service after that. The fare is $1.00, or 50 cents for senior citizens, people with disabilities, and youths 6 to 17. Children 5 and younger, when accompanied by an adult, ride for free. One-day $3.00 shuttle passes are available.

The Barnstable Villager
(800) 352-7155
thebreeze.info
Starting at the Hyannis Transportation Center, this year-round shuttle travels to Barnstable Village and to the Barnstable County Complex. It makes stops at the Cape Cod Mall (see our Shopping chapter) and other shopping areas on Route 132 in downtown Hyannis. It also goes to Barnstable Harbor, where passengers can catch a whale-watching boat (see our Whale-Watching chapter) and stops at the Barnstable Municipal Airport.

Hyannis Area Shuttles
(800) 352-7155
thebreeze.info
The Hyannis Beaches Breeze and the Hyannis Villager service the Hyannis area. The Beaches Breeze shuttle circulates through the downtown area, the ferry docks, and Kalmus and Veterans Beach. The Villager circulates through downtown and out to the Star Market.

SeaLine Breeze
(800) 352-7155
thebreeze.info
A year-round bus service, the SeaLine runs between Hyannis and Falmouth, connecting with the Whoosh Trolley in sum-

mer and taking over the Woods Hole route when the Whoosh is not running. It makes stops in Centerville, Osterville, Marstons Mills, Mashpee Commons, Falmouth, and Woods Hole.

Yarmouth Breeze
(800) 352-7155
thebreeze.info

This shuttle leaves the Hyannis Transportation Center and travels along Route 28 through Yarmouth to Seagull and Smugglers Beach.

H2O Breeze
(800) 352-7155
thebreeze.info

Instituted in 1996, this minibus runs down Route 28 from Hyannis to Orleans. It runs six trips a day all year, increasing to hourly trips in summer, and you can get on at regular stops or just flag the driver down! The entire round-trip ride takes an hour or so one-way.

Provincetown Shuttle
(800) 352-7155
thebreeze.info

This is the most popular shuttle service on the Cape. It runs from the campgrounds in North Truro to Provincetown and Herring Cove Beach.

BY BICYCLE

Cycling is a popular way to get around Cape Cod, especially in summer. One advantage is that the terrain is relatively flat. You can pedal through villages and towns or get away from vehicular traffic by taking one of the Cape's pretty bike trails (see our Biking section in the Hiking and Biking Trails chapter). The 25-mile Cape Cod Rail Trail, which follows the old rail beds, runs from Dennis to Wellfleet and goes through Nickerson State Park. The Cape has dozens of bicycle rental businesses that can put you on two

wheels; you can get mountain bikes, kid trailers, even bicycles built for two. Most bike rental places also sell bicycles, accessories, and parts, in addition to renting equipment such as helmets and child passenger seats.

Bicycling is a must on the islands during the summer, as well as in some towns on the Cape. The roads can get clogged, often bringing traffic to a standstill, especially on weekends and during special events. Falmouth, Chatham, and especially Provincetown are ideal for biking around, saving you the headache of finding a parking space.

BY RAIL

Years ago rail was the most common way to get to the Cape and to your town of choice. Today, sadly, rail service is all but gone after Amtrak eliminated the famous Cape Codder line. At this writing there are no plans to revive it. On the bright side the old rail beds from Dennis to Wellfleet have been converted into a great bike trail! (See the By Bicycle section, above, and our Hiking and Biking Trails chapter.) Also, a remnant of the old Cape Codder line that runs from Hyannis to Sandwich has been used in the past by the Cape Cod Railroad for sightseeing trips with a dining car (see our Tours and Excursions chapter); it is a lovely ride that winds through cranberry bogs and woodlands through the untouched center of the Cape.

BY BOAT

We've saved the best until last. Traveling to the Cape on the water may be the most relaxing way to get here. Several ferry companies offer fast, reliable transportation between various ports to the Cape and islands. It is important to make a reservation, especially if you plan on crossing with your car, because ferries get booked during peak season months in advance. Summer reservations, for example, are often booked by early winter of the preceding year. There are last-minute cancellations, but be prepared to wait for hours. (Don't forget to book your return reservation as well.) All island-bound ferries offer sufficient pay-per-day parking.

The Steamship Authority
Woods Hole Wharf, Woods Hole
(508) 693-9130, (508) 477-8600
www.steamshipauthority.com
The Steamship Authority is the only company offering year-round ferry service from Woods Hole and New Bedford to points on Martha's Vineyard, and from Hyannis to Nantucket. It's also the only ferry that transports cars. Keep in mind that taking your car to the islands can be very expensive, and it's usually not necessary because you can rent one upon your arrival. Better yet rent a bicycle or moped (see our Martha's Vineyard and Nantucket chapters). We advise you to check the schedule for boat departures as they change seasonally. The one-way fare from Woods Hole to Martha's Vineyard is $5.50 for adults, $2.75 for children ages 5 to 12, and free for children younger than 5. Ferry service from New Bedford costs $10.00 one-way for adults; ages 5 to 12 are $5.00. Ferry service from Hyannis to Nantucket costs $13 one-way. The Steamship Authority also offers a Fast Ferry to Nantucket from Hyannis and the cost is $26 round trip.

Island Queen
75 Falmouth Heights Road, Falmouth
(508) 548-4800
www.islandqueen.com

Even if you're taking a ferry ride on an overcast day, be sure to wear layers and sunscreen. Even if you can't see the sun, you could be burned by the glare off the water—and the wind is certain to be chillier than it is on shore.

For $10.00 round-trip ($5.00 for children), you can take the 600-passenger *Island Queen* from Falmouth Harbor to Martha's Vineyard from Memorial Day weekend to Columbus Day. The trip is a leisurely 35 minutes each way, and food service is available on board, along with a full bar. The passenger-only vessel makes seven trips each day in summer, and reservations are not needed. The *Island Queen* is also available for charters.

Hy-Line Cruises
Ocean Street Dock, Hyannis
(508) 778-2600, (888) 778-1132
www.hy-linecruises.com
Hy-Line offers the only service between Hyannis and Martha's Vineyard from early May through late October. The trip takes about an hour and a half, with scheduled departures throughout the day, seven days a week. A round-trip fare for Hyannis to Martha's Vineyard costs $27.00 for adults and $13.50 for children ages 5 to 12. The company also services the Hyannis to Nantucket route and offers interisland service between Nantucket and Martha's Vineyard. It takes less than two hours to journey by ferry from Hyannis to Nantucket. Fare is $27.00 for adults and $13.50 for children. Hy-Line's High Speed Ferry, the *Grey Lady,* makes the crossing from Hyannis to Nantucket in about an hour, and a round-trip ticket costs $58 for passengers 12 and older and $41 for children ages 5 to 12. It's a good idea to call ahead for reservations, especially if you plan to travel during a holiday weekend or during July and August. Ferries leave from Dock One, Ocean Street, Hyannis.

Freedom Cruise Line
Route 28, Harwichport
(508) 432-8999
www.nantucketislandferry.com
Sailing from Saquatucket Harbor in Harwichport, Freedom Cruise Line offers daily passenger service to Nantucket, and you can bring along your bicycle and pet too. The trip takes about one and a half hours,

The Island Queen *runs seasonal service between Falmouth and Martha's Vineyard.*
ISLAND COMMUTER CORP.

and round-trip fare is $46 for adults and $37 for children; one-way fare is $29 for adults and $25 for children. Bicycles are $10 round-trip. *Freedom* is an 80-passenger ferry, so reservations are strongly advised. There are also restrictions on how many "overnighters" the line can leave overnight on the island, so reservations are necessary. There is free parking for day-trippers.

Bay State Cruise Company
Pier at the World Trade Center, Seaport Boulevard, Boston
(508) 487-9284, (617) 748-1428
www.baystatecruises.com

Bay State Cruises offers two flavors of ferry service from Boston to Province-town: fast and fun, or leisurely and fun. Choose the *Provincetown Express* if you are headed to P'town for, say, the week-end, and you'd rather unwind from the week on a smooth-sailing catamaran than on the interstate. The *Provincetown*

Express offers three daily departures. Stake out a spot on the enclosed lower deck with comfortable, climate-controlled seating, or choose the open upper deck (with windscreen) for those who want a taste of the sea breeze. Sailing time is 90 minutes to Provincetown. Those who think that getting there is half the fun might opt for the *Provincetown II*. It's Boston's largest passenger cruise ship and tries to evoke the grandeur of days of yore. Relax on the sundeck for the three-hour cruise while you plan the rest of your day in Provincetown. You'll have three-and-a-half hours to explore Provincetown if you just want a day trip, or you can buy one-way passage. Round-trip fares aboard the *Provincetown Express* are $55 for adults, $50 for seniors, $45 for children, and $10 for bicycles. Aboard the *Provincetown II,* round-trip fares are $29 for adults, $23 for seniors, $19 for children, and $10 for bicycles.

Captain John Boat Lines
State Pier, off Water Street, Plymouth
(508) 747–2400, (800) 242–2469
www.provincetownferry.com

If you can only spare time for a day trip, but you don't want to spend half of your time in the car, this seasonal day-trip service from Plymouth to Provincetown may be perfect for you. Leave the State Pier in Plymouth and enjoy a narrated tour of the harbor, breakfast or drinks, and a one-and-a-half hour sail across the bay. Once there, you are set free for four-and-a-half hours of exploring Provincetown. You can't bring your car on the boat, but you can bring your bicycle along for $3.00. They offer one trip daily from mid-June through August. It leaves Plymouth at 10:00 A.M. and returns at 6:00 P.M. Round-trip fare for adults is $30, seniors are $25, and children under 12 are $20.

Falmouth-Edgartown Ferry
278 Scranton Avenue, Falmouth
(508) 548–9400
www.falmouthferry.com

As the name implies this ferry will take you directly to Edgartown (most ferry service takes you to Oak Bluffs or Vineyard Haven). Sailing time aboard the *Pied Piper* is roughly one hour. They offer five round-trips daily, with six on Friday. Round-trip fares are $30.00 for adults, $24.00 for children younger than 12, and $8.00 for bicycles. There is a $14.00 per day parking charge. Reservations are required.

Vineyard Fast Ferry
Roger Williams Way, Quonset Point,
Rhode Island
(401) 295–4040
www.vineyardfastferry.com

If you're headed directly to Martha's Vineyard and would like nothing more than to avoid traffic congestion on the Cape, look into this seasonal fast-ferry service that debuted in 2003. It's ideal for vacationers coming from southern New England who would rather spend ninety minutes making the trip by water than waiting for hours in traffic. The dock at Quonset Point is roughly 15 miles from T. F. Green International Airport in Providence, Rhode Island, 15 miles from the Amtrak terminal in Kingston, Rhode Island, and about eight minutes from I–95. You'll ride aboard *The Millennium*, a 128-foot, high-speed, three deck catamaran. Two daily round-trips are scheduled for Monday through Thursday, three for Friday through Sunday. Round-trip fares are $48.00 for adults, $36.00 for children, and $8.00 for bikes for the ninety-minute trip from Quonset to Oak Bluffs. There is an $8.00-per-day charge to park your car. Reservations are strongly recommended.

[Facing page] *Treat yourself to an out-of-car experience by leaving your vehicle behind when traveling to the islands.* HYANNIS AREA CHAMBER OF COMMERCE

HISTORIC CAPE COD

Open the pages of any American history book, and you will read the Cape's story, from the Viking explorations on these shores nearly one thousand years ago to the landing of the Pilgrims in Provincetown in 1620. We read of the first Thanksgiving when a peace treaty was signed between the Wampanoag tribe and Plymouth Governor John Carver, and the Pilgrims gave thanks for their first year in the New World. Here, on this curved sandbar, the seeds of democracy were sown when the Pilgrims, anchored in Provincetown Harbor, signed a precursor to the constitution, the Mayflower Compact.

The Pilgrims were actually headed for the northern Virginia territory, which at the time stretched up to near the Hudson River, before they were forced to steer northward by ocean storms.

Cape Cod has come to occupy a unique niche in our nation's consciousness. The Cape's harbors resonate with salty tales of sea captains and whaling merchants, pirates and moon-cussers. Well-known nature writers such as Henry David Thoreau, John Hay, and Henry Beston have described the wonder and mystery of the Cape's natural beauty and its changing seasons. And the glamour and controversy of the Kennedy era, of Hyannisport and Chappaquiddick, have added to its allure.

The old times may have gone, but the legacy of Cape Cod remains and is visible no matter where you turn. Stop by any town meeting, and you will see that the

Cape's history is of paramount importance to the Cape Codders who continue to fight for their identity, their independence, and the preservation of the Cape's natural environment and recognition of its unique heritage.

PEOPLE OF THE FIRST LIGHT

The history of the Wampanoag Indians—the word Wampanoag means "People of the dawn or first light"—dates well before Western explorers set foot on these sandy shores. Some theories suggest that their ancestors traveled from Asia to North America via the Bering Strait at the end of the ice age. Others, because there is no linguistic link, dispel that idea. The best guess is that Native American Indians arrived upon this newly formed land about 10,000 years ago to settle in this area. We do know that somewhere between 7,000 and 9,000 years ago, a small band of Native Americans came to the eastern shore of the Upper Mill Pond in Brewster. In 1987 archaeologist Fred Dunford from the Cape Cod Museum of Natural History uncovered artifacts at this prehistoric archaeological site that have placed the native inhabitants in the Stony Brook Valley firmly within what is called the Middle Archaic Period. An exhibit at the museum displays the artifacts recovered during the field research.

Ancestors of the present-day Mashpee Wampanoag were Algonquin-speaking people who shared cultural traditions with a number of groups in southern New England under the name of Massachusetts-Narragansett. As members of the Algonquin

---

[Facing page] *This statue of Iyanough, Hyannis's namesake, sits on the Hyannis Village Green.*
HYANNIS AREA CHAMBER OF COMMERCE

Indian Nation, the Wampanoag Indians of the Cape were broken down into five major tribes: Nausets of the Lower Cape; South Sea in the Barnstable and Mashpee areas; Suconessets of Falmouth; Shaumes of Sandwich; and the Manamets in the Bourne and Sagamore areas. These tribes were further broken down into subtribes, such as the Nobscusset Indians of Dennis, who were members of the Nauset tribe.

THE VIKINGS

There are many tales of Norse explorers arriving in this area beginning more than a thousand years ago, but there has yet to be definitive proof of such exploration. One such legend tells that Norsemen visited the Cape and islands around A.D. 986, though they did not make landfall. Bjarni Herjulfsson was the little-known explorer who made the journey, and if the story is true, then he discovered America about 500 years before Columbus. Upon his return to his native Iceland, Herjulfsson told his story, and it became incorporated into Norse lore to be retold for years to come. One of those listening to the tales was Leif Ericson, son of Eric the Red. Around the year 1000, Leif borrowed his father's ship and sailed south, past Newfoundland and Nova Scotia, to arrive at what some historians believe was Cape Cod. The story goes that he sailed his vessel up a river that flowed in two directions, possibly Bass River, and made his camp at an inland lake where he could anchor his vessel, possibly Follins Pond at the head of Bass River in Yarmouth/Dennis. Despite these explorations, however, Native Americans were the sole inhabitants of the area until the 1600s.

The first recorded description of these people was provided by Giovanni di Verrazzano, who, in 1524, spent several weeks exploring the area between Block Island and Buzzards Bay. Verrazzano described the people as being handsome, well dressed, and friendly. "These people are the most beautiful and have the most civil customs that we have found on this voyage," writes Verrazzano. "They are very generous and give away all they have. We made great friends with them and they painted and decorated their faces with various colors, showing us that it was a sign of happiness."

OTHER EARLY EXPLORERS

The year 1602 saw a sail on the horizon, growing larger as it approached, a sail that represented the first of many to arrive along these shores over the next decades. The English explorer Bartholomew Gosnold landed at a number of places along the Cape and islands and discovered the treacherous shoals that guarded the easternmost section of the Cape. Gosnold and his crew chose one of the Elizabeth Islands off Woods Hole to establish a settlement, but it failed shortly thereafter. He noted that game, fish, and berries were plentiful, and they traded with Native Americans for tobacco, deerskins, and fish.

By far the most complete description of Indian life on the Cape comes from the journal of Samuel de Champlain, who in 1606 paid an extended visit to the area. He sailed along the coast approaching Cape Cod from the north and followed the shoreline, recording the depth of the bays and the features of the land, finally anchoring in Stage Harbor, Chatham. It seems that Champlain felt less admiration for the Native Americans because his party had several conflicts with the natives, resulting in the death of at least one sailor. The damage done, Champlain and crew departed to explore other parts of North America. For years afterward other notable explorers such as Henry Hudson and John Smith avoided these shores, probably because tales of the battle at Stage Harbor had no doubt circulated.

THE PILGRIMS

It was not until November 1620 that European explorers would try again to settle this virgin outpost. This was the month when the *Mayflower* arrived in Provincetown Harbor. The ship had been headed for Virginia, but had been blown off course and had landed well north of its intended destination. We call the voyagers Pilgrims, but they called themselves Separatists. The religious movement that brought them to American began in 14th-century England and was based on the premise that no man needed a priest between himself and God, no person should be involved in ritualistic worship, and everyone was under the obligation to lead his life as simply as possible.

The way the Pilgrims recounted their voyage, after their ship encountered the dangerous shoals off the coast of Cape Cod, they rounded the tip to the north and entered the safe haven of Cape Cod Bay. After the *Mayflower* anchored in Provincetown Harbor and before explorations were initiated, the Mayflower Compact, a charter for a democratic settlement, was signed on board on November 11, 1620. Led by Captain Myles Standish, a group explored the surrounding coast and voyaged southward, eventually coming ashore across the bay on the sand flats of Eastham where they first encountered Indians. Today the beach is still called First Encounter Beach to signify the spot where shots were fired and arrows launched. The Pilgrims rejected Provincetown as a place to settle because, despite the vast harbor, there was no readily available fresh water. They traveled across Cape Cod Bay as far as Plymouth, where they found a protected harbor with high ground overlooking it, suitable for a permanent settlement.

Most versions of American history start with the Pilgrims' arrival at Plymouth Rock on Christmas Day in 1620. But the hostile greeting they received from the Indians near Eastham suggests an earlier activity in the area: It's thought that the Indians were retaliating, presumably for the Pilgrims' previous pilfering of their corn reserves at a site in Truro that

Three Mayflower *passengers lie in Eastham's Old Cove Cemetery, located about a mile north of the Orleans-Eastham rotary on U.S. Route 6. The graveyard is on the right just after Shore Road. Here you can see legible gravestones dating from the 1700s. Gravestone rubbing is not permitted without permission of the Eastham Historical Society. Call (508) 255-8725.*

today is known as Corn Hill. One thing we do know: The Pilgrims would return to Cape Cod again and again. Many of these early settlers were instrumental in preparing the way for the settlement of a number of the earliest towns in Sandwich and, more specifically, Eastham. Each of these towns would develop its own independent history, carving out its own niche in the growth of Cape Cod. Meanwhile the Native American Indians were a race already in decline. Epidemics of smallpox, introduced just three or four years before the arrival of the Pilgrims by other exploring groups, had reduced their ranks considerably. Ignorant of the laws of the new settlers, these natives unwittingly handed over large tracts of land for a pittance, not realizing their mark on the white man's strange parchment was legal and binding.

Religion played a large role in the settlement of the different towns. Though most of the earliest settlers were Congregationalists, there were also Quakers among them, and later Methodists and Baptists. Though these settlers left other places to land here in search of religious freedom, many off them found themselves embroiled in the same old religious arguments. And when the settlers were not arguing about religion, they were squabbling over land and where one person's property ended and another's began. With the building of a meetinghouse and the hiring of a minister to preach, a handful of families

CLOSE-UP

The Cape Cod Canal

When William Bradford and Myles Standish were exploring the area around Plymouth in 1626, they discovered that two rivers, the Manomet on Buzzards Bay and the Scusset on Cape Cod Bay, were separated by only a short distance of land. The Pilgrims realized the advantage to trade and transportation of digging a canal that would connect the two bodies of water; however, the idea was not acted upon. In 1776 General George Washington, hoping to avoid a British blockade and to enhance security, sent an engineer to conduct the first feasible study of the area, but still no canal was constructed.

Well into the late 1800s, attempts to organize this mammoth construction project continued to be thwarted until 1904, when New York financier Augustus Belmont considered the project. He purchased the Boston, Cape Cod and New York Canal Company. By July 1907 his newly formed Cape Cod Construction Company moved its first shovelful of dirt, and digging was under way. Over the

next seven years, the men and machinery removed earth. In 1912 two large dredges began digging toward each other from Bourne and Sandwich.

Workers completed the Buzzards Bay Railroad Bridge in September 1910 and finished the two vehicle bridges within the next two years. The finished canal became the world's widest sea-level canal at 480 feet across. It was 17.4 miles long and 34 feet deep. On July 29, 1914, exactly seven years to the day since work first began, the Cape Cod Canal officially opened, heralded by a parade of ships and boats, among them Augustus Belmont's private 80-foot yacht and the U.S. Navy destroyer *McDougall,* which carried Assistant Secretary of the Navy Franklin Delano Roosevelt. The Cape Cod Canal beat the opening of the Panama Canal by 17 days.

In 1915 canal traffic numbered more than 2,600 vessels, but it never achieved the volume of traffic that Belmont had hoped for. When a German submarine

would form an application for incorporation. The church spurred incorporation, and incorporation spurred more settlers, and thus the towns were born and grew and prospered.

The Cape has more than three-and-a-half centuries of documented history. Each of the 15 towns displays its history like a treasured heirloom. Cemeteries, old churches, historic dwellings, and museums all help to preserve and illuminate Cape Cod's colorful history.

UPPER CAPE

Bourne

It was in Bourne that the Pilgrims established their first trading post in 1627. In a paradox of sorts, this township holds the unique position of being both the oldest and yet the newest town on the Cape. Originally settled as part of Sandwich (established 1687), the present town of Bourne was incorporated in 1884 when it

attacked and sank the *Perth Amboy* off Nauset Beach in Orleans, President Woodrow Wilson ordered a readily compliant Belmont to permit the government to operate the canal. Eventually Belmont sold the canal to the American government for $11.5 million, and the Army Corps of Engineers took charge of its operation and maintenance. Although the canal was technically a success, it never brought the commercial prosperity to Upper Cape towns that its planners anticipated.

During the Great Depression the National Industrial Recovery Act of 1933 provided $4.6 million to build the present three bridges, employing some 700 workers for two years. These modern bridges were completed in 1935. The Bourne and Sagamore Bridges, with a span of 616 feet, became among the longest continuous truss bridges in North America. The railroad bridge, at 544 feet, remains the third-longest vertical-lift drawbridge on the continent. You can admire the workmanship of the bridges from the 7-mile paved service road that lines both sides of the canal.

If you are taking a boat ride through the Cape Cod Canal, you'll move along at a good clip in the direction of the tide but seem to be fighting an uphill battle when you go against it. One reason for this is that Cape Cod Bay waters are about 5 feet higher than Buzzards Bay waters, so a tremendous current is created as they merge and flow through the narrow passageway. Average high-tide waters move through the canal at 4 to 5 miles per hour. When high tides are accentuated by a full moon or other conditions, the water's speed can reach more than 7 miles per hour.

If you'd like to learn more about the canal, take a tour of the Corps of Engineers headquarters at Taylors Point in Buzzards Bay (508-759-4431), or stop by the visitor center on the Cranberry Highway. If you wish to read about the canal, we recommend *The Cape Cod Canal* by Robert Farson.

broke away from Sandwich after some two-and-a-half centuries of dissension. It is named for Jonathan Bourne, a prominent citizen who made his fortune and reputation in the whaling industry.

A largely agricultural and fishing community, Bourne's motions for separation from Sandwich never seemed to pass at town meetings, so aggrieved citizens in the outlying villages petitioned the state legislature. Because these areas attracted prominent summer visitors

from New York, New Jersey, and Boston, there was no lack of advice and perhaps influence. When the towns separated, Sandwich lost its warm-water coast, harbors, shellfish beds on Buzzards Bay, and a number of industries, such as Keith & Ryder, which made stagecoaches and railroad cars.

One of the most important events of Bourne history was the building of the Cape Cod Canal and the Bourne Bridge, which spans this man-made waterway.

The idea of building a canal was first raised by Governor William Bradford of Plymouth. He had noticed that the Manomet River from the south and Scusset Creek from the north nearly cut through the neck of the peninsula of Cape Cod. Indeed local Indians took advantage of these waterways to traverse the Cape, carrying their canoes the short distance in between the two rivers. In 1627 the Plymouth settlers established Aptucxet Trading Post on the banks of the Manomet River for the purpose of trading with the Dutch from New Amsterdam (New York) to the south as well as with Indians in the area. The trading post was closed in the late 1650s (see our Attractions chapter for more information), but the idea of a canal resurfaced again and again. General Washington inquired about such a waterway during the American Revolution. The building of a canal would make the trip from New York to Boston by sea so much quicker and safer: A huge number of ships were shipwrecked around the treacherous shores of Cape Cod and the islands. Various plans were presented throughout the 19th century, but it was not until the early 20th century that shovel moved dirt and the canal was dug. (See the Close-up on the canal in this chapter.)

Like most Cape towns, Bourne consisted mostly of farmers and fishermen in the early years and, in the 19th century, industrial workers, who labored at grist and flour mills, a comb and button factory, and lumbering. Trade necessitated transportation, and the coming of the railroad to Buzzards Bay in the 19th century spawned a tourist industry that still thrives today, though the railroad in now defunct. The villages of Bourne were popular with wealthy people who summered here and built handsome estates along the beautiful shore. President Grover Cleveland purchased a summer house called Gray Gables, where he would come to relax and escape the pressures of Washington. Cleveland was an avid sportsman and loved hunting and fishing on the Cape

with his good friend, renowned 19th-century actor Joseph Jefferson, who owned a summer home on Buttermilk Bay called the Crow's Nest.

Sandwich

The very first of Cape Cod's 15 towns to be incorporated was Sandwich, settled in 1637, when permission was granted to Edmund Freeman of Saugus to establish a settlement comprising 60 families. In that year Freeman and nine other men from Saugus (now Lynn, Massachusetts, a city north of Boston) arrived to tame this area known as Manomet, which was close to the Aptucxet Trading Post in what is now the town of Bourne. These 10 men became known as the "10 men of Saugus" and were joined by some 30 other families from Plymouth, Lynn, and Duxbury.

Pilgrims Myles Standish and John Alden journeyed down from Plymouth in 1639 to establish the bounds of this growing settlement. The town became incorporated with the name of Sandwich because a number of its residents had originally come from Sandwich, England. At that time the new township of Sandwich also included all the land that would later become Bourne.

The first settlers were largely Congregationalists, but Quakers came to town shortly afterward, seeking converts. Some settlers did convert, but the Quakers were persecuted in town, and many left for other parts. Pockets of Quakers remained in Sandwich, however, to take their place in the town's history, and are still there.

The earliest settlers were chiefly farmers who also raised cattle and sheep. Because Sandwich lacked an adequate harbor, the maritime history of the town was limited to local fishing and reaping the harvest of the occasional beached whale. Local sailors and ship captains typically sailed from ports of other towns, such as neighboring Barnstable and Falmouth, each of which had decent harbors.

Sandwich did contribute with its share of saltworks, but the town remained mainly a farming community, earning its living from the soil rather than from the sea.

The 19th century brought change and unthinkable prosperity to Sandwich. In 1825 Deming Jarves established the Boston and Sandwich Glass Works, which he figured would utilize two of Sandwich's more abundant natural resources: sand and trees. Unfortunately the sand was found to be the wrong type for producing the glass Jarves had in mind. Sand had to be imported to Sandwich! By 1850 the plant employed 500 workers and was producing a half-ton of glassware each week. Besides standard glassware, the company also created artistic pieces. Jarves enticed some of the world's greatest glassmakers to relocate from Europe to Sandwich to fashion these intricate, decorative works of art.

The same year glassmaking came to Sandwich, Keith & Ryder opened for business to produce wagons, stagecoaches, and, later, railroad freight trains. This highly successful company remained in business for 102 years, employed many Sandwich residents, and produced the vehicles that helped America expand westward.

The decade of the 1880s saw Sandwich's future grow dim. In 1884 Bourne and her six villages separated from Sandwich, taking away residential tax dollars as well as the Keith & Ryder company. Four years later, in 1888, the major blow came when the glass company closed its doors because of competition. People were out of work, and Sandwich's economy crumbled. The ripple effect closed local businesses, which in turn put more people out of work, thus closing more businesses. A number of people moved away to start again elsewhere.

Fortunately Sandwich has survived intact and remains a charming village that attracts many visitors with its numerous historical buildings. Visitors also come to see the Sandwich Glass Museum (see our Attractions chapter), which traces the history of the town's glassworks and displays one of the largest collections of blown, pressed, cut, and engraved Sandwich glass in the United States.

Falmouth

Falmouth was officially settled in 1660 by a dozen families led by Isaac Robinson and John Hatch, both Barnstable Congregationalists fed up with the religious persecutions of the day, particularly of Quakers. The original name for this area was the Indian term Suckanesset, or Succonessitt, which translated as "black clam" or "the place of the black shells." In 1690 the town was renamed Falmouth after an English seaport.

Falmouth was the site of a handful of small battles with the British during both the American Revolutionary War and the War of 1812, and in each case the Falmouth men prevailed. During the American Revolution Falmouth was one of the few Cape towns fired on by the British. In 1779 the British attempted to loot the town of its supplies and weaponry, but their advances were repelled. Frustrated, the British decided to teach the Falmouth patriots a lesson by burning their town. The marauders were met by 200 members of the Cape militia who prevented an attack. One year earlier the waters off Falmouth saw perhaps the first naval victory in American history. The British had been off shore capturing Falmouth ships, ransacking them, and confiscating their supplies. Colonel Joseph Dimmick, who had been training the Falmouth militia on the village green, took three whaleboats out against the British navy and won back a schooner that the British had hijacked earlier!

During another war, in 1814, the British ship *Nimrod* sailed into waters off Falmouth. Its captain demanded that the town's cannons, which were positioned in the village square, be handed over. Captain Weston Jenkins of the Falmouth militia flatly refused to comply, and the pages of history state that his reply to the British was, "Come and get 'em!" This, of course, prompted heavy fire, and a number of buildings in town were hit, including the Elm Arch Inn and the Nimrod Inn. Both establishments proudly wear their battle scars today—a cannonball-sized hole still exists in a wall at the Nimrod Inn.

The town was ideally suited to fishing and farming and a whaling fleet was based in Woods Hole, where there remains a stone building on Water Street once used to make candles from sperma- ceti whale oil. Shipbuilding was an impor- tant maritime trade, and at one point Falmouth's 300 households included 148 headed by sea captains.

Agriculture thrived here, and cran- berries and strawberries were leading crops. In fact around the turn of the 20th century, the Town of Falmouth was the leading producer of strawberries east of the Mississippi. (Many Cape Verdeans who had come from the Por- tuguese islands off the coast of Africa to work in the fishing and whaling industry sought agricultural work here and even- tually bought land and settled in the area.) Salt harvested from seawater was also an important "crop."

Falmouth set aside its village green in 1749 as common land for the town's 600 residents. Once used for grazing livestock and military training, the expanse now adds charm as well as its proud history to the town.

Across the street from the village green is the First Congregational Church, built in 1708. Its 807-pound bell was made by Paul Revere and cost the town of Fal- mouth $338.94. Falmouth is also home to Nobska Light, built in 1828; Marine Biologi- cal Laboratory, established in 1888; and Woods Hole Oceanographic Institute, established in the late 1930s.

Mashpee

The history of Mashpee reflects the white man's attempt to allow the Native Indians

of the area to "own" their own village and manage their own affairs. Though these intentions were probably good ones, in truth it is a tale of one race of people try- ing to decide what another race wants. The results, though not completely disas- trous, were at best off the mark.

Centuries before the Pilgrims landed in Provincetown, the Wampanoag Federa- tion was well established in southeastern Massachusetts. The federation consisted of approximately 30 tribes of peaceful people who had a complex social struc- ture. These native Indians grew crops, hunted, fished, traded amongst them- selves, and pretty much lived without war, religious persecution, economic and social hardships, and the other trappings that troubled the European settlers' lives. Among these people the Massipees of the South Sea tribe lived in the vicinity of the present town of Mashpee.

The town's history is complex and very different from the other 15 Cape towns because it is the only one in which native people acquired legal title to their lands. As white settlers began to hoodwink the Indians out of their native lands, three men stepped forward as missionary minis- ters to level the playing field. Those men were Samuel Treat in Eastham, Thomas Tupper in Bourne, and Richard Bourne in Mashpee. Though not an ordained minis- ter, Bourne arrived in Mashpee in 1660 in an attempt to convert the natives to Christianity and to establish a native Indian church. Bourne had the back- ground, contacts, and desire to help native people establish the "Kingdome of Marshpee." He realized early on that the only way to gain rights for the Indians was to get them to adopt some of the white man's ways, primarily the church and an understanding of their law.

The year 1684 saw the building of the present Indian Meeting House (see the Attractions chapter), now standing as the Cape's oldest church. In 1685, the year of Bourne's death, the General Court voted that no property within the plantation could be sold without the consent of the native residents. Despite this, the Native Americans were not prepared for self-government within an essentially foreign society, and the overseer system imposed by Plymouth virtually made the natives slaves on their own lands. In the 1700s the tribe numbers dropped critically. In 1767 the area had 21 shingled homes, 52 wigwams, and 291 people; 100 years later, the population stood at 331 people. During the American Revolution 70 Mashpee Indians were killed fighting against the British.

Throughout the remainder of the 18th and 19th centuries, the town of Mashpee sought its freedom from the oversight of Plymouth. Assisting in that cause were Indian pastors Blind Joe Amos and William Apes. In 1834 the district of Mashpee was established, but the overseer system remained in effect. Immigration in the form of blacks, natives of the Cape Verde Islands off the coast of Africa, and even captured Hessian soldiers who had fought with the British in the American Revolution added to the bloodlines and began to reduce the numbers of pure-bred Indians. Finally, in 1870, Mashpee was incorporated as the Cape's 14th town.

Freedom was still something to be achieved, even with the incorporation. Advisory boards, convinced that the natives could not manage their affairs, continued to meddle. The last of these advisory councils finally released its grip in 1970, during the year marking the town's centennial celebration. Recent years have seen legal suits initiated by the Town of Mashpee as well as the Wampanoag Tribal Council, coupled with unprecedented development, the most of any town in the state for several consecutive years. Today the Mashpee Wampanoags continue to advocate for their rights and are currently seeking federal recognition.

Its Indian heritage is still solidly a part of Mashpee, and those who want to learn about it can visit the Indian Museum and Tribal Council on Route 130, the Indian church and cemetery on Route 28, and the town archives on Great Neck Road. Or you can attend the Pow Wow in July (see our Annual Events chapter). Plimouth Plantation in Plymouth is also a good source of information on the culture of the Wampanoag people.

i

The town of Mashpee was originally set aside by the Plymouth Colony as an Indian village and designated as a plantation for the Wampanoag Indians displaced by the settlers building towns on their ancestral lands. Today you can visit the Archives Building, home of the Mashpee Historical Commission. For more information, contact the Mashpee Chamber of Commerce at (508) 477-0792.

MID-CAPE

Barnstable

Barnstable was one of the first three towns settled on the Cape, incorporated in 1639 along with Sandwich and Yarmouth. Named for Barnstaple, England (the colonists were not known for their spelling), the town's many place names actually reflect the early presence of Native Americans of various tribes. The villages of Cotuit, Cummaquid, and Hyannis can trace their names to Indian roots. Hyannis, for example, is named for Iyanough (also spelled Iyannough, or Iyanno, or a number of other ways), the Cummaquid sachem who extended kind hospitality to early settlers. His grave, off Route 6A in Cummaquid along the north shore of Barnstable, is marked (look for the sign), and a bronze statue of him stands at the village green on Main Street in Hyannis, as it rightly should.

Another statue in town is of statesman and patriot James Otis Jr. It stands in front of the Barnstable County Court-

IN THIS CEMETERY LIE
THE MORTAL REMAINS
OF
CAPT. JOHN PERCIVAL
KNOWN AS 'MAD JACK'
BORN APR. 3, 1779
DIED SEPT. 17, 1862

IN COMMAND OF
'OLD IRONSIDES'
ON 52,279 MILE VOYAGE
AROUND THE WORLD
1844 — 1846

BARNSTABLE TERCENTENARY 19

house on Route 6A in Barnstable Village, in sharp contrast to the statue of Iyannough in the southern village. Though each man came from the same land, they lived in two entirely different worlds. The relationship between these two cultures was summarized well by local historian Donald Trayser, who observed, "Fear of the Indians was natural, but on the Cape unjustified." How true, for even during the King Philip War of 1676–77, which saw Massachusetts and Rhode Island Indians fighting against white settlers, relations between white settlers and the Cape Indians remained friendly.

Though the first white man to settle in the area was a parson, John Hull of Weymouth, Massachusetts, the founding of Barnstable in 1639 is credited to the Reverend John Lothrop, a Congregational minister who had been persecuted and imprisoned in England before emigrating to America with 25 followers. The group originally settled in Scituate, and within five years moved to Barnstable, then known as Mattakeese, where the vast salt marshes at Great Marsh offered unlimited food and bedding for livestock. The settlement originally stretched as far west as to include Falmouth. The southern part of the town was settled in 1660, in the area of the village of Hyannis. In 1685 the county of Barnstable was established with the town of Barnstable serving as the county seat. At the point of the town's bicentennial celebration in 1839, there were 4,000 residents. Imagine, a bicentennial in 1839 when there were 24 states still to be admitted to the Union!

Along Route 6A in Barnstable Village you can view a historic marker at Sacrament Rock, the site of the first communion served by Reverend Lothrop to his congregation. Unfortunately the historic rock was dynamited to make way for Route 6A but it has been cemented back together complete with a plaque telling of the history and relocated on the side of the road in Barnstable Village. Not far away is Lothrop Cemetery, where the good reverend's remains became one with the earth many years ago.

Another marker on Route 6A identifies the home of Thomas Hinckley, an original settler of Barnstable who was a colonial governor in 1681. Barnstable is distinguished by a number of individuals and families who influenced the region and, in some cases, the nation. A marker in West Barnstable shows the home of James Otis, a chief justice of the State Court during the Revolutionary War. His son, James Otis Jr., was credited with delivering a speech that set the stage for the great rebellion. He participated in many significant events in colonial history, such as protests against the Stamp Act and the Townshend Acts, and was a good friend of John Adams.

At the intersection of Routes 149 and 6A in West Barnstable is a cemetery containing the grave of Captain "Mad Jack" Percival, one of Barnstable's most famous citizens. Percival was captain of the warship *Constitution* ("Old Ironsides") from 1844 to 1847. The famous vessel is now on permanent display in Boston Harbor.

Like the other Mid-Cape towns, Barnstable was settled by farmers. In addition to livestock, early farmers raised corn, rye, onions, and flax. By the 19th century fishing, shipping, and coastal trading were the foundation of its economy. The town boasted some 800 shipmasters, 104 in the village of Centerville alone. Osterville's Crosby Boatyard is famous for the Cape Cod catboat designed there. The West Barnstable Brick Company was active from 1860 to 1927, producing 100,000 bricks a day.

Cobb's Hill West Cemetery in Barnstable is the burial site of many of the

[Facing page] *In West Barnstable's Lothrop Hill Cemetery, you'll find the intriguing headstone of Capt. John Percival, apparently better known as "Mad Jack."* HYANNIS AREA CHAMBER OF COMMERCE

early families in the area, and the West Parish church built in 1717 along Route 149 in West Barnstable stands as a proud monument to the world of 18th-century Cape Codders.

Yarmouth

Next time you're feeling sorry for yourself, think about one of Yarmouth's founding fathers, Anthony Thatcher. Here was a man who lost everything, only to rebuild his life over again and again, and in the process help to build a town. Before leaving England he lost his first wife and five of his nine children. Remarried, he and his wife and his four remaining children set sail for the New World in 1635. Though they arrived without mishap, a subsequent boat ride from Ipswich to Marblehead ended in the loss of his four children. Of all those on board, only he and his wife survived. With everything lost the Thatchers arrived at Yarmouth in 1639 to found that town along with Thomas Howes and John Crow. John Thatcher, Anthony Thatcher's son, born in 1638 at Ipswich, would father 21 children to help populate the new township, his house is directly across the street from the Yarmouthport Post Office on Route 6A.

The lands of Yarmouth had long been settled by Indians of the Mattakeese and Nobscusset tribes before Pilgrim Stephen Hopkins came south from Plymouth to build a house here in 1638. The new town, which was most likely named for Great Yarmouth in England, was originally a huge area encompassing the present towns of Yarmouth and Dennis. With its salt marshes, thick woodlands, and rich soil, the north side was settled first. Lands were quickly acquired from the Indians, and a sturdy community began to grow. The Indians found themselves being boxed in, and the areas were set aside for them at Long Pond, Scargo Lake, and along Bass River and Parker River. Burial grounds at Long Pond and Scargo Lake are marked with plaques; the one at Long Pond reads: ON THIS SLOPE LIE BURIED THE LAST NATIVE INDIANS OF YARMOUTH.

Yarmouth was a farming community in the 18th century and was renowned later for its maritime activity until the locomotives came to Cape Cod and the age of steam eclipsed the age of sail. Many ships from Yarmouth were engaged in the Indo-China trade. Secum and Taylor shipbuilders built the legendary *Red Jacket*, which made a record transatlantic crossing in 13 days.

Saltworks and cordage works sprung up on the Bass River. Settled by a Quaker named David Kelly, South Yarmouth became known as Quaker Village or Friends Village, and the townsfolk erected a meetinghouse there around 1809. Though other towns were less tolerant of Quakers, Yarmouth eventually accepted the "heretics," and their settlement played a large part in the development of the town. As early as 1721 an east parish of the Yarmouth Congregational Church was established in the area now known as Dennis. In 1793 this east parish, all of Yarmouth east of the Bass River, separated from the town to become the town of Dennis.

Yarmouth is an architectural historian's dream, for it has two historic districts comprising 650 buildings, many of which are on the National Register of Historic Places. The age of the area and the sophistication of its residents are reflected in its varied architectural styles: Federal, Gothic, Greek Revival, and Victorian. Of course, the traditional Cape house—full Cape, half-Cape, and three-quarters Cape—is well represented along the historic routes.

[Facing page] *The Olde Colonial Courthouse in Barnstable Village, site of* Tales of Cape Cod, *was built in 1774 and is the oldest wooden courthouse on Cape Cod.*
HYANNIS AREA CHAMBER OF COMMERCE

A final note on Yarmouth: It seems it also has a chapter in the Norse sagas. As the tale goes, Leif Ericson's brother Thorvald visited these shores at the beginning of the 11th century and met up with Indians at Bass Hole in the northern part of Yarmouth. In a battle with the Indians, Thorvald was killed and buried at the beach. Thorvald's grave has never been found.

Dennis

To understand the early history of the town of Dennis, you must first study the history of Yarmouth, for Dennis was settled as part of Yarmouth in 1639. Of Old Yarmouth's three earliest settlers, Anthony Thatcher, Thomas Howes, and John Crow, two of the three—Howes and Crow—settled in what would later become Dennis. In 1721 the east parish of Yarmouth was established in the area now known as Dennis Village, and four years later a minister came to this east precinct of Yarmouth to become the church's preacher. That young minister was Rev. Josiah Dennis, a Harvard graduate who was born in Northern Ireland and arrived in Massachusetts around the year 1700 at the age of seven. Josiah Dennis would preach at the east church until his death in 1763. His successor, Nathan Stone, was the minister at the time of the separation from Yarmouth and the town's incorporation in 1793. It was suggested that the new township be named Dennis in honor of its first minister, rather than Nobscusset for the Indians of the area. Coincidentally the last Nobscusset Indian died in 1793, the year of incorporation.

Many of the early residents had been farmers in England and were attracted to the area by the abundance of salt-marsh hay for their cattle. Early settlers practiced shore whaling and utilized "drift whales" that floated ashore. As whale oil became more valuable, whales were methodically pursued. Watch houses were built at Sesuit and Nobscusset harbors to provide an alert when the great creatures were in the bay. Long boats were sent out, and the whales were herded into shallow water, where they became stranded. As whaling grew into an industry, harpooning, a skill developed in Scandinavia, was employed from boats offshore.

Around the time of the American Revolution, large-scale farming dropped off for lack of land, and many people moved to western Massachusetts. As the deepwater harbors of Nantucket and New Bedford began to dominate the whaling industry, Dennis turned to fishing, coastal trading, and shipbuilding. Fishing wharves lined the southern coastline, and Dennisport basked in the sweet aroma of fish drying on fish flakes. Some 400 shipmasters hailed from the town. Shiverick Shipyards in East Dennis produced eight magnificent clipper ships, all of which were recognized in the Golden Age of Sail. Mastered and crewed largely by Dennis men, these vessels helped to open up routes to the Orient and brought much fame and fortune to the town and its residents. Important as a fast means of transportation, particularly around Cape Horn during the California Gold Rush, these hardworking vessels were often in service for 25 to 30 years. A marker on Sesuit Road denotes the site of the shipyard.

Two major Cape industries, cranberry cultivation and saltworks, were both pioneered in Dennis. During the time the British were blockading American ports, the Continental Congress offered a reward to anyone who could invent an efficient means of producing salt. Capt. John Sears of East Dennis stepped forward in the latter quarter of the 18th century to invent and eventually patent a solar evaporation vat that actually distilled salt from seawater. Though the brunt of many a joke, his "odd" experiments worked, and a profitable industry grew from his backyard hobby. Very soon saltworks were everywhere, lining every available beachfront area around the Cape. Meanwhile, in 1816, Henry Hall of North Dennis observed that wild cranberries flourished in areas where sand blew over them. He replicated the conditions and is considered to be the first person to cultivate cranberries.

LOWER CAPE

Brewster

Much of the history of Brewster was made beyond the boundaries of the town on the oceans of the world. Brewster raised more deepwater ship captains per capita than all other 19th-century American towns. Many of these ship captains operated slightly outside the law of the day. For instance during the War of 1812, Brewster's seafaring men defied President Thomas Jefferson's embargo against Britain. There were fortunes to be made crossing the Atlantic, and these men of Brewster were not about to let a presidential decree stand in the way!

Brewster was originally settled as part of Harwich in 1656 by John Wing, formerly of Sandwich. Early settlement was in West Brewster, around Route 124, in the area of the present Brewster Stone. A church founded here in 1700 has pews still marked with the names of original members. By the mid-1700s, bad feelings existed between the north and south precincts of Harwich, as each end of the town was so different in its makeup. The ship captains and the fortunes they made were on the north side, whereas the working class, including fishermen and farmers, dwelt on the south side. By 1803 each town went in its own direction, the southern part keeping the name Harwich, the northern part opting for the name Brewster to honor *Mayflower* Pilgrim William Brewster.

In the center of Brewster, an old cemetery behind the Unitarian Church is the final resting place of many notable historic figures, including Captain David Nicker-son, who was in Paris during the French Revolution. According to local legend, he was handed a baby—supposedly the Lost Dauphin of France, the son of Marie Antoinette and Louis XVI. He was begged to bring the child to America and asked to name the child Rene Rousseau, which he did. The child grew up to be a sea captain and, at the age of 25, was lost at sea. It is Cape custom for a young man lost at sea to have his name inscribed on his father's headstone, so upon Capt. Nickerson's stone (who was lost at sea a few years later) is also the name Rene Rousseau.

Brewster has more than one connection with France. During the French Revolution, 1794 to be more exact, Captain Elijah Cobb's ship was seized. Cobb obtained an audience with Robespierre to plead his case for the release of his ship. Robespierre saw Cobb's side of the argument and released the ship just days before he himself was executed. Cobb would later become a prisoner of war during the War of 1812 and be released in a prisoner exchange.

In 1815 Brewster Captain Jeremiah May orchestrated plans to take Napoleon to America, but the plans fell apart when the former emperor was captured.

Although Brewster has a strong maritime history, the Cape Cod Museum of Natural History permits an unusual glimpse of prehistoric life in this town. The first people who lived in this area would have seen a vast plain covered with pine forests, grasslands, and rivers, with bogs where Cape Cod Bay is now, for the shoreline was miles away from its present location, nearly out to Georges Bank. As glaciers melted the sea level rose and covered the land area, which is now the continental shelf. Prehistoric people settled around the river mouths such as Stony Brook in Brewster. Stone tools, spears, knives, and hide scrapers have been found at the town's Upper Mill Pond. In 1619 a plague killed as many as 90 percent of the native people. Written history kept by the Pilgrims and early colonists in Plymouth and on Cape Cod reflects a decimated and vulnerable native culture; European settlers, on the other hand, were strong in numbers but considerably divided by economic and religious differences.

Brewster was in 1870 the birthplace of prolific Cape writer Joe Lincoln. Through his novels many people were first introduced to Cape Cod and its history.

Harwich

Like all of Cape Cod, Harwich was home to local Indians, in this case the Nauset Indians of Harwich, consisting of the Sauquatuckett tribe to the north and the Monomoyick tribe to the south. These Indians lived in unspoiled beauty, undisturbed for many centuries and even for the couple of decades after the settlement of Yarmouth to the west and Eastham to the east. This land was the Cape's last wilderness until white settlers began to arrive toward the end of the 1650s.

In 1656 John Wing became the first settler to tame these wilds. He was a converted Quaker from Sandwich who apparently tired of the persecutions in that town and left to build a life elsewhere. He settled in part of the old Harwich that would eventually become what is Brewster nowadays. Wing was followed by John Dillingham and later, Gersham Hall, who in the 1660s became the first to settle in the southern area of old Harwich (the section that would remain the Harwich of today). More families followed, and by 1690 there were enough living in the area to establish a church. In 1694 this area became incorporated as Harwich and contained the present towns of Harwich and Brewster as well as parts of Eastham and Orleans.

Harwich of the 18th century was a town in separation. Residents in the southern part of town grew weary of traveling to the church parish in the north, so in 1744 they appealed for the building of a church in the south. Two years later permission was granted, and a church was built. This southern parish later saw itself being split into some 15 splinter churches as a religious revolution of sorts took place in town. These religious groups included Congregationalists, Baptists, New Lighters, Come Outers (those who "came out" against slavery), and Standpatters (those who were not abolitionists).

In the 18th century the town itself began to come apart. The areas known as Portonumecot and Namecoyick became parts of Eastham in 1772, later becoming South Orleans. About a quarter of a century later, the remaining part of Harwich split in two, the northern part becoming Brewster in 1803.

The earliest settlers were farmers who occasionally shored a whale. Harwich would later become one of the Cape's major fishing ports, reaping huge harvests of cod and mackerel. Other industries included the fishing for alewives, or young herring, from a number of streams as well as the harvesting of cranberries from the many bogs. This latter industry was developed in town by Alvin Cahoon, who was instrumental in making cranberries a harvestable crop. Meanwhile Harwich's Major Nathaniel Freeman gave the saltworks industry on the Cape a big boost by utilizing windmills to pump seawater into the salt vats. In fact so profound were Harwich's contributions to the industry that it became home of the Massachusetts Salt Works Company, established in 1797. The industry peaked during the 1830s, only to see its decline a decade later, when salt mining in the Midwest provided a more cost-effective alternative.

Two structures in Harwich of historical interest are the South Harwich Methodist Church on Chatham Road and the Captain James Berry House on Main Street, both on the National Register of Historic Places. You can see other historic sites at the Herring River in West Harwich and Muddy Creek between Harwich and Chatham.

Chatham

If the 13th-century Flateyjarbok (Flat Land Book) does in fact provide an accurate account of Norse expeditions around A.D. 1000, then the first visitors to Chatham could most likely have been Vikings from Iceland. If these Norse sagas are true, then Bjarni Herjulfsson sailed right past these shores more than a thousand years ago. The earliest accepted historic record, though, indicates that Samuel de Champlain anchored in Stage Harbor in 1606 to repair a broken rudder. Though Champlain and his crew were only able to navigate the treacherous shoals with the aid of Monomoyick Indians of the area, fear between the two groups once Champlain's men had set up camp on shore resulted in bloodshed. With a fixed rudder the French left the harbor to explore Canada. Champlain named the locale Port Fortune after the misfortune he had encountered there.

Fourteen years later Chatham provided the Pilgrims with their first glimpse of land since leaving England. Shoals off Monomoy Island drove the ship to the north, however, rather than to their intended southern route to Virginia. Chatham remained unsettled until 1664, when William Nickerson of Yarmouth arrived in the area to stay. Since 1656 Nickerson had been acquiring land from the Monomoyicks, though it wasn't until 1672 that he actually received a deed of any kind. By 1682 he possessed about 4,000 acres of land—nearly all of Chatham!

In Nickerson's time the area was known as Monomoit, and he had a difficult time attracting settlers to this remote area of the Cape. Besides the Indians there was also the threat of attack by pirates. The Monomoyicks turned out to be friendly neighbors to the settlers who determined to "brave the wilds." At one time it was considered under Yarmouth's jurisdiction and, later, under that of Eastham. Though not a town, this area of Monomoit was allowed to separate from Eastham in 1679 to become what was termed a "consta-blewich," meaning Monomoit could collect its own taxes but had no representation in the Colony Court. Monomoit's only chance at incorporation was in establishing a church and then in attracting a minister to this wilderness outpost. After a number of preachers came and went (no less than eight including one who drowned), Rev. Hugh Adams arrived in 1711, and, in June 1712, the town was incorporated. The stipulation was that the town had to be incorporated with an English name, so Chatham was chosen.

Chatham was the site of one of the worst smallpox epidemics on the Cape. During the winter of 1765–66 some 60 people, 10 percent of the population, contracted the disease. Thirty-seven people died, including the town doctor.

Chatham has one of the most dangerous coastlines along the Northeast. As Champlain learned in 1606, Chatham is guarded by treacherous shoals that have caused many a shipwreck over the centuries. In 1808 two wooden lighthouses were constructed at the mouth of the harbor to warn approaching ships. They crumbled over the eroded cliff and were replaced in 1841 and again in 1879 and 1881. Today one of the towers, Chatham Light, still serves as a navigational aid. The other tower was moved north to Eastham to become Nauset Light. The terrible shipwreck called the Monomoy Disaster of 1902 took place just south of Chatham Light off the Monomoy Islands. Twelve men lost their lives on Shovelful Shoals in a fierce winter storm that March morning. Sole survivors Captain Elmer Mayo and Captain Seth Ellis became heroes, each man putting his own life in harm's way with the slightest hope of saving the life of another. Their tale of heroism is told on a monument standing in front of Chatham Light.

Orleans

The history of the Cape town of Orleans is sprinkled with French seasoning. Though it's not known for sure, the origin of the town's name seems to point to Louis Philippe de Bourbon, the Duke of Orleans in France. The Duke was in exile during the French Revolution and had visited America one month before the Cape town was incorporated. Thirty-three years later he would become the king of France.

Originally settled as the south precinct of Eastham in 1710, the area was known as Pochet. The first meetinghouse was built in 1718 to become the South Parish of Eastham. Graves in the nearby cemetery date back to 1719. Orleans broke away from Eastham and was incorporated in 1797 to become one of only two towns on Cape Cod to not bear an English name (the other town is Mashpee). Before the white settlers this land belonged to the Nauset Indians, more specifically the subtribes known as the Monomoyick and the Potonamiquoit (there are numerous spellings for this second tribe). Leif Ericson of the Norse sagas may have visited Nauset Beach along Orleans's Atlantic coast around the year 1000, Bartholomew Gosnold stopped here in 1602 and named this place Cape Cod for the many codfish he found, and the French explorer Samuel de Champlain visited these outer shores in 1606.

The first recorded European shipwreck on the East Coast occurred off Nauset Beach in December 1626 when the ketch *Sparrowhawk* wrecked in a storm. During the 19th century the remains of the historic vessel emerged from the dunes and are now housed in a museum in Plymouth.

One of the smallest towns on the Cape, Orleans borders Cape Cod Bay to the northwest, the Atlantic Ocean to the east, and the waters of Pleasant Bay to the south. The land itself is marked by many bays, ponds, and creeks. The town is also the site of the Cape's first canal, Jeremiah's Gutter, a hand-dug trench that connected Boatmeadow River and Town Cove. Extremely high tides would flood the low-lying lands between the two bodies of water—in fact Gosnold mistakenly concluded that the Cape

north of this spot was actually an island cut off from the rest of the peninsula by this gulf of water. Dug in 1804 Jeremiah's Gutter (named for the resident Jeremiah Smith who owned land through which it traveled) was useful during the War of 1812 when British ships were blockading Cape ports. After the war its use diminished, and the canal was left to fill in with silt.

The French returned to Orleans in 1898 in the form of the French Cable Company. The company managed an undersea cable that connected the Cape town with Brest, France. A second cable then ran from Orleans to New York. Many important news items were received at Orleans first before being referred on to New York and the rest of the country, such as the loss of the steamer *Portland* in 1898, Lindbergh's flight across the Atlantic in 1927, and Germany's invasion of France in 1940. Along with the cable came workers from France to man the company's building. Many of these French remained in Orleans and raised families here.

Orleans has an extraordinary distinction—it has been attacked by both the British and the Germans. During the War of 1812, the HMS *Newcastle* anchored off Rock Harbor, and its captain demanded payment of $1,000 to spare the town's saltworks. The offer was refused, and so commenced the Battle of Rock Harbor. British sailors attempted a landing but were driven away by the town's militia. The ransom was never paid.

On July 22, 1918, during World War I, a German U-boat surfaced off Nauset Beach to fire on and sink three barges and a tugboat, the *Perth Amboy*. An estimated 146 rounds were fired in the one-sided exchange. At least one of the submarine's shells landed on the beach, the only assault on American soil during the war. When word of the attack was received at the Chatham Air Station, three planes were sent up to launch a counterattack. Without weaponry the best the Yanks could do was toss a monkey wrench at the fleeing sub.

In 1984 the 470-foot Maltese freighter *Eldia* grounded on Nauset Beach. It had unloaded its cargo of sugar in New Brunswick and was riding light off Cape Cod when high winds and heavy seas blew it onto shore. Although the 28-member crew was evacuated with no loss of life, few will forget the bizarre sight of a giant ship on Nauset Beach, a sight that hearkened back to the old days when this coastline snatched many a passing ship to wreck upon her shoals.

Eastham

The decade of the 1640s saw the Pilgrims in Plymouth considering their future and whether they wanted to stay in Plymouth. Some thought of relocating their settlement to the outer lands of Cape Cod, and in 1643, a committee was formed to investigate that very possibility. Among those in the party who journeyed to the outer Cape was Thomas Prence, who came across to the New World on board the vessel *Fortune* in 1621. Upon their return to Plymouth, the committee decided to pack up their belongings and take their chances in the land known as Nauset, now known as Eastham.

Settlement commenced in 1644. The boundaries were vague at best, at first consisting of everything east of Old Yarmouth and including the towns of Brewster, Harwich, Chatham, Orleans, Wellfleet, Truro, and, of course, Eastham. The township was known as Nauset until 1651 when it was renamed Eastham. This land was reserved for the Old Comers, those Pilgrims who voyaged across the Atlantic on the first three ships to carry settlers—the *Mayflower, Fortune,* and *Anne.* Joining Prence were John Doane, Nicholas Snow, and Josias Cook, as well as Richard Higgins, John Smalley, and Edward Bangs. Eastham is the only Cape Cod town founded entirely by people from Plymouth Colony. It's interesting that Pilgrims should return to Eastham, as it was the site of their first contact with Native Indians at First Encounter Beach in December 1620, just before they sailed the *Mayflower* across the Bay to settle at Plymouth. Founding father Thomas Prence would later become Governor of Plymouth Colony from 1655 until his death in 1673.

The first meetinghouse was erected in 1646 on the north side of Town Cove. The much-loved Reverend Samuel Treat came to Eastham in 1693, and his ministry would span the next 45 years. Besides preaching to the white settlers, Treat also ministered to more than 500 Native Americans, or "Praying Indians," and wrote services in their language. He enlisted Native preachers and lived up to his name by treating the Indians with the respect they were owed.

Harwich, which at the time included Brewster, separated from Eastham very early on with its settlement in 1656. Chatham departed next, when that area became a constablewich in control of its own destiny in 1679. Truro broke away from Eastham in 1709. Around 1720, a north parish was established in the area of Wellfleet and a south parish at what was later to become Orleans. The divisions were made official in 1763 when Wellfleet became its own town and in 1797 when Orleans followed suit. Eastham, once the most populated town on the Cape, became the least populated. Over the century since its settlement, so many trees had been cut that the once-rich Eastham topsoil was stripped away by the savage ocean winds. Scrub pine took hold where vast forests of oak once stood. Farmers turned from their barren soils to the seas and became fishermen. Those who did remain behind on shore became dairy farmers.

Old Cove Cemetery is Eastham's oldest cemetery. Three Pilgrims are buried here. In the mid-1800s a small plot was added nearby for the graves of many children who died when a terrible epidemic of smallpox struck the town. The small cemetery was so deeply associated with grief and tragedy that people shunned it, and it became overgrown with weeds and briars and was long forgotten. Only recently have the 22 headstones dating from 1836 to 1892 been rediscovered.

Henry Beston's famous book, *The Outermost House,* published in 1928, relates the year he spent in his beach cottage on the Great Dune of Eastham. Although the cottage was destroyed by the blizzard of 1978, its place in literary history is commemorated by a placard at Coast Guard Beach.

Wellfleet

When the settlers arrived at Nauset in 1644 to purchase lands from the Indians of the area, they asked them who owned the northern lands from Wellfleet toward Provincetown. The Indians, perhaps not understanding the question and possibly not identifying with the European notion of ownership, answered "nobody." So the settlers announced, "Then we own it!" And so began the settlement of Wellfleet, known then as Billingsgate, at that time merely the north precinct of the town of Eastham.

The lay of the land at Wellfleet was much different than it is today. Land masses that are now attached to the mainland were actually islands back then. Other 17th- and 18th-century islands that once supported homes and communities are now gone, swept away by the tides. Such is the case with the island of Billingsgate, which over the years was devoured by the waves. Strangely much

of the settlement of the area occurred on the islands rather than on the mainland. A north parish meetinghouse was erected in the area in 1723. As early as 1734 the residents here applied for town status, but it would be another three decades before their application was approved. In 1763 the town was incorporated, briefly, as the town of Poole, later changed to Wellfleet. Some say that the name "Wellfleet" may have come from "Wallfleet," after the Wallfleet oyster bed located in Blackwater Bay in England. Samuel de Champlain, who visited these Wellfleet shores back in the early 17th century, named the harbor *Port aux Huitres* (no need to look to your French dictionary, *huitres* does in fact translate as oysters). Of course, "Wallfleet" (or Wellfleet) sounds a lot like "whale fleet" too—another possible source for the town's name.

It is only a mile between Wellfleet's shores on the outer beach of the Atlantic Ocean and Cape Cod Bay. Wellfleet Harbor was once known as Grampus Bay for the blackfish, or pilot whales, that stranded themselves there. When the oyster beds died of in 1770 because of an epidemic of some sort, Wellfleet men became commercial fishermen, lobstermen, and whalers. Seed oysters were imported after the Revolutionary War, and the beds thrived again, making Wellfleet the largest producer of oysters in the state. During the early 19th century, salt vats were big business, and the town had some 40 saltworks during the 1830s, producing roughly 18,000 bushels of salt on an annual basis. The Wellfleet wharf business grew during the mid-1800s, catering to the fishing industry.

In 1717 off the shores of Wellfleet, the pirate known as Black Sam Bellamy was returning to the Cape on board his vessel *Whydah* when the ship was caught in a storm and sank. The location of the wreck baffled salvagers and historians until, in 1982, a treasure salvager located the wreck of the infamous ship. The bronze ship's bell with THE WHYDAH GALLEY 1716 inscribed on it was brought to the surface,

From 1872 to 1914, 13 Life-Saving Stations were built approximately every 8 miles along Cape Cod's eastern shore. They provided rescue and shelter for shipwreck victims. Today you can visit the Beachcomber Restaurant in Cahoon's Hollow, Wellfleet, a converted lifesaving station on the bluffs overlooking the Atlantic Ocean.

along with hundreds of pieces of gold and other treasures. Artifacts from the *Whydah* can be seen at a museum on Provincetown's MacMillan Pier.

Wellfleet is the site from which one of the first trans-Atlantic wireless telegraph messages was sent in 1903. The year before, a huge station was built on the cliff overlooking the ocean. This miracle of science that allowed messages to travel across the invisible airwaves was the invention of Italian physicist Guglielmo Marconi, who began experimenting with sending wireless messages in his teenage years. Besides that first telegraph message of 1903 (from President Theodore Roosevelt to King Edward VII of England), the Wellfleet wireless station also received a distress message from the sinking *Titanic* in April 1912.

The following are some of Wellfleet's other claims to fame: The steeple of Wellfleet's First Congregational Church is the only town clock in the world that keeps ship's time (see our Attractions chapter). In the 1870s Captain Lorenzo Dow Baker of Wellfleet introduced bananas to the United States and established the L. D. Baker Company in 1881, which later became the United Fruit Company. Wellfleet resident Luther Crowell invented the square-bottom paper bag.

Truro

The history of Truro can be traced to three hills: Corn Hill, the Hill of Storms, and the Hill of Churches. In November 1620 the *Mayflower*, with its passengers and crew, found its way to Provincetown Harbor. An expedition that included Captain Myles Standish and William Bradford explored the lands of this lonely outpost in search of food and water and possibly a good place to settle. In the area of Truro, upon a hill now known as Corn Hill, the Pilgrims stumbled across what appeared to be an abandoned Indian encampment. Here they found Indian gravesites and unearthed buried baskets filled with ears

The thin pieces of wood used in overlapping rows that form the sides and roofs of Cape Cod houses are white cedar shingles. White cedar is preferred over red cedar by most Cape Codders because it takes on a handsome, silvery sheen, whereas red cedar eventually turns brown. White cedar is also lighter, softer, and easier to split and shave.

of corn. They took this corn, and it became the seeds of the Pilgrims' first planting. Also in Truro the Pilgrim expedition located their first fresh water supply since leaving England, at Pilgrim Spring, which can still be seen on a Cape Cod National Seashore walking trail.

Truro was originally settled as part of the Nauset tract in the mid-17th century, later incorporated as Eastham. A group known as the Pamet Proprietors bought the land from the natives in 1689, and by 1697 farms were established in this remote area of the Cape, first called Pamet after the Native American tribe there. Pamet was granted municipal privileges in 1705 and called Dangerfield because of the treacherous coastline. When Dangerfield officially separated from Eastham in 1709, the township was renamed Truro for the English town in Cornwall, which, with its rolling hills and lonely moors, resembled this area. The first meetinghouse was built in 1710 on the Hill of Storms. This meetinghouse was dismantled in 1840. The hill is also the site of North Cemetery, where the town's oldest stones can be found.

Truro was primarily a fishing and whaling town. At first whaling was done from shore and later from boats. In the 18th century Truro was a leader in this industry, with vessels visiting the African coast and the whaling grounds of the Pacific. One particular Truro whaler, Ichabod Paddock, was even recruited to teach Nantucketers his techniques. (He must have been a good teacher!) Truro's history has always reflected a relationship with the sea. It had

Dune Shacks

One of the more evocative vistas on the Cape are the outer dunes that run between Truro and Provincetown. Over the years these lovely, wild dunes have attracted all manner of artists, adventurers, and eccentrics. In the 1930s and '40s, squatters cobbled together numerous shacks out of driftwood and scraps in these dunes. Eighteen of these haphazard shacks have persisted to this day, largely because of the fascination many people have with their present and former inhabitants, and the fierce devotion to this singular way of life of those who still live among the dunes. Located along a 2-mile ridge of dunes, a few miles from bustling Provincetown, these austere lean-tos still have no power or water. Their extraordinary location and solitude have attracted an impressive roster of artists and writers

over the years, from Eugene O'Neill and Tennessee Williams to Jackson Pollock, e.e. cummings, Norman Mailer, and Annie Dillard.

Seventeen of the shacks were added to the National Register of Historic Places in 1989 and now fall under the auspices of the National Park Service. The Cape Cod National Seashore and the Peaked Hill Trust, a nonprofit community organization, are responsible for maintaining nearly all of the shacks. When the National Park Service took over the shacks back in the early 1960s, they signed long-term leases with the current inhabitants. At press time many of these leases were up, and it is unclear what the long-term fate of the shacks will be.

If you're an artist or writer, you can apply for a brief, inspiring stay in one of

two good harbors, Pamet River Harbor and East Harbor (which is now the freshwater Pilgrim Lake, where the Pilgrims were thought to have anchored when they first arrived). Pamet River Harbor was the site of a thriving wharf business that grew from Union Wharf, built in 1829. The town had a sail loft and a shipbuilding yard built in 1830 on the Pamet River, where brigs and many Grand Banks schooners were built. The successful Union Company Store, which specialized in ship chandlering and general merchandise, epitomized the flavor of this fishing haven, and many townsfolk owned shares in the store and thereby shared in the town's victories.

But a series of events would send the

town into a downward spiral. First was the terrible gale of October 2, 1841, which would see the loss of 57 Truro men (10 percent of the town's able seamen) and seven of the town's eight fishing vessels. Then, in the 1850s, erosion began to claim the harbor. Citizens saw that erosion could eventually allow the Atlantic Ocean to cut right through Truro, creating an island of North Truro and Provincetown (the North Truro we know today is well south of Pilgrim Lake, up on the hill; this area is now called Beach Point). To avoid this the entrance of East Harbor was blocked to become a lake. Then came the big blow when the Union Store went out of business in 1860. A growing 1840 population of

the shacks. The Provincetown Community Compact manages one of them, called the C-Scape Dune Shack. You may contact them about applying at (508) 487-3684, or by writing P.O. Box 819, Provincetown, MA 02657. The Peaked Hill Trust runs another artist-in-residence program, which awards two-week stays to eligible artists in several other shacks. You may contact them at (508) 487-3635, or write them at P.O. Box 1705, Provincetown, MA 02657.

If a glimpse of the unparalleled light and views in the outer dunes is all you're after, you can access the area from Race Point Road or Snail Road. Off Snail Road follow a trail up to the top of the dunes, and you can see a few shacks in the distance. You can also view them if you hike east from Race Point Beach. An easier way to catch a glimpse is to visit the Cape Cod National Seashore's Province Lands Visitor Center (508-487-1256). It has a wraparound observation deck offering a 360-degree view, including several dune shacks. It's located on Race Point Road, off U.S. Route 6 in Provincetown, and is open from mid-April until Thanksgiving. An even easier option: Art's Dune Tours. Most vehicles aren't allowed on the dunes, but you can enjoy the views from the air-conditioned comfort of one of Art's Suburbans. They take groups on narrated, two-hour tours among the dunes, which include plenty of colorful history lessons about the shacks. Call (508) 487-1950, or visit www.artsdunetours.com. Tickets should be purchased in advance, and tours leave from the corner of Standish and Commercial Streets in Provincetown. Do remember, however, that these are either private residences or are being inhabited by artists in search of solitude.

about 2,000 had been cut in half by 1880. Migration cut that number in half again to about 500 people by 1930 as residents moved away to earn a living elsewhere.

The Hill of Churches is the spot where the Methodists of Truro built their meetinghouse in 1826. Methodists had first arrived here in the 1790s. The Congregationalists then decided to build their new church on the very same hill in 1827. It was built on this high ground to serve as both a worship center and as a beacon for ships. Its bell was cast by Paul Revere's son and cost $320, and the windows were made of Sandwich glass. In 1830 the Town Hall, or Union Hall, was constructed on the same hill, and its architecture resembles that of a church. The spires of these buildings can still be seen among the trees as you drive through Truro on U.S. Route 6.

Highland Light in North Truro, also known as Cape Cod Light, is Cape Cod's oldest lighthouse. The 80-foot tower, which sits atop a 120-foot cliff, was built in 1797 and rebuilt in 1857. Cliff erosion threatened the structure's future, so in 1996 the historic lighthouse was moved to its present location. In November 1778, during the days of the American Revolution, the British man-of-war *Somerset* wrecked along the Truro coast at Dead Man's Hollow in a gale. Some 480 British sailors were saved as the vessel cleared the outer bars and wrecked along the beach. The people of Truro and Province-town divided up the spoils of the wreck, stripping the vessel of all its cargo and equipment. The British were eventually marched to Boston to confront the revolutionary forces, and the *Somerset*'s doctor is said to have stayed on in Truro and married a local woman.

Provincetown

At the very end of the Cape, at Province-town, is where the history of Massachusetts began. Though English explorer John Smith sailed past this spot in 1614 without a thought of making landfall, Provincetown has the historic distinction of being the landing place of the *Mayflower*'s Pilgrims on November 21, 1620. The Pilgrims then went on to Plymouth where they established a successful settlement America. Perhaps even more historically significant, while the vessel was moored in the harbor, the Pilgrims drafted and signed the Mayflower Compact, a document that became the foundation of democratic government in America. It spelled out the Pilgrims' plans for self-government—a government of, by, and for the people (sound familiar?). The Pilgrims spent five weeks in the Provincetown, Truro, Wellfleet, and Eastham area before they realized that the Cape's tip did not offer all they needed for settlement—namely fresh water and a protected harbor. Though some members wished to remain in this area, eventually all the Pilgrims got back on board the *Mayflower*, raised anchor, and continued along the coast to eventually land in Plymouth. Incidentally, several Pilgrims who had died on the crossing were buried in Provincetown.

Long before the Pilgrims came, however, the tip of the Cape had attracted native tribes and foreign explorers. Norse legends claim Vikings were the first discoverers of the New World, and Leif Ericson's brother, Thorvald, may have landed here during the first years of the 11th century to repair a damaged keel, naming the place Keelness.

Because of its remoteness the tip of the Cape was one of the last parts to be settled. The area earned a somewhat unsavory reputation because of the smugglers, looters, and gamblers who came here before its actual settlement. Much carousing was done here! No civil order was in place, and anyone who docked here to participate in whatever illegalities took place in the few coastal shacks did so in a land where laws simply did not exist. When nearby Truro was incorporated in 1709, this land to the north named "Cape Cod" was thrown into the package in an attempt to bring some order to this faraway land. Eventually a permanent, though undisciplined, settlement did take hold. Law and order took hold as well, and this port town would quickly get down to business.

The township of Provincetown was incorporated in 1727, and the people immediately turned their attention to the sea and became expert fishermen and whalers. By 1760 a dozen whaling ships called Provincetown Harbor their home port. These whaling boats, always in search of good crews, found them in the Azores, Canary Islands, and Cape Verdes. By the middle part of the century, Provincetown had a tremendous fishing and whaling fleet and was considered one of the most prosperous ports in the country. Seventy-five wharves sprouted up along Commercial Street in this Cape Cod seaport, which was third behind only New Bedford and Nantucket in terms of whaling. The famous whaler *Charles W. Morgan*, now on prominent display at Mystic Seaport, Connecticut, was a Provincetown whaler that worked up until 1921, well after the quest for the leviathan had ended in most other ports. Experienced Portuguese fishermen joined the whalers who had made Provincetown their home, and by the turn of the 20th century, the port town had evolved into a flourishing fishing village with a Portuguese flavor. Today the annual Portuguese Festival, held the last weekend in June, celebrates the town's proud fishing tradition.

Provincetown also has the distinction of being the longest continuously running art colony in the country. In 1899 it became the site of an important art colony when Charles Hawthorne opened the Cape Cod School of Art. Art schools and galleries sprung up in this salty yet beautiful fishing village. That art legacy lives on with the many art schools and galleries in Provincetown today. This harbor community also attracted writers such as Eugene O'Neill, Sinclair Lewis, and John Dos Passos. In 1915 O'Neill, who in his early years worked on fishing boats, joined the Provincetown Players, a group who presented plays in an old fish house on Lewis Wharf in the East End of town. O'Neill went on to earn three Pulitzer Prizes and a Nobel Prize in 1936.

There are several historic monuments in Provincetown, the most impressive being the Cape Cod Pilgrim Memorial monument, constructed by the U.S. Army Corps of Engineers and funded by descendents of the Pilgrims. President Theodore Roosevelt laid its cornerstone in 1907, and President William Howard Taft attended its dedication ceremony in 1910. At 252 feet high, it is the tallest all-granite structure in the United States. A bronze plaque at the western end of Commercial Street commemorates the landing site of the *Mayflower*'s Pilgrims in 1620, and the Pilgrim bas relief on Bradford Street behind Town Hall depicts the signing of the Mayflower Compact in Provincetown Harbor.

Today Provincetown's fishing industry is a shadow of its heyday in the 1850s, and the main source of income is tourism. Commercial Street attracts thousands of visitors each year to its many shops, fine restaurants, and exciting nightlife. Provincetown is a colorful place, a vibrant mix of artists, fishermen, craftspeople, professionals, and retirees. An integral part of this mix is Provincetown's gay and lesbian population who call this town home because of its accepting attitude, easy-going lifestyle, and respect for the individual.

Provincetown continues to be a fishing community boasting a proud Portuguese heritage. The Portuguese have played a large part in the town's history, as have the Norsemen who explored these shores nearly 1,000 years ago; the Pilgrims who landed in 1620; the smugglers and gamblers of the 17th century; the playwrights, artists, and bohemians of the last century; and the gay and lesbian population and the many washashores who have more recently made Provincetown their home—all have contributed to making Provincetown the fascinating place it is today. A trip to Cape Cod is not complete without a visit to the town at the tip.

HOTELS, MOTELS, AND RESORTS

Cape Cod is a peninsula of great diversity, and that characteristic holds true when it comes to the accommodations it offers its visitors. From elegant waterfront resorts to no-frills economy motels, there is a place for every budget and lifestyle.

Cape Cod has several large contemporary four-star resorts where you'll be awash in amenities, as well as hotels and motels that are moderately priced and offer fewer amenities but are perfectly acceptable. Many of the Cape's resorts, hotels, and motels offer suites in addition to rooms with the standard two double beds or one king-size bed.

For the most part you will get what you pay for on the Cape. Private beaches, spacious rooms, and water views do come with a price. Still, bargains exist, especially in the off-season. Years ago the Cape would shut down after Labor Day, but more and more people are discovering the relaxing pace and tranquility of the Cape in the late fall, winter, and early spring, so many hotels, motels, and resorts are stretching out their seasons, with some staying open year-round.

Autumn has become a popular season on the Cape. Visitors can enjoy the Cape's beauty at substantially lower prices, and there are plenty of packages available to make the Cape even more attractive. Rates at some accommodations can be as much as 50 percent less than summer rates, and the indoor pool is just as refreshing and the outside sights are just as breathtaking in the off-season.

In this chapter we present hotels, motels, resorts, and hostels for your consideration; we also provide a short section on kennels, should you need a place for your pet to stay. If you're interested in

other kinds of accommodations, see our Bed-and-Breakfasts, Inns, and Cottages; Vacation Rentals; and Campgrounds and State Parks chapters. We've narrowed your search a bit because there are thousands of rooms to choose from; in fact according to the Cape Cod Chamber of Commerce, there are more than 37,000 rooms available for rent on Cape Cod during the season between Memorial Day and Columbus Day. Your best bet is to begin by deciding how you plan to spend your time while you're here, then pick the area that offers the activities you're looking for.

If you plan on bringing bicycles, there are a number of hotels on or near bike trails, such as the Cape Cod Rail Trail, which stretches from the Mid- to Lower Cape, or the Shining Sea Bike Path on the Upper Cape (see our Hiking and Biking Trails chapter). If you plan on bringing a sailboard, there are a number of excellent hotels on the waterfront near Kalmus Beach in Hyannis, home to world-respected windsurfing and championship events weekly. If golf is your bag, you've come to the right place, as many resorts and hotels offer golf packages. Of course cost is a consideration as well, so we've rated each entry for price (see the code at the beginning of this chapter).

It's best to make reservations before arriving on Cape Cod, as the area's accommodations fill up quickly, not only during the summer season, but also during the weekends in spring and fall. This is especially true if you are planning to visit during special events, such as the Falmouth Road Race weekend or our local sailors' favorite, Fugawi Weekend. That's not to say you can't arrive without reservations and find a great room—it just might take a few stops. In this case your best bet would be to travel along Route 28 through Yarmouth, an area that has one of the highest concentrations of hotels and motels you'll find on the Cape.

The Cape's summer season is not only its busiest season but also its costliest as far as accommodations go. Many of the Cape's hotels and motels are only open during a handful of months (typically Memorial Day to Columbus Day) and have to reap a year's worth of income in less than a half-year's time. The July Fourth and Labor Day weekends are the bookends of what is usually a pretty steady tourist season. Still, June can be a very busy month, too.

Children are welcome at all facilities unless we mention otherwise. You can nearly always expect to pay your bill with a major credit card; we let you know if an accommodation does not accept credit cards. Most facilities offer in-room televisions, telephones, and air-conditioning, but most accommodations do not allow pets. we do, however, make references to the ones that do welcome pets.

Most motels and hotels try to meet the needs of smokers and nonsmokers with restricted areas and/or rooms, but others have a comprehensive nonsmoking policy. We mention in the listings below those hotels and motels that prohibit smoking entirely on their grounds. However, if nothing is mentioned, assume smoking is permitted in certain areas of the hotel, motel, and resort. A number of places also have wheelchair-accessible facilities, and we indicate these in the entries below.

HOTELS, MOTELS, AND RESORTS

PRICE CODE

To help you select a hotel, motel, or resort in your price range, we have established the following key based on the average cost of a night's stay in a double-occupancy room during the season, minus tax and special charges. Massachusetts charges a state tax, as do the individual Cape towns, which equates to about 9.7 percent added to your bill.

$	Less than $75
$$	$75 to $110
$$$	$111 to $175
$$$$	$176 or more

Upper Cape

Bay Motor Inn   **$–$$$**
223 Main Street, Buzzards Bay (Bourne)
(508) 759–3989
www.capecodtravel.com/baymotorinn
Nestled in three acres of beautifully landscaped grounds, this family-owned and operated motor inn has been providing vacationers with affordable accommodations for nearly 40 years. Bring your bike, fishing rod, and walking shoes, because just across the street is the famous Cape Cod Canal with miles of paved trails alongside it. Friendly owners Fred and Irene Carbone will make you feel at home in your air-conditioned rooms, complete with fresh flowers. Popular with families, retirees, and especially fishermen, the Bay Motor Inn offers 17 clean units that include poolside, efficiency, and cottage units. According to Fred, the most popular choice of guests are the Cape "Coddages," freestanding cottage units complete with cable TV, air-conditioning, phones, and tiled bathrooms. You'll be close to a wide assortment of attractions and restaurants, or you can simply spend the day lounging by the wheelchair-accessible pool, playing tennis at the nearby courts, or just watching the boat traffic on the canal. Pets are allowed, but Fred and Irene ask that guests do not leave dogs unattended during the day (just down the road is a veterinary service that will watch your pet for a small fee). The Bay Motor Inn is open from April 1 to November 1.

Best Western Bridge-Bourne Hotel $$
100 Trowbridge Road, Bourne
(508) 759-0800, (800) 675-0008
www.bestwesterncapecod.com

Sites and attractions from Provincetown to Boston are within about an hour's drive of this comfortable lodging, and the sunsets are stunning over the nearby Cape Cod Canal. Buses to and from Logan Airport in Boston and the Woods Hole ferries to Martha's Vineyard depart practically from the front door of the hotel.

This 43-room hotel with attractive modern rooms sits high above the Cape Cod Canal and features an indoor heated pool, hot tub, and eight deluxe suites with Jacuzzis and kitchenettes. Function rooms are available for weddings and other events, and the on-side Trowbridge Tavern can chase away any hunger or thirst. Children 12 and younger stay free in their parents' room. It is open year-round.

Dan'l Webster Inn $$$-$$$$
149 Main Street, Sandwich
(508) 888-3622, (800) 444-3566
www.danlwebsterinn.com

One of the Upper Cape's most distinguished facilities, the Dan'l Webster Inn offers three dining rooms—the Music Room, the Heritage Room, and the Conservatory (see our Restaurants chapter)—an English-style tavern, and an outdoor swimming pool, all set in the midst of the historic and beautiful Sandwich Village. This colonial inn is a reproduction of the original tavern, built in 1692, that served as a parsonage and Patriot headquarters during the Revolutionary War. It was patronized by statesman Daniel Webster during the town's mid-19th century heyday, hence its name.

Guests have their choice of guest rooms and suites at the inn or in two older homes, the Fessenden House on the property and the Quince Tree Inn 1 block away. Furnishings throughout are antiques or period reproductions. Dan'l Webster Inn offers many types of accommodations, ranging in style from the formally elegant Daniel Webster Suite with a fireplace and massive canopied bed to double-bed rooms in the Jarves Wing. All guest rooms are individually decorated and feature private baths; some have a Jacuzzi. Pampering includes fresh flowers, chocolates, turned-down beds, and silk bathrobes. While staying here you are within strolling distance of Sandwich's many museums and other historic attractions, including the Hoxie House and the Grist Mill on Shawme Pond. The Dan'l Webster Inn is open year-round.

Sandwich Lodge & Resort $$-$$$
54 Route 6A, Sandwich
(508) 888-2255, (800) 282-5353
www.sandwichlodge.com

Located in the oldest town on Cape Cod, the Sandwich Lodge & Resort is comfortable for the whole family and close to nearly all of Cape Cod's wonders. This affordable full-service hotel along beautiful Route 6A has 68 rooms including 4 efficiencies, 15 two-room suites, and 2 honeymoon suites. Set on nine acres, the Sandwich Lodge & Resort offers both indoor and outdoor pools, a laundry, a game room for the kids, a whirlpool, and meeting rooms for those mixing business with pleasure. Table tennis, billiards, badminton, volleyball, horseshoes, and shuffleboard fill the void between dips in the pools. In the morning fresh bakery items await you in the main lobby adjacent to the indoor pool. The lobby offers artwork for sale by local artists. Just down the road is the historic district of Sandwich with its many museums as well as the 76-acre Heritage Plantation. On the grounds of the Sandwich Lodge & Resort is a restaurant, which serves lunch and dinner.

[Facing page] *The lodging options in Cape Cod range from no-frills motels to elegant waterfront resorts with their own private beaches.* THE RED JACKET RESORTS

Sandwich Lodge & Resort is open year-round. Pets are allowed in certain rooms for an extra charge.

Shady Nook Inn & Motel $$–$$$$
14 Route 6A, Sandwich
(508) 888-0409, (800) 338-5208
www.shadynookinn.com
One of the closest motels to the Shawmee Forest and minutes away from Heritage Plantation, the immaculate Shady Nook Inn, run by Jim and Sharon Rinaldi, showcases colorful flower beds, well-manicured lawns, and a lovely pool area. The 30 rooms, including 7 efficiencies, offer king- and queen-size beds and doubles, cable TV, and full baths. All rooms are spacious and have refrigerators. You will want to take a look at Jim's display of Coca-Cola memorabilia in the office area. Convenient to historic Sandwich Village and nearby beaches, the Shady Nook Inn is open year-round.

The Earl of Sandwich $–$$
378 Route 6A, East Sandwich
(508) 888-1415, (800) 442-EARL (3275)
www.earlofsandwich.com
Built around a tranquil duck pond in a country setting, the Earl of Sandwich boasts lush gardens, a pool, and homey, comfortable rooms. Many rooms have canopied beds, most have air-conditioning and refrigerators, and all have private baths, color cable TV, and telephone. A complimentary continental breakfast is included with your stay. Owner Brian Clifford displays some of his impressive hand-crafted reproductions of antique brass and copper lanterns in the lobby. The Earl of Sandwich is located within a short drive from area beaches, shopping, and the many historical sites in nearby Sandwich. Rates are reasonable, especially during the off-season. Be sure to call ahead if you plan on bringing the family pet. Pets are welcome but with some restrictions.

Spring Garden Inn $$–$$$
578 Route 6A, East Sandwich
(508) 888-0710, (800) 303-1751
www.springgarden.com

A place of solitude and beauty, the Spring Garden Inn is located along a quiet section of the Old Kings Highway at the east end of Sandwich. Set on a hillside overlooking a tranquil 2,500-acre conservation area, the inn offers marvelous views of marsh stretching out toward the Scorton River. Pine-paneled rooms with beam ceilings are comfortable and clean with private baths, coffeemakers, refrigerators, cable TVs, private phones, and air-conditioning and heat. The motel also features a two-room suite in the original living quarters of the inn, built in the 1940s, and two garden efficiency apartments. The efficiency studio features a queen bed, pull-out sofa, and a full-size, fully equipped kitchen. The one-bedroom efficiency apartment has a kitchenette and dining table, and leads to a garden patio area. Families will enjoy the swimming pool and a spacious backyard for the children. Scorton Creek is a great spot for canoeing and fishing. Complimentary continental breakfast is served each morning. Flower beds accent the grounds, and window boxes are bright with red geraniums and white petunias. The inn is open from the beginning of April to the end of November.

Spring Hill Motor Lodge $$–$$$$
351 Route 6A, East Sandwich
(508) 888-1456
www.sunsol.com/springhill
The Cape Cod–style Spring Hill Motor Lodge has exceptionally well-maintained grounds spotted with colorful junipers. Owners Trevor and Regina Aldhurst have given the lodge a resort atmosphere. Its 24 comfortable, spacious rooms are equipped with all the modern amenities—color cable TV, direct-dial telephone, coffeemakers, refrigerators, and individually controlled heat and air-conditioning. The lodge also features a heated pool privately nestled among the pines and surrounded by a large deck ideal for sunning, a lighted "tournament quality" tennis court, and a separate basketball hoop and picnic area with tables. Bright one- and two-bedroom contemporary

cottages feature custom kitchens, cathedral ceilings, French doors, and bay windows overlooking the manicured grounds. Guests may take advantage of the Route 6A antiques, craft, and gift shops, as well as nearby beaches, fishing, and golfing. Spring Hill Motor Lodge is open from April to November.

Sea Crest Oceanfront Resort & Conference Center $$$–$$$$
350 Quaker Road, North Falmouth
(508) 540–9400, (800) 225–3110
www.seacrest-resort.com
This resort/conference center has 700 feet of white-sand waterfront on sparkling Buzzards Bay. The Sea Crest offers you the opportunity to indulge in everything from tennis to swimming, dancing to dining. From May through late October, kayaks, sailboards, and sailboats are available to let you explore the inlets of the bay at your leisure. Windsurfing instruction is also offered during the summer months.

Enjoy water-view dining in the Sea Crest's Oceanfront Dining Room, or grab a bite at the Surf Lounge. If you'd rather soak up some rays, try the Cabana Bar, which has an outdoor (and an indoor) pool. You can snack or lunch there too. In addition you can enjoy the resort's exercise room, game room, whirlpool, sauna, and its two all-weather tennis courts. If you're bringing the kids, you'll be happy to know that during July and August, the day camp staff holds activities for children.

Many of the 266 rooms have water views and balconies; all rooms come with double or king-size beds, irons and ironing boards, cable TV, telephones with data ports, and hair dryers. Available space is sometimes limited by conferences. The resort has numerous conference rooms for those who have to work for a living. For those who can tear themselves away from the meetings and the gorgeous beachfront, Falmouth's downtown and harbor are about a 10- to 15-minute drive away. Sea Crest is a year-round facility.

Nautilus Motor Inn $$–$$$
539 Woods Hole Road, Woods Hole (Falmouth)
(508) 548–1525, (800) 654–2333
www.nautilusinn.com
This motor inn rests atop a hill overlooking Woods Hole Harbor, where ferries and oceanographic research vessels motor in and out. The views here are spectacular (yes, that's Martha's Vineyard you see across the water). Situated close to Falmouth and the village of Woods Hole, which has great restaurants and marine-science attractions, this 54-room facility has a nice outdoor pool, a spacious sundeck, and tennis courts. All rooms have balconies or patios, some with lovely views of Vineyard Sound. Your morning coffee at the Nautilus is complimentary. The inn is open April through October.

The Admiralty Inn $$–$$$
51 Route 28, Falmouth
(508) 548–4240, (800) 341–5700
www.vacationinnproperties.com
The Admiralty Inn of Falmouth has an outdoor pool with gazebo and bar, an indoor heated pool, a whirlpool, and an on-site restaurant. Its central location makes it convenient to the beaches of Falmouth and the various island ferries that leave from Falmouth Harbor and Woods Hole. Open year-round, the Admiralty has 98 air-conditioned rooms, including 28 townhouse suites. Eight of the rooms are wheelchair accessible. Rooms and suites feature private baths and include a wet bar, refrigerator, and coffeemaker, and the two-story townhouse suites offer two TVs, a VCR and a Jacuzzi.

Best Western Falmouth Marina Tradewinds $$$
26 Robbins Road, Falmouth
(508) 548–4575, (800) 341–5700
www.vacationinnproperties.com
The views you'll have of Falmouth Harbor are outstanding. From your room you can watch sailboats making their way in and out of the busy harbor and the big, white

Island Queen ferry pulling away from her slip bound for Martha's Vineyard. Harbor views, a swimming pool, and proximity to restaurants and attractions all make this large facility a popular one. From its 63 rooms choose a double room or suite with a living room, kitchen, bedroom, and bath. Rooms are spacious and comfortable and have coffeemakers, refrigerators, and wet bars. The facility is open mid-April through October. During the off-season in September and October, room rates are about half those you'd pay in summer. The world-renowned Falmouth Road Race in August passes right by the property (see our Sports and Recreation chapter).

Coonamessett Inn $$-$$$
311 Gifford Street, Falmouth
(508) 548-2300
www.capecodrestaurants.org
The tradition and charm of a New England inn is yours at the Coonamessett. Long adored by the locals for its beauty and grace overlooking Jones Pond, the Coonamessett has been for decades a Falmouth favorite for weddings, special occasions, and dining out. Known more for its fine restaurant (see our Restaurants chapter), the Coonamessett also offers spacious suites. Splendid views of gardens and the grounds meet you each morning. The inn is located near all the beauty and adventure the Cape has to offer. This gracious and glorious inn is open year-round.

Falmouth Inn $$-$$$
824 Route 28, Falmouth
(508) 540-2500, (800) 255-4157
www.falmouthinn.com
One of Falmouth's larger hotels, the Falmouth Inn is a single-floor facility catering to those who seek value as well as convenience. Located in the center of Falmouth on Main Street, the Falmouth Inn offers 123 spacious rooms that include color TV with free HBO, direct-dial telephone, year-round temperature control, indoor corridors, game room, and an outdoor courtyard. The retractable roof of the heated indoor-outdoor pool is unique

for Cape Cod. You may enjoy the soothing pleasures of a sauna. On-site is a restaurant and cozy lounge. Falmouth Inn is near all of Falmouth's marvelous assets, including Main Street shops and restaurants, beaches, Falmouth Harbor, and the *Island Queen* ferry. In the fall and spring, the hotel offers rates that are nearly half that of summer rates, as well as special rate packages that include two meals. Inquire about getting a preferred tee time at the Falmouth Country Club golf course. The inn is open year-round and welcomes pets. There is no charge for children younger than 18.

Inn on the Square $$-$$$
40 Route 28, Falmouth
(508) 457-0606, (800) 676-0000
www.innonthesquare.com
In a town with so many long-established accommodations, this relative newcomer has a lot to offer, including an indoor heated pool and a dining room and lounge area (Tavern on the Square, which is open to the public). The dining room is open for breakfast, lunch, and dinner. This inn is close to the Bonanza Bus Line terminal and the Shining Sea Bike Path, as well as the many shops, museums, and restaurants of Falmouth. The wheelchair-accessible inn has 72 attractive rooms and suites. All rooms have double beds. The Inn on the Square is open year-round.

Shore Way Acres Inn $$-$$$
59 Shore Street, Falmouth
(508) 540-3000, (800) 352-7100
www.shorewayacresinn.com
In a classic New England setting along Shore Street, with its colonial homes and centuries-old elm trees, rests Shore Way Acres Inn. At one end of the street and only a few minutes walk away is the picture-perfect Surf Drive town beach were you can look out across Vineyard Sound to Martha's Vineyard. The street's other end empties onto Main Street, where you will find, well, everything. Shore Way Acres offers several options for accommodations. If you enjoy the cozy comfort of a

country inn, you'll feel very much at home in one of the fully restored 18th-century Sea Captain's houses with their traditional furnishings and yesteryear charm. If you appreciate the style of a conventional hotel, you'll enjoy a tastefully appointed room in one of the contemporary buildings. All guest rooms include private bath, telephone, cable TV, and individual air-conditioning and heat control. Many rooms offer special features such as a full kitchen, decorative fireplace, coffeemaker, refrigerator, sitting area, balcony, and private terrace. There's a lot here to keep you busy. Besides a sauna and an outdoor and an indoor pool (enclosed with large windows overlooking the beautiful grounds), there are also badminton, croquet, and volleyball courts; lawn swings; a Victorian gazebo; umbrella tables; and barbecue grills on-site. Nearby you'll also find tennis courts, golf courses, horseback riding, fishing, and bike-riding facilities. You can get discounted ferry tickets in the lobby, and the desk staff will help you make arrangements for group activities. Excellent value packages for weekends, honeymoons, and reunions are offered at the Shore Way Acres with meals provided. The inn is open year-round.

Green Harbor Waterfront Motor Lodge $$–$$$
134 Acapesket Road, East Falmouth
(508) 548-4747, (800) 548-5556
www.gogreenharbor.com
If you like to be close to the water, you'll like Green Harbor's beachfront accommodations. This East Falmouth fixture rests on the Green Pond inlet, which eventually empties into Vineyard Sound and is perfect for kayaking or canoeing. Green Harbor has 40 pleasantly appointed units. Each waterfront guest room offers one queen and one double bed, a private full bath, cable TV, telephone, and microwave, refrigerator, and individually controlled heat and air-conditioning. Waterfront vacation cottages feature three bedrooms, working fireplace, full kitchen, and yes, three televisions. In all about half of the

accommodations feature a full kitchen. The family-run facility, which caters to mostly families, has an outdoor pool as well as a 1-foot-deep kiddie pool. There are docking facilities available for your use if you plan to arrive on your own boat. Other on-site amenities include volleyball and shuffleboard courts, charcoal grills, and a boating beach. Rowboats and paddleboats are also available for guest use. The lodge is open from May to November. Green Harbor allows pets as long as they are not left unattended in the room.

New Seabury Resort $$$$
Rock Landing Road (off Great Neck Road S.), Mashpee
(508) 477-9111, (800) 999-9033
www.newseabury.com
Established in 1962, this exclusive oceanfront resort with 3 miles of beach frontage is one of the premier resorts on Cape Cod. More than 100 one-bedroom/one-bath or two-bedroom/two-bath condo villas with full kitchens are available, some offering fantastic ocean views. New Seabury is an adults' playground with two great golf courses, one of which is one of the best in New England; two outdoor pools; numerous tennis courts; bike and hiking trails; a restaurant; a lounge; and an on-site marketplace with paths of crushed clam shells. New Seabury has one wheelchair-accessible unit. Open from March to the end of October.

Mid-Cape

Centerville Corners Motor Lodge $$–$$$
1338 Craigville Beach Road, Centerville
(508) 775-7223, (800) 242-1137
www.centervillecorners.com
A short walk from popular Craigville Beach on Nantucket Sound, Centerville Corners Motor Lodge is ideally located in the lovely, whaling Captain's Village of Centerville. From here you are within minutes of the Kennedy Compound in Hyannisport, the ferryboats to the islands,

elegant restaurants, and the Main Street historic district of Hyannis. Kayakers will delight in paddling the nearby Centerville River. Bring your bikes; from the motel you can pedal into Osterville or Hyannis with relative ease.

This 30-year-old lodging blends colonial charm with gracious modern amenities. Each spacious room is equipped with color cable TV, direct-dial telephones, two double beds, newly tiled baths, and individually controlled air-conditioning. Each day, in season, continental breakfast is served in the motel's coffee shop. The indoor heated pool and saunas overlook the large, private grounds, which you are free to use for picnics, barbecues, croquet, badminton, or just relaxing with your favorite book.

Additionally Centerville Corners Motor Lodge is right across the street from the legendary Four Seas ice-cream parlor and just a short stroll to the 1856 Penny Candy Store and the Centerville Historical Society Museum. Dogs are permitted with prior approval. Golfers should ask about the motel's package deals.

Check around for golf packages when looking for a place to stay on Cape Cod. Many hotels, motels, and resorts offer golf packages that include accommodations for two nights, two rounds of golf, and dinner discount certificates.

Trade Winds Inn   **$$–$$$**
Craigville Beach Road, Craigville
(Barnstable)
(509) 775-0365, (877) 444-7966
www.twicapecod.com
Set upon a hill that runs down to Craigville Beach on one side and Lake Elizabeth on the other, this inn on six acres provides some of the very best views of Nantucket Sound. You can choose from three buildings housing 35 rooms—the Ocean View in the main building offering (you guessed it) ocean views, and the Sea Breeze and Sea Shore buildings without ocean views. All the rooms at this motel-with-a-bed-and-breakfast-feel have air-conditioning, and a good many of them come with a patio or balcony.

Tucked away along the east end of Craigville Beach, it is just a five-minute drive to the fine restaurants of Hyannis, the Cape Cod Melody Tent (see our Arts chapter), the ferries to the islands, and Hyannis's Main Street shops. The inn serves a continental breakfast in season and has a patio with umbrella tables. Enjoy Trade Winds' private beach on Nantucket Sound (complimentary beach chairs are provided), putting green, and outstanding, friendly service. Open from April to the end of October, the inn's off-season rates are nearly half of summer rates.

The Anchor-In   **$$$**
1 South Street, Hyannis
(508) 775-0357
www.anchorin.com
You can't get much closer to Hyannis Harbor than this! The Anchor-In offers a great location with outstanding views, super rooms, immaculate grounds, and a delightful staff. Just 60 feet from the water's edge in downtown Hyannis, the Anchor-In is within walking distance of restaurants, island ferries, excursion boats, and shopping. Hyannis Marina, many boats, and a public boat launch are within sight. Most of the 48 rooms, whether standard, deluxe, or executive, have a private deck and a harbor view and sleep four comfortably. Four executive rooms can accommodate six, and two of those executive rooms also features Jacuzzis. All rooms are spotlessly clean, comfortable, and attractively furnished; two rooms are fully wheelchair accessible. A large private pool and lawn, complete with a huge grounded anchor to support the inn's name, overlook the harbor.

Open year-round, the Anchor-In caters to international guests from around the world (primarily the UK, Germany, France, and Canada) who are often surprised and delighted to see their country's flag flying from the Anchor-In poolside flagpole—just one more added touch of hospitality.

Days Inn $$-$$$
867 Route 132, Hyannis
(508) 771-6100, (800) 368-4667
Open from mid-February to the end of November, this 99-room Days Inn offers a central location convenient to shopping, restaurants, and the airport. Just down the road in one direction is the Hyannis Golf Course; in the other direction is downtown Hyannis with its Kennedy Museum and Memorial. On-site are two pools (indoor and outdoor), a whirlpool, and an exercise room featuring treadmill and Nautilus. Five rooms are wheelchair accessible. An on-site coffee shop serves complimentary coffee from 7:00 to 10:00 A.M. A complimentary continental breakfast is also served. The inn is adjacent to the Cape Cod Mall and is a favorite accommodation for families as well as business travelers. Off-season rates drop significantly, and the Days Inn also participates in several discount programs.

Harbor House Inn $$$
119 Ocean Street, Hyannis
(508) 771-1880, (800) 211-5551
www.harborhouseinn.net
You will enjoy the best of everything that Hyannis has to offer at the Harbor House Inn. They are directly across the street from Hyannis Harbor, Cape Cod's most scenic waterfront area. All the units at the Harbor House are minisuites, each with either two full, two queen, or a king-size bed and either a balcony or patio. Large. light, and modern, each unit also contains a separate full kitchen, remote-control color TV, and individual heat and air-conditioning. Interestingly each suite also has windows with screens and a screen door should you wish to enjoy the salt breeze off the harbor—you don't find that too often on Cape Cod. The inn is a 100 percent nonsmoking accommodation. A continental breakfast is offered each morning. Within a short walk of the inn is

downtown Main Street with its great shops, boutiques, fine restaurants, and lounges. It is a very short walk to the ferries to the islands. The inn is open April to November.

Hyannis Harbor Hotel $$-$$$
213 Ocean Street, Hyannis
(508) 775-4420, (888) 810-0044
www.hyannisharborhotel.com
Breathe in the salt air, bathe in the sun, and watch the boats sail in and out of Hyannis Harbor while you relax on the sundeck by the beautifully landscaped outdoor pool and Jacuzzi. If it's raining, how about a dip in the heated indoor pool? At the Hyannis Harbor Hotel, you're directly across Ocean Street from picturesque Hyannis Harbor, just steps from the island ferries to Nantucket and Martha's Vineyard, as well as fishing chargers and sightseeing excursions. You are also only a short walk to Veterans Beach, the JFK Memorial, JFK Museum, downtown shopping, and many harborside restaurants.

A lot of effort has gone into ensuring that each of the 136 rooms has a Cape Cod style. Airy and open, many of the rooms offer balconies overlooking the scenic harbor and inviting outdoor pool area. Open from early May to late October.

Hyannis Inn Motel $$-$$$
473 Main Street, Hyannis
(508) 775-0255, (800) 922-8993
www.hyannisinn.com
The Hyannis Inn Motel is located right in the center of downtown Hyannis. Family-run for nearly 50 years, this motel is a good choice for active visitors who want easy access to everything Hyannis has to offer. With its reasonable rates and comfortable accommodations, it also appeals to visitors looking for an inexpensive Cape Cod vacation. Everything you will need is within walking distance—shops, attractions, island ferries, excursion tours, and whale watching—and beaches are but a few miles away. The 77 rooms are clean, well-maintained, and all feature what you would normally expect, like

remote-control cable color TV, direct-dial phone with data ports for your computers and voice mail, individual climate controls, and outside decks. They also have larger, deluxe rooms with sofa and refrigerator. For your special enjoyment there are a limited number of whirlpool rooms. Swim a few laps in the heated indoor pool, enjoy the sauna, and relax on the sundeck. You can start your day at their Bluebird's Restaurant, which serves breakfast, and unwind later in the day at the Elbow Room Cocktail Lounge, serving good cheer. They do have a wheelchair-accessible room. Children younger than 5 stay free. The motel is open from the beginning of February to mid-November.

If you plan on traveling to Martha's Vineyard or Nantucket, consider one of the hotels located on Ocean Street, Hyannis, directly across from picturesque Hyannis Harbor and the ferries to the islands.

Hyannis Travel Inn $$–$$$
18 North Street, Hyannis
(508) 775-8200, (800) 352-7190
www.hyannistravelinn.com
With 83 rooms, indoor and outdoor pools, saunas, and an oversized whirlpool (large enough for all your friends and then some), this well-maintained Hyannis facility is a good value for couples and families who want to be close to the many Hyannis attractions. Minigolf, the Cape Cod and Hyannis Railroad, shops, restaurants, beaches, and the John F. Kennedy Museum are all within a five-minute walk. Slightly longer walks will get you to the island ferries, the Hyannis waterfront district, and the Cape Cod Melody Tent (see our Arts chapter). Amenities include a continental breakfast with coffee, muffins, bagels, and juice plus discount coupons for area restaurants. The motel is closed for 10 weeks between Thanksgiving and February.

International Inn $$$
662 Main Street, Hyannis
(508) 775-5600
www.cuddles.com
How does a cuddle and bubble sound to you? We suppose that would depend on who's asking the question. Described as the most romantic accommodation in the Hyannis area, the International Inn is as centrally located as it is romantic: You'll find it at the west end of Main Street, just a short stroll from the Cape Cod Melody Tent (see the Arts chapter) and all the shops and sites along the popular main drag of Hyannis. A favorite spot for couples celebrating wedding anniversaries, the Inn's Cuddle and Bubble Plaza Suite is a sought-after getaway around Valentine's Day. This three-room suite includes a romantic king-size canopy bed, a wet bar, and an even wetter 5-by-7 foot sunken Jacuzzi. Besides bubble-laden Jacuzzis, the International Inn boasts the Gazebo Garden Room Restaurant, indoor and outdoor swimming pools, and saunas for men and women.

Ramada Inn Hyannis $$–$$$
1127 Route 132, Hyannis
(508) 775-1153, (800) 676-0000
www.ccrh.com
This 196-room Ramada has a lovely glass-walled pool area visible from the front lobby, and right off the pool is an inviting lawn with lounge chairs and an attractive dining room that serves breakfast, lunch, and dinner. Its central location makes it convenient for shopping and fine dining. Only a short walk to the Cape Cod Mall and hundreds of other shops and stores in the numerous other plazas along Route 132, you can leave your car parked and avoid heavy traffic along this popular stretch. Those not in the shopping mood will enjoy the Ramada's convenient location, near just about everything else in Hyannis, and close to U.S. Route 6, which takes you anywhere else you may want to explore.

The Ramada offers 20 post-and-beam design loft suites, 16 with efficiency units.

Each loft suite is two stories with a king-size bed on the first floor and a double-bed sofa on the second floor, two bathrooms, and an outside deck. They don't have a health club on the premises, but if you show your room key at a nearby health club, you have access to all their equipment. There's a good-size game room for the kids and across the hall a lounge for the adults. Open year-round.

Sheraton Hyannis Hotel & Resort $$$
West End Rotary, Hyannis
(508) 775-7775, (800) 843-8272
Across the street from the Cape Cod Melody Tent, this resort features an 18-hole par 54 golf course—a spectacular 2,600-yard course. If you are a golfer, look into their golf packages featuring unlimited use of the course. A full-service hotel/conference center, Sheraton Hyannis offers everything from concierge service to a beautiful 60-foot indoor pool and Schooner's restaurant, serving lunch and refreshments.

Most of the Sheraton's 224 rooms have views of the golf course or an attractive courtyard and offer double, king, and suite units. On premises you'll enjoy the Oyster Bar Cocktail Lounge. There is an on-site health club, which has free weights, Nautilus equipment, step and pool aerobics classes, sauna and massage, as well as the premier health spa on Cape Cod. Off-season midweek rates are about half the in season amount. Ask about their holiday and weekend packages. It is open year-round.

Americana Holiday Motel $
99 Route 28, West Yarmouth
(508) 775-5511, (800) 445-4497
www.americanaholiday.com
Conveniently located along Route 28 in West Yarmouth, near the Hyannis line, is the Americana Holiday Motel. This motel has 136 rooms, each with a full-size private bath and air-conditioning. A dozen or more beaches are close by, yet the Americana boasts three (yes, three) swimming pools—one indoor and two outdoor. The motel also has a sauna, steam room, and whirlpool bath to help you unwind. There's an on-site putting green and shuffleboard court for the adults and a game room and playground to keep the kiddies entertained. This family-owned and -operated establishment also has a coffee shop on-site serving free coffee all day and a continental breakfast each morning (which, during the off-season, is free with your stay). The Americana's attractive rates become incredible during the off-season (from the beginning of April to mid-June and from early September to mid-November) when they dip down into the $50s! Dinner discounts are offered at select local restaurants, and the first two children in your party younger than 12 stay free. The Americana is open from the beginning of April to mid-November.

Bayside Resort $$–$$$
225 Main Street, West Yarmouth
(508) 775-5669, (800) 243-1114
www.baysideresort.com
Refrigerators, cable TV with free in-room movies, and movies on demand make you feel at home. Many of the rooms have a sundeck and overlook Lewis Bay, where you can view one of the most beautiful inlets on the Mid-Cape. They also offer romantic Jacuzzi suites for two. There is an oversized whirlpool and sauna in the indoor pool area that also boasts a fully equipped fitness center. Bayside has the advantage of a pub, especially one within steps of the indoor tropical pool. Outside, the picturesque pool area has a great view of Lewis Bay and they have filled the large deck area with plenty of lounge chairs for your relaxation. They have also created the ambience of the beach without leaving the resort with an outdoor beach volleyball court and a sandy beach park, a perfect place to both start and end your day. Bayside Resort is open year-round.

Cape Point Hotel $$-$$$
476 Route 28, West Yarmouth
(508) 778-1500, (800) 323-9505
www.capepointhotel.com

Centrally located along West Yarmouth's popular Route 28, the Cape Point is an attractive accommodation with pretty flower gardens and reasonably priced rooms for families and budget-conscious travelers. A waterfall in the lobby greets you upon your arrival. The facility includes a lovely outdoor pool, a regal indoor pool with a balcony overhead, a children's pool, Jacuzzi, exercise room, and video game room to kept he kids entertained. Standard rooms have two queen-size beds, cable TV, refrigerator, and telephone. Deluxe rooms offer the same amenities but are approximately one-third larger and have a love seat–sofa that pulls out to a single bed. They also seemed to be located closer to the indoor pool. Two-bedroom family suites offer an extra special touch without taking an executive-size bite out of the family budget. Wheelchair-accessible accommodations are available. Open year-round, the inn also has a coffee shop and a lounge, the Sports Loft, on-site.

Green Harbor $$$$
182 Baxter Avenue, West Yarmouth
(800) CAPE COD
www.greenharborresort.com

Because it is surrounded by salt water on three sides, there's really no sense in mentioning the wonderful water views. Almost as beautiful as the water views are the lovely eight-acre grounds of grass and sand and gardens bursting with flowers. As for the accommodations, the 52 units here range widely in style from suites to cottages to villa townhouses. Some units are in separate cottages; others are in the main motel building. Some rooms have decks and patios, and villas have decks overlooking the ocean. An oversize outdoor pool and deck offer a change of scenery for those who have been spending time down on the private beach. An on-site minigolf course keeps the kids in the swing of things, and bikes, canoes,

and rowboats are all available. The angler in you will enjoy the jetties off the beaches. Or just pull up a chair and relax watching the tide rise and fall. Golfers take note: Green Harbor is a Red Jacket Resort. As their guest you can take advantage of other Red Jacket Resort amenities . . . like the Blue Rock Golf Course (see our Golf chapter). Green Harbor is open May to mid-October.

The Mariner $$-$$$
573 Route 28, West Yarmouth
(508) 771-7887, (800) 445-4050
www.mariner-capecod.com

This is a Cape golf resort of a unique kind. You see, the golf portion of the package includes a challenging nine-hole minigolf course. A putter is all you need, and that's provided. So are the golf balls. And the cost for a round is minimal, much less than the other miniature golf courses in the area. As for the motel itself, it has 100 clean, air-conditioned rooms with in-room refrigerators and safes for all the valuable sand dollars you'll find combing the beaches of Nantucket Sound. At the Mariner you'll also find a 50-foot heated indoor pool, a 55-foot heated outdoor pool, whirlpool, saunas, and a barbecue area. Yarmouth's Sea Gull Beach is only a five-minute drive away, and Hyannis (and the island ferries) is no more than 10 minutes down Route 28. There are numerous dining opportunities within a couple of miles, from casual to fine. The Mariner is open from early February to early December, and children stay for free.

Tidewater $$-$$$
135 Route 28, West Yarmouth
(508) 775-6322, (800) 338-6322
www.tidewaterml.com

A well-respected 100-room motel, the Tidewater is on four acres bordering a conservation area overlooking Mill Creek Bay and Mill Pond. One mile east of downtown Hyannis, it provides a location central to the many attractions of Yarmouth, island ferries, and the airport. Ideal for families and couples, this lodge has amenities that include a large indoor pool as well as an outdoor pool, hot Vita spa, sauna, coffee shop, and a game room that has table tennis, darts, and board games. Beaches are a short drive away, as is just about everything else, from movies, minigolf, and restaurants to outlets and shops. A large outdoor grassy area has picnic tables, a recreation area with volleyball net, sandbox, swings, and play equipment for the kids. The rooms feature remote control cable TV, with movies, telephone, and individually controlled heat and air-conditioning. Enjoy one of their new deluxe Jacuzzi rooms as your day comes to an end. The rooms, which have two double or one king-size bed, are clean, nicely furnished, and have refrigerators. Most of the property is nonsmoking. Wheelchair-accessible rooms as well as bed-and-breakfast packages are available. There is no charge for children younger than 17 staying with an adult. Tidewater is closed in January.

All Seasons Motor Inn $$
1199 Route 28, South Yarmouth
(508) 394-7600, (800) 527-0359
www.allseasons.com
Voted the Best Mid-Cape Motel 11 years in a row by the readers of *Cape Cod Life*, this high-quality resort has earned its reputation for excellent service. All 114 rooms have remote control color cable TV with VCRs, refrigerators, coffeemakers, hair dryers, individually controlled air-conditioning and heat, and private room safes. Many of the rooms have private balconies or patios that overlook the outdoor pool and garden courtyard, and all rooms are smoke-free. An indoor pool, whirlpool, sauna, exercise room, game room, and solarium are all accessible from your room through indoor corridors. You can also enjoy breakfast in the skylight dining room or greenhouse. Poolside lunch is available in season. All Seasons' location allows for easy access to many of the Cape's favorite attractions. Warm-water-sound beaches and fine dining are close. The popular golf courses of

Yarmouth and Dennis are within a short distance. The All Seasons Motor Inn has a spacious three-acre setting with gorgeous gardens and well-manicured lawns. Six wheelchair-accessible rooms are available. A year-round facility, the inn offers low off-season rates.

Blue Rock Golf Resort $$-$$$
Off Great Western Road, South Yarmouth
(508) 398-6962, (800) 237-8887
www.bluerockresort.com
We've golfed here dozens of times and still we've yet to master this devilishly tricky par 54 course with a number of water holes. The Blue Rock Golf Course has 18 holes, a pro shop, golf school, driving range, and putting green (see our Golf chapter for more information). The Blue Rock is a 40-room motel with either double or deluxe king accommodations. Rooms have temperature control and panoramic views of the golf course. After you've hit the course you can hit the heated outdoor pool, Jacuzzi, Grille Room restaurant, or on-site lounge. While you're waiting for your tee time, enjoy some tennis or a good book on your private patio or deck. Off-site you have access to a nearby private beach and biking paths. This Red Jacket inn is open from April to the end of October. There are golf packages (and other packages) available.

Blue Water $$$-$$$$
South Shore Drive, South Yarmouth
(508) 398-2288, (800) 367-9393
www.bluewater-resort.com
At this oceanfront hotel you can choose from among two swimming pools, a putting green, a tennis court, and, of course, the waters of Nantucket Sound. This Red Jacket facility has a dining room lounge that serves breakfast and lunch. Rugosa roses and sand dunes enhance the attractive well-kept grounds. The 83 units include clean, attractive rooms with two double beds, some efficiencies, three cottages, and a house with an in-room whirlpool. Some units are wheelchair

accessible. During the summer Blue Water offers supervised children's activities. Ask about the Blue Water's terrific package deals throughout the year. Children younger than 12 stay for free.

The Dunes Motor Inn $-$$
170 Seaview Avenue, South Yarmouth
(508) 398-3062, (800) 237-5070
www.thedunescapecod.com
Resting just 300 yards from the beach, the Dunes is a hidden Cape Cod treasure. The facility has 34 guest rooms, all decorated in Cape Cod scenes, and two cottages. The rooms have two double, king-, or queen-size beds, private baths, air-conditioning, cable television, and in-room phones. Efficiency units have two double beds along with a full kitchen set-up, and there's even a two-bedroom family suite. An on-site coffee shop serves a continental breakfast for a minimal charge. There's a heated outdoor pool available, and if that's not enough, the refreshing waters of Nantucket Sound are just a short walk away. The Dunes enjoys a high volume of repeat clientele during the summer and off-season. It is open from May to Columbus Day.

Gull Wing Suites $$
822 Route 28, South Yarmouth
(508) 394-9300, (800) 676-0000
www.ccrh.com
If you are looking for more room and want to stay in a suite, Gull Wing Suites has 136

Planning to bring your Windsurfer? Consider any one of the fine accommodations along South Shore Drive in South Yarmouth. Here the warm waters of Nantucket Sound lap at the shore outside your door and the prevailing winds of summer offer world-class windsurfing right from the beaches in front of the Red Jacket Beach Resort, (508) 398-6941.

---

contemporary minisuites with a sitting area, color TV, refrigerator, wet bar, and individual climate control. It is perfect for budget-conscious families who want extra room and deluxe treatment. Open year-round, the Gull Wing is a family resort with clean, comfortable rooms and a heated indoor pool, outdoor pool, whirlpool, sauna, Jacuzzi, and a game room for the kids. It also offers you a great location from which to visit area attractions, historical sites, and beautiful beaches. The Gull Wing welcomes children 18 and younger free when accompanied by an adult.

Ocean Mist Resort $$-$$$$
97 South Shore Drive, South Yarmouth
(508) 398-2633, (800) 248-MIST
www.capecodtravel.com/oceanmist
Ocean Mist's 63 rooms are either deluxe or loft suites. The beautiful, contemporary deluxe rooms feature wet bars or efficiencies. All have individual heat and air-conditioning controls and remote-control cable television. Their loft suites feature dramatic cathedral ceilings and wet bars. Most have skylights and two private balconies with panoramic views of the ocean. Ocean Mist has a heated indoor pool and a coffee shop. Restaurants are close by, and Hyannis shopping and dining, golf courses, and historic sites are within a few miles.

Red Jacket Beach Resort $$$-$$$$
South Shore Drive, South Yarmouth
(508) 398-6941, (800) 672-0500
www.redjacketinns.com
The Red Jacket has everything, including a 1,000-foot sandy waterfront beach as well as frontage on Parker's River salt marsh. Water views are everywhere from the dining room, outside swimming pool, and, of course, the rooms, some of which are practically on the beach.

If it's land sports that you prefer, their tennis courts and basketball and volleyball courts are sure to please. Their jogging

At the Red Jacket Beach Resort you can swim in the heated outdoor pool and still have a beautiful view of the oceanfront. RED JACKET BEACH RESORTS

route provides an excellent view of the oceanfront as you wind past a lovely garden gazebo during your workout. A great place for families, the resort offers a supervised children's program of sports and activities. Kayaks are available for rent. In addition to their private beach, both the outdoor and indoor pools are heated. They also have a whirlpool spa and sauna to add to the enjoyment of your stay. You can also elect to stay in one of 13 townhouses.

Surfcomber $$$$
107 South Shore Drive, South Yarmouth
(508) 398-9228
www.surfcombermotel.com

The Surfcomber provides peace and quiet right by the water's edge. Sunbathing and swimming will be your occupation for the week, yet if you ever tire of the saltwater swimming, there is a heated outdoor swimming pool within earshot of the ocean waves. Four rooms look right out over the water. Many rooms offer private balconies overlooking the well-maintained grounds and pool, and approximately half of the rooms are efficiencies with a sink, fridge, and four-burner stove. The staff is friendly and often know the guests by name because so many visitors return year after year. Surfcomber is open from May to Columbus Day.

Colony Beach Motel $$-$$$
413 Old Wharf Road, Dennisport
(508) 398-2217
www.colonybeachmotel.com

With its charming colonial architecture and Cape Cod allure, this motel right on the sound is a perfect place to start the summer. You can choose from 47 rooms, including oceanfront and ocean-view efficiency units with a fully equipped kitchen and dining area, motel units, or nonefficiency suites with a living room. Among the amenities are a private beach and a heated outdoor swimming pool. Children 3 years of age and older are welcome. It's open mid-May to mid-October.

Want to stay in a waterfront hotel but don't know where to start? Try Chase Avenue in Dennisport, where you can find beachfront accommodations like the Corsair Resort, the quaint 'By the Sea' Guests Bed & Breakfast, and the Edgewater Resort, all offering sea, sand, comfort, and the convenience of fine restaurants and nearby kids' activities.

The Corsair and Cross Rip $$$-$$$$
41 Chase Avenue, Dennisport
(508) 398-2279
www.corsaircrossrip.com

These two Dennisport motels, resting side by side on Nantucket Sound, form a family-owned and -operated oceanfront resort on three acres of prime Nantucket Sound real estate. Together they offer an abundance of amenities, including two outdoor pools (one at each facility), two outdoor Jacuzzis, and two large sundecks overlooking the ocean. Recreation buildings across the street feature an indoor pool, a game room, a toddler area with plenty of toys, a barbecue area, and an outdoor play area for the kids.

There are many types of rooms from which to choose. All rooms at the Cross Rip, except for the economy units, have kitchenettes. You may want to go for a two-room oceanfront suite. The Corsair offers minisuites with two double beds and a galley kitchen, and oceanview suites featuring two rooms, a galley kitchen, and two baths (in the Captain's Suite). Open from late March through October, the complex also offers a pair of four-bedroom houses for rent across the street with access to the amenities.

The Edgewater Beach Resort $$-$$$$
95 Chase Avenue, Dennisport
(508) 398-6922
www.edgewatercapecod.com

Situated on more than five acres of waterfront at the farthest reaches of Dennisport, the Edgewater offers 89 units, all with balconies and views of either the ocean in all its glory or the attractive central courtyard and putting green. Some of the units have kitchenettes, but for those staying in the other 73 units, there are many fine restaurants within a 10- to 15-minute drive. The Edgewater has, arguably, the finest pool in the area: a magnificent oversized indoor-outdoor pool complete with a whirlpool and sauna. A note on the pool: half of it is glass contained, with a sliding glass door that cuts the inside portion off from the outside portion in the event of inclement weather. Also on-site are a fitness center and two shuffleboard courts.

Pelham House Resort Motel $$$–$$$$
14 Sea Street, Dennisport
(508) 398-6076, (800) 497-3542
www.pelhamhouseresort.com
For more than 60 years, the Pelham House has been a fixture at the end of Sea Street. It has everything you want in a Cape Cod vacation: a beautiful, private sandy beach on the warm waters of Nantucket Sound, 35 modern oceanview rooms with private decks, a large saltwater swimming pool, tennis, free breakfast, and warm hospitality. There's also a bar for poolside or before-dinner cocktails. All rooms include color cable TV, individually controlled heat, private baths, and refrigerators. Most rooms have two double beds; deluxe beachfront rooms have two queens, and king- and queen-size beds are available in the penthouse suites.

The owners, the McCarthy and Collins families, pride themselves on the individual attention each guest receives. In particular Bob McCarthy Sr. makes sure that each day is a "new" production at the Pelham House Resort.

The resort is ideal for family reunions, conferences, meetings, and especially weddings in the spring and fall. In true Cape Cod fashion, a large tent is erected for these happy occasions on the resort's expansive lawn on a knoll overlooking the sound. Open April to November, rates vary with season. Ask about their seasonal packages, which include full breakfast buffets.

The Soundings Seaside
Resort $$$–$$$$
79 Chase Avenue, Dennisport
(508) 394-6561
www.thesoundings.com
A huge complex right on the water, the front section of its main building is distinguished by colonial architecture accented with four Greek Revival Doric columns. The Soundings has two swimming pools to complement its 360 feet of waterfront—one a heated indoor pool and the other one actually on the beach with a poolside snack bar to boot. Other amenities include sauna, Jacuzzi, a putting green where you can loosen up before playing Dennis's two 18-hole golf courses (see our Golf chapter), and an on-site coffee shop serving breakfast to start the day off right.

This oceanside facility has 100 rooms, each with individually controlled air-conditioning. Room options are plentiful: You can choose from pavilion rooms at the inner courtyard, deluxe ocean-view, and deluxe on-the-ocean rooms, efficiency units, and a penthouse with a full kitchen. The Soundings' season runs from May 1 to mid-October and families are, of course, most welcome.

Lower Cape

Ocean Edge Resort $$$$
2660 Route 6A, Brewster
(508) 896-9000, (800) 343-6074
www.oceanedge.com
Truly a landmark resort, Ocean Edge is distinguished by the impressive Gothic and Renaissance Revival stucco mansion and stone carriage house standing tall and stately beyond a beautifully manicured lawn. Once part of the vast Roland Nickerson estate, the main 400-foot-long building is the Ocean Edge Conference Center and is every bit as grand inside as out, with carved wood-paneled walls and Oriental rugs. The resort takes up 380 acres on both the north side (where the

mansion is) and the south side along Route 6A. Attached to the main building by enclosed walkways is a 90-room hotel that offers room service among other amenities. Behind the main building, beyond the tennis courts and pool are condominiums, some of which have ocean views. Across the road is the Villages, a huge residential and rental condominium community with a golf course, pool, Linx Restaurant, and the Reef Cafe at its center. You can book anything from suites to three-bedroom condos; some rooms have fireplaces, and all have cable TV and phones.

People flock here for the world-class golf (see our Golf chapter), tennis schools and clinics (fees are in addition to room rates, but golf and tennis packages are available), and for the abundance of other recreational activities. The resort has six pools, four outdoor and two indoor, and a 1,000-foot private beach for guests to use. Ocean Edge also offers children's activities in summer and year-round concierge services to help you plan activities. The elegant mansion is home to the comfortable, wood-paneled downstairs Bayzo's Pub, which serves light fare, and the adjacent Ocean Grille for fine dining.

Wychmere Village $$-$$$
767 Route 28, Harwichport
(508) 432-1434, (800) 432-1434
www.wychmere.com
A great place for a family getaway, Wychmere Village is a causal, family-style compound of 24 comfortable units tucked away on three acres of pine groves and gardens. Your hosts, Larry and Judy, are more than gracious. The motel features a spacious sundeck, pool, picnic area with charcoal grill, and badminton and shuffleboard courts. The beaches are two minutes away, and Saquatucket Harbor, with its boats, ducks, and geese, is a mere 200-yard jaunt. Choose from a variety of room types, including traditional motel units, efficiencies, two-bedroom suites, and a two-bedroom cottage. All rooms have a country decor, are air-conditioned,

and feature cable TV, refrigerators, and complimentary maid service. Nonsmoking units are available. Wychmere Village is open from early April through December.

Chatham Bars Inn $$$$
297 Shore Road, Chatham
(508) 945-0096, (800) 527-4884
www.chathambarsinn.com
Built in 1914 as a hunting lodge by a wealthy Boston family, this resort still maintains its elegance and grandeur. The inn's impressive main house, which looks out over the water, has 40 rooms, with another 165 in buildings just outside the main house and across the street along the shore. All the rooms are inviting and purposely understated—decorated with lots of wicker and floral prints and fabrics—and nearly all of them have a balcony that offers breathtaking views of the Atlantic Ocean and Pleasant Bay. The 25 acres of grounds boast every conceivable sport from tennis to shuffleboard, along with a private beach and a heated outdoor pool. How about a game of volleyball? There's a concierge available daily in summer and on weekends in the off-season to help you plan excursions and other activities. Three restaurants complete the idyllic picture. The Chatham Bars Inn offers a number of off-season packages.

Pleasant Bay Village
Resort Motel $$$-$$$$
1191 Route 28, Chatham
(508) 945-1133, (800) 547-1011
Painstakingly renovated over the last decade by innkeeper Howard Gamsey, this 58-room facility is set on six acres of beautiful grounds, with Japanese and other stunning gardens, waterfalls cascading into an ornamental pond of koi fish, and private woodland. Pleasant Bay Village's efficiencies and suites are furnished in contemporary style. Original art from some of Cape Cod's well-known artists adorns the walls, and every accommodation, from rooms to two-bedroom suites, is comfortable, private, and quiet. One

room is wheelchair accessible. Wake up to complimentary morning coffee and newspapers. Full breakfasts are available, as is lunch beside the outdoor heated pool and, in summer, dinner for guests. Children are welcome, and the facility, open from mid-April through October, is nonsmoking.

The Seafarer of Chatham $$–$$$
Route 28 and Ridgevale Road, Chatham
(508) 432-1739, (800) 786-2772
www.seafarerofchatham.com
Owners Don and Lynn Cahoon say they offer "the privacy and comfort of a modern motel with the charm of a country inn." The Seafarer, situated along Chatham's historic district, has one of the Cape's loveliest (and quietest) settings, where welcoming lounge chairs and old-fashioned Adirondack chairs nestle among lavish flower gardens.

Each of the 20 ground-level rooms in the blue-trimmed, brick building have been hand-stenciled in the authentic colonial manner with decorative borders and have tiled baths. Coffee and tea service are offered. Children are welcome at the Seafarer, which is open April through November.

Wequassett Inn $$$$
Route 28 at Pleasant Bay Road, Chatham
(508) 432-5400, (800) 225-7125
www.wequassett.com
This resort is almost a village unto itself. The 22-acre estate, which takes its name from a Native American word that means "crescent on the water," actually comprises 20 buildings, including one built in 1740. Each of the 104 rooms and suites has views of Pleasant Bay, Round Cove, or the woods and is furnished in Early American or country pine. So exquisite is the decor that many rooms have won national design awards.

Tennis buffs can stay in one of three villas, just steps away from four all-weather tennis courts. The inn also has its own dock and offers a sailing program for novices to salty-dog sailors. (The inn even

has a rental fleet of Hobie Cats and Sunfish.) If you're not in the mood for salt water, take a dip in the awesome 68-foot heated pool

Golfers will be happy to learn the Wequassett is affiliated with the exclusive nearby Cape Cod National Golf Club, allowing guests to arrange for tee times at the private course.

The staff here is attentive but far from stuffy, and a concierge is available to help you with everything from dinner reservations to fishing excursions. The Wequassett is open from mid-April to mid-November.

The Cove $$$
13 Route 28, Orleans
(508) 255-1203, (800) 343-2233
www.thecoveorleans.com
The sparkling waters of Town Cove lap at the shore of this attractive year-round complex, which features beautifully landscaped gardens and patios, a heated outdoor pool, and, of course, terrific water views. Many of the 47 rooms have views of Town Cove, and many have private decks. All are equipped with heat and air-conditioning, queen- or king-size beds, private baths, phones, TVs, refrigerators, and coffeemakers. Nonsmoking rooms are available, and children are welcome. Book a waterfront room or, for an extra special stay, a room at the Inn at the Cove. It has 10 rooms and suites (eight with fireplaces, some with full kitchens), all warm and cozy with Shaker-style furnishings. Visit the waterfront gazebo, where you can commune with the terns and gulls, and watch sailboats tack by. An added bonus: Guests get a free 90-minute boat tour around Town Cove, an experience not to be missed!

Nauset Knoll Motor Lodge $$$
237 Beach Road, East Orleans
(508) 255-2364
www.capecodtravel.com/nausetknoll
Resorts can boast that they are located on the water, but only a few can say they are located on the ocean. Situated on a

knoll overlooking Nauset Beach and the Atlantic, every room commands a superb view of the ocean. Here you can relax with the rhythmic sounds of the Atlantic Ocean's crashing surf. Four acres of man-icured grounds assure privacy. The Nauset Knoll consists of 12 spacious rooms, all on ground level, cooled by the sea breeze. Each room has an 8-foot picture window facing the ocean, ceramic tiled bathroom with tub and shower combina-tion, color TV, and baseboard hot-water heat. Operated under the supervision of the National Park Service, the Nauset Knoll is the only motel on the Atlantic Ocean within the Cape Cod National Seashore. If you need more, the lodge is just a short drive to fine dining and the attractions of the lower Cape. We'll give you a tip about this place: Try to plan a fall stay at the lodge. You will have the beach all to yourself, you'll enjoy the warm fall waters that have heated all summer, and if you're a birder, you'll enjoy the best birding of the year along the dune uplands. Children are welcome at Nauset Knoll, which is open from mid-April to late October.

Orleans Holiday Motel   **$$–$$$**
Route 6A, Orleans
(508) 255–1514, (800) 451–1833
www.orleansholiday.com
Open year-round in Orleans, the Orleans Holiday Motel has 45 contemporary, clean rooms in a great location just outside of town. The motel offers accommodations with two double beds, one queen-size bed, or two queen-size beds. Rollaway beds and cribs are also available. Each room is fully carpeted and includes air-conditioning, heat, bath with tub and shower, direct-dial phones, color cable TV with HBO, and a refrigerator.

During the summer months, this is a great place to stay. The pool has an extra-large shallow section for children. The nicely landscaped backyard area is ideal for barbecues and picnics. It's close to family dining—across the street from a Chinese restaurant and next door to the Egg and I breakfast spot and the local favorite, the Lobster Claw Restaurant. A complimentary continental breakfast is served in the motel lobby every morning from 8:00 until 11:00 A.M. Most rooms are nonsmoking.

Seashore Park Inn   **$$–$$$**
Canal Road, Orleans
(508) 255-2500, (800) 772-6453
www.seashoreparkinn.com
Centrally located, this 62-room, family-oriented resort features a large indoor pool in a huge glass-walled room that you may have a hard time tearing the kids away from. That is, until they realize how close this property is to area attrac-tions. The Seashore Park Inn is near restaurants, shops, the Cape Cod National Seashore, and other beaches, as well as the Cape Cod Rail Bicycle Trail. A continental breakfast is served every morning in the sunny cafe over-looking the outdoor pool. Many of the rooms are efficiency units, with refriger-ators, stoves, and a second sitting area with a sleep sofa. All the rooms have two double beds, telephones, cable tele-visions with remote controls, and the efficiencies have two TVs. Most of the rooms offer balconies or patios. The facility is 100 percent nonsmoking. Open from April through November, the Seashore Park Inn offers off-season rates as well as money-saving weekly rates any time of year. Children younger than 17 stay free.

Captain's Quarters Motel and
Conference Center   **$$–$$$**
U.S. Route 6, North Eastham
(508) 255-5686, (800) 327-7769
www.captains-quarters.com
With 70 rooms, tennis courts, an outdoor heated pool, and access to the bike path, this family-run facility has a lot to offer. Rooms all have wall-to-wall carpeting, air-conditioning and heat, refrigerators, phones, color cable TVs, and queen-size or double beds. Enjoy a complimentary breakfast in the lounge area, which fea-

tures a delightful hand-painted mural of nearby Nauset Light Beach. You can also help yourself to fresh popcorn later in the day. Families find this a good place to make their home base as they explore the Outer Cape. For business people the Captain's Quarters offers conference facilities. It's open from April to November.

Eagle Wing Motel   **$$$**
960 U.S. Route 6, Eastham
(508) 240-5656, (800) 278-5656
www.eaglewingmotel.com
All 19 rooms in this little gem, located near the Cape Cod National Seashore, have private baths, air-conditioning and heat, refrigerators, cable TV, and phones. Most have king-size beds. A back deck stretches the length of the building so guests can enjoy the quiet backyard, which borders a wetland sweet with birdsong in spring and summer. There's a large outdoor pool, and morning coffee is available. Ideal for couples looking for quiet, clean, and comfortable surroundings, the Eagle Wing provides all the amenities of a large facility while maintaining the feel of a guesthouse or inn. The motel, which is completely non-smoking, is open May through October.

Four Points Hotel   **$$$**
U.S. Route 6, Eastham
(508) 255-5000
www.fourpoints-eastham.com
The Four Points Hotel, part of the Sheraton chain, has 107 recently renovated guest rooms, including two suites, all beautifully appointed. The indoor atrium and pool are soothing, steamy balm at the end of a long day (there are also men's and women's saunas and an outdoor pool). The fitness room is stocked with up-to-date equipment. The on-site restaurant serves breakfast and dinner (daily in summer, but weekends only in the off-season), and the Regency Lounge is open for late-night cocktails. There's also a tavern by the indoor pool. Four Points is open year-round and is great for families or business travelers.

Midway Motel & Cottages   **$$-$$$**
5460 U.S. Route 6, North Eastham
(508) 255-3117, (800) 755-3117
www.midwaymotel.com
Right on the scenic 25-mile Cape Cod Rail Trail bike path, in the heart of the Cape Cod National Seashore and close to the Wellfleet Bay Wildlife Sanctuary, this homey complex is made up of four separate buildings, nicely spaced and set back from the road. There are a total of nine motel units, an efficiency, a three-bedroom cottage that can sleep six, and a one-bedroom cottage that can accommodate two to four people. All rooms have full baths, cable TVs, air-conditioning, ceiling fans, coffeemakers, refrigerators, and microwave ovens. The three-acre property has a play yard for children, and, for all ages, volleyball, horseshoes, and shuffleboard. Complimentary coffee is served each morning in the cozy common room. The Midway is open March through October.

Viking Shores Motor Lodge   **$$**
U.S. Route 6, Eastham
(508) 255-3200, (800) 242-2131
www.vikingshores.com
Centrally located within the Cape Cod National Seashore Park, Viking Shores not only offers a relaxing atmosphere in a wooded natural setting, but also direct access to the 26-mile Cape Cod Bike Trail, which is great for biking, rollerblading, running, or simply walking. Each of the 40 modern rooms are comfortable and feature cable TV, private baths, refrigerators, telephones, and individually controlled heat and air-conditioning. Outside, barbecue grills and picnic tables are sprinkled throughout the landscaped grounds. Nauset Beach and Coast Guard Beach on the Atlantic Ocean are just minutes away. If you enjoy tennis, don't forget your racquet to play on their courts. And the heated pool offers you the opportunity to just sit back and relax. If that's not enough, your hosts, Kevin and Leslie Holland, will make sure you enjoy yourselves. They can assist you with bike rentals and have enough bikes to accommodate family groups. They

are also happy to suggest a nature trail, guided walk, or a local seafood restaurant. The Audubon Sanctuary at Wellfleet Bay is less than a mile from the Viking Shores, and Ben & Jerry's is just down the street—always a plus when on vacation. A complimentary continental breakfast is served each morning in the commons area. The Viking Shores Motor Lodge is open April through October.

The Even'Tide $$–$$$
650 U.S. Route 6, South Wellfleet
(508) 349-3410, (800) 368-0007
(Massachusetts only)
www.eventidemotel.com

This friendly, family-owned motel is set so far back among the woods that you may feel like you're vacationing in the middle of a forest—if forests came complete with a 30-by 60-foot indoor pool. All the rooms at this year-round facility come with a refrigerator, cable TV, clock radio, coffeemaker, and heat and air-conditioning controls. The most popular units are the queen-size rooms with their pretty custom-made oak furnishings. Eight cottages, five of them A-frames with wood-stoves, are also available, and most have decks. Biking enthusiasts take note: The Cape Cod Rail Trail runs right through the backyard. An outdoor play area, complete with basketball court and horseshoe pit, beckons children and adults will appreciate the sundeck.

Mainstay Motor Inn $$
2068 U.S. Route 6, South Wellfleet
(508) 349-2350, (800) 346-2350
www.mainstaymotorinn.com

The Mainstay is convenient to everything. Tennis courts are within walking distance, the Cape Cod National Seashore is a scallop shell's throw away, Wellfleet Harbor's marina is practically in the front yard, and whale-watching boats in Provincetown are a few miles away. When you're tired of sightseeing, relax by the Mainstay's indoor pool, or soak in the Jacuzzi. Each of the 30 rooms here has a king- or queen-size bed or two double beds with a full bath,

refrigerator, and outdoor deck. Some rooms are efficiencies with microwave ovens as well, and there is also a three-room cottage available for rent by the week in season. A complimentary continental breakfast is served daily in the coffee room, which also houses the Mainstay's free lending library. It's open year-round.

Wellfleet Motel & Lodge $$–$$$
U.S. Route 6, Wellfleet
(508) 349-3535, (800) 852-2900
www.wellfleetmotel.com

With a total of 65 rooms, the Wellfleet Motel & Lodge is right on the Cape Cod Rail Trail bike path and just across the street from Audubon's Wellfleet Bay Sanctuary (see our Hiking and Biking Trails chapter). All the rooms—40 in the lodge and 25 motel units—are equipped with refrigerators and coffeemakers, and microwave ovens are available for a small fee. There's both an indoor and an outdoor pool, with a barbecue beside the latter. Chose from seven different types of rooms, including suites. The lodge has a coffee shop with a full breakfast menu, and the facility is open year-round.

Horizons Beach Resort $$–$$$
190 Route 6A, North Truro
(508) 487-0042, (800) 782-0742
(outside Massachusetts)
www.horizonsbeach.com

In a quiet, rural setting just a short drive away from the shops, restaurants, and attractions of Provincetown and only a mile from Cape Cod National Seashore, Horizons Beach Resort offers 75 efficiency units, some right on the beach and the rest a short stroll away. All have air-conditioning, heat, cable TV, kitchens, refrigerators, and coffeemakers. Beachfront units have private decks with stunning views of Cape Cod Bay. Relax on the 480-foot, private beach on Cape Cod Bay, or take a dip in the beachside pool. Horizons is open from early April to early November and also offers two-room condominium units with fireplaces.

Topmast Motel $$-$$$
209 Shore Road, North Truro
(508) 487-1189
www.capecodtravel.com/topmast
This two-story motel, right on Cape Cod
Bay and surrounded by conservation land,
enjoys incredible views. Choose from a
total of 33 units: beachfront motel or efficiency units with stoves, sinks, refrigerators, and microwave ovens, or poolside
rooms with views of the landscaped
grounds. Beachside rooms have private
balconies overlooking the private beach,
which is cleaned daily, and the outdoor
pool is surrounded by chaise longues and
picnic tables. You can get breakfast all
day at the poolside eatery, Harbor Lights
(see our Restaurants chapter), along with
lunches and a Friday night fish fry. Run for
more than 30 years by the Silva family,
this well-kept facility is the only beachfront motel in the area with its own
restaurant. Topmast is open May 1 to
mid-October.

Best Western Chateau Motor Inn $$$
105 Bradford Street West, Provincetown
(508) 487-1286, (800) 528-1234
www.bwprovincetown.com
High atop a hill at the west end of town,
this 54-room facility enjoys sweeping
views. It's run by the Gordon family, and
it's as meticulously kept as their Beachfront property (see next entry). The rooms
are all newly done in classic Cape decor,
and each has a large TV, refrigerator, and
air-conditioning. Some rooms are even
equipped with private safes. There's a
large heated pool, restaurant, and lounge,
lovely gardens, and a number of decks
overlooking the water. Kids stay free, and
here guests get complimentary morning
coffee and muffins. It's open from early
May to mid-October.

Best Western Tides Beachfront $$$
837 Commercial Street, Provincetown
(508) 487-1045, (800) 528-1234
www.bwprovincetown.com
The Gordon family, which has owned this
two-story chain motel for many years,
devotes its considerable experience and
energies to the care of the tidy, comfy,
oceanfront motel and its guests. (The
lawns alone—greener than we've ever
seen—will be your first clue to the staff's
special care of the motel.)

The 64 rooms are several notches
above your standard motel fare, clean and
comfortable, with air-conditioning, heat,
and cable TV. Almost half the rooms literally sit at the water's edge, so you can
wake up in the morning and walk through
the sliders to the surf. The motel also has
a fenced-in pool, badminton courts, and
plenty of free parking, and an on-site
restaurant (open to the public) that serves
breakfast and lunch only. A boon for families: Children younger than 18 stay free!
Best Western Tides Beachfront is open
from early May to mid-October.

HOSTELS

If you're a back-to-basics type of person
who would rather spend money on, say, a
nice dinner or some pricey souvenirs than
empty your wallet on a fancy hotel, a hostel may be for you. And you won't be
alone. What was once the primary lodging
choice of the young and the broke
has become a frugal favorite among all
generations.

Beds are simple and often in dormlike
settings, and lockouts (those times when
you must vacate your room) and curfews
are strictly enforced. The American Youth
Hostels (AYHs) have lockouts timed
between 9:00 A.M. and 5:00 P.M.; nightly
curfew is 11:00 P.M. Reservations are necessary. Check-in is between 5:00 and 10:00
P.M. All AYHs offer free on-site parking and
bike storage.

The cost of a night's lodging is around
$20—a far cry from the usual motel room
rate of $70 to $150 or more.

The area has four AYHs—in Eastham,
North Truro, Martha's Vineyard, and Nantucket—and non-AYH members can stay
at them by simply paying the modest
additional fee for an introductory mem-

bership (also see our Nantucket and Martha's Vineyard chapters). AYH accepts VISA and MasterCard and offers discounts to area attractions. There's also a privately owned hostel in Provincetown. Below we give descriptions of the Cape hostels.

Hostelling International $
75 Goody Hallet Drive, Eastham
(508) 255-2785, (888) 901-2085
www.capecodhostels.org

The first things you'll notice as you drive through the three acres of grounds are the handmade wooden signs welcoming visitors in different languages. A nice touch, for hostels do attract a number of international travelers. This hostel offers 50 beds in eight cabins ($18.00 to $24.00, plus $3.00 for nonmembers). Two family cabins, which offer two double beds and two bunk beds and sleep six, are also available.

Guests can use the screened-in porch common room, picnic tables, grills, communal kitchen, volleyball and basketball courts, and game room. The grounds are lovely and wild, with birds singing in the trees and a gentle breeze blowing across the patio. The hostel is open mid-May through mid-September.

Hostelling International $
111 North Pamet Road, North Truro
(508) 349-3889
www.capecodhostels.org

There's a reason this hostel is perched high atop the sand dunes: It was once a Coast Guard Station known as Little America. Now this hostel's known by that name too. Its location within the Cape Cod National Seashore will give you unbeatable views of the coastline, cranberry bogs, beaches, and beautiful Cape Cod sunrises. The 42 beds are set up in a multilevel house. Rates are $17 to $25. It's open from late June through August.

Outermost Hostel $
28 Winslow Street, Provincetown
(508) 487-4378

This privately owned hostel has 30 beds in five whitewashed cabins—nothing to write home about but a steal at $18.50 per night. The hostel has a common living room and kitchen in one cabin. The expansive yard offers grills and picnic tables. The Outermost has no lockouts and no curfew. It's open mid-May to mid-October.

KENNELS

If you need a place for your dog or cat to stay—perhaps you got your signals crossed on whether your chosen accommodation allows pets, or maybe you'd like to take a couple of days and visit the islands, sans pooch—the Cape has a number of kennels. Here are a few of the best.

The Animal Inn
Route 130, Sandwich
(508) 477-0990

This veterinarian-owned facility has heated individual kennels, sheltered outdoor runs, and a separate kitty quarters. It offers grooming, obedience training, an on-premise vet clinic, and even a soothing sound system. The manager lives on the property, so your pets are always watched over.

Pleasant Bay Animal Hospital
Route 137 and Queen Ann Road, East Harwich
(508) 432-5500

This facility offers boarding and grooming as well as medical services. In business as an animal hospital for nearly 30 years under the ownership of Dr. Christopher Donner, Pleasant Bay began offering boarding several years ago. It has separate, air-conditioned accommodations for dogs and cats. Dogs get individual attention and are walked three times a day (or more if an owner chooses) on four and a half acres of property.

Derbyfield Country Kennel
556 Depot Street, North Harwich
(508) 432–2510

The owners reside at this kennel, which offers separate heated accommodations for dogs and cats and indoor/outdoor runs. Cats get extra-large, shelved cages so they can jump from level to level, and all pets get a treat at the nightly bed-

check time. Grooming and pickup and delivery are also available, as are premium pet supplies; special diets can be accommodated.

Nauset Kennels
2685 Nauset Road, North Eastham
(508) 255–0081

In business since 1972, this reputable facility offers indoor and outdoor runs, three outdoor play yards, and separate quarters for dogs and cats, with insulated floors and even air-conditioning. Nauset Kennels also does grooming and offers pickup and delivery. The owners live on premises.

BED-AND-BREAKFASTS, INNS, AND COTTAGES

One hundred and fifty years ago, travelers to various destinations on Cape Cod sought out lodging at day's end, seeking a hearty meal and a good night's rest in pleasant surroundings. Today travelers not only still look forward to the comfort of an inn at day's end, but many have made those inns destinations in themselves. Bed-and-breakfasts are usually private residences where the owners rent bedrooms (and sometimes suites) and offer a continental or full breakfast; inns are generally larger and often serve three-course gourmet meals for breakfast that could nourish you for the whole day. Because our bed-and-breakfasts and inns are often housed in older buildings, you get a firsthand taste of Cape history. It can be like stepping back in time—without giving up any modern comforts! In fact in exploring their amenities, we were impressed with recent remodels that include Jacuzzis, gas fireplaces in rooms, and data ports for those who can't leave the laptop at home. We are also proud to say that Cape Cod bed-and-breakfasts offer unsurpassed hospitality. Their loyalty to an era when accommodations were more intimate and more individualized provides a sense of community and an experience to be remembered. And though their architectural styles and ambience are as diverse as the 15 Cape Cod towns, if you are looking for a home-away-from-home for your stay, you'd do well to consider a stay at one of the Cape's many bed-and-breakfasts or inns.

Another option on the Cape is to stay in a cottage. Cottage colonies are clusters of small, individual cottages or cabins that may share a common kitchen and gathering space or may be self-contained with private bathrooms and small kitchens. Families with young children may find that cottage colonies are a good choice, because they aren't adorned with antique furnishings, as the inns often are, and there's plenty of space to run around in. Most are housekeeping cottages, meaning you clean up after yourself, and many require that you bring your own linens; be sure to ask exactly what the cottage supplies when you make your reservations.

Whatever type of accommodations you chose, it's likely to be an old one, each forming a small piece of our history. With the Atlantic Ocean to our east, Nantucket sound to the south, and Cape Cod Bay to our north, it's no wonder that many of our historic homes were built by sea captains. In the 1700s and 1800s, young men often went to sea, and many traveled to the far corners of the world, returning with their wealth to build homes (estates in their day). Brewster, for instance, is referred to as the Sea Captains' Town, where, it is said, 99 sea captains lived at one time. Towns like these also were dotted with large, rambling homesteads.

Today many such homes are bed-and-breakfasts. Private bathrooms have been enlarged to include showers and tubs, and, in keeping with modern desires, Jacuzzis have been added to many of the homes. Furnishings ranging from antiques to period reproductions grace common rooms, and in the guest rooms, canopied and four-poster beds offer a romantic atmosphere. Wide-planked floors, narrow hallways, steep ship's staircases, and fireplaces add to the country charm of each accommodation.

Historic houses with antique furnishings and civilized amenities such as crystal wine glasses and hand-stitched quilts don't mix well with boisterous children, so some bed-and-breakfasts don't allow children; others have age restrictions (we've heard of age cutoffs ranging from 6 to 18). We indicate those inns that welcome children and also let you know if these have age restrictions for their younger guests.

The Cape offers a variety of accommodations beyond the conventional. Rates also vary; the ones we give here include either a full or continental breakfast. Some establishments offer what they call "hearty" or "extended" continental breakfasts, which usually means fresh squeezed juice, homemade muffins and breads, granola, and a fruit course. Some of the innkeepers we've talked to are accomplished gourmet cooks who offer luscious breakfasts that far exceed expectations. The more ambitious ones offer multi-course gourmet treats that change each day of your stay and may include a main plate of elegant crepes, quiche, French toast, or whatever the innkeeper has chosen for the day. Some innkeepers have even had their recipes published in national magazines and cookbooks.

Most of the bed-and-breakfasts and inns we visited offer private bathrooms; the days of the shared bathroom seem to be in the past. Innkeepers are highly concerned about the privacy of their guests, and for that reason, some have in-room phones and televisions, whereas others pride themselves on being places where guests can escape ringing phones and the otherwise ubiquitous tube. Often, inns and bed-and-breakfasts compromise by offering TV and phones only in common areas. Most establishments do not allow pets, but we'll let you know if they do. Most innkeepers can make arrangements at a local kennel if you do need to bring your pet.

Our innkeepers take pride in their intimate knowledge of Cape Cod and will tell you everything they know if you ask. Remember that each establishment is as personal and unique as its innkeepers, who are more than willing to share their expertise and knowledge with you to make your visit more memorable. So ask them for recommendations about things to do in the area, places to visit, and the best restaurants. One good tactic: Ask

Not every hotel, bed-and-breakfast, or cottage is near the water. If being within walking or biking distance of the beach is a priority for you, be sure to ask about proximity to beaches before you book a place to stay.

your innkeepers where they go when they want to eat out and where they take friends who are visiting them from off-Cape. And don't be surprised if you find yourself developing a friendship with your hosts; many such relationships have been formed over long chats.

About smoking: Most inns and bed-and-breakfasts do not allow it. More and more patrons are demanding a smoke-free atmosphere, and the small, intimate nature of most inns makes it difficult, if not impossible, to set aside indoor smoking areas. Because there is usually no lack of patios, decks, lawns, and porches at such establishments, smokers in most cases will be able to find some outdoor area where they can light up. If a smoking policy is not mentioned in our write-up, assume it's outdoor smoking only. In rare cases smoking may be prohibited anywhere on the property, and we'll mention it if the policy is that strict.

A few Insiders' insights: Most establishments have cancellation penalties and restrictions. Calling to cancel less than two weeks before your arrival (especially in season) will almost guarantee that you won't get your deposit back (or that it will be applied to a future stay). Some establishments will give refunds in the event of cancellations only if they are able to rerent your room. Most accommodations require a two-night minimum stay during the peak season, three nights on holiday weekends. Some, however, have minimum stays as long as five nights in July and August. Cottages are generally rented by the week in season. Innkeepers are much more flexible in the off-season—before June and after September, or anytime besides July and August, depending on the establishment—and off-season rates are usually drastically reduced.

If you'd like help booking accommodations, check out the reservation services listed at the end of this chapter. Many of them specialize in inns and bed-and-breakfasts.

Most innkeepers accept major credit cards, but we'll let you know if a specific lodging does not. We'll also note when an inn is open year-round, or, if not, what months it is open. Many old inns find it difficult to meet handicapped access codes because of the historic nature of their buildings, but if an inn has wheelchair-accessible features, we'll mention that.

If you're planning to stay on Martha's Vineyard or Nantucket, see our special chapters on those islands later in the book for information on their accommodations.

And, please, respect the house rules, so you'll be warmly welcomed the next time you come!

PRICE CODE

The following key to room rates should help you get a quick fix on the range of prices available. The key is based on the average cost of a night's stay in a double-occupancy room during the peak summer season, minus tax and special charges, if any. State and local room tax combined is generally 9.7 percent.

$	Less than $100
$$	$100 to $150
$$$	$151 to $200
$$$$	$201 or more

BED-AND-BREAKFASTS AND INNS

Upper Cape

Wood Duck Inn   **$$**
1050 County Road, Cataumet (Bourne)
(508) 564-6404
www.woodduckinnbb.com

If you are a nature lover, especially a birder, looking for a serenely private getaway, this is the place for you. The Wood Duck Inn Bed and Breakfast is located in Cataumet, a seaside hamlet and one of the "villages" of Bourne. It offers a country setting on a peaceful rural road that meanders past fields and cranberry bogs. From the spacious, well-manicured lawn, you'll have sweeping views looking out toward 40 acres of cranberry bogs that connect with miles of wooded conservation area; if you walk farther out, you'll come to a large pond; beyond that you'll find Red Brook Harbor on Buzzards Bay. If you do walk through the grounds, or farther, you'll find the birding is great. But you don't necessarily have to go on a hike to spot wildlife. You might see foxes, coyotes, ospreys, or blue herons right from your guest-room window. The inn, built in 1848 by a sea captain's son, offers two suites and one comfy guest room, each with a private outside entrance—and easy access for the less mobile. The interior decor is tasteful and consists of charming country antiques, handmade quilts, and stenciling. The Cottage Room includes a microwave, refrigerator, television, phone, and private bath. The other two suites also come with television and phone and include a kitchenette, sitting room, private bath, and separate bedroom. The appropriately named Treetops Suite is more like a condo-efficiency complete with games and CDs to play on the stereo, and the Garden Suite is ideal for a romantic couple with its king-size antique featherbed and sweeping views of the bog and the inn's spectacular gardens.

Each morning your hosts and resident innkeepers, Dawn and Phil, leave a wonderful hot breakfast at your door, which you can enjoy at your convenience. "Our guests want to come and go as they please, and they love their privacy," notes Phil. "This allows them to take a relaxing morning walk and have a bite to eat before they leave and upon their return."

Though the Wood Duck Inn is out in the country, it is just 10 minutes from Falmouth center and the island ferries, 90 minutes to Boston, and 90 minutes to Provincetown at the tip of the Cape. The suites are private and spacious enough to welcome "peaceful" children. It is also a fine location for a country-style Cape Cod wedding. The inn is open year-round. No credit cards.

Bay Beach $$$$
1-3 Bay Beach Lane, Sandwich
(508) 888-8813, (800) 475-6398
www.baybeach.com

Overlooking captivating Cape Cod Bay, Bay Beach is your private window onto a world of luxury and exceptional beauty. Recognized by the American Bed and Breakfast Association as one of the top inns in North America, Bay Beach is truly an exceptional accommodation. One of the keys to its success is the professionalism, hospitality, and superb taste of owners Emily and Reale Lemieux. Each of the six spacious rooms is exquisitely decorated for elegant comfort in wicker, rattan, and rich color. Each room has a private bath, air-conditioning, a stereo with CD player, and refrigerator; three have Jacuzzis, and all have private decks. The views from this modern, oceanfront bed-and-breakfast are incredible—on a clear day you can see the Pilgrim Monument across the bay at Provincetown. This secluded, beachfront compound is just minutes from a wide variety of activities, including fishing, swimming, golf, biking, and walking trails. One room is wheelchair accessible. An extensive continental breakfast is served featuring homemade breads and fresh fruits. Children 16 years of age and older are welcome at the Bay Beach, which is open from May to the end of October.

The Belfry Inne and Bistro $$$-$$$$
8 Jarves Street, Sandwich
(508) 888-8550, (800) 844-4542
www.belfryinn.com

The Belfry Inne (ca. 1879) exemplifies an era renowned for gentility and grace.

From beneath a timeworn façade, innkeeper Chris Wilson has uncovered original cornerboards, fishscale scalloped shingles, and other fancy artistry from the Victorian age. This stately structure, once a rectory, is captivating. Splendid period detail, such as the original Eastlake newel post, Sandwich-glass double door, and other architectural features, have been faithfully restored.

The Inne, which encourages respite and relaxation, comprises two properties—the Drew House, an 1882 Victorian manor house, and the Abbey, a former church built in 1900. The Drew House, a true painted lady, features eight bedrooms, working fireplaces, and private baths, some with whirlpools. The Abbey has been transformed into six fabulous bedroom suites each distinctly decorated and named Monday through Saturday, from the book of Genesis. They feature gas fireplaces, ultra-massage whirlpools for two, king/queen beds, balconies, TV, and air-conditioning. Extra touches such as skylights, vintage bathtubs, hand-selected antiques, and down-filled duvets increase the feel of elegance. From a queen-size iron bedstead to a mahogany shell–painted headboard, each furnishing in each room has been restored to its late 19th-century charm. The inn features a full restaurant, the Belfry Bistro, where diners can savor delicious international cuisine and enjoy piano music nightly. The Belfry Bistro, located in the Abbey, specializes in intimate dinners for 2 or can cater an elegant affair for 85. A full guest breakfast is served buffet style daily; specialties include house-made granola and Inne-baked pastries and breads. Chris will most likely join you for coffee and help you plan your day's itinerary while on Cape Cod. A picture-postcard property in the heart of Sandwich center, the Belfry is close to all that historic Sandwich offers. Shops, museums, and the nature center are all within a short walk. The Belfry is open year-round. Children are welcome, but no pets are allowed.

The Captain Ezra Nye House $$
152 Main Street, Sandwich
(508) 888-6142, (800) 388-2278
www.captainezranyehouse.com

This homey bed-and-breakfast, built in 1829, displays the international flavor of a sea captain's home. You'll enjoy seeing the china collections, original art, Sandwich glass (of course), and a prominent painting of the *Independence,* Captain Nye's ship.

The inn has two common rooms and a lovely formal dining room where a large breakfast is served. There are six immaculate, antique-furnished rooms with private baths, some with hand-stenciling and four-poster beds. One room has a working fireplace. A suite with a private entrance has a queen-size bed, two rooms, and a private bath. Children age 10 and older are welcome at this year-round inn along historic Main Street, just a pleasant, leisurely stroll to all local sights.

Inn at Sandwich Center $$-$$$
118 Tupper Road, Sandwich
(508) 888-6958, (800) 249-6949
www.innatsandwich.com

This vintage Federal-style house was built during the mid-1700s and has, over the years, been beautifully restored to its original elegance. It features a beehive oven with a ca. 1750s fireplace and wide-planked floors, and is furnished with wonderful period pieces, including a beautiful oak hutch handcrafted locally by West Barnstable Tables. As the name implies, the Inn at Sandwich Center is conveniently located in town, just steps from the Sandwich Glass Museum, the Thornton Burgess Society Museum, Shawnee Pond, and Heritage Plantation. The inn itself is listed in the National Register of Historic Places.

There are five guest rooms, all tastefully appointed, most with fireplaces, some with lovely four-poster beds; all have private baths. Central air-conditioning makes things even more comfortable. There is a small library to browse through, and in the parlor, comfy chairs are available so that you may enjoy a good book. A continental breakfast is served each morning.

The Inn at Sandwich Center is open year-round and is nonsmoking. Ask about the inn's holiday packages. Children older than 12 are welcome.

Isaiah Jones Homestead $$-$$$
165 Main Street, Sandwich
(508) 888-9115, (800) 526-1625
www.isaiahjones.com

An elegant 1849 Victorian in charming Sandwich Village is furnished almost entirely with antiques. And, even though a few of the pieces in the Gathering Room are museum quality, innkeepers Jan and Dan Klapper are quick to point out that the comfy furniture is meant to be used and not just admired. Here you'll be able to enjoy rich Oriental items, antiques, and all the decorative drama of the Victorian era, including a curved main stairway and 11-foot ceilings. Built at the height of Sandwich's 19th-century prosperity, the rooms here are named for important Sandwich citizens, such as Thomas Dexter, who built the gristmill in 1654 in the center of town, and Deming Jarves, who was the founder of the Sandwich Glass Factory. All seven rooms are elaborately appointed, some with canopied and four-poster beds, two with a whirlpool, and three with working fireplaces. Each has a private bath. The Klappers serve a hearty breakfast that may include fresh scones, hot breads, egg strata, fresh fruit, and juices. After breakfast retire to a chair on the front porch overlooking Main Street to make plans for the day. There's much to do and see within walking distance, and Dan will assist you in making your plans. Tea, iced tea, and lemonade are served in the afternoon. Children 12 and older are welcome at this year-round inn.

The Village Inn at Sandwich $$
4 Jarves Street, Sandwich
(508) 833-0363, (800) 922-9989
www.capecodinn.com

This inn at the corner of Main and Jarves Streets evokes an earlier time, with its pretty flower gardens, wraparound porches with rockers, and rooms with hand-painted furniture. Built in the 1830s during Sandwich's industrial boom, which rendered it among the Cape's wealthiest towns, this home was restored about 12 years ago as an inn. It features eight guest rooms, two sitting rooms, and a dining room with a small wet bar for guests. Six rooms have queen-size beds and private baths, and two rooms have twin beds and a shared bath. Complimentary breakfast of French toast with strawberries or puffed pancakes is served. The inn, which welcomes children 12 and older, is open year-round.

Chapoquoit Inn $$-$$$$
495 Route 28A, West Falmouth
(508) 540-7232, (800) 842-8994
www.chapoquoit.com
This inn, surrounded by extensive gardens with a splendid array of seasonal flowers, affords you the perfect place to relax and unwind. You are encouraged to take advantage of the attractive and spacious living room. The entranceway is a typical Greek Revival affair, with pilasters, entablature, and half-length sidelights. Windows are simply framed and contain the old six-over-six sash, and a wonderful old arched window is located in the gable. A sunlit breakfast room opens to a deck overlooking a gazebo and the gardens. Choose one of the spacious guests rooms, lovingly decorated for your comfort with linens, colorful quilts, and an abundance of pillows. Each room has a character of its own and is furnished with various antiques, family mementos, and beautiful prints of Falmouth locations by local artist and family friend Karen Rinaldo. The master bedroom has pretty bay windows and a canopied king-size bed accented by a regal wall coloring. There are eight rooms in total, and all have private full baths. Wake up to the aroma of freshly brewed coffee and a breakfast of fresh fruit, muffins, breads, and a hot specialty each day served cafe style. Spend your days at Chapoquoit Beach, within walking distance; Old Silver Beach; or one of the ten other beaches in the area. The sunsets are

glorious on the tidal creek across the street. The inn is close to Falmouth Center and the island ferries. Chapoquoit Inn is open year-round. Children 12 and older are welcome.

The Inn at West Falmouth $$$-$$$$
66 Frazer Road, West Falmouth
(508) 540-7696, (800) 397-7696
www.innatwestfalmouth.com
Nestled among cedar trees high on a hill overlooking Buzzards Bay, this turn-of-the-20th-century shingle-style building will welcome you back to another era. The inn, with eight elegantly appointed guest rooms, offers seclusion, sweeping vistas, and magnificent sunsets. Once a country estate, the Inn at West Falmouth is furnished in Oriental, English, and continental antiques, and discriminating travelers will certainly revel in the sheer beauty and charm of this inn. Each guest room has a fireplace, private balcony, and a marble whirlpool tub. Relax with an afternoon sherry on the large screened-in porch while you take in the spectacular views of Buzzards Bay and the surrounding gardens. Breakfast is served in the dining room, where a wall of French doors and stained glass lead windows lead to an outside deck overlooking a heated pool and red-clay tennis court. The Inn at West Falmouth is open year-round.

Woods Hole Passage $$-$$$
186 Woods Hole Road, Woods Hole/
Falmouth line
(508) 548-9575, (800) 790-8976
www.woodsholepassage.com
The Woods Hole Passage is a quiet retreat located along the road that connects Falmouth with Woods Hole. It may be in one of the best locations on Cape Cod if you are looking for an active, outdoor-filled visit. Woods Hole is just minutes away and offers fine waterfront dining, and Falmouth, with its great variety of fashionable stores and beaches, is about the same short distance away in the other direction. But if you're looking to get outside, take an easy stroll to one of our

favorite spots on Cape Cod, Quisset Harbor, and the elevated rock outcrop affectionately known as the Knob (see our Hiking and Biking Trails chapter). If you are looking to bike, the inn is down the road from the famous Shining Sea Bike Path. Your host Deb Pruitt has assembled a handy map that highlights the varied walking and bike paths nearby and the roads that lead to the local beaches.

Woods Hole Passage itself was originally part of the adjoining larger estate. It is a rustic, century-old carriage house with a newly renovated barn on spacious grounds surrounded by old shade trees, and it has a lovely garden with a fish pond. The four guest rooms are located in the renovated carriage house. We would describe the rooms as "country modern," and what impresses first is how clean and airy the rooms are with their lace curtains and graciously appointed furnishings. All have private baths, air-conditioners, and queen-size beds with attractive bedspreads.

Deb prepares a hearty homemade breakfast of fruit, muffins, or sticky buns plus a main dish, all served on small private tables in the guest room overlooking the expansive lawn or on the patio in the summer. If you do want to venture to the islands for the day, a "breakfast-to-go" can be arranged. Woods Hole Passage is open year-round and it is a nonsmoking inn that welcomes children by prior arrangement.

Palmer House Inn $$$-$$$$
81 Palmer Avenue, Falmouth
(508) 548-1230, (800) 472-2632
www.palmerhouseinn.com

This is a Victorian charmer on one of Falmouth's more secluded tree-lined streets. Lace curtains at the stained-glass windows, rich woodwork, polished hardwood floors, and antique furnishings create an overall sense of warmth. This large and immaculate facility has delightful touches pointing to a time of class and elegance (you'll love the scented fine linens and the plump pillows), but the inn also provides

such modern-day amenities as bubbling whirlpool tubs and firm mattresses. The inn has 12 guestrooms: 8 in the Queen Anne–style main house and 4 in the guesthouse. Every room has a private bath, ceiling fan, and air-conditioning.

The tasteful touches provided by innkeepers Joanne and Ken Baker are numerous. The gourmet breakfast is a full sit-down meal that may include Belgian waffles and apricot sauce, Swiss eggs with pastry, or chocolate-stuffed French toast. The inn is open year-round and welcomes children age 10 and older.

The Village Green Inn $$$-$$$$
40 Main Street, Falmouth
(508) 548-5621, (800) 237-1119
www.villagegreeninn.com

Elegant accommodations, 19th-century charm, and warm hospitality await you at this inn, which is listed in the National Register of Historic Places. This handsome lodging was originally built as a Federal-style home in 1804 and in 1894 was remodeled in the Victorian style. It is tastefully decorated in soft colors with antiques and reproductions, creating a restful and comfortable atmosphere. Don and Diane Crosby are your charming hosts, greeting you with a warm smile and instantly making you feel at home. They'll even loan you bikes so you can explore the Shining Sea Bike Path just a half-mile away. From the front porch you can hear the chiming of the Paul Revere bell from the church tower across the green, a daily reminder of the role Falmouth patriots played in the birth of this nation. At the Village Green Inn you have your choice of five guest rooms, including a fabulous, spacious, sunny suite. All rooms have air-conditioning, cable TV, and a private bath, and two rooms have working fireplaces. Rosewood wainscoting and lace at the windows add to the historic flavor here. There is a lovely formal parlor offering complimentary glasses of sherry. Two large porches adorned with white wicker furniture and hanging geranium plants invite you to relax with lemonade and freshly baked cookies as you enjoy the view of the historic village green. A full complimentary breakfast in the dining room includes fruit, eggs, and baked goods, and afternoon sherry or lemonade is served out on the porch. Closed in February. The inn welcomes children 12 and older.

The Wildflower Inn $$$-$$$$
167 Palmer Avenue, Falmouth
(508) 548-9524, (800) 294-5459
www.wildflower-inn.com

The five rooms here at this Victorian-style inn are named after flowers (Jasmine, Moonflower, Geranium, Beachrose, and Forget-Me-Not). Each room is different—a white wrought-iron bed in one room, a four-poster canopied bed in another. Some have antiques; all are filled with flowers. Each room has a private bath, and two rooms have whirlpools. Also on-site is a cottage, fashioned from the old stables with a full kitchen, living room, and loft bedroom, along with a full bathroom complete with tub. Each morning a gourmet breakfast is served in the inn's gathering room or on the wraparound porch; it features granola, blended frozen juice, baked goods, and a hot entree of, say, wildflower crepes or flower-stuffed pancakes (stuffed with edible flowers!). The Wildflower Inn is closed during the winter season. The inn welcomes children in some of the guest rooms.

The Beach House at Falmouth Heights $$-$$$
10 Worcester Court, Falmouth Heights
(508) 457-0310, (800) 351-3426
www.capecodbeachhouse.com

The Beach House bed-and-breakfast at Falmouth Heights is a breath of fresh air. Eight special rooms and a cottage are decorated with playful, hand-painted murals, and each room has a whimsical seaside theme (i.e., the Wave Room, the Fish Room, the Lighthouse Room, the Floral Room). Each is furnished with hand-crafted furnishings and a comfy reading chair, and has a private bath. Full of color and personality, each room except one has a queen-size bed (the one without has a king that converts into comfortable twin beds). You'll enjoy your full continental buffet breakfast of home-baked goodies each morning in the kitchen cafe, where the mural makes you feel like you're sitting in an outdoor garden. If you do want to enjoy your breakfast outdoors, there are private tables overlooking the private pool or you may go to a poolside table. Your innkeepers Lynn and Woody Rollins and their resident assistant innkeeper Bonnie Bird have created a uniquely comfortable ambience at the Beach House. Tucked away behind the house and hidden by shrubbery is their private swimming pool. Have we mentioned the beach? Well, the beach is right there; you can hear the waves of Vineyard Sound gently break on the sand. Besides being close to the beach, the Beach House is also within walking distance of the island ferry, Falmouth Harbor, shopping, and restaurants. The Beach House regularly entertains international travelers and is open from the beginning of May to Columbus Day (and on other holiday weekends before and after). Children 12 and older are welcome.

Grafton Inn $$$-$$$$
261 Grand Avenue S., Falmouth Heights
(508) 540-8688, (800) 642-4069
www.graftoninn.com

Completely renovated and updated to its 19th-century Victorian roots, the Grafton sits on the oceanfront at Falmouth Heights, providing incredible views of Martha's Vineyard across the water. The 11 guest rooms, 10 of which have water views, are furnished with king- or queen-size beds. Private baths are available in each room, as is air-conditioning and individual heat controls for those chilly fall evenings. Thoughtful amenities include extra pillows, fluffy towels, French-milled soaps, homemade chocolates, and fresh flowers. Morning brings a hearty breakfast of eggs Benedict, Belgian waffles, pecan and cinnamon buns, and coffee. Afternoon saunters by with wine and cheese, a good book on the sun-filled porch, or perhaps a walk along the beach. Evening might find you at one of the many area restaurants, at the theater, or perhaps lounging back at the inn talking with new or old friends. The goal of innkeepers Liv and Rudy Cvitan is "to provide busy professionals a rejuvenating retreat," and they do that well. Open from mid-February to mid-December, the inn welcomes children 16 and older.

Inn on the Sound $$-$$$$
313 Grand Avenue, Falmouth Heights
(508) 457-9666, (800) 564-9668
www.innonthesound.com
If you can imagine yourself awakening to a million-dollar view of Vineyard Sound with the island of Martha's Vineyard in the near distance, then the Inn on the Sound is for you. Nine of its 10 guest rooms have magnificent water views, and every room has its own individual character. The decor is casual contemporary with natural oak features, ceiling fans, and the homey touch. All of the rooms have private baths; four have private decks. Guests often reserve a specific room as each room varies in both size and view. Your hostess, Renee Ross, has graced the inn with her exquisite taste and professionalism, which comes from her long experience as an interior designer and her work in the hospitality, catering, art, and framing businesses. Hot coffee and tea are always available. The Inn on the Sound is located almost on the finish line of the Falmouth Road Race, up the hill from the beaches at Falmouth Heights, and close to fine dining. The Inn is a quiet treat for visitors looking for a restful, peaceful, and soothing stay. They also provide guests with beach chairs and towels. Well-behaved adults 18 and older are welcome. The inn is open year-round.

The Moorings $-$$
207 Grand Avenue S., Falmouth Heights
(508) 540-2370, (800) 398-4007
The sun, the surf, the beach: It's all here at the Moorings along Grand Avenue South in Falmouth Heights. Water views abound; you can sit on the 40-foot porch for hours and just stare at Vineyard Sound. At night you can watch Martha's Vineyard sparkle across the dark water, or watch the twinkling island ferries go to and from in their graceful parade across the waves. The Moorings is within walking distance of the harbor and nearby restaurants. The famed Falmouth Road Race ends a few hundred feet short of its front door, and the beach is directly across the street. The inn, which has an antiques-filled Victorian decor, is well suited to families and couples. It has eight charming guest rooms, each with a private bath. You can choose between a room with a double bed, or a king, or a double and a twin, or even a double and two twins. Enjoy a grand complimentary breakfast buffet that may include fresh fruit with vanilla yogurt, homemade bread, granola, French toast, and omelets, and will probably satisfy you till dinner. The Moorings was built in 1905. It is open mid-May to the end of October, and children are welcome.

Mid-Cape

The Josiah Sampson House $$
40 Old Kings Road, Cotuit
(508) 428-8383, (877) 574-6873
www.josiahsampson.com
Built in 1793 in the Federal style of the times, the Josiah Sampson House offers six spacious and comfortable guest rooms, each with private modern bath and decorated with fine antiques and period reproductions. Innkeepers Carol and Leonard Carter have named the rooms for their original use. The Library Room, which now has a queen-size bed, was in fact Josiah Sampson's library and still boasts a collection of books. The Queen's Room has two twin canopy beds and offers excellent views of the yard complete with romantic gazebo. The Rose

Room, so called for its vibrant decorating scheme, has a beautiful queen-size canopy bed. Each room has its own fireplace in authentic 18th-century style. Breakfast is served each morning in the dining room or on the garden-view porch. As a finishing touch to your day, relax in the hot tub. The Josiah Sampson House is open year-round.

Honeysuckle Hill $$-$$$
591 Route 6A, West Barnstable
(508) 362-8418, (866) 444-5522
www.honeysucklehill.com
Built in 1810 in the Queen Anne style by the Fish and Goodspeed families, this inn, which is listed in the National Register of Historic Places, is surrounded by lush green lawns and colorful gardens. The guest rooms are light, lovely, and laden with antiques, white wicker, featherbeds, and Battenburg lace. Each room is air-conditioned and has an ultraluxurious oversized marble shower, complemented by English toiletries and fluffy terry robes. This comfortably renovated house has all the grace of its heritage: wide-planked floors, ship's captain's staircase, wonderful ceiling angles, and narrow halls. At Honeysuckle Hill you'll enjoy your morning coffee, complimentary newspaper, and a full breakfast in the sunny dining room. The menu changes daily and offers such gourmet specialties as Dutch babies, the Captain's eggs, or Grand Marnier French toast, accompanied by fruit and freshly baked muffins. Then you can retire to the front porch to plan your day or just sit and soak up the heat of the sun.

Your hosts, Bill and Mary Kilburn, are very gracious and take pride in offering you excellent accommodations. The inn is open year-round and welcomes children age 12 and older. When inquiring about a stay, ask about their special package rates.

Ashley Manor $$-$$$$
3660 Route 6A, Barnstable
(508) 362-8044, (888) 535-2246
www.ashleymanor.net
A sweeping driveway invites guests to the lovely two-acre estate. The oldest part of the Manor is said to date from 1699, and, despite the many additions since, it still retains its link to its colonial past with wide-board floors, hand-glazed wainscoting on the walls, wide hearth fireplaces, a beehive oven, and even a secret passageway. Spacious guest accommodations and six guest rooms, including two double-bed rooms and four suites, are carefully designed to conform to the age and history of the manor house. All have air-conditioning and private baths and feature distinctive wallpaper; all but one have a working fireplace; some of the rooms have canopy-draped beds, and some have whirlpools.

The Manor is furnished with handsome antiques, Oriental rugs, and graceful country furniture. A backyard gazebo and fountain garden highlight the parklike private grounds and a tennis court. Within walking distance of Barnstable Village center and the harbor, the Ashley Manor is a gem of an inn and is open year-round. Children 14 years of age and older are welcome.

Beechwood $$$
2839 Route 6A, Barnstable
(508) 362-6618, (800) 609-6618
www.beechwoodinn.com
This Queen Anne–style home has been fully and authentically restored, hearkening back to an era of grace and elegance when there was time to sit, relax, and rejoice in the simple pleasures of life. Guests from around the world delight in the sprawling lawn, the 10-foot privet hedge, and century-old weeping beech tree that lent the inn its name. The inn also features a wraparound veranda with comfortable rockers, antique-filled rooms, and huge canopied beds in the six guest rooms. The rich tones of natural wood throughout the inn are set off beautifully by Oriental rugs, armoires, and antique furnishings. Built in 1853, this Victorian home has fireplaces in the dining room and parlor, where afternoon tea, cocoa, and coffee are served. Some rooms also have fireplaces, and some have seasonal views of Cape Cod Bay. All rooms have

private baths. Innkeepers Ken and Debbie Traugot serve a three-course gourmet breakfast that draws rave reviews for such items as raspberry bread, banana-chocolate chip muffins, and more than 30 different entrees, including tomato pastry puff eggs and apple harvest pancakes. The Beechwood, which is just down the road from Barnstable village, its harbor, and area beaches, is open year-round. The inn welcomes children age 12 and older.

The Lamb and Lion Inn $$–$$$
2504 Route 6A, Barnstable
(508) 362-6823, (800) 909-6923
www.lambandlion.com

Veteran innkeeper Alice Pitcher has blended the warmth of a classic Cape Cod inn with the comfort and convenience of a small luxury hotel. Set back off historic Route 6A, this 240-year-old estate, barn, and inn surround a central courtyard featuring a lovely outdoor pool with year-round hot tub. It's a fun, airy inn with a Caribbean island feel, until you enter the colonial-era common room of the main house and stand on the wideboard floors in front of one of the many fireplaces. Then you'll know you're in the best of two worlds.

The Lamb and Lion Inn offers a variety of rooms, all opening onto the courtyard. Some have private entrances, others have private decks for afternoon lounging. They even offer a family-style suite, the "Barn-stable," in a converted ca. 1740 barn with three loft sleeping areas, living room, kitchen, and barbecue deck. All the rooms are spacious, very clean, and have private baths, cable TV, and telephones with data ports.

The Innkeeper's Pride, elegant accommodations set apart from the other guest rooms, offers a fireplace, sunken tub, and kitchen. Fresh baked breads and muffins, granola, and juices are served in the morning, either on the sun porch or poolside. Dogs are allowed (actually, Alice's Yorkshire Terriers are the real innkeepers). Children are encouraged, and the courtyard and pool area offer a perfect spot for

kids (as well as adults) when the beaches are too windy. The Lamb and Lion is open year-round. The inn also hosts family celebrations, catered luncheons, small wedding parties, and small group meetings.

Acworth Inn $$–$$$
4352 Route 6A, Cummaquid (Barnstable)
(508) 362-3330, (800) 362-6363
www.acworthinn.com

The Acworth, originally built in the 1860s, blends 19th-century traditional architecture with French country-style comfort. The five guest rooms are bright and airy, each with a private bath. Each room has its own special charm. Air-conditioning is available, and two of the rooms have working fireplaces. Our favorite room, the Orleans Room, is a luxury suite with whirlpool tub, fireplace, and sitting room—perfect for a romantic getaway or honeymoon.

The Acworth Inn is centrally located to fine dining, shopping, and outdoor activities. The inn is open year-round and is nonsmoking.

Simmons Homestead Inn $$$–$$$$
288 Scudder Avenue, Hyannisport
(508) 778-4999, (800) 637-1649
www.capecodtravel.com/simmonsinn

Hyannisport is home to the Simmons Homestead Inn, a historic sea captain's home that was built in 1820 by Lemuel Simmons. It was a private estate until 1987, when it was restored and converted into a country inn. In the process the original wide-pine floors and all the original woodwork were refinished. The property is attractive, with a great rolling backyard and a sitting porch. The interior decor is eclectic, reflecting the personality of its fun-loving innkeeper Bill Putnam. The inn has 14 rooms, some furnished with canopied four-poster beds, brass beds, or white wicker. Each room has a private bath, one has a private deck, and two have working fireplaces. And if you like plants and animals of the brass and ceramic variety, you will be right at home. Eclectic and fun in decor, all the rooms have their own animal theme (as in giraffe, elephant, cat, etc.). There's even a hot tub and a spacious billiards room. There are a dozen 10-speed mountain bikes available for guests to use. In the morning guests will find a full country breakfast in the dining room (the late Dinah Shore once cooked breakfast here for the guests). A social hour with wine takes place at 6:00 P.M. to get the guests in the evening mood, and a single-malt "tasting hour" is also held weeknights during the cooler months. The Simmons Homestead is the perfect setting for a Hyannis-based stay that will include shopping, dining, entertainment, beaches, and boat excursions, all within a short drive. Open year-round, the inn welcomes children and pets.

Sea Beach Inn $
388 Sea Street, Hyannis
(508) 775-4612
www.capecodtravel.com/seabeach

This comfortable inn was once an 1860 sea captain's home. Located within sight and sound of the gently lapping waters of Nantucket Sound on Sea Street Beach, the inn has five guest rooms in the main house and another four in the carriage barn. Three of the five rooms in the main house have private baths, and the rooms in the rustic carriage barn are perfect for families. Visitors from all over the world find their way to the Sea Beach Inn, and many are repeat customers who enjoy hosts Neil and Elizabeth Carr's down-to-earth, cozy manner. Sea Beach Inn is perfect for those who seek the charm of a bed-and-breakfast and yet desire affordable lodging. It's also an easy walk to some of Hyannis's best eating establishments, as well as the Melody Tent for first-rate nightly entertainment. An efficiency unit is also available, and a pleasing continental breakfast is included. The Inn is open from May through Columbus Day, and children are welcome any time.

Sea Breeze Inn $-$$
270 Ocean Avenue, Hyannis
(508) 771-7213
www.seabreezeinn.com

The Sea Breeze Inn displays a nautical flair, and with its superb location so close to the beach, you'll feel the sea breezes firsthand. Besides the proximity to the beach, the inn is also near all Hyannis activities, including the Cape Cod Melody Tent, restaurants, golf, and island ferries. The 14 bright and airy rooms in the main building feature antique canopy beds, private baths, and air-conditioning. The inn also features a rooftop widow's walk with tables, chairs, and a beautiful view of Nantucket Sound. The inn also has one cottage. A generous continental breakfast of muffins, bagels, cereals, and fresh fruit is served in the large, pleasant dining room of the main house. The inn is open year-round, and children are welcome.

Captain Farris House $$-$$$
308 Old Main Street, South Yarmouth
(508) 760-2818, (800) 350-9477
www.captainfarriscapecod.com

This jewel of a house was built in 1845 in a historic section of South Yarmouth known as Bass River. A perfect blend of antique and contemporary, the inn has eight magnificent rooms, each one a romantic getaway, lovingly detailed with modern amenities; private baths, some with Jacuzzis; beautiful antique king- or queen-size beds; cable TVs with VCR and in-house videos; bathrobes; and air-conditioning. Two suites upstairs feature sunken bathrooms, queen-size beds, living rooms, and upscale European flair. One room offers a queen-size four-poster bed, Jacuzzi, and a walk-out sundeck. Two of the large rooms upstairs have four-poster canopied beds and fireplaces. The Captain Farris House is in the National Register of Historic Places. Three-course breakfasts are served either in the dining room or outside in the courtyard or on the veranda. Candlelight dinners are served to guests during the off-season with advance notice. Afternoon refreshments are also served. Next door is the Elisha Jenkins House, which has a huge suite. The inn is open year-round, and children 12 and older are welcome.

Crook' Jaw Inn
$$-$$$
186 Route 6A, Yarmouthport
(508) 362-6111, (888) 389-4253
www.crookjawinn.com

From the moment you step inside, there is a distinctive feeling to this ca. 1798 Cape Cod sea captain's house. It boasts a wealth of "early settler" details, seven fireplaces, pegged hardwood wide-planked floors, a ship's captain's staircase, and narrow hallways. The common room with fireplace and the dining room beckon you to relish the days when travelers gathered around to exchange tales. You will find modern conveniences here, including private baths, a whirlpool in the downstairs guest room, and air-conditioning, mixed in with the spare loveliness of colonial-era antiques. The library includes a broad array of subjects and titles from the innkeepers' own collection. Karen and Jim Dowcett are your hosts. Jim is a college professor of composition and world music, and Karen is from the world of theater and community studies. Each morning guests can linger over a breakfast of frittatas, soufflés, fresh berries from the summer garden, and home-baked scones. Within walking distance are some great dining spots, including the oldest inn on Cape Cod, the Olde Yarmouth Inn (see our Restaurants chapter), which was established as a stagecoach stop in 1696.

The Crook' Jaw, which is listed in the National Register of Historic Places, features featherbeds and Egyptian cotton linens, and the five guest rooms are uniquely designed, offering furnishings that span continents and centuries. The Crook' Jaw also has a gorgeous patio. The inn is open year-round.

Liberty Hill Inn
$$-$$$
77 Route 6A, Yarmouthport
(508) 362-3976, (888) 821-3977
www.capecod.net/libertyhillinn

Yarmouthport is a tranquil Cape Cod village with a history dating back to 1638, when the first settlers attempted to conquer the vast wilderness (the town was incorporated in 1639). Located in the heart of the village, the inn is just a short, leisurely stroll away from picturesque country lanes, outstanding restaurants, interesting antiques and gift shops, and a number of historical attractions. Built by a shipbuilder in 1825, this handsome Greek Revival building with nine lovely guest rooms evokes the elegance of past centuries with its wide floorboards, chandeliers, and antiques. Some rooms have four-poster beds, some have lovely lace canopy queen-size beds, and all have private bathrooms and air-conditioning. Two rooms with whirlpools are available, and like most older homes, fireplaces are in some of the rooms. Your hosts serve a sumptuous breakfast at your own table under a crystal chandelier. The Liberty Hill Inn is a beautiful place that allows seasonal glimpses of Cape Cod Bay. It is centrally located and near fine dining, shopping, and attractions. The inn is open year-round, and children are welcome. One room is wheelchair accessible.

Wedgewood Inn
$$$
Route 6A, Yarmouthport
(508) 362-5157
www.wedgewood-inn.com

The Wedgewood Inn, located on a knoll overlooking Yarmouthport village, has been featured on the cover of *Colonial Homes* and in the Italian magazine *Dove*. For years it has been voted one of the top inns in the mid-Cape by readers of *Cape Cod Life* and was recently chosen by the editors of *Yankee Magazine's Travel Guide to New England* as one of the best inns in the region. Built in 1812, this elegant inn is a proud representative of the 19th-century world of our Cape Cod ancestors. The grounds are beautiful, featuring tiered lawns traced with Yankee stone walls and large old maple trees. DISTINCTIVE LODGING reads the gold beveled lettering on the Wedgewood blue sign out front, and distinctive lodging is what you will receive. The nine guest rooms are breathtaking, with handmade quilts on the beds and shuttered windows; seven of them have working fireplaces. You'll also find authentic and reproduction antiques throughout. The deluxe accommodations in double rooms and suites offer comfort, privacy, and air-conditioning. One east-facing suite has a large bedroom, sitting room, private bath, and porch with a view of the gardens and gazebo.

Wonderful full breakfasts featuring Belgian waffles and blueberry muffins will help you begin the day on the right foot. And if you need any help planning your agenda of antiquing, bike riding, sightseeing, or anything else, your hosts, innkeepers Gerrie and Milt Graham, who couldn't be nicer, can help you plan your fun-filled Cape Cod activities. The Wedgewood Inn, which is open year-round, welcomes children 10 and older.

The Four Chimneys Inn $$–$$$
Route 6A, Dennis
(508) 385–6317, (800) 874–5502
www.fourchimneysinn.com

Built in the late 1870s, this three-story Victorian house on historic Route 6A has eight guest rooms, all named for herbs and wildflowers, such as Bayberry, Teaberry, Blueberry, and Rosehip. The first two floors, decorated in Victorian fashion, feature 11-foot-high ceilings edged with plaster moldings and centered with medallions and paddle fans. Oversized windows are trimmed with wide woodwork, and the entrance has a beautiful freestanding staircase. Painted wide-board floors and stenciling give the third-floor bedrooms country ambience. Each room is as different as its name: Some have cherry four-poster beds, others have wicker beds, and still others have antique oak or pine beds. Two rooms feature canopy beds. Four rooms offer views of Scargo Lake just across the street. All rooms have private baths, and most have televisions. You can readup on the house's history in the detailed account kept in the common room.

An expanded continental breakfast is served on the screened porch or in the dining room if the weather is cool. Lush grounds surround the property, which is

One of the advantages of staying at a small inn or bed-and-breakfast is the proximity to at least one Insider and in most cases two. Innkeepers are usually very happy to answer questions and give advice about where to shop, dine, and sightsee. Not only do they live here, but they've also had the benefit of reports from other guests. Take advantage of their knowledge and experience.

just a couple of minutes' ride away from area beaches and a leisurely stroll down Main Street to Dennis village and its many antique shops. The Four Chimneys Inn is open from mid-February to mid-December and welcomes children 8 and older.

Isaiah Hall Bed and Breakfast Inn $$–$$$
152 Whig Street, Dennis
(508) 385–9928, (800) 736–0160
www.isaiahhallinn.com

Along quiet Whig Street you'll find the wonderful Isaiah Hall Bed and Breakfast, named for a 19th-century cooper, whose brother Henry is credited with developing cranberry cultivation on Cape Cod back in 1814. Isaiah Hall, realizing how successful these cultivated cranberries would become, began producing barrels in large volume. In fact Isaiah's barrel size is still the accepted unit of measure for the cranberries that are bought and sold today on the open market.

This 1857 Greek Revival farmhouse has 10 rooms, individually decorated in quintessential Cape Cod style with charming antiques, quilts, and Oriental rugs. All have private baths, eight have queen-size beds that are canopied or boast bedsteads of white iron or brass, four have balconies, and one has a fireplace. One room is a suite. These rooms are in the main and carriage houses, the latter featuring stenciled walls, white wicker, and knotty pine walls. All the rooms have air-conditioning, TVs, and VCRs.

A delightful extended continental breakfast of home-baked breads, muffins,

and local jams is served each morning at the dining room's gorgeous 12-foot cherry table. After breakfast take a stroll through the wonderful gardens or perhaps down to Corporation Beach for a day of sun, sand, and surf. Later you can walk to America's oldest summer theater, the Cape Playhouse, or over to Dennis village. The inn is open from the end of April to late October, and children 7 and older are welcome.

The Lighthouse Inn $$$$
1 Lighthouse Inn Road, West Dennis
(508) 398-2244
www.lighthouseinn.com

The Lighthouse Inn began life in May 1855 as the Bass River Light, the Cape's 15th lighthouse. At that time it consisted only of the very center section of the inn today. Though it closed briefly from 1880 to 1881, it remained an important southside lighthouse until 1914, when the opening of the Cape Cod Canal made it obsolete. In 1989 it was recommissioned and is today a working lighthouse from May to October each year. We were given a tour of its tower once, and the view from the top is spectacular.

It is a compound of sorts situated all by itself down at West Dennis Beach. Accommodations run the gamut from basic rooms and suites in the Main House to oceanfront cottages with decks, fireplaces, and comfortable furnishings that sleep as many as six people. Each room and cottage has a TV, telephone, refrigerator, in-room safe, hair dryer, and private bath. Weekly cottage rentals also include daily breakfast and dinner.

On-site there is a tennis court, an outdoor heated swimming pool, a restaurant (also known as the Lighthouse Inn—see our Restaurants chapter), a nightclub (the Sand Bar, which is described in our Nightlife chapter), and a private beach with a network of private jetties from which you can cast your line for the blue-fish that run these waters in June. There are arts and crafts classes and sandcastle-building contests and other daily, supervised activities for children ages 3 and older. The Stone family operates the inn from mid-May to mid-October.

'By the Sea' Guests Bed & Breakfast $$
57 Chase Avenue (also Inman Road Ext.), Dennisport
(508) 398-8685, (800) 447-9202
www.bytheseaguests.com

'By the Sea' Guests is one of the few Cape Cod bed-and-breakfasts with its own private beach. Family operated, this lovely 12-room inn has withstood storms and hurricanes off Nantucket Sound and still offers you a quiet and comfortable beachfront lodging experience.

It's almost as if things haven't changed since 1964. Helen and Dino Kossifos continue the tradition of family hospitality and friendly service. You can still awaken to a hearty continental breakfast of hot coffee, specialty tea, hot and cold cereals, home-baked rolls, pastry, and fresh cut fruits served on the wraparound veranda overlooking Nantucket sound. In addition homemade brownies, carrot cake, cookies, and fresh fruits are available to the guests throughout the day and evening.

Of the 12 rooms 4 are oceanfront and 4 have ocean views. One suite is wheelchair accessible. All rooms have color TVs, small guest refrigerators, ceiling fans, individually controlled thermostats for cooler evenings, and private ceramic-tiled bathrooms with glass showers, including two with soaking tubs. The rooms are warm, cozy, and comfortable. Barbecue grills and beach chairs are available for your use. 'By the Sea' Guests is open from the beginning of May to the beginning of December. They welcome well-behaved children and allow outside smoking only. Whether you take a morning stroll or view a

---

[Facing page] *Area bed-and-breakfasts offer gracious hospitality and historic surroundings.*
HYANNIS AREA CHAMBER OF COMMERCE

memorable sunset from the private beach, 'By the Sea' offers just that . . . sea, sand, comfort, and convenience.

The Rose Petal Bed & Breakfast $$
152 Sea Street, Dennisport
(508) 398-8470
www.rosepetalofdennis.com

One end of Sea Street in Dennisport leads to the waters of Nantucket Sound, and the other leads to the Rose Petal Bed & Breakfast tucked away in the neighborhood of century-old houses. The Rose Petal was built in 1872 as the residence of Almond Wixon, whose family was among the original settlers of Dennisport. Wixon himself was among those lost aboard the *Cross Rip* lightship in February 1918, which drifted away on an ice floe, never to be seen again.

Innkeepers Dan and Gayle Kelly completely restored the house in 1986. The Kellys offer guests a choice of three cozy second-floor rooms. Two rooms feature queen-size brass beds (covered with hand-stitched quilts), antiques, and private baths. The third has a private entrance off a large deck and an antique, queen-size iron bed, and shares a first-floor bath with the hosts. The elegant dining room is the setting for a full homemade complimentary breakfast featuring home-baked pastries along with your entree. Complimentary beverages are available in the guest refrigerator. The many beaches of Dennisport are close by, and two Dennis golf courses are just a 5- to 10-minute ride away. It's open year-round, and children of all ages are welcome.

Lower Cape

Beechcroft Inn $-$$$
1360 Route 6A, Brewster
(508) 896-9534, (877) 233-2446
www.beechcroftinn.com

This old inn is full of character. The 10 rooms are nicely but simply done with antique furnishings, quilts, and tasteful artwork—mostly vintage prints and needlepoint. All the rooms are named

after wildflowers indigenous to the Cape; our favorite is the third-floor Queen Anne's Lace, which has a small private deck and a breathtaking view of Cape Cod Bay.

The 1828 building was originally Brewster's first Universalist Meeting House and was converted to an inn 140 years ago. The owners also run an English tea room, the Brewster Tea Pot, on the premises, which bodes well for delicious breakfasts. Guests have use of two sitting rooms. The inn is open year-round, and children age 10 and older are welcome.

The Brewster
Farmhouse Inn $$$-$$$$
716 Route 6A, Brewster
(508) 896-3910, (800) 892-3910
www.brewsterfarmhouseinn.com

The Brewster Farmhouse Inn offers the best of both worlds: the charm of an 1846 Federal-style farmhouse and all the modern amenities. Each of the eight guest rooms has its own special charm. The distinctively decorated rooms have seating areas, fine linens, down comforters, TV with HBO, air-conditioners, and private bathrooms with hair dryers, toiletries, and thick terry-cloth robes. The Shaker Room has a working fireplace, and the Garden Room has a private deck. Outside, beyond the spacious rear deck surrounded by hedges, hydrangeas, and gardens, there's a heated pool and a hot tub that can be used year-round. The two-acre property has an apple orchard and is right across the road from the historic windmill on the grounds of the Drummer Boy Park where Sunday evening band concerts are held in the summer. It is also just a short stroll to the nature trails at the Cape Cod Museum of Natural History.

Carol and Gary Concors, who bought the inn in 1996, both love to cook, so you can look forward to a full gourmet breakfast every morning served in the cathedral-ceiling common room or outside on the deck. They also serve afternoon tea with homemade pastries—the perfect pick-me-up after a day of sightseeing or sunbathing! Children older than 16 are welcome. The inn is open year-round.

The Candleberry Inn $$-$$$$
1882 Route 6A, Brewster
(508) 896-3300
www.candleberryinn.com

This beautifully restored, 250-year-old house has a rich history, which innkeepers Gini and David Donnelly decided to honor by naming each of the guest rooms for a former owner, including Captain Frank B. Foster and one-time town moderator and state senator D. George Copeland. They've also redecorated in keeping with the understated, traditional feel of the house, and the inn is adorned with lovely antiques and family heirlooms, Oriental rugs, period paintings, homemade quilts, and lace canopies on the beds. The house features original wide floorboards, wainscoting, and window glass with "bubbles and waves," all of which contribute to the authentic colonial ambience. The nine guest rooms all have private baths; six, including one suite, are in the main house, and another three are located in the newer carriage house, including a luxury suite complete with Jacuzzi and private terrace. Guests are treated to a full breakfast in the dining room or outside on the brick porch, which has a view of lush gardens. The inn is open year-round and offers tempting winter rates; children 10 and older are welcome.

Chillingsworth $$
2449 Route 6A, Brewster
(508) 896-3640
www.chillingsworth.com

A well-kept secret on the Lower Cape is that the renowned restaurant Chillingsworth (see our Restaurants chapter) also has a bed-and-breakfast component, in the form of three elegant rooms furnished with antiques. Two are large, with sitting areas, and all three have private baths, air-conditioning, and cable TV. Guests are treated to a full breakfast each morning and wine and cheese in the afternoon, and get club privileges at Ocean Edge resort (see our Hotels, Motels, and Resorts chapter) just down the street. They're also within walking distance of a private beach—and, of course, steps away from elegant French cuisine served at Chillingsworth Restaurant (see our Restaurants chapter). Chillingsworth is open from mid-May through November.

Old Sea Pines Inn $-$$
2553 Route 6A, Brewster
(508) 896-6114
www.oldseapinesinn.com

The Old Sea Pines Inn in Brewster was once the center of a 300-acre estate known as the Sea Pines School of Charm and Personality. It continued as a school until the 1970s when innkeepers and owners Stephen and Michele Rowan envisioned this lovely mansion as a bed-and-breakfast inn. From the outset they have carefully maintained its original turn-of-the-20th-century style and integrity. Besides the structure itself, the charming decor adds to the inn's appeal: You'll love the Priscilla curtains, rocking chairs, green wicker furniture, brass and iron beds, and framed old photographs dotting the wallpapered walls. Some of the inn's 22 rooms, especially the 5 with shared baths, are small, but they are a great bargain and still include the inn's terrific full breakfasts. You can also opt for one of the more modern rooms in the adjacent North Cottage. Next to the spacious living room is the large, completely restored formal dining room, which opens to a spacious outdoor dining deck surrounded by trees and overlooking the inn's lawns and gardens.

Many couples choose to be married at the Old Sea Pines Inn or to hold their receptions here. The charming, private setting of the Wedding Garden is perfect for ceremonies. Receptions are held on the entire ground floor, which include two spacious, adjoining dining rooms that open up into a large area with dance floor. The inn, open year-round, also does rehearsal dinners and weddings. Good news for families: Young children are welcome in the inn's two family suites.

The Ruddy Turnstone $$-$$$
463 Route 6A, Brewster
(508) 385-9871, (800) 654-1995
www.theruddyturnstone.com

Set back from the road on three acres of land, this lovingly restored 200-year-old house offers a tranquil respite from the rest of the world, yet is centrally located. Shops, attractions, and beaches are only a short drive away, but as innkeeper Sally Swanson puts it, "It's really quiet here." The Ruddy Turnstone has five guest rooms, all with private baths and queen-size beds. Three rooms are in the main house, and two are in the carriage house, where Sally and her husband Gordon (Swanie) formerly ran an antiques shop. There are still plenty of antiques furnishing the rooms and common areas. One common room has a television, fireplace, board games, and books, but the rooms are TV-free. Guests are treated to a full country breakfast either in the dining room or on the porch. The expansive backyard with gardens and fruit trees runs down to the marsh. The hammocks out back are popular spots for relaxation, or you can play horseshoes. Bring your binoculars to view the wide array of birds that call the marsh home, or borrow one of the available pairs at the inn. Magnificent views of Cape Cod Bay, lowlands, and barrier beach offer visitors a glimpse of Cape Cod's natural beauty. The Ruddy Turnstone is open most of the year, but closes in January and February. Children 10 and older are welcome.

Augustus Snow House $$$
528 Main Street, Harwichport
(508) 430-0528, (800) 320-0528
www.augustussnow.com

The Augustus Snow House, built in 1901, is one of the most awe-inspiring examples of turn-of-the-20th-century architecture around. It's ideally located in the old sea captain's village of Harwichport, 1 block from the inn's own private beach on the warmer waters of Nantucket Sound, within 30 miles of Falmouth to the west, and an easy drive to Provincetown.

The Victorian inn has a wraparound veranda with screened-in gazebo, round turrets, and gabled dormers. As you enter the house, you can't help but notice the mirrored oak fireplace in the common room, as well as the fine oak woodwork and rich Victorian wallpaper. Behind you an impressive staircase leads past stained-glass windows to five spacious guest rooms. Each is tastefully, elegantly decorated and graced with well-crafted reproduction fireplaces. All rooms have remote controlled TVs, air-conditioning, and private baths; three have Jacuzzi tubs. The bathrooms have unusual features: Yours might have a marble or tin sink, claw-foot tub, or a marble commode. All add to the charm of a stay at the Augustus Snow House.

Each day brings a different full breakfast served at individual tables in the sun-filled dining room or outside in the gazebo. In the afternoon guests may also enjoy refreshments served with all the elegance of breakfast. The Augustus Snow House offers a charming setting for weddings and other special occasions. It is open year-round and offers lower rates from mid-October through early May.

Cape Winds-by-the-Sea $$
28 Shore Road, West Harwich
(508) 432-1418
www.capewinds.com

Cape Winds is a pearl of a getaway. If you've ever imagined sitting on a porch in a rocker listening to the gentle swells in Nantucket Sound, this is the place for you. The inn sits across the lane overlooking the water in a quiet residential seashore community, only a few houses away from a town beach. Every room has a view of the sound, and all have private baths, refrigerators, and televisions.

But the view is only the beginning. There's the warm hospitality of the innkeepers, Ed and Judi Shank. There's the six guest rooms in the homey house, which are accented by handmade quilts, wainscoting trim, and ship lap wall coverings. The Brewster and Chatham studio rooms feature a stove, sink, and refrigerator. Leave your beach chairs and towels at home; you can borrow them here. Continental breakfast is included. Children of all ages are welcome. The inn is open year-round. No credit cards.

Dunscroft by-the-Sea $$$-$$$$
24 Pilgrim Road, Harwichport
(508) 432-0810, (800) 432-4345
www.dunscroftbythesea.com

The Dunscroft, built as a private estate in 1920, exudes casual elegance. There's a lovely ocean breeze here, as the inn is only a stroll away from a mile-long private beach on Nantucket Sound. The bright rooms are furnished with fine linens, beautiful beds—canopied, four-poster, and sleigh beds—plump pillows, and lace curtains. All are air-conditioned and have private baths, some with walk-in showers, some with standard tub and shower, and others with Jacuzzi and shower. In the evening you will find candles lighting your room and a crisply turned-down bed, and you can drift off to sleep to the sound of the waves on the beach.

Eight of the inn's guest rooms are in the main house, and four of these have private entrances. Just beyond the brick patio and garden is a separate suite with a fireplace. Guests enjoy a full breakfast in the dining room, and they can relax in the comfortable common room with French doors that open onto an enclosed sun porch. Once you walk into the large, sunny gathering room with grand piano, television, and library, you may just stick around all day. The inn, which is near Main Street shops, is open year-round.

Harbor Breeze Inn $-$$$
326 Lower County Road, Harwichport
(508) 432-0337, (800) 455-0247
www.harborbreezeinn.com

Near Allen Harbor and a short stroll from a town beach is the Harbor Breeze Inn, a relaxing little hideaway with a cottagelike feel. A series of cedar-shake rambling additions behind the main Cape Cod–style house form the guest wing, which is surrounded by a colorful garden courtyard. In a quiet, residential neighborhood, Harbor Breeze is just a half-mile away from shops and family activities. In season flowered walkways lead to 10 guest rooms, which tastefully blend the charm of wicker, wood, and country florals with quality comforts—private decks and entrances, modern baths, cable TVs, air-conditioning, refrigerators, and king-, queen- or twin-size beds. Some have fireplaces as well. The grounds are pretty, with ivy, lilacs, perennial beds, and shady pines complemented by hanging baskets of flowers. A charming breakfast room, which overlooks the pool, is the site for a hearty continental breakfast that always includes something home-baked. Guests are welcome to borrow beach towels, beach blankets, and small coolers. Children of all ages are welcome here, and double suites for families are available—but the unique layout allows plenty of privacy for couples without children. Open year-round, Harbor Breeze offers special packages in the off-season and some good deals in summer as well.

The Captain's House Inn $$$$
377 Old Harbor Road, Chatham
(508) 945-0127, (800) 315-0728
www.captainshouseinn.com

The stately white 1839 Greek Revival–style mansion, the attached carriage house, new luxurious "Stables," and the 200-year-old "bow roof cape" called the "Captain's Cottage" provide 19 luxuriously appointed guest quarters. Each has its own personality; most have queen- or king-size canopied four-poster beds, sitting areas, and fireplaces; some have whirlpool tubs and TVs with VCRs; and all have private bath, air-conditioning, and telephone. Select rooms also include whirlpools.

Enjoy a gourmet country breakfast and English afternoon tea served in the dining room, which overlooks the gardens. A continental breakfast is available in the privacy of your room upon request. The whole complex is beautifully appointed with antiques, period wallpaper, and furnishings. It is exceedingly well run. The Captain's House Inn is open year-round.

Carriage House Inn $$$-$$$$
407 Old Harbor Road, Chatham
(508) 945-4688, (800) 355-8868
www.capecodtravel.com/carriagehouse
Located a quarter mile from Pleasant Bay
and the ocean in this picturesque seaside
village, the inn is a traditional Cape home,
tastefully furnished with antiques, family
mementos, and a baby grand piano in the
parlor. The six bright and airy guest rooms
feature queen-size beds, private bathrooms, and air-conditioning. The carriage
house rooms offer fireplaces, private
entrances, and sliding glass doors that
open to private, flower-bedecked sitting
areas. All bathrooms are modern, with
roomy vanities and oversized showers.
Breakfast is served under the crystal
chandelier in the formal dining room or at
individual tables in the adjacent sunroom.
The atmosphere at the inn is relaxed and
casual. The Carriage House Inn is open
year-round and welcomes children age 13
and older.

The Cranberry Inn $$$$
359 Main Street, Chatham
(508) 945-9232, (800) 332-4667
www.cranberryinn.com
Settle into comfort at Chatham's oldest
lodging, a grand 1830s Greek Revival
building updated with modern comforts
such as private baths, air-conditioning,
telephones, and remote-control televisions
in every room. The decor is traditionally
New England, and the inn's 18 guest
rooms are each carefully decorated with
antiques and reproduction furnishings.
Eight of the guest rooms feature fireplaces. The common rooms include a
reception room with baby grand piano,
fireplace, and fresh long-stemmed roses.
The Tavern, with a wood-burning fireplace,
is a cozy spot for evening cocktails. A full
country breakfast is served in the cheerful
dining room—on a chilly morning you may
wish to sit near the fireplace.

The inn's location on the quiet outskirts
of the village is convenient for walking to
the beach, shops, restaurants, and the
many art galleries in Chatham. Directly

behind the inn is a lovely, natural cranberry
bog and nature trail leading to Old Mill
Pond. Guests are welcome to walk with
care and in the winter season may enjoy
seeing the abundance of wildlife that
migrates through this part of Cape Cod.
The Cranberry Inn is open year-round and
welcomes children age 12 and older.

Cyrus Kent House $$$-$$$$
63 Cross Street, Chatham
(508) 945-9104, (800) 338-5368
www.cyruskent.com
Tasteful, classy, and historic, the Cyrus
Kent House is tucked away on a quiet
street walking distance of town. This
stately 1877 home has 11 rooms, all with
private baths, televisions, phone, and air-
conditioning; four have fireplaces. With tall
windows that let in lots of light, the rooms
have an airy feel and are beautifully done
in muted tones that enhance the historic
ambience. Framed wildflower prints hang
on the walls above four-poster beds, and
fresh flowers grace each room. Two suites
contained in the adjacent carriage house
make perfect honeymoon hideaways.

In summer iced tea is served on the
porch, and in winter there are evening
wine-and-cheese gatherings in the large
living room, which has a marble fireplace
and piano. A continental-plus breakfast is
served each morning in the dining room or,
in warm weather, on the deck that overlooks the lawn. The inn is open year-round
and welcomes children age 10 and older.

The Moorings Bed &
Breakfast $$$-$$$$
326 Main Street, Chatham
(508) 945-0848, (800) 320-0848
www.mooringscapecod.com
Welcome to the home of Admiral Charles
Rockwell—well, former home—but the
spirit of the 19th-century seafarer lives on
in this grand old house, built in 1860. The
living room, which the Admiral designed
to resemble the interior of a ship, features
gorgeous wood paneling, a carved man-
telpiece, and arched doorways. It's the
perfect place to curl up with a book or

play cards at the table by the bay window. The main house has five charming guest rooms. We especially like the second-floor Admiral's Room, which has a working fireplace framed by a beautiful, hand-carved mantel with built-in mirror.

Behind the house are one-, two-, and three-bedroom efficiency units and a private cottage (rented by the week) with its own deck, full kitchen, and a washer/dryer. Guests in all the rooms gather each morning for a generous continental breakfast in the dining room, and guests are welcome to use one of the inn's bicycles or borrow a beach chair. All this is within easy walking distance of both shops and beaches. The main house is open year-round. Children cannot be accommodated in the main house, but they are welcome in some of the other units.

Port Fortune Inn $$$
201 Main Street, Chatham
(508) 945-0792, (800) 750-0792
www.portfortuneinn.com

Innkeepers Mike and Renee Kahl, who bought the property in 1996, decided to revive the name the inn used in the 1930s. Port Fortune was also Chatham's original name, bestowed by explorer Samuel de Champlain in 1606. The Kahls completely redid all the existing rooms and added two lovely, spacious rooms in the second floor of the building, which was a restaurant and now houses the reception area and the breakfast room. The new rooms have ocean views; all the rooms have queen-size beds, private baths, air-conditioning, and telephones, and are furnished with antiques and reproductions.

Most of the inn's 12 rooms are in the larger building next door, which is also home to a large, sunny common room furnished with antiques and equipped with a fireplace for chilly evenings. In fine weather sit outside on the brick terrace and enjoy the ocean breezes. The inn, located in the quiet Old Village section of town just down the road from Chatham Light, is open year-round and welcomes children 12 and older.

The Queen Anne Inn $$-$$$$
70 Queen Anne Road, Chatham
(508) 945-0394, (800) 545-INNS
www.queenanneinn.com

Built in the 1840s by a sea captain for his daughter, the Queen Anne Inn has been an inn since 1874 and is one of Chatham's loveliest treasures. Innkeeper Guenther Weinkopf offers personal, classy touches. All of the rooms are furnished with antiques, many dating from the inn's early years. Each of the 30 rooms have a private bath, TV, and telephone; some rooms have balconies and fireplaces or hot tubs, or you can stay in a luxury suite that has all the extras. With three clay tennis courts, the inn offers tennis packages, and it also has an outdoor pool, an indoor whirlpool, and a fine restaurant, which offers the guests a breakfast and also serves dinner to guests and the public May through December. Children are welcome. The inn is open all year except January and half of February.

High Nauset $$$
227 Beach Road, East Orleans
(508) 255-1658
www.highnauset.com

Sitting atop a high knoll overlooking the Atlantic Ocean, High Nauset is just 350 steps from Nauset Beach, one of the prettiest coastlines found anywhere on Cape Cod. This seaside home, which abuts the Cape Cod National Seashore, features four new sun-filled guest rooms on the second floor, which take advantage of the panoramic ocean views. Each of the guest rooms has a spacious private bath with tub and shower combination, cable TV, individually controlled heat, ceiling fan, and a large picture window framing a view of the sparkling sea. Two of these bright and airy guest rooms feature a queen-size bed, and two feature a king-size bed. Two separate entrances lead to the guest rooms and the guest living quarters, the perfect place to enjoy a delicious continental breakfast of homemade treats. A private lawn provides a great place to relax while you listen to the sounds of pounding surf and migrating birds. High Nauset is open year-round, and children 12 and older are welcome.

The Nauset House Inn $–$$$
143 Beach Road, East Orleans
(508) 255-2195, (800) 771-5508
www.nausethouseinn.com

This is one of the nicest inns we've ever seen. The Nauset House, on the road to Nauset Beach, has 14 charming guest rooms, imaginatively yet simply done, furnished with antique and hand-painted furniture. Rich shades of antique blue, green, and berry coat the wide floorboards, and wood paneling and antique quilts hang beneath hand-stenciled wall borders. Four-poster beds are invitingly covered with quilts and pillows. The large common room in this 1810 house is set up with several intimate sitting areas for sociable conversation or solitary reading by the fireplace. Past the brick-floored breakfast room is an enchanting greenhouse conservatory where ivy climbs the glass walls, fragrant camellias grow near wicker chairs, and grapes ripen on the arbor above the entrance.

Innkeeper Diane Johnson's breakfasts are well worth the extra charge and so popular that she has compiled several cookbooks for those who want to try making her specialties, such as ginger pancakes, Portuguese omelets, fruit torte, and oatmeal butterscotch muffins. The inn is open April through October and welcomes children 12 and older.

The Parsonage Inn $$
202 Main Street, East Orleans
(508) 255-8217, (888) 422-8217
www.parsonageinn.com

Built around 1770, this house still has its original wide floorboards and the tranquil feel of the 18th-century parsonage that it once was. The eight guest rooms, each with a private bath, are furnished with country antiques and decorated simply with hand-stenciling, quilts, and fresh flowers. Each room is a bit different, but all are quietly pretty. We especially like the room called the Barn, in the adjacent outbuilding, which features old, rough-hewn beams and a fence-post bed, along with its own refrigerator and sitting area.

Innkeepers Ian and Elizabeth Browne serve a hearty morning meal in the charming little breakfast room or outside on the brick patio. You can also opt to take breakfast in your room. The offerings usually include pancakes, waffles, or French toast. Later in the day enjoy refreshments in the parlor, play the piano, or relax in front of the fire. Just a mile and a half from Nauset Beach, the Parsonage is also close to shops, restaurants, and galleries and is open year-round. Children older than 6 are welcome.

Ship's Knees Inn $$
186 Beach Road, East Orleans
(508) 255-1312
www.capecodtravel.com/shipskneesinn

This restored 1820 sea captain's home is just steps away form Nauset Beach and enjoys beautiful ocean views and ocean air. The rooms are cozy and comfortable, with a homey, old-fashioned feel of the braided rug variety and no pretenses. Most rooms have TVs, air-conditioning, and refrigerators. You can also opt for one of two heated cottages with decks, fireplaces, kitchens, and living rooms.

A continental breakfast is served on the patio, which gets a lovely sea breeze, or in the common room. The inn has a pool and tennis courts, is open year-round, and welcomes children 12 and older.

Eastham Windmill Bed & Breakfast and Gallery $$
55 Samoset Road, Eastham
(508) 240-3111
www.windmillgallery.com

Owners and innkeepers Bob and Barbara Cronin, former educators, have worked wonders in restoring this quaint 1900s historic house into an inn and art gallery. If you like to be around folk art, you'll love the Windmill, which emanates a homey, folksy appeal. The downstairs is the gallery displaying Barbara's original watercolors and painted tiles. The upstairs has been converted into two charming and cozy guest rooms, each with private bathrooms. You won't find fancy antiques; instead the rooms are adorned with Barbara's unique hand-painted Americana furniture.

The Windmill Bed & Breakfast is located across from the Eastham Windmill, the oldest windmill on Cape Cod. It's easy to understand why they named one of their two guest rooms the Windmill View Room. The Horton Room, named for Chester Horton, a well-known Eastham resident who built the house at the turn of the 20th century, spans the rear of the bed-and-breakfast portion of the home and has a sitting area and pleasant view of the property's grape arbor and ornamental plantings. It is furnished with a queen-size bed, a single bed, and Barbara's hand-painted furniture. The rooms can be connected, making it ideal for family vacations or couples traveling together. A continental breakfast is served daily. The inn is also conveniently located within walking distance to Salt Pond, the National Seashore Visitors Center with its scenic nature trails; it's also close to First Encounter Beach on the bay side and Coast Guard Beach on the Atlantic. The inn and gallery are open year-round. Children are welcome.

The Over Look Inn $$-$$$
3085 U.S. Route 6, Eastham
(508) 255-1886
www.overlookinn.com

Nestled in a wood across from the entrance to the Cape Cod National Seashore, this 1869 place is beautifully decorated with imaginative colors blending nicely with antique furnishings. The front parlor, for instance, is decorated in a rich berry color that complements the mahogany furniture. Lace curtains let in plenty of sun. The inn has 11 guest rooms, each with private bath. Out back is a renovated 18th-century barn that houses three lovely suites. Innkeepers Pam and Don Anderson stayed here on their hon-

eymoon—little did they know they would soon be running it! Don's Danish heritage shines through in the country breakfast and afternoon tea. The Over Look Inn is right next to the Cape Cod Rail Trail bike trail (see our Hiking and Biking Trails chapter)—around the corner is a friendly bike shop where you can rent bikes—and a short pedal away from beaches and area attractions such as the Eastham Windmill. The inn is open year-round.

Whalewalk Inn $$$-$$$$
220 Bridge Road, Eastham
(508) 255-0617, (800) 440-1281
www.whalewalkinn.com

Elegant and accommodating, the Whalewalk Inn offers 16 guest rooms and suites in five buildings, all beautifully decorated in pastel colors and furnished with antiques and reproductions, original art, baskets, throw pillows, and fresh flowers. Innkeepers Elaine and Kevin Conlin and their staff go out of their way to please you. Browse through the inn's library of books, menus from area restaurants, and other resources. In the morning help yourself to coffee, and then sit down to a full breakfast in the sunny dining room. Relax in one of several common areas. Some rooms have sitting rooms and private entrances, and some have fireplaces; all have air-conditioning.

To the rear of the main 1830s house is the Guest House, with two suites and a main room (families traveling together often rent the whole building); the Saltbox, a charming cottage with a fireplace and private patio; and the newly built Carriage House, which has six rooms. The three-and-a-half-acre grounds feature impeccable lawns with comfortable Adirondack chairs. The Whalewalk is open from April through November and select winter weekends, and welcomes children 12 and older.

The Penny House Inn $$$
4885 U.S. Route 6, North Eastham
(508) 255-6632, (800) 554-1751
www.pennyhouseinn.com

Bright as a shiny penny, this welcoming house, set on two acres of land, offers 11 comfortable rooms, each with a private bath. In fine weather sit outside on the roomy brick terrace and watch birds alight in the trees. Don't miss the full breakfast in the dining room, which features the home's original 1690 wide wooden floorboards. "We have people come and ask if they can buy our floorboards," laughs innkeeper Margaret Keith. She points out that the house actually has two sections— the old 1690 portion and what she calls the new section, which dates from 1750.

The rooms, which all have cute names like A Penny Earned and A Pretty Penny, are of varying sizes and rates. All rooms have air-conditioning, TVs, and minirefrigerators. The Penny Serenade has a private entrance and private deck overlooking the terrace—a perfect honeymoon suite! If you want a fireplace, ask for the roomy Captain's Quarters. Guests enjoy a small sitting room, with refrigerator and wet bar, and the Great Room. Open year-round, this inn offers guests afternoon tea in winter and cookies and lemonade in summer. The Penny House is nonsmoking, and children older than 8 are welcome.

Blue Gateways   **$$**
252 Main Street, Wellfleet
(508) 349-7530
www.bluegateways.com
The history of this 1700s building, listed on the National Register of Historic Places, includes a stint as a tea room in the 1920s and an earlier incarnation as a bed-and-breakfast run by two ladies in the 1940s. Within walking distance of Wellfleet Harbor and the galleries, shops, and restaurants of Wellfleet Center, Blue Gateways has three guest rooms, all with private baths and furnished with antiques. Guests are treated to a continental breakfast each morning on the all-season sunporch and have use of the backyard, a downstairs living room with a fireplace, and an upstairs common room with a refrigerator and wet bar. There is a cable TV and VCR in the sunporch. Blue Gateways is closed

November through April and welcomes children age 12 and older.

Oyster Cove Bed & Breakfast   **$$$$**
20 Partridge Way, Wellfleet
(508) 349-2994
www.oystercove.com
How can anyone go wrong when choosing accommodations with names like the Beach Suites or the Captain's Studio (our personal favorite, with breathtaking views overlooking Wellfleet Harbor)? Your hosts, Dick and Sandy Nichols, built this large three-level deck home on waterfront property owned by their family since the 1930s. It offers you views of Indian Neck, Great Island, Chipman Cove, and of course Wellfleet Harbor, home of the world-famous Wellfleet oyster. Bring your kayak and explore to your hearts content. Or walk the shoreline of Ducke Creeke. Nature is at your doorstep. And when you're hungry for civilization again, you can head to the many art galleries in Wellfleet.

This spacious contemporary home features French doors, open ceilings with exposed beams, and polished concrete floors. Each living area, which opens onto a large outside deck, includes cable TV with VCR and a CD/radio system. The lower level Beach Suite is unique in that it includes three large bedrooms, and guests can rent one, two, or all of them. It also features a large bathroom with two sinks and tub with shower, and a living/dining area with wet bar and kitchenette, making it ideal for couples, families, or groups of up to six people. All beds are queen size.

A gourmet continental breakfast of Sandy's muffins and scones, fresh fruit, and hot coffee is served daily. Dick is more than happy to help you plan your whale-watching, fishing, or sailing excursions, or your activity of preference. Oyster Cove is open year-round.

Kalmar Village   **$$$**
674 Shore Road, North Truro
(508) 487-0585, (617) 247-0211 (off-season)
www.kalmarvillage.com

Kalmar is a perfect family retreat—truly a little village—that's been in the same family since the 1960s. It features a 400-foot private beach, a pool, barbecue, and well-maintained grounds awash in fragrant lilac and rosa rugosa. Kalmar is just steps away from the Provincetown border and close to the National Seashore. Rates include maid service and cable TV, and there's even a laundry on the premises.

Kalmar has a total of 55 units but is extremely popular and usually gets booked at least a year in advance. If you can't finagle getting one of the cottages—the epitome of Cape Cod charm—consider one of the efficiency units. Kalmar Village is open mid-May through late October.

The Moorlands $$–$$$
11 Hughes Road, North Truro
(508) 487-0663
www.themoorlands.com

It's off the beaten track, but once you find the Moorlands, we promise you'll have no problem returning again and again. Built by Captain Atkin Hughes about 100 years ago, the house has been lovingly restored to Victorian splendor and updated to include such modern amenities as in-room phones, ceiling fans, TVs, and refrigerators.

The hosts serve a continental breakfast daily in the dining room, and you can chat with new friends or curl up with a book in the parlor. Music lovers take note: The Moorlands has a music room with a variety of instruments you are welcome to play, including a piano, organ, guitars, and bass. Accommodations at this year-round inn vary: Choose from three guest rooms (all with private baths), a two-room suite, three-room apartment, two 1950s-style cottages, or the 18th-century restored carriage house, which has a full kitchen, TV and VCR, private bath, and even a five-person hot tub! It's open year-round, and children are welcome in the cottages.

The Brass Key $$$$
67 Bradford Street, Provincetown
(508) 487-9005, (800) 842-9858
www.brasskey.com

Expanded and renovated in 1997, the inn has a total of 33 rooms, all with private baths, telephones, TV/VCRs, refrigerators, even seersucker robes and hair dryers. Some rooms have private Jacuzzis, others have deluxe showers with wall jets, and a number of rooms have fireplaces, either wood or gas fired. An elaborate continental breakfast is served each morning. The Brass Key has an outdoor pool as well as a large, in-ground hot tub set in a gorgeous brick-lined courtyard; you can ask for one of the rooms that opens onto the hot tub or the pool. Although the complex now has frontage on three streets, it still maintains its original intimacy. With six outbuildings and the gatehouse, the property is personalized by host Michael Mac-Intyre's one-of-a-kind touches—vaulted skylights, a teddy loft, a rooftop widow's walk, tasteful antiques, wrought-iron lamps, a collection of decoys, and, of course, brass keys.

A five-night minimum is required during the busy season (mid-June through mid-September). There is one wheelchair-accessible room. The inn is open from mid-April through mid-November and winter holiday weekends. No children younger than 16.

The Inn at Cook Street $$–$$$
7 Cook Street, Provincetown
(508) 487-3894, (800) COOK-655
www.innatcookstreet.com

This cozy little inn, opened in 1996, offers three guest rooms, two suites, and an adjacent cottage, all with private baths and nice touches such as stuffed animals, flowers, and framed photographs taken by one of the innkeepers. All have TVs, and some have decks, either private or shared; the suites are equipped with refrigerators. Our favorite is the Hobbit Suite with its sloping ceilings and private deck overlooking the lush backyard, where Adirondack chairs beckon. Sit for a while and watch the carp in the small fish pond. Innkeepers Paul Church and Dana Mitton serve up a hearty continental breakfast and genuine hospitality. Molly, the resident golden retriever, will greet you with a friendly, gentle nuzzle. The inn is open year-round.

Land's End Inn $$$-$$$$
22 Commercial Street, Provincetown
(508) 487-0706, (800) 276-7088
www.landsendinn.com

Land's End is a celebration of art and architecture. With sweeping water views as a backdrop, the interior is filled with an incredible collection of vases, lamps, woodcarvings, and Tiffany lamps. Oriental rugs and unusual antique furniture abound, and each of the 16 guest rooms—all with private baths—is unique. Perched on top of Gull Hill at the far end of Commercial Street and reached by climbing an enchanting brick path that twists and turns, the inn is a remarkable piece of architecture—sort of Victorian contempo-rary. The main building dates back to 1904, and a wraparound porch and rear addition are recent but in keeping with the turn-of-the-20th-century feel of the place, as are the terraced gardens on the two-acre grounds. The inn is open year-round.

ShireMax Inn $$
5 Tremont Street, Provincetown
(508) 487-1233, (888) 744-7312
www.p-townlib.com/shiremax

Innkeeper Jack Barnett named his inn after his two Samoyed huskies, Shire and Max. Jack is a dog lover, and his inn in the quiet west end of town is one of only a handful of places that welcomes pets. (The inn charges an additional $5.00 per night per room for pets, and you must get approval in advance to bring your well-behaved pet.)

The seven rooms are large and homey and are stocked with everything from irons and ironing boards to beach chairs and towels. Four have private baths; three share. The room in the far back of the main house offers a private bath, private entrance, and sundeck. Two separate apartments are also available; each has a VCR and TV, telephone, full kitchen, and private sundeck. Guests are served an expanded continental breakfast on the deck, which is a great place to sunbathe in the afternoon. A minimum stay of five nights is required in July and August; the apartments are rented by the week. The ShireMax is open year-round.

Three Peaks Guest House $$
210 Bradford Street, Provincetown
(508) 487-6424

Style and distinction mark the character of Three Peaks Guest House. Built in the early 1870s and renovated to conform to the original integrity of the period, Three Peaks is one of the most outstanding examples of Victorian architecture in Provincetown.

You'll recognize its uniqueness as you approach through gardens along a flower-lined walkway and as you step onto the front porch graced with upholstered wicker rockers. You enter through the original wide double doors and find your-self in a foyer with high ceilings and an open staircase to the second floor. The six guest rooms have color TV, refrigerators, and either ceiling fans or in-season air-conditioning. All have their own color scheme complemented by distinctive tow-els in large and modern baths. A continen-tal breakfast is served each morning.

Three Peaks is open year-round and offers some marvelous rates during the winter months. It is a nonsmoking house, but the spacious porches accommodate smokers. Children are welcome, but no pets please: three cats and a dog are already in residence!

Windamar House $$$
568 Commercial Street, Provincetown
(508) 487-0599
www.provincetown.com/windamar

This elegant former sea captain's house, ca. 1840, sits behind a white picket fence that encompasses manicured lawns and lush English gardens. Inside antiques and original artwork mesh perfectly with fine wallpapers and coordinating fabrics.

This is one of the finest accommoda-tions in Provincetown, just a 15-minute walk to the center of town yet so far removed that you'll swear you're alone in paradise. The inn has six guest rooms, each with its own motif. Two rooms have private baths. Our favorite is the Studio, with its cathedral ceiling and an entire wall of glass overlooking the gardens and grape arbor. The Windamar also has two furnished apartments, including a penthouse with stunning panoramic views of Cape Cod Bay and Provincetown Harbor. Located in Provincetown's quiet East End, the inn is open year-round and provides free on-site parking. No credit cards.

Want to spend a night in a lighthouse? You can, at Race Point Lighthouse, located at the Cape's tip in Provincetown. It has several bedrooms in the keeper's house that you can reserve for a night, a weekend, or longer. You'll need to bring your own bed linens, towels, food, and drinking water, but you'll also be surrounded by the beauty of the Cape Cod National Seashore. Rooms rate are around $145 a night. Call (508) 487-9930, or visit www.race pointlighthouse.net.

COTTAGES

You may want to consider staying in a cottage: usually a freestanding, small house that sits in a colony of look-alike units. Cottages provide a more rustic environment. Some provide a communal outdoor pool with recreation and barbecue area. Usually they come with a kitchenette, microwave, television, and a small yard area, and some may be on or near the water.

Upper Cape

Pine Grove Cottages   **$**
358 Route 6A, East Sandwich
(508) 888-8179
www.pinegrovecottages.com
There aren't many settings like the one you'll find here: a pretty three-acre pine grove, set back from historic Route 6A in a truly peaceful environment. The charming heated cottages—there are 10 of them—sit side by side on the property and have ample space between them to ensure privacy. In fact you can have your own private Cape Cod one-room cottage, perfect for two people, for half the cost of an average motel room. These are immaculate accommodations and can, in some cases, house as many as six people. The

deluxe cottages have two bedrooms, a living room with sleep sofa, TV, and a fully equipped kitchen. Pine Grove specializes in hosting families and accommodating reunions or other large gatherings. The owners—Vic, Kim, and David—all have families of their own and know what to expect from yours. "All you really need to bring along on your vacation is your family and your personal belongings," says Kim. "We've got the rest."

The cottages rent by the night or the week. For about $65 a night you can rent a rustic cottage with color TV and efficiency area. The complex has a swimming pool and a play area for young children, and they provide cribs, baby baths, barbecue grills, linens, and towels. Pine Grove Cottages are available from May through November.

Lower Cape

Linger Longer by the Sea   **$$-$$$**
261 Linnell Landing Road, Brewster
(508) 896-3451, (508) 896-7714
www.lingerlongerbythesea.com
At the edge of Cape Cod Bay, the 1907 main building with its lawn ringed by a moss-covered stone wall conjures up visions of turn-of-the-20th-century seaside grandeur. It now houses six apartments

and is flanked by 10 cottages, 7 of which also sit directly on the bay. Relax on your private deck and watch the sun set over the shimmering flats at low tide, go to sleep to the calming sound of water lapping the beach outside your door, and step out for a morning swim. You'll definitely want to linger here.

All units have fully equipped kitchens, color TV, living rooms, bedrooms, and bathrooms with tubs and showers. Cribs and high chairs are provided free on request. You'll have the benefit of a private beach, and the cottages have picnic tables and charcoal grills. Tired of the beach? Take a walk at nearby Nickerson State Park, or ride the Cape Cod Rail Trail bike path. Also close by are shops and restaurants. Linger Longer is open from early April through November. Most of the units are winterized, so you'll be cozy and warm during off-season visits. Cottages 8 and 9 have fireplaces.

Cranberry Cottages $$
785 U.S. Route 6, Eastham
(508) 255-0602
www.sunsol.com/cranberrycottages
Owners Lisa and Guy Grant are sticklers about offering their guests the best in carefree and comfortable accommodations. Snugly tucked away among locust trees, these cottages are so far apart that privacy is never an issue. Among the 14 cottages there are several options: one-room efficiencies, two-bedroom housekeeping cottages, or nonhousekeeping units, which come with maid services and have no kitchen facilities, though they are equipped with coffeemakers. If you visit during the off-season, you'll be glad to know that the cottages are individually heated for nippy autumn and winter nights. The cottages are open year-round, and in season they're rented by the week only.

The Colony $$$
Chequessett Neck Road, Wellfleet
(508) 349-3761
Welcome to the simple life. Built as a private club in 1949 by one of the founders of Boston's Institute for Contemporary Arts, this collection of masonry and wood-frame duplexes, scattered along a wooded hillside overlooking the water, has been run as a cottage colony since 1963. With bedrooms that double as sitting rooms during the day, the cottages have fireplaces, galley kitchens, glass- and screen-enclosed dining porches, and patios or decks. Some of them have original art by well-known artists and have counterparts in museums. You'll find fresh flowers in your room and have the benefit of daily maid service.

The Colony is open from late May through September. The cottages, which are available as one- or two-bedroom units, are rented by the week. Children are welcome.

Surf Side Cottages $$$
Ocean View Drive, South Wellfleet
(508) 349-3959
www.surfsidevacation.com
Talk about location! Scattered along the sand dunes and fragrant pines of Cape Cod National Seashore, Surf Side is part of an idyllic summer community, where children run free down sandy dirt roads and the only sound late at night is the roar of the tide. This is quintessential Outer Cape, where the sharp beach grass blows on high dunes overlooking white beaches. With knotty pine interiors, screened porches, fireplaces, kitchens, bathrooms, barbecues, and heat, these 17 cottages are equipped with everything you need—there's even a laundry facility! These are some of the only Oceanside accommodations in this area, perfect for families, and they book fast. Try for the Ocean Breeze or Surf View cottages, the two closest to the water. Pets are permitted off-season (before Memorial Day and after Columbus Day) for an additional charge. Surf Side is open from early April through November.

Days Cottages $$
271 Shore Road, North Truro
(508) 487-1062
www.dayscottages.com
If these pretty-as-a-picture waterfront

cottages look familiar, it's because they have been immortalized through the years by dozens of artists in countless paintings and postcards.

What began as nine cottages in 1931 has grown to 23—all exactly alike. Each blooms with the name of a different flower (such as Larkspur and Dahlia) and offers comfy living rooms with stunning water views. Remember, however, that these cottages are so popular with returning guests that it's nearly impossible to book one for less than a week during the season. The on-site self-service market stocks everything you'll need, from postcards to pomegranates. The cottages are open May through October. No credit cards.

RESERVATION SERVICES

Reservation services can make planning your vacation much easier. Instead of calling around to see which establishments have openings—especially if you haven't started planning way in advance—enlist the help of one of the Cape's reservation services. Most deal with hotels, inns, and bed-and-breakfasts, though some specialize in the latter. The following reservation services are among the best around. Most do not charge; others charge a modest fee. We indicate any fees in the individual write-ups.

Bed and Breakfast Cape Cod
16 Arey's Lane, P.O. Box 1312,
Orleans, MA 02653
(508) 255-3824, (800) 541-6226
www.bandbcapecod.com
In early 1998 Orleans Bed & Breakfast Associates merged with Bed and Breakfast Cape Cod to create a reservation service that represents more than 130 inns and bed-and-breakfasts throughout Cape Cod, Martha's Vineyard, and Nantucket. Properties, which are all inspected and approved annually, range from modest to luxurious. You're sure to find an accommodation that suits your taste, be it an intimate bed-and-breakfast or an inn with

a restaurant. There is a one-time $10 fee for the services here, and they do mean one time: If you used their services a decade ago and call again this year, the fee you paid back then is still good.

Bed & Breakfast Reservations
(617) 964-1606, (978) 281-9505, (800)
832-2632 (outside Massachusetts)
www.bbreserve.com
In business since 1985, Bed & Breakfast Reservations has been providing visitors to New England with carefully selected accommodations in eastern Massachusetts. They represent some of the most beautiful inns, bed-and-breakfasts, and guesthouses from Cape Cod to the North Shore, Boston and in between. They also have a select few special accommodations for travelers looking to include Maine, New Hampshire, or Vermont in their itineraries.

With just one phone call, Bed & Breakfast Reservations will help you select from a fine list of approved accommodations to match your needs and comfort level. You can choose from a list of charming host homes, historic inns, private suites, cozy summer cottages, or furnished apartments—if you want to spend a few days in Boston.

After looking down their list of inns, we're sure you'll experience a pleasant stay in any one of the inns they represent. A two-night minimum stay is required for reservations. Your reservation is guaranteed in writing for the number of nights requested. A $20 agency fee is charged. Bed & Breakfast Reservations is a year-round service.

In Town Reservations
4 Standish Street, Provincetown
(508) 487-1833, (800) 677-8696
www.intownreservations.com
In Town handles house rentals by the week, month, or season, handling a huge number of annually inspected properties in Provincetown and North Truro. The firm also books reservations at inns, bed-and-breakfasts, guesthouses, motels, and condominiums—all for no fee!

VACATION RENTALS

Cape Cod, with its miles and miles of beaches, quaint villages, delicious restaurants, numerous attractions, challenging golf courses, and thousands and thousands of rental properties, has all the makings of an ideal summer vacation. Summer gatherings with family and friends, outdoor picnics, oceanside clambakes, after-dark cocktails by the flickering July candlelight...these memories and many more can be harvested from a vacation spent at a cottage or home located down near the ocean's edge.

Though the Cape is probably best known for its summer season when the beaches become the most popular attractions, Cape Cod is also an excellent place to spend a week or two during the shoulder seasons of spring and autumn when the air is cooler and the rents are lighter. We year-rounders even enjoy the snows of January and February, especially when it graces the marshes of meandering icy streams and accents the climbing dune cliffs. Several communities have even begun playing host to holiday festivities and special New Year's celebrations.

Recent years could be best described as an owner's market. Rentals have been snatched up quickly, often before the season starts in June. Although scanning the newspapers can yield some good rental leads, your best bet is to contact local real estate agents. Even if you're planning an off-season rental, prepare early. Many owners close up their property around Columbus Day and would rather not have to go through the cleaning routine again for the sake of a last-minute one-week rental. Along those lines you sometimes can negotiate a better deal on a rental by agreeing to rent for the month or the season because it's much easier for the owners. One possibility is to join together with some friends and agree to an extended rental. Each group can then take a week or two weeks over the month or season.

The warm summer months provide a variety of rental properties from cottages to houses to condominium units. A rental cottage is usually a three-season small house. Many cottage rentals, even long-term ones, do not supply linens (such as sheets or towels), paper goods, or toiletries. Some offer housekeeping and laundry services for an extra fee. Almost all weekly rental units of any kind rent from Saturday to Saturday.

When you think of condominiums and time-shares, think upscale apartments, almost always fully furnished and often part of a waterfront or waterview complex. Time-share units are owned by a person or company who then rents out the unit for various periods of time. Time-shares should only concern you if you plan on buying into one.

To make your vacation run more smoothly, remember that the price you'll pay is based on several factors, including location (those near or on the water are, of course, the most expensive), length of stay, how long in advance your reservation was made, and the time of year of your visit. July is the Cape's busiest month in terms of rentals. August, September, and October are also very busy months on Cape Cod. Columbus Day weekend can find almost every hotel room filled as visitors enjoy the Cape's most colorful shades.

If you do want to rent a cottage for a week, especially during July, plan on calling well in advance. Many rental offices are busy in January and February booking rentals for the coming summer season. In-season rates are the priciest; those in shoulder seasons (right before or immediately following the busy summer season) can drop as much as 30 percent; off-season rates (if the accommodations are available) can be as much as 50 percent off seasonal prices.

It would be impossible to mention all the resorts and rental agencies on the Cape, but we've put together a list of those that offer the finest in vacation rentals. Keep in mind that many of these agencies are also full-service real estate companies (see our Relocation chapter) and will be more than happy to answer any questions—and perhaps sell you a property once you've acquired a taste for Cape Cod. Many of those who join the ranks of the year-rounders begin as summer renters who get hooked and later buy a cottage. Once you begin to spend some time here you'll find leaving the Cape increasingly difficult.

Usually the rental properties contain a fully equipped kitchen, but it is important to remember that the Cape includes such a range of properties that "fully equipped" can mean different things depending on the situation. For instance where a dishwasher may be considered standard issue for a year-round house, it is not always available in a small cottage that may have been built 50 years ago, before dishwashers were an option. A microwave oven may or may not be available. Blenders, electric can openers, and the like should all be determined up front if such items are considered a must. Also, you may want to inquire as to whether the stove and oven are electric or gas.

Televisions, VCRs, telephones, whether the cottage has a tub or just a shower (families with small children who are used to taking baths will want to know) are all items to be questioned before you send in your deposit. By the way, the typical deposit on a vacation rental is 50 percent due upon making reservations, with the balance due before your arrival. Before you book always ask about cancellation policies and whether pets, visiting guests, and/or smoking are allowed. If a particular item is important to you, or when in doubt, it's better to ask than run the risk of being disappointed when you arrive.

Finally, if you cannot find what you're looking for in this chapter, call the chamber of commerce in the town in which you're interested (chamber of commerce phone numbers are listed in the Area Overview chapter). The local chambers are more than happy to offer you more information so you can plan that perfect summer vacation.

UPPER CAPE

Cape Coast Realty
**18-B MacArthur Boulevard, Bourne
(508) 759-9517
www.capecoastrealty.com**
You can choose from approximately 70 waterfront and water-view homes for rent in Bourne, Sandwich, and Falmouth. The rate for a small cottage is about $850 per week; a private luxury home rents for around $2,000 per week.

When contacting agents about vacation rentals, ask if they list any "quirky" ones. Sometimes you can find older cottages or homes with quaint or out-of-the-ordinary accommodations at bargain prices.

Beach Realty
**133 North Shore Boulevard, East Sandwich
(800) 886-4998
www.beachrealtycapecod.com**
This office carries approximately 200 property listings in five beach areas from Sagamore to Sandy Neck. Properties differ in size, and most of them rent by the week, though vacation rentals area available. Homes rent for $525–$3,500.

Kinlin Grover GMAC Real Estate
**Various locations and numbers
www.vacationcapecod.com**
Kinlin Grover GMAC is the leader in Cape Cod vacation rentals. Through their eight

Sunday traffic going off the Cape is the worst. Most regulars say you have to be off the Cape before 10:00 A.M. to beat the backup at the bridges. We recommend extending your visit to Cape Cod, and leaving after 6:00 P.M. when traffic is not so bad.

offices and Web sites (also try www.kinlin grover.com) they service more visitors than any other rental company on the Cape. With locations in Osterville (508-428-3100), Falmouth (508-540-8881), Sandwich (508-833-3330), Brewster (508-896-7004), Harwich (508-432-9300), Chatham (508-945-5566), East Orleans (508-255-2200), and Wellfleet (508-349-9000), Kinlin Grover GMAC Real Estate is sure to have the rental property you are looking for.

Barrett Real Estate
178 Route 28, Falmouth
(508) 548-2000
www.capecodrealestate.com/barrett
With an inventory of 500 vacation rentals from cottages to waterfront homes, this office has listings in Falmouth, Bourne, and Mashpee, including Popponesset. Homes and condos are rented by the week or full season.

Donahue Real Estate
850 Main Street, Falmouth
(508) 548-5412
www.falmouthhomes.com
This active rental office lists approximately 250 rental properties, including, houses, condominiums, duplexes, and apartments, many with three and four bedrooms. Most of these properties are in Falmouth, and they are available for one week to a full season.

Many rental agencies have specific properties designated for family reunions or weddings.

Ermine Lovell Real Estate
881 Palmer Avenue, Falmouth
(508) 548-0711
www.capecodrealestate.com/lovell
With many inland and waterfront properties, including 8- or 11-bedroom houses, this nearly 70-year-old real estate office offers vacation rentals exclusively in the Falmouth and Woods Hole areas.

Real Estate Associates
563 Route 28A (at Route 151), North Falmouth
(508) 563-7173
www.realestateassc.com
Real Estate Associates has more than 100 houses, condominiums, and cottages in waterfront, water-view, and beach locations. Within Falmouth, Bourne, Mashpee, and Sandwich (many along Buzzards Bay and Vineyard Sound), properties range from 1- to 10-bedroom homes. This three-decades-old business also has offices in West Falmouth, Pocasset, Falmouth, Mashpee, and Sandwich.

New Seabury Rentals
12 Mall Way, Mashpee
(800) 388-7686
www.newseaburyre.com
Nearly all the rental properties lie within the 2,000-acre New Seabury Resort. The number of available homes and condominiums varies year by year but averages about 200 a season. Some are waterfront and range from two- to four-bedroom units. Country club, golf, tennis, and beach memberships are available. Membership fees allow you to utilize the pool and health club.

MID-CAPE

Craigville Realty
648 Craigville Beach Road, Craigville
(508) 775-3174
www.craigvillebeach.com
In business since 1951, Craigville Realty has more than 200 rental properties, mostly homes and cottages in Centerville, Hyan-

nis, West Hyannisport, and Craigville. They range from modest to exclusive, from $750 to $10,000 per week, including some waterfront. Craigville also rents properties for two weeks and has some properties available for the full summer season.

Century 21 Shoreland Real Estate
724 Main Street, Hyannis
(508) 771-2008
www.shorelandre.com
Shoreland deals primarily with rentals from Mashpee to Harwich on a year-round basis, and the Barnstable villages of Osterville, Cotuit, and Hyannis for seasonal rentals. The company specializes in short-term corporate relocation rentals and also offers weekly seasonal rates. The properties range from efficiencies to six-bedroom homes. Summer weekly rates range from a low of $700 to upwards of $12,000 for a beachfront house.

Waterfront Rentals
20 Pilgrim Road, West Yarmouth
(508) 778-1818
www.waterfrontrentalsinc.com
You can rent estates, homes, and condos from Bourne to Truro through this 18-year-old agency that offers a wide selection of mid- and lower Cape properties. Approximately 160 properties are available for weekly, seasonal, or year-round rental and range from one- to nine-bedroom facilities. These rental properties range from $800 to $3,000 per week. Videos of properties can be viewed at the office.

James E. Mischler, Realtors
Intersection of Routes 28 and 134, West Dennis
(508)) 394-3330, (800) 863-3330
www.capecodrealestate.com/mischler
This mid-Cape office, established by Jim and Rita Mischler in 1979, has some 400 vacation properties in the Dennis, Yarmouth, and Harwich areas. These quality properties, which include vacation homes as well as cottages, rent for between $600 and $5,000 a week—the former being an efficiency, and the latter a five-bedroom home on the water.

Peter McDowell Associates
585 Route 6A, Dennis
(508) 385-9114, (888) 385-9114
11 Route 28, Dennisport
(508) 394-5400, (800) 870-5401
www.capecodproperties.com
This full-service real estate company has been servicing the Dennis area for nearly 40 years. It offers about 200 summer rentals from Barnstable to Yarmouth. Rental properties are available for a week, two weeks, a month, or for the whole summer season.

Although the Cape is best known for its summer season, Cape Cod is also an excellent place to spend a week or two during the off-seasons. The weather may be cooler, but the rents are considerably less.

Steele Associates
1372 Route 134, East Dennis
(508) 385-7311
www.steelerealty.com
This family-owned company, in its 16th year in business, offers more than 50 rental homes in beach areas from Barnstable to Orleans. Rentals are weekly, monthly, or seasonal. Besides a busy summer rental season, Steele Associates also offers rentals during the off-season months of September and October. Summer weekly rentals range from $750 to $4,000 (for waterfront), and houses generally range from two to four bedrooms.

LOWER CAPE

Kinlin Grover GMAC Real Estate
1990 Route 6A, Brewster
(508) 896-7004, (800) 338-1851
www.vacationcapecod.com

With eight offices handling seasonal rentals, Kinlin Grover GMAC Real Estate is one of the Cape's largest real estate companies. It has an excellent selection of rental properties available by the week, for two weeks, the month, or on a seasonal basis. Properties include homes, cottages, and condominiums in the lower Cape towns from Brewster to Provincetown. Kinlin Grover GMAC Real Estate also has rental offices in Osterville (508-428-3100), Falmouth (508-540-8881), Sandwich (508-833-3330), Brewster (508-896-7004), Harwich (508-432-9300), Chatham (508-945-5566), East Orleans (508-255-2200), and Wellfleet (508-349-9000).

Great Locations Real Estate
2660 Route 6A, Brewster
(508) 896-2090, (800) 626-9984
www.greatlocationsre.com
Great Locations offers exceptional vacation rentals, including a large selection of condominium rentals at Ocean Edge Resort in Brewster. The properties Great Locations handles are primarily in the Brewster and Dennis areas. Prices range from $800 to $3,700 per week in season, the latter being the price of a three-bedroom house on the water. Monthly and seasonal rentals are also available through this high-quality vacation rental outfit.

Peterson Realty
255 Main Street, West Harwich
(508) 432-1220
www.petersonrealty.com
Peterson Realty offers about 125 rentals ranging from summer cottages to year-round homes in the Harwich, Dennis, Yarmouth, and Chatham areas. Its vacation rentals are also available by the week, month, and season.

Sylvan Realty
1715 Route 28, West Chatham
(508) 945-7222
www.sylvanrentals.com
This agency specializes in rentals of

some 200 individually owned cottages and homes in the Chatham and Harwich areas. Fully furnished beach cottages are available on a weekly, monthly, and seasonal basis.

Pine Acres Realty
938 Main Street, Chatham
(508) 945-7443
www.pineacresrealty.com
This company truly lives up to its motto, "Bringing people and houses together since 1948." Choose from more than 150 Chatham properties rented by the week, season, or year. Rentals run from $800 to $5,000 for a waterfront estate.

The Real Estate Company
207 Main Street, East Orleans
(508) 255-5100
www.capecodvacation.com
The Real Estate Company manages more than 350 vacation rentals on the Lower Cape. Their Web site allows access to their entire inventory of vacation homes, which rent from between $200 and $6,000 per week.

American Heritage Realty
414 Chatham Road, South Orleans
(888) 296-4313
www.capecodforrent.com
With a 37-year reputation for excellence, American Heritage is one of the lower Cape's leading real estate and vacation rental firms. It serves Orleans, Harwich, Brewster, Chatham, Eastham, and Wellfleet. The Web site address says it all: Cape Cod for rent.

Anchor Real Estate
U.S. Route 6, North Eastham
(508) 255-4949
www.anchor-realestate.net
A well-respected real estate office on the lower Cape, Anchor Real Estate and its owner Suzanne Goodrich have received a number of awards over the years. The office has some 200 quality summer vacation rentals. An average rental is

about $1,200 for a three-bedroom, two-bath house within a half-mile of the water. Unique services include convenient linen rentals for tenants and bed-and-breakfast reservations.

Beachfront Realty
139 Commercial Street, Provincetown
(508) 487-1397
www.beachfront-realty.com
Beachfront deals with properties in Provincetown. The company represents more than 50 accommodations for weekly rental and approximately 30 for seasonal rental. Weekly rates run from $900 to $4,000.

Harborside Realty
162 Commercial Street, Provincetown
(508) 487-4005, (800) 838-4005
www.harborside-realty.com
Harborside Realty handles 200 Provincetown properties, from basic quaint cottages at $850 a week to the most trendy three-bedroom private homes at about $3,500 a week. Properties are available by the week, month, and for the summer season.

Hordes of young people flock to the Cape to work at restaurants, attractions, and shops during a typical summer. In the interest of saving money, sometimes far too many people bunk down in a house for the summer—and unwind after their shifts in the early morning hours. Make sure to ask your rental agent if the place you're looking at is located near one these rowdy party houses.

Pat Shultz and Associates
406 Commercial Street, Provincetown
(508) 487-9550
www.patshultz.com
Pat Shultz and Associates has been handling Provincetown rentals since 1970. Over that time it has established itself as a major player in both residential and commercial rentals. A friendly four-member staff promises to find the perfect rental for your needs—weekly, monthly, seasonally, or annually. Properties range from $750 studios and $850 one-bedroom apartments to $2,700 two-bedroom units and $5,500 waterfront houses.

CAMPGROUNDS AND STATE PARKS

Cape Cod is a paradise for those who enjoy water sports, fishing, hiking, biking, and any of the other outdoor activities for which it is so well known. The Cape has a number of picturesque campgrounds and state parks that allow visitors to enjoy a peaceful outdoor experience amid unspoiled surroundings. Whether it's in a tent or an RV, camping Cape Cod style takes you out of the rhythm of everyday life and gives you a chance to lead a freer lifestyle—at least for a while. You'll go home refreshed—and you'll save scads of money, because camping is the best deal going on the Cape. For less than $30 a night you can pitch a tent in a quiet, rustic environment on the edge of the dunes or deep in woodland.

In this chapter we've included information on both public and private campgrounds. Cape Cod has more than 3,700 campsites in 20 campgrounds and three state parks with 80 campsites. As there is a diverse range of campgrounds, visitors will be sure to find accommodations to suit their style of camping. Peak season on the Cape is from the close of schools (around mid-June) until Labor Day, with peak weeks from early July to mid-August. During this time reservations are essential at most campgrounds.

TIPS TO GET YOU STARTED

Whether you are an experienced camper or a first-timer, decide on what kind of camping experience you want: back to nature, family oriented, in the woods, or close to town. Note that there is no wilderness camping on Cape Cod.

Second, consider your choices. Some people prefer to camp at smaller, more remote campgrounds and like to "rough it." In this case consider the quiet solitude of the campgrounds near the National Seashore and surrounding areas in the Lower Cape. To others camping is merely an affordable way to spend time on the Cape, and you may want to be near more lively areas, in which case the privately owned campgrounds in the Upper and Mid-Cape areas will probably suit your needs.

You'll always be close to water, so that shouldn't be a consideration, but there is a difference between the campgrounds on the Upper Cape and those located on the Lower Cape. Many campgrounds located in the Upper Cape have such amenities as swimming pools, game rooms, and organized activities and tend to be more self-contained, while the smaller campgrounds on the Lower Cape may not have these amenities but are closer to bike paths, hiking trails, and other areas of natural beauty. All campgrounds listed offer suitable tent sites and/or RV camping and provide flush toilets, and most offer electrical and water hookups. Individual offerings are outlined in the entries below, as are costs. Although the listings below are as up-to-date as we can make them, you may want to use the phone numbers given to verify current fees and services.

CAMPGROUNDS

Upper Cape

Bay View Campground
260 Route 28 (MacArthur Boulevard), Bourne
(508) 759-7610
www.bayviewcampground.com
Perched on one of the highest points of land on Cape Cod, this 430-site campground is a perfect spot to enjoy beautiful sunsets and take advantage of the recreational opportunities in the area. Bay View is 20 minutes by car from both Falmouth and Sandwich. Walkers, runners, and in-line skaters will enjoy the nearby canal bike path, and nearby, within a mile, is Adventure Isle, which has miniature golf, amusement rides, batting cages, and a go-cart track. Needless to say, Bay View is extremely popular with families.

The campground offers so much leisure activity you may find it difficult to fit it all in. Bay View has areas for tennis, basketball, volleyball, shuffleboard, and horseshoes, plus two playgrounds, three large in-ground swimming pools, and a baby pool. In the recreation hall you can play table tennis, pool, and video games. Bay View has a full-time recreation director who organizes daily activities for all ages, from teen dances with pizza to arts and crafts, water volleyball, magic shows, baseball, and family wagon rides and dances.

Each site has a picnic table, fireplace, and hookups for water and electricity (full hookup sites have 30 amps); most have sewer hookup. A cable TV connection costs extra. Facilities include showers and toilets, ice, gas, and wood. You can buy RV supplies such as hoses and awnings at the office.

The campground is open from May to October. Reservations are accepted in early January for the upcoming season. The in-season rate for two people is $39.00 plus $3.00 for children younger than 18 and $10.00 for those 18 and older. The off-season rate—for May and June and Labor Day to October—is $31.00 Pets are welcome but must be restrained, and you'll need to bring their current rabies vaccination certificate.

Bourne Scenic Park
Bourne Scenic Highway (U.S. Route 6 and Route 28), Buzzards Bay
(508) 759-7873
www.bournerecauth.com
For location Bourne Scenic Park rivals the best accommodations on Cape Cod. Situated on the banks of the world's widest sea-level canal, this 475-site facility offers shady woods and proximity to shops and grocery stores. And the scenery is extraordinary: gigantic white cruise ships and tankers glide past your campsite along the canal and occasionally give a massive blast on their horns.

From the park bikers and strollers have several access points to the popular canal service road bike path where people push baby strollers, walk dogs, bike, and in-line skate all day long. In the summer the park offers hayrides and live entertainment, including bands and DJs. You can swim in the park's large saltwater pool.

Operated by the Bourne Recreation Authority, the Scenic Park has electric and water hookups, a dump station, playgrounds, a recreation hall, a volleyball court, and activities for children throughout the summer. The country store sells basic supplies, including ice and wood.

In season the rates are $28 per day with electricity hookup and $25 without, or

---

During peak weeks in the summer, most campgrounds require a reservation. Many also require a minimum length of stay during weekends in July and August. For instance a minimum stay of two nights may be required over weekends, and a three-night stay might be required on holiday weekends. In July and August seven-night stays are required at some area campgrounds.

$260 for two weeks. In the off-season, a two-week stay costs $140 ($95 per week) with electricity. Please note that from late June until September, reservations may be made for one or two weeks only.

Each December birders brave the cool weather and wind to scour the hinterlands of Cape Cod for every single bird they can see or hear. And to no one's surprise, seabirds consistently top the National Audubon Society's annual bird count on the Outer Cape. The 2002 count turned up 47,256 birds of 136 species. The 4,512 dunlins, a close relative to the sandpiper, were the most common, followed by northern gannets (3,909), herring gulls (3,542), and razorbills (3,432). The birders also spotted 83 great blue herons.

Dunroamin' Cottages and Trailer Park
5 John Ewer Road, Sandwich
(508) 477-0859, (508) 477-0541

A family-run business since 1952, Dunroamin' offers 60 trailer sites for self-contained vehicles, plus four cottages, on 35 acres next to Peter's Pond. The cottages, which book early, are right on the pond, which offers great freshwater fishing, and all guests of Dunroamin' are welcome to use the park's rowboats. There's a swing set and basketball hoop, and the park is a good, safe place for children to ride their bikes. Pets are allowed in the trailer park provided they're vaccinated, restrained, and kept off the beach. Trailer sites include hookups for water, electricity, and sewerage. Daily rates, based on a party of four, are $30 daily, $200 weekly, and $750 monthly. Cottages, which can accommodate five to six people, have weekly rental costs of about $630 to $685 in season, and between $450 and $515 in the off-season. The park, in South Sandwich off Cotuit Road, just 6 miles from the village of Sandwich and 9 miles from the

Sagamore Bridge, is open mid-April to mid-October for trailers and mid-June to mid-September for cottage rentals.

Peter's Pond Park
185 Cotuit Road, Sandwich
(508) 477-1775
www.peterspond.com

For campers who return year after year, this facility is as close to owning waterfront property on Cape Cod as you can get without paying taxes. A 100-acre campground situated on a lovely freshwater lake, Peter's Pond Park offers swimming, fishing, and boating. It abuts a large conservation area with walking trails and has playgrounds, playing fields for baseball and volleyball, horseshoes, a convenience store, and adult and teen recreation halls. The campground, which has been in the DeGraw family for more than 70 years, offers 475 large sites, one-third of which are for tent camping, and the rest are for RVs. Wheelchair-accessible facilities are available. You can cook on individual charcoal and gas stoves. Campers are only a few miles from beaches, museums, the Cape Cod Canal, and antique and gift shops in Sandwich and Mashpee. Pets are allowed if you abide by the park rules and have a valid rabies certificate for your animal.

The park rents tepees, cabins, docks, and rowboats by the week (daily off-season). The rates run from $29 to $65 per night. The campground is open from mid-April until mid-October.

Waquoit Bay National Estuarine Research Reserve
Washburn Island, Mashpee/Falmouth
(508) 457-0495, ext. 100
www.waquoitbayreserve.org

Camping on the 300-acre Washburn Island in Waquoit Bay should be considered a privilege as well as a luxury. This beautiful island is now managed by the state, and campers must have permits (see information below). Eleven sites are available, nine for families and two for a group of no more than 25. The reserve offers a group rate of $25. Facilities consist of composting toilets and outhouses; the island has no electricity or fresh water. Only hibachis and Coleman-type stoves can be used for cooking. Access to the island across a narrow tidal channel is possible only by private boat—your own. Camping ends in mid-October.

Permits cost $5.00 per night for Massachusetts residents, $6.00 for out-of-staters. For more information call the number above or write to the Waquoit Bay Research Reserve, P.O. Box 3092, Waquoit, MA 02536.

Sippewissett Campground & Cabins
836 Palmer Avenue, Falmouth
(508) 548-2542, (800) 957–CAMP
www.sippewissett.com

This 40-year-old, family-owned campground offers a home base from which to reach the shops, restaurants, and historic sites in Falmouth. In fact campers can pick from seven great beaches, two windsurfing beaches, fishing, golf, boating, and hiking trails that are no more than 15 minutes away by car.

The campground has an activity center, a playground, and a volleyball area. Most of the 120 sites (60 for tents and 60 for RVs) are wooded, and all have picnic tables and fire pits. This shady campground offers 24-hour security, emergency assistance, and a coin-operated laundry. Dogs are not permitted here from Memorial Day to Labor Day.

Nightly charges for families are $31 in season. Electric and water hookups are $2.00 per day. The off-season rate is $24 and $26 with water and electricity. Off-season rates apply at the beginning and end of the season, which runs from mid-May to mid-October.

Mid-Cape

Campers Haven Ltd.
184 Old Wharf Road, Dennisport
(508) 398-2811
www.campershaven.com

This place emphasizes family fun. The fes-

Most of the campgrounds that are in areas that allow campfires have wood available. For a few dollars you can get a good-sized bundle that should last you a few nights of toasting marshmallows.

tivities here include free movies, sing-alongs, story hours, candy bingo, beach barbecues, minigolf, volleyball, basketball, horseshoes, potluck suppers, and two playgrounds, one for little tykes and another for older children—all included in the rock-bottom price. Some of the warmest waters on the Cape are just seconds away, so enjoy their private beach on Nantucket Sound.

Choose from among 265 shaded sites. All include water, electricity, cable TV, and gray water disposal (many sites have full sewage disposal). Rates are $45 per day, or $295 per week. The park is open from April to Columbus Day and is limited to RVs and campers only.

Grindell's Ocean View Park
61 Old Wharf Road, Dennisport
(508) 398-2671

This is an RV aficionado's dream come true—a real village within one of the prettiest stretches of the Cape. The park has 160 sites for RVs up to 34 feet long; book early if you want to stay right on the ocean. All sites have three-way hookups and concrete patios.

You can also opt for one of the 11 white and weathered-gray cottages, all with bathrooms, electricity, wooden decks, and lots of privacy, on the ocean or nestled among the pine trees. Spend the day relaxing on the private saltwater beach, or try your luck at fishing—cast a line off the breakwater right outside your door.

The park has two pay toilets, hot-water showers, and a fully stocked grocery store. The park is open from mid-May through the end of September; rates are $40 a night for a waterfront site, $30 one row back. In July and August sites are

rented by the week only: $250 for waterfront sites and $200 for sites one row back. Cottages are available by the week during July and August for $320 to $500 per week. Reservations are a must from mid-June through Labor Day. Grindell's does not accept credit cards or pets.

Lower Cape

Shady Knoll Campground
1709 Route 6A, Brewster
(508) 896-3002
www.shadyknoll.com

With 100 wooded sites for tents and RVs, Shady Knoll is close to bay beaches, the bike trail, and shops, and is within walking distance of a small grocery store. Located near the Route 137 junction, Shady Knoll offers free hot showers, full hookups, fireplaces, laundry facilities, a playground, game room, lounge, and campground store. Campfires are allowed, and movies are shown nightly during the summer. Reservations are requested. Weekends in July and August require a three-night minimum stay. Shady Knoll is open May 15 to October 15. Rates are $23.00 to $42.50 a night, depending on the number of people and whether you need electric or sewer hookup. Pets are allowed, provided you take them with you when you leave your site.

Sweetwater Forest
Off Route 124, Brewster
(508) 896-3773
www.sweetwaterforest.com

Don't let the winding, bumpy dirt driveway fool you—that's as rough as it gets around here. One of the largest and oldest campgrounds on Cape Cod, Sweetwater is a sprawling spread of 250 sites situated lakefront and in 60 acres of woodland. You can rent a canoe or a rowboat and cruise around the lake, fish off the dock, or play horseshoes on the beach—you can even arrange for a pony ride! There are five different playgrounds, as well as a new 18-hole minigolf course. And in case you forgot to bring enough reading material, Sweetwater offers a free lending library.

Sites are available with partial or full hookups, and there's a separate area just for tents. Each site has its own fireplace. Four modern comfort stations with free hot showers assure that you won't have far to go when you have to go. Rates start at $25 per day for a family of 4 with no hookup, $35 for full hookup, which includes cable TV with the electric hookup. Reservations are recommended during the summer and on holiday weekends, and pets are allowed. Though the grounds officially close from November through April, self-contained camping is allowed during these months.

Atlantic Oaks
3700 U.S. Route 6, Eastham
(508) 255-1437
www.atlanticoaks.com

Just a half-mile from the Cape Cod National Seashore's visitor center, this modern campground meets the needs of RVers and tent campers alike (though the emphasis here is on the former). The 135 large wooded sites include 100 drive-throughs with full electric and water hookups and cable TV. Other amenities include metered gas service, free hot showers, laundry facilities, nightly movies during the summer, and, to keep the kids entertained, a playground. Dogs are allowed here, provided that they are taken with you when you're away from the camp. You might want to bring your bicycles, as Atlantic Oaks abuts the Cape Cod Rail Trail.

[Facing page] *Camper's Haven Ltd., located in Dennisport, has its own private beach on Nantucket Sound.* © PETER PELLAND/PELLAND ADVERTISING

The grounds are protected (not that they need to be, in sleepy Eastham) by a 24-hour security gate. Rates are $33.00 to $47.50 per night at this year-round campground. Winter camping (November through May) is by reservation only.

Paine's Campground
180 Old County Road, off U.S. Route 6, South Wellfleet
(508) 349–3007
www.campingcapecod.com

The emphasis here is on tent camping, and those who really want to get away from it all can choose a secluded site, whether in the "single and couples" section or in the quiet "couples only" section. Both are very private areas, though no water or electricity is available. This is just one of the special amenities the Paine family has offered dedicated campers since 1958.

Campers with children are placed in a family section. Many of these sites will accommodate multiple tents. Although Paine's preference is for tents, there are some hookup sites with water and 15-amp service; these are grouped together and suitable for tents, pop-ups, and pick-up campers. Seven sites have also been converted for RVs, with electric and water hookups, but there are no sewer hookups or dump stations. All hookup sites cost an extra $4.00 fee per day. Base rates are $26.00 per night for two people; add $13.00 per night for each extra adult and $5.00 per child. Off-season rates drop to $20.00, $10.00, and $4.00 respectively. Larger group sites can accommodate family reunions and other small to large groups. No water or electric is available to the group sites. Several private shaded "lug-in" sites are available for those who want to simply unwind under the fragrant pines. Reservations for any site are strongly recommended, and there is a no-pets policy. Paine's Campground is open May though the end of September.

Maurice's Campground
80 U.S. Route 6, Wellfleet
(508) 349–2029
www.mauricescampground.com

This place redefines "rustic." The 200 tent, trailer, and RV sites, as well as four cottages and seven cabins, are set in the middle of a large pine grove, far from the hustle and bustle of U.S. Route 6. Each site is spacious and has a picnic table. The general store offers pick-your-own lobster—perfect for a clambake! (Local ordinances forbid open fires in the area, but you can bring your own hibachi.)

The cottages, always in demand, can sleep two to four people and have insulated walls, fully equipped kitchens, and maple furnishings. The cabins, which can accommodate two or three people, are similar in construction to the cottages but do not accommodate cooking. Three utility buildings provide plenty of sanitary facilities, including metered hot-water showers (a quarter and a bar of soap will do the job!).

The site fee is $27 per day for two adults with no hookups. Electric and water hookups are an extra $4.00. Weekly rates for cottages start at $525; cabins rent for $80 nightly. Reservations are strongly recommended for July and August. There is a no-pets policy. The campground is open Memorial Day to Columbus Day.

Horton's Camping Resort
71 South Highland Road, North Truro
(508) 487–1220, (800) 252–7705
www.hortonscampingresort.com

The 200 sites here come in one size—large—but in choice of sunny, shaded, or wooded areas. Some tent site have partial hookups (electricity and water) for a nominal additional fee. RV owners can choose from 72 sites with hookups, most on an open grassy area, though you can opt for a wooded site (the latter does not provide electric, water, or sewer connections). Horton's, open from May to Columbus Day, is close to the Cape Cod National Seashore and other Lower Cape attractions. Camp amenities include a playground, access gate, and camp store. It's located close enough to Coast Guard Beach that you can walk or bike there and avoid parking fees.

Site fees start at $22 per night for tent sites and work their way up to $33 for those with full hookups. About 10 sites have sweeping water views that take in Highland Light and Pilgrim Monument in Provincetown; these premium sites are $26 with no hookup. The same rate applies to several more secluded sites reserved for adults camping without children. There's no charge for the sea breezes. No open fires or dogs. Reservations are strongly recommended from July through Labor Day.

North Truro Camping Area
48 Highland Road, North Truro
(508) 487-1847
www.ntcacamping.com

This is camping at its finest: 350 tent, trailer, and RV sites surrounded by 22 acres of native pines and rambling hills, smack-dab in the middle of the Cape Cod National Seashore. Think of it as your year-round vacation home, replete with flush toilets, metered hot showers, a Laundromat, private picnic tables, ceramic tile rest rooms, and even free cable hookups for your portable TV! Saunter over to the ocean or bay beach, both less than a mile away, or hike and bike the nearby trails.

Free cable television connection is provided with electric hookup. No open fires, and no pets during the season. Weekly stays are discounted by 10 percent; stay for a month, and the discount increases to 15 percent. The basic site fee is $22.00, plus $8.00 for complete hookup. Reservations are not taken over the phone. Open mid-June until January 1.

Dunes' Edge Campground
386 U.S. Route 6, Provincetown
(508) 487-9815
www.dunes-edge.com

Only in Provincetown would the roads of a campground have such cute names as Bunny Trail, Blueberry Lane, Cranberry Bowl, and Beach Plum Road. Dunes' Edge, nestled beneath the shadow of Horses Head, one of the tallest hills in town, is as idyllic, clean, and quaint as you're going to get short of starting our own outdoor hideaway.

Most of the 85 tent sites and 15 trailer spaces offer the utmost in privacy. The campground offers hot showers, laundry facilities, and a store, as well as close proximity to the Cape Cod National Seashore, which actually borders Dunes' Edge. The rates are $30 per day for one or two people in season, and $25 in the off-season. The limit is six people per site. Your pet—one per site, welcome as long as it's leashed—stays free! Reservations are highly recommended. Personal checks are accepted for the initial deposit only, then only cash or travelers' checks are accepted. No credit cards. Open May through September.

STATE PARKS

Within Massachusetts' state-owned campgrounds you'll discover some of America's best camping experiences. There are 27 exceptional state forests and parks in Massachusetts, and three of them are on Cape Cod—Nickerson State Park, Scusset Beach State Reservation, and Shawme-Crowell State Forest. Campsite reservations for Scusset Beach State Reservation and Nickerson State Park may be made for the period between Memorial Day and Labor Day weekend. Reservations may be made as early as six months in advance for a stay of seven or more consecutive days. Shorter stays of two to six days can be reserved after March 1.

Scusset Beach State Reservation
Scusset Beach Road, Buzzards Bay
(508) 888-0859, (877) 422-6762
(ICAMPMA) (reservations)
www.reserveamerica.com

What a great place to spend a vacation! Barely a few hundred yards from a beautiful sandy beach on Cape Cod Bay, Scusset Beach State Reservation offers pleasant walking trails and immediate access to the 7-mile long Cape Cod Canal bike path. Deer, foxes, upland game birds, and rabbits make their homes in the 330-acre preserve.

Fishing enthusiasts can cast their lines from a stone jetty at the end of the canal or from the banks of the canal, and there's also a wheelchair-accessible fishing pier. Scusset has 98 campsites, most in the open, including three wheelchair-accessible sites. Fresh water and dumping stations are nearby.

The campground is open year-round; however, after Columbus Day the water is turned off in the public facilities, and only self-contained vehicles are permitted until early April. The seasonal nightly rate is $12 for a tent site, $17 for an RV site. Large groups or clubs with self-contained RVs might be interested in reserving the 3.5-acre field with grills and tables.

Stays are limited to no more than two weeks between Memorial Day and Labor Day, and reservations are required. Off the beaten path, Scusset is located at the end of Scusset Beach Road, which runs parallel to the canal. To get on this road, make a three-quarter turn around the Sagamore rotary coming from Boston on Route 3.

Shawme-Crowell State Forest
Route 130, Sandwich
(508) 888-0351, (877) 422-6762
(ICAMPMA) (reservations)
www.reserveamerica.com

The cool, wooded setting for Shawme-Crowell State Forest offers a summer haven for tent campers and RV owners. Just a half-mile away from scenic Route 6A, it's close to the canal bike path and Sandwich's marina, museums, and restaurants. Campers here have beach privileges at Scusset Beach on the opposite side of the canal.

Encompassing 742 acres, Shawme-Crowell is the fourth-largest park in Massachusetts. It has 280 sites, all with their own picnic tables and fireplaces. Scattered throughout are clean rest rooms, hot showers, and sewage-disposal sites. The park has no on-site hookups for water or electricity. A convenience store carries firewood, ice, and other camping goods.

Overseen by friendly park rangers, this quiet, uncongested campground is open year-round for both tents and RVs—the first state park to adopt this year-round policy (previously, the park allowed only self-contained vehicles in winter). The nightly fee for four adults (children are free) is $10. Two vehicles are allowed per site.

Nickerson State Park
3488 Route 6A, East Brewster
(508) 896-3491, (877) 422-6762
(ICAMPMA) (reservations)
www.reserveamerica.com

This beautiful park, one of the state's largest, is Cape Cod's crown jewel. The 1,900-plus wooded acres that make up the bulk of the park once belonged to Roland Nickerson, a multimillionaire who founded the First National Bank of Chicago. The Nickersons, who lived farther west on Route 6A in an opulent estate now known as Ocean Edge Resort (see our Hotels, Motels, and Resorts chapter), had a hunting lodge on the acreage that now makes up the State Park. The Nickersons hosted private hunts at their "Bungalow Estates," as they referred to their rustic playground. Nickerson's wife, Addie, donated the land to the state in 1934 in honor of their son, a victim of the 1918 influenza epidemic, and in honor of her husband.

The park features eight kettle ponds formed by ice-age glaciers. A kettle pond that you see today may be gone next season. The ponds are completely dependent on ground water and precipitation, and the water levels fluctuate from year to year. You can spot many rare species of plants and wildflowers growing around the edges of kettle ponds, but remember it's against the law to trample or pick them.

You could spend a month here and still have things to do. Boat or swim in Cliff Pond, the largest in the park, or try your luck fishing at one of the four trout-stocked ponds. (Note there are no lifeguards.) Bird-watchers will be pleased to know Nickerson is a regular stop on the migration route of such feathered friends as larks, woodpeckers, wrens, warblers, and thrushes. It's also a watering hole for cormorants, Canada geese, great blue herons, ducks—even the occasional common loon. You may also spot owls, osprey, hawks, eagles, and such woodland animals as red foxes, skunks, chipmunks, white-tailed deer, and non-poisonous snakes. The Cape Cod Rail Trail, which is great for bicycling, passes right through the park, with a few loops branching off through different areas of the park. And that's just in season! Nickerson is open year-round, and winter visitors can ice-fish, ice-skate, and when

Once a private hunting reserve of a wealthy landowner with a penchant for exotic game, Nickerson State Park (Route 6A, Brewster, 508–896–3491) now offers 1,955 acres of parkland for the public's enjoyment. A system of bike and walking trails weave their way through the park's woods and around its eight ponds.

there is snow, cross-country ski on marked trails. The park is an easy walk or drive from bay beaches, and beach walks are among the many interpretive activities led by park naturalists in season.

Nickerson State Park offers 420 camping sites at $12 per night, but does not offer electric or RV hookups. The sites are large enough to handle two tents and two cars. The rate is for four adults per site. Reservations are required, and there is an $8.50 processing fee. Open mid-April through mid-October.

RESTAURANTS

Cape Cod offers spectacular sunsets, an abundance of outdoor activities, live theater, music, art galleries, and museums of all types. But that's not all. Our oceanfront paradise also happens to be well known for its fine restaurants.

Indeed there's a restaurant here to suit every mood, taste, whim, and budget. To help you choose the restaurant that suits your palate and your pocket, we've prepared descriptions of our favorite restaurants on Cape Cod. We focus on restaurants that offer dining experiences you won't find elsewhere. We'll tell you about places that offer such regional favorites as Chatham cod, Monomoy mussels, Wellfleet oysters, famous Cape Cod chowder—and of course, lobster. Although not all of the Cape's restaurants specialize in seafood, most do serve lobster, and we highly recommend it, whether boiled, baked, broiled, stuffed, stewed, sautéed, served in salads, fried in cakes, or simmered the way we like it— with basil, wine, and tomatoes and served with clams, scallops, shrimp and mussels. Delicious!

If you're not in the mood for such regional dishes, you have lots of other choices. What's remarkable about the Cape is the incredible variety of eating establishments on this relatively small spit of land. Have a yen for Chinese? Are you itching for Mexican? How about Japanese sushi? Or a plate filled with good old American fried chicken? We've got all that too.

You'll find descriptions here of one-of-a-kind restaurants that serve dinners to suit any taste, as well as of cheerful breakfast eateries and perfect places to break for lunch. Most of those listed accept major credit cards (we note the ones that don't), and, unless otherwise stated, all are wheelchair accessible. Many offer early-bird dinner specials, usually to those seated by 5:30 P.M. with discounts ranging

anywhere from 10 to 30 percent off the regular price. Because not many restaurants offer bargains in the summer, these specials are very popular. We'll tell you about those too.

One of the nice things about eating out on the Cape is that most restaurants maintain a casual and comfortable "come-as-you-are" dress code, so to enjoy the relaxed atmosphere of these restaurants, you need dress no more formally than "Cape Cod casual," typically an ensemble of shirt, shorts, and sandals. Some restaurants, such as the Paddock in Hyannis or Chillingsworth in Brewster, afford you the opportunity to dress up more formally. We'll let you know when more formal dress might be appropriate.

Many restaurants are packed during the height of the tourist season (July Fourth to Labor Day) and on weekends and holidays. In summer reservations are a must at fine restaurants, and a wait is common at those that maintain a first-come, first-served policy. You may even have to wait a bit when you've made reservations, as even the most efficient restaurant can get backed up with lingering diners. This is, after all, the Cape, where no one is in a hurry! But remember: If we've recommended the eatery, the wait is worth it.

And if you're thinking of a smoke while you're waiting, you should know that more and more restaurants are now smoke-free, some by choice, others by law. Most Cape towns now have ordinances prohibiting smoking, not only in public places, but in restaurants and bars as well. If it's an issue for you, we suggest you call ahead to check on the individual establishment's smoking policy, or check with the local chamber of commerce to see if there are any town-wide restrictions. In many cases you will have to step outside if you want to smoke.

We have followed our usual geographical order in presenting the restaurants in this chapter. Note that some entries are described as seasonal. These establishments are closed for the winter months, usually from late fall through April or May.

PRICE CODE

The following price code is meant strictly as a guideline. The code is based on the average price of dinner for two, excluding appetizers, alcoholic beverages, dessert, tax, and tip. (Tipping is customarily 15 to 20 percent.)

$	Less than $20
$$	$20 to $35
$$$	$36 to $50
$$$$	$51 and more

UPPER CAPE

The Chart Room $$
One Shipyard Lane, Cataumet (Bourne)
(508) 563–5350

The staff at the Chart Room, located at Kingman Marina, is expert at accommodating weary and rumpled mariners looking for a good meal. And that's what they find at this three-decade-old casual-style restaurant with an excellent reputation for consistency and good seafood—baked stuffed lobster, lobster salad, scrod, sole, bluefish, striped bass, halibut—in addition to steaks and chops. The freshly made quahog chowder is perfect—not too thick, not too watery, full of flavor. Desserts, such as apple pie and ice cream puffs, are made locally. The Chart Room opens around Memorial Day for weekends only until mid-June, then it's open daily through the summer; after Labor Day and up to Columbus Day it's open only on weekends. The Chart Room serves lunch and dinner and there's an afternoon bar menu as well. Call and ask for directions—this one's a little hard to find, but well worth the trouble.

Lobster Trap Restaurant $
290 Shore Road, Bourne
(508) 759–3992

For more than 25 years, the Lobster Trap Restaurant has been satisfying tourists and locals alike with its great seafood. Open from Memorial Day through September, the Lobster Trap is a busy lunch spot and is packed at dinnertime. On the menu are popular dishes such as fish and chips, broiled haddock, chowders, steamers, and, of course, lobster, as well as many other kinds of broiled, boiled, and fried seafood. Special treats may include such tasty dishes as broiled swordfish tips. Burgers and chicken dishes are also served. The restaurant has a casual atmosphere—eat on paper plates with plastic forks on a large deck overlooking scenic Buzzards Bay. This seasonal restaurant is open for lunch and dinner seven days a week. No credit cards.

Stir-Crazy $
626 Route 28, Pocasset (Bourne)
(508) 564–6464

If you enjoy Asian food, do yourself a big favor and stop off for dinner or take-out at this small restaurant on MacArthur Boulevard (Route 28) for some Cambodian cooking. The food is redolent with exotic flavors and spices and features healthy ingredients such as fresh vegetables, rice, and homemade noodles. Although the food can be spicy, it is not too hot unless you request it that way. It is open for dinner from Tuesday to Sunday and serves lunch only on Friday. Stir-Crazy closes during the month of January.

The Bridge Restaurant $$
21 Route 6A, Sagamore
(508) 888–8144

Many travelers pass right by the Bridge Restaurant, which sits at the foot of the Sagamore Bridge, but if you want to enjoy a great meal just before leaving the Cape, get off U.S. Route 6 at exit 1 and you'll find the restaurant right across from the exit ramp. Specializing in New England and Italian dishes, the most popular meal at the Bridge is the pot roast, but many also love the fresh-fish entrees. The restaurant is open for lunch and dinner year-round, except Thanksgiving and Christmas Day.

Sagamore Inn $
1131 Route 6A, Sagamore
(508) 888-9707
www.sagamoreinn.com

Locals love the real Cape Cod feel and family atmosphere at the Sagamore Inn. There are three main reasons why the parking lot is always jammed: (1) the service is excellent; (2) the staff, mostly native Cape Codders, is fun-loving; and (3) Shirley's mouth-watering pot roast (we're serious!) is on the menu. The shrimp, lobster, and homemade lasagna are superb, as are the freshly made desserts, such as chocolate mousse and a delicious carrot cake. The Sagamore Inn is open for lunch and dinner daily except Tuesday from April through mid-November.

Aqua Grille $$
14 Gallo Road, Sandwich
(508) 888-8889
www.aquagrille.com

Veteran Cape Cod restaurateurs the Zartarian family (the Paddock Restaurant in Hyannis) and German chef Gert Rausch have joined to create a quality dining experience with a global flair at moderate prices in a casual waterfront atmosphere. Aqua Grille is located at Sandwich Marina and Cape Cod Canal, and if you are in the mood for enjoying Cape Cod favorites such as native fish and lobster in a waterfront setting, this is your place. Appetizers are delicious and unusual (like the bay shrimp quesadillas, stuffed with cilantro and Vermont goat cheese, served with pico de gallo and ancho chile crème fraiche). Gert's special grilled-fish entrees are enhanced by chipotle aioli, sauce béarnaise, tomato and basil stew, dill mayonnaise, remoulade, and roasted red bell pepper sauce. The restaurant has a special

children's menu. Complementing the menu is an extensive wine and drink list. The Aqua Grille can also accommodate special-occasion functions such as rehearsal dinners and weddings. It's open daily April to November for lunch and dinner.

The Bee-Hive Tavern $$
406 Route 6A, East Sandwich
(508) 833-1184

The day the Bee-Hive opened in 1992, it was so mobbed it ran out of food and had to close two hours early! Credit the business savvy of owners Bob King and Tobin Wert, who have built success around cozy seating, reliably good food, and a personable staff. The menu offers a mix of specials, traditional entrees, and fresh seafood. The fried oysters are absolutely wonderful! Rolls and desserts are baked on-site, and the homemade Bee Sting ice cream with buttercrunch bits makes a memorable dessert. The Bee-Hive is open daily year-round for lunch and dinner and serves breakfast on Sunday only. The Bee-Hive is usually busy, but it's worth the wait.

Bobby Byrne's Pub $
Tupper Road, Sandwich
(508) 888-6088
Mashpee Commons, Mashpee
(508) 477-0600
www.bobbybyrnes.com

When locals are in a mood to relax, Bobby Byrne's is the place they head to, as this friendly pub lives up to its billing as "an eating, drinking, and talking establishment." Savory sandwiches, hamburgers, and nightly specials will certainly hit the spot, and their freshly made soups and lighter fare are always popular. Its casual atmosphere and reasonable prices, along with large bar and wide-screen TV, draw fans of the Patriots, Red Sox, Celtics, and Bruins and friends who just want to get together to catch up on the latest. Bobby Byrne's serves lunch and dinner daily year-round. There's another Bobby Byrne's in Hyannis (see the listing below in our Mid-Cape section).

Captain Scott's $
71 Tupper Road, Sandwich
(508) 888-1675

If you are looking for casual dining, then try Captain Scott's, a small eatery with great food and prices easy on the wallet. You can really stretch your dollar here with the daily specials, which usually run from about $5.00 to $12.00 per entree. You have your choice of indoor or outdoor seating, or you can order take-out. Captain Scott's, near the town marina, features early-bird specials and a daily special. In addition to the fish and ships and fried smelt, the chicken and Italian entrees are very popular. Captain Scott's is open daily year-round for lunch and dinner.

The Dan'l Webster Inn $$$
149 Main Street, Sandwich
(508) 888-3622
www.danlwebsterinn.com

This is a Cape Cod dining encounter of the more formal kind. The award-winning Dan'l Webster (see our Hotels, Motels, and Resorts and Nightlife chapters) offers American cuisine, fine service, and exemplary wine list, and elegant ambience. We recommend dining in the Conservatory, a glass-walled area that offers a lovely view of a linden tree and gardens. Seafood entrees are always delicious here, but the chicken potpie has been the consistent top seller through the years. This year-round restaurant, open daily, serves lunch and dinner. The 21-page wine list, which has received the *Wine Spectator*'s award of excellence, includes superb French, Italian, German, and American varieties.

Horizons on Cape Cod Bay $$
98 Town Neck Road, Sandwich
(508) 888-6166

After taking in the panoramic view across Cape Cod Bay as far as Provincetown, you can understand why Horizons in Sandwich is so popular. Sit indoors or out on a deck (bring your sunglasses on a bright day), and order from a menu that's as casual as the atmosphere. You'll find the traditional seafood fare you'd expect from a place this close to the water. Horizons has early-bird specials and a children's menu, and most items are available on a take-out basis. It serves lunch and dinner daily from April to early November. The downstairs Cape Cod Bay Room is open for special functions, but book it early. Horizons will also arrange traditional clambakes on the beach.

Marshland $
109 Route 6A, Sandwich
(508) 888-9824

This local favorite might look inconspicuous, but the long bench outside is a tip-off to its popularity—there's often a line here. The wait is seldom long, however, and the food is terrific, especially breakfast. Daily specials, quick service, and booth seating make this a popular meeting place, so expect a friendly hubbub in the restaurant. Everything on the menu is homemade, and the baked stuffed shells, lasagna, meat loaf, and broiled scrod with crab sauce are particularly good. If you're in a rush, you can grab some coffee and a fresh muffin or cinnamon roll in the coffee shop. Marshland is open daily year-round. Breakfast, lunch, and dinner are served Tuesday through Sunday, with breakfast and lunch only on Monday. It has a second location at 315 Cotuit Road in Sandwich. No credit cards.

Seafood Sam's $-$$
6 Coast Guard Road on the Cape Cod Canal, Sandwich
(508) 888-4629
Route 28, Falmouth
(508) 540-7877
Route 28, South Yarmouth
(508) 394-3504
Route 28, Harwichport
(508) 432-1422
www.seafoodsams.com

It was the summer of 1974 when "Sam's Seafood" first opened their doors to a restaurant so small there was no seating, only take-out. With four of the original employees now owners in successful cooperation of four restaurants on Cape Cod, now called Seafood Sam's, they can seat between 50 and 350 people depending on which location you visit. The largest of the four is located on the Cape Cod Canal in Sandwich, the smallest in Harwichport on Route 28, each with its own distinctive feel. One thing is for sure, no matter which restaurant you visit, you will receive fast service, reasonable prices, and a delicious offering of the best seafood, fresh daily, made to order. Specials are offered weekly, and all meals are served with your choice of rice pilaf or French fries and their own creamy coleslaw. The menu has been expanded over the years to include chicken, hot dogs, pasta, and veggies, to name a few items. The Seafood Sam's in Sandwich has a full liquor license and a large dining room in casual surroundings, perfect for families. In Falmouth Seafood Sam's serves beer and wine and a full line of tasty desserts for a mouth-watering finale to your meal. For more information on their other locations, please check the Mid-Cape and Lower Cape listings in the restaurant sections. All Seafood Sam's restaurants are open from March through October for lunch and dinner.

6A Cafe $
415 Route 6A, East Sandwich
(508) 888-5220

What a perfect gem! This cozy, personable diner-style cafe offers excellent food at unbelievably low prices. Adding to the fun atmosphere, an electric train circles the dining room overhead, not unlike the train that travels along the tracks crossing Route 6A not far from the cafe. You can order anything from pizza to burgers. 6A Cafe offers specials on weekdays. This comfortable, spotless cafe serves breakfast and lunch daily from 6:00 A.M. to 2:30 P.M.

Sweet Tomatoes $
148 Route 6A, Sandwich
(508) 888-5979

This is pizza with pizzazz! From the crust to the creative toppings, these Neapolitan pizzas are full of flavor and healthy ingre-

dients, and you can watch them being assembled. How about a white Greek pizza with feta cheese, spinach, and garlic, or maybe a white pizza with shrimp, garlic, onion, and capers? Whatever you decide, don't wait until you're hungry to call in an order because they often need half an hour to an hour to fill orders. Sweet Tomatoes is open Thursday through Sunday in the off-season for dinners and nightly during July and August.

Box Lunch $
781 Main Street, Falmouth
(508) 457-ROLS
www.boxlunch.com

The menu at Box Lunch boasts more than 50 "rollwiches"—sandwiches built on a thin round of pita bread then rolled up tight for easy eating. These sandwiches have such names as the Monument, which features heaps of turkey, ham, Swiss cheese, Durkee's dressing, lettuce, tomato, and avocado, and Jaws II, which is an oversize monstrosity featuring a half-pound of rare roast beef, horseradish, onions, and mayo (this one bites back!). There are meatless selections as well, such as the Organic Pocket. Other year-round Box Lunch locations can be found in Hyannis, Falmouth, South Dennis, North Eastham, Wellfleet, and Provincetown (each is individually owned). Recently Box Lunch locations in Wellfleet, North Eastham, and Falmouth have begun to serve breakfast as well. This is great food that won't cost you a lot of bread! (See our Mid- and Lower Cape sections.)

Chapoquoit Grill $$
410 West Falmouth Highway, Route 28A, Falmouth
(508) 540-7794

This is a real locals' favorite, so you may have to wait to be seated, even on a weeknight. Our advice is to head for the bar, which is a delightful place, and start the evening off with a beverage. The food here is excellent, and the menu puts a spin on the concept of eclectic.

The Coonamessett Inn $$$$
311 Gifford Street, Falmouth
(508) 548-2300
www.capecodrestaurants.org

A classic country inn, the Coonamessett has been a Falmouth favorite for decades. The restaurant has four attractive dining rooms, one with a fireplace, and two with lovely views of Jones Pond behind the inn. Popular menu items include traditional regional favorites, such as herb-crusted Chatham cod, a heart-healthy special of the day, and freshly made soups, such as roasted eggplant soup and butternut-squash bisque. There is also a choice of vegetarian entrees, and all desserts are freshly made. The Coonamessett Inn is open daily year-round serving lunch, dinner, and Sunday brunch.

Flying Bridge Restaurant $$
220 Scranton Avenue, Falmouth
(508) 548-2700
www.capecodrestaurants.org

If you're looking for good food, delightful outdoor seating, and a fabulous view of Falmouth's busy inner harbor, you'll find it here. The menu offers a nice mix of native seafood, Italian dishes, steaks, burgers, sandwiches, and chef's specialties. Lobster, swordfish, and fresh-caught tuna are always popular. This large restaurant, which is heavily booked for weddings and special functions, offers seating on two levels, and about half of its seating is outdoors. You can dine here daily in season for lunch and dinner, with late-night hours on weekends. As they say, the only thing they overlook is Falmouth Harbor.

Golden Swan $$
323 Main Street, Falmouth
(508) 540-6580

For a quiet, moderately priced restaurant with a German flavor and a diverse menu, stop in at the Golden Swan. Local customers enjoy the well-prepared veal, shrimp, and chicken dishes, complemented with an ample wine and beer list.

Come in before 7:00 P.M. on Saturday evening for the early-bird specials. Golden Swan is open for dinner daily year-round.

Hearth 'N Kettle $
Route 28 (at Colonial Shopping Center), Falmouth
(508) 548-6111
www.hearthnkettle.com

The family-owned Hearth 'N Kettle has built a rock-solid reputation among locals for good food and a flexible menu at affordable prices. In their more than 20 years of "Cape Cod cooking," the Hearth 'N Kettle family has offered a wholesome and hearty cooking style that is a mixture of original and traditional recipes. The emphasis is on tender chicken, select meats, and Cape Cod fresh seafood. Open for breakfast, lunch, and dinner daily, the Hearth 'N Kettle Restaurants serve a hearty breakfast menu, a brunch menu, early-bird entree specials (served from noon to 6:00 P.M.), kids' meals, and of course a variety of soups, salad platters, sandwiches, and a full diner menu . . . talk about giving the people what they want! H&K restaurants are located on the Main Streets of Falmouth, Hyannis, South Yarmouth, Orleans, Plymouth, Weymouth, and South Attleboro (see other listings in our Mid-Cape and Lower Cape sections).

Oysters Too $$-$$$
876 Route 28, East Falmouth
(508) 548-9191
www.oysterstoo.com

This is another favorite restaurant among Falmouth locals, perhaps because head chef Tom Pandiscio knows and appreciates the importance of his regular customers. A special menu is prepared to showcase an interesting variety and the best seasonal items. The atmosphere is relaxed, and the fireplace offers just the right ambience. There's live piano music on Friday and Saturday evenings. The restaurant is open year-round, but closed on Monday and Tuesday during the winter.

Peking Palace   **$$**
452 Main Street, Falmouth
(508) 540-8204

This newly renovated restaurant is always packed, and it's no wonder. The pan-Asian cuisine is excellent, creatively prepared, and served in generous portions, even the take-out. The lunch and dinner menus focus on Mandarin, Szechuan, and Cantonese, with an assortment of chicken and beef dishes, plus a new sushi bar. Peking Palace is open daily year-round until midnight.

The Quarterdeck   **$$-$$$**
164 Main Street, Falmouth
(508) 548-9900

What a cozy, laid-back place to duck into for a bite to eat! The fried calamari, seafood, pasta, and vegetarian entrees are great, but be on the lookout for something new when the chef is feeling creative. The Quarterdeck has a nautical decor, friendly staff, and a large choice of beers with a decent wine list, which includes Portuguese selections. It is open seven days a week for lunch and dinner year-round.

Regatta of Falmouth
by the Sea   **$$$-$$$$**
217 Clinton Avenue, Falmouth
(508) 548-5400

This award-winning restaurant, owned and operated by the very charming and colorful Brantz and Wendy Bryan, has so much to offer: a unique and beautiful waterfront location at the entrance to Falmouth Harbor, absolutely wonderful food and service, and an exceptional wine list, predominantly French. Simply put, meals here are works of art, beautifully cooked and impeccably served. With 18 windows facing Vineyard Sound, it doesn't matter where you sit in the Regatta by the Sea, you are guaranteed an unsurpassed close-up view of the Falmouth waterfront. Rich lavenders and pale pinks lend an elegant summery feel to the contemporary French-inspired decor. The menu offers all manner of delights,

including the freshest seafood and American, European, and Asian cuisine.

Dinner is served nightly May through mid-September, and reservations are suggested. If you want a good tip: The Regatta by the Sea offers elegantly delicious early-bird three-course dinners, modestly priced, from 4:30 to 5:15 P.M. daily. The regular menu is served from 4:30 P.M. until closing. Dress at the Regatta by the Sea is attractively formal or attractively informal, in accordance with their guests' good taste.

Captain Kidd Waterfront Tavern   **$$**
77 Water Street, Woods Hole
(508) 548-9206

There's the Woods Hole Oceanographic Institute, then there's the other Woods Hole institution, the Captain Kidd, which opened shortly after Prohibition ended. Don't miss it. You can settle down at the bar, in the lounge complete with a fireplace, in the waterfront dining room, or outside on the patio or dock overlooking Eel Pond. The menu features fresh seafood, including scrod, tuna, and lobster brought in by local fishermen. The Kidd serves lunch and dinner daily year-round.

Fishmonger's Cafe   **$$**
56 Water Street, Woods Hole
(508) 540-9148

Where else besides Woods Hole could you enjoy a good ol' bowl of clam chowder beside a working drawbridge? Watching the little bridge being raised and lowered for boat traffic passing into Eel Pond within a few feet of the restaurant is a fascinating pastime at Fishmonger's. In fact all of Woods Hole's remarkable sights, marine and otherwise, are part of the view from this restaurant's windows. The casual gourmet menu focuses on natural foods, grains, fresh fish, and homemade soups, plus a number of vegetarian entrees—all excellent—as well as daily special dishes. The Fishmonger is open for breakfast (except Tuesday), lunch, and dinner daily.

The Landfall $$$
2 Luscombe Avenue, Woods Hole
(508) 548-1758

At the Landfall you can enjoy fresh seafood while you watch the sailboats and fishing vessels coming and going in the harbor and the ferries pulling into their Woods Hole berth only a few hundred feet away. The restaurant's nautical decor complements its surroundings, and it makes sense to order fresh seafood here, especially the clam chowder, scallops, lobster, or seafood platter, as well as the seafood specialties, such as swordfish with lobster medallions and asparagus with hollandaise sauce. The key lime pie is a delicious dessert, a great way to round off your meal. It is open for lunch and dinner daily from April through October.

Shuckers $$
91-A Water Street, Woods Hole
(508) 540-3850

This is a super-casual place to meet, eat, and order a Nobska Light beer. Shuckers is a lively place, and everything is prepared on the premises. The bartenders are fun, and the seafood is exceptional—look for the twin lobster special and the mussel stew. Shuckers has a raw bar and outdoor seating overlooking Eel Pond and is open for lunch and dinner daily from Memorial Day until two weeks after Labor Day.

Cherrystones $$
413 Route 151, Mashpee
(508) 477-4481

Warm and inviting with pine paneling, booths, tables, and a rustic Cape Cod decor, Cherrystones is a great family place. The menu is typically Cape Cod, too, featuring hearty home-style cooking. The quahog chowder is delicious, and the sliced leg of lamb is cut-with-a-fork tender and costs considerably less than you'd pay at most other places. For dessert the lemon cake with raspberry sorbet and the crème de menthe parfait are wonderful. This well-run, family-owned place is open for dinner daily year-round.

Nearly 16,000 people are employed by restaurants on the Cape during the high summer season. That's nearly 16 percent of the Cape's total workforce.

Cooke's Seafood $-$$
7 Ryan's Way, Mashpee
(508) 477-9595
Route 132, Hyannis
(508) 775-0450
www.cookesseafood.com

Cooke's has been serving award-winning broiled and fried seafood since 1977. Known for their excellent seafood platters, their fried clams consistently rank with the best on Cape Cod. Both locations are open daily from March to the end of November for lunch and dinner.

The Flume $$
13 Lake Avenue, off Route 130, Mashpee
(508) 477-1456

The Flume has an enviable reputation for serving excellent food based on countless happy customers who have satisfied themselves with such traditional dishes as codfish cakes, finan haddie, chicken pie, chocolate cream pie, and apple brown Betty. Everything here is homemade and delicious, but seafood gets the rave reviews. Casual and family oriented, the Flume is open from April 1 until the end of November and serves dinner Tuesday through Sunday from 5:00 to 9:00 P.M. (Sunday from noon to 8:00 P.M.) in July and August. Dinner is served Wednesday through Sunday the rest of the year. The restaurant is usually crowded, but it's a pretty spot so you won't mind the wait.

Persy's Place $-$$
Route 28, Mashpee
(508) 477-6633

If you or your companions are picky about breakfast or lunch, Persy's Place will be a treat for you. The *Boston Globe* has written that "Persy's has the largest breakfast menu in New England," and we certainly

If you are looking for some peace and tranquility, you may be surprised to learn that Cape Cod is host to a number of tea rooms. The Tea Shoppe in Mashpee Commons (508–477–7261), offers more than 40 choices of teas. At the Dunbar Tea Shop, located at 1 Water Street in Sandwich (508–833–2485), you can savor your tea while delighting in a cucumber and cream cheese sandwich.

agree there is something for everyone here. The menu features many made-from-scratch and hard-to-find specialties, such as Persy's own corn-beef hash and pan-fried codfish cakes. Most breakfasts come with a slab of their famous home-made cornbread and Boston baked beans. And don't forget their lunch menu, featuring three homemade chowders, four quiches, and 21 great deli sandwiches. The restaurant seats abut 110, plus there is seating in an enclosed porch and outdoors. It is open year-round for breakfast and lunch. Persy's is easy to find on Route 28, between Routes 130 and 151 (the rotary at Mashpee Commons). It is open from 7:00 A.M. to 3:00 P.M.

Popponesset Inn $$
Shore Drive, Mashpee
(508) 477–1100
One of the loveliest oceanside dining spots on Cape Cod. The 250-seat restaurant, located at the New Seabury Resort, is in tremendous demand for weddings and other private functions such as clambakes, oceanside buffets, and barbecues, but it's also open to the public. The menu offers dependably good, light entrees. The Popponesset Inn is open for lunch and dinner daily. Reservations are suggested.

Siena $$
Mashpee Commons, Routes 28 and 151, Mashpee
(508) 477–5929
www.siena.us

The contemporary, warmly tinted interior of this new restaurant is a great setting for enjoying its sophisticated Italian cuisine. The open kitchen, complete with wood-fired grill, keeps the place lively. Wood-grilled clams are a great place to start, and the entrees range from grilled swordfish to spaghetti and scallops drizzled with scallions and caramelized onions in a white wine sauce. Open daily for lunch, dinner, or a late-night meal.

MID-CAPE

The Regatta of Cotuit $$$$
Route 28, Cotuit
(508) 428–5715
The Regatta of Cotuit is undoubtedly one of the area's finest restaurants. Take our word for it: This sophisticated year-round dining establishment will delight you in the presentation, taste of your meal, and the impeccable service. The exciting New American cuisine with French, Continental, and Asian accents is inventive, with rock-solid skills and a deft imagination that will have you saying "unbelievable food."

Housed in a historic 18th-century stagecoach inn, the restaurant has eight lovely candlelit dining rooms (five on the main floor and three on the second), which provide the intimate atmosphere that fosters a most memorable dining experience. Each beautifully appointed room has an elegant, earthy ambience. The distinguished wine list is everything you would expect from a world-class restaurant. In fact owners Wendy and Brantz Bryan's fervent dedication to a cuisine that encompasses such diverse creations as pan-seared sushi-grade tuna with wasabi ginger lime vinaigrette, marinated cucumber noodles, pickled lotus root, and fresh Vietnamese spring rolls is a worldly breath of tastes.

For ultimate luxury the filet mignon topped with Great Hill blue cheese and crispy leeks served with a cabernet demi-glace is sumptuous. A full bar is offered in the small turn-of-the-20th-century piano bar. Dine early: The Regatta offers early three-course dinners, modestly priced, from 4:30 to 5:45 P.M. The regular menu is served from 5:00 P.M. until closing. Dress at the Regatta is attractively formal or attractively informal, in accordance with their guests' good taste. Reservations are encouraged. The Regatta of Cotuit is open year-round for dinner.

Hearth 'N Kettle $
23 Richardson Road, Centerville
(508) 775-8878
Route 132 and Bearses Way, Hyannis
(508) 771-3000
1196 Route 28, South Yarmouth
(508) 394-2252
www.hearthnkettle.com
Locals and visitors to the Mid-Cape area can enjoy breakfast, lunch, and dinner at Hearth 'N Kettles in Centerville, Hyannis, and South Yarmouth.

The Centerville location has a bakery on-site where you can pick up your morning muffins and pastries or a cake for a special occasion.

Located along popular Main Street in Hyannis, the Hearth 'N Kettle is a great place to duck in for breakfast, a business luncheon, or dinner year-round. It closes only on Christmas Day. The restaurant offers a menu steeped in traditional New England dishes with some surprises.

The South Yarmouth Hearth 'N Kettle is also open year-round for breakfast, lunch, and dinner. Kids will enjoy watching ducks in the pond behind the restaurant— visible through the many back windows. You can find other Hearth 'N Kettle locations in Falmouth and Orleans as well as off-Cape in Plymouth, Weymouth, and Attleboro. (See our write-ups in the Upper and Lower Cape sections too.)

The Dolphin Restaurant $$
3250 Route 6A, Barnstable
(508) 362-6610
The Dolphin is one of the many bright spots along Route 6A in Barnstable village. With low ceilings and a cozy fire-

Four Seas Ice Cream on South Main Street in Centerville is a Cape Cod institution, serving up award-winning ice cream for more than 60 years. Ice cream is made on the premises daily, using fresh ingredients. It's named for the "seas" that border the Cape: Nantucket Sound, the Atlantic Ocean, Cape Cod Bay, and Buzzards Bay.

place, this third-generation family restaurant has changed little over the decades. The menu includes seafood, steaks, some veal and duck, sandwiches, burgers, and good daily specials. The calamari is also good, and so it the lively conversation at the bar. The Dolphin, which seats about 125, is open daily for diner and every day except Sunday for lunch. Reservations are recommended.

Alberto's Ristorante $$$
360 Main Street, Hyannis
(508) 778-1770
Serving fine Northern Italian cuisine featuring freshly made pasta, this restaurant has definitely made its mark on Main Street in Hyannis. The elegantly decorated restaurant is bright, comfortable, consistent, and well managed. Alberto's Italian hospitality will have you coming back again and again, whether for stuffed pasta, seafood dishes, or sirloin. Or perhaps you'd like to try the seafood ravioli filled with lobster, scallops, shrimp, and ricotta, Romano, and Parmesan cheeses. Daily and early-bird specials are offered, and Alberto's boasts an extensive wine list. If you're planning a large gathering, Alberto's dining rooms can be comfortably arranged for up to 200 people. Alberto's is open daily for dinner year-round. Reservations are suggested.

Baxter's Boathouse Club $$
177 Pleasant Street, Hyannis
(508) 775-4490
www.baxtersboathouse.com
When tourists ask the locals where to find

a waterfront restaurant in Hyannis, the answer is often "Go to Baxter's." It's a perfect choice for a casual meal or cocktails in a waterfront setting—the view of the harbor is fabulous. If you are arriving by boat, you can tie up at the small dock, or you can stay on your boat and be waited on (talk about service!). The *Governor Brann,* a converted Maine ferryboat, is tied alongside the restaurant and seats more than 200 people. Kids get a kick out of feeding the seagulls and ducks looking for a snack. Fried clams are the most popular menu item, and, in addition to seafood, Baxter's also serves steaks, sandwiches, and burgers. Baxter's serves lunch and dinner daily from April through Columbus Day. The bar stays open until the wee hours.

The Black Cat $$-$$$
165 Ocean Street, Hyannis
(508) 778-1233

Many places advertise that they buy their fish fresh each day, but the Black Cat maintains that they buy their fish twice a day. Open year-round, seven days a week, the Black Cat features upscale, American-style food. Its large and varied menu covers seafood, pasta, and beef, and features several sautéed dishes. In the spring and fall, the Black Cat accepts reservations, but in the busy summer season, you may experience a slight wait for a table, as this restaurant is popular with both locals and tourists. It has an outdoor patio seating overlooking Hyannis Harbor and features live entertainment Friday through Sunday.

Bobby Byrne's Pub $
Route 28 and Bearses Way, Hyannis
(508) 775-1425
www.bobbybyrnes.com

This favorite Mid-Cape restaurant is open year-round, serving lunch and dinner daily, as well as brunch on Sunday. Specials are offered throughout the week. Bobby Byrne's has two other Cape locations, on Tupper Road in Sandwich and at Mashpee

Commons in Mashpee. (See the write-up in the Upper Cape section of this chapter.)

Cooke's $
Route 132, Hyannis
(508) 775-0450
www.cookesseafood.com

Cooke's is one of those casual establishments that help define the Cape season—when Cooke's opens its doors in mid-March, you know the summer crowds aren't too far away. Cooke's has a reputation for serving great seafood, especially fried clams; also try the fish and chips and fresh scallops, and see if you don't agree that this place serves up some of the best seafood on the Cape. Don't fret if you aren't a fish aficionado—Cooke's also has standard favorites such as burgers. They're open daily for lunch and dinner from March to the end of November. There's another Cooke's at 7 Ryan's Way (508-477-9595) in Mashpee.

The Gourmet Brunch $
517 Main Street, Hyannis
(508) 771-2558
www.theoriginalgourmetbrunch.com

Not for the indecisive, this menu has many omelets from which to choose, made possible by the combination of such tasty additions as sausage, bacon, asparagus, peppers, cheese, bean sprouts, and even peanut butter. Or order waffles or a specialty item such as Brunch Supreme, which is made with puff pastry, ham, artichoke hearts, poached egg, cheese sauce, and crabmeat. Belgian waffles and quiches round out the breakfast selections, and a glass of champagne with strawberries makes for a festive brunch indeed. You can order breakfast at any time, but don't overlook the lunch menu. Soups, clam chowder, hot and cold sandwiches, and salads are standouts. The offerings continue beyond the menu with daily blackboard specials. The restaurant is open for breakfast and lunch daily year-round. No credit cards.

The Naked Oyster Bistro
& Raw Bar $$-$$$
20 Independence Drive, Hyannis
(508) 778-6500
www.nakedoyster.com

This sleek eatery, secreted behind a bland exterior among a strip of office buildings, forsakes the nautical theme favored by legions of other Cape restaurants; all the better to focus squarely on fresh, excellent seafood. This hip place, with a long mahogany bar, feels like it should be in New York City and is perfect for a cocktail and oysters Rockefeller (oysters with spinach, cheese, Pernod, and bacon).

The regular menu includes appetizers such as tuna sashimi and calamari marinara, and entrees like Misto Di Mare: sautéed shrimp, sea scallops, mussels, little neck clams, and baby calamari steamed in fennel saffron bouillabaisse over linguini. There are also several steak entrees and a few offerings for vegetarians. But people really come here for the raw bar: the "naked" dishes are considered the best offerings here, but the "dressed" options are also well done. Everything is complemented by an extensive list of wines by the glass. For the ultimate raw-bar indulgence, go with the chilled Seafood Tower: four little neck clams, four naked oysters, four chilled shrimp cocktails, one lobster tail cocktail, tuna sashimi, and half a bottle of Veuve Cliquot Champagne. Open year-round for lunch Monday through Friday and dinner Monday through Saturday.

The Paddock $$-$$$
West End Rotary, Hyannis
(508) 775-7677
www.paddockcapecod.com

The Paddock Restaurant has been serving elegant cuisine in a casual, friendly setting for more than 40 years. Aside from beautiful surroundings, great service, and hospitality, the Paddock offers a delicious menu and an extensive wine list. Owners John and Maxine Zartarian operate the restaurant (they met as college students working at the Flying Bridge in Falmouth), and their two sons are also involved in the family business. The menu offers a wide selection of seafood, pasta, poultry, steaks, and the house specialty—the two-pound baked, stuffed lobster. A children's menu is available upon request. The Paddock Restaurant can also comfortably accommodate up to 150 people for cocktail parties or up to 125 people for dining. The Paddock is open from April through mid-November for lunch and dinner.

The Roadhouse Cafe $$-$$$
488 South Street, Hyannis
(508) 775-2386
www.roadhousecafe.com

You'll be hard-pressed to find a critic of the Roadhouse Cafe. It seems as if everybody loves it, and what's not to love? The lobster bisque has huge chunks of lobster; the chicken homard, rolled with lobster and Swiss cheese, is manna from heaven; and some patrons say the cafe has better Italian cuisine than most Italian restaurants. The bistro tavern area looks a bit like backwoods Maine with its fireplace and beamed ceiling; you can sit at bar stools or booths enjoying fabulous piano music, and order from either the bistro or the Roadhouse's menu. The Back Door Bistro presents the finest musicians on the East Coast as part of its Monday Night Jazz. The live entertainment adds a perfect touch to this fun restaurant (see our Nightlife chapter). The Roadhouse Cafe is open for dinner daily year-round; reservations are recommended.

Sam Diego's $$
950 Route 132, Hyannis
(508) 771-8816
www.samdiegos.com

Sam's offers you delights from south of the border. The place has a fiesta atmosphere, and the food is fun, fun, fun! Free chips and salsa arrive shortly after you sit down, giving you something to munch on as you peruse the extensive menu and wait for a golden Margarita. If you ask for the hot stuff, they've got it. Sam Diego's is one of the best Mexican places on the

Cape. It offers an enjoyable and comfortable dining experience, reasonable prices, and a convenient location with plenty of parking. People of all ages seem to enjoy the food and atmosphere. Save room for the fried ice cream—it's almost a meal in itself. Sam Diego's is open for lunch and dinner daily year-round.

Mama Angie's $$
416 Route 28, Yarmouth
(508) 771-6531
You want to eat out but you can't decide where? Try Mama Angie's. The menu is varied, featuring favorites like prime rib and lobster with specialties like seafood fettuccine. Families love this friendly place. There are crayons on the table and place mats to draw on. The kids' masterpieces might even earn a spot on the restaurant's "Wall of Fame." But once the families clear out, Mama Angie's becomes a great place for couples looking for a quiet late meal. With a great children's menu and some excellent early-bird specials, Mama Angie's is sure to please everyone.

Blackrock Tuscan Grille $$$
633 Route 28, West Yarmouth
(508) 771-1001
www.blackrocktuscangrille.com
If you're in the mood for beef, then you'll want to get on down to the Blackrock Tuscan Grille on Route 28 in West Yarmouth. Besides serving 100-percent certified Angus beef, the Blackrock Tuscan Grille focuses on Tuscan cuisine, with a fair amount of seafood thrown in for good measure. Getting back to the beef, there's prime rib, New York sirloin, veal chops, and filet mignon, just to name a handful of entrees. Dinner is served daily year-round, with live entertainment nightly during the summer. The bar opens at 3:00 P.M. and the restaurant at 4:00 P.M.

Captain Parker's Pub $
668 Route 28, West Yarmouth
(508) 771-4266
www.captainparkers.com

Locals and visitors alike flock to Captain Parker's. Enormous portions, great-tasting food, and a huge list of specials are a few reasons this place is often crowded. In fact you're likely to see familiar faces if you come here more than once. Entrees include baked stuffed scrod served with Newburg sauce and London broil, and don't leave without trying their award-winning chowder. Captain Parker's Pub is open daily year-round for lunch and dinner, and the prices are always reasonable. Check out their Sunday brunch.

902 Main $$$
902 Route 28, South Yarmouth
(508) 398-9902
www.902main.com
Gilbert and Kolleen Pepin offer fresh local foods from a seasonal menu at this promising new restaurant. The interior of the unassuming brick building is tastefully decorated, complete with a fireplace and a small, dark-paneled bar. Entrees include sautéed lobster with white truffle risotto, asparagus, and lemon-thyme butter sauce, or pan-roasted native cod. Top it off with summer indulgences like crème brûlée, chocolate soufflés, or a key lime tart. 902 Main also hosts occasional wine dinners, at which wines are paired with specially devised menus. Open daily for dinner.

Seafood Sam's $-$$
1006 Route 28, South Yarmouth
(508) 394-3504
6 Coast Guard Road on the Cape Cod
Canal, Sandwich
(508) 888-4629
Route 28, Falmouth
(508) 540-7877
Route 28, Harwichport
(508) 432-1422
www.seafoodsams.com
A restaurant with delicious seafood, fast service, and reasonable prices, Seafood Sam's has been a favorite local eatery since 1974. With four restaurants conveniently located in the Upper, Mid-, and Lower Cape, each restaurant offers the

same daily specials of the traditional fried summer seafood and burger variety. Eat in or call for take-out, Seafood Sam's is open daily for lunch and dinner from March through October.

Skippy's Pier I   **$$**
17 Neptune Lane, South Yarmouth
(508) 398-9556
Why come to Skippy's? For starters it has a great view of Parkers River. It has seating for 250 people, including deck seating for 120. It's relaxing, comfortable, and clean, and it has reasonable prices. All the seats have water views, and the sunsets are gorgeous. Skippy's serves grilled-chicken Caesar salad, seafood from the raw bar, scrod, clams, scallops, burgers, and pasta dishes. Open for lunch and dinner daily. The restaurant is closed in January.

Abbicci   **$$$**
43 Route 6A, Yarmouthport
(508) 362-3501
www.abbiccirestaurant.com
This outstanding contemporary Italian restaurant specializes in native seafood, pasta, and veal. It has a reputation for consistently high-quality food and service and excellent small-production wines, mostly from Italy and California. A regularly changing menu ensures that Abbicci is never predictable, but it's doubtful anyone would object if it were. The osso bucco, pan-seared halibut with fresh tomato and white wine sauce, and homemade fresh stuffed ravioli are always popular. You may want to start off with mussels and fried calamari. Time-honored methods and recipes are carried through to the desserts. The restaurant serves lunch, dinner, and a popular Sunday brunch. Take advantage of the daily early-evening specials. Reservations are suggested. Abbicci is open daily year-round.

Inaho   **$$-$$$**
157 Route 6A, Yarmouthport
(508) 362-5522
Inaho means "ear of rice" in Japanese, and as a symbol of good harvest or prosperity,

the image is apt indeed for this Japanese restaurant. Inaho has been drawing rave reviews from locals and visitors alike for its beautifully prepared food, especially fish. Co-owner Alda Watanabe says the sushi and tempura are popular. Another often-ordered item is shabu-shabu, a beef and vegetable dish that is brought to the table and cooked much like a fondue. The restaurant has a full sushi bar and is open for dinner year-round. It is closed on Monday.

Oliver's   **$$**
Route 6A, Yarmouthport
(508) 362-6062
www.oliverscapecod.com
Generous portions, consistent food quality, and a large, varied menu offer plenty of reasons to dine at Oliver's year after year. Entrees range from seafood to chops to Italian dishes. In addition to regular offerings, you can order from a seasonal menu that changes four times a year. Veal Oliver is the house specialty, and desserts include cheesecakes, mud pie with fudge sauce, and Ben and Jerry's ice cream. Oliver's serves lunch and dinner daily, except Thanksgiving and Christmas Day. They close on Labor Day, too, so owners Glen, Rick, and Dale Ormon can throw a party for their staff.

Contrast Bistro & Espresso Bar   **$$**
605 Route 6A, Dennis
(508) 385-9100
www.contrastbistro.com
Opened in 1997, this snazzy little eatery is done in bold colors, and the food has as much flair as the decor. For lunch or dinner choose from fresh salads; hearty soups; sandwiches served on thick-sliced, crusty breads with a garnish of fruit; lavish pizza; and cod cakes. Contrast is open daily for lunch and dinner.

Gina's by the Sea   **$$**
134 Taunton Avenue, Dennis
(508) 385-3213
This intimate family-owned restaurant, complete with fireplace, knotty pine walls, and homespun ambience, has been serving

customers since 1937 and is a favorite among many loyal patrons. The minute you walk in the door, you'll be greeted by the tantalizing aroma of garlic and marinara sauce. The menu features classic Northern Italian dishes and comforting desserts. Chances are you'll have a bit of a wait, so relax at the laid-back bar or take a stroll on the beach, just steps away, until your table's ready. Gina's is open for dinner from the beginning of April through the end of November and adds lunch service through July and August.

The Red Pheasant $$-$$$
905 Route 6A, Dennis
(508) 385-2133, (800) 480-2133
www.redpheasantinn.com

Clearly one of the high points along the mid-Cape's fine dining circuit, the rustic and romantic Red Pheasant is considered one of the Cape's finest. The menu is a delectable blend of game, lamb, and seafood. Tables at the Red Pheasant, which is housed in a 200-year-old barn with wide pine floors and two fireplaces, are adorned with locally crafted pottery, glassware, and fresh flowers. The service is impeccable, and the food is second to none. Chef Bill Atwood, who runs the Red Pheasant with his charming wife, Denise, creates such wonderful dishes as pan-roasted salmon and crab hash, and boneless roast Long Island duckling. Dessert could include a trio of mousse in petit chocolate cups. The award-winning wine list (it has received the Award of Excellence since 1987 by *Wine Spectator*) is prodigious—there are more than 300 from which to select.

The Red Pheasant has great ambience any time of year, but the Garden Room is especially nice in summer, and in winter, a table near the fireplace is cozy. The Red Pheasant serves dinner only, and reservations are strongly suggested.

Scargo Cafe $$
799 Route 6A, Dennis
(508) 385-8200
www.scargocafe.com

This is one of our favorite spots for lunch or dinner. What was once a sea captain's house (and, with all its wainscoting and wood paneling, quite a lovely one at that) is now home to one of the Mid-Cape's finer casual restaurants. The cafe has two cozy dining rooms and a glassed-in atrium and greenhouse. The menu offers familiar favorites such as pasta marinara, fettuccini Alfredo, baked Cape scallops, and crab in puff pastry. Scargo has great appetizers, such as shrimp seafood stuffed mushrooms or mussels Montana. The dessert pièce de résistance is the house specialty, Grapenut Custard, absolutely the best in New England according to *Bon Appetit* magazine. Children's and early-bird menus are also available. Reservations are accepted for parties of six or more. Scargo serves lunch and dinner daily year-round.

The Marshside $$
28 Bridge Street, East Dennis
(508) 385-4010

We know of some people from just south of Boston who will make a day trip to Dennis just to have lunch at the Marshside. A stone's throw north of the intersection of Routes 6A and 134, this is a restaurant that attracts tourists as well as locals and maintains a passionate following. You may want to start off with a wingdings appetizer—no summer vacation is complete without one. Dine on baked stuffed shrimp or the surf and turf, but save room for an after-dinner slice of pecan, mud, or banana cream pie! Besides seafood entrees, the restaurant also serves lighter fare, such as burgers. Marshside caters to the kids with a special kids' menu and coloring books.

Owner Mary Lou Goodwin will most likely be around to greet and seat you—ask for table with a view of the marsh full of wildlife and Sesuit Harbor beyond. High tide comes right up to the back of the restaurant. The Marshside serves breakfast, lunch, and dinner daily and is open year-round so you can see the marsh during all four seasons.

Red Cottage $
36 Old Bass River Road, South Dennis
(508) 394-2923
Here you'll find home cooking at its best. Open all year for breakfast and lunch, the Red Cottage is famous for its home fries. No simple sliced-and-fried taters here. Instead the potatoes are tossed with ham, mushrooms, tomatoes, green peppers, and onion, then smothered with hollandaise sauce. Equally delicious are the crepes and Belgian waffles. The Red Cottage also features an extensive "lite side" menu, complete with a listing of fat grams per serving. Open Tuesday through Sunday (daily in July and August), it's a busy place on weekend mornings but well worth the wait.

Christine's $$
581 Route 28, West Dennis
(508) 394-7333
www.christinesofcapecod.com
Always a popular spot, Christine's offers an eclectic mix of Lebanese and Italian dishes, steak, and seafood. Lovers of Italian cuisine will relish the shrimp scampi. Chicken Christine is an excellent choice, or you might opt for the fried or baked seafood specials. Christine's is also famous for its Sunday brunch, a spectacular array of more than 20 goodies served on a buffet that includes a carving station. Reservations are only accepted for parties of six or more. Open year-round, Christine's serves dinner daily in summer. It's also a great place to go for live entertainment (see our Nightlife chapter).

The Lighthouse Inn Restaurant $$$
1 Lighthouse Road, West Dennis
(508) 398-2244
www.lighthouseinn.com
Located within the Lighthouse Inn (see our Bed-and-Breakfasts, Inns, and Cottages chapter), this spacious restaurant is reminiscent of the classic Cape Cod restaurants of bygone years. Resting right on the water, the windows along the south-facing wall are many and offer breathtaking views of Nantucket Sound.

Peaked ceilings give the restaurant an airy feel. Service is quick and efficient. The food here runs from the traditional (steamed lobster, filet mignon) to such innovative and enticing delectables as almond-encrusted salmon and chicken breast coated with hazelnuts. Situated on the site of the current West Dennis Lighthouse (formerly the Old Bass River Light; see our Attractions chapter), the Lighthouse Inn serves breakfast and dinner daily. Reservations are suggested.

Bob Briggs' Wee Packet $$
79 Depot Street, Dennisport
(508) 398-2181
www.weepacket.com
It may bear an unusual name, but Wee Packet is more like a big package of fun at unbeatable prices. Think of it as eating in someone's house filled with Formica-topped tables, seashells, and driftwood. It has exposed views of the kitchen and blue-plate specials such as broiled scallops and baked stuffed bluefish. Convenient to all those summering in Harwichport and Dennisport, Wee Packet serves breakfast, lunch, and dinner from mid-May through September.

Clancy's $$
8 Upper County Road, Dennisport
(508) 394-6661
www.clancysrestaurant.com
This restaurant has a friendly ambience and plenty of delicious food. Clancy's itself is quite a dish: It sits on the banks of Swan River, and the views are almost as wonderful as the food. (The view of the water is spectacular off the sundeck—no extra charge!) Here you'll be able to get your fill without breaking the bank, even if you order the popular Steak Lucifer, a meld of sirloin, lobster, and asparagus topped with béarnaise sauce. Lunch and dinner are served daily, and there is a Sunday brunch.

Ebb Tide Restaurant $$$
94 Chase Avenue, Dennisport
(508) 398-8733
www.ebbtiderestaurant.com

This family-owned restaurant, in business for more than 40 years, is a favorite among those who live in or visit the Dennisport area. Within walking distance to the hotels and motels that line beach-fronted Chase Avenue, the Ebb Tide is a great place to enjoy traditional New England cuisine in a lovely setting. All-white linen with rich, royal blue accents, the restaurant's interior is elegant without being stuffy, and it's family friendly. The menu features lots of fresh seafood, steak, and other appetite pleasers. It's open for dinner May through Columbus Day.

You may notice that your waiter or waitress has an accent that is anything but local. Students come from around the world—many from Ireland—for a "J-1 summer" on the Cape. J-1 is the name of the student visas they have in order to work in the United States.

LOWER CAPE

The Bramble Inn   **$$$$**
2019 Route 6A, Brewster
(508) 896-7644
www.brambleinn.com
This well-regarded restaurant offers fine dining in an intimate setting. Each of the five small, unpretentious dining rooms is set with linen, antique china, candlelight, and fresh flowers, and the food is worth of the ambience. The Bramble Inn serves four-course dinner with a menu that changes every two weeks, always offering about eight different choices. Some of the most popular specialties prepared by chef/owner Ruth Manchester are rack of lamb, assorted seafood curry, and roasted boneless chicken breast served with a whole lobster and Champagne sauce. For dessert indulge in such home-made confections as white chocolate coeur la crème with raspberry sauce and flourless chocolate cake. Although there is no dress code, many patrons do show up in their best clothes, so you might feel more comfortable trading your jeans for something a bit dressier. Reservations are required.

Brewster Coffee Shop   **$**
Route 6A, Brewster
(508) 896-8224
This is a great place to meet a friend for breakfast or lunch any time of the year. Homey and friendly, the shop serves up terrific omelets, pancakes, and other breakfast specialties. Lunchtime features burgers, chowder, and fresh fish. Fresh coffee is served all day in big white mugs. No credit cards.

Brewster Fish House   **$$$**
2208 Route 6A, Brewster
(508) 896-7867
This small, well-established restaurant serves some of the best seafood on the Cape, reasonably priced and delightfully innovative. You'll have a huge menu of wonderful entrees from which to choose, enhanced by an ample wine list. Famous for its fresh fish specialties, the restaurant also features several nonseafood specials every night. The decor is simple but comfortable. Be forewarned: There is often a wait to get in because the restaurant has limited seating and does not take reservations. The food is worth the wait! The Fish House serves lunch and dinner daily in season.

Brewster Inn and Chowder House   **$$**
1993 Route 6A, Brewster
(508) 896-7771
As the name suggests, this restaurant serves some of the best chowder you'll ever taste. The home cooking here is superb. Winter specials include lean, juicy Yankee pot roast and flaky broiled Chatham scrod, and the burgers can't be beat. Mom's apple pie was almost as good as the one you'll get here. The dining room is small and homey, and the service friendly.

The Brewster Inn and Chowder House serves lunch and dinner daily year-round.

Chillingsworth $$$$
2449 Route 6A, Brewster
(508) 896-3640
www.chillingsworth.com

Long considered the Cape's finest (and most formal) restaurant, Chillingsworth is the pinnacle of innovative French cuisine. In the main dining room of this colonial home, chef/owner Robert Rabin offers constantly changing, seven-course prix fixe candlelight dinners, served at two seatings in season (one in the off-season), amid priceless French antiques. Feast on at least a dozen variations of appetizers and entrees, including roast lobster over spinach and fennel with lobster basil sauce, and seared tuna tournedos with foie grax and morel sauce. The desserts are heavenly; one connoisseur of tiramisu we met insists Chillingworth's is the best around.

Jackets are preferred for men in the main dining room, and women will want to dress to the nines. Chillingsworth is open from mid-May through November. It serves dinner nightly in season and weekends only in spring and fall. In addition to fine dining in the elegant main restaurant, the Chillingsworth Bistro offers casual, a la carte bistro dining in the Greenhouse for both lunch and dinner as well as Sunday brunch. Reservations are preferred.

For those who want to stay close to fine cuisine, Chillingsworth also offers elegant accommodations in three antique-appointed rooms (see our Bed-and-Breakfasts, Inns, and Cottages chapter).

Cobie's $
3260 Route 6A, Brewster
(508) 896-7021

Launched in 1948, Cobie's is a veritable institution around here, and faithful patrons come back year after year for some of the best fried seafood anywhere. With white-clapboard, clam-shack ambience, this is one of the most comfortable outdoor eateries you'll find. It's open-air, but there is a roof over the picnic tables, which are freshly painted and kept squeaky-clean. Right off the Cape Cod Rail Trail near Nickerson State Park, Cobie's is a popular stop for seafood-craving cyclists and campers. Cobie's is open daily for lunch and dinner from late May through mid-September.

Laurino's $$
3668 Route 6A, Brewster
(508) 896-6135

Here's a great place to bring the family. It serves huge portions of such Italian dishes as chicken Lauro (boneless chicken breast with scallops, sun-dried tomatoes, mushrooms, and tarragon cream) and seafood cioppino served by super-friendly servers at penny-pinching prices. Laurino's also has a nice selection of pizza and Italian grinders (sandwiches on a hard roll), and a special children's menu. If that's not enough to keep the little ones entertained, Laurino's also has a video room. Laurino's serves lunch and dinner daily year-round.

Cape Sea Grille $$$
31 Sea Street, Harwichport
(508) 432-4745
www.capeseagrille.com

You will find delicious creative American cuisine at the Sea Grille. The menu focuses on fresh seafood, seasonal produce, and sophisticated—not fried!—preparation. The beautifully restored sea captain's estate exudes casual elegance with its hardwood floors and an open, airy interior.

The Country Inn $$$
86 Sisson Road, Harwichport
(508) 432-2769
www.countryinncapecod.com

This year-round inn specializes in classic dishes such as roast prime rib, filet mignon, lamb chops, and duck, plus fresh seafood. Each night entrees are presented with a companion wine, if you'd like to educate your palate while eating your fill. Enjoy the wide vistas available from the dining room. Each season is uniquely lovely at the Country Inn, which is actually three ca. 1700s homes joined together in the early 1900s as the private home for a working farm. This is one of the few places where you'll find desserts such as flambéed strawberries Romanoff and bananas Foster, so indulge!

400 East $$
Intersection of Route 39 and Route 137, East Harwich
(508) 432-1800
www.the400.com

Ask anyone where to find the best burger in town, and you'll be pointed to 400 East in East Harwich. The triple-decker clubs and chicken teriyaki are also quite good but nobody makes a bigger, juicier, or tastier burger. The menu bulges with dozens of other choices too. The restaurant is publike, with dark woods, captain's chairs, comfy booths, and super-friendly waitstaff. 400 East serves lunch and dinner daily year-round.

Jake Rooney's $$
Route 28 and Brooks Road, Harwichport
(508) 430-1100

Talk about an extensive menu—Jake Rooney's has a seven-pager with something for everyone. Along with fresh seafood, chicken, burgers, and steaks, the restaurant serves Southwestern, Greek, and other international dishes. House specialties include aged Black Angus steak and lobsters—you can choose the latter out of Jake Rooney's lobster tank, which doubles as great entertainment for the kids! The restaurant has a casual publike atmosphere, with antique paintings providing a nice touch. You'll find yourself wanting to come back, and you can any time of year. Jake Rooney's is open daily for lunch and dinner plus brunch on Sunday year-round.

L'Alouette $$$
787 Route 28, Harwichport
(508) 430-0405

Beloved by regular patrons for more than a decade for its sophisticated French food, L'Alouette also boasts a cozy atmosphere and cordial, attentive staff. The rack of lamb with garlic crust is a particular favorite, along with roast duckling accented with a sweet orange sauce. For dessert try the crème brûlée, for which the restaurant is known, or (if you're a die-hard chocolate addict) the chocolate truffle cake with raspberry sauce. Open year-round, the restaurant offers good deals in the winter for those who eat early. Dinner is served Tuesday through Sunday in season and Wednesday through Sunday in winter. Reservations are requested.

Seafood Sam's $-$$
Route 28, Harwichport
(508) 432-1422
Route 28, South Yarmouth
(508) 394-3504
Route 28, Falmouth
(508) 540-7877
6 Coast Guard Road on the Cape Cod Canal, Sandwich
(508) 888-4629
www.seafoodsams.com

Seafood lovers will want to visit this small roadside clam shack. Since 1974 Seafood Sam's has been serving Cape Codders and visitors the tastiest and healthiest seafood dinners, either broiled or fried (in a special low-fat oil). Seafood Sam's has three other locations in the Upper Cape and Mid-Cape; please check listings in those sections. They are open daily for lunch and dinner.

The Gingerbread House $$
141 Division Street, Harwich
(508) 432-1901, (800) 788-1901 (reservations)
www.gingerbreadhousecapecod.com

This charming little eatery specializes in Polish fare, making it a refreshing change. Where else can you get kielbasa omelettes or pierogies stuffed with mushrooms or potatoes and cheese? Owner Stacia Kostecki also serves a traditional English daily tea, with a special house blend tea alongside assorted finger sandwiches and homemade, melt-in-your-mouth scones with real clotted cream imported from England. Afternoon tea and dinners are served by reservation only. It's open for breakfast Thursday through Sunday 8:00 A.M. to 2:00 P.M.

Raspberries $
30 Earle Road, Harwich
(508) 432-1180
This is an ideal place to go for breakfast, especially for hearty appetites. The breakfast buffet here is bountiful and a great deal: $9.95 on weekdays or $11.95 for Sunday brunch. Indulge in pancakes, scrambled eggs, French toast, home fries, eggs Benedict, ham, quiche, pastries, muffins, fresh fruit ... the list goes on and on. Raspberries is open for breakfast from June through mid-September.

Chatham Bars Inn $(grill)
297 Shore Road, Chatham $$(tavern)
(508) 945-0096 $$$$(dining)
www.chathambarsinn.com
You can choose among three restaurants here. The seaside Beach House Grill is an ideal choice for an alfresco lunch of lobster rolls and chardonnay. Sit on a deck that is literally anchored in the sand, or if the wind is too much, opt for the glass-enclosed dining room. Lunch features the typical Cape Cod staples: burgers, salads, and fried clams. (To befit the posh Chatham Bars Inn, the fried clams are served with remoulade sauce instead of tartar sauce.) You can dine here for breakfast and lunch daily during the season. The restaurant is open daily July through September.

The Main Dining Room of the Chatham Bars Inn, plush and pricey, is your second choice. Open for breakfast and dinner only, with a menu that changes daily, the restaurant offers four-course a la carte classic New England cuisine and 6- to 10-course wonders. With attentive service and a refined, unhurried atmosphere, this is fine dining as it should be. Linger over each course as you gaze out over the spectacular views of Pleasant Bay and the open Atlantic at the Chatham spit. And save room for a fabulous, homemade dessert.

Men are requested to wear jackets and ties. Dinner is served May through November.

Less formal than the Chatham Bars Inn's Main Dining Room is the North Beach Tavern, where the food is every bit as good as what's dished out in its more pricey sister eatery. Relax over a casual lunch or dinner inside near the fireplace. Many people come here simply to savor coffee and dessert. The tavern is open daily year-round.

Chatham Cookware Cafe $
524 Main Street, Chatham
(508) 945-1250
The perfect place to stop for a snack, or more, while shopping your way down Main Street. Filling breakfast sandwiches are served on Portuguese muffins, along with bagels, yogurt, and Danish. If there are any left when you stop by, opt for the vanilla nutmeg muffin dipped in butter. They also serve a range of thick sandwiches. You can't go wrong with the Farley: smoked turkey, avocado, cheddar, cucumbers, hummus, sprouts, and lettuce served on a French baguette. They also have cold drinks, coffee, and lemonade to pep you up. Enjoy your purchases at a few air-conditioned tables inside, or carry it with you. They also have a freezer section of prepared foods that might come in handy if you need to throw a dinner together on short notice: salmon puffs, lobster strudel, spanikopita, and more. Duck in for breakfast or lunch daily.

Chatham Squire $$
487 Main Street, Chatham
(508) 945-0945
www.thesquire.com
Home to Chatham's only raw bar, the Squire offers a delightfully eclectic menu focused on fresh fish and shellfish, and the food is out of this world. In addition to the dining room, the Squire has a large pub where you can get munchies. Locals have been eating here since 1968, and the waitstaff knows just about everyone by first name. Add yours to the list! It's open year-round for lunch and dinner.

Chatham Wayside Inn $$$
512 Main Street, Chatham
(508) 945-5550, (800) CHATHAM
www.waysideinn.com
This lovely downtown inn has several dining rooms and serves breakfast, lunch, and dinner, and you can't miss with any of them. The breakfast menu includes classic items such as French toast, waffles, omelets, fresh fruit, and muffins. Lunch might be crab cakes or lobster risotto Florentine, but if you're in the mood for simpler fare, order a burger, sandwich, or fish and chips. Save your appetite for dinner here, which might be rack of lamb—hailed by more than one world traveler as the best anywhere—grilled Atlantic salmon, or barbecue-grilled swordfish. The restaurant is closed on Monday in the off-season.

Christian's $$
443 Main Street, Chatham
(508) 945-3362
www.christiansrestaurant.com
Christian's is housed in a lovely old building and offers two levels with distinct personalities. Downstairs the wood paneling and beams are painted antique blue, and the tables are covered in florals and lace. Upstairs old books line the walls and a grand piano (enjoy the music nightly) stands near a mahogany bar and leather sofa and chairs. The restaurant places an emphasis on American and continental dishes with a flair. One favorite dish is the Sea of Love: lobster, shrimp, and scallops sautéed with basil, artichoke hearts, mushrooms, and sun-dried tomatoes, tossed with penne noodles. Christian's is open for lunch and dinner in season, and dinner only in the off-season, daily during the season, and Thursday through Monday from January through March. Reservations are suggested.

Impudent Oyster $$$
15 Chatham Bars Avenue, Chatham
(508) 945-3545
www.impudentoyster.com
With a lively, friendly atmosphere, this restaurant is a favorite among locals.

Everyone orders (and loves) the oysters Rockefeller. Also recommended; the mussels in white wine sauce, the sole picatta, and the pesca fra diablo. Exposed beams, plants, and skylights make this eatery attractive, and unlike its namesake, the service is anything put impudent. The Impudent Oyster serves lunch and dinner daily year-round.

Larry's P.X. $
1591 Main Street, West Chatham
(508) 945-3964
Very early risers will gravitate here along with local anglers, who often stop by for their first cup of java when Larry's opens at 4:00 A.M. If you're a late riser, take heart—this place serves breakfast all day! You can also get burgers, soup, and sandwiches. It's not fancy by any stretch, but it's comfortable, clean, and friendly. And if you want to know what's going on around town, this is a good place to come. You can order food until 3:00 P.M. Larry's P.X. is open daily except Thanksgiving and Christmas days, and is closed January and February.

Pate's Restaurant $$
1260 Main Street, Chatham
(508) 945-9777
In business since 1957, this restaurant still cooks its food in an open hearth, exactly as it's been doing since it opened. Most locals will tell you to order the swordfish or prime rib (one patron we know dares you to find anything fresher). Legend has it that this was summer-resident Tip O'Neill's favorite restaurant. From the cars parked outside each summer, you can tell it's a favorite of a lot of people. Pate's serves dinner and is open nightly.

Twenty-Eight Atlantic at the Wequassett Inn $$$-$$$$
2173 Route 28, Chatham
(508) 432-5400
www.wequassett.com
This place is posh and serves sophisticated New England cuisine with international touches. The prime location overlooking Pleasant Bay offers you the

rare pleasure of ocean views while dining. The classy, understated interior is quietly luxurious, while the food trumpets its sophistication. Each course is an event, from appetizers like tempura soft-shelled crab, to entrees such as saffron-smoked mussel risotto or Chatham Day Boat Scallops, to desserts like Flight of Crème Brûlée, artfully presented in a series of porcelain soup spoons. They also have some of the more inventive vegetarian options around. Reservations are accepted, and dress is "smart casual." Twenty-Eight Atlantic is open year-round for lunch and dinner.

Vining's Bistro $$$
595 Main Street, Chatham
(508) 945-5033
www.viningsbistro.com

One of our very favorite restaurants, the Bistro features an unusual, ever-changing menu with an emphasis on wood grilling, which adds incredible flavor to meats, chicken, and vegetables. No dish is ordinary here, where specials may include such innovations as baked pumpkin and sage raviolis; wood-grilled chicken breast stuffed with figs, pine nuts, and spinach; or grilled pork tenderloin with corn-bread stuffing and grilled apples. And of course there are always great pastas. Ask for a window seat, as the restaurant is on the second floor, and it's fun to look down at the folks strolling Main Street—or to gaze up at the moon! The Bistro is open for dinner during the summer.

Barley Neck Inn $$$, $$(pub)
5 Beach Road, East Orleans
(508) 255-0212
www.barleyneck.com

This grand old 1857 sea captain's mansion was lovingly restored by Joe and Kathi Lewis, who run an upscale, fine-dining restaurant along with a more casual, but still classy pub. The fine-dining portion of the restaurant has several dining rooms, the most intimate being the Taylor Room, named for the mansion's original owner,

Captain Joseph Taylor. Specialties include roasted duck breast with apple and cranberry chutney and broiled salmon medallions. For starters we recommend the Cape Cod crab cakes, though you can't go wrong with the scallops ravioli. Save room for dessert.

If you're in the mood for something more casual, check out Joe's Beach Road Bar & Grille, where the menu includes gourmet pizza and lots of native seafood, and a huge stone fireplace warms chilly nights. There's also entertainment year-round (see our Nightlife chapter).

The Barley Neck Inn is open for dinner daily year-round. Dining room hours vary in the off-season, so call ahead. Reservations, in any case, are a good idea for the dining room.

The Binnacle Tavern $$
20 South Route 28, Orleans
(508) 255-7901

Tucked back off Route 28, this casual, pub-like eatery, decorated with an impressive assortment of nautical antiques, is popular for its gourmet pizzas and homemade pasta dishes. It's so popular, in fact, that in season you'll probably have to wait to be seated. Sidle up to the small bar, if you can, and be patient; the wait is worth it. We highly recommend the pizzas, with topping as basic as pepperoni and cheese or as adventurous as Gorgonzola and currants or shrimp and apples. Our favorite is the vegetarian. The pastas are delicious, too, and we once savored a cup of lobster bisque here that was the best we'd ever tasted. The Binnacle is open daily in season for dinner. Reservations are not accepted.

Captain Linnell House $$$
137 Skaket Beach Road, Orleans
(508) 255-3400
www.linnell.com

This classic 1854 mansion, which seems magically to appear as you round a curve in the road toward Skaket Beach, is well worth finding. Since 1988 owner/chef William Conway has been creating award-winning cuisine such as sautéed oysters in a champagne-ginger sauce, and shrimp and scallops sautéed in tarragon lobster butter. The roast pork tenderloin is excellent, and the bourbon lobster bisque is a must! Conway is smart to serve children smaller portions, and he entices patrons with free chowder and dessert if they're seated by 5:30 P.M. Open year-round, the restaurant serves dinner seven days a week in season, with a reduced schedule in winter; call for hours then.

The Cheese Corner and Deli $
56 Main Street, Orleans
(508) 255-1699

A favorite lunch spot among locals, this small shop has only a handful of indoor tables and in the summer a second handful on the patio. The soups and salads are made from scratch, as are the breads, and the sandwiches are tasty. The shop also carries an array of gourmet and Scandinavian foods and gifts, imported and domestic cheeses, and homemade dinner entrees. Call ahead and your lunch will be ready for you. It's open year-round.

Cottage St. Bakery $
2 Cottage Street, Orleans
(508) 255-2821

Tucked away on a little street off Route 28, opposite the Christmas Tree Shop, this charming little bakery turns out scrumptious muffins, cookies, coffeecakes, and scones, among other specialties. Come here for the perfect birthday cake or just the perfect muffin. Try the Dirtbombs, generous nutmeg-smothered pastries. Sit down at a table or buy something to take home. The bakery is open daily year-round and does catering, wedding cakes, and mail order.

Hearth 'N Kettle $
Route 6A and West Road (at Skaket Corners), Orleans
(508) 240-0111
www.hearthnkettle.com

One of the five Hearth 'N Kettle restaurants on the Cape, this Orleans location serves breakfast, lunch, and dinner year-round. The Orleans Hearth 'N Kettle is a favorite among both locals and visitors for good reason. The food is always good, the prices reasonable, and the service friendly and prompt. It's also child-friendly: Kids not only have their own menu, but get coloring books, crayons, and special cups as well! Other H&Ks are in Falmouth, Centerville, Hyannis, and South Yarmouth (see the listings in the Upper Cape and Mid-Cape sections). The restaurant has a full bar and is all non-smoking. It's open daily.

The Hot Chocolate Sparrow $
Route 6A, Orleans
(800) 922-6399
www.hotchocolatesparrow.com

The Sparrow is the hot spot in town for espresso, cappuccino, or just plain coffee. Even that is anything but plain—every day there are a half-dozen flavors from which to choose. In warm weather try one of their frozen coffee-chocolate drinks. There's an array of munchies to go with your coffee, including muffins, cookies, and coffeecake. And then there's the chocolate. Homemade at the Sparrow's mother store in North Eastham are incredible truffles, fudge, caramels, toffee, and chocolates. All candy is sold by the pound or piece, and gift tins and packages are available as well. And, yes, they do mail orders. Open daily year-round, the Sparrow also serves ice cream, bagels, soups, and panini sandwiches.

Hunan Gourmet III $$
Bayberry Plaza, 225 Route 6A, Orleans
(508) 240-0888

Craving Chinese? You'd be hard-pressed to find better anywhere on the Cape. Hunan Gourmet III is perhaps best-known

---

[Facing page] *The Captain Linnell House offers top drawer meals in an 1854 mansion.*

for its all-you-can-eat buffet, a seemingly endless feast including sesame chicken, garlic noodles, vegetable lo mein, chicken with black bean sauce, shrimp and scallop medley, you-shell shrimp, almond cookies, dumplings, chicken teriyaki, pork fried rice, egg rolls, boneless ribs, fruit salad, and the ubiquitous Jell-O. Insiders know how to avoid the wait by getting to Hunan Gourmet III at 5:00 P.M. when the buffet first opens. You can order from the menu anytime from lunchtime to closing (later hours on Friday and Saturday). Luncheon specials also available daily, and the restaurant is open year-round.

Land Ho! $$
38 Main Street, Orleans
(508) 255-5165
www.land-ho.com

This is a favorite haunt of locals, just as it's been since owner John Murphy took it over in 1969. This wood-paneled pub is a comfortable place to sit and chat over a meal, and is brightened by red-and-white checked tablecloths and hundreds of original, wood-carved signs hanging from the ceiling. The blackboard specials are always good, as are the chowder, kale soup, and burgers. The stuffed quahogs are terrific, and the crab cakes are always great too. Actually we've never had a bad meal here, which may explain why we come here again and again. The Ho! is open for lunch and dinner daily all year. It's also a cool nightspot (see our Nightlife chapter), and serves a limited food menu until midnight.

The Lobster Claw $$
Route 6A, Orleans
(508) 255-1800
www.capecodtravel.com/lobclaw

For 34 years the Berig family has been delighting guests with a wonderful family dining experience on Cape Cod. This is seafood the way it should be served, from their chowder to the steamed clams, to the four varieties of lobster

If you find yourself looking for a place to eat after 9:00 P.M. on the Cape—and you're not in Hyannis or Provincetown—your choices are limited. Most restaurants stop serving food at 9:00 P.M. The Land Ho! restaurant, right on Route 6A in Orleans, is a beacon at that point. It serves their full menu until 10:00 P.M. and serves appetizers, burgers, and soups until midnight. Call (508) 255-5165 for more information.

dinners (boiled, Lobster Newburg, deep-fried lobster meat, and baked stuffed lobster), all served with French fries and coleslaw. Other meals of chicken and steak are certainly available, but why would you come to Cape Cod and go to the Lobster Claw to order steak? Then again the lunch menu is made up of American classics—hamburger, turkey breast sandwich, and hot dogs—and the place is still packed. The early-bird dinner special is served from 4:00 to 5:30 P.M. and you get a free chowder, beverage, and choice of ice cream, Jell-O, or pudding with any regular priced dinner. The Lobster Claw is open April through October, 7 days a week, serving lunch and dinner from 11:30 A.M.

Nauset Beach Club $$$
222 Main Street, East Orleans
(508) 255-8547
www.nausetbeachclub.com

The Northern Italian delicacies served here are delicious. Everything is tasty, especially the dishes made with locally caught fish. The risotto is superb, the appetizers terrific, and the desserts make a heavenly finish to a great meal. The restaurant, housed in a former duck-hunting cottage on the way to Nauset Beach, has a warm atmosphere, with terra-cotta walls, a tiled bar, and low lights. Dinner is served every evening during the season, and Tuesday through Saturday from late November through mid-May.

Old Jailhouse Tavern $$
28 West Road, Orleans
(508) 255–JAIL

Occupying the former home of Orleans constable Henry Perry (the stone room was actually used as a jail), this jailhouse rocks year-round with regulars who find the food, ahem, arresting. You'll find all the basics here: spinach and Cobb salads, quiche and burgers, shrimp cocktail, flour tortilla pizza, and chicken parmagiana. Then there's the menu's most unusual dish: toast Nelson, which is French bread smothered with bacon, onion, shrimp, scallops, crabmeat, Parmesan cheese, and hollandaise sauce. We promise you'll want to visit this jailhouse year-round; it's open for lunch and dinner daily.

The Orleans Inn $$$
21 Route 6A, Orleans
(508) 255–2222
www.orleansinn.com

Right on Town Cove the Orleans Inn enjoys spectacular water views from its lovely dining room and handsome bar area. The 1875 building, once home to the Snow family, has been lovingly restored to its former grandeur by the Maas family and is truly a pleasure to visit. The view from the dining room is breathtaking in any season, and the decor is elegant yet understated. The menu features well-prepared classics like prime rib, lobster, baked cod, and the inn's signature dish, flounder stuffed with seafood and served with béarnaise sauce. Save room for something decadent from the dessert menu.

During summer the inn offers outdoor dining overlooking Town Cove with a view of Nauset Marsh in the distance.

The lunch menu stars tempting wrap sandwiches and seafood. You can order lunch until 4:00 P.M., a wonderful option for lazy, throw-away-the-schedule vacation days.

A new raw bar offers grilled seafood as well as steamers, shrimp, and oysters served deckside. Spend some time down-stairs in O'Hagan's Irish Pub, where the martinis are famous and the ambience friendly (see our Nightlife chapter for details). Orleans Inn is open daily year-round for lunch and dinner.

The Yardarm $-$$
Route 28, Orleans
(508) 255–4840
www.capecodtravel.com/yardarm

The Yardarm, an eating and drinking pub, is upbeat and often compared with an English-style pub. Sports play a significant role in the Yardarm, so allow for some cheering during games. A favorite with locals and visitors, the Yardarm is famous for its seafood chowder, fish and chips, and signature prime rib dinner. It's open year-round, serving lunch beginning at 11:30 A.M. and dinner at 5:30 P.M., featuring creative "whiteboard" specials and a kids' menu. The Yardarm is located just five minutes from Nauset Beach and across the street from Orleans Town Cove.

Box Lunch $
Seatoller Shops, U.S. Route 6, Eastham
(508) 255–0799
50 Briar Lane, Wellfleet
(the Original Box Lunch)
(508) 349–2178
217 Main Street, East Orleans
(508) 240–3278
353 Commercial Street, Provincetown
(508) 487–6026
www.boxlunch.com

Once you try one of the Box Lunch's locally famous "rollwiches"—meats, cheeses, salads, and spreads on thin, pitalike bread rolled up for easy eating—you'll be hooked. There's a huge variety, everything from the Ferdinand, a quarter-pound of roast beef, three melted cheeses, onion, tomatoes, and mayo; to the Organic Pocket, bulging with cheeses, sprouts, avocado, tomatoes, lettuce, and creamy Italian dressing. You can call your order in for a fast take-out or eat there at one of the outdoor picnic tables; it's open daily all year.

Eastham Lobster Pool $$
4380 U.S. Route 6, Eastham
(508) 255-9706
www.lobsterpool.com

Landlubbers beware: Though you can choose from several dishes, including steaks and burgers, the thing to order here is fish. In fact the menu offers so many choices that it's seven pages long. Don't want it fried? How about grilled, baked, or poached in fat-free, lemon-herb sauce? Or go for lobster: This is a great place to get it. The fish is local, guaranteeing the finest in freshness. If the weather is nice, sit outdoors instead of at the barrackslike communal wooden tables indoors. The entire menu is available daily in season from midday until late night. In business more than 40 years, the Lobster Pool is open for lunch and dinner April 1 through October.

Aesop's Tables $$$
Main Street next to Town Hall, Wellfleet
(508) 349-6450

We love the layout of this lovely restaurant, which occupies a big, old mansion in the center of town. Aesop's has no less than six dining rooms, plus the intimate parlor-style Upstairs Bar, with its comfy window seats and soft couches and armchairs. In summer you can dine on the terrace. Much of the menu of trout, lobster, and salmon is determined by market availability (no frozen fish here), and some of the herbs are organically grown in Aesop's own herb gardens. In fact one of the most popular choices here is Monet's Garden Salad, a heaping serving of all kinds of greens and all things natural, including exotic edible flowers, tossed with goat cheese and pine nuts—a true work of art! The appetizers here include baked oysters and littleneck clams steamed with sausage and chilies. Try to save room for the Death-by-Chocolate dessert; we also recommend the wedding cake special, which is always different and always incredible. Aesop's Tables is open daily from mid-May to late October for dinner and late June to the end of September for lunch.

Bayside Lobster Hutt $$$
Commercial Street, Wellfleet
(508) 349-6055

It's rumored that if you show up wearing a tie, you won't be allowed in. And tipping? Absolutely forbidden! That's how informal this former oyster-shack-turned-lobster-pound is. For more than 25 years, Bayside has been serving lobster in the rough; order your food, sit at one of the large communal tables, and join your dining companions as you crack away. (The neighbors at the table may be strangers when you arrive, but there's something about lobster juice running down chins that bonds people.) For kids who refuse to crack a crustacean, there's a burgers-hot-dogs-and-fries menu. Bring your own beer or wine. Bayside is open for dinner from late June through early September.

Bookstore and Restaurant $$
Kendrick Avenue, Wellfleet
(508) 349-3154
www.bookstorerestaurant.com

This comfortable eatery, which enjoys spectacular views of Wellfleet Harbor, is so popular we can almost guarantee that you'll have to wait for a table in summer and sometimes in the fall as well. But all those people can't be wrong—they know

Summertime dining on Cape Cod is never complete without a visit to a local clam shack. Whether for lunch, dinner, or take-out, nothing beats the flavor of heaping plates of fried clams after a day outdoors. On Cape Cod fried clams are usually served whole, with their bellies. If you're used to clam strips, the bellies may come as a pleasant surprise. Arnolds on Route 6 in Eastham is a popular spot to get great fried clams. Call (508) 255-2575, or visit www.arnoldsrestaurant.com.

this is the place to go for great food at reasonable prices and water views to boot. Open year-round for breakfast, lunch, and dinner, the Bookstore really does have a bookstore around back. Stop there if you love hunting for bargains among shelves and shelves (not to mention boxes) of old books. Then bring your appetite to the dining room for baked stuffed lobster, grilled swordfish, or fish and chips, to name just a few of the many seafood specialties on the menu. There's even a raw bar, and for landlubbers there are pastas, soups, sandwiches, and salads. For lunch order a sandwich that comes with curly fries—they're terrific! In fine weather try for a table on the deck, and enjoy the gentle breeze off the harbor. It's open daily all year.

The Duck Creeke Tavern Room $$
70 Main Street, Wellfleet
(508) 349-7369
www.innatduckcreeke.com

The Duck Creeke Tavern Room offers fun and fine food from around the globe, with great live music in the background. The Chart Room, overlooking the pond at the rear of the building, has its surface decorated with marine charts of the local waters and is a favorite gathering place in the evening for locals and visitors alike (see our Nightlife chapter). You need not be staying at the Inn at Duck Creeke to eat in one of its two restaurants, the other being Sweet Seasons. We prefer this one for its simplicity in both food (pizza, chowders, and pasta) and decor, if you can call a bar made out of antique doors simple. The tavern serves dinner Tuesday through Sunday during the season; it's closed from mid-October through late May.

Finely J.P.'s $$
U.S. Route 6, Wellfleet
(508) 349-7500

It would be easy to pass right by this tiny restaurant as it almost looks like a cottage, but we recommend you stop. Since it opened 10 years ago, Finely J.P.'s has received rave reviews for such dishes as oven-poached salmon with ginger and soy sauce, Wellfleet paella, cataplana with Cajun andouille sausage (a Portuguese dish made with lobster, clams, and spicy sausage), and their famous Caesar salad. Vegetarians will like the lasagna, made with pesto, ricotta, zucchini, and grilled tomatoes. Finely J.P.'s is open for dinner seven days a week in summer, and Thursday through Sunday the rest of the year.

Wellfleet Dairy Bar & Grill $
U.S. Route 6, Eastham-Wellfleet line
(508) 349-7007
www.intermissiongrill.com

Be sure to ask about their dinner and movie special. It couldn't be any easier here, as the Wellfleet Dairy Bar & Grill is located at the Wellfleet Cinemas and Wellfleet Drive-In Theater. A casual family dining spot, it's a great place to meet friends before or after the movies or any other time. There's always something for the kids on their kiddy menu, like hamburgers, some chowdah, or fish and chips. The parents can grab a beer. Air-conditioning or patio dining is also available. Don't forget there is take-out too! Order your dinner to go, and eat it under the stars at the Drive-In Theater (see the Arts chapter). The Grill is open every day in the summer from 11:30 A.M. Call (508) 349-7007 for take-out orders and off-season hours.

The Lighthouse $$
Main Street, Wellfleet
(508) 349-3681

This casual restaurant, right in the center of town, is one of those old standbys we return to again and again. The food is not fancy but good and reasonably priced, and the atmosphere is friendly. It's a great place to take kids. The young ones can get hot dogs and be happy as clams, and you can eat clams, fish and chips, burgers, chili, or one of the blackboard specials. It's a great place to meet friends any time of day. The Lighthouse is open year-round for breakfast, lunch, and dinner. It also has a bakery (508-349-1600).

Moby Dick's $$-$$$
U.S. Route 6, Wellfleet
(508) 349-9795

You can't miss this eatery along Route 6, and you shouldn't. Decked out in a satisfying amount of nautical decor and boasting a friendly staff—many of them hail from abroad—Moby Dick's has good seafood, traditionally prepared. Be careful not to fill up on a delicious fried Outer Cape onion before the main course arrives, which is likely to be from local waters: fresh Monomoy Steamers, Cape Sea Scallops, or a lobster in-the-rough dinner, complete with drawn butter and corn on the cob. Or you could opt for Moby's Clambake Special: lobster, native Monomoy steamed clams, and corn on the cob. There's also the requisite amount of fried seafood, burgers, chicken sandwiches, BLTs, and more. Open for lunch and dinner from 11:30 A.M. to 10:00 P.M. in season.

Used by North American Indians before the Pilgrims arrived in 1620, the cranberry is one of only three major native North American fruits—Concord grapes and blueberries being the other two.

P.J.'s Family Restaurant $
2616 U.S. Route 6, Wellfleet
(508) 349-2126

A local institution since 1971, P.J.'s serves great chowder, homemade kale soup, and onion rings, along with broiled scallops, fish and chips, hot dogs, and lobster. There's nothing like one of their huge fish sandwiches followed by some soft-serve ice cream. The take-out window at P.J.'s is always bustling; place your order, and sit outside at a picnic table. Or you can sit inside in the comfortable dining room. The restaurant serves lunch and dinner daily from mid-April through mid-October.

Serena's $$
U.S. Route 6, South Wellfleet
(508) 349-9370

If you're looking for great Italian food in a family-friendly atmosphere, this is the place. In addition to traditional favorites like lasagna (choose from meat or vegetarian) and pastas, the menu offers plenty of seafood—what else would you expect on the Outer Cape? If you like spicy dishes, try the Seafood Fra Diavolo, billed as "hot as the devil" with mussels, littlenecks, Wellfleet oysters, scallops, scrod, squid, and jumbo shrimp swimming in a wine and marinara sauce and spiced either regular, hot, or very hot. Our preference is the broiled Wellfleet scallops, sweet and done to perfection in butter and lemon wine sauce. Serena's welcomes young diners with a children's menu. It is open daily for dinner only from mid-April to mid-November.

Sweet Seasons Restaurant and Cafe $$-$$$
70 Main Street at the Inn at Duck Creeke, Wellfleet
(508) 349-6535
www.innatduckcreeke.com

Sweet Seasons Restaurant provides a stylish and airy ambience in which to enjoy some fine, fine dining. If you're hungry for a great garden soup or lobster bisque, or if you're craving Wellfleet oysters and portobello mushrooms, then Sweet Seasons is your place. Entrees like fresh scallops, seasonal shrimp, and Seafood Caldo (shrimp, mussels, and cod in a Portuguese vegetable, tomato, and citrus broth) will have you returning. Sweet Seasons is also an ideal setting for weddings and family reunions. (For lodging arrangements on the property, see the listing for the Inn at Duck Creeke in our Bed-and-Breakfasts, Inns, and Cottages chapter.)

Van Rensselaer's Restaurant & Raw Bar $$
U.S. Route 6, South Wellfleet
(508) 349-2127

This restaurant has a strong local following, and it's easy to see why. VR's, as most locals call it, serves wholesome food in a casual setting at reasonable prices. Popular breakfast items include the Homegrown—scrambled eggs with fresh basil and tomato, served with fresh fruit. The dinner menu, enhanced by a terrific salad bar, lists specialties such as mixed seafood grill, seafood fettuccine, and steak tenderloin au poivre. The menu also includes a number of vegetarian dishes, and there's a children's menu too. Van Rensselaer's is open May 15 through the end of October for breakfast and dinner, daily in season, and on weekends in the fall. All items are available for take-out, and the early-bird specials are from 4:30 to 6:00 P.M. The restaurant is right across from the National Seashore's Marconi Station.

The Wellfleet Beachcomber $-$$
1120 Cahoon Hollow Road, Wellfleet
(508) 349-6055
www.thebeachcomber.com

When you mention the word Beachcomber on Cape Cod, everyone knows you are talking about the Beachcomber in Wellfleet. This Cape Cod institution serves up the best in great food and live music (see our Nightlife chapter) in the unique setting of Cahoon Hollow overlooking the Atlantic Ocean. Featuring Wellfleet oysters and steamers at the raw bar on the patio and a complete menu with daily specials, plus a kids' menu and arcade, the Beachcomber is the place to be. A take-out window allows you to climb the dune path from the beach, order your lunch, and return to Cahoon Hollow Beach, in the Cape Cod National Seashore. The Beachcomber is open from Memorial Day weekend to Labor Day from 11:30 A.M. to 1:00 A.M.

Adrian's $$
535 U.S. Route 6, Truro
(508) 487-4360
www.adriansrestaurant.com

Perched high atop a bluff overlooking Cape Cod Bay, Adrian's features fantastic views and fantastic food. Owners Adrian and Annette Cyr regularly travel to Italy, where they gather and fine-tune recipes for their loyal following. (The wood-fired brick pizza oven, in fact, was brought from Italy—brick by brick!) The thin-crust pizzas here are meals in themselves, featuring such enticing combinations as lamb and feta, and shrimp, garlic, and artichokes. The homemade pastas are served in two sizes, regular and large, and the Gorgonzola cappelletti, with a sage, butter, and Parmesan sauce, cannot be beat. For dessert indulge in tiramisu. During the season Adrian's serves wonderful breakfasts, including such delectables as cranberry pancakes with orange butter. You can have breakfast and dinner at Adrian's daily from mid-May through Columbus Day weekend.

Harbor Lights $
Route 6A, Truro
(508) 487-3062

Here is a place for bountiful breakfasts. The best of the best is the stack of Big, Fat Blueberry Pancakes, as the menu accurately describes them. The pancakes are indeed big and fat, but they are also extremely light and quite satisfying. (The blueberries, by the way, are fresh.) Or opt for simple eggs and home fries, or any of the numerous daily specials, such as Mexican omelets oozing with cheese and chili. You can have breakfast here daily through the lunch hours. Harbor Lights also has a good lunch menu and offers a fish fry on Friday evenings. It's open from early May to Columbus Day. No credit cards.

Jams $
Truro Center, Truro
(508) 349-1616

For many people Memorial Day marks the official start of the season on the Cape. It also marks the day Jams opens its door after months of hibernation. The sandwiches, named after Cape Cod sites and sights, are a bit pricey but mouth-watering and very filling. The Long Nook, for example, features tarragon chicken salad with lettuce and tomato; the Bikini has provolone, lettuce, tomato, onions, sprouts and creamy Italian dressing. The newly renovated store also carries wine, coffee, newspapers, and toiletries. Jams offers breakfast, lunch, and take-out and closes its doors in September.

Montano's $$
481 U.S. Route 6, Truro
(508) 487-2026
www.montanos.com
This great family-oriented restaurant serves creative Italian specialties, fresh seafood, and wonderful steaks. Hearty appetites will be satisfied here, as entrees come with unlimited garden salad, potato or pasta, and homemade bread. Chef/owner Bob Montano includes some innovative chicken and veal dishes among the many menu offerings—there's something for everyone here. If you love steak, go for such dishes as Steak Montano (18 ounces of sirloin topped with roasted garlic butter) or the trademark Steak Umbriago, 18 ounces of sirloin smothered with sautéed onions, roasted peppers, garlic, mushrooms, and olives and served in a wine sauce. Montano's is open daily year-round for dinner.

Terra Luna $$$
104 Shore Road, Truro
(508) 487-1019
With its cathedral ceiling, barnboard walls, exposed beams, tin-and-wood roof, and whimsical pieces of art, this eatery knows the importance of being different. And it shows on the menu and blackboard specials, which feature New American and Mediterranean cuisine. Favorites here include shrimp linguine, clams, and andouille sausage, polenta with grilled Portobello mushroom ragu, and Tuscan bread salads. Terra Luna serves dinner daily from mid-May through mid-October.

The Whitman House $$
U.S. Route 6, Truro
(508) 487-1740
www.whitmanhouse.com
Great food, great service, homey atmosphere—this is one of those restaurants you'll find yourself returning to again and again. And that's exactly what the Rice family, who's been running the Whitman House since 1962, wants. For starters cheese and crackers, along with homemade bread, are brought to the table before you order. The menu has something for everyone including prime rib au jus, baked stuffed shrimp, charbroiled swordfish, and, of course, lobster. The 175-seat Whitman House Restaurant serves dinner daily beginning at 5:00 P.M. and offers an early-dinner menu until 6:00 P.M.

Bubala's by the Bay $$
183 Commercial Street, Provincetown
(508) 487-0773
www.capecodaccess.com/bubala's
This funky restaurant, open for breakfast, lunch, and dinner, features an eclectic menu that ranges from burgers and fajitas to seafood dishes like grilled tuna wasabi and Caribbean fish cakes. There are also vegetarian entrees, and a late-night menu. It has a heated patio on the water and quite a selection of fancy martinis. It's open May through October.

Ciro & Sal's $$$
4 Kiley Court, Provincetown
(508) 487-6444
www.ciroandsals.com
Once a coffeehouse for artists back in the '50s, Ciro & Sal's is considered one of the better Italian restaurants on the Lower Cape, especially when it comes to such Northern Italian delicacies as Abruzzese (scallops, clams, shrimp, fish, mussels, and squid sautéed with plum tomatoes, fresh garlic, and herbs over pasta) and Vitello Scaloppine Alla Marsala. For desserts nothing beats the homemade cannoli. And it would be hard to beat the atmosphere: Nestled in a low-ceilinged plaster

and brick-walled cellar off Commercial Street, Ciro & Sal's is filled with raffia-wrapped Chianti bottles hanging from the rafters and the sound of arias in the air. It's open daily for dinner during the busy season and weekends only from November through May starting at 5:30 P.M.

Front Street $$$$
230 Commercial Street, Provincetown
(508) 487-9715
www.frontstreetrestaurant.com

One of the town's most popular and romantic restaurants—bistro may be a better word—Front Street is hidden in the brick-lined cellar of a Victorian house. Chef Donna Aliperti changes the menu weekly, showing off her culinary craft with such dishes as avocado latkes, curried apple-carrot bisque, tea smoked duck, and her famous braised lamb shank. The wine list is extensive, and the waitstaff knows just how to serve (they are there, but they never hover). Front Street serves dinner daily during the season.

The Lobster Pot Restaurant $$$
321 Commercial Street, Provincetown
(508) 487-0842
www.ptownlobsterpot.com

Ask anyone in town where to go for the best seafood, and everyone will tell you the Lobster Pot. The wait can be long in the summer, because the Pot, as everyone calls it, doesn't accept reservations. Wait it out. The seafood is the freshest available, and Tim McNulty's clam chowder (now available frozen for take-out) has won more "best of" awards than anyone can remember. (Some of the awards can be spotted in the Top of the Pot, the small bar/dining area overlooking the bay and a great place to sit.) The menu is extensive, but almost everyone orders lobster. The Pot usually has multiple sizes in stock (check the tank as you enter), and despite popular rumor, the bigger the lobster does not mean the tougher the meat. The Lobster Pot is open daily for lunch and dinner April through December.

The Martin House $$$
157 Commercial Street, Provincetown
(508) 487-1327
www.themartinhouse.com

This highly acclaimed restaurant focuses on regional food with an international influence. The menu, which changes four times a year, always offers lots of seafood—Wellfleet oysters are one of the chef's favorite ingredients—along with game, Angus beef, and vegetarian dishes. Housed in an 18th-century building by the water's edge, the Martin House has a number of intimate dining rooms with five fireplaces used in the cooler months and an outdoor garden patio for warm-weather dining. Open February through December, the Martin House serves dinner seven days a week May through October, and Thursday through Monday the rest of the year.

Even at the height of the Cape's busy tourist season in July and August, there are ways to avoid the crowds. Many fine restaurants offer early-bird specials to entice you to dine before 5:30 P.M. Call ahead and ask when you should come to take advantage of the early-bird special. In addition to avoiding a wait, you might get a free bowl of chowder with your order, reduced menu prices, or both.

Michael Shay's Rib and
Seafood House $$
350 Bradford Street, Provincetown
(508) 487-3368

This friendly, sparkling restaurant serves great steaks, chicken, and seafood in a pretty dining room overlooking Provincetown Harbor. You know it's child-friendly by the small basket of toys near the door for parents who may have forgotten to bring diversions for their little ones. It's open daily for breakfast, lunch, and dinner year-round, but the best deal is the Friday night fish and clam fry, when for a ridiculously low price you can feast on unlimited plates of fish or clams, lightly breaded and fried, and served with coleslaw and French fries.

Napi's   **$$**
7 Freeman Street, Provincetown
(508) 487-1145, (800) 571-6274
www.napis-restaurant.com
In 1973 Helen and Napi Van Dereck built this restaurant, and today, more than a quarter-century later, its nickname, "Provincetown's most unusual restaurant," still sticks. Napi's is a work of art, with walls built from pieces of discarded Boston factories and decorated with salvaged bric-a-brac, artwork, and antiques. The menu is nearly novella length, offering international dishes such as Brazilian shrimp, scallops Provençal, Russian oysters, and Thai chicken and shrimp. We love the Syrian falafel melt—in fact we love this restaurant!

Napi's is open year-round. During the summer season, Napi's serves dinner nightly from 5:00 P.M. October through April Napi's also serves lunch and dinner starting at 11:30 A.M. An early-bird menu is available from 5:00 to 6:00 P.M. daily. You'll find free, limited parking adjacent to the restaurant on the corner of Bradford Street.

Sal's Place   **$$**
99 Commercial Street, Provincetown
(508) 487-1279
www.salsplaceprovincetown.com
Not as relentlessly hip as some of the other Commercial Street locales, this Provincetown fixture tucked away in the quiet West End is a find nonetheless. If you have your druthers, you'll dine on the deck overlooking the water. If a chill has set in, choose a table in one of the two indoor dining rooms under a bower of Chianti bottles. Chef-owner Jack Papetsas has been in charge of the food since 1964. You'll love the generous servings of classic southern Italian specialties. Reservations are recommended. Open for dinner May through October.

N I G H T L I F E

Cape Cod can you find a crusty fisherman and a suited professional drinking a pint or two at the same bar... and finding something in common to talk about.

Throughout the Cape bars are required by law to close at 1:00 A.M., and some close earlier, especially on weekdays or during the off-season. Last call varies anywhere from 15 minutes to a half-hour before closing. Wine and beer are sold only in package stores (the Cape term for liquor stores) and at some convenience stores. Throughout most of Massachusetts, including the Cape, package stores must close by 11:00 P.M. Many Cape liquor stores close by 10:00 P.M.

If you're the type who feels complimented when a doorman asks for your ID, you'll love the Cape. But bouncers aren't just being polite. The state drinking age is a strictly enforced 21. Be sure to bring your ID because, unless bars have a special 18-plus event, they won't let you in the door without proof that you are at least 21.

The legal blood-alcohol limit in Massachusetts is .08 percent. That's understood to be about the equivalent of one beer an hour for the average person. If you refuse a breath test for your blood alcohol, your license can be revoked for up to 180 days.

One thing the Cape doesn't have is an abundance of public transportation. Unlike nightlife in a more urban atmosphere, you won't find a line of cabs or a subway stop in front of the local clubs at closing time. If you want to try cabbing it, be sure to call ahead and set up a pickup time. However, a designated driver often is the best option for getting to and from your destination.

The cozy, back roads charm of the Cape requires full attention for drivers, especially as there are few streetlights. With many people riding bikes or walking, even late into the evening, the Cape is no place to drink and drive. In recent years

paying customers, to last the year. Balancing these hot spots are the more reserved, but equally casual, environs for those looking only to unwind.

From relaxing piano bars, to hopping clubs playing the latest pop music, to casual bars with a couple of acoustic guitars in the background, there is a lot to cover in such a short time. Some towns are less nocturnally active, satisfied in offering just a few after-dark spots to keep things interesting. As the Cape itself has always hosted an eclectic mix of patrons, so too does its nightlife. Only on

Massachusetts has stepped up efforts to curb drinking and driving. During summer months Cape police add dozens of officers to their departments, in part to increase traffic enforcement during the peak season.

For those interested in exploring Cape nightlife, we present here some of the bright spots you'll find from Bourne to P-town. Listings in this chapter predominantly cover bars, clubs, and restaurants that offer live entertainment. See our Arts chapter for theater, concerts, and other evening activities, and check local newspapers for special events such as dances and dinners sponsored by local churches and fraternal organizations. Because many of the nightspots we mention are also great dining establishments, look for more details on their cuisine in our Restaurants chapter.

If you're interested in hearing some blues, jazz, and other good music, try Joe's Twin Villa. This former speakeasy is located on Old Mill Road in Osterville and has reportedly attracted certain Kennedys and Schwarzeneggers to its dance floor. Call (508) 428-9861 to see what musicians are playing.

And even with all the hot spots available, you don't have to spend all your time inside. The Cape is a perfect place for a summer stroll. From the energy and carnival-like atmosphere of a walk down Commercial Street in Provincetown to the sight of Chatham Light piercing the evening fog as it sweeps its beams across the broken barrier beach, some of the most intoxicating nightlife on Cape Cod has no cover charge.

UPPER CAPE

The Courtyard Restaurant and Pub
1337 County Road, Cataumet (Bourne)
(508) 563-1818

The Courtyard Restaurant pushes back the dinner tables at 9:00 P.M. on Friday and Saturday nights to make way for dancing and live entertainment that runs the gamut from contemporary jazz and blues to light rock and Top 40. Entertainment is provided Tuesday, Wednesday, Friday, and Saturday evenings year-round. The crowd, which often ranges in age from late 20s to early 50s, takes in the music of local groups. This place is a favorite with locals, especially on weekend afternoons in the summer as patrons gather around the fishpond at the outside tiki patio bar to listen to music and partake in the excellent selection of American fare on their menu.

Dan'l Webster Inn
149 Main Street, Sandwich
(508) 888-3622, (800) 444-3566
www.danlwebsterinn.com

Candlelit rooms, dining fireside or in the gardens of a moonlit conservatory—the Dan'l Webster Inn offers all these. (See our Hotels, Motels, and Resorts and Restaurants chapters.) Colonial charm and elegance combine here to provide a perfectly quiet evening in the Cape's oldest town. Whether a late dinner in the restaurant (they serve till 9:00 P.M. daily) or a visit to the Tavern at the Inn Grille & Wine Bar, an authentic replica of the two-centuries-old tap room where Daniel Webster made regular visits, you'll have a positively exceptional experience at the Dan'l Webster Inn. The Tavern serves up outstanding ales and microbrewed favorites as well as fine wines from the Wine Bar. You can order from the tavern menu until midnight. Located in historic Sandwich center, the Dan'l Webster is a beautiful setting for a romantic evening on the town.

Sandwich Tavern
290 Route 130, Sandwich
(508) 888-2200
www.sandwichtavern.com

Talk about mixing it up—this is a sports bar (with 18 TVs showing at least six different events at one time), tavern, restaurant (serving sandwiches, salads, pizza), and game room (featuring Keno, darts, and four full-size pool tables). On Thursday, Friday, and Saturday nights the dance floor is where popular local bands perform, and locals get out to kick up the dust.

The Flying Bridge
220 Scranton Avenue, Falmouth
(508) 548-2700
www.capecodrestaurants.org/flying bridge

Definitely one of Falmouth's brightest and best, the Flying Bridge is a large facility that offers harbor-front drinks and dining nightly, and live entertainment and dancing in the upstairs lounge on weekends (see our Restaurants chapter). The lounge is open from May through September, and live entertainment is provided during the summer months. Local bands perform top 40 and jazz until 12:30 A.M. on Friday and Saturday.

Liam Maguire's Irish Pub and Restaurant
273 Main Street, Falmouth
(508) 548-0285
www.liammaguire.com

At this Irish pub and restaurant, you'll get lively entertainment nightly in season when owner Liam Maguire takes the stage with his guitar to perform traditional and contemporary Irish folk music and requests such as "Danny Boy," "Green Fields," and "My Wild Irish Rose." International Irish music greats Tommy Makem and Paddy Reilly usually appear once a year to the delight of those of us who wear our green and orange with pride. The restaurant is open year-round and

serves both Irish and non-Irish food until 10:00 P.M. The pub has a number of Irish beers on tap. Every time we visit here, we have clam chowder and Guinness, a great combination which satisfies an affinity for two very special places.

The Nimrod
100 Dillingham Road, Falmouth
(508) 540-4132
www.thenimrod.com

This colonial tavern still bears scars from British cannon fire (it's in what is now the men's room, if you're interested). Such reverence to history hasn't kept the Nimrod from staying with the times, however. It offers live music, mainly jazz, nightly. It also serves solid lunches and dinners. Entrees include grilled native swordfish with lemon shallot butter, oven-roasted salmon with a blue cheese crust, charbroiled New York sirloin, and shrimp marsala. Lunches include stuffed quahogs, salads, and simple pastas and sandwiches. And what's with the name? We're told the Nimrod was a fearless warrior of the biblical era. To this day the name is awarded to the British Navy's most powerful weapon. Open for lunch and dinner daily.

McGann's Pub
734 Route 28, East Falmouth
(508) 540-6656

McGann's will remind you of a genuine Irish pub—except of course for the karaoke on Thursday and the live music on Friday and Saturday evenings, which tends to be alternative rock. McGann's caters to a cross-section of ages. In season, though, it's a hot spot for the college-age crowd, which comes to dance and enjoy the live music.

Silver Lounge
412 Route 28A, North Falmouth
(508) 563-2410

Driving toward Falmouth on Route 28A, you'll come upon the Silver Lounge in North Falmouth. This place has been a favorite hangout for years and is one of the few that serves food until 1:00 A.M. Eat in the railroad car, then join the crowd at the piano bar in the lounge, always a focal point for local gatherings. The pianist plays Thursday through Saturday from 8:30 P.M. to midnight.

Surf Lounge at the Sea Crest Resort
350 Quaker Road, North Falmouth
(508) 540-9400

This oceanfront resort is a great place for an evening out if you want romantic dinner overlooking Buzzards Bay followed by some music and maybe a little cheek-to-cheek dancing. Live entertainment runs Thursday through Sunday from Memorial Day to the end of September and includes everything from a disc jockey to bands performing blues, show tunes, or Top 40.

Woods Hole Community Hall
Water Street, Woods Hole
no phone

The Woods Hole Community Hall is a nice place to spend an evening of contra dancing, watching theater (see our Arts chapter), or listening to great folk music. The intimacy of the Community Hall permits you to sit within feet of performers. There's no central phone number to call for information, so you'll have to watch local papers for upcoming events.

Mashpee Commons
Mashpee Rotary, Routes 28 and 151, Mashpee
(508) 477-5400
www.mashpeecommons.com

Grab your lawn chair and spend a summer evening enjoying free music and entertainment at Mashpee Commons, a retail center that sponsors some 35 outdoor concerts and performances a season and has become an important entertainment center on the Cape. Call the above number for a schedule of events (see our Annual Events chapter for more details).

MID-CAPE

The New Driftwood Coffee House
2150 Main Street, Marstons Mills
(508) 771-9000
www.newdriftwood.com

The New Driftwood Coffee House hearkens back to those 1960s coffeehouses featuring folk music and beat poets. It's the largest folk and acoustic venue on the Cape and features top local and national folk-singing talent. They have concerts the first Saturday of most months. Call for a schedule.

Blue Anchor Cafe & Sushi
453 Main Street, Hyannis
(508) 771-9464
www.yings.net

The Blue Anchor offers European, American, and Asian cuisine for dinner in its large candlelit dining room, but the main attraction is arguably the dance floor and live entertainment. You'll want to call for an entertainment schedule, but regular entries include jazz, soul, reggae, karaoke—even some Sinatra. Open for dinner daily.

Hyport Brewing Co.
720 Main Street, Hyannis
(508) 775-8289
www.hyportbrew.com

Open year-round, the Hyport Brewing Co. offers flavorful beers for locals and tourists. Catch any televised sporting event on their five satellite TVs and surround-sound stereo system. Monday night madness at the Hyport means you hang out with the rest of the locals and listen to the live music of the house favorites Zach and the Fatman, who perform in the lounge. There's live music Friday and Saturday nights until the 1:00 A.M. closing, but it's the beer that they brew and the popular menu they serve that keep people coming back. Try the Flounder—a sample of six delicious Hyport brews served on a Flounder platter.

Kendrick's
72 North Street, Hyannis
(508) 771-9700
Kendrick's is a hot spot of action in Hyannis. A two-level layout to this restaurant/bar, not to mention one of the largest fish tanks in the region, gives this restaurant a cozy feel. Mix in live bands and you have a nightspot that draws from miles around.

The 19th Hole
11 Barnstable Road, Hyannis
(508) 771-1032
The 40-and-younger crowd flocks to the 19th Hole, a happening sports bar with darts, pool, and a jukebox.

The Paddock
20 Scudder Avenue, Hyannis
(508) 775-7677
www.paddockcapecod.com
The lounge at the Paddock (see our Restaurants chapter) is packed on Friday and Saturday nights with people coming to hear pianist and organist Ray Rasicot, who makes musical magic on a piano and Hammond B3 organ as he performs everything from "Georgia on My Mind" to the music from *The Phantom of the Opera*—and he encourages audience participation. A Cape performer for more than 30 years, Rasicot plays Friday and Saturday in season.

Roadhouse Cafe
488 South Street, Hyannis
(508) 775-2386
www.roadhousecafe.com
For another guaranteed good time, try the Roadhouse Cafe. The owner's dad is Lou Columbo, the highly regarded jazz musician, so it's no surprise that the Lou Columbo Jazz Ensemble takes the floor here on a regular basis (every Monday night, as a matter for fact, year-round). "He's very outgoing and entertaining,"

says Dave Columbo of his trumpet-playing father. Top area pianists are featured on other evenings. How old is the crowd? "Twenty-one up to 80," says Dave Columbo.

RooBar
586 Main Street, Hyannis
(508) 778-6516
www.theroobar.com
This lively restaurant features an open kitchen, slick mood lighting, and a happening bar scene. The martinis are smart, and more than 130 kinds of wine are there for the choosing. The menu changes with the chef's latest inspiration, but likely items include Portuguese seafood stew, margarita shrimp, and a slew of interesting, affordable pizzas. Open daily for dinner.

Mill Hill Club
164 Route 28, West Yarmouth
(508) 775-2580
Attention, sports fans: Do 23 televisions sound like a dream? It's reality at the Mill Hill Club. The diversions here include pool tables, video games, and six bars. Regional and local bands perform regularly. If male and female bikini contests and DJ dance parties are more your style, you'll find them here, too. Many of the events are 18-plus and often require a cover charge.

Oliver's
Route 6A, Yarmouthport
(508) 362-6062
www.oliverscapecod.com
If you're overdue for a good time, get yourself down to Oliver's in Yarmouthport (see our Restaurants chapter), near the town line with Dennis. The lounge seats about 45, and there's live entertainment summers on Friday through Sunday nights and in the off-season on Friday and Saturday nights. The late-30s to 50s crowd comes to dance to music from the 1970s and '80s. Oliver's is a locals' favorite, but Cape visitors will also feel welcome.

Captain's Club Bar & Grill
243 Lower County Road, Dennisport
(508) 398-5673
www.captainsclubbargrill.com
If you're looking for a hot nightspot with a young and sometimes wild crowd, Captain's Club offers Boston-based and local blues and classic rock bands year-round. It's open nightly from Memorial Day to Labor Day and Friday and Saturday off-season.

Clancy's
8 Upper County Road, Dennisport
(508) 394-6661
www.clancysrestaurant.com
On the banks of the Swan River, Clancy's caters to those seeking soothing background music while wining and dining (see our Restaurants chapter). Five nights a week a year-round pianist plays everything from jazz to contemporary favorites.

Improper Bostonian
Route 28, Dennisport
(508) 394-7416
This summertime-only venue is open Wednesday through Saturday from Memorial Day to Labor Day weekend and offers live bands at least two nights a week, usually Friday and Saturday, and a DJ the rest of the time. The music is a meld of jazz, rock, pop, and blues. The Saturday afternoon happy hours are very popular. The Improper Bostonian attracts a young—early 20s to late 30s—crowd.

Michael Patrick's Publick House
435 Route 28, Dennisport
(508) 398-1620
During the summer you can hear Irish music nightly at Michael Patrick's Publick House. In the fall the live music switches over to contemporary dance favorites (with a dance floor to go with them) from the '50s through the '90s, on Friday and Saturday nights only. Sundays from 4:00 to 8:00 P.M. are reserved for jazz. Michael Patrick's is a place for all ages.

Christine's
581 Route 28, West Dennis
(508) 394-7333
www.christinesofcapecod.com
By day Christine's is humming with busloads of hungry tourists looking for good food (see our Restaurants chapter). At night it's hopping with locals who cram the 300-seat showroom for concerts by top draws. There's something happening seven nights a week during the summer with live concerts. During the off-season, Christine's offers local bands and dancing on Saturday nights.

Sand Bar
4 Lighthouse Road, West Dennis
(508) 398-2244
No visit to the Cape would be complete without spending an evening with Philo Rockwell King, better known as Rock King, who has been playing to royal (and somewhat older) audiences at the Sand Bar, on the road to West Dennis Beach, for more than 40 years. King does everything from bouts of boogie-woogie to jokes. King holds court Wednesday through Saturday (weekends only Memorial Day through the end of June).

Sundancer's
116 Route 28, West Dennis
(508) 394-1600
This casual venue attracts a youngish crowd, and features local rock bands most nights in season. On summer Sundays the focus here is live reggae music—and yes, they are located on the Bass River which adds ambience to the Caribbean beat.

LOWER CAPE

The Reef Cafe
Route 6A, Brewster
(508) 896-7167
Located just off Route 6A on the grounds of Ocean Edge Resort, the Reef features easy-listening bands on Friday and Saturday nights summer through fall.

The Woodshed
1989 Route 6A, Brewster
(508) 896-7771

Adjacent to the Brewster Inn and Chowder House, the Woodshed is a great place to unwind and take in some local color, along with great acoustic rock. As its name implies this is a rustic venue and definitely casual. It can get noisy, but the crowd is relaxed and fun loving.

Cape Cod's Irish Pub
126 Route 28, West Harwich
(508) 432-8808
www.capecodsirishpub.com

Traditional Irish music fills the air every evening from 9:30 to 10:30 P.M.; then, after a short break, the band changes gears and covers music from Paul Simon to the Beach Boys to U2. Irish superstars such as Tommy Makem and the Clancy Brothers have been known to stop in at the Irish Pub, located right next to the Herring River Bridge. The Pub, which often holds a St. Patrick's Day party in August, is open from Memorial Day through Columbus Day.

Jake Rooney's
Route 28 and Brooks Road, Harwichport
(508) 430-1100

This year-round restaurant (see our Restaurants chapter) has live entertainment six or seven nights a week in summer and on weekends in the off-season. The mix includes karaoke, sing-alongs, and local bands that play good-time music from the '50s, '60s, and '70s. One popular regular is Jimmy Craven, a guitar soloist who often invites people to come up and jam with him, making for some entertaining evenings. There's a dance floor, but if you want to sit it out, you can play keno. Jake Rooney's is also a good place to watch the big game, as there are several large-screen TVs here.

Campari's Bistro Bar & Grill
323 Route 28, North Chatham
(508) 945-9123
www.camparis.com

Campari's is one of the few dining establishments on the Lower Cape that features live jazz and easy listening music on most evenings year-round. The restaurant is divided into two sections, the elegant bistro and bar to one side and a more casual grill to the other.

Chatham Bars Inn
Shore Road, Chatham
(508) 945-0096, (800) 527-4884
www.chathambarsinn.com

Seeking sophisticated entertainment? All summer the Chatham Bars Inn holds a dinner dance on Saturday nights. Jackets are required, and the ability to waltz, fox trot, and cha-cha-cha doesn't hurt. Slightly more casual, family-oriented events are held in the Beach House Grill in summer.

The Chatham Squire
487 Main Street, Chatham
(508) 945-0945
www.thesquire.com

Half tavern and half nice restaurant, the Squire has several bars, with the tavern side being the liveliest. Although the Squire has live bands only occasionally, it has a jukebox, pool tables, and the only raw bar in town. This year-round establishment has a congenial atmosphere where locals gather in the off-season. Check out the tavern's great collection of license plates.

Sou'Wester Steak House
1563 Route 18, Chatham
(508) 945-4424

Here's a great place to kick up your heels. The Sou'Wester's dance floor is open all year Thursday through Saturday; bands are usually rock 'n roll or blues.

Upstairs at Christian's
443 Main Street, Chatham
(508) 945-3362
www.christiansrestaurant.com

This cozy, book-lined second-floor space is a year-round piano bar, with entertainment seven nights a week in summer and on Friday and Saturday in the off-season.

Between 1945 and 1957 five drive-in theaters opened on Cape Cod. Today the large outdoor screen at the Wellfleet Drive-In is the only one remaining. It opened in 1957 with a screening of Desk Set *starring Spencer Tracy and Katharine Hepburn.*

Wequassett Inn
Route 28 at Pleasant Bay Road, Chatham
(508) 432-5400
www.wequassett.com

The lounge here hosts a pianist on weekends in summer. It's an upscale, civilized place to hear music that accompanies your conversation rather than drowning it out. Men are required to wear jackets.

Joe's Beach Road Bar & Grille at the Barley Neck Inn
5 Beach Road, East Orleans
(508) 255-0212
www.barleyneckinn.com

The high-ceilinged, barn-like lounge at the Barley Neck has a beautifully redone mahogany bar and a great old stone fireplace. Sink into comfortable armchairs and listen to some of the best piano music you'll hear anywhere. Jim Turner is a regular at the ivories here, playing Friday through Sunday in the summer. There is also the occasional evening of dinner theater. You can get great munchies here—see our Restaurants chapter.

Land Ho!
Route 6A, Orleans
(508) 255-5165

This popular pub, hung with hundreds of original signs, has live bands two nights a week in summer—the nights vary. When there's no live music, the well-stocked jukebox is always playing.

The Beach Break Grill & Lounge
Main Street, U.S. Route 6, Eastham
(508) 240-3100

The Beach Break Grill & Lounge (see our Restaurants chapter) features a menu of light bites and live entertainment, usually jazz or blues, during the summer. With an outdoor deck, this venue attracts a crowd in their 30s through 50s.

First Encounter Coffeehouse
Samoset Road, Eastham
(508) 255-5438
www.firstencounter.org

Many big names, including Wellfleet's own Patty Larkin and Livingston Taylor (James' brother), got their start and still perform at this well-known coffeehouse located in a church. The building itself is an 1899 yellow clapboard and stained-glass church (the meeting room of the Unitarian church is turned into the coffeehouse, and its location has earned it the name "Chapel in the Pines"). Concerts are given the second and fourth Saturday night of each month. If you're late you won't stand a prayer of getting in—the seating is limited to 100 people.

Rick's Outer Bar
Town Center Plaza, U.S. Route 6, North Eastham
(508) 255-4959

Rick's attracts a lively crowd who come to listen and dance to DJs on weekends all summer. In the off-season this year-round local hangout is a good place to play darts, listen to the jukebox, or watch the game on a large-screen TV.

The Beachcomber of Wellfleet
Cahoon Hollow Road, Wellfleet
(508) 349-6055
www.thebeachcomber.com

Ask any local where to find the best music on the Lower Cape, and you will be pointed to the Beachcomber. The former 1897 lifesaving station sits almost at water's edge and attracts a collegiate crowd, especially after a day on the beach. The music here ranges from loud to louder, with popular acts including local favorites the Incredible Casuals, the

Skatalites, and the Samples. It's open weekends in June and daily from late June to Labor Day from 11:30 A.M. to 1:00 A.M. There is a cover charge for live entertainment on Friday, Saturday, and Sunday, with two shows on Saturday and Sunday at 4:00 and 9:00 P.M.

Bookstore and Restaurant
50 Kendrick Avenue, Wellfleet
(508) 349-3154
www.bookstorerestaurant.com

This popular restaurant (see our Restaurants chapter) across from Mayo Beach features occasional live music. Downstairs is the Bomb Shelter Pub, which has a jukebox, darts, pool tables, large-screen TV, and a local, sports-loving crowd. It's open year-round.

The Duck Creeke Tavern Room
70 Main Street, Wellfleet
(508) 349-7369
www.innatduckcreeke.com

With its fireplace and authentic beams, this tavern, housed in an 1800s building, is a great place to savor live music. There's entertainment—including jazz, pop, and Latin ensembles—on special evenings during the summer.

Wellfleet Town Pier
Commercial Street, Wellfleet

Dancing in the dark? Why not? And throw the stars in for good measure! On Wednesday evenings in July and August, the Wellfleet Town Pier becomes a stage for square dancing complete with a live caller. The fun starts around 7:30 P.M. and lasts until 10:00 P.M.

Bubala's by the Bay
185 Commercial Street, Provincetown
(508) 487-0773

Open mid-April through October, this funky restaurant has live entertainment nightly in July and August, usually jazz, but sometimes folk rock.

The Boatslip
161 Commercial Street, Provincetown
(508) 487-1669

Music rarely gets louder than this, and the dance floor is one hot spot for a mostly male crowd. The club has indoor and outdoor dance floors with entertainment Thursday through Sunday. There's also a mixed lesbian and gay tea dance most afternoons in season on the outdoor pool deck. It's open April through October.

Cafe Mews
429 Commercial Street, Provincetown
(508) 487-1500
www.mews.com

In summer this year-round waterfront restaurant offers live entertainment, usually a cabaret act, on Friday, Saturday, and Sunday. Some of the best entertainment, however, is in the off-season. October through May, Cafe Mews hosts an open-mike coffeehouse.

Club Euro
258 Commercial Street, Provincetown
(508) 487-2505

Once home to a Congregational church and movie theater, this club uses the pulpit/stage to host some of the best acts in world music, jazz, blues, funk, and reggae, along with cabaret and drag acts. The room itself is a sight to see: murals of deep-sea denizens, including 3-D mermaids, awash in an ocean of greens and blues. Repeat performers include such favorites as Taj Mahal and Buckwheat Zydeco. The crowd is hot and hip. It's open Memorial Day through mid-October, as long as the weather stays warm.

Governor Bradford
312 Commercial Street, Provincetown
(508) 487-2781, (508) 487-9618

Right in the center of town, this local hangout has chess and backgammon sets, pool tables, and pinball machines along with live entertainment just about every

night in season. Usually it's karaoke at least several nights a week and live bands Saturday and Monday nights. It's open year-round.

Pied Bar
193A Commercial Street, Provincetown
(508) 487-1527
www.thepied.com

Many people consider this the quintessential lesbian dance club; *Time* named it one of the best women's bars in the country! The recently revamped bar is all about the dance floor: new sound, new lights—quite a scene. Open Memorial Day to Halloween, the Pied Bar features an after-tea dance every evening at 6:30 P.M. in season, and a girl party every night after 10:00 P.M.

[Facing page] *Located right on the beach, the Beachcomber of Wellfleet attracts a young crowd and great music to liven up summer nights.* SUSAN BLOOD AND THE BEACHCOMBER

SHOPPING

Shopping on Cape Cod is an experience as unique as the Cape itself. Although there are some large chain stores, the majority of retail shopping here is done in scores of smaller, independent shops that populate every Cape town.

We do get the latest fashions here, but Cape clothing stores are especially strong in classic designs and offbeat clothes just right for artistic types. We've got gourmet shops, jewelers, outdoor shops, shoe stores, bookshops, and wonderful gift shops. Many of our gift shops double as galleries, making it easy to find that special, one-of-a-kind wall hanging, basket, vase, or planter. (If you're in the market for art, be sure to check our Arts chapter for galleries.)

Shopping on the Cape is an adventure. It's also a personal, pleasant experience with friendly shopkeepers and clerks just as likely to strike up a conversation about the weather or current events as the latest fashions or home décor. In a tight-knit economic community, shopkeepers and business people present a united front, so that the lady at the plant shop will recommend the potter down the street, who'll tell you about the stained-glass artist next door, who'll send you to the fabric shop in the next town over.

There are a few sizable retail centers besides Cape Cod Mall, which completed a massive renovation in 2000. Busy Route 132 in Hyannis is also home to three other shopping plazas right nearby. On the Upper Cape the open-air Mashpee Commons, now with more than 90 shops plus several banks and eateries, is a beautifully designed area that makes shopping a pleasure. In Falmouth there's the Falmouth Mall with 20 stores. These large centers certainly come in handy—and sometimes

you're just in the mood for a mall-type shopping experience—but some of our happiest hours have been spent ducking in and out of Main Street shops in towns such as Chatham, Orleans, and Sandwich. And don't miss downtown Hyannis, which has some great shops that some people overlook because they're concentrating on the large retail hubs on Route 132. The Village of Osterville has its own little downtown. On the north side of the Cape, Barnstable Village, West Barnstable, and Sandwich all offers some great shops. Sandwich's lovely Main Street is lined with plenty of shops you can walk to, and Woods Hole is another quaint area you should check out if you're in the Upper Cape area. Yarmouthport has a quiet Main Street on Route 6A, with a cluster of stores and antiques shops in one central area.

For a really different shopping experience, spend a day in Provincetown, where Commercial Street is as funky and colorful as Greenwich Village—only with a small-town, seaside flavor. This is the place to go for the offbeat and the outrageous, along with the artistic and spiritual. But don't forget to wear good walking shoes: It can take a good portion of the day just to get from one end of Commercial Street to the other! Wellfleet has a nice downtown, with an emphasis on galleries mixed with a few choice shops. Eastham's shopping scene is a bit scattered geographically, but it's a worthwhile excursion. They're just not all in one place, so you do need a car.

Orleans is the real retail hub of the Lower Cape. Many residents of surrounding towns come here regularly to do their grocery shopping, pick up dry cleaning, buy flowers, and just shop. It's the kind of town where you're bound to run into someone you know, and even if you don't you'll get the same warm, comfortable feeling because it's such a friendly town. It has a nice downtown area where you can park your car and stroll down the brick-paved sidewalks.

Chatham is also a great walking town, though there are shops beyond the down-town area you may want to drive to. Main Street Chatham has a genteel, relaxed feel—no hustle-bustle here. In summer spend a Friday afternoon browsing on Main Street, and hang on to your parking space so you can stay for the outdoor concert on the green! Harwich is sprawl-ing, with shops all along Route 28 and in other areas of town. Harwichport is a good place to start, because much of it is walkable. Brewster, likewise, has a couple of little centers, with a cluster of shops near the Brewster General Store (which is itself a must-see), another cluster a mile or so east (including Brewster Book Store), and, to the west, the Lemon Tree complex of shops (which we recommend you check out).

Shopkeepers accept many forms of payment—cash, personal checks (with proper ID), travelers' checks, and credit cards. Not all shops take all credit cards, but most accept at least one or two.

About business hours: Although most stores are open seven days a week during the season (Memorial Day to Labor Day), many shops—especially those on the Lower Cape—have sporadic off-season hours or are open only on weekends in winter. We'll let you know if that is the case, and, of course, we'll tell you when a shop is closed in the off-season. Other-wise, you can assume the store is open all year. It's always a good idea to call first in the really quiet months such as January, February, and March; even shops that are open all year sometimes close for a week or two in the dead of winter for cleaning, painting, or redecorating so they'll be ready for another busy summer. Happy shopping!

GENERAL SHOPPING

Upper Cape

Tanger Factory Outlet Center
Bourne Bridge Approach, Buzzards Bay
(800) 406-8435, (207) 439-6822
www.tangeroutlet.com
This small collection of outlets has been known to slow us down considerably when we're heading off Cape. There's a great Liz Claiborne outlet (508-759-7771), plus outlets for other quality names including Levi's, Izod, and Nine West. Look for the sign just before you get onto Route 25 in Buzzards Bay. It's open every day.

Cape Cod Factory Outlet Mall
1 Factory Outlet Road, Sagamore
(508) 888-8417
www.capecodoutletmall.com
This is a nice collection of 21 well-known manufacturers, including Bass (508-888-8652), Oshkosh B'Gosh (508-833-2242), Buck-A-Book (508-833-1119), Corning Revere (508-888-3262), and Carter's (508-888-7413). Other well-known outlets here include Samsonite, Reebok, Casual Corner, Petite Sophisticates, and the Museum of Fine Arts Catalog Clearance Outlet. The mall also has kiosks for leather goods, clothing, and jewelry. The mall is open daily year-round and is just off exit 1 as you're heading onto the Cape on U.S. Route 6. It's right at the base of the Sag-amore Bridge.

If the weather is overcast or rainy, Cape crowds move from the beaches to shop-ping centers like Hyannis and Route 28 in Yarmouth. This is the perfect oppor-tunity for you to take advantage of the Cape's public transportation services to avoid spending even a moment of your vacation stuck in traffic. See www.the breeze.info for more information.

Christmas Tree Shop
Route 6A, Sagamore
(508) 888-7010

Don't you just love a bargain! People have been known to lose track of time in this store and to emerge dazed and happy, carrying bags filled with all kinds of things they didn't know they needed. The bargains here are irresistible! This growing chain was started by a Cape family more than 30 years ago, and it's been a draw for locals and tourists alike ever since. The Christmas Tree Shop carries a huge, ever-changing inventory of gifts and housewares, including lamps, lawn furniture, greeting cards, food and gourmet items, paper goods, linens, and, of course, Christmas items, all at near-wholesale prices. The inventory is always fresh and interesting and the staff pleasant and helpful. The Sagamore shop, with its unusual thatched roof, is a regional attraction; other Christmas Tree Shops are located in Falmouth, Hyannis, West Dennis, West Yarmouth, Yarmouthport, and Orleans. The shops are open daily.

Pairpoint Glassworks
851 Route 6A, Sagamore
(800) 899-0953
www.pairpoint.com

In keeping with the glassmaking history of the area, established in the 1800s by Boston & Sandwich Glass Co., Pairpoint produces and sells beautifully fashioned handblown and pressed glass. Pairpoint makes vases, candlesticks, sun catchers, cup plates, and stemware, along with authentic reproductions of early American glass originals found in museums. You can watch glassblowers at work Monday through Friday; the shop is open daily.

The Old Cranberry Barn
348 Route 6A, East Sandwich
(508) 888-7699

This is the place to stop if you're interested in furniture, furniture, and more furniture. They specialize in antique and reproduction pieces from Europe. You'll find armoires, servers, buffets, tables, and chairs, both painted and unpainted. Open May to December, daily in summer. Call ahead for off-season hours.

Sandwich Lantern Works
17 Jan Sebastian Way, Sandwich
Industrial Park
(888) 741-0714
www.sandwichlantern.com

Handmade on the premises, the handsome brass and copper onion lights sold here are replicas of those once carried on whaling vessels. Pre-1800s lanterns, wall sconce, and chandeliers to hang indoors or outdoors are also available. This shop is open Monday through Saturday.

Titcomb's Bookshop
432 Route 6A, East Sandwich
(508) 888-2331

It would be easy to spend hours in this shop. Its three floors have all manner of cozy places to sit and peruse the large selection of new, used, and historical books. Titcomb's specializes in rare books, local authors, and regional history, and their wide range of children's selections includes the popular American Girl series (you'll find everything from books, trading cards, and albums to project books, posters, and theater kits). Titcomb's is one of the few stores to carry Tasha Tudor prints—many of them signed! It also carries greeting cards and orders and ships books. It's open daily.

Toy Chest and Hobby Shop
4 Merchants Road, Sandwich
(508) 833-8616

This cute shop for children carries popular brands such as Lego, Brio, and Playmobil along with books, hobby pieces, stuffed animals, baby toys, and lots of arts-and-crafts items for children. The store also sells educational puzzles, books, model planes, boats, and cars. It's open Monday through Saturday, with Sunday hours during the Christmas holiday season.

Made on Cape Cod

If you want to really take home a piece of Cape Cod, seek out products that are made here. Besides being a vacation paradise, the Cape is home to many creative and enterprising people whose products have achieved success locally and regionally, and in some cases, nationally. Here is a sampling of some of our favorite Cape-made products:

Cape Cod Potato Chips: Made in Hyannis, these goodies are probably the best-known Cape product. Founded by Chatham's Steve Bernard in 1980, the company was later bought by Eagle Snacks, then a division of Anheuser-Busch. When that firm decided to downsize in 1996, Bernard bought his old company back and became a local hero, because his action saved the plant from closing. It's more than just a great name; these are really good chips. For a fun field trip, take the kids on a free tour of the Cape Cod Potato Chips factory on Breed's Hill Road between 9:00 A.M. and 5:00 P.M. daily, Monday through Friday. You may also call them at (508) 775-3358 or look them up on the Web at www.capecodchips.com.

Barnstable Bat Company: Baseball fans will cheer for these bats, which are used by the Cape Cod Baseball League as well as some Major League teams. They make great gifts for non-pros, too, especially because you can have them engraved. Made of white northern ash, the bats bear the Cape Cod logo and start at around $50 for an adult bat (engraving included) and $40 for a youth bat. The company, launched in 1992, is located at 40 Pleasant Pines Avenue in Centerville, where the showroom is open Monday through Friday and some weekends in summer. Call them at (888) 549-8046 to check hours or request a brochure. They do a lot of mail-order business, and you can also order off their site at www.barnstablebat.com.

Cape Cod Metal Polishing Cloths: These specialty cleaners have become famous well beyond the bridge since being developed by William Block, an antique brass restorer in Dennis, in 1992. Packaged in a distinctive tin, the cloths are sold nationwide, in Canada, and in Europe. People who have tried them swear by them, and we'll second that. For store locations call (508) 385-5099, or stop by most any hardware store on Cape Cod. For more information check out www.capecodpolish.com.

Cape Cod Lavender Farm: A little-known treasure on the Lower Cape is the Cape Cod Lavender Farm in Harwich. Tucked away down a bumpy dirt drive off a dead-end road off Route 124 (look for the lavender sign about a block north of Harwich Center), this family-run business produces soaps, oils, lotions, and candles, all scented with lavender grown on the premises. Walking into the small shed that serves as a shop is a heady experience; the lavender fragrance is almost overwhelming, but wonderfully so. You'll want to stay and curl up on a lavender-scented pillow. Take one home instead, or choose a lavender sachet, or a bouquet of dried lavender. If you can't get there, call (508) 432-8297 for a brochure; the Sutphin family is happy to do mail-order, or order over their Web site at www.cape codlavenderfarm.com.

Bean & Cod
140 Main Street, Falmouth
(508) 548-8840
www.beanandcod.com
This is a combination sandwich shop and elegant gift store. Both attractive and appetizing gifts are everywhere: Houseware items, such as glasses, trays, place mats, and lamps, adorn the walls and displays; intriguing gourmet food baskets, custom-filled with cheese, crackers, teas and coffees, and regional products adorn the sandwich deli counter, where you can choose from a menu of soups, sandwiches, and a daily special.

The Bean & Cod will ship wherever you want. The New England Bucket contains pancake mix and syrup from Vermont, baked beans, Lake Champlain chocolate, and New England clam chowder. If you need a present for a formal or special occasion, you'll find it here. It's open daily all year. The store also carries cookbooks, food mills, and other cooking equipment.

The Black Dog General Store
214 Main Street, Falmouth
(800) 626-1991
www.theblackdog.com
The iconic Black Dog has finally jumped Nantucket Sound! In 2003 this Martha's Vineyard cottage industry (see our Martha's Vineyard chapter), though seemingly omnipresent already, established a presence on the mainland (here in Falmouth and out in Provincetown). Now those unfortunate individuals who won't be making it over to the Vineyard can still buy their very own been-there T-shirt. Or sweatshirt. Or leash. Or coffee mug. This store, modeled after the Vineyard Haven mother-ship emporium, features all the Black Dog apparel and accessories you—and your dog—will ever need.

Howlingbird Studio
91 Palmer Avenue, Falmouth
(508) 540-3787
www.howlingbird.com

This silk-screening studio that hand prints on canvas bags, long- and short-sleeve T-shirts, sweatshirts, and hats is popular with Woods Hole Oceanographic Institute scientists and tourists alike. The animal and organism-themed prints tend toward the scientific rather than cutesy—a nice change of pace. Howlingbird is open daily year-round, with shorter hours in winter. Its retail shop in Woods Hole is open May through Christmas. Items are stocked and ready for printing, some are already printed, or you can bring in your own article. If the screen you select is in use, your order can be printed immediately.

Soft as a Grape
251 Main Street, Falmouth
(508) 548-6159
www.softasagrape.com
This well-established business carries T-shirts, shorts, and other casual apparel, including floral limited-edition designs in dresses, hats, tees, and sweaters. The store, which carries some jewelry, barrettes, and trinkets, is open daily year-round. You'll find other Soft as a Grape shops in Plymouth, Sagamore, Mashpee, Hyannis, Chatham, Orleans, Provincetown, and Edgartown.

Uncle Bill's Country Store & Flower Shop
Route 28A, North Falmouth
(508) 564-4355
This favorite for Falmouth shoppers carries a little bit of everything—greeting cards, collectibles, homemade jams, penny candy, and jewelry. You can also pick up fresh or silk flowers here. Special collections include Byers Choice carolers, Old World Christmas, and decorations for all holiday seasons, especially Christmas. The store has a huge variety of teddy bears and also stocks a large number of cranberry and cranberry-design products, among them linen, pottery, food, cookbooks, and children's toys. The store is open every day of the year except Thanksgiving and Christmas.

Under the Sun
22 Water Street, Woods Hole
(508) 540-3603

Under the Sun has been in business in Woods Hole for nearly 30 years and has always emphasized local artists and artisans who make jewelry, glassware, pottery, and other functional and artistic pieces. They also carry a selection of comfortable shoes: Birkenstock, Teva, Dansko, and others. The shop is open daily in season and Monday through Saturday in the winter.

Mashpee Commons
At the Mashpee Rotary between Routes 28 and 151, Mashpee
(508) 477-5400
www.mashpeecommons.com

With more than 90 businesses, including four banks, 11 eateries, and several nationally known chains, Mashpee Commons has been praised in national design magazines for its attractive, functional, and unique retail shopping area. Some of its best-known businesses include Gap, Williams-Sonoma, Puritan Clothing Store, P.A. Company, Regal Cinema, Talbot's, Banana Republic, and Gap Kids, along with a cigar shop and the Sporting Life sporting goods store. Between shop-hopping, recharge at Starbuck's coffee house. For the health-conscious, Fountain of Juice serves all kinds of fruit smoothies. Mashpee Commons sponsors 50 annual outdoor concerts and activities throughout the year, including hayrides, Christmas caroling, and pops symphony performances. Mashpee Commons is open daily all year, with longer evening hours in summer. Keep reading for more information on some of the other shops in Mashpee Commons.

Cape Cod Toys
Mashpee Commons, Mashpee
(508) 477-2221

It's a toy store, and this shop has nearly every toy imaginable—or at least, all the best ones! Lego, Gund stuffed animals, European educational toys, great beach toys, and instructions on how to make a sand dragon are a mere sampling of the delights inside this shop. The shop has something for children of all ages, including the wee ones.

Homecomings
Mashpee Commons, Mashpee
(508) 477-8519

You'll find everything imaginable for the kitchen, from small appliances to gourmet coffees and utensils. Homecomings sells regional food such as New England chowder, corn relish, beach plum jelly, and cranberry vinegar in a lobster bottle. The shop also carries cookbooks, jelly beans, and contemporary gift items.

In Massachusetts you can generally buy clothing without incurring a sales tax. A 5 percent tax is added to purchases of more than $175.

Kensington's
Mashpee Commons, Mashpee
(508) 477-4006

Here's a store for the young and restless, or just the restless: Nantucket bags, all kinds of luggage, everything for the beach (from portable chairs to coolers), backpacks, current and historical maps, journals, and countless other upscale items related to travel—even a tide clock. Items are priced from very reasonable to expensive.

Signature
Mashpee Commons, Mashpee
(508) 539-0029
www.signaturecraftgallery.com

This is an American Craftsman Gallery, a designation that indicates all goods are American made. The items are distinctive as well, for nearly every piece of jewelry, artwork, and stemware at Signature is one of a kind. Fascinating art objects in glass and metal, unique pieces of jewelry in gold and semiprecious stones, and even garden sculpture are displayed here, creating a gallery atmosphere in a unique shop. Signature is open daily year-round.

Mid-Cape

Black's Handweaving Shop
597 Route 6A, West Barnstable
(508) 362-3955

Here's your chance to watch weavers at their looms as Bob Jr. and Gabrielle Black create beautiful throws, shawls, scarves, and place mats in their shop, which is attached to their home (0.7 mile west of Route 149). Bob makes jacquard coverlets and throws and can personalize larger pieces by weaving names and dates into them. The Blacks are custom crafters, so you can choose your own colors and designs. They weave about 90 percent of the shop's goods; the rest is the work of other hand weavers. The Blacks have been weaving since the 1940s; they opened the shop in 1954 and over the years have woven pieces for customers worldwide. The shop is open daily.

Claire Murray
770 Route 6A, West Barnstable
(508) 375-0331, (800) 252-4733
www.clairemurray.com

Located in a beautifully restored barn, this Claire Murray shop offers the same beautiful, distinctive, handmade rugs, needlepoint, gift items, home accessories, and cotton throws as the Osterville shop (see listing) and the Nantucket shop. Also available are rug-hooking and cross-stitch kits, as well as lessons. The shop is open daily.

Tern Studio
Route 149, West Barnstable
(508) 362-6077

If you love wood—really fine wood, worked by a real craftsman—come visit Tern Studio, where Albert Barbour handcrafts fine wood furniture and one-of-a-kind wood turnings. Barbour uses all New England wood and often employs green wood for his turned pieces, then ages the finished pieces. The gallery is full of hand-turned bowls, candlesticks, and vases—each a unique piece of art. You may also find a few pieces of furniture, but because most of the furniture Barbour produces is custom work, it doesn't stay in the studio for long. Photos of his pieces in their new homes line the walls of his studio. "My idea is, don't make the same thing twice," says Barbour, who has been plying his craft for more than two decades. "I don't want to become a factory." No chance of that; these far-from-factory creations must be seen to be appreciated. Tern Studio is open year-round, usually five days a week. But bear in mind that Barbour is also a furniture doctor. As some of his patients are too large to move, he makes house calls (on-Cape only). Call ahead to make sure he's around if you don't want to risk limiting your visit to peering in the windows at his lovely work.

West Barnstable Tables
2454 Route 149, West Barnstable
(508) 362-2676
www.westbarnstabletables.com

In their 33rd year of business in this large, year-round showroom, Stephen Whittlesey and Richard Kiusalas produce handmade custom furniture in a primitive style that retains and emphasizes the color and texture of the natural wood, much of which is about 100 years old, salvaged from New England houses, barns, and boats. The shop also converts antique windows into frames for mirrors. Trestle, Shaker, farm table, and pedestal legs accent the distinctive tables. They display unique folk art cupboards created from antique wood and found pieces such as ship portholes. It's open daily.

The Whippletree
660 Route 6A, West Barnstable
(508) 362-3320
www.thewhippletree.com

Housed in a beautiful, 225-year-old barn, the Whippletree is filled with gifts and home accessories with a country flavor, including cotton coverlets, dried flowers and wreaths, greeting cards, candles, and hand-carved birds. Some popular collectible lines include Cats Meow, Snowbabies, and Squashville. You can also select gifts for the holidays and items for children and babies. The Whippletree is open seven days a week from June to December and Thursday through Sunday the rest of the year.

Claire Murray
867 Main Street, Osterville
(508) 420-3562, (800) 252-4733
www.clairemurray.com
Claire Murray's handmade rugs are so beautiful you won't want to walk on them. Actually some of the smaller ones make great wall hangings! The colors are rich and the designs delightful on these heirloom pieces. You can buy finished rugs— prices range from $99 to $4,000—or a kit. Some patterns are simple enough for beginners; others are a challenge to accomplished rug makers. Kits average about $130. Classes are available in rug hooking, needlepoint, cross-stitch, and knitting; call for more information and class schedules. The shop, which is open daily all year, also carries needlepoint and counted cross-stitch kits, gift items, wearable art, home accessories, and cotton throws. And look for Claire Murray's beautifully illustrated book: It makes a great gift. There's a Claire Murray shop on Nantucket, on Martha's Vineyard in Edgartown, and in West Barnstable (see listing above). For a catalog call the 800 number.

Joan Peters of Osterville
885 Main Street, Osterville
(508) 428-3418
www.joanpetersofosterville.com
Interior designer Joan Peters brings together the elements of her own original paintings, wall coverings, hand-painted furniture, sinks, and tiles to create a distinctive, coordinated look. She'll even paint floors to match the rest of a room's decor and fill a living space with unique accent pieces such as teapot chandeliers, mirrors, and custom shades. She custom designs carpets, and her hand-painted sinks and tiles are not only designed and painted on-site but also fired in kilns at the studio. Open Monday through Saturday.

Oak & Ivory
1112 Main Street, Osterville
(508) 428-9425
www.oakandivory.com
This shop is owned and operated by a sixth-generation Nantucketer who makes classic Nantucket baskets on the premises. It also carries antique reproductions of tables, chairs, hutches, chests, and side chairs. For a gift that represents the Cape's maritime history and traditions, you can't improve on the whimsical handmade Sailor's Valentine seashell boxes or the lightship baskets in precious metals and original scrimshaw. The shop is open daily in summer and in December and closed Sunday the rest of the year.

The Shoe Salon
837 Main Street, Osterville
(508) 428-2410
www.theshoesalon.com
You'll find shoes by Cole Haan, Dansko, and Jack Rogers, along with accessories such as jewelry, handbags, and even a select few sweaters. "We try to bring the unusual—we're not a me-too store," explains owner Pamela Boden. In addition to dressier shoes, the store carries men's and women's Mephisto walking shoes, which have been handmade in France for more than 30 years. Boden describes them as "the Mercedes-Benz of walking shoes." The shop is open Monday through Saturday. A second Shoe Salon is located on Main Street in Chatham (508-945-0292).

Yankee Accent
23 Wianno Avenue, Osterville
(508) 428-2332
A cross between a gift shop and a gallery, this nearly 30-year-old business with a nautical focus carries prints and originals by well-known local artists such as Kathy O'Neil and Nancy Braginton-Smith. It also carries gifts for the home and books by New England authors. The store is open daily from May to January and on Saturday only the rest of the year.

Cape Clockwork
1694 Route 28, Centerville
(508) 771-1082
www.capeclock.com
Wendell Sharp, a certified master clock-maker, relocated his shop—the largest clock dealership on the Cape—from Yarmouth in the fall of 1998. He carries 20 or so grandfather clock designs plus a complete selection of Sligh and Howard Miller wall and mantel clocks, Chelsea ship clocks, and Swiss music boxes. He is a dealer for the Wellfleet Clock Company, which makes tide clocks and shelf and wall clocks. Sharp's motto: "If you need a clock repaired/Old or new/Bring it in/Wendell knows what to do." He is open daily in season and closed Sunday off-season.

1856 Country Store
555 Main Street, Centerville
(508) 775-1856
www.1856countrystore.com
As the local children know, if you've only got a nickel in your pocket, you can still buy something sweet at this charming and historic country store in the heart of Centerville. Whether you're after penny candy, a daily paper, or a souvenir of your vacation on Cape Cod, you'll find it here. And as you can tell from the benches out front marked Democrats and Republicans, the Country Store is a gathering place for adults (registered, opinionated, and otherwise), teenagers, and kids. On a hot day this is where you'll find a cold soda, and on cold days, a cup of hot coffee.

The gift selection ranges from the popular Westerwald pottery (a line that features each village in Barnstable) to homemade jams, hand-dipped candles, and note and greeting cards. From gossip to Gummy Bears, the Country Store has it all! It is open daily.

Andi Carole Contemporary Fashions
20 Sea Street, Hyannis
(508) 771-7539
This classy boutique sells gorgeous designer clothing for women—clothes by small designer labels you won't find anywhere else. One of those designers is Andi Carole herself, a talented lady known locally for her crusade against litter and for her beautiful dresses with clean, flattering lines. She uses European fabrics with an emphasis on natural fibers, and the quality of the material shows in each piece. These dresses just fall so beautifully. "The thing about my dresses is you've got to see them on," says Carole, who opened this shop after a decade of designing in Europe. Everything she sells in the store is American made, including accessories and jewelry.

Cape Cod Mall
Routes 132 and 28, Hyannis
(508) 771-0200
www.simon.com
The largest mall on Cape Cod—really, the only "real" mall—Cape Cod Mall is anchored by Filene's, Macy's, and Sears, along with mini-anchor Best Buy. Major retailers at the mall include Bath & Body Works, Banana Republic, Gap, Gap Kids, Express, Eddie Bauer, Ann Taylor Loft, Abercrombie & Fitch, and Victoria's Secret. Their 400-seat international Food Court features Au Bon Pain, D'angelo, Manchu Wok, McDonald's, Sarku Japan, Freshens Yogurt, and Sbarro. There's also a Hoyt's Cinema 12.

Cape Cod Mall is a totally nonsmoking facility and hosts many special events throughout the year. The stores are open Monday through Saturday 9:30 A.M. to 9:30 P.M., Sunday 11:00 A.M. to 6:00 P.M.

[Facing page] *Centerville's 1856 Country Store is a great place to pick up a souvenir of your trip to the Cape.* HYANNIS AREA CHAMBER OF COMMERCE

Columbia Trading Company
1 Barnstable Road, Hyannis
(508) 778-2929
www.columbiatrading.com
If it has anything to do with boats, you'll find it here. This shop, right near the corner of Main Street, deals in out-of-print and rare nautical books, marine antiques, ship models, and marine artifacts. Literally they offer thousands of new, used, and rare books on whaling, shipwrecks, Coast Guard history, boat building, sailboat racing, and navigation. It also has marine art for sale. The shop is open Monday through Saturday, year-round.

Nantucket Trading Company
354 Main Street, Hyannis
(888) 790-3933
www.nantuckettrading.com
If you like adding color and style to your kitchen, treat yourself to a shopping spree here. We love browsing in this spacious, two-level store, which carries glassware, dishes, cookware, and a huge assortment of kitchen gadgets along with specialty foods such as Nantucket Coffee, tea, spices, garlic, vinegars, and Cape's Kitchen pasta sauces and salsas. You'll also find terrific serving bowls, salad sets, cutting boards, place mats, and napkins. This is a great place to shop for a gift, and the store's bridal registry is a neat alternative to the more traditional crystal and china registry. It offers UPS shipping and free gift wrapping. Nantucket Trading Company, which also has a location in Falmouth at 208 Main Street (508-548-5881), is open daily all year, with expanded evening hours in the summer.

Puritan of Cape Cod
408 Main Street, Hyannis
(508) 775-2400, (800) 924-0606
www.puritancapecod.com

In business nearly 90 years, this family-owned retail clothing store represents three generations of commitment to Cape Cod and has a very traditional feel. We especially appreciate the attentive service we always get here. Where else can you get free alterations, free gift wrapping, and a lifetime guarantee? Puritan carries a complete line of men's and women's clothing including sportswear and performance shoes. Puritan also rents and conditions skis.

The company introduced its own beautiful four-color Cape Cod tartan plaid several years ago and offers men's and women's clothing in this handsome material. Puritan has other locations in Chatham, Orleans, Falmouth, and Mashpee Commons, plus a seasonal shop in Wellfleet. The stores are open daily.

The Mill Store
39 Route 28, West Yarmouth
(508) 775-3818
This store has a large selection of unfinished furniture and craft items and is simply a fun place to explore if you are feeling creative or thinking it's time to make some changes in your personal space. Prices are excellent, and the store is open daily. The Mill Store has other locations in Dennisport, West Harwich, and Plymouth.

The Picket Fence
4225 Route 6A, Cummaquid
(508) 362-4865
www.thepicketfence.com
Behind a picket fence is the Picket Fence, a great old barn filled with unique decorative items and collectibles. You'll find hand-painted furniture, pottery, original dolls, and a terrific assortment of holiday decorations. We always make a point of coming here at least once before Christmas. It's a fun place to browse, and it's friendly too. In

[Facing page] *Main Street, Hyannis, has seen many improvements over the last few years, and, as the biggest town on the Cape, boasts many shops and restaurants.* HYANNIS AREA CHAMBER OF COMMERCE

November you will often find free hot cider and cookies greeting you.

The shop closes after Christmas and opens again in spring.

Pondside Gifts & Boutique
1198 Main Street, Route 28, South Yarmouth
(508) 760-1190
www.pondsidegifts.com

This unique gift store and boutique is located in the Hearth 'N Kettle Plaza on Route 28 (see our Restaurants chapter for other locations of the Hearth 'N Kettle Restaurants) and offers a great selection of gifts that are ideal for wedding presents or gifts for any occasion. Their lovely pilgrim glass vases and lamps are made with gold and lead crystal and have a beautiful cranberry color. In the boutique they've got evening bags and attractive button-down cardigan sweaters printed with images of colored lighthouses of Massachusetts. The store is open year-round Monday through Saturday from 9:00 A.M. to 5:00 P.M., but during the summer until 5:30 P.M. (6:00 P.M. on Friday).

The Silver Unicorn
941 Route 28, South Yarmouth
(508) 394-8401

If you are looking for a keepsake of your visit to the Cape, stop in at the Silver Unicorn where you'll discover an extensive line of nautical jewelry—bracelets, charms, rings, and earrings in gold and sterling silver—with a Cape Cod theme (maps, lobster traps, and whale tails). The shop also sells nautical glass sculpture. It's open daily.

Wild Birds Unlimited
1198 Route 28, South Yarmouth
(508) 760-1996
www.wbu.com

Bird lovers flock to this store for bird feeders (priced from $3.00 to $300.00) and plenty of seed and suet. But why stop there? The bird-themed paraphernalia goes on and on: hand-carved birds, jewelry, music boxes, clothing, songbird tapes, videos, books, and all kinds of edu-

cational materials. Do you want a birdbath? Wild Birds Unlimited has standing and hanging baths in wood, iron, concrete, ceramic, and plastic that can be hung from trees, mounted on a deck, or placed in your gardens. The store is open seven days a week.

Yankee Crafters Inc.
48 North Main Street, South Yarmouth
(508) 394-0575

Thousands of pieces of handcrafted wampum (cylindrical beads made from shells, once used by Native Americans as ornaments and currency) jewelry—rings, pins, earrings, and bolas—are offered at very reasonable prices. Also among the collections are Scandinavian jewelry, linens, calendars, crystal, and Norwegian trolls. The building is listed on the National Register of Historic Places. Yankee Crafters is open daily.

The Barn & Co.
358 Route 6A, Yarmouthport
(508) 362-3841

Make a point of stopping by to admire this ca. 1840 barn filled with fold art and country-style crafts by local and regional artists. You'll find Hearts Content hand-painted clothing and slate welcome signs, Brewster native Mary Beth Baxter's primitive cards and prints, Marstons Mills' Dust of the Earth pottery, dried floral arrangements, and everybody's favorite—angels—in cloth, ceramics, and porcelain. Local basketmakers produce handsome items in Shaker, traditional, and Nantucket lightship designs. The shop, also great for Christmas ornaments, is open year-round.

Parnassus Book Service
Route 6A, Yarmouthport
(508) 362-6420
www.parnassusbooks.com

Housed in an 1840s building, Parnassus is a book lover's dream come true. There are books everywhere—filling the floor-to-ceiling shelves, stacked on the wooden floor, piled in boxes. New books are mixed in with old, arranged in a unique categorized system that is purposely left unlabeled—owner Ben Muse likes customers to explore. But he's always happy to help you look for a particular book, and if he doesn't have it, he'll try to find it elsewhere. A long-time book scout, he'll generally come through. The shop carries extensive collections in such subjects as maritime history, fine arts, antiques, and Cape Cod and colonial American history; it also carries many publications you won't find anywhere else, such as old town reports. It is open Monday through Saturday year-round.

Armchair Bookstore
619 Route 6A, Dennis
(508) 385-0900
www.armchairbookstore.com
We love browsing in this bright, homey shop, which has a huge selection of titles in hard- and softcover along with wonderful gift items, cards, and toys. The family-run shop stocks literary fiction, history, nature, and wonderful children's books, among many other categories. Armchair is open seven days a week, year-round.

Lady Bug Knitting Shop
612 Route 6A, Dennis
(508) 385-2662
www.ladybugknitting.com
In business since 1982 this shop concentrates on knitting only. In the Kings Grant complex, the shop carries lots of yarn, needles, and supplies, and books on knitting. Owner Barbara Prue offers knitting classes for all levels. The shop is open year-round, daily in summer and Monday through Saturday the rest of the year.

Linda Burke
633 Route 6A, Dennis
(508) 385-8102
Linda Burke specializes in clothing that is classic and comfortable. The store's motto is irresistible: "We wear 20 percent of our clothes 80 percent of the time. Our goal is to be that 20 percent." The store maintains a customer registry that makes wardrobe building easier and gift giving error proof. Owner Linda Burke does all

A great way to pick up antiques, art, and collectibles—and gain an education in the process—is at auction. If you're unfamiliar with the auction scene, attend one or two as a spectator before going to bid. Established more than 45 years ago, the Robert C. Eldred Company on Route 6A in Dennis is the oldest auction house on the Cape. The company holds at least 12 sales throughout the year; call (508) 385-3116, or visit www.eldreds.com for a free schedule. The Sandwich Auction House (508-888-1926, www.sandwichauction.com) holds auctions the first and third Saturday of each month.

the alterations herself—you won't find this kind of service in larger stores. The shop is open year-round.

Ross Coppelman Jewelers
1439 Route 6A, Dennis
(508) 385-7900
www.rosscoppelman.com
To say Ross Coppelman's gold and silver creations are unique would be an understatement. This jewelry is lush, extravagant, bold, and beautiful. Unusual and classic gemstones are displayed in striking settings, many of them inspired by ancient Egyptian, Aztec, and Roman designs but with a contemporary flair. Just west of the Route 134 junction, the shop has two showrooms of gold and silver jewelry and a workshop where it is created. Coppelman, who opened his business in 1971, designs and produces custom jewelry, including wedding rings, and also resets stones. The shop is open daily in summer, and Monday though Saturday the rest of the year.

Tobey Farm and Garden Center
352 Route 6A, Dennis
(508) 385-2930
Tucked inside this 300-year-old working farm—one of the best stops on the Cape for fresh fruits and vegetables—is a small

shopping area featuring exquisite, reasonably priced dried floral wreaths and centerpieces made from German statice, lavender, eucalyptus, rosebuds, and yarrow. Freshly baked pies and a variety of locally bottled jams and jellies are irresistible. It's open mid-April through Christmas. Don't miss their Halloween celebration, which includes hayrides for children.

Lower Cape

Brewster Book Store
2648 Route 6A, Brewster
(508) 896-6543, (800) 823-6543
www.brewsterbookstore.com
This delightful little shop is filled to the brim with hardcover and paperback books with a strong local-author and local-interest section and a terrific children's section. It also sells unusual cards and stationery. The shop holds regular book signings, especially with local authors, and offers a story time for little ones on Tuesday and Friday at 10:00 A.M. It's open daily.

Brewster General Store
1935 Route 6A, Brewster
(508) 896-3744
www.brewsterstore.com
Erected as a Unitarian church in 1852, the Brewster General Store is a landmark and a tradition. Revered by locals and visitors alike, it's a friendly, take-your-time kind of place where you grab a cup of coffee, a doughnut, and a newspaper and sit out on the porch on one of the benches (actually old church pews) and watch the world go by. You can also buy linens, mugs, teapots, cookbooks, jams, and T-shirts, among a great assortment of items. Children love coming in to pick out penny candy and put dimes in the turn-of-the-century player piano that gives the place a rollicking ragtime sound. On Sunday mornings the store fills up with folks getting their papers, and the coffee flows.

Upstairs you'll find antique linens, old milk bottles, sheet music, books, artwork, and other unique items. In summer the

shed in the back of the store opens as the Brewster Scoop, serving up the finest in ice cream and low-fat yogurt. The shop is open daily.

The Cook Shop
Lemon Tree Village Shops
1091 Route 6A, Brewster
(508) 896-7698
www.cookshopcapecod.com
This store has enough cooking implements, gourmet foods, gadgets, and decorative items to keep you browsing for hours. You'll find top-of-the-line cookware, coffeemakers, waffle irons, gourmet foods, and everything you need to impress your friends in the kitchen. Don't miss the second floor, which is packed with dinnerware, cutlery, containers, baskets, and linens. The shop is open daily.

Great Cape Cod Herbs
2628 Route 6A, Brewster
(508) 896-5900
www.greatcape.com
Proprietor Stephan Brown runs the Cape's only all-natural herbal apothecary in a rambling old stable. Here more than 170 Western and Chinese herbs are stored in glass containers on rough-hewn shelves. You'll also find books on herbs and natural healing. Brown grows many of the herbs himself and uses them in his unique holistic teas, which, he claims, might cure such ailments as urinary tract problems, ulcers, sinusitis, and sleep disorders. Vegetarian alert: Peta's Place, an on-site cafe, serves up organic, vegetarian lunches. The shop is open daily.

Handcraft House
3966 Route 6A, Brewster
(508) 240-1412
www.handcrafthousegallery.com
One of our favorites, Handcraft House (which really is in a former residence) serves as a showcase for owner Eileen Smith's beautiful watercolors, many of them Cape landscapes. But it also carries a variety of fine, handcrafted items largely by New England craftspeople. You'll find

The Brewster General Store, located on Route 6A, is the perfect place for coffee, donuts, and the paper. ERICA BOLLERUD

colorful hand-woven scarves, iron-forged candlesticks, wood marquetry boxes, glass sun catchers, and jewelry, among many other items. The shop is open daily in season, on weekends in late fall, and is closed from January to mid-April.

Hopkins House
2727 Route 6A, Brewster
(508) 896-9337

You may have a hard time distinguishing between the old and the new in this shop, located in a historic home and filled with a blend of antiques, reproductions, and folk art by owner Mary Beth Baxter, who has a knack for creating paintings that look as if they've been waiting a century for you to discover them. Her delightful designs turn up on wood, furniture, Christmas ornaments, cards, and even T-shirts. The attached bakery, run by Baxter's daughter, sells irresistible scones, muffins, sticky buns, and breads. Check out the themed herb

and flower gardens out front—one planted specifically to attract butterflies—and the potting shed out back for plants. The shop is open Tuesday through Sunday through Christmas and closed January to mid-May.

La Bodega
Lemon Tree Village Shops
1075 Route 6A, Brewster
(508) 896-7340
www.capelabodega.com

This shop not only has lovely and unusual women's clothing, but a wide array of beautiful imported jewelry and gifts. In fact it began with more of an emphasis on jewelry and gifts, but has gradually shifted its focus to clothing and accessories. Owners Nancy and Foster Phillips, who launched the shop in 1982 (its first location was in Dennis), travel extensively and bring back treasures to sell in the shop, mostly from Mexico and South America. The shop is open year-round.

Lemon Tree Pottery
Lemon Tree Village Shops
1069 Route 6A, Brewster
(508) 896-3065
www.lemontreepottery.com
Opened in 1965, this shop has over the years blossomed into a showcase of pottery, ceramics, jewelry, and other beautiful things. One specialty is very evident outside the shop and throughout the Lemon Tree complex of shops: lawn ornaments—everything from fountains to rabbits and cats. The shop also sells terra-cotta herb markers, dream catchers, wonderful jewelry, ceramics, wind chimes, and hand-dipped tapers. The shop is open daily.

Linda's Originals
220 Route 6A, Brewster
(508) 385-2285, (800) 385-2284
The Yankee Craftsmen
220 Route 6A, Brewster
(508) 385-4758, (800) 385-4758
www.my-collectibles.com
Perched side-by-side on a hill, these two stores have been delighting collectors for a decade. Linda's Originals carries a wide range of hand-painted clothing and hand-crafted items and the largest selection of afghans on the Cape. The store is also home to the Cats Meow, a captivating collection of miniature handcrafted buildings. (This is the only place in the country where you can buy items from the Cats Meow Cape Cod Collection, such as the Cape Playhouse, Scargo Tower, and the Chatham Lighthouse.)

The Yankee Craftsmen truly lives up to its name: The rooms abound with collectible items made by crafters from the Cape and worldwide. It also has one of the largest collections of Byers Choice Carolers in the country as well as Harbour Lights lighthouses. In the summer be sure to visit the lavish, award-winning flower gardens. The shops are open daily.

The Strawberry Patch
2550 Route 6A, Brewster
(508) 896-5050

This red-shuttered old horse barn is the exclusive home of Hand-tiques, the name owner Mary Anne Boyd coined for her unique array of gifts. Many of the goods are displayed in antique display cases: A cast-iron stove holds cookie cutters, and old post office boxes cradle candles.

In business since 1971, the shop carries lovely U.S.-made cotton throws, pillows, and tablecloths, along with kitchenware, dolls, gifts, candy, and Christmas decorations. Befitting a former equine home, the shop features several selling stalls, including the Teacher Stall (everything for a teacher or classroom). A separate sale barn offers first-quality goodies at discounts of up to 50 percent. The Strawberry Patch is open daily.

Sydenstricker Galleries
490 Route 6A, Brewster
(508) 385-3272
www.sydenstricker.com
The colors are bold and bright, the designs sharp and striking. The glass made here is so dazzling that several American embassies serve dessert to their guests on Sydenstricker plates, inspired by the art of ancient Egypt. Two sheets of glass are fitted into a terra-cotta mold; the first sheet is decorated by sifting powdered glass through a stencil. A five-hour fusing locks in the color. Choose from dishes in various sizes (some with a signature rippled edge), complete place settings, rectangular serving plates, candy dishes, even ashtrays. Two showcases are filled with glass paperweights. You can watch the glass being made Tuesday through Saturday from 10:00 A.M. to 2:30 P.M. The shop is open daily.

Allen Harbor Nautical Gifts
335 Lower County Road, Harwichport
(508) 432-0353, (800) 832-2467
www.capecodnauticalgifts.com
Even landlubbers will enjoy the incredible selection of items found here. There are jigsaw puzzles and calendars commemorating various Cape Cod landmarks, T-shirts,

watches, and jewelry (including an unusual charm bracelet that spells out "I love you" in colorful cloisonné ship flags), doormats, and decorative household treats. Allen Harbor also sells a great selection of tide clocks and wind and weather instruments. The shop, which also does mail order, is closed weekends during the off-season except at Christmastime.

Cape Cod Bonsai Studio
1012 Route 28, Harwich
(508) 432-8400
www.capecodbonsai.com
Owner Michael Novik has planted his love and knowledge of gardening in Harwich, and the results are growing beyond belief. Four greenhouses contain an abundance of bonsai trees—dwarf juniper, elm, box-wood, and Japanese cherry—and tropical plants for sale in individual ceramic planters or in meticulously arranged groupings. You can also purchase acces-sories, including training wire, traditional ceramic planters, and selected pieces of suiseki, stone forms resembling mountains that are also used as planters. The prices are reasonable, and Novik's helpful advice will allay any fears nongreen thumbers may have. He also offers courses and workshops in bonsai care and training. It's open by appointment in the off-season.

Cape Cod Cooperage
1150 Queen Anne Road, Harwich
(508) 432-0788
The Cooperage is a step back in time and a must-see for anyone who wants a glimpse of living Cape Cod history. This big old barn is the only place where cranberry boxes and rough-sawed fish boxes (both used today by people as storage containers) are made by hand, just as they were more than 100 years ago. The store also offers an incredible selection of hand-painted furni-ture and staves, every conceivable arts-and-crafts notion, bevies of birdhouses, and old-fashioned kids' toys, such as pull-along ducks and rabbits and hobbyhorses. During season you can also buy fresh-picked cran-berries. It's open daily all year.

Honeycomb Hollow
69 Route 28, West Harwich
(877) 430-7444
www.honeycombhollowcandles.com
If you love candles, you shouldn't miss this shop, where owner Judy Bissonette makes beeswax candles by hand. You'll find not only rolled tapers, but also handmade scented beeswax jar candles and votive candles. Other beeswax and honey prod-ucts, including skin-care products, hand-dipped chocolates, and honey bears, line the shelves. The shop is located in the Khorikian Plaza not far from the Dennis line. It's open daily all year.

Monahan and Company
540 Route 28, Harwichport
(508) 432-3302
www.monahanjewelers.com
The oldest family-owned jewelry store in the country, Monahan still carries on the tradition started by founder Jeremiah Monahan in 1815: quality jewelry at fair prices. Monahan and Co. designs and manufactures hundreds of styles of nauti-cal and seashore related jewelry. They also custom design nautical pieces in 14K and 18K gold and platinum. Monahan and Co. is open daily May through October and weekends in the off-season.

Pewter Crafter of Cape Cod
791 Route 28, Harwichport
(508) 432-5858
www.pewtercraftercapecod.com
Here at the Cape's only pewter studio, artist and craftsman Ron Kusins displays the simple beauty of a metal that was for a time overlooked. The shop features unique jewelry, vases, plates, cups, and other items done in traditional and contempo-rary styles that are both decorative and functional. It's open Tuesday through Sat-urday in season; calls are welcome for appointments.

The Potted Geranium
188 Route 28, West Harwich
(508) 432-1114
www.pottedgeranium.com

Every room of this old Cape Cod house is filled with wonderful home accessories, folk art, crafts, and gifts. It's the kind of shop that puts you in a good mood the moment you walk in the door. You'll find such items as pewter bookmarks made in Chatham, locally produced weathervane Christmas ornaments, hand-painted mirrors, baskets, ceramics, linens, Vera Bradley bags, and even paper jewelry. If a new mom or baby is on your gift list, visit the baby room for blankest, layettes, clothes, and wooden toys. The former kitchen makes a fitting home for flavored teas and coffees, kitchen utensils and linens, and a sampling of jellies and jams from the Chatham Jam and Jelly Shop. Open daily in season the shop is closed during the month of March and Wednesday in the off-season.

Wychmere Book and Coffee
521 Main Street, Harwichport
(508) 432-7868
www.wychmerebooks.com

This lovely shop, opened in 1997, is roomy and organized and provides a cozy sitting area with self-serve coffee and cookies—refreshments are on the honor system, just leave your money in the teapot! Curl up in one of the inviting window seats if the resident dog hasn't claimed them. Along with a great assortment of bestsellers, and new and classic books, the shop sells cards and gifts and hosts regular author appearances, book discussions, and children's story hours. It's open daily in summer and closed Tuesday in the off-season.

Yankee Doodle Shop
181 Route 28, Harwich
(508) 432-0579
www.yankeedoodleshop.com

For more than 45 years, this has been one Yankee Doodle Dandy of a shop! Room after room of finished and unfinished quality country furniture, all made right on the premises, are offered at prices so low you'll question the price tag. The front porch, for instance, is home

to at least 12 kinds of rockers, with prices averaging $75. Yankee Doodle markets a wide selection of cast-iron doorstops and reproduction mechanical banks, hard-to-find wooden cupolas, folk art—even authentic spinning wheels! In the off-season it's open Friday and Saturday only.

Ben Franklin
631 Main Street, Chatham
(508) 945-0655

This is one of an increasingly rare breed of retail shop: an old-fashioned five-and-dime store. It carries a wide variety of merchandise from art supplies and toys to greeting cards, mugs, and T-shirts. We love to come here because it looks, feels, and even smells like the stationery-variety store we remember from childhood. Kids gravitate to this shop because it sells baseball cards, model kits, and basics such as Play-Doh and Silly Putty, and adults like it because it sells grown-up basics such as desk blotters, calendars, and magazines. The shop is closed Sunday in the off-season.

Cabbages & Kings Bookstore
628 Main Street, Chatham
(508) 945-1603

What a delightful shop! It has one of the largest children's sections we've come across in any bookstore and sells toys as well. We always have a tough time getting our little ones out of this store. Adults will appreciate not only the nice selection of quality books but also the unique greeting cards and stationery. The store will even gift wrap. It's open daily year-round.

Chatham Candy Manor
484 Main Street, Chatham
(508) 945-0825, (800) 221-6497
www.candymanor.com

People from all over the world have visited Chatham Candy Manor for the caloric concoctions that they make in small batches then hand-dip every day in the same tradition started more than 50 years ago by the store's founder, Naomi Turner. The selection is endless: chocolate-dipped fruits (including apricots, strawberries, and pineapples in dark or milk chocolate), hazelnut puree and chocolate treats shaped like scallops, and our favorite cranberry cordials (fresh fruit melded with bonbon crème and liqueur, then covered with pure chocolate). Even the barley lollipops are kettle cooked and poured by hand. When holiday season comes around, watch for demonstrations of candy-cane making. Mail order is available; call for a brochure and price list. The shop is open daily.

Chatham Glass Company
758 Main Street, Chatham
(508) 945-5547
www.chathamglass.com

Glassblower Jim Holmes is the force behind the vibrant contemporary glass pieces you'll find here. The bud vases evoke jeweled candied apples, and the kaleidoscopic bowls and sleek candlesticks would liven up any table. Holmes's work is carried by several fancy department stores, but you can skip the middleman by finding your own one-of-a-kind piece right here. If your taste is more traditional, this is also the place to order the small, colonial-style "bulls-eye" glass window panes that you may have been admiring in local historical homes. Look in on the working studio if you want to see how it's all done. Open Monday through Saturday.

Chatham Jam and Jelly Shop
10 Vineyard Avenue, Chatham
(508) 945-3052

You can't leave Cape Cod without a jar of beach plum jam, and this is just the place to get it. The shop, in a residential area just off Route 28, sells more than 75 varieties of homemade preserves, and several concoctions (wild beach plum, cranberry, and wild blackberry) are from fruit hand-picked on Cape Cod. The shop offers—even encourages—taste sampling, so you can't go wrong. Gift sets and mail order are available. It's open Monday through Friday.

The Dead Zone
647 Main Street, Chatham
(508) 945-5853

Since 1990 the Dead Zone has been paying homage to the legion of Deadheads—devout followers of the band the Grateful Dead. Inside you'll find reminders of the '60s and '70s: tie-dyed clothes in wild colors, irreverent bumper stickers, incense, and love beads. The shop is open daily.

Pentimento
584 Main Street, Chatham
(508) 945-0178

This shop has wonderful ambience—maybe it's the fact that it sells indulgent items such as luxurious clothing form designers like Sigrid Olsen and Eileen Fisher, pretty blank journals, fine stationery, scarves, and jewelry. It also carries whimsical picture frames, bejeweled sandals, clever totes, and home accessories. It's closed January, February, and March.

Scrimshaw by Marcy
333 Old Harbor Road, Chatham
(508) 945-0782

Animal activists need not worry: The scrimshaw sold here is antique and was made long before any whale protection laws were put into effect. There's a nice selection, including whales' teeth with elaborate engravings and what are known as Sailor's Valentines—octagon-shaped boxes with elaborately decorated shell lids that natives on Barbados made and gave to sailors, who in turn gave them to loved ones upon their return home. The "scrimshaw" bookmarks, made from antique ivory piano keys, make unique gifts and are a great bargain at $20; a catalog of designs is available. It's open Monday through Saturday from May to Columbus Day and by chance or appointment the rest of the year.

The Whale's Eye
653 Route 28, Chatham
(508) 945-3084

Housed in an old barn, the Whale's Eye has an array of beautifully hand-painted furniture and mirrors. All the work is by Suzanne and John Rocanello, who opened the shop in the barn adjacent to their home in the late 1970s and soon after began marketing their creations at craft shows all over the Cape (see our Annual Events chapter). At the shop you'll see chests, boxes, tables, and mirrors, many painted with nautical scenes. The Rocanellos do a lot of custom work, and if you bring in a fabric swatch or wallpaper strip, they'll be happy to use colors that will work with your decor. The shop is open daily in summer and a bit sporadically in spring and fall. "If the barn door is open, we're here, " says Suzanne, but it's best to call first. It's open by appointment only in the winter.

Yankee Ingenuity
525 Main Street, Chatham
(508) 945–1288, (888) 945–9123
www.yankee-ingenuity.com
Half gallery, half gift shop, Yankee Ingenuity carries unusual item in a wide range of prices, making it an ideal place to shop for a gift for any occasion. You'll find hand-carved animal figurines with fishing poles in their paws and fish dangling from their lines, cunning birdhouse ornaments, unusual mirrors, beautiful Cape Cod photography, clocks, desk accessories, oversized stuffed animals, even Tiffany-style lamps. The shop is filled with interesting and beautiful things, from Impressionist-print umbrellas to jewelry, letter openers, and desk chimes. It's open daily.

Yellow Umbrella Books
501 Main Street, Chatham
(508) 945–0144
www.yellowumbrellabooks.com
Yellow Umbrella has been offering locals and tourists the latest in fiction and non-fiction bestsellers, used books, and works by local authors since 1979. The store also has an extensive section of books about Cape Cod. It carries rare and out-of-print books, used hardcover and paperback books, and will do special orders. Be sure to visit the outdoor bargain racks—any book is a buck. It's open daily year-round.

The Baseball Shop
26 Main Street, Orleans
(508) 240–1063
Score a home run every time if you're looking for the latest in all things baseball. The store stocks more than 1,000 different baseball caps as well as trading cards, bumper stickers, autographed material, and select clothing. It's open year-round, daily in season and closed Tuesday in winter.

Beth Bishop Shop
Route 28, Orleans
(508) 255–0642
Locals will tell you that Beth Bishop "is always in style." Known for its service and wide selection of fine-quality dresses, sportswear, beachwear, sleepwear, and outerwear, it's been a favorite Cape-wide clothing store since 1985. At Beth Bishop you can create a wardrobe of great pieces that work alone or together, from weekday to weekend. The shop is open year-round.

Bird Watcher's General Store
36 Route 6A, Orleans
(508) 255–6974, (800) 562–1512
www.birdwatchersgeneralstore.com
This is a store for the birds—literally. Since 1983 owner Mike O'Connor's entire focus is on the needs of both birds and birdwatchers. This is the place to buy a bird feeder—the store carries more than 100, not to mention tons of bird feed to fill them! You can't be a bird-watcher without binoculars, and Bird Watcher's carries some 40 types. It also stocks a comprehensive selection of bird books, T-shirts, socks, door knockers, welcome mats, sun catchers, magnets, gift wrap, and note cards—all focused on birds. Even if you aren't into our feathered friends, you must stop here: Tell the super-friendly staff a joke, and they'll give you a gift. Now that's something to crow about! The shop is closed Thanksgiving and Christmas.

Booksmith/Musicsmith
Skaket Corners
Route 6A and West Road, Orleans
(508) 255-4590

This is a great place to shop if you're into books and your other half is into music. You'll both be happy browsing here, as half the store is devoted to hardcover and softcover books, and the other half is compact discs and tapes. The store also sells calendars, magazines, cassettes, and videos and has a great children's corner in back, complete with a small table and chairs where little ones can sit and read. It's open daily year-round.

Crazy Horse Tack and Gift Shop
125 Route 6A, Orleans
(508) 240-2244, (800) 243-4003

Horse-crazy folks around here come galloping to this shop, which sells all sorts of equine products, from saddles and bridles to riding apparel, jewelry, and toys. There's a nice selection of gift items such as coffee mugs, key chains, and books, so if you've got a horse lover on your gift list, this is the place to go. The shop sells both English and Western tack and apparel and also carries plenty of horse-care products. It's open year-round.

Focalpoint Studio
Post Office Square, Main Street, Orleans
(508) 255-6617, (800) 696-6617
www.focalpointstudio.com

For nearly 30 years, Focalpoint has been specializing in family portraits, which are often done at the beach. If you're vacationing, what better way to remember your stay here? Local photographer/owner Bob Tucker has created traditional portraits for hundreds upon hundreds of families and sparkling candids at more than 500 weddings. Focalpoint will also produce photo images on T-shirts, mouse pads, and other items. They offer framing services, color laser copies, and fax service. It's open year-round.

Every Saturday from June to October, you can buy the freshest Cape Cod-grown fruits and vegetables, cultivated mushrooms, local honey, herbs, and flowers—even freshly caught fish—at the Orleans Farmers' Market, Old Colony Way, near the Dunkin' Donuts.

The Goose Hummock Shop
Route 6A, Orleans
(508) 255-0455
www.goose.com

Outdoor enthusiasts find the Goose Hummock Shop ideal for one-stop shopping. From bait and fishing equipment to camping gear, firearms, clothing, canoes, kayaks, and bicycles, it's all sold and serviced by a knowledgeable staff either here or in the store right behind the main one. Don't need any sand eels today? Then stop in for a tides chart and map—they're free! The shop is open daily.

Kemp Pottery
9 Route 6A, Orleans
(508) 255-5853

Here's your chance to see a potter at work, as this is not only Steve Kemp's store but also his studio and has been since 1978. His varied designs, often inspired by nature, include lamps, sinks, tiles, bird feeders, fountains, and sculpture, and many of them are made with Nauset Beach sand. Kemp also does unique bas relief signs, several of which can be seen at the Cape Cod Museum of Natural History in Brewster. His functional pieces, including dinnerware, are lead-free and safe for the oven, dishwasher, and microwave. The Kemps also have a shop in West Brewster on Route 6A. Open daily in season, Monday to Saturday off-season.

Kid & Kaboodle
115 Route 6A, Orleans
(508) 240-0460

At last, a store that sells good children's clothing at reasonable prices! Whether you need a gift for a baby shower, play clothes for your toddler, or a christening gown for your grandchild, this is the place to come. If you're shopping with little ones, they can play with the toys in the back room while you browse, but don't forget to visit that room yourself, as it's filled with great bargains! Kid & Kaboodle also carries maternity clothes and rents baby furniture. It's open daily

Oceana
1 Main Street Square, Orleans
(508) 240-1414

If you love beautiful things, you'll want to browse here. It's the kind of shop that inspires you to slow down and take your time, so tranquil is the ambience. Oceana carries lovely jewelry, candlesticks, nature books, and original art, wall hangings, rugs, and hand-painted tables, along with many other items. Oceana Kids, located next door, is filled with nature-oriented toys, rubber stamps, and wooden toys. Don't miss these shops; they are open daily.

Orleans Whole Foods Store
46 Main Street, Orleans
(508) 255-6540

This is a true health food store, where you can buy grains and cereals in bulk, and purchase freshly ground peanut butter, vitamins, and a wide variety of organic products, including produce. It's also a great place to grab a quick lunch, as the store makes healthy sandwiches, soups, and sometimes pizza—sit on the bench out front and watch the world go by. But don't overlook its gift shop potential: This good-for-you shop carries a nice selection of books, with an emphasis on spiritual topics, self-help themes, and cooking; lovely, unusual greeting cards; and Crabtree & Evelyn soaps and lotions—not to mention calendars and T-shirts. It's open daily.

XO Clothing Shop
85 Route 6A, Orleans
(508) 255-4407

We confess: We didn't really want to tell

you about this shop, which sells quality women's clothing at fabulously low prices. It's one of those shops you only tell your best friends about. But owner Diane Smith does such a good job keeping up with her inventory that we figure there must be room for a few more Insiders to discover her shop. Not only are the prices great, but Diane and her staff are friendly and helpful.

The Chocolate Sparrow
4205 U.S. Route 6, Seatoller Shops, North Eastham
(508) 240-0606

Anyone who appreciates really good chocolate will love this shop—the aroma alone is heavenly. You'll find excellent fudge, dipped chocolates, and decadent truffles, all made here. If you come at the right time, you can watch them being made. The Chocolate Sparrow also has a Wellfleet location (508-349-1333), open only in summer, and a coffee bar-chocolate shop in Orleans, the Hot Chocolate Sparrow (see our Restaurants chapter). The shop is open daily.

Collectors' World
U.S. Route 6, Eastham
(508) 255-3616, (800) 421-4270
www.collectorsworldcapecod.com

This is one of those shops where you'll find yourself wandering around and losing all track of time. The shop carries both antique and new collectibles, including dolls, gnomes, model cars, lighthouses, and cottage figurines. It also sells quality jewelry and unusual wooden toys for children. The shop is open year-round, but hours are sporadic in winter.

The Glass Eye
U.S. Route 6, Main Street Mercantile, Eastham
(508) 255-5044
www.theglasseyegallery.com

We love browsing in this lovely shop on a sunny day, when light gleams off all the colored glass. And when it's cloudy, this shop will brighten your day. All the stained-glass work displayed in the gallery is by owner John Knight, but the shop also carries blown glass, handcrafted jewelry, and gift items from a variety of other artists, many of them local. In addition to glasswork the gallery sells wonderful hand-made paper creations by co-owner Donna Knight, who often offers papermaking demonstrations. Be sure to visit the working stained-glass studio downstairs. Scrap glass is free for the asking, and you can even take lessons in the off-season. The shop is open daily through Christmas and closed on Sunday from January to spring.

Sunken Meadow Basketworks & Pottery
125 North Sunken Meadow Road, North Eastham
(508) 255-8962

In an airy studio set among pine trees is a collection of gorgeous handmade baskets created by owners Hugh and Paulette Penney, who focus on form rather than function. Some are functional as well, but that's secondary to the rich colors, patterns, and textures they feature. Hugh Penney's unique basketry wall hangings are beautiful, incorporating grape vines for a wild, natural look ideal for giving any room a focal point with both color and texture. You'll also find pinch pottery and handmade jewelry by Paulette at very reasonable prices. The shop is open year-round, daily in spring, summer, and fall but with more sporadic hours in winter. In general, however, it's good to call ahead, "just to be sure" the Penneys are on the premises.

The Eclectic Company
14 Commercial Street, Wellfleet
(508) 349-1775

This aptly named shop offers a diverse assortment of unusual home accessories, clothing, and jewelry. You'll find darling hand-painted furniture, colorful ceramics, linens, and unique accents for your home, such as garden accessories. It's open daily in summer and on weekends in spring and fall; the shop closes after Columbus Day and reopens again in May.

Herridge Books
11 East Main Street, Wellfleet
(508) 349-1323

The books here are in such great shape that many customers cannot believe they are used. The store stocks the very best in dozens of genres from architecture to zoology. Don't miss the lower level, reached via a yellow stairway with an unusual handrail made from an oar; you'll find some wonderful old volumes there. Bird lovers will relish the limited-edition Audubon prints that are based on originals and sanctioned by the Audubon Society. Don't forget to check out the small but delightful collection of hand-colored postcards sitting at the front register. Herridge Books is open daily in summer, weekends only in late fall, and closed January to mid-April.

Jules Besch Gallery
275 Main Street, Wellfleet
(508) 349-1231

Proprietor Michael Tuck's store bears testimony to his belief that letter writing need not be a lost art. Glorious blank and versed cards for everyday and special occasions line the walls of his gallery, along with beautifully colored blank stationery sold by the sheet. Wooden racks hold luxurious wrapping paper, also sold by the sheet. The gallery also carries and array of inkwells and ink, and fountain and quill pens. You'll also find handcrafted mirrors, framed with scraps of driftwood, shards of broken Blue Delft china, lobster claws, skate egg cases, and other seashore treasures. It's closed in January, open weekends only from mid-February through mid-May, and keeps regular hours the rest of the year.

The Kite Gallery
75 Commercial Street, Wellfleet
(508) 487-0232
www.thekitegallery.com

The sky's the limit in this festival of everything fancy and high-flying. The pickings are far from slim: The shop has a huge selection of professional stunt kites, single-

line kites, and colorful (and, in some cases, elaborate) windsocks and flags. The Kite Gallery is closed in the off-season.

Salty Duck Pottery
115 Main Street, Wellfleet
(508) 349-3342

Katherine Stillman's wheel-thrown pottery has a free and easy quality to it. Most of the plates and cups are designed with free-form pears (an homage to the pear tree in front of her studio, perhaps?) and abstract designs. All her wares are lead-free and can go from oven to dishwasher. We also give Katherine credit for her open-door policy: If you want to buy something and she's not there, simply leave cash or fill out a charge slip. Her trust is as beautiful as her pottery.

The Secret Garden
Main Street, Wellfleet
(508) 349-1444

It's not a secret any longer: This two-story garden is overrun with charming garden art, folk art, twig love seats, garden goodies, crushed-velvet hats, birdhouses, animal marionettes, and an eclectic selection of jewelry. Kids go bonkers for the animal- and fish-shaped change purses from Tibet.

The Wellfleet Collection
Main Street, Wellfleet
(508) 349-0900

This gallery/shop is a delightful browse. Filled with tastefully arranged artwork, quilts, pottery, folk art, linens, jewelry, and antiques, the shop represents the works of largely New England–based artists and craftspeople, including Cape artists. Open daily Memorial Day to Columbus Day, it's open Saturday in late fall through Christmas and closed January to Easter, when it reopens for weekends.

Wellfleet Flea Market
U.S. Route 6, within the Wellfleet
Drive-in, South Wellfleet
(508) 349-0541
www.wellfleetfleamarket.com

This outdoor extravaganza and Cape Cod institution since 1957 features up to 300 vendors selling everything from imported dresses, leather bags, and fleece vests to used books, antiques, and handmade furniture, all at great prices. Items we've found here include old license plates, new sweatshirts, designer men's shirts, used paperback books, great old prints, and shampoo! It's open from 8:00 A.M. to 4:00 P.M. Saturday and Sunday mid-April through October. During July and August the Flea Market is open Saturday, Sunday, Wednesday, and Thursday. It's also open on holiday Mondays! Admission is $1.00 per carload on Thursday and $2.00 per carload on Wednesday, Saturday, and Sunday in season. If you stay long enough to get hungry, you can grab a bite at the snack bar. There are rest rooms for your convenience too. Many of the vendors accept credit cards; many are also open to price haggling.

Atlantic Spice Company
Routes 6 and 6A, North Truro
(800) 316-7965
www.atlanticspice.com

Trust us when we say we're going to send you someplace spicy. This warehouse sells row after row of spices and herbs, from allspice to vanilla beans and everything in between. You can buy in bulk (1- or 5-pound packages), or if you're unsure of the potency of a particular spice, you can buy a smaller sampler bag or ask for a taste. Atlantic also sells a wide range of teas (loose and in tea bags), shelled nuts, seeds, and baking items. The shop is open Monday through Saturday all year.

Susan Baker Memorial Museum
46 Route 6A, North Truro
(508) 487-2557

Everyone has a right to his or her own idiosyncrasies, and Susan Baker is no exception. Not wanting to wait until she dies to have her own memorial museum, she opened this pop palace in 1984. Once you spot Susan's work, you won't forget her startling and brightly colored pieces that are sometimes three-dimensional, sometimes satirical, sometimes in the form of printed booklets (her oh-so-cute but crudely drawn cats and dogs are big sellers). Who says art can't be fun? The shop is open daily in season and erratically off-season (ring the bell at the side door if you'd like to see the collection in the off-season).

The Whitman House Quilt Shop
U.S. Route 6 at Great Hollow Road, North Truro
(508) 487-3204, (877) 487-3204
www.whitmanhousequilts.com
It would be easy to call this store, sitting next to the Whitman House (see our Restaurants chapter), a class act: The building is a former schoolhouse and the oldest structure in Truro. The specialty here is Amish quilts, new and old, with prices that are more than reasonable. The two floors also showcase modern-day cranberry glass, teddy bears, a profusion of potpourri, brass beds, and dolls. It's closed in the off-season.

Adams Pharmacy
254 Commercial Street, Provincetown
(508) 487-0069
Come to Provincetown's only drugstore to revel in the charm of a small-town apothecary. Adams was founded in 1870, and except for the products found on the shelves and the dates on the newspapers in the rack, we bet little has changed (except, perhaps, the prices of prescriptions and over-the-counter drugs). Adams even has one of those long steel lunch counters you never see anymore. A great way to learn about the town is to sit and order coffee early one morning, when the old-timers gather to exchange stories (both real and exaggerated) of days gone by. The store is open daily.

Cabot's Candy
276 Commercial Street, Provincetown
(508) 487-3550
www.cabotscandy.com
Candy stores are a dime a dozen in Provincetown, but none comes close to Cabot's. The Cicero clan began making fudge and saltwater taffy on the premises in 1969, and they are the only ones making taffy this way on the Lower Cape. Stand inside or in front of the huge picture window and watch as a massive spool of taffy is tamed into individually wrapped bite-size pieces. (Ask for a free sample.) The flavors sometimes change, but you can be sure of finding cranberry, grape, chocolate, cherry, piña colada, peanut butter, licorice, and orange-pineapple. Cabot's also sells sugar-free taffy. It's open only holidays and weekends in the off-season.

Exuma Fine Jewelry
283 Commercial Street, Provincetown
(508) 487-2746
www.exumajewelry.com
A fixture in Provincetown for more than 30 years, Exuma specializes in custom jewelry, creating classic and modern designs in 14- and 18-karat gold and platinum. Rings are big here—gorgeous settings of sapphires, rubies, emeralds, and diamonds, to name just a few, glitter in the cases. Jeweler and craftsman Gunter Hanelt, originally from Germany, favors clean, uncomplicated designs that never go out of style. The showroom, located diagonally across from Town Hall, is open year-round, daily in summer, six days a week (closed Wednesday) through Christmas and on weekends only in January through March.

Galadriel's Mirror
246 Commercial Street, Provincetown
(508) 487-9437
This store is truly a gem—or more accurately, a lot of gems! You won't be able to resist running your fingers through the bowls of polished stones and touching the jagged edges of brilliant minerals. You'll find jade, rose quartz, topaz, and other stones along with gold and silver jewelry. Take your time in here; there's a lot to see, and browsing among such beautiful things

will put you in a tranquil mood. The shop, a fixture in Provincetown for nearly 30 years, is open year-round.

Good Scents
361A Commercial Street, Provincetown
(508) 487-3393
www.goodscents.com

This small store is filled with all you need to pamper yourself (or someone else)—lovely scented soaps, shampoos and lotions, along with bath brushes, luxurious robes, and massage oils. Choose from a variety of skin-care products, and have lotions, shampoos, and bath gels custom-scented with essential or perfume oils. Take them home, and you'll know why they call this shop Good Scents. The shop happily makes up gift baskets and does mail order, It's open daily in season, closes for the month of January, and has limited hours in the early spring.

> **i** *For an out-of-the-ordinary shopping treat, visit Marine Specialties at 235 Commercial Street in Provincetown. This small warehouse stocks a broad range of stuff, from Army-Navy surplus items, to camping and sailing supplies, to just plain strange odds and ends from closeout sales everywhere.*

Mad Hatter
360 Commercial Street, Provincetown
(508) 487-4063

Hats off to this ingenious store, a meld of whimsical and functional. Though Mad Hatter sells jackets, shirts, and scarves, people head here for the crowning touch. Choose from zany headgear, such as a multicolored beanie with a propeller, or more traditional, classic designs. You can also get custom-made hats here. The shop is open daily in season and weekends from the beginning of January through mid-March.

Northern Lights Hammocks
361 Commercial Street, Provincetown
(508) 487-2385
www.northernlightshammocks.com

Tootsies tired? Don't shop 'til you drop: Take a break by sampling one of the many hammocks here. The friendly staff will try to get you to sample the swinging, sway-ing set, whether it be one made of rope, cotton, wood, or canvas. (Your feet will thank you.) Some of the hammocks here are true works of art. One Mexican import features a polished wooden base that could harmonize with the decor of even the chicest home. The shop is open daily in season and weekends only off-season, and has a breezy deck location right on the beach.

Now Voyager
357 Commercial Street, Provincetown
(508) 487-0848
www.nowvoyagerbooks.com

Best known for its collection of gay and lesbian books, Now Voyager also has the latest in fiction and nonfiction and a large mystery section. It has a sampling of CDs, cassettes, and videos as well as used books. The shop closes for a winter break in the month of January.

Provincetown Bookshop
246 Commercial Street, Provincetown
(508) 487-0964

Open since 1964 this year-round shop is filled floor to ceiling with hardcover and paperback books, everything from poetry and plays to best sellers with a good selection of Cape Cod books. Enter through the sliding wood door, and you feel instantly at home. A great shop for browsing. It's open daily.

Small Pleasures
359 Commercial Street, Provincetown
(508) 487-3712

If you love antique jewelry, this is a must-see shop. The lovely glass-topped display cases are packed with vintage treasures. You'll find rubies, emeralds, diamonds, and moonstones in unique, original settings. The store also carries a selection of old silver spoons, tongs, and other small items. The pleasure will be yours. It's open May through October.

Tailwaggers
205 Commercial Street, Provincetown
(508) 487-6404
www.provincetown.com/tailwaggers
A full-service pet palace, Tailwaggers offers all sorts of unusual dog and kitty treats, food by the can or bag, leashes and collars, beds and brushes, combs, and other grooming aids. For pups that get chilly in winter, Tailwaggers offers an extensive line of winterwear. With such great toys for both felines and canines, the shop has been called a toyshop for pets. The wall behind the cash register is devoted to pictures of people with their satisfied pets. Tailwaggers is the only store in town to offer thirsty critters their own water dish. Open daily in season, Tailwaggers is closed Tuesday, Wednesday, and Thursday off-season.

ANTIQUES

There are those who come to the Cape not only for its lovely beaches but also for its proliferation of great antiques shops—and we don't blame them! Every town has more than a few places to browse among old things, with some dealers specializing in certain items such as pattern glass, early American furniture, or old tools, and others carrying a smattering of diverse items. A number of antiques cooperatives and centers have sprung up on the Cape, providing one-stop shopping for those who like variety.

Listing every antiques shop could easily fill a whole book, so we've focused on our favorites here. You're sure to find others as you travel the Cape, particularly on the north side, where historic Route 6A is an antique lover's paradise.

Many antiques stores are open year-round, though off-season hours vary greatly. And antique dealers being the independent souls they are, it's not uncommon to find that they've suddenly decided to take the morning off, even on a day you'd expect them to be open. So it's a good idea to call ahead before you venture out.

Upper Cape

The Old House
294 Head of the Bay Road, Buzzards Bay
(508) 759-4942
The Old House, built around 1724, is a wonderful antique itself. The shop has been in business for more than 60 years and carries vintage collectibles such as Early American pressed glass, blown glass, and china. The gift shop across the street specializes in new goods—linen calendars, Vermont country toys, and character mice. The two shops are open from April to the end of December, every day except Sunday.

Pocasset Exchange
710 County Road, Pocasset (Bourne)
(508) 563-2224
A longtime Bourne antiques shop set off Route 28 at the corner of County Road and Barlows Landing Road, the Pocasset Exchange carries antiques, vintage jewelry, collectible linens, and odd lots of glass and china, furniture, and household objects. The Exchange is open Thursday, Friday, and Saturday from April through November.

Horsefeathers Antiques
454 Route 6A, East Sandwich
(508) 888-5298
Owner Jeanne Gresham has created a distinctly Victorian and feminine feeling in this lovely shop, which carries table and bed linens, antique lace and trim, and a mix of everyday and special items such as china teacups and paper valentines.

Antique christening gowns and other children's clothing are usually available. The shop is usually open 10:00 A.M. to 5:00 P.M. daily year-round, but it's best to call first in the off-season, when hours vary.

The Weather Store
146 Main Street, Sandwich
(800) 646-1203
www.theweatherstore.com
New Englanders have a long history of trying to understand, predict, and maybe even outsmart the weather, which can be downright unpredictable in these parts. Testament to that history, this store is filled with antique weather instruments such as weather vanes, barometers, thermometers, books, and compasses, along with marine antiques such as spyglasses and 19th-century maps. The store is open Monday through Saturday from April through Christmas and by appointment other times.

Aurora Borealis Antiques
194 Lakeview Avenue, Falmouth
(508) 548-8280
Here you'll find a quality line of Staffordshire, Orientalia, prints, furniture, nautical pieces, lamps, silver, and glass, along with ephemera and books. The shop is open by appointment.

If you want to get the most out of your antiquing adventures, contact the Cape Cod Antiques Dealers Association for a listing of their members. Visit them on-line at www.ccada.com, or e-mail info@ccada.com.

The Village Barn
606 Route 28A, West Falmouth
(508) 540-3215
This lovely old barn, built around 1850, is home to eight dealers with an eclectic assortment of antiques on two floors, including some wonderful glass and china, furniture, and linens. One dealer specializes in Cape Cod souvenirs and old advertising. The Village Barn, located in an area home to several other antiques shops, is open year-round, 10:00 A.M. to 5:00 P.M. daily in season and generally weekends only from January to March, depending on the weather.

Mid-Cape

Sow's Ear Antique Company
4698 Route 28, Cotuit
(508) 428-4931
The Sow's Ear is in a 1729 house that is considered the oldest in Cotuit. A browser's delight, this period home is filled with 18th- and 19th-century furnishings and accessories. Here you might find unusual furniture, rugs, baskets, dolls, decoys, vases, silver, folk art, or other treasures. Blended among the antiques are some new items, such as candles and light fixtures. Located right next door to the Cahoon Museum of American Art, the shop is open year-round, Tuesday through Sunday, 10:00 A.M. to 5:00 P.M.

The Farmhouse
1340 Main Street, Osterville
(508) 420-2400
This lovely mid-18th-century building is full of a wide and ever-changing variety of antiques and collectibles from the early 1800s through the 1920s. There's lots of furniture, glass, silverware, artwork, and lamps. Furniture and accessories are arranged the way they would be in a house—one room is set up as a living room, another a dining room, and one as a bedroom, complete with shelves of fine, old linen tied up with ribbons. The shop is open daily 10:00 A.M. to 5:00 P.M. year-round.

Stanley Wheelock
870 Main Street, Osterville
(508) 420-3170
This established Osterville business is

known for its general line of American, English, and Continental furniture, decorative accessories, china, glass, and fine prints. It is open Monday through Saturday from April through December and by chance or appointment from January through March.

Maps of Antiquity
1022 Route 6A, West Barnstable
(508) 362-7169
www.mapsofantiquity.com

You could spend your whole day in this store looking through old maps. These are hand-printed maps from the skilled hands of a craftsman or artist. Maps of Antiquity mostly offers 19th-century maps but it also has some earlier ones, including those of Massachusetts townships and other New England states. European and world maps, railroad maps, coastal charts, and early U.S. maps are also part of the collection. If you can't find a specific map in their inventory, the store may be able to order it. The shop is open seven days a week, 10:00 A.M. to 5:00 P.M. Memorial Day weekend to early fall and then most weekends until the year ends.

West Barnstable Antiques
625 Route 6A, West Barnstable
(508) 362-2047

The ample inventory of furniture includes many desks, tables, and occasional pieces, particularly in primitive and Shaker styles. The shop's Chinese exports, artwork, painted pieces, and stoneware are also worth a look, and the shop has some sports memorabilia as well. It is open daily in season, and Friday through Monday from January through March.

Constance Goff Antiques
161 Route 6A, Yarmouthport
(508) 362-9540, (508) 362-5300 (winter)

A genteel air pervades this orderly shop, which features lovely 19th-century furniture and accessories including rugs and lamps along with jewelry, silver, and a large selection of English Flow Blue and White Ironstone. The shop, now in its 26th year, is open Monday through Saturday from mid-June to mid-September, Wednesday through Saturday in the spring and fall, and by chance or appointment.

Maritime Antiques
205 White Rock Road, Yarmouthport
(508) 362-1604
www.rcmaritimeantiques.com

This well-regarded shop specializes in nautical pieces and is a regular stop for collectors of maritime paraphernalia. You'll find scrimshaw, ship models, paintings, bells, flags, and Civil War memorabilia. It's open mostly by chance or appointment, so call ahead.

Antiques Center of Cape Cod
243 Route 6A, Dennis
(508) 385-6400
www.antiquecenterofcapecod.com

This huge center has almost 285 dealers selling everything from wooden iceboxes to old dolls. In addition to the main building, with 18,000 square feet on two floors (be sure to go upstairs, where some real treasures are displayed), there is now a consignment warehouse in back. Certainly the largest antiques center on the Cape, this place can be a bit overwhelming to the uninitiated, but odds are you won't leave empty-handed. Put on your walking shoes and check it out! It's open daily all year except January through March, when it's closed on Wednesday.

Red Lion Antiques
601 Route 6A, Dennis
(508) 385-4783

With 17 dealers crammed into two floors, the Red Lion can only be described as eclectic. One dealer specializes in antique clocks and repairs them as well. You'll also find assorted china, silver, and collectibles. It's open daily year-round, except January through March, when it's closed on Wednesday.

Lower Cape

Kingsland Manor
440 Route 6A, Brewster
(508) 385-9741
This place will take your breath away. Aptly named, Kingsland Manor is filled with an impressive and varied collection of antiques from Tiffany silver to Victorian furniture. The shop houses quite a lot of large furniture, including some unusual pieces, as well as smaller items. There's a collection of old canes with ivory and brass handles and a case full of military miniatures. A courtyard with a fountain leads to two outbuildings also filled with unusual and classic antiques. It's open year-round, seven days a week except Thanksgiving, Christmas Day, and New Year's Day.

The Spyglass
2257 Route 6A, Brewster
(508) 896-4423
This fascinating shop specializes in 18th- and 19th-century marine antiques. You'll find barometers, globes, sextants, writing boxes, maps, and navigation charts, as well as early American furniture and folk art. Open daily. Call ahead during the winter months.

The Barn at Windsong
245 Bank Street, Harwich
(508) 432-8281
This lovely old barn houses the wares of seven dealers, making it a browser's delight. You'll find linens, lace, children's prints, collectibles, silver, Staffordshire, and primitives, among other items. The shop is open daily, May through October.

Harwich Antiques Center
10 Route 28, West Harwich
(580) 432-4220
This two-building complex has some 157 dealers displaying furniture, paintings, decoys, antique tools, cranberry memorabilia, silver, and cut glass. There's a large assortment of majolica, along with porcelain, dinnerware, linen, and quilts. Located across the street from Friendly's close to the Dennis town line, the center is open daily all year, with evening hours in summer.

Chatham Antiques
1409 Route 28, South Chatham
(508) 945-1660
Here's a wonderful selection of antiques displayed in an antique setting! It's an authentic old Cape farmhouse (ca. 1674) filled with early American Furniture, clocks, paintings, china, pewter, silver, and glass. This friendly shop, in business 20 years, is open May through October on weekends and by appointment in the off-season months.

House on the Hill
17 Seaview Street, Chatham
(508) 945-2290
You'll find a delightful collection of baseball cards and sports memorabilia, political pins, toys, old advertisements, postcards, and Cape Cod memorabilia here, along with glass, china, and small furniture. The shop keeps extended hours in summer, usually until dusk, and is open by chance or appointment the rest of the year.

Countryside Antiques
6 Lewis Road, East Orleans
(508) 240-0525
Tucked away off Main Street on the way to Nauset Beach (look for Lewis Road on the right after Fancy's Farm Stand), this shop is filled with beautiful imported furniture, both antique and reproduction, as well as some wonderful accessory accents. Owners Richard and Deborah Rita travel abroad several times a year to find the best English, Irish, and Scandinavian antique and reproduction furniture to fill their shop and the annex in the barn behind the main store. Countryside is open May through early December and by chance or appointment after that.

Pleasant Bay Antiques
540 Route 28, South Orleans
(508) 255-0930
www.pleasantbayantiques.com
This shop, housed in a 200-year-old barn and a portion of the attached house, is filled with some of the loveliest early American furniture you'll find anywhere, including tables, highboys, desks, and four-poster beds. You're likely to find grandfather clocks, elegant secretary desks, and dining tables. Don't miss the decoy room, and be sure to go up in the loft, which is filled with antique chairs. The shop is open year-round.

Farmhouse Antiques
U.S. Route 6 and Village Lane, South Wellfleet
(508) 349-1708
What a fun shop to wander through! This old farmhouse is jammed with Orientalia, vintage linen, decorative pieces, and more ephemera—postcards, trading cards, advertising ads, and magazines—than you'll know what to do with. You can also find restored antique lamps, lighting fixtures, and original pieces by local artist Diane Vetromile, who has been known to cover an entire table with buttons to fabulous effect. Truly an experience for adventurous treasure-hunters, the shop is open daily year-round.

West End Antiques
146 Commercial Street, Provincetown
(508) 487-6723
Launched in 1994 this well-regarded old shop offers a great collection of old Provincetown souvenirs, advertising, and memorabilia, children's collectibles, clocks, and lots of lovely glass, particularly Depression glass. It also has china and art pottery, especially Roseville. Open daily in summer, except for Sunday. It is open weekends in spring and late fall and closed January to March.

ATTRACTIONS

In this chapter we cover those destinations that reveal the Cape's rich history, natural beauty, and unique charm. These are historic landmarks, museums, and attractions dedicated to promoting an awareness and enjoyment of Cape Cod.

Don't worry, we're not talking tourist traps. Thankfully there aren't many of those around Cape Cod. Sure, some of these attractions are very popular—the museums, in particular, are sure to be busy on a rainy summer's day. Still many of these attractions and museums are off the beaten track and well worth discovering.

From Aptucxet Trading Post along the Cape Cod Canal to Pilgrim Monument in the heart of Provincetown, interesting, fun, educational, and inspiring places beckon. So visit some of these attractions, such as the Cape Cod Museum of Natural History in Brewster, where you can immerse yourself in a wave tank, or get up close and personal with a lighthouse on Monomoy Island. And in Provincetown you can see treasures of the world's only pirate shipwreck at the Expedition Whydah Sea Lab and Learning Center on MacMillan Pier.

There are hundreds of organizations across Cape Cod that offer the visitor a glimpse into the past or provide a better understanding of the Cape's heritage. Among them are historic homes, sea captain's mansions, and historical buildings, including windmills, churches, meetinghouses, and homesteads. Some are open during certain times of the year, whereas others are year-round sites. In any season, though, you're sure to have a wide choice of activities that invite you to connect with our rich past. In fact Cape Cod has turned into a year-round classroom, designed to enlighten participants of all ages about our remarkable peninsula.

Following is a list of Cape Cod's many attractions, including a walk through the pages of the Cape's history as provided by the many museums and historic sites scattered about the old carriage routes of the Cape's 15 proud towns. But don't forget to turn to other chapters—Kidstuff, Sports and Recreation, Beaches, and Boating and Water Sports, to name a few—for other interesting stops along the way.

UPPER CAPE

Aptucxet Trading Post
24 Aptucxet Road, Bourne
(508) 759-9487
www.bournehistoricalsoc.org

Aptucxet (pronounced Ap-tuc-set) is the site of a Pilgrim trading post, the first of its kind in the New World. Situated on the banks of what is now the Cape Cod Canal, this replica trading post (built in 1930) has interesting displays that include a collection of prehistoric tools from the Wampanoag tribe and a rune stone supposedly chiseled by Vikings. Also on the grounds is a Victorian railroad station built by the Old Colony Railroad in 1892 for President Grover Cleveland (President Cleveland had a summer place in Bourne) and a Dutch-style Jefferson windmill shipped here from the Netherlands and once owned by 19th-century actor and Bourne resident Joseph Jefferson. The trading post also features a recently renovated saltworks. The Aptucxet Trading Post is open Tuesday through Saturday 10:00 A.M. to 4:00 P.M., Sunday 2:00 to 5:00 P.M. from May through Columbus Day; in July and August the hours are the same, and it's open daily including holidays. Groups of 10 or more can arrange special tours. Admission is $3.50 for adults, $2.00 for senior citizens, and $2.50 for children ages 6 to 18.

Bourne Historical Center/Bourne Historical Society
30 Keene Street, Bourne
(508) 759-8167
www.bournehistoricalsoc.org

This is a late 19th-century colonial Revival building of architectural significance, designed as a library by noted architect Henry Vaughn (1845–1917). There is an exhibition gallery with changing exhibits relating to the history of Bourne, including paintings, photographs, furniture, and other artifacts. The building also houses the Bourne Archives, which makes Bourne one of the few towns on the Cape with its own archive building. The house is open Monday and Tuesday from 9:00 A.M. to 3:00 P.M. and by appointment, and there is no admission fee.

Briggs-McDermott House and Blacksmith Shop
22 Sandwich Road, Bourne
(508) 759-6120

This Greek Revival-style house, furnished with 1830–1910 period furniture, is maintained by the Bourne Society for Historic Preservation. On the National Registry of Historic Places, the house is located across from the Bourne Public Library and is significant because it features a dazzling Charles Raleigh–painted ceiling, as well as some of his paintings. An adjoining blacksmith shop—a restored shop with working forge, artifacts, tools, and wagons—is said to be where President Grover Cleveland had his horses shod. The house and working blacksmith shop are open for tours from June 15 through Labor Day weekend on Tuesday from 1:00 to 4:00 P.M.

Benjamin Nye Homestead
85 Old County Road, East Sandwich
(508) 888-4213
www.nyefamily.org

The Benjamin Nye Homestead offers yet another peek into the lives of the Pilgrims

Rhododendrons, known for their large flowers and splendid colors, are considered native to Cape Cod. The name Rhododendron comes from the Greek rhodo *meaning "rose" and* dendron *meaning "tree." Rhododendrons bloom the last week in May and the first few weeks in June. They may be seen throughout the Cape, but especially at the Heritage Museums & Gardens in Sandwich, where Charles O. Dexter used between 5,000 and 10,000 seedlings to produce new varieties of rhododendrons known as Dexter Rhododendrons.*

and the many generations that settled on the Cape after them. The house dates back to at least 1685, but many believe the structure first went up in the 1670s. One certainty is that the home was much smaller than it is today. The original structure was expanded into a saltbox-style house and then enlarged into a colonial dwelling. It was a private residence until 1958 and has been operated as a museum since 1972. Furnishings and displays in the rooms reflect different periods of its history, and parts of the upstairs are left exposed to show the house's original construction. On occasion the museum offers special demonstrations of hearthside cooking, spinning, and candle making. To this day the Nye Family Association, which runs the museum, makes new discoveries in the house, uncovering old floors and locating other original items that have been tucked away over the centuries. The museum is open from mid-June through mid-October, and an admission fee of $3.00 is charged for adults and $1.00 for children.

Dexter Grist Mill
Town Hall Square, Town Hall, Sandwich
(508) 888-4910

A working 17th-century gristmill with primitive wooden gears, the Dexter Grist Mill features a 54-inch French Buhr millstone. For the first 15 years after the incorporation of Sandwich, the residents of this first Cape Cod town had to travel to Plymouth to have their corn ground. Thomas Dexter of Sandwich remedied that situation by building a mill on this site in 1654 to the delight of all residents. A stream running through the village was dammed to create a picturesque pond and herring run, which give migrating herring a pathway from Cape Cod Bay to Shawme Pond. Dexter Mill offers a tour complete with fresh ground corn and is open daily 10:00 A.M. to 4:00 P.M. in the summer, with limited hours in September and October. After Columbus Day the mill closes until June 15. Admission is $1.50 for adults and 75 cents for children. You can also combine a trip to the mill with a visit to the Hoxie House (see below) for $4.00 for adults and $2.00 for children.

Heritage Museums & Gardens
Grove and Pine Streets, Sandwich
(508) 888-3300
www.heritagemuseumsandgardens.org
This immaculately maintained museum complex has 76 acres of grounds with outdoor gardens, paths, sprawling lawns, and the renowned Dexter collection of rhododendrons. An antique car collection, a military museum with antique guns and flags, and a folk art museum with permanent and special collections delight visitors from around the world, as does a ride on a colorful restored 1912 carousel. The grounds also feature the Old East Windmill, which was built at Orleans in 1800 and moved to Heritage Plantation in 1968. The complex has a gift shop and cafe and hosts numerous special events and outdoor concerts. A shuttle bus with a wheelchair lift provides transportation around the grounds. The museum is open 9:00 A.M. to 6:00 P.M. daily, Thursday until 8:00 P.M., from mid-May through mid-October. The admission fee is $12.00 for adults, $10.00 for senior citizens (60-plus), $6.00 for children ages 6 to 16, and free for children 5 and younger.

Hoxie House
Route 130, Sandwich
(508) 888-1173
The Hoxie House is Cape Cod's oldest saltbox-style house and is a classic historic home, built around 1675 for the Reverend John Smith, his wife, Susanna, and their 13 children. It is named for Abraham Hoxie, a Sandwich whaling captain who bought it in the 1850s. Remarkably its occupants lived without electricity, plumbing, or central heat until the early 1950s. In the late 1950s the town purchased the Hoxie House, restored it to its original condition, and added period furnishings. The museum is open daily from June through mid-October from 10:00 A.M. to 5:00 P.M. There is an admission fee of $2.50 for adults and $1.50 for children. You can also purchase combined admission for the Hoxie House and the Dexter Grist Mill (see above) for $4.00 for adults and $2.00 for children.

Sandwich Fish Hatchery
Route 6A, Sandwich
(508) 888-0008
More than a quarter of a million fish, primarily trout, are raised here to stock the state's various ponds. You can track the stages of fish development and even feed them. Admission is free. The hatchery is open year-round from 9:00 A.M. to 3:00 P.M. daily (see our Kidstuff chapter).

Sandwich Glass Museum
129 Main Street at Tupper Road, Sandwich
(508) 888-0251
www.sandwichglassmuseum.org
In 1825 Deming Jarves arrived in Sandwich to open the Boston and Sandwich Glass Company. Over the next 60 years this company provided many Sandwich residents with jobs and brought much prosperity to the town. Displays of exquisite antique glass at the Sandwich Glass Museum will delight both professional collectors and casual visitors. This museum contains one of the largest collections of blown, pressed, cut, and engraved Sandwich glass in the

United States. It provides a wonderful picture of the glass-making industry and the town during its heyday through artifacts, equipment, old photographs, and records. The museum has a gift shop and offers excellent lectures and exhibits throughout the year. It is open April through December from 9:30 A.M. to 5:00 P.M. daily; February through March it's open from Wednesday through Sunday 9:30 A.M. to 4:00 P.M. Adults enter for $3.50 and children 6 to 16 years of age for $1.00. It closes for the month of January. Groups of 10 or more are eligible for a group discount price of $2.50 per adult—call for details.

Thornton Burgess Museum
4 Water Street (Route 130), Sandwich
(508) 888-6870
www.thorntonburgess.org

The Thornton W. Burgess Museum is located on beautiful Shawmee Pond in the historic center of Cape Cod's oldest town. Thornton W. Burgess, born in Sandwich in 1874 and renowned author of some 170 books, penned the popular children's series *Old Mother West Wind,* as well as *The Adventures of Peter Cottontail.* Although it is geared toward children (see our Kidstuff chapter), the museum's collection of Burgess books, photographs, and memorabilia should also be fascinating to adults. If you are looking for something sure to please the middle school-age children, Thornton W. Burgess also offers an activities-packed summer program for kids (also see our Kidstuff chapter). The museum has a gift store and offers many special activities, including its Victorian Christmas Celebration in December. The museum is open daily from April through October Monday through Saturday, 10:00 A.M. to 4:00 P.M., Sunday 1:00 to 4:00 P.M. and weekends in December. Both the museum and the Green Briar Nature Center & Jam Kitchen are run by the Thornton W. Burgess Society, a nonprofit organization founded in 1976 "to inspire reverence for wildlife and concern for the natural environment." The society requests a donation for admission to the museum.

Bourne Farm
Route 28A and Thomas Flanders Road, West Falmouth
(508) 548-8484

This 1775 farm is a former working farm that has been beautifully restored so that you can enjoy and learn about the early days of farming in Falmouth. Call to make an appointment for a tour. They offer seasonal guided walks, special nature programs, and an annual Pumpkin Day Festival the Saturday of Columbus Day weekend (see our Annual Events chapter).

Falmouth Historical Society
55 Palmer Avenue, Falmouth
(508) 548-4857
www.falmouthhistoricalsociety.org

The Historical Society maintains and operates the Julia Wood House and the Conant House at this site, the latter offering a display of memorabilia of Katharine Lee Bates who penned the poem "America the Beautiful." You will also find antique glass, silver, china, Revolutionary War exhibits, and whaling memorabilia. The Julia Wood House is a Georgian-style building that is furnished as a house museum. Built by a doctor, one of its rooms is furnished as a doctor's office. The Conant House features displays on Falmouth's coastal trading and whaling eras, and a barn houses other exhibits. Both houses are on the National Register of Historic Places and are open mid-June to mid-September Monday through Thursday from 10:00 A.M. to 4:00 P.M. and Sunday from 1:00 to 4:00 P.M. The Historical Society also offers guided walking tours in the summer. Admission to the two museum houses is $3.00 for adults and $1.50 for children.

During his lifetime Paul Revere made only 37 church bells. The First Congregational Church on Main Street in Falmouth boasts one, cast in 1796, by the famous patriot.

Marine Biological Laboratory
Water Street, Woods Hole
(508) 289-7623
www.mbl.edu

A one-hour tour includes a video followed by a guided side trip to view wonders of the sea. You can also take a walking tour of the campus. Free tours are held Monday through Friday from late June through August. Children younger than 5 are not admitted. Reservations are required one week in advance of your visit because tours are limited to 15 people. The tours are free and are scheduled for 1:00, 2:00, and 3:00 P.M.

Woods Hole Historical Museum
573 Woods Hole Road, Woods Hole
(508) 548-7270

This museum is actually a complex of three buildings, the main one being the William Bradley House, the third-oldest house in the village of Woods Hole. It was owned by 19th-century ship captain William Bradley, who was lost at sea. The structure houses the Woods Hole Historical Collection of paintings, portraits, photographs, and records. Because the exhibits change annually, it's an interesting visit even if you have been there before. The two other buildings, moved to the grounds in 1996, are a boat barn and an 1890s workshop that at one time belonged to a doctor who puttered with various hobbies, including etching and fly-tying. Late June through September the houses are open Tuesday through Saturday from 10:00 A.M. to 4:00 P.M.; closed January through mid-June. Admission is free, though donations are gratefully accepted.

Woods Hole Oceanographic Institute's Exhibit Center
15 School Street, Woods Hole
(508) 289-2663, (508) 289-2252
www.whoi.edu

Ever wonder how they discovered the wreck of the *Titanic*? This is the place to learn about that and other oceanographic feats. See videos of deep submersible *Alvin*, explore interactive exhibits about whale and dolphin research, and watch colorful footage of the life that lives along deep-sea hydrothermal vents. The exhibit center is open April through December, daily Memorial Day through Labor Day. A $2.00 donation for those 10 and older is requested. You can also take a guided tour of the WHOI dock area and other research facilities. These tours leave from the WHOI Information Office at 93 School Street Monday through Friday at 10:30 A.M. and 1:30 P.M., and last about 90 minutes. Call to reserve a spot because space is limited.

Cape Cod Children's Museum
577 Great Neck Road South, Mashpee
(508) 539-8788
www.capecodchildrensmuseum.pair.com

Here families can have fun together while discovering new things about the world around us. Exhibits, workshops, and special events stimulate curiosity and spark the desire to learn. The museum offers daily programs, a planetarium, and science exhibits. It's the perfect rainy-day activity. Open year-round, the summer hours are 10:00 A.M. to 5:00 P.M. Monday through Saturday, and noon to 5:00 P.M. on Sunday. Admission is $5.00 for those ages 5 through 59 and $4.00 for children ages 1 to 4 and seniors 60 years and older (see our Kidstuff chapter).

Indian Meetinghouse and Burial Ground
Route 28 and Meeting House Road, Mashpee
(508) 477-1536

Dating back to 1684 this structure is the oldest church building on Cape Cod. It was built by a Native American congrega-

---

[Facing page] *In Woods Hole, Nobska Point Light stands tall over Vineyard Sound.*

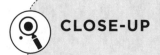

Cape Cod Lighthouses

Extending more than 50 miles into the Atlantic Ocean, Cape Cod has always been difficult to navigate because of its rugged coastline, dangerous sand bars and rip tides, and few safe harbors to enter in a storm. Over the past 300 years, there have been more than 3,000 shipwrecks on the Cape, mainly along the treacherous outer shore between Provincetown and Chatham.

Cape Cod has had more than 20 lighthouses operating along its shores during the past 200 years. Before the days of the Cape Cod Canal, during the 19th-century heyday of busy shipping between Boston and New York, lighthouses were essential to protect ships from dangerous shoals. Lighthouse keepers were needed to tend the kerosene lamps, and the brave men of the U.S. Lifesaving Service manned lifeboats in an attempt to save lives when ships foundered in storms off the Cape Cod coast, often called the Graveyard of the Atlantic. Today seven lighthouses still operate, and several decommissioned lights still stand along the coastline.

Nobska Point Light, Woods Hole

Nobska Point Light Station is extremely picturesque and may appear familiar because it is frequently photographed. It towers over the waters of Vineyard Sound and serves as a beacon for Woods Hole Harbor and as a guide for mariners traveling between the Cape Cod mainland and Martha's Vineyard Island. The light is easily accessible, and the view from the grounds looking across Vineyard Sound to Martha's Vineyard is breathtaking. To get to Nobska

Point Light from Falmouth, turn left at the intersection of Route 28 and Woods Hole Road, and follow Woods Hole Road about 3 miles to Church Street. Turn left, and Nobska Lighthouse will appear about 1½ miles on the left. Limited parking is available opposite the light.

Stage Harbor Light, Chatham

This light used to serve as a beacon for Chatham's "Old Harbor," or Stage Harbor. In 1933 the original tower was disconnected and sold to the government. It remains as private property today and is occasionally opened during specially scheduled events. It provides a great backdrop upon entering and leaving Stage Harbor on a seal cruise. Stage Harbor Light is inaccessible by road. Off Route 28 in Chatham, turn right at Barn Hill Road, and continue one-half mile to Harding Beach Road. Turn right, and continue to Harding Beach parking lot. You'll walk more than 1 mile along the beach to the light. Or you can view it from the end of Champlain Road in Chatham.

Chatham Light, Chatham

Today Chatham Light is also Chatham Coast Guard Station, a very important lifeboat station along this dangerous shore. There is ample parking at this site for a magnificent view of the Atlantic Ocean and the North Beach break, known as Chatham Spit. Coin-operated telescopes along the bluff give you an enhanced view of the barrier beach beyond the entrance to the little harbor. The beach is easily accessible by stairs leading down from the parking lot. Look carefully, and you might see seals sunning themselves on the beach any time of year. To get to Chatham Light, drive east on Main Street, Chatham, to the junction with Shore Road. Turn right, and drive half a mile. Lighthouse parking is opposite overlook parking area.

Monomoy Light, Chatham

Monomoy Point Light is at the southern tip of Monomoy Island some 8 miles from the mainland. The Cape Cod Museum of Natural History is the only organization that can give you permission to enter the lighthouse and enjoy the expansive view of the entire island from atop the lighthouse tower. You can stay overnight with a naturalist in the keeper's quarters for an unforgettable wilderness experience by calling the Cape Cod Museum of Natural History (508–896–3867); the cost is $180 per person. Reservations are required on a first-come first-served basis, and the museum runs two or three overnight excursions per month May through September. The island is only accessible by boat. The light itself is at the south end of the 5-mile-long island.

Nauset Light, Eastham

Nauset Beach Light was, until recently, located atop a bluff overlooking the Atlantic Ocean. Thanks to the efforts of friends of the lighthouse and the funds they raised, the light tower and keeper's home (which is privately owned) was moved just west of its former site on property of the Cape Cod National Seashore to protect it from encroaching beach erosion. This working lighthouse is visible 15½ miles out to sea. It's not tough at all to get to Nauset Light. Take U.S. Route 6 through Eastham, and at the traffic lights at Cape Cod National

Seashore Visitor Center, turn right onto Nauset Road. Follow Nauset Road, and it will merge with Doane Road; follow Doane to the intersection with Ocean View Drive. Bear left onto Ocean View Drive; 1 mile down the road is Nauset Light Beach parking lot.

Three Sisters Lighthouses, Eastham

Nauset Beach Light Station was first established in 1839 with the construction of three small brick towers. Because of the three separate structures, the light station has always been known as the "Three Sisters of Nauset." The Three Sisters have been moved back about a half-mile from the shore and are arranged in an attractive parklike setting, standing as a monument to all lighthouses still in existence. Directions: Same directions as to Nauset Light. Park in the beach parking lot and walk inland a quarter of a mile along a paved trail parallel to Cable Road. You'll find the Three Sisters at the end of the trail.

Highland Light, Truro

Also known as Cape Cod Light, this is the Cape's first lighthouse, built in 1797 at the request of George Washington. The light was rebuilt in 1857, and this is the 66-foot tower that you see today. This lighthouse's other claim to fame is that it was moved away from the eroding high dune cliffs during 1996 and part of 1997 to save it from falling into the ocean. One of the most important lights on the East Coast for mariners, it is also a favorite destination for photographers and travelers. The current beacon, with more than 620,000 candlepower, is the most powerful light in New England and shines about 20 miles to sea. You can get to Cape Cod Light from U.S. Route 6 in North Truro. Turn

onto Highland Road, which is more than 3 miles north of Truro Center. At the end of Highland Road, turn right onto Lighthouse Road, and you'll see the parking lot.

Race Point Lighthouse, Provincetown
Built in 1876, this lighthouse was manned by a lightkeeper until 1972, when the light station was automated and the last keeper vacated the house. After the light station was automated (it now runs on solar power), the lightkeeper's house fell into disrepair. In recent years the New England Lighthouse Foundation has com-

pleted a splendid renovation of the house, which is now used as a retreat for scientists and artists. It is not easily accessible; you can only reach it by four-wheel-drive vehicle or on foot, if you want to enjoy a ramble along the outermost shoreline. It takes some extra effort to get to the Race Point Light. From U.S. Route 6, turn right at the traffic lights onto Race Point Road, follow it to the end, and park in the parking lot at Race Point Coast Guard Station. Heading west, you must walk along the beach for about 2 miles.

tion of "Praying Indians" in Santuit and the wood for it was hauled by ox cart from Plymouth. It was moved to the present location in 1717 and the ancient cemetery surrounding it has a number of old headstones. The church is open in the summer for worship and memorial services. Otherwise it is only open by appointment. Call the above number to make an appointment and to determine any fees.

Indian Museum
Route 130, Mashpee
(508) 477-1536

This building was erected by descendants of Richard Bourne, the 17th-century minister and missionary who undertook the cause of the Native Mashpee Indians. The recently renovated museum contains local artifacts and a diorama depicting Wampanoag home life. Guides are all Wampanoag Indians, and the tribe runs the museum. Next to it is a herring run that helps migratory saltwater herring make their way up the Mashpee River to Mashpee Lake. The museum is open year-round, Monday through Friday, 10:00 A.M. to 2:00 P.M. and Saturday by appointment. Admission is free, although donations are accepted.

MID-CAPE

Cahoon Museum of American Art
4676 Route 28, Cotuit
(508) 428-7581
www.cahoonmuseum.org

Located in a 1775 Georgian colonial farmhouse, the Cahoon Museum is best known for its collection of fanciful primitive paintings by the late Ralph and Martha Cahoon. The building—worth a visit in itself with its wide-planked floors, narrow doorways, and ship captain's staircase—was actually the Cahoon's home and studio for 37 years. In addition to the Cahoon paintings, the permanent collection features 19th- and 20th-century American art. The museum also offers special exhibitions, gallery talks, classes, and a gift shop. It is open Tuesday through Saturday year-round, except January, when it closes for a month. Admission is $3.00; children younger than age 12 are free.

Osterville Historical Society
Parker and West Bay Roads, Osterville
(508) 428-5861
www.osterville.org

The Osterville Historical Society operates

a colorful museum within the Jonathan Parker House, which was built as a half-house in 1824. The exceptional displays include a large painting of George Washington at Valley Forge by Jean Baptiste Adolphe Gilbert, a Victorian Room, and a children's room that contains dolls, toys, and two beautiful doll houses, one made in 1870. The Osterville Room contains maps and other archival material about the village. Displays of Sandwich glass, period furniture, Early American pottery, pewter, and historical documents are also popular with visitors. Behind the Jonathan Parker House rests a boathouse containing historic Crosby catboats and Wianno Seniors and Juniors—all these styles of boats were designed in Osterville. Also on the grounds is the mid-18th-century Cammett House, which is the second-oldest house in Osterville and provides a look at early architecture, including a root cellar and beehive oven. From June through September the Historical Society museum is open from Thursday through Sunday, 1:30 to 4:30 P.M.

Centerville Historical Society
513 Main Street, Centerville
(508) 775-0331
Founded in 1952 this society maintains the Mary Lincoln House with late Victorian displays, including a child's room, a doll and quilt room, and a colonial kitchen. Also on view are the personal collections of Charles Ayling, including Sandwich glass, military collections, Dodge MacKnight paintings, Elmer Crowell bird carvings, and furniture. Other displays include marine artifacts, including tools, excerpts from ships' logs, and the wheel from the steamer *Portland,* which was lost on November 27, 1898, in a gale subsequently called the Portland Gale after the steamer. The Centerville museum is noted for its fine collection of period clothing, including shoes, jewelry, and accessories. The house is open from 1:30 to 4:30 P.M., Wednesday through Saturday, mid-June through mid-September. Admission is $2.50 for adults, $2.00 for seniors, $1.00

for children ages 6 to 17, and free for children younger than 6.

John F. Kennedy Hyannis Museum
397 Main Street, Hyannis
(580) 790-3077
www.hyannis.com
The John F. Kennedy Hyannis Museum is a multimedia exhibit designed to open a window on the days that JFK, a Hyannis-port summer resident, spent on Cape Cod. Opened in 1992 the JFK museum features an 80-photo collection that spans his life, a video narrated by Walter Cronkite containing vintage footage, and an oral history. The museum is near the John F. Kennedy Memorial (see the listing below), the Kennedy Compound in Hyannisport, and St. Francis Xavier Church, where the Kennedy family has worshiped since the 1930s. The museum is open daily mid-April through October from 9:00 A.M. to 5:00 P.M., except on holidays and Sunday when they open at noon. November through early December and mid-February through mid-April the museum is open Thursday through Sunday only, 10:00 A.M. to 4:00 P.M., except Sunday and holidays, when they open at noon. Admission is $5.00 for adults and $2.50 for seniors and those ages 10 to 16; children younger than 10 are admitted free.

John F. Kennedy Memorial
Ocean Street, Hyannis
(508) 790-6320
This monument to our fallen president and fellow Cape resident was opened in 1966. Situated along a quiet section of Ocean Street in Hyannis, it looks out over Lewis Bay. This touching memorial is a stone monument adorned with Kennedy's image and a fountain where visitors can remember our 35th president. It is open year-round, and the fountain gladly accepts your pennies and your best wishes.

Barnstable Court House
Route 6A, Barnstable
(508) 362-2511
www.barnstablecounty.org

This granite building, constructed in 1832, has two cannons on the front lawn that were hauled to Barnstable by oxen to defend the town's saltworks during the War of 1812. Also on the front lawn is a life-size statue of James Otis Jr., who was known as "the Patriot" because of his speeches that rallied people to the Patriot cause before the American Revolution. Otis, who was a good friend of President John Adams, delivered a number of speeches in Boston and elsewhere that helped to move the colonies closer toward revolution. A fiery individual, he was once severely injured in a brawl, and in 1783 a bolt of lightning killed him. Six buildings compose the governmental complex of Barnstable County (including the House of Correction), which has been the seat of the county court since 1685.

The Olde Colonial Courthouse
Rendezvous Lane at Route 6A, Barnstable
(508) 362-8927
Built in 1772, this courthouse is where the seeds of independence were planted. At this site on September 27, 1774, more than 1,500 people disrupted a court session to protest a British ruling determining how jurors were to be selected. The protest ended peacefully. The building also served as a Baptist church for more than a hundred years. Today the building is the home of Tales of Cape Cod, an organization dedicated to the preservation of local history. There are no set hours; in fact the building is only open for special events or by appointment by calling the number listed above. Admission is free.

Sturgis Library
3090 Route 6A, Barnstable
(508) 362-6636
Along historic Route 6A in Barnstable Village, you can find what is believed to be the oldest library building (ca. 1644) in the country. The library has a number of spe-

cial collections documenting the rich history of Cape Cod and the islands, including the Henry Crocker Kittredge Maritime Collection, the Lothrop Genealogy and Local History Collection, the Cape Cod Collection, and the Sturgis Library Archives. A trained genealogist and research librarian can assist you in using the resources in the collection. The library is open year-round; hours are Monday, Wednesday, and Friday 10:00 A.M. to 5:00 P.M.; Tuesday 1:00 to 8:00 P.M.; Thursday 1:00 to 5:00 P.M.; Saturday 10:00 A.M. to 4:00 P.M. It is closed Sunday.

West Parish Meetinghouse
2049 Meetinghouse Way (Route 149),
West Barnstable
(508) 362-4445
When the first Congregationalists arrived to the settlement of Barnstable in 1646, they set to work on building a meetinghouse on Cobb Hill at Barnstable Village. Though this original building no longer exists, the West Parish Meetinghouse, built in 1717, attests to a flourishing congregation that divided itself into east and west parishes. The East Parish Meetinghouse is long gone, but the West Parish building stands today as a proud reminder of those early years. Paul Revere cast the bell, and the 1723 gilded cock weather vane earned the church its nickname the "Rooster Church." They believe it is the oldest Congregational church meetinghouse still in use today.

Iyanough's Grave
Off Route 6A, Cummaquid
no phone
Monuments to the American Indian Sachem Iyanough appear all around Barnstable. The village of Hyannis and the section of the village of Osterville known as Wianno are both derivations of his

---

[Facing page] *Exhibits at the JFK Hyannis Museum focus on the Cape years of President Kennedy.* HYANNIS AREA CHAMBER OF COMMERCE

name. The village green in Hyannis features a statue of the chief. Another monument to Iyanough is his gravesite, just north of Route 6A in the village of Cummaquid. In 1621, when he was in his mid-twenties, the chief died of exposure after being chased into a swamp by Pilgrim Myles Standish, who at the time believed Indians were endangering settlers. Iyanough, however, has displayed only good relations with the settlers. In the mid-19th-century, a farmer plowing his field discovered Sachem's grave. A sign along Route 6A marks the spot.

Captain Bangs Hallet House
Strawberry Lane (off Route 6A),
Yarmouthport
(508) 362-3021
www.hsoy.org

Owned and operated by the Historic Society of Old Yarmouth, the oldest section of the Captain Bangs Hallet House was built in 1740. The main section was then added in 1840. The site is named for Capt. Bangs Hallet, who lived here after retiring from the China trade and acquiring the house from Captain Allen H. Knowles in 1863. Tours of the building take place Thursday through Sunday at 1:00, 2:00, and 3:00 P.M. from June through mid-October. Call ahead to arrange group tours. Admission is $3.50 for adults and 50 cents for children.

The Edward Gorey House
8 Strawberry Lane, off Route 6A,
Yarmouthport
(508) 362-3909
www.edwardgoreyhouse.org

Edward Gorey, a prolific and distinctive artist, illustrator, and author, lived out the last years of his life here, in what he called the "Elephant House" (because the gray shingles resembled elephant hide?). It is now a small museum dedicated to preserving his work and introducing it to fresh eyes. Best known for his animated opening credits to the PBS series *Mystery* and for dark curios like *The Gashlycrumb*

Tinies, this is a great place to learn about his life and interests. You'll see countless drawings, adolescent diaries—even his favorite yellow sweater. You'll also learn about his work in the Cape theater community, and at least one room will be a hit with the little ones: Gorey was an ardent advocate of animal welfare, so one room is devoted to animals and suitable for kindergartners. Open Wednesday through Sunday. Admission is $5.00 for adults, $3.00 for students and seniors, $2.00 for ages 6 to 12, under age 6 free.

Winslow Crocker House
250 Route 6A, Yarmouthport
(508) 362-4385
www.hsoy.org

A Georgian design, this house was built in 1780 at West Barnstable and moved to Yarmouthport. It has elaborate paneling, a large central chimney, a bowed roof, and a fine collection of decorative arts from the 1600s to 1800s. Owned and operated by the Society for the Preservation of New England Antiquities, the newly restored Winslow Crocker House is open Saturday and Sunday from June through mid-October. Hourly tours begin at 11:00 A.M. with the last tour beginning at 4:00 P.M. Admission is $4.00.

Judah Baker Windmill
River Street, South Yarmouth
(508) 382-2231, ext. 237
www.hsoy.org

Resting along the banks of the Bass River at the end of Willow Street on River Street is the Judah Baker Windmill, built in 1791. It wasn't always located in South Yarmouth. It was once a Dennis windmill built near Grand Cove. After changing hands a few times during the course of the 19th century, it eventually landed in the hand of Capt. Braddock Matthews, who moved the windmill to its current South Yarmouth location in 1863 and named it for the man who built it, Judah Baker. It remained in operation until 1891.

This small Yarmouthport home is where noted illustrator Edward Gorey spent his Cape years. It is now a museum devoted to his work and interests. ERICA BOLLERUD

ZooQuarium
674 Route 28, West Yarmouth
(508) 775-8883
www.zooquariumcapecod.net
This must be the wildest place on the Cape! Half zoo, half aquarium, the ZooQuarium has displays and exhibits of all things native to our area. The featured attraction: sea lion and seal shows presented daily in the summer at 11:00 A.M. and 1:00, 3:00, and 5:00 P.M. But there's so much more. One large room houses tanks of local pond and sea-life exhibits. Outside there is a petting zoo with llamas and sheep. The ZooQuarium is open daily from mid-February to late November. Admission is $9.00 for visitors ages 10 and older and $6.00 for children ages 2 to 9 (see our Kidstuff chapter for more information).

Cape Museum of Fine Arts
Route 6A, Dennis
(508) 385-4477
www.cmfa.org
The Cape Cod Museum of Fine Arts is home to a growing public collection of paintings, sculpture, and works on paper by a wide variety of artists associated with Cape Cod—from serene maritime paintings, to work produced at the artists' colony of Provincetown in the early 20th century, to contemporary art. The collection features artwork by Hawthorne, Diehl, Gammell, Hofmann, Vickrey, Hunter, McCurl, and others. A gift shop is on the premises. The museum is open year-round. From mid-May through Columbus Day, you can visit Monday through Saturday from 10:00 A.M. to 5:00 P.M., and Sunday from noon to 5:00 P.M. Adult

admission is $7.00, people younger than 18 enter free. Admission by donation Wednesday from 10:00 A.M. to 1:00 P.M. (See the Arts chapter for more information on their gallery shows.)

The Cape Cod Potato Chip Company is a success story that has made Cape Cod a household word among people who appreciate a quality potato chip. You can visit the factory on Breed's Hill Road in Hyannis any weekday from 9:00 A.M. to 5:00 P.M. For more information call (508) 775-3358, or visit www.capecodchips.com.

Congregational Church of South Dennis
218 Main Street, South Dennis
(508) 394-5992

Known as the Sea Captain's Church because so many of its members were shipmasters, this church was built in 1835. The south parish of the Dennis church was established here in 1794 and later broke away from the north in 1817. The current church replaced a small meetinghouse built in 1794. The church features the oldest operating pipe organ in the country and a chandelier of Sandwich glass that was once fueled with whale oil. The organ, built in 1765, was installed in the mid-19th century and attracts pipe organ enthusiasts from around the world. Behind the church is a cemetery with many stones bearing the names of ship captains as well as the words LOST AT SEA.

Josiah Dennis Manse and Old West Schoolhouse
77 Nobuscusset Road at Whig Street, Dennis
(508) 385-2232, (508) 385-3528 (for tours)

This 1736 saltbox was the home of the town's founding father, Reverend Josiah Dennis, who lived here until his death in 1763. Look closely at the front of this house, and you'll see that the windows on the left side are lower than the windows on the right, suggesting that this was once a half-Cape house expanded at a later date. The manse is now a museum featuring artifacts of early Dennis life, with a children's room and spinning and weaving exhibit. A maritime room holds models, paintings, and equipment from the Shiverick Shipyards, which produced eight large clipper ships during the mid-19th century. On the grounds is a 1770 one-room schoolhouse. The museum, which is owned by the town, is open in July, August, and September on Tuesday from 10:00 A.M. to noon and Thursday afternoons from 2:00 to 4:00 P.M. Admission is free, but donations are accepted.

Nobscusset Indian Burial Ground
Route 6A, East Dennis
no phone

Although this burial ground is rather difficult to locate, it's well worth the effort. Along the banks of Scargo Lake, known to the Native Americans as Nobscusset Pond, lies the Nobscusset Indian burial ground. There are no stones to see, only a plot of land encircled with a granite and iron fence, and a plaque that identifies the spot as THE BURIAL GROUND FOR THE NOBSCUSSET TRIBE OF INDIANS. The tribe's 17th-century sachem, Mahantampaine, is buried here. To find the burial ground, look for a clearing in the bushes a few hundred feet west of the Scargo Lake town landing on Route 6A.

Old Bass River Light (West Dennis Light)
1 Lighthouse Inn Road, West Dennis
(508) 398-2244
www.lighthouseinn.com

Now the center section of the Lighthouse Inn at West Dennis Beach (see our Bed-and-Breakfasts, Inns, and Cottages chapter), the Old Bass River Light was originally constructed in 1855, becoming the Cape's 15th lighthouse. Though closed briefly from

1880 to 1881, it continued operation until 1914, when the opening of the Cape Cod Canal rendered it obsolete. In 1989 the lighthouse was reactivated as the West Dennis Light by the Stone family, who owns and operates the Lighthouse Inn. They also operate the light itself, which blinks each evening from May 1 to October 31.

Scargo Tower
Off Scargo Hill Road, East Dennis
no phone

Scargo Tower is a 28-foot-high brick observatory sitting atop the 160-foot-high Scargo Hill, so you can imagine the view on a clear day. Provincetown Monument across Cape Cod Bay can be seen, as can the white cliffs of Plymouth. In perfect atmospheric conditions you can just make out a suggestion of Nantucket to the south. Built in 1902 and called Tobey Tower to honor early settler Thomas Tobey, it was given to the town of Dennis in 1929 and renamed Scargo Tower in favor of the Nobscusset Indian Princess of the same name. Below the tower and hill rests Scargo Lake, which during the summer hosts swimmers, sailboats, and canoes. Scargo Tower is open to the public and is a great place to stargaze.

LOWER CAPE

The Brewster General Store
1935 Route 6A, Brewster
(508) 896-3744
www.brewsterstore.com

This 18th-century general store is definitely worth a stop. With a Norman Rockwell ambience and a pinch of Aaron Copeland thrown in for good measure, the classic building has attracted many local painters who've captured its New England flavor with oils and watercolors. Inside you'll find a variety of items for sale, and the kids will have a blast filling bags with candy. The store is open daily year-round, 6:00 A.M. to 10:00 P.M. in the summer, and 6:30 A.M. to 5:30 P.M. in the winter.

For a real treat take in a movie at Cape Cinema on Route 6A in Dennis. Get there early enough to admire the colorful interior ceiling designed by Rockwell Kent, then settle in for the screening, which is usually of the independent variety. This is where The Wizard of Oz *premiered in 1940. For more information call (508) 385-2503, or visit www.capecinema.com.*

Brewster Historical Society Museum
3341 Route 6A, Brewster
(508) 896-9521

The Brewster Historical Society's museum has exhibits honoring the maritime history of Brewster and features memorabilia relating to the town, including an early-20th-century barber shop, a ca. 1860 dollhouse, and much more. The focus of the exhibit is ever changing. It's open only on weekends from June 15 to June 30 and September 1 through 15, and open Tuesday through Friday in July and August from 1:00 to 4:00 P.M., or by appointment.

The Historical Society also operates the Old Higgins Farm Windmill (see our listing below) and Harris-Black House, both at 785 Main Street, Drummer Boy Park, Route 6A in Brewster. Both are open during the same hours as the Brewster Historical Society Museum.

Cape Cod Museum of Natural History
869 Route 6A, Brewster
(508) 896-3867, (800) 479-3867 (Massachusetts only)
www.ccmnh.org

This museum is one of the best resources in the area for learning about the Cape's natural history. With two floors of exhibits, this museum provides visitors with a good idea of the flora and fauna of Cape Cod. Here you can discover the nature of Cape Cod through interactive exhibits, live animals, fresh and saltwater aquaria, and a touch tank to give you an up-close vantage point. Learn about coastal erosion, the archaeology of Cape Cod, or see what keeps bees so busy in a working beehive. Many displays are geared toward children, but people of all ages can learn something new here. Behind the museum is a vast salt marsh. The museum has walking trails, lectures, a library, a gift shop, and special exhibits—including an impressive marine room. The museum is open daily in the summer, from 10:00 A.M. to 4:00 P.M. Call for off-season hours. Admission is $7.00 for those ages 13 and older, $3.50 for children 3 to 12, and free for youngsters age 2 and younger.

Crosby Mansion
Crosby Lane (off Route 6A), across from Nickerson State Park, Brewster
(508) 896-3491, (508) 896-1744

Many consider the Crosby Mansion to be one of the Cape's hidden gems, wrapped in a love story more than a century old. This gracious home was built in 1888 by Albert Crosby for his wife, Matilda. Interestingly the structure was built around the original four-room Cape house in which Crosby was born. Aside from being a residence, the building has been used as a music school, a summer camp, and for weddings. A continuous slide show, exhibits, and tour allow you to learn about the Crosby family and life in the 1890s. Local volunteers put countless hours into preservation of the building. The house is maintained by the Friends of Crosby Mansion, and there are no set hours, although there are usually open houses held on Sunday during the summer, and the house is usually opened for the Brewster in Bloom weekend, usually the last weekend in April or the first weekend in May (see our Annual Events chapter). You can call the number above to arrange a tour of the building; there is no fee to tour the house.

New England Fire & History Museum
1439 Route 6A, Brewster
(508) 896-5711
www.nefiremuseum.org

See how fires were fought in the old days and witness firsthand the Chicago Fire of 1871 through the use of an award-winning diorama. This museum has more than 30 hand-drawn and horse-drawn firefighting implements on display, as well as more than a thousand other items, including the personal fire helmet collection of famed Boston Pops conductor Arthur Fiedler. There is also a replica of an apothecary shop and an original Brewster blacksmith shop. The museum is open from 10:00 A.M. to 4:00 P.M. on weekdays from Memorial Day to Labor Day and only on weekends after Labor Day through Columbus Day. Admission is $7.00 for adults, $6.00 for seniors, $3.00 for children ages 5 through 12, and $1.00 for each child younger than 5.

Old Higgins Farm Windmill
785 Route 6A, Brewster
(508) 896-9521

Built in 1795, this smock-type windmill was moved from Ellis Landing in Brewster to its current location at Drummer Boy Park in 1974. It ground its last bushel of grain around 1900 and is today maintained by the Brewster Historical Society, which opens it to the public from June to September. The windmill is open weekends for two weeks in June from June 15 through June 30, and then again for two weekends in September between September 1 and September 15. In July and August the windmill is open Tuesday through Friday, 1:00 to 4:00 P.M. The visit is free, but donations are welcome.

Stony Brook Grist Mill
Off Stony Brook Road, Brewster
no phone

This area was home to many mills over the centuries, beginning with the very first gristmill built by Thomas Prence in 1663. Near Prence's grist mill a fulling mill was also built in the 1600s. The fulling mill burned down in 1760, and the gristmill did the same in 1871. The country's first factory-produced woolen cloth was produced at a woolen mill built here in 1814. A new gristmill was constructed over the remains of the original in 1873, and it is this mill that today sits alongside Stony

Brook. The mill is open to the public May through August. Adjacent to the mill is the Brewster herring run, where the annual migration of herring, also called alewives, occurs each spring.

Brooks Academy Museum
80 Parallel Street (at Routes 124 and 39), Harwich
(508) 432-8089

The Harwich Historical Society operates this museum, which is named for its builder, Sidney Brooks. It offers a comprehensive exhibit on Cranberry history and culture in addition to collections of Native American artifacts; Sandwich glass; early tools, implements, and toys; and historical documents, including genealogical information. Brooks Academy was known in the 1840s as the Pine Grove Seminary and was one of the first schools of navigation in the country. The building was sold to the town of Harwich in 1869 and used as a public school. The museum is open June through September from 1:00 to 4:00 P.M. Tuesday through Friday. The rest of the year it is open only by appointment. We were told that Thursday is the best day to call if you have questions or want to set up a tour. Admission is free, but donations are welcomed. They also offer special programs on Saturday. For instance a walking tour of historic Harwich takes place on certain Saturdays during the summer months.

Atwood House and Museum
347 Stage Harbor Road, Chatham
(508) 945-2493
www.chathamhistoricalsociety.org

Built in 1752, the Atwood House is one of the oldest houses in Chatham. It was home to five generations of Atwoods and features a gambrel roof. Since 1926 the house has been the home of the Chatham Historical Society. The museum's eight rooms, containing many historic collections and furnishings, include the Joseph C. Lincoln Room, which is a repository of the prolific Cape author's books and memorabilia. The museum also holds murals by 20th-century artist Alice Stall-knecht Wight, an antique Fresnel lens from Chatham Light, antiques, Sandwich glass, and an international collection of seashells and artifacts. It is open June to the end of September, Tuesday through Friday from 1:00 to 4:00 P.M. Admission is free for members and children accompanied by adults; nonmembers are $5.00 and students over 12, $2.00.

Chatham Fish Pier
Aunt Lydia's Cove (off Shore Road), Chatham
no phone

Just down the road from the Chatham Light is the Chatham fish pier, where there's always a small crowd gathered on the visitors deck. Not only does the pier offer a great view of Chatham's harbor and outer beach with the Atlantic beyond, but when the fishing boats unload their catch, both children and adults get a fascinating glimpse of the Cape's best-known industry.

Chatham Light
Shore Road, Chatham
no phone

In 1808 two wooden lighthouses were built on a cliff in Chatham east of the location of the current Chatham lighthouse—a cliff that no longer exists. These first two Chatham lights were range lights, meaning they were movable and could be aligned in such a way that mariners approaching Chatham by sea could find the channel to the harbor by lining up the two lights. By 1841 the cliff had eroded so much that both lighthouses tumbled to the beach below. Another pair of lighthouses—these made with brick and mortar—were constructed to replace the old ones, but the cliff continued to erode at a rate of 20 feet per year until these were also destroyed in 1879 and 1881. To replace this second set, two iron lighthouses were built. One is the current Chatham Light; the other was moved to Eastham in 1923 to become the current Nauset Light. Chatham Light overlooks the Chatham Break, a mile-wide hole in the barrier beach that stretches back to the mainland and Nauset Beach in Orleans. The break occurred in early 1987 during a fierce nor'easter.

Old Godfrey Windmill
Near Chase Park, Chatham
no phone

This wind-powered grist mill was built along Stage Harbor Road in 1797 by Colonel Benjamin Godfrey. The mill ground corn until 1898. Over the course of the 20th century, it was twice damaged by storms and was closed until 1956 when it was given to the town. The mill was then moved to its current location at Chase Park. It is open every day except Tuesday throughout July and August. This is one of those look-see attractions with no admission fee charged.

The Railroad Museum
153 Depot Road, Chatham
no phone

On the appropriately named Depot Street is Chatham's Railroad Museum. It was built in 1887 and operated as a train depot until 1937, servicing more than 20,000 passengers per year. It was donated to the town in the 1950s and is today a museum offering a wide variety of railroad-related items that are sure to delight railroad buffs. The building, listed in the National Register of Historic Places, offers displays of antique equipment and memorabilia as well as a caboose dating form 1910. It is open Tuesday through Saturday, 10:00 A.M. to 4:00 P.M., mid-June through mid-September. There is no admission fee, though donations are accepted.

Centuries ago, Route 6A was a simple trail, no more than a cart path for early settlers. As towns flourished and commerce grew, Route 6A became an extension of the Kings Highway of the Plymouth colony and now is the major route for those traveling the north side of Cape Cod. Ranked among the top scenic byways in the country, Route 6A extends 34 miles from Bourne to Orleans.

French Cable Station Museum
Corner of Cove Road and Route 28, Orleans
(508) 240-1735

Built in 1890, this is the U.S. terminal for the first trans-Atlantic cable laid between the United States and France via Newfoundland. The cable was 3,000 miles long and was used to transmit news of such important events as Lindbergh's trans-Atlantic flight in 1927 and the invasion of France by the Germans in 1940. Many of the original French cable operators immigrated to this country and settled in the area. The cable station was guarded by Marines during World War II because it provided an important link with U.S. operations in Europe. The station was closed in 1959, but all the original cables, instruments, and other equipment are still in place. It is open during July and August, Monday through Saturday from 1:00 to 4:00 P.M.; June and September, Friday through Sunday 1:00 to 4:00 P.M.; and at other times by special request. No admission fee is charge, though donations are accepted.

Jonathan Young Windmill
Route 28, Orleans
(508) 240-3775

This fine windmill was built in 1720 in South Orleans and moved in the mid-1800s to Orleans Center. It was then bought by private interest in 1897 and relocated again, this time to Hyannisport. In 1983 the windmill was donated to the Orleans Historical Society and moved back to Orleans and place at Town Cove Park, where it was restored. The windmill is open to the public weekends from 11:00 A.M. to 4:00 P.M. during the summer months. No admission fee is charged. This is a beautiful place to have a picnic.

Orleans Historical Society Museum and Meeting House
3 River Road, Orleans
(508) 240-1329

Opposite Orleans Town Hall, this Greek Revival-style meetinghouse is a former

Universalist church built in 1834. Acquired by the Orleans Historical Society in 1971, it now houses collections of historic photographs, paintings, toys, costumes, china, and farm implements. It also has displays of Native American artifacts and Coast Guard lifesaving equipment, as well as items salvaged from one of the most infamous New England shipwrecks, the November 1898 wreck of the *Portland*, which resulted in the loss of all 176 people aboard. One of the many interesting items here is a letter from Capt. Richard Raggot of the British Navy dated September 30, 1814, containing the British demand for $1,000 to protect the town's saltworks from destruction (see our Historic Cape Cod chapter). The museum is open in July and August, Thursday through Saturday from 10:00 A.M. to 1:00 P.M. and Thursday evenings from 6:30 to 8:30 P.M. Admission is free.

Cape Cod National Seashore Salt Pond Visitor Center
U.S. Route 6A, Eastham
(508) 255-3241
www.nps.gov/caco
Here you can learn about the geological and natural elements that make up the outer shores of Cape Cod. The Salt Pond Visitor Center, part of the Cape Cod National Seashore, is generally open daily year-round from 9:00 A.M. to 4:30 P.M. The summer has extended hours to 5:00 P.M. At press time Salt Pond was undergoing a major renovation. For more information about the Visitor Center, see our chapter on the Cape Cod National Seashore.

Eastham Grist Mill
U.S. Route 6, Eastham
no phone
Resting upon the town green in Eastham is the oldest and most widely known of all the Cape Cod windmills. The Eastham Grist Mill was built in Plymouth in the 1680s, which means that the corn it ground most likely found its way into the mouths of the sons and daughters of Pilgrims. It was later moved to Truro during

Combine the magic of a Cape Cod vacation and the thrill of a train ride as the Cape Cod Central Railroad (508–771–3800 or www.capetrain.com) takes you on a ride from downtown Hyannis to the Cape Cod Canal. The train travels through beautiful bogs and past natural woodlands and lush marshes, giving you a nice long look at the natural beauty of Cape Cod.

the end of the 18th century by floating it across Cape Cod Bay. In 1798 it was moved to Eastham. The mill remained in operation until the turn of the 20th century. It was first opened to the public in the 1930s and restored in the 1960s. Nowadays it is open weekdays from 10:00 A.M. to 4:00 P.M. and Sunday 1:00 to 5:00 P.M. during the summer months when visitors can see its original wooden machinery that still operates today—what craftsmanship! Admission is free, but donations are accepted.

Eastham Schoolhouse Museum
U.S. Route 6 at Nauset and Schoolhouse Roads, Eastham
(508) 255-0788
www.easthamhistorical.org
This one-room schoolhouse was built in 1869 as an elementary school. Around the turn of the 20th century, the town had three such one-room schoolhouse. These were later joined to form the Eastham Central School, which operated until 1936. After two of the original schoolhouses deteriorated in the mid-1900s, the old original schoolhouse was restored to its late-19th-century one-room status and serves as a museum of the Eastham Historical Society. It still has two doors marked as separate entrances for boys and girls. Exhibits include farming and household implements, Native American artifacts, and displays pertaining to area history. The museum is open weekdays in July and August and Saturday in September from 1:00 to 4:00 P.M. Admission is free.

Edward Penniman House
Fort Hill Road, Eastham
(508) 255-3421
www.nps.gov/caco

Located within the boundaries of the Cape Cod National Seashore, the Penniman House in the Fort Hill area of Eastham showcases the fortunes made by the Cape's whaling captains. Retiring from the sea in 1876, Captain Edward Penniman built this impressive Victorian mansion on a knoll with a cupola overlooking the Atlantic Ocean. In front of the house there is a gateway made of two huge whale jawbones marking the entrance to the property. You can tour the house during the summer season. The Penniman House is open from May through September, Tuesday through Friday from 1:00 to 4:00 P.M. Just call ahead to register if you plan on visiting. Guided tours are available in May and June on Monday and Saturday starting at 10:00 A.M. Admission is free.

First Encounter Beach
Samoset Road, Eastham
no phone

At First Encounter Beach along the Cape Cod Bay side of Eastham's shore is a granite boulder with a plaque marking this location as the site of the Pilgrims' first encounter with Native Americans. Unfortunately this first encounter was not a friendly one. The Pilgrims, on their third day of exploring this new land, awoke to a volley of arrows that they answered with a volley of musket fire. Both parties departed, uninjured. Future relations between the two peoples would be much more cordial.

Nauset Light
Beach Road, Eastham
(508) 240-2612
www.nausetlight.org

Highland Light to the north had one tower. Chatham Light to the south had two towers. So, to mark the cliffs of Eastham, Nauset was given three lights. The first three lighthouses built on the cliff here were small brick towers constructed in 1837. These three lighthouses surrendered to cliff erosion in 1892, and their remains can be seen along Nauset Beach from time to time, especially in the early spring after winter storms wash away tons of beach sand. Three new towers, taller and made of wood, were constructed on the cliff to replace the original towers and were known as the Three Sisters. Two of these lighthouses were sold to private interests in 1918; otherwise they would have fallen over the rapidly eroding cliffs. The third light worked the cliff alone until 1923 when it, too, was sold. During that year the site saw the installation of the current Nauset Light, formerly one of the Chatham Twins. In 1996 Nauset Light was moved back from the cliff, as it was about to suffer the fate of the original brick lighthouses. As for the Three Sisters, they have been reunited and are now on display along Cable Road, just up the street from Nauset Light. Nauset Light is open for Sunday tours during the summer. Call for times.

Swift-Daley House and Tool Museum
U.S. Route 6, Eastham
(508) 240-1247

Built in 1741 by Joshua Knowles, this bow-roofed home has wide floorboards, a minister's cupboard, original wainscoting, and an 8-foot-wide fireplace. The house once belonged to Nathaniel Swift, one of the principals of the Swift Meat Packing Company. Its eight rooms are filled with period furnishings, including artifacts and clothing from the colonial through the Victorian eras. It is open weekdays from 10:00 A.M. to 4:00 P.M. in July and August. The Tool Museum behind the Swift-Daley House, has a display that includes numerous tools and implements collected in the area, including remnants of saltworks and cranberry-growing operations. The hours are the same as those for the Swift-Daley House. Admission to both is free.

First Congregational Church
Main Street, Wellfleet
(508) 349-6877

This church holds the distinction of being the only church in the world known to keep ship's time, thus revealing Wellfleet's proud history as a seafaring town. For those not familiar with ship's time, the 24-hour day is divide up into six four-hour segments, representing a four-hour watch on board a ship. The first watch begins at 12:00 and concludes at 4:00 when the second watch begins. On each half hour during the watch, the bells chime: one bell at 12:30, two bells at 1:00, three bells at 1:30 and so on until eight bells are chimed and then the cycle begins again. Wellfleet's First Congregational Church was built in 1850 and contains an 1873 Hook and Hastings organ. Call to arrange a visit.

Marconi Wireless Site
Marconi Site Road (off U.S. Route 6), Wellfleet
(508) 349-3785

Many believe this to be the site of the initial transatlantic wireless message; in fact the first such message was sent from England to Greenland in 1901, more than a year before the South Wellfleet Wireless Transmitting Station sent its first message. Regardless this site, now know locally as Marconi Wireless Site or Marconi Station, does hold its place as the site of the first wireless message sent across the Atlantic from the United States. On January 19, 1903, the airwaves crackled atop this windswept Wellfleet cliff—helping to change long-distance communications forever. Developed by the Italian physicist Guglielmo Marconi, the first Wellfleet telegraph transmitted a message from President Theodore Roosevelt to King Edward VII of England. On the evening of April 14, 1912, the station received the distress call from the *Titanic*. The station at South Wellfleet would only be in service until 1917 as cliff erosion was already threatening. Although erosion has destroyed much of the site, a plaque commemorates the site, and you can still view the footings of some of the towers (these towers stood more than 200 feet high) as well as a model of how the station looked in 1903.

Wellfleet Historical Society Museum
266 Main Street, Wellfleet
(508) 349-9157
www.wellfleethistoricalsociety.org

Wellfleet Historical Society Museum is located in a mid-19th-century general store. Its collection, focusing on the town's history, includes lifesaving equipment and medals, oystering, and early medicine. The exhibits highlight prominent Wellfleet residents, such as Lorenzo Dow Baker, founder of the United Fruit Company empire, who was the first to import bananas into the United States in 1870; Luther Crowell, who invented a machine that made the square-bottomed paper bag; Sarah Atwood, one of the country's first female lighthouse keepers; and Clarence John Bell, a horse-and-buggy era doctor who delivered 2,500 babies in Wellfleet. The museum is open Tuesday through Saturday from late June through early September, 1:00 to 4:00 P.M. Call for a schedule of walking tours. There is a nominal admission of $1.00; children younger than 12 get in free.

Highland Light (Cape Cod Light)
Highland Road, Truro
(508) 487-1121
www.trurohistorical.org

This is the nation's first lighthouse. The original Cape Cod Light first stood watch on these sandy cliffs in 1797 and was lit by whale-oil lamps. By 1857 the tower was in danger of falling down, so the current Highland Lighthouse was constructed that year. Remarkably the original whale-oil lamps were in use until the turn of the 20th century, when they were replaced by a modern lamp system. The light system was updated with electricity as recently as 1932. Sitting atop the cliffs of Truro and with a range of some 20 to 30 miles, the light is the first seen by transatlantic mariners as they approach the northeast coast. The 80-foot tower was moved back from the cliff in 1996 and thus saved from the erosion threatening to destroy it. It stands today not only as a monument to our Cape Cod heritage, but also to contemporary Cape Codders who saved this landmark from destruction. After all, is Cape Cod truly Cape Cod without the majestic sweep of Highland's beam? We think not.

Highland Light is open May through October daily for guided tours from 10:00 A.M. to 5:45 P.M. Admission is $3.00 for the tower, and $5.00 for the tower and adjoining museum. Children must be 51 inches tall to tour the tower.

The 10-team Cape Cod Baseball League is a popular draw on late summer afternoons throughout the Cape. The players hail from colleges and universities around the country, use only wooden bats, and take aim for the big leagues. Games are played from mid-June to mid-August and are free. For more information visit www.capecodbaseball.org.

Jenny Lind Tower
Off Lighthouse Road, North Truro
no phone

In the mid-1800s Jenny Lind was a legendary opera singer dubbed the "Swedish Nightingale" because of her sweet soprano voice. In 1850 showman P. T. Barnum had his private army of reporters churning out news stories about Lind a half-year before her arrival in America, whipping the country into a frenzy comparable to 1964's Beatlemania. Legend has it that her concert in Boston was so oversold that crowds rioted, forcing Lind to sing (for free) high atop a 55-foot stone tower at the Fitchburg Railroad Depot. In 1927, when it was announced that the tower was

going to be destroyed, a wealthy Boston attorney shipped it, piece by piece, to a parcel of land he owned in North Truro. Today the tower and the land are part of the Cape Cod National Seashore. Though the tower is not officially open to the public, you can see it from the parking lot of the Highland Light as well as from the Highland Golf Links.

Truro Historical Society Museum at the Highland House
Highland Light Road, North Truro
(508) 487-3397
www.trurohistorical.org

A turn-of-the-20th-century hotel (built in 1907) houses the Truro Historical Society's collections. These include Native American artifacts, items dating from the 17th century, lifesaving equipment, 17th-century weaponry, antique fishing and whaling equipment, household items, shipwreck items, Sandwich glass, and historic photographs. The museum is open June through September, seven days a week, 10:00 A.M. to 5:00 P.M. Admission is $3.00; children younger than 12 are admitted free. The museum is just a stone's throw from the Highland Lighthouse.

Truro Vineyards of Cape Cod
Route 6A, North Truro
(508) 487-6200

Take a break from sightseeing and indulge in a few sips of local wine. Tour the vineyard, which thrives on the Cape's sandy soils and temperate breezes, and the winery. It's produced some well-regarded wines, from gutsy reds and sweet dessert wines to mellow "deck" wines. Tastings are casual affairs, held under a white tent behind the lovely 1830s farmhouse that houses the gift shop. It carries their wines, as well as cooking oils, marinades, jams, and all the wine accoutrements you could ever need. Tastings and tours are from noon to 5:00 P.M. daily Memorial Day through Thanksgiving, Friday through Sunday during the shoulder seasons.

Wreck of the *Frances*
Head of the Meadow Beach, Head of the Meadow Road, Truro
no phone

This is a unique historic site in that it is a 19th-century shipwreck that can still be seen out in the water off Truro's Head of the Meadow Beach. A 120-foot German bark, the *Frances*, wrecked here on the evening of December 26, 1872. Though all hands were saved by a crew of Truro volunteers headed up by Captain Edwin Worthen, the keeper of the newly-built Highland Lifesaving Station, Captain Kortling of the *Frances* died of illness three days later. Today the black iron hull of the *Frances* pokes up occasionally above the Atlantic waves and serves as a memorial to the more than 1,000 shipwrecks that have occurred along the outer Cape over the past three-and-a-half centuries.

Expedition Whydah Museum
MacMillan Wharf, Provincetown
(508) 487-8899
www.whydah.com

The museum is devoted to the only pirate ship ever discovered and authenticated. A fascinating story of pirates unfolds as the museum tells the story of the wreck of the *Whydah*, its discovery by local diver Barry Clifford, and the priceless artifacts recovered from the wreck found off Wellfleet, Cape Cod. The museum is open from Memorial Day weekend through Labor Day weekend, 10:00 A.M. to 7:00 P.M. daily; during September and October the museum is open only on weekends. Adults are charged $5.00, children cost $3.50, and children younger than 6 enter free.

Old Harbor Lifesaving Station
Race Point Road, Provincetown
(508) 487-1256
www.nps.gov/caco

Race Point is now home to the Old Harbor Lifesaving Station that once protected the shores of Chatham. Built in 1898, it was one of the 13 stations that lined the outer Cape beaches from Provincetown to Monomoy Point until the Lifesaving Ser-

vice became part of the Coast Guard in 1914. The Old Harbor Station was decommissioned in 1944 and sold off to private interests. It was acquired by the National Park Service in 1973 and moved up the coast on a barge in the winter of 1978, just ahead of the devastating blizzard. Now it rests at Race Point overlooking the Atlantic. Its boat room contains a surf boat and various lifesaving apparatus. The station is open to visitors during July and August from 1:30 to 3:30 P.M. daily and 6:00 to 8:00 P.M. Thursday for their popular lifesaving drill presentation (see our Cape Cod National Seashore chapter).

Pilgrim Monument and Provincetown Museum
One High Pole Hill Road, Provincetown
(508) 487-1310
www.pilgrim-monument.org

The tallest granite structure in the United States, this 252-foot tower commemorates the Pilgrims' arrival in this town in 1620. It was completed in 1910 and features a granite block from every state in the union at the time. Theodore Roosevelt attended the laying of the cornerstone in 1907. This is a beacon for the area, visible from the Cape Cod Canal on a clear day. For a spectacular view of Cape Cod Bay and the area, you can climb the 116 steps and 60 ramps to the top. The museum has displays of Native American artifacts and antique china, pewter, and silver. Other items of particular interest pertain to expeditions by Antarctic explorer Admiral Donald MacMillan, a native son of Provincetown, and to the life of playwright

Whale watching is still one of our biggest visitor attractions (see our Whale Watching chapter). Each year whales travel thousands of miles so they can keep coming back to the same feeding and calving grounds. The whales seen off Cape Cod's Stellwagen Bank are usually migrating from Nova Scotia to New England and Florida waters.

Eugene O'Neill, whose plays were first performed in this town. The museum is open April through November at 9:00 A.M. each day. Last admission is at 4:15 P.M. in the off-season and 6:15 P.M. in July and August, and the doors are closed 45 minutes later. Parking is free; an admission fee of $7.00 is charged adults; children's admission is $3.00 for those ages 4 to 12.

Provincetown Art Association and Museum
460 Commercial Street, Provincetown
(508) 487-1750
www.paam.org

The Provincetown Art Association and Museum was established in 1914 during the early years of Provincetown's art colony. Four galleries feature exhibits by established and emerging Outer Cape artists, as well as Art Association members. Also on display are works from the very impressive 1,700-piece permanent collection, including works by Hawthorne, Motherwell, Knaths, Hensche, Hofmann, Moffett, Bultman, and other painters closely associated with Provincetown who were colorful members of this artists' colony. There is a museum store, library, artists' archives, and a museum school on the premises. It's open all year on weekends from noon to 5:00 P.M. In July and August it also has evening hours from 8:00 to 10:00 P.M. An admission fee of $3.00 is charged adults and teens, and children 12 and younger and seniors are charged $1.00. Members enter free.

Race Point Lighthouse, Long Point Lighthouse, Wood End Lighthouse
Province Lands, Provincetown
(508) 487-9930
www.racepointlighthouse.net

Provincetown has three lighthouses guiding ships along its dangerous coastline toward the safety of Provincetown Harbor. All three are at the farthest reaches of Cape Cod, where roads give way to ever-shifting dunes of sand. Race Point Light was built in 1876, replacing the original lighthouse built here in 1816. The current Race Point Lighthouse is 41 feet tall. Long Point Light, at 36 feet, was originally installed along this lonely shore in 1827 and was replaced by the current Long Point Lighthouse in 1875. Today it is powered by solar energy. Between Race Point and Long Point rests the 45-foot-tall Wood End Light, which was built in 1873. Its light is also solar powered. All three have foghorns, which make for an interesting sound in foggy weather. You can spend a night, weekend, or week at the keeper's house. Call for prices and availability.

KIDSTUFF 👫

ape Cod is a wonderful place to be
a kid. We've met countless adults
who say their idyllic childhood
vacations here are part of why they return
to the Cape—sometimes permanently.

What are the attractions for little people? Obviously there are the beaches.
Everyone—not just children—loves running
in the sand, splashing in the surf, building
sandcastles, and hunting for seashells and
beach rocks. Cape Cod kids have their own
giant sandbox to play in year-round—well,
most of the year, although some tykes we
know enjoy a romp by the bay even in
January! But there's plenty to do on the
Cape beyond beaches, from bumper cars
and miniature golf to nature centers and
museums. Kids can watch jam being made
at the Green Briar Nature Center in Sandwich, feed the turtles and fish at the Cape
Cod Museum of Natural History in Brewster, catch a sea lion show at the ZooQuarium in Yarmouth, or climb aboard a seal
cruise on Beachcomber Boat Tours.

There's so much for kids to do on the
Cape that to detail everything would take
a whole book. So we decided to simply
offer a selection of what we consider to
be the best and the brightest. We know
you'll already be planning trips to museums (see our Attractions chapter), so we
reserved this space for places especially
geared toward children.

If you're looking for suggestions and
ideas for kids who love the outdoors, such
as biking, hiking, swimming, and sunning,
turn to our Hiking and Biking Trails chapter or our Beaches chapter. During the
summer, the Cape is alive with the sounds
of music and puppet theaters and kiddie
shows; take a look at our Arts chapter for
more about these.

Also included in this chapter are
descriptions of summer camps, sports
clinics, and creative centers that have
become dependable outlets for youthful
curiosity and energy. You're sure to find
some that inspire your children.

One last word. If you and your other
half must get away for some time alone,
babysitting services are available (see our
Education and Child Care chapter). Most
hotels and accommodations keep a list of
reliable sitters they've recommended in
the past. The Children's Place (508–240–
3310), a regional family resource center in
Eastham (serving the Lower Cape towns
from Brewster to Provincetown), keeps a
list of recommended babysitters. And if
you're staying on the Lower Cape (namely
Provincetown), the Council on Aging
(508–487–7080) also offers a babysitting
service. Senior citizens will watch your
kids (either in their homes or at your
place) for a reasonable hourly rate, which
depends on the number of children and
the amount of notice given. It's not an all-
day arrangement but perfect for parents
who want to get away for a few hours of
sightseeing or dinner.

AQUARIUMS AND ANIMAL FARMS

Upper Cape

The Aquarium of the National Marine Fisheries Service
166 Water Street, Woods Hole
(508) 495–2001

Please touch the specimens! That's the
rule stressed here at the public aquarium
of the Northeast Fisheries Science Center.
Children can feel around three touch-
tanks and pick up such deep-sea wonders
as sea cucumbers, lobsters, and starfish.
They can also look at creatures close up
under a magnifier and come eye-to-eye
with marine life through the glass of 16
display tanks. They can see seals too:
Feedings are held at 11:00 A.M. and 4:00

P.M. Student volunteers are on hand to answer kids' queries in summer. The aquarium is open Monday through Friday 11:00 A.M. to 4:00 P.M.

> Have a stuffed animal fan in your family? They'll probably enjoy a visit to Fuzzy McGoo's Teddy Bear Factory at 569 Main Street, Hyannis. Choose a floppy bear, stuff it yourself (with the help of a stuffing machine), pick out an outfit and a name, and you've got a new companion. For more information call (508) 771-4755, or visit www.fuzzy mcgoos.com.

Marine Biological Laboratory
7 MBL Street, Woods Hole
(508) 289-7623
www.mbl.edu
A visit here requires advance planning but is well worth it. Geared for children 10 and older, an hour-long tour includes a video followed by a guided side trip to say hello to squid, sponges, crabs, and coral. The facility gives tours at 1:00, 2:00, and 3:00 P.M. Monday through Friday from late June through August. Reservations one week in advance are required as tours are limited to 15 people. For safety reasons children younger than 5 are not permitted in the Marine Resources Center, although they may view the video presentation. The tour is free.

Sandwich Fish Hatchery
Route 6A, Sandwich
(508) 888-0008
Fishing around to do something really different? Adults and kids alike will enjoy the Sandwich Fish Hatchery, where more than a quarter of a million fish are raised to stock the state's various ponds. Kids will be able to track the stages of fish development and feed the critters (bring quarters!). Admission is free. It's open year-round, 9:00 A.M. to 3:00 P.M. daily.

Mid-Cape

ZooQuarium
674 Route 28, Yarmouth
(508) 775-8883
www.zooquariumcapecod.net
As its name implies, this place is half zoo and half aquarium—and all fun! One huge room in the ZooQuarium houses tanks of fish, frogs, and turtles. From there you walk out into the huge backyard, where you'll think you're miles from the commercial bustle of Route 28. This is another world, where llamas, sheep, pigs, and other animals wander in roomy pens and come over for a nuzzle or a nibble of corn. The nearby classroom, with its touch-and-tell displays, is a fun place to learn. Don't miss the sea lion shows, which are held at 11:00 A.M. and 1:00, 3:00, and 5:00 P.M. during July through Labor Day and at 11:00 A.M., and 1:00, 2:30, and 4:00 P.M. in the off-season. Hunter, Willow, and Rufus love to perform, especially for children. And don't miss the Zoorific Theater, a hands-on live animal education program staged at 10:00 A.M., noon, 2:00, and 4:00 P.M. July through Labor Day and at 10:15 A.M., noon, 1:45, and 3:15 P.M. during other months of operation. The ZooQuarium is open daily from mid-February to late November; in summer, the hours are 9:30 A.M. to 6:00 P.M. and in the off-season 9:30 A.M. to 5:00 P.M. Admission is $9.00 for those age 10 and older and $6.00 for children ages 2 through 9.

MUSEUMS AND NATURE CENTERS

Upper Cape

Green Briar Nature Center and Jam Kitchen
6 Discover Hill Road, East Sandwich
(508) 888-6870
www.thorntonburgess.com
You're still in Burgess country here: Remember the Old Briar Patch? That ficti-

tious locale comes to life at this nature center, which abuts 57 acres of conservation land. Kids can visit frogs and turtles at the Smiling Pool and wander on the nature trails to look for signs of other critters. The Jam Center, established in 1903, is a kitchen nestled back in the woods where jams and jellies are still made the right way—by hand. Take a tour of the kitchen and see them being made, then buy some to take home. You can also take one of the center's regularly offered jam-making classes—available for both children and adults—and take home the fruits of your own labor. Green Briar is open daily April through December, Tuesday through Saturday January through March. Admission is by donation.

Heritage Museums & Gardens
Grove and Pine Streets, Sandwich
(508) 888-3300
www.heritagemuseumsandgardens.org

This is a perfect outing for parents and the kids-in-the-stroller set. You'll get to see everything—lush gardens and some magnificent collections including 32 antique cars and folk art—while giving the little ones a good workout. The old-fashioned, hand-carved 1912 indoor carousel gives free rides with paid admission. Admission is $12.00 for adults ($10.00 for those older than 60), $6.00 for ages 6 through 16, and free for children 5 and younger. Admission is free for members of Heritage Plantation. It's open daily 9:00 A.M. to 6:00 P.M., Thursday until 8:00 P.M. from May through mid-October.

Thornton Burgess Museum
4 Water Street, Sandwich
(508) 888-4668
www.thorntonburgess.org

The life and career of the Sandwich native and children's author who wrote thousands of stories and 170 books, including *The Adventures of Peter Cottontail* and the beloved Old Mother West Wind series, is chronicled here through memorabilia and exhibits. The cottage

The National Marine Life Center cares for stranded marine animals. Their visitor center, with exhibits and activities about whales, dolphins, seals, and sea turtles, is worth the trip, and admission is free. Open to visitors daily from late May to September. Call (508) 743-9888, or visit www.nmlc.org.

where the museum is housed was the home of Burgess's eccentric aunt, a teacher who talked with plants and wildlife. So it's only natural that this is a place where kids can also get close to plants—in the touch-and-smell herb garden. In the see-and-touch room, kids are invited to guess what they're handling—is it a rubber snake? A feather? Story hours (Burgess's tales, of course) are given on the front lawn regularly throughout the summer. The museum is open daily April through October; hours are 10:00 A.M. to 4:00 P.M. Monday through Saturday, and 1:00 to 4:00 P.M. on Sunday. Admission is $2.00 for adults, $1.00 for children.

Cape Cod Children's Museum
577 Great Neck Road South, Mashpee
(508) 539-8788
www.capecodchildrensmuseum.pair.com

Learning is especially fun here. Attractions include a Starlab Planetarium, a puppet theater, and a dress-up toddlers castle. But the biggest draw here is the 30-foot pirate ship on which you'll always find scores of Bluebeard wannabes scurrying up and down the three levels. The museum also has two indoor sandboxes with a specially designed implement that allows kids to write with sand. Monthly thematic programs with activities three times daily are held year-round. The museum is open 10:00 A.M. to 5:00 P.M. daily and noon to 5:00 P.M. on Sunday. Admission is $5.00 for those age 5 and older and $4.00 for children ages 1 through 4 and for those older than 60.

Lower Cape

Cape Cod Museum of Natural History
896 Route 6A, Brewster
(508) 896-3867
www.ccmnh.org

Although this wonderful facility is great for people of all ages, it is family oriented and very child-friendly. Take the little ones downstairs to a room full of hands-on exhibits, fish tanks, and demonstrations that will entertain them for hours. They can observe the world of nature close up through whale displays, marine life exhibits, and window birdfeeders. The museum also has an interesting gift shop packed with educational yet entertaining souvenirs. The museum offers walking trails and numerous classes, programs, and tours. It is open daily during the summer; call for off-season hours. Summer hours are 10:00 A.M. to 4:00 P.M. Admission is $7.00 for those ages 13 and older; $3.50 for children 3 to 12, and free for those age 2 and younger. (Tip: If you have children and live here or spend a significant portion of time here, a CCMNH membership is a great investment!)

New England Fire & History Museum
1439 Route 6A, Brewster
(508) 896-5711
www.nefiremuseum.org

Children have always been fascinated by fire engines, and here they can view a whole history of them. Kids can climb on antique fire trucks and a fireboat, and eye an animated diorama of the Great Chicago Fire. The complex also has blacksmith and apothecary shops and a picnic area. The museum is open from 10:00 A.M. to 4:00 P.M. weekdays and from noon to 4:00 P.M. weekends from Memorial Day to Labor Day; after Labor Day it's open weekends only through Columbus Day. Admission is $7.00 for adults, $6.00 for senior citizens, $3.00 for ages 5 through 12, and $1.00 for children younger than 5.

Railroad Museum
153 Depot Road, Chatham
no phone

Take the kids here for a look at old cars and cabooses, models, relics, and photos. (The museum is on the National Register of Historic Places.) The constantly playing soundtrack of wheels and whistles adds to the railway atmosphere and appeals to kids who love those noises! Donations are accepted. It's open Tuesday through Saturday 10:00 A.M. to 4:00 P.M. mid-June through mid-September.

Wellfleet Bay Wildlife Sanctuary
U.S. Route 6, Wellfleet
(508) 349-2615
www.wellfleetbay.org

This Outer Cape treasure offers many fascinating programs that let you sample the Cape's different habitats, from coastal heathlands to meadows, from fresh and saltwater inlets to barrier beaches and, of course, to observe the wildlife that inhabit those areas. Both on-site programs at the sanctuary and off-site programs that include nearby Nauset Marsh and Monomoy Island are offered. Learn about monarch butterfly migration, participate in sea turtle treks, or cruise Nauset Marsh for a while, then get off the boat and explore tidal flats for crabs and snails or dig for clams and sea worms. Programs include interactive field trips, guided walks, cruises, and informative lectures by

---

They're strange looking, they're harmless, and they are more closely related to spiders than to true crabs. Horseshoe crabs are recognized by their brown, rounded shell and spinelike tail or telson. The horseshoe crab has inhabited the earth for 200 to 350 million years and has remained essentially unchanged in form.

[Facing page] *There are many opportunities for fun and learning, even away from the beach.* STEVE BEAUDET, CAPE COD SEA CAMPS

Rainy Day Doings

The gardeners among us welcome rainy days, knowing that without enough moisture the Cape would be bereft of many of the plants and flowers that make it beautiful. For those on vacation, however, a rainy day can be challenging, especially if there are children involved. You might be content to curl up in your cottage with a good book listening to the rain drum musically on the roof, but a few hours of that will drive even the calmest child stir-crazy. Coloring books and puzzles will work only so long—after that you'll be forced to pile the family into the car in search of adventure. Here are a few of our favorite rainy-day activities; many of them are listed in this chapter.

Libraries: Every town has one, and on rainy days, the children's librarians expect crowds and often schedule extra activities accordingly. See the Yellow Pages in the phone book or look in the gray pages under individual towns for the address and phone number of the library nearest you.

Bookstores: We love to browse in bookstores on rainy days. A few of our favorites are Parnassus Books in Yarmouthport (great for old books), Armchair Bookstore in Dennis (which has an especially appealing children's section), and Cabbages and Kings (another great one for kids) in Chatham.

Cape Cod Museum of Natural History: This Brewster museum will keep chil-dren—and adults—amused for hours. It is busier than usual on rainy days, but the plus side is that you're sure to meet other families to chat with.

Cape Cod Mall: Expect crowds at this Hyannis mall on rainy days, but at least it's a diversion. There are plenty of shops, plus three anchor stores (see our Shopping chapter) and a lively food court. Just about everybody on the Cape goes shopping when it rains, but at least at the mall you can park your car instead of driving from shop to shop—driving can be a real nightmare on a rainy summer day.

Arcades: If you can stand the noise, bring your kids to Ryan Family Amusements, located in Cape Cod Mall and in South Yarmouth and Buzzards Bay.

Movies: Look for matinees, which are generally cheaper than evening shows. If you've got access to a VCR, rent a movie and stay in. Stock up on popcorn first!

Bowling: This is more popular than you might think, and it's a great family activity, especially when skies are not sunny.

Beaches: As long as it's not stormy, there's nothing wrong with a walk at the beach in the rain. We especially like going to the beach when there's a light mist falling, and fog gives the shorline a mystical, ethereal look. Best of all, there are no crowds!

Audubon naturalists. You can sign up for an organized program or just come to walk the beautiful trails or the tidal flats at low tide (bring a pail, hike up your pants—or wear shorts—and start exploring). The sanctuary trails are open 365 days a year from 8:00 A.M. to dusk. The nature center is open daily, 8:30 A.M. to 5:00 P.M. through Columbus Day, and closed Mondays after Columbus Day. Admission is free for Massachusetts Audubon members. The fee for nonmembers is $5.00 for an adult, $3.00 for a child 12 and younger and senior citizens.

MINIGOLF AND AMUSEMENTS

Upper Cape

Adventure Isle
343 MacArthur Boulevard (Route 28), Bourne
(508) 759-2636, (800) 53-KARTS
www.adventureisle.com
You could spend days at this large complex, located 2 miles south of the Bourne Bridge on Route 28, and still not have enough time to do—and ride—everything. In addition to a minigolf course and a driving range, the complex has a go-cart track, minibikes, bumper cars, bumper boat lagoon, batting cages, a video arcade, a 25-foot super slide, and the newest attraction, laser tag. Adventure Isle is open daily mid-April through October from 10:00 A.M. to 11:00 P.M. in summer, and 10:00 A.M. to 6:00 P.M. in the fall.

Sandwich Minigolf
159 Route 6A, Sandwich
(508) 833-1905
www.sandwichminigolf.com
This 28-hole course is built on a former cranberry bog, and the architectural trademarks of the Cape, such as covered bridges, windmills, whales, and sea horses, are incorporated in its designs. Best of all: The course features the world's only floating green! It's open daily mid-May through mid-September. The cost for 18 holes is $6.00 for those 13 and older and $4.50 for children younger than 12; to play 28 holes it's $8.00 for older players and $6.50 for children younger than 12.

Mid-Cape

Cape Cod Storyland Golf
70 Center Street, Hyannis
(508) 778-4339
This 2-acre, 18-hole course is one of the largest minigolf courses in New England. It's designed as a miniversion of the Cape, with each hole representing a Cape Cod town complete with reproductions of historic buildings, ponds, and waterfalls. When you've had enough putting around, take a spin on the bumper boats. It's open daily from mid-April through the end of October. Admission is $7.00 for adults and $6.00 for ages 12 and younger.

Strawberry season on the Cape usually begins around the second week of June, though it's very dependent on spring weather. If you want to indulge in some picking during your visit, check with Andrews Farm (508-548-5257), 398 Old Meeting House Road, East Falmouth, or Coonamessett Farm (508-563-2560), 277 Hatchville Road, East Falmouth, to see what's ripe for picking. Picking on the first day of the season will get you the largest, plumpest berries. Remember to wear long pants and sunscreen while picking—it will make it easier to enjoy the berries when you're done!

Pirate Adventures
Ocean Street Dock, Hyannis
(508) 430-0202, (508) 255-8811
www.pirateadventurescapecod.com
Pirate Adventures is pure fantasy—an old-fashioned, swashbuckling adventure your children will remember for years to come. With costumed pirate actors, painted faces, and sailor sashes, the little mated aboard the pirate ship *Sea Gypsy* cast off on a pirate adventure. There's underwater treasure to find and a secret map that leads you there. But before the crew gets to pull up the booty, they may have to fire the water cannons in order to save

the ship and capture the treasure. There is lots of fun to be had, as the crew sings sea chanteys, takes the time-honored oath of loyal sailors, and participates in storytelling and a gang effort to find the treasure. This popular adventure runs frequent trips from the Ocean Street Docks in Hyannis and Town Cove, next to the Goose Hummock, in Orleans beginning late June and running through Labor Day. There are six excursions daily between 9:30 A.M. and 5:00 P.M. Reservations are required. Admission is $17 for ages 3 and older, $12 for 2 and younger.

Ryan Family Amusements
Cape Cod Mall, Route 132, Hyannis
(508) 790-2524
1067 Route 28, South Yarmouth
(508) 394-5644
200 Main Street, Buzzards Bay
(508) 759-9892
www.ryanfamily.com
Ryan Family Amusements offers all kinds of arcade games, pinball, Skee-ball, and video games along with children's games such as ride-on horses, air hockey, and basketball.

Pirate's Cove Adventure Golf
723 Main Street, South Yarmouth
(508) 394-6200
This 36-hole course even has a pirate ship in a fake pond surrounded by waterfalls and cliffs. Kids can win fun prizes in keeping with the theme, such as pirate eye patches, tattoos, and flags. Pirate's Cove is open daily from mid-April through late October. Admission is $7.50 ($6.50 for ages 12 and younger). In the summer, Pirate's Cove is open from 9:00 A.M. to 10:00 P.M.; in the fall it's usually open 10:00 A.M. to 4:00 P.M.

Lower Cape

Bud's Go-Karts
369 Sisson Road, Harwich
(508) 432-4964

Unique to the Lower Cape, this long-established go-cart center, easy to find on the corner of Route 28 and Sisson Road, rings all summer with the delighted shrieks and shouts of children going FAST! and loving it. You can get on the course for $5.00. In the summer it's open daily from 9:00 A.M. to 11:00 P.M.

Grand Slam Entertainment
322 Route 28, Harwich
(508) 430-1155
Batting cages—including one with fastballs as fast as 90 miles per hour!—are ready and waiting for your little sluggers. There are also bumper boats and arcade games. A good time to ride the boats is on a hot day, when the lines will be short because everyone else will be at the beach and the bumper rides will splash (and cool) you. Activities are priced by tokens—one token, for example, buys you 10 pitches in the batting cage. Tokens purchased singly cost $1.50, but in multiples they cost less: $1.25 when you buy five, $1.00 if you buy 10, and 90 cents if you purchase 22. Grand Slam is open 9:00 A.M. to 10:00 P.M. daily, April through September.

Trampoline Center
296 Route 28, Harwich
(508) 432-8717
Boiiinnnng! Up they go! Kids will have a great time jumping to their hearts' content. A dozen large trampolines in a fenced-in outdoor area are set at ground level, so even the smallest of small fry can fly high. Remember to follow the two rules: no shoes and no flips. The center is open 9:00 A.M. to 10:00 P.M. (or 11:00 P.M. if lots of people are bouncing) daily from mid-June through Labor Day. The cost is $4.50 for 10 minutes.

Cape Escape
14 Canal Road, Orleans
(508) 240-1791
Right near the Orleans Rotary, this fun (and we accent fun) little minigolf center features 18 holes set in nautical surroundings, complete with waterfalls, ponds,

boats, and a water wheel. It's also right next door to two kid-friendly restaurants, Wendy's and Friendly's, and across from a great two-story gift store, Cape Tradewinds, and a bike rental shop. Cape Escape Mini-Golf is open daily from 9:00 A.M. to 10:30 P.M., April through Columbus Day. The cost is $7.00 for adults and $6.00 for children 12 and under.

Gift Barn Mini Golf
U.S. Route 6, Eastham
(508) 255-7000
Just 1 mile north of the National Seashore Visitor Center, this family-run complex offers an 18-hole minigolf course. It has an arcade with pinball, video games, and redemption games—kids love them, because they get to pick out their own prizes. It's open daily June through September, but there's also a great gift shop with lots of stuff for kids that's open springtime until Christmas Eve. And the Red Barn Pizza is right next door if you want to mix gift shopping with minigolf and a meal. The minigolf is open 9:00 A.M. to 10:00 P.M. and costs $3.00 per person; replays are $1.50.

PLAYGROUNDS

Children love playgrounds, and there are plenty of them on the Cape. Just find an elementary school and you're sure to find a playground. Remember, these are open to the public only when school is not in session. Some towns have playgrounds that are not at schools, a great plus because they are more accessible. Here are a few of our favorites:

Barnstable: Behind Barnstable West Elementary School on Route 6A is a wonderful, castlelike wooden playground that will keep kids busy for hours.

Yarmouthport: On Route 6A at the end of Union Street is a wide-open, grassy park where kids can run, plus a playground. It features a fun train, climbing tower with a twisty-tunnel slide, swings, and tires for climbing.

Looking for a twist on the normal sightseeing tour? Try Cape Cod Duckmobiles. They offer tours of downtown Hyannis and Hyannis Harbor on restored U.S. military amphibious vehicles. These narrated tours take you from land to sea and back to land. Tours leave from 427 Main Street, Hyannis. Tickets are $14 for adults, seniors and students are $11, and children younger than age 5 ride free. For more information call (888) 225-DUCK, or visit www.duckmobile.com.

Dennisport: Tucked away on Hall Street, a side street behind the Dennisport Public Library on Route 28, not far from the Harwich line, is a lovely park with a gazebo, and next to it, a great little playground. It features a fun train, climbing tower with a twisty-tunnel slide, swings, and tires for climbing.

Harwich: Behind the elementary school on South Street is the Castle in the Clouds, a wonderful, community-built structure with towers, bridges, and slides. Just a short walk across the yard is a great preschool play area, with a wooden train, tires to climb on, swings, and plenty of sand.

Chatham: Across the street from the Railroad Museum on Depot Road, behind the Chatham Elementary School, is the Play-a-Round Playground, a multilevel wooden structure of twisting turrets, chutes, slides, and bridges. It includes a playing area for disabled children and a fenced-in area for wee ones.

Orleans: Our favorite for simplicity is the parklike play area on Eldredge Parkway, across from the police station and next to the tennis courts. It has swings, slides, a sandbox, lots of room to run, and a couple of simple climbers, and it's perfect for preschoolers. If your kids are a bit older and seeking something more challenging, go down the street to Orleans Elementary School and walk behind the school to the big wooden structure with bridges and tunnels.

One of the most rewarding two hours spent on the sea is aboard the 50-foot research vessel and floating classroom, the R/V Tiger Shark. You'll learn to identify and handle a variety of sea creatures; work with marine naturalists to collect marine life in a jellyfish catch, plankton tow, and lobster and crab trap pull; and bottom dredge with a beam. By the end of your SEAfari you will have a greater appreciation of marine life. Trips leave three times daily from the Ocean Street Docks in Hyannis, mid-June through September. Tickets are $28 for adults and $20 for children ages 3 to 12. For more information call (508) 775-1730, or visit www.t-shark.com.

Wellfleet: At Baker's Field across from Mayo Beach (on Kendrick Avenue, just past the harbor) is a sandy, spacious playground with something for all ages, including a huge structure with ladders, bridges, and slides. It's a perfect alternative if your kids are bored with the beach. They won't be bored here!

TOURS

Cape Cod Central Railroad
252 Main Street, Hyannis
(508) 771-3800, (888) 797-RAIL
www.capetrain.com
Kids will love taking a ride on this line, especially for the thrill as the whistle blows. The rhythm of the train and the spirit of the crew will whisk you away on an exhilarating journey by rail to the Cape Cod Canal and back. You'll pass cranberry bogs, woodlands, and marshes, but just getting there is all the fun. The scenic trains operate late May through late October daily except Monday (holidays excluded). Tickets are sold the day of your trip, and no reservations are taken. Trains depart from Hyannis at 11:00 A.M. and 2:00 P.M. (Sunday 2:00 P.M. only). It

takes just less than an hour to get to the canal. The train turns around there and completes the two-hour ride back to Hyannis (see our Tours and Excursions chapter for more details). Tickets are $15.00 for adults, $13.00 for seniors (62 and older), $9.00 for children ages 3 to 11, and children younger than 3 are free. The railroad also offers a "Family Supper Train." Enjoy kid- and adult-appropriate food as well as activities and entertainment during your two-hour journey. Reservations are required for this trip. They run Tuesday evenings in July and Monday and Tuesday evenings in August. Adults are $38.95, and children younger than 12 are $24.95.

Cape Cod Potato Chip Company
Breed's Hill Road, Hyannis
(508) 775-7253
www.capecodchips.com
Is there a kid anywhere who doesn't love potato chips? They'll love seeing them made even more. The company offers free tours daily year-round—and, yes, you get free crunchy samples at the end. Bet you can't visit just once! It's open year-round 9:00 A.M. to 5:00 P.M. Monday through Friday.

READ ALL ABOUT IT

When searching for activities for your children on the Cape, don't overlook libraries which offer a lot more than just books. Cape libraries tend to be social centers—busy, stimulating places that offer many programs and activities—especially those for children! Almost all the libraries on the Cape offer summer reading programs in which youngsters keep track of the books they read. In addition there are craft classes and story hours—a real boon for the parents of preschoolers. Wherever you are on the Cape, you're not far from a library, check the Yellow Pages for the ones nearest you. Here are just a few of our favorites. Library hours and days of operation change according to season.

Upper Cape

Sandwich Public Library
142 Main Street, Sandwich
(508) 888-0625
www.sandwichpubliclibrary.com
The library holds story hours three days a week for toddlers and preschoolers; call for times and registration. The library also offers a variety of children's activities throughout the year, including a summer reading club.

Mid-Cape

Sturgis Library
3039 Route 6A, Barnstable
(508) 362-6636
www.sturgislibrary.org
This lovely old library offers story time. A preschool story hour is held Friday at 10:00 A.M. from September to June. Pre-register to make sure your child gets a sticker with his or her name on it. The library also offers story/craft programs, puppet shows, and a variety of other pro-grams. Call for dates and times.

Lower Cape

Eldredge Public Library
564 Main Street, Chatham
(508) 945-5170
www.eldredgelibrary.org
Regular story hours are held during the summer on Saturday at 11:15 A.M. for ages 5 and 6. A number of special programs are scheduled throughout the year, including storytellers, folksingers, craft classes, and holiday parties; call for dates and times. The library has a great children's room with a preschool play area, board games for older children, and a study area.

Eastham Public Library
190 Samoset Road, Eastham
(508) 240-5950
www.easthamlibrary.org

This library has a nice children's room, with a terrific play area for little ones and a helpful children's librarian. Story hours are held all year on Friday at 10:30 A.M. The library offers a variety of children's activities during the summer, including writing, drama, and crafts classes.

Provincetown Public Library
330 Commercial Street, Provincetown
(508) 487-7094
www.ptownlib.com
Toddler story time is held at 10:30 A.M. on Wednesday all year, and a story time for all ages takes place Saturday at 10:30 A.M. all year. The summer reading program includes all sorts of classes such as acting, puppet making, crafts, and science. The library, which has a great (and very active!) children's room, always has a col-orful theme to give recognition to children who participate in the reading program.

SUMMER CAMPS AND CREATIVE CENTERS

Many a Cape Cod resident has childhood recollections of learning to swim and sail at a Cape Cod summer camp. With its numer-ous beaches, ponds, and woods, this area is ideal for providing youngsters with outdoor education and recreation. The Cape also has outlets for youthful energies at its sports clinics and art-fostering creative centers. One affordable alternative to day camps are the recreation programs spon-sored by each town. Offerings vary from town to town, but generally include arts and crafts, swimming, tennis, and other sports. Some even have golf and sailing! Each town varies in its policy for allowing participation by nonresidents, most allow nonresidents to sign up, with lower fees for residents. Fees vary as well—the town of Orleans offers its summer recreation pro-gram free to both residents and visitors, but most other towns charge at least nomi-nal fees; all the programs are bargains. Contact your local town recreation depart-ment for specific information.

Upper Cape

Camp Burgess for Boys-Camp Hayward for Girls
75 Stowe Road, South Sandwich
(508) 428-2571
www.ssymca.org
Set on 400 acres of land in an area that encompasses three ponds, these two camps—Burgess for boys and Hayward for girls—are traditional overnight camps for children ages 7 to 15 run by the South Shore YMCA. The waterfront facility allows for sailing, windsurfing, waterski-ing, basketball, volleyball, and tennis. The camps feature a 30-foot climbing tower and offer low- and high-ropes courses. Also offered are classes in arts and crafts, photography, rocketry, and horseback rid-ing. Sessions run two weeks in July and August and cost $900 per camper for the two weeks.

Camp Lyndon Cape Cod YMCA
Stowe Road, South Sandwich
(508) 428-9251
www.ymcacapecod.org/lyndon.htm
A day camp for boys and girls from ages 4 to 12, Lyndon offers archery, games, sports, sailing and boating, a ropes chal-lenge course, arts and crafts, kickball, and soccer. Swimming (including instruction) and horseback riding (ages 6 to 12) are part of the program. Camp Lyndon and its sister camp, Camp 132 in West Barnstable, are very popular and fill quickly. We advise contacting Camp Lyndon in March if you'd like your child to participate in one of their two-week summer programs. Two weeks at Camp Lyndon costs $348. Bus transportation is available.

Camp Farley 4-H Outdoor Education Center
615 Route 130, Mashpee
(508) 477-0181
www.campfarley.com
This 32-acre camp on beautiful freshwater

Mashpee-Wakeby Pond has both day and overnight programs for children ages 4 to 15. Activities range from arts and crafts to boating, canoeing, and horseback riding. Environmental and nature programs are also included. Kids will love the miniature farmyard with goats, sheep, pigs, and chickens. Day camp rates vary by age from $100 to $225 per week. The camp offers weeklong sessions for $350 to overnight campers in grades 3 to 10.

Mid-Cape

Fair Acres Country Day School
35 Fair Acres Drive, Marstons Mills
(508) 420-3288
With pretty Shubel Pond at its doorstep, this day camp for children ages 4 to 9 offers cer-tified Red Cross swimming instruction, arts and crafts, nature studies, sports, tennis, and drama. Call Monday through Friday between 9:00 A.M. and 1:00 P.M. for details.

YMCA Camp 132
2245 Route 132, Barnstable
(508) 362-6500
The Y offers a weeklong summer day pro-gram for children ages 5 to 12 at its well-equipped facility. Children participate in arts and crafts, archery, sports, swimming (including lessons), and Friday field trips (to the Boston Aquarium and to whale watch, for example). Rates vary by age. YMCA membership is not required, but you save 5 percent by belonging to the association.
    The Y also has an active swim team, offers swimming lessons for children ages 6 months and older, and offers youth basketball.

Camp Wingate-Kirkland
White Rock Road, Yarmouthport
18 Woodridge Road, Wayland, MA 01778 (winter)
(508) 362-3798, (508) 358-5816 (winter)
www.campwk.com

Since the late 1950s this coeducational overnight youth camp has offered sports, water activities, arts and crafts, camp craft, music, and drama. Children can choose from a seven-week session or one of the two three-and-a-half-week sessions.

Cape Cod Gymnastics
341 Hokum Road, Dennis
(508) 385-8216
www.capecodgymnastics.com
Open year-round with a variety of classes, Cape Cod Gymnastics offers a nine-week summer program for children 8 and older that culminates with a week of intensive daily training. Other classes are available for children as young as preschool ages, including one for preschoolers and parents to take together. The gym-dandy class is geared to 5- and 6-year-olds, and a variety of other classes are offered for different ages and abilities. Classes are offered between 9:00 A.M. and 8:00 P.M. for different skill levels. Day camps are roughly $450 per week.

Lower Cape

Brewster Day Camp
3570 Route 6A, Brewster
(508) 896-6555
www.brewsterdaycamp.com
Set on a four-acre campus near Nickerson State Park, the Brewster Day Camp offers art, archery, boating, exploring, field sports, games, nature activities, Red Cross swimming lessons, and sailing. There are off-campus trips to places like WaterWhizz, Adventure Isle, and the Providence Zoo, and children can opt for lessons in horseback riding, golf, and tennis. One- to five-day programs are offered (with a few overnights) for children from kindergarten through eighth grade. Sign up by the week, with the full session running for eight weeks from late June through mid-August. A five-day session costs $345.

Brewster Whitecaps Baseball Clinic
Community Center Field, Brewster
(508) 896-3424, (508) 896-9661
www.brewsterwhitecaps.com
Batter up! From mid-June through July the Brewster Whitecaps team sponsors week-long clinics on the art of baseball. Kids learn everything from how to bunt to how to hit a home run. Open to children ages 6 to 13, the clinics meet at Cape Cod Regional Technical School field, the home field for the Brewster Whitecaps. Cost is $50 per week.

Cape Cod Museum of Natural History
Route 6A, Brewster
(508) 896-3867
www.ccmnh.org
The emphasis here is on—what else—the great outdoors. The museum offers one- and two-week day camps for children in grades 1 through 6 in which they learn about everything from birds to dinosaurs. They even get to set up their own fresh-water and saltwater aquariums. Twice a week the museum holds preschool classes for ages 3 to 4. They offer a natural history summer camp calibrated to the interests of those age 3 through grade 7. Typical activities include catching insects, building bird feeders, making sun clocks, and learning about bird banding, coyote tracking, geology, and astronomy. Call for a schedule.

Cape Cod Sea Camps
P.O. Box 1880, Route 6A, Brewster, MA 02631
(508) 896-3451
www.capecodseacamps.com
Established in 1922, Cape Cod Sea Camps is the oldest residential camp on the Cape. With beautiful grounds that stretch to Cape Cod Bay, it offers a seven-week residential camp for ages 7 to 17 and a day camp for ages 5 to 17. Instruction covers all sorts of water sports, including sailing, swimming, windsurfing, waterskiing, and canoeing. They offer both day and overnight programs.

Woodsong Farm Equestrian Center
121 Lund Farm Way, Brewster
(508) 896-5555
www.woodsongcentral.com
If your child is crazy about horses, check out Woodsong Farm's summer programs. For beginners there's Pony Kids, offered two, three, or five days a week for ages 5 to 14. Experienced riders ages 9 to 18 can enroll in Horsemasters for five days a week. Both programs cover all aspects of horsemanship. Lessons are available year-round at the center, which also boards horses and has its own tack shop. Group lessons cost $285 per week.

Chatham A's Baseball Clinic
Veteran's Field, Veteran's Field Road
(off Main Street behind the middle
school), Chatham
(508) 945-5199
www.chathamas.com
The weekly training programs conducted by the Chatham A's team helps kids ages 6 to 17 master the dos and don'ts of baseball. Classes are held at the field, between Main Street and Depot Road (the entrance is on Main Street) from mid-June through August and cost $50 per week for ages 9 to 12, $90 for ages 13 to 17.

Creative Arts Center
154 Crowell Road, Chatham
(508) 945-3583
www.capecodcreativearts.org
Budding da Vincis and Cassatts will love the year-round classes in drawing, painting, pottery, photography, sculpture, and jewelry making. Classes are flexible and open to a wide range of ages and skill levels. Price varies per program.

Academy of Performing Arts
5 Giddiah Hill Road, Orleans
(508) 255-5510
www.apa1.org
More than 20 instructors teach classes ranging from dance (ballet, jazz, line, and tap) to drama and creative writing for children and adults. How about clown classes? Or sign up for classes in how to play a musical instrument, everything from piano, cello, and flute to saxophone, viola, and guitar. Courses run two weeks in July and August with a graduation ceremony—a public performance to show off newfound talent. (Don't worry, everyone applauds.)

Orleans Cardinals Baseball Clinic
P.O. Box 504, Orleans, MA 02653
(508) 255-0793
www.orleanscardinals.com
The Cardinals offer what is perhaps the finest baseball clinic on the Cape—and it's very affordable. The weeklong morning clinics for boys and girls ages 6 through 13 begin in mid-June and continue through the first week of August. Cost is $55 for the first week and $50 for each additional week. This fee includes an Orleans Cardinals Clinic T-shirt.

Wellfleet Bay Wildlife Sanctuary
291 U.S. Route 6, P.O. Box 236, South
Wellfleet, MA 02663
www.wellfleetbay.org
Kids who are avid about nature will appreciate the one-week Natural History Day Camp Programs at this Massachusetts Audubon site. The activities are calibrated to different ages, but they all have an intense focus on animals and their habitats. Each week focuses on different marine or animal life, their habitats, and the children's exploring and observing skills. Younger kids learn about animal tracks, older kids go on canoe trips and snorkel in Cape Cod Bay. The camp runs from late June through August for children in prekindergarten programs through grade 4.

[Facing page] *Gaining confidence on the water at Cape Cod Sea Camps.* STEVE BEAUDET, CAPE COD SEA CAMPS

ANNUAL EVENTS

alendars ready? Before you decide when you want to visit Cape Cod, you might want to take a look at just what's going on. You'll have a lot to look at too. Cape Cod has come a long way since the days when it was known as just a summer playground. Now it's a year-round vacation resort with events planned for all twelve months of the year.

Arrive in May and you'll find yourself at the largest sailboat regatta on the East Coast, the Figawi Race from Hyannis to Nantucket (be sure to make early reservations for their posh charity ball). In June Cape Cod Heritage Week will lead you through the towns of the Cape, where you'll discover a treasure chest of cultural, historical, and environmental riches. Flip the calendar to December, and you'll find yourself strolling amid merry crowds through some of America's most charming colonial villages decked out in Christmas card perfection.

During Cape Cod's busy summer season, you can sit down to a banquet of lobster rolls, clam chowder, and strawberries dished up at many of the time-honored festivals designed by local residents in celebration of our cultural heritage.

Perhaps no event on Cape Cod surpasses the joyousness of the Portuguese Festival held in Provincetown the last weekend in June. In July Independence Day fireworks, patriotic banners, and parades mark the official start of summer, when arts and crafts fairs abound and village greens around the Cape host evening concerts. The circus and fairs come to town, and the annual Wampanoag Pow Wow brings together Native American Indians from across the nation for three days of tribal dances and events. At the end of August you can hear the cool strains of jazz when the New England Jazz Festival comes to Mashpee.

Autumn is a truly magical time here—more so if you're visiting Bourne for its Farm Pumpkin Day or Falmouth for Harvest Day. Museums and sanctuaries also offer an opportunity to explore the seasonal changes through programs and activities every day of the year.

Also occurring throughout the year, Cape Cod's many charity events help maintain institutions vital to the social fabric of the Cape and give you great opportunities to have fun. You can play croquet on the lawn of the stately Ocean Edge Resort or listen to the Boston Pops Esplanade Orchestra at the Village Green in Hyannis.

We suggest that you call the Cape Cod Chamber of Commerce, or the chamber of commerce or board of trade in the town you will be visiting, for an up-to-date listing of weekly events. Most towns have a local newspaper that publishes a weekly calendar section, most often on Friday. The *Cape Cod Times*, the Cape's daily newspaper, does a fine job covering the whole area with a weekly supplement, *Cape Week*.

The following listing of events is arranged chronologically by month and then roughly be geography, so Provincetown festivals, for example are listed toward the end of the month. The year begins appropriately with New Year's celebrations.

JANUARY

Cape-wide

New Year's Eve Celebrations
Various sites throughout the Cape
(508) 790-ARTS
Almost every town on Cape Cod, including Falmouth, Mashpee, Hyannis, Orleans,

and Provincetown, have fireworks displays, costume parades, and fun for the whole family. Chatham has one of the largest First Night events, appropriately named Chatham First Night, with a celebration of the arts from noon until the midnight fireworks go off. Cape-wide celebrations have been in high demand. You can purchase First Night buttons at the local chamber of commerce (listed in our Area Overview chapter), at participating community stores, or by calling the Arts Foundation at the number above.

FEBRUARY

Upper Cape

Cape and Islands Orchid Society Show
Sea Crest Resort, 350 Quaker Road, Falmouth
(508) 548-2221
This annual show is sponsored by the Cape and Islands Orchid Society the last weekend in February. It includes exquisite blooming orchid displays, informative demonstrations on growing orchids and building greenhouses, and, of course, orchids for sale. The aroma alone is worth the admission: $5.00 for adults, and $3.00 for seniors and children.

Mid-Cape

Hyannis Marathon, Half Marathon, 10K, Relay
Hyannis
(508) 775-0143
This event, usually held in late February, starts and finishes at the Sheraton Hyannis Resort Hotel. Some 300 marathoners, 1,500 half marathoners, 500 10Kers, and 50 relay teams wend their way along a scenic course that passes Craigville Beach, Hyannis Harbor, Lewis Bay, the John F.

Kennedy Memorial, and the Kennedy Family Compound. The marathon is a Boston Marathon qualifying event.

Presidents Day Antique Show and Sale
Barnstable High School Field House
West Main Street, Hyannis
(508) 775-2280
Scheduled each year for the Saturday and Sunday of Presidents Day weekend, this show features more than 40 regional dealers who offer an array of antique furniture, glass, and china. The doors open at 10:00 A.M. This is a major fund-raiser for the Hyannis Public Library. Admission is $4.00.

APRIL

Upper Cape

Woods Hole Model Boat Show
Woods Hole Historical Museum, 579 Woods Hole Road, Woods Hole
(508) 548-7270
www.woodsholemuseum.org
You don't have to be an enthusiast to enjoy yourself at this event, held in late April. Stroll through an indoor exhibit of large model boats, or join the enthusiasts down at Eel Pond for regattas featuring radio-controlled models of vintage yachts from the 1930s.

If you are lucky, you can sometimes spot whales from land. April is one of the best times for seeing humpback and finback whales. Race Point or Hatches Harbor in Provincetown are good places to look, because nearshore water there is deep enough for marine mammals. Whales can also be seen occasionally right inside Provincetown Harbor. For more information we recommend you call the Center for Coastal Studies, (508) 487-3622.

Mid-Cape

Daff O'Ville Days
Various sites in Osterville
(508) 428-9700

Sponsored by the Osterville Business and Professional Association, this village-wide celebration takes place during the last week in April. Events include an Arbor Day celebration, Mad Hatter Tea Party, bagpipe music, wine tastings, and a book sale. The fun continues with outdoor grills, a fashion show, and an antique car display. Special children's events keep the little ones busy, and daffodils beautify the village. There is plenty of free parking.

Lower Cape

Brewster in Bloom
Various locations in Brewster
(508) 896-3500
www.brewsterinbloom.com

An annual and eagerly awaited spring event, Brewster in Bloom has grown from a small festival celebrating Brewster's beautiful daffodil display. The festival is four days of fun and games, including such activities as a golf tournament, dance, flea market, road race, parade, band concert, arts and crafts fair, food tasting, inn tour, and children's activities. And all the while there are more than 100,000 blooming daffodils lining the streets! The event takes place the last weekend in April, sometimes falling into the first days of May. Tickets are required for certain events, like the golf tourney and the dance; otherwise, most of the Brewster in Bloom activities are free.

MAY

Cape-wide

Cape Cod Maritime Days
Various sites throughout the Cape
(508) 362-3828
www.capecodcommission.org/hdn

History galore! Maritime Week is a major Cape-wide event that highlights the landmarks and sites comprising Cape Cod's wealth of maritime history. This mid-May celebration is coordinated by the Cape Cod Commission, which arranges lighthouse tours, Coast Guard open houses, special cruises, walks, and lectures throughout the week. In Yarmouthport a village that was once a major port, for example, you can take self-guided walking tours of sea captains' homes and attend open houses at museums, getting from place to place via the free trolley service. All events are free.

Upper Cape

Annual Cape Cod Canal Striped Bass Fishing Tourney
Bourne
(508) 759-6000
www.capecodcanalchamber.org

The Canal Region Chamber of Commerce and area tackle shops sponsor this popular nine-day tournament. It starts the third Saturday of the month, prime time for some of the best bass fishing in the canal area. Sign up to win cash awards and prizes. Entrance fees are $30 for adults and $15 for children 14 and younger.

Rhododendron's Blooming
Heritage Museums & Gardens, Grove and Pine Streets, Sandwich
(508) 888-3300
www.heritagemuseumsandgardens.org

One of the largest and best collections of rhododendrons is found in Sandwich, and many are in bloom the last week in May and during the first two weeks in June. You may participate in tours and lectures, and shop for plants at the plant sale. And, of course, view the multitude of beautiful rhododendron colors. Admission to Heritage Museums & Gardens is $12.00, seniors $10.00, ages 6 to 16 $6.00, ages 5 and younger free.

Herb Festival
Green Briar Nature Center, 6 Discovery
Hill Road, East Sandwich
(508) 888-6870
www.thorntonburgess.org
Benefiting the Thornton Burgess Society, this free event held over three days in mid-May offers lectures on herbs, special demonstrations, exhibits, and wildflower garden walks. You can get a taste of the herbs at a wonderful luncheon (reservations are required) and buy plants just in time to start your own herb garden.

Woods Hole Illumination Weekend
Woods Hole
(508) 548-8500
This event, held over a weekend in late May, provides a great introduction to charming Woods Hole. Harbor tours, carriage rides, Coast Guard rescue enactments, and music under the stars will keep you occupied while you're waiting for the main attraction: nightly illuminations of boats and businesses throughout Woods Hole Village, Eel Pond, Great Harbor, and Little Harbor. Best of all, it's all free!

Mid-Cape

Figawi Sailboat Race & Charity Ball
Hyannis
(508) 778-6100, (800) 4HYNNIS
www.figawi.com
The Figawi regatta, which takes place over Memorial Day weekend, is a great Cape Cod celebration that kicks off the summer season in style. Generally considered the largest sailboat race on the East Coast, the Figawi usually draws more than 200 boats in a highly competitive (for some!) race from Hyannis to Nantucket. A cocktail party greets contestants at Nantucket, and the following day is filled with an awards ceremony, afternoon clambake, and evening Memorial Day party. The reverse Figawi from Nantucket to Hyannis is followed by another party and another awards pres-

In the spring Pilgrim Heights in Truro is one of the best places on Cape Cod to see hawks. Look for broad-winged hawks, sharp-shinned hawks, American kestrels, and northern harriers. You might spot red-tailed hawks too, which are present year-round. If you are interested, Wellfleet Bay Audubon Sanctuary (508-349-2615), leads hawk walks through the spring months.

entation. It's just party, party, party! And if you'll be here earlier, you can join the fun a whole week earlier at the black-tie Figawi Charity Ball (508-771-3333), the kickoff event held the preceding weekend at the Sheraton Hyannis Hotel and Resort. Proceeds aid local charities.

Johnny Kelley Half Marathon and
Five Miler
Hyannis
(508) 775-8877
www.johnnykelleyroadrace.com
This annual half marathon and 5-mile race is named for the man who ran in more Boston Marathons than any other runner. This race benefits the Cape Cod Hospital Foundation and is run on Sunday of Memorial Day weekend (see our Sports and Recreation chapter).

Lower Cape

Spring Fling
Downtown Chatham
(508) 345-5199
www.chathamcapecod.org
Chatham gets a little crazy with spring fever in May with its annual Spring Fling. There's a wild and crazy hat parade, clowns, jugglers, a pet show, and face painting. Sponsored by the Chatham Merchants Association, this family-oriented event is held on the Saturday of Mother's Day weekend.

Arts and Crafts Shows
Nauset Middle School, Route 28, Orleans
(508) 385-4899
The Artisans' Guild of Cape Cod hosts five arts and crafts shows during the year; the first takes place on Memorial Day weekend (the others are held in early July, early August, mid-October, and late November). Some shows are held on the front lawn of Nauset Middle School, others are held in the school's gymnasium. There is plenty of parking available at the school, and there is no admission fee.

JUNE
Upper Cape

Strawberry Festival
St. Barnabas Church, Falmouth
(508) 548-8500
About a century ago Falmouth was one of the largest producers of strawberries in the eastern United States. Today locals mark this late June event on their calendars, and it seems that everyone in town shows up on the Village Green across from the St. Barnabas Church to feast on fresh, luscious strawberries from Tony Andrews Farm in East Falmouth. You can also buy crafts and baked goods throughout the day.

Willowbend Children's Charity Pro-Am
Willowbend Country Club,
100 Willowbend Road, Mashpee
(508) 539-5030
www.willowbendproam.com
The greatest names in golf, including Greg Norman, Tom Watson, and Nick Faldo, have competed in this annual Pro-Am with such pro sports stars as Doug Flutie and Hall of Fame hockey defenseman Bobby Orr. The event, held the last Monday in the month, benefits children's programs on the Cape (see our Sports and Recreation chapter). Tickets are $15.00; children younger than 12 are $5.00.

Mid-Cape

Annual WCOD Chowder Festival
Cape Cod Melody Tent, West Main Street, Hyannis
(508) 775-5678
www.106wcod.com
Sample delicious chowders cooked up by some of Cape Cod's best restaurants at the Annual WCOD 106FM Chowder Festival, but be sure to get to the Melody Tent before the chowder buckets run dry. From noon to 5:00 P.M. enjoy chowder, listen to live entertainment, and enjoy kids' activities. Tickets are $10.00 in advance for adults, and $4.00 for children younger than 10. The event is usually held toward the end of June, but the exact date depends on the Melody Tent entertainment schedule.

Lower Cape

Brewster Historical Society Antiques Fair
Drummer Boy Field, Route 6A, Brewster
(508) 896-9521
You're bound to find something special to purchase among the more than 75 dealers selling their wares at this very popular show and sale. It's held on the last Saturday of June on the Drummer Boy Park grounds, and as a special bonus the on-site Old Higgins Farm windmill is open free to the public for the event. The fair runs from 9:00 A.M. to 4:00 P.M. and admission is $4.00; ages 12 and younger are free.

Portuguese Festival
Provincetown
(508) 487-0086
Provincetown celebrates its Portuguese and fishing heritage with a festival the last weekend of June. There is music galore, a kid's fishing derby on Friday from 10:00 A.M. to noon, a parade at 5:00 P.M. on Saturday, and live music and dance performances throughout the weekend. The

Blessing of the Fleet occurs on Sunday, and that event begins with a noon procession from St. Peter's Church to MacMillan Pier. Parking is limited in Provincetown, but you should be able to find a place in one of the town parking lots if you get there early. There is no charge to attend the parade and the blessing of the fleet; however, a $3.00 donation is requested for some of the activities.

JULY

Cape-wide

Independence Day Fireworks and Events
Various locations throughout the Cape
Many towns across the Cape offer spectacular fireworks displays to celebrate Independence Day. Plan to arrive by dusk at one of the following locations: Falmouth Heights, Hyannis Harbor, Orleans Rock Harbor, and Provincetown Harbor. Hyannis also hosts a July 4th boat parade in the harbor, Falmouth has a blessing of the fleet, and Harwich has a July 4th Family Fun Day with a craft fair and entertainment. Chatham, Orleans, Wellfleet, and Provincetown have parades. The Community of Jesus in Orleans (508-240-2400) holds a Star Spangled Spectacular Festival complete with a band concert and fireworks.

Upper Cape

Concerts in the Park
Buzzards Bay Park, Buzzards Bay
(508) 759-6000
The music ranges from country and western to jazz and from show tunes to rock and roll at this music series held at Buzzards Bay Park gazebo. Bring a blanket or lawn chair and join the fun every Thursday night from 7:00 to 9:00 P.M. during July and August. Admission is free.

Barnstable County Fair
Route 151, East Falmouth
(508) 563-3200
www.barnstablecountyfair.org
A Cape Cod tradition for 138 years, the Barnstable County Fair regularly attracts more than 100,000 people for nine days packed with fun, food, and education. There are incredible exhibits, amazing entertainment, awesome animal shows, and food and craft events at which adults and children win prizes for baked goods, canned goods, homegrown fruits and vegetables, quilts, and other handiwork as well as for the best sheep, pigs, cows, rabbits, poultry, and so on. Top-name entertainment fills the evenings. A petting zoo, carnival rides, and games make the Barnstable County Fair really exciting for kids. It's a Cape Cod classic held the third week in July. Regular admission is $8.00 for those 13 and older; children younger than 12 enter free. Check out the three-day pass for $18.00.

Annual Arts & Crafts Street Fair
Main Street, Falmouth
(508) 548-8500
Hosted by the Falmouth Village Association, this event features more than 200 artisans and craftspeople displaying their wares. Booths line both sides of Main Street, and they close the street to vehicle traffic. You'll also find plenty of food and fun entertainment throughout the day. The Street Fair, held on a Wednesday during early July, starts at 10:00 A.M. and goes until 6:00 P.M.

Mashpee Wampanoag Pow Wow
Barnstable County Fair Grounds, Route 151, Mashpee
(508) 477-0208
Open to the public, this event is sponsored by the Mashpee Wampanoag Tribal Council and features tribal dances and other activities, such as the native fireball game, princess contests, a road race, traditional clambake, and American-Indian crafts. This

popular three-day event attracts American Indians from many other states and always takes place the first weekend in July. Admission is charged.

Annual Sandcastle Competition
South Cape Beach, Mashpee
(508) 539-1400

South Cape Beach is the site of this annual sandcastle competition sponsored by Leisure Services from 9:00 A.M. until noon the second Saturday in July. There are five categories: 5 to 7 years of age, 8 to 10, 11 to 13, 14 to 16, and family. Try your hand at sculpting sand. You are allowed three hours to produce your masterpiece; judging is at noon. The competition is free though pre-registration is requested for those who want to compete.

Mashpee Night at the Pops
Mashpee Commons, Mashpee
(508) 539-2345

Mashpee puts together an unbeatable combination: the Cape Cod Symphony Orchestra featuring conductor Royston Nash and a fireworks display. Just bring your own chair. It's sponsored by the Mashpee Community Concert Committee. It's generally held on the last Saturday in July. Admission is free.

Clambakes are a classic Cape Cod tradition. It's a major undertaking: It requires digging a pit and lining it with stones. A fire is built in the pit. Once it has burned to ash, the hot rocks are covered with seaweed. Oysters, scallops, fish, and lobster—often corn and potatoes, too— are piled on, covered up, and steamed for an hour or so. Want someone else to do the work? Compass Rose Clambakes will cater a clambake for you. Call (508) 566-1000, or visit www.compassrose clambakes.com.

Mid-Cape

St. George's Grecian Festival
St. George Greek Orthodox Church,
Route 28, Centerville
(508) 775-3045

This three-day fair in mid-July features fantastic food like you've never tasted before. Besides the wonderful Greek food (ah, the stuffed grape leaves and Retsina wine!), there's a great crafts fair and bake sale as well as high-spirited dancing and a guided tour of the majestic domed Greek Orthodox Church. There are different booths and food tents. Free admission and parking.

Lower Cape

Sunday Evening Concerts
Drummer Boy Park, Route 6A, Brewster
(508) 385-8504

Every Sunday evening throughout the summer musicians offer free outdoor concerts at the Gazebo at Drummer Boy Park on Route 6A. Have a wonderful time listening to folk, classical, Big Band, or contemporary music, depending on the night, and enjoying the view of Cape Cod Bay off in the distance. Concerts start at 6:00 P.M. and last about two hours.

Annual Harwich Professional Arts and Crafts Festival
Brooks Park, Oak Street, Harwich
(508) 385-8689, (800) 441-3199

This early-July event features more than 100 professional craftspeople and artisans offering their handcrafted works of art for sale. The arts and crafts festival is held over two days. There is no admission charge. A similar event is held in August (see listing in next section).

Band Time in Chatham
Kate Gould Park, off Main Street, Chatham
(508) 945-5199
www.chathamcapecod.org

This is good old-fashioned Cape Cod family fun. On Fridays from July 4 through Labor Day, Kate Gould Park fills with thousands of people who happily listen to the Chatham Band play various traditional tunes, including such favorites as the "Bunny Hop" and the "Hokey Pokey" for the kids. Bring a blanket, lawn chairs, and maybe some bug spray. The music is free, but you may want to purchase balloons and refreshments. Concerts start at 8:00 P.M.

AUGUST

Upper Cape

Peter Rabbit's Animal Fair
Thornton Burgess Museum, Route 130, Sandwich
(508) 888-6870
The Thornton Burgess Society sponsors this fair geared to younger folk, who will love the live animal exhibits, pet rabbit show, music, refreshments, and games. Burgess items are available for purchase. There is no admission fee to the fair, which takes place the second weekend in August.

Falmouth Road Race
Falmouth
(508) 540-7000
www.falmouthroadrace.com
More than two decades ago, a group of runners decided to run from Woods Hole to a bar in Falmouth Heights. Thus began what has become an international road race that is second only to the Boston Marathon in New England popularity. The Falmouth Road Race attracts thousands of onlookers and some 9,500 runners from across the country and around the world to sample its challenging 7.1-mile course the second weekend of August. The race starts at 10:00 A.M. (see our Sports and Recreation chapter for more information).

Mid-Cape

Centerville Old Home Week
Various sites in Centerville
(508) 775-1787
Among the special moments of the Centerville Old Home Week are a reunion dinner, an ice-cream social with legendary Four Seas ice cream, lectures, a road race, band concerts, and a bonfire at the beach. A good time is always had by all. Old Home Week takes place in mid-August, and proceeds benefit the Centerville Library.

West Barnstable Village Festival
Library and Community Building, Lombard Field, Route 149, West Barnstable
(508) 362-2262
Look for fun and community spirit with book sales, children's games and activities, a photography contest, raffles, antique cars, and plenty of food. This event is held in the middle of the month, and most activities are free.

Pops by the Sea
Hyannis Village Green, Hyannis
(508) 362-0066
This is it—the most popular concert on the Cape! The Boston Pops Esplanade Orchestra comes to town with conductor Keith Lockhart to perform some wonderful late-afternoon music, both classical and popular tunes as well as patriotic marches and sing-alongs. Held at the Hyannis Village Green, the concert usually takes place on the first Sunday of the month and is sponsored by the Arts Foundation of Cape Cod. Lawn seats cost $15 ($20 the day of the concert) and premium seats cost $50.

Dennis Festival Days
Various sites in Dennis
(508) 398-3568, (800) 243-9920
www.dennischamber.com

The annual Dennis Festival Days is a weeklong, end-of-summer (usually the third week of the month) celebration held at various locations in town. Activities include kite-flying and sandcastle-building contests, an antique auto parade, church suppers, historic tours, a chalk art contest, river cruises, hayrides, farm tours, flower shows, an arts and crafts fair, and fireworks at West Dennis Beach. One highlight that always brews excitement is the Annual Great Beer Race, in which waiters and waitresses from local restaurants weave through an obstacle course carrying pitchers of beer on trays.

Lower Cape

Craftsmen Fair
Drummer Boy Park, Route 6A, Brewster
(508) 385-2970
The Society of Cape Cod Craftsmen has been sponsoring this popular juried crafts showcase for more than 50 years, making it the second-oldest crafts organization in New England! The three-day craft celebration features about 50 craftspeople. It is held in early August from 10:00 A.M. to 5:00 P.M. all three days and admission is free.

Annual Harwich Professional Arts and Crafts Festival
Brooks Park, Oak Street, Harwich
(508) 385-8689, (800) 441-3199
Held at the beginning of August, this event features more than 100 professional artists and craftsmen offering their hand-crafted works of art for sale. This crafts festival is held over two days. There is no admission charged.

Annual Pops in the Park
Eldredge Park, Orleans
(508) 225-1386
www.popsinthepark.com
Grab your lawn chair or blanket, pack a picnic dinner, and enjoy the music. The Annual Pops in the Park, held at Eldredge Park in Orleans, is an outdoor concert by the Cape Symphony Orchestra, conducted by Royston Nash. It's always an enchanted evening of music and fun. The concert is held the third or fourth Saturday of the month. Tickets cost $55.00 for table seats, $25.00 for chair seats, $18.00 for the lawn, and $5.00 for children ages 6 to 17.

Fine Arts Work Center Annual Benefit Auction
24 Pearl Street, Provincetown
(508) 487-9960
You'll find a little bit of everything here—from works of fine art to jewelry to furniture to clothing. Merchandise and services are donated to this live auction by area merchants and residents. The event is held mid-August and proceeds from the auction help support the Work Center's fellowship programs. Admission to the auction is free.

Carnival Week
Various locations in Provincetown
(508) 487-2313
www.ptownchamber.com
Just when you thought you had seen it all in P-town, along comes Carnival Week! Sponsored by the Provincetown Business Guild, this weeklong celebration, usually held the third week in August, features musical productions, guesthouse parties, balls, nightclub entertainment, and an outrageous parade complete with floats and entertainers. A splendid time is guaranteed for all!

[Facing page] *The Boston Pops visits the Cape to put on the extremely popular annual concert, Pops by the Sea, on the Hyannis Town Green.* HYANNIS AREA CHAMBER OF COMMERCE

Provincetown AIDS Support Group
Annual Auction
Provincetown Town Hall
(508) 487-9445

This Provincetown auction is held every Labor Day weekend and is attended by tourists, residents, and even some celebrities who bid on everything from works of art to furniture and jewelry. Proceed benefit the town's AIDS support programs. Nearly every Provincetown artist contributes artwork to this worthy cause.

SEPTEMBER

Upper Cape

Bourne Scallop Fest
Buzzards Bay Park, Buzzards Bay
(508) 759-6000
www.capecodcanalchamber.org

For more than 30 years Bourne has hosted the largest scallop festival on the East Coast during the third weekend in September. Thousands converge on Buzzards Bay Park over three days to sample the seafood and attend the crafts fair. There are children's games, rides, plenty of entertainment, and, of course, scallops! It's $3.00 to enter, and there are plenty of things to spend your money on, like great food and local handmade crafts.

Volunteers throughout Massachusetts turn out each year on the third Saturday in September for COASTSWEEP, a statewide beach cleanup organized by Massachusetts Coastal Zone Management. Participants collect marine debris and record the types of trash they find. This information is then used to help reduce further marine debris problems. Call (617) 287-5570 for a calendar of events or to volunteer.

Cape Cod Kennel Club Show
Barnstable Fair Grounds, Route 151,
East Falmouth
(508) 394-1681

Any AKC-licensed dog that meets eligibility requirements is allowed to enter; applications must be submitted three weeks before the show. More than 1,000 dogs representing more than 125 breeds compete. Spectator tickets are $5.00 for adults and $2.00 for children age 12 and younger.

Mid-Cape

Cape Cod Glass Show
Cape Cod Community College, off
Route 132, West Barnstable
(508) 888-0251

The Sandwich Glass Museum has sponsored this mid-September glass show for more than 15 years. Nearly 50 glass dealers from throughout the United States display samples of antique and contemporary glass. Pieces from as far back as the 18th century are displayed, as well as popular depression glassware, art glass marbles, and more. Of course rare and not-so-rare Sandwich glass is also on display. Proceeds from this event benefit the Sandwich Glass Museum. Admission is $6.00.

Lower Cape

Annual Bird Carvers' Festival
Cape Cod Museum of Natural History
869 Route 6A, Brewster
(508) 896-3867
www.ccmnh.org

The Annual Bird Carvers' Festival is one of the oldest wildlife-carving exhibitions in the country. It is usually held on the third weekend of September. At the event, which is a fund-raiser for the Cape Cod Museum of Natural History, experience a world of decoys and miniatures as well as nature walks, carving demonstrations, birds of prey exhibits, and birdhouse-building tips. Admission is charged.

Harwich Cranberry Harvest Festival
Various locations in Harwich
(508) 430-2811
www.harwichcranberryfestival.com

Since it started as part of the National Bicentennial Celebration in 1976, the Harwich Cranberry Harvest Festival has grown into a week-and-a-half-long town-wide extravaganza. The week is filled with many events, including a carnival, a parade, fireworks, a road race, an arts and crafts festival, a classic car show, sailboat races, softball games, food tasting ... the list goes on and on. This is the postsummer event you cannot miss! The festival is held the third weekend in September.

A Taste of Harwich
Cape Cod Regional Technical School
Route 124, Harwich
(508) 432-1600
www.harwichcc.com

Get a taste of Harwich, all under one roof. This evening event, sponsored by the Harwich Chamber of Commerce, allows you to sample fine cuisine from a number of Harwich restaurants. A Taste of Harwich takes place during the Harwich Cranberry Harvest Festival.

Eastham Windmill Weekend
Various locations in Eastham
(508) 240-7211
www.easthamchamber.com

This is Eastham's big day! Windmill Weekend is a community celebration, featuring a parade, road race, games, sand castle competition, entertainment, antique car show, kids' activities, and an arts and crafts show. The whole event focuses on the Eastham gristmill, which was built in Plymouth way back in the 17th century. The celebration usually takes place the weekend after Labor Day. The mill is opened to visitors during the festivities

(see our Attractions chapter). U.S. Route 6 is closed for a few hours for the parade, so pay attention to the date if you are planning on passing through!

Truro Treasures Weekend
Truro
(508) 487-8514
www.trurotreasures.org

This celebration of Truro has been going on for more than 10 years now and seems to get bigger every year. It takes place during a long weekend in late September and features a historic home tour, a classic and antique car exhibit, an arts and crafts fair at the Truro Central School, a flea market at Atlantic Spice, a pancake breakfast, grape stomping at the Truro Vineyards, a treasure hunt and face-painting for the children, and is topped off with a favorite local tradition: the "Dump Dance," complete with live music.

Great Provincetown Schooner Regatta
Provincetown
(508) 487-3424
www.provincetownschoonerrace.com

Four classes of sailing vessels—ranging from 19 feet to more than 65 feet in length—compete in this race. Held on a weekend in early September, it starts off with a Parade of Sail along the Provincetown waterfront, followed by the noon start of the regatta.

Provincetown Art Association Annual Consignment Auction
460 Commercial Street, Provincetown
(508) 487-1750

Every year since 1979 this auction has been an art lover's dream come true. The items put on the block here are consigned by collectors, assuring only first-rate works of art by area artists. Dealers and collectors from around the country attend. There is no charge to attend this mid-September auction. Proceeds from the live auction help fund the Provincetown Art Association's programs and exhibitions.

OCTOBER

Upper Cape

Annual Harvest Day
Main Street, Falmouth
(508) 548-1191
www.falmouth-capecod.com
What better way to spend a crisp fall day than at Falmouth's Annual Harvest Day? The Cape Cod Farmers Market, face painting, pumpkin totem pole, pumpkin decorating, dried-flower arrangements—they all add up to lots of autumn fun. The Village Association sponsors this affair the first Saturday of the month.

Cape Cod Marathon
Falmouth
(508) 540-6959
www.capecodmarathon.com
This marathon, which begins and ends at Falmouth's Village Green, attracts more than 1,000 participants. Sponsored by the Falmouth Track Club and run the last week in October, it's considered a Boston Marathon-qualifying event (see our Sports and Recreation chapter). The race starts at 8:30 A.M.

Mashpee Oktoberfest
Mashpee Commons, Routes 151 and 28,
Mashpee
(508) 539-1400
www.mashpeechamber.com
Mashpee adds to the autumn fun with its very own two-day Oktoberfest complete with an arts and crafts show and rides for the children. There are sidewalk sales, a parade, car show, authentic German food and music, and live entertainment. The festivities are presented by Mashpee Leisure Services, Mashpee Commons, and the Mashpee Chamber. This great family event is held early in October from 10:00 A.M. to 5:00 P.M. Admission is free.

Mid-Cape

Yarmouth Seaside Festival
John Simpkins Elementary School
Route 28, South Yarmouth
(508) 778-1008
www.yarmouthcapecod.com
The town of Yarmouth goes all out for this major event. Come enjoy a parade, arts and crafts, plenty of food, music, children's rides, demonstrations, races, competitions, and a fireworks display. The festival is scheduled each year for Columbus Day weekend.

Lower Cape

Wellfleet Oyster Festival
Wellfleet
(508) 349-0330
www.wellfleetoysterfestival.org
Main Street is closed to cars during the weekend after Columbus Day to accommodate this two-day food and crafts fair. Shellfishermen and -women serving up their local specialties are the main attraction, but the art auction, live music, 5K road race, kayak race, historic walking tours, gallery talks, and a town-wide parade keep everyone busy. It culminates with the Sunday finals of a two-day "Shuck-Off" competition, in which shellfish harvesters show off their speed and skills.

Women's Week
Various sites in Provincetown
www.womeninnkeepers.com
Women's Week, usually held midmonth near Columbus Day, is a weeklong festival of music, comedy shows, readings, fashion shows, auctions, and a Saturday night prom. Many art galleries also hold events and exhibitions honoring women. Women's Week is sponsored by the Women Innkeepers of Provincetown.

[Facing page] *Fall means ripe cranberries, just in time for Thanksgiving feasts.* HYANNIS AREA CHAMBER OF COMMERCE

NOVEMBER

Lower Cape

Annual Holiday Craft Fair
Cape Cod Regional Technical High
School, Route 124, Harwich
(508) 771-2600, ext. 232
This is a big one! Held annually at the
Cape Cod Tech, this craft fair features
more than 125 artisans from up and down
the East Coast. The fair, which features all
handcrafted items, takes place over two
days, and admission is free.

Chatham by the Sea
Various sites in Chatham
(508) 945-1122
www.chathamcapecod.org
Chatham celebrates the holiday season
early with Chatham by the Sea, which
kicks off mid-November with candy-
cane making demonstrations, arts and
crafts fairs, a dinner dance at the
Chatham Bars Inn, and, of course, the
arrival of Santa Claus. The event runs
through New Year's Eve, culminating
with the First Night celebration (see
January listings).

Annual Lighting of the Monument
1 High Pole Road, Provincetown
(508) 487-3424
www.ptownchamber.com
Every winter volunteers drape Provincetown's Pilgrim Monument with some
5,000 lights, turning the world's tallest
granite structure into the world's tallest
granite Christmas tree (more than 250
feet tall—see our Attractions chapter).
The monument is lit in November, the
day before Thanksgiving, and remains lit
nightly through New Year's Day. Carols
and refreshments at the town hall complete the scene.

DECEMBER

Cape-wide

Christmas Strolls
There's perhaps no more wonderful way to
catch the holiday spirit than a Christmastime stroll through one of the Cape's picturesque villages. The museums, historic
homes, bed-and-breakfasts, and stores all
open their doors to the public with good
holiday cheer. Expect to see Santa com-
manding the attention of wide-eyed children and to hear carolers filling the air with
traditional holiday song. Besides getting
you in the spirit, the strolls are also a great
way to get your holiday shopping done.

Many towns and villages have Christmas strolls; they are generally planned for
early December. Here are some of them:

Sandwich Stroll (during Christmas in
Sandwich; see listing below)

Falmouth Christmas Stroll (during
Christmas by the Sea; see listing below)

**Hyannis Christmas Stroll and Harbor
Lighting**

Barnstable Village Christmas Stroll

Dennis Christmas Stroll

Yarmouthport Christmas Stroll

**Osterville Village Christmas Open
House**

Harwich Stroll (during Christmas
Weekend in the Harwiches)

Chatham Christmas Stroll

Upper Cape

Christmas in Sandwich
Various sites in Sandwich
(508) 759-6000
Here is small-town New England at its
loveliest. The celebration runs for more
than two weeks, starting with carols and a
stroll throughout the village to view the

Christmas lights that twinkle in and around the village's historic homes. The celebration continues with church fairs, music, plays, open houses at museums, bed-and-breakfasts, shops in the village, exhibits, and demonstrations. Christmas in Sandwich is sponsored by the Canal Region Chamber of Commerce.

Christmas by the Sea Weekend
Various sites in Falmouth
(508) 548-8500
www.falmouth-capecod.com
Falmouth's Christmas by the Sea is a gala three-day celebration. It features Christmas caroling at Nobska Lighthouse, concerts and other performances, bazaars, Santa's arrival by boat, and the lighting of the Falmouth Village Green, complete with caroling. The festivities include the annual Christmas Parade down Main Street to the Village Green on Sunday.

Mid-Cape

Hyannis Christmas Harbor Lighting and Stroll
Bismore Park, Ocean Street, Hyannis
(800) 4HYNNIS
www.hyannis.com

Hyannis is ablaze with Christmas cheer from the gaily lit harbor homes and buildings to the holiday boat parade in Hyannis Harbor. Highlights of the three-day festivities include free harbor tours, free chowder, hot chocolate, and other goodies. The boat parade is usually held during the first week of December, followed in the next few days by the Hyannis Christmas Stroll on Main Street. Come enjoy the holiday decorations, hayrides, special activities, and free refreshments. Santa Claus makes an appearance. Don't miss the lighting of the Village Green!

Lower Cape

Christmas Weekend in the Harwiches
(508) 432-1600, (800) 441-3199
www.harwichcc.com
In mid-December the town of Harwich gets into the Christmas spirit with three days of strolls, entertainment, open houses, and fun activities for the whole family. At Brooks Park there is a Christmas tree lighting and carol singing. The events are sponsored by the Harwich Chamber of Commerce, which can be reached at the two numbers above.

THE ARTS 🖼

Cape Cod offers visitors and residents alike a varied and rich cultural experience with a cosmopolitan twist. Cape Cod is famed for its summer theater, whose illustrious history begins with the first performed play of Eugene O'Neill and continues with spectacular productions at places such as the marvelous Cape Playhouse in Dennis, which has attracted (and continues to attract) world-class talent like Helen Hayes, Julie Harris, and Tallulah Bankhead. If you're a music lover, you can enjoy hot sounds at the Beachcomber and Jazz by the Sea or soaring symphonies at various venues when the Cape Cod Symphony Orchestra performs.

You'll find that the Cape is rich in the visual arts too. The spectacular landscape, the laid-back lifestyle, and the unique light have been an irresistible draw for painters. Craftspeople and artisans have come too. Fine art galleries abound, such as Cummaquid Fine Arts, Tree's Place in Orleans, or the Blue Heron Gallery in Wellfleet.

Indeed the Cape is one of New England's largest centers of the arts. It has some 125 different arts organizations, according to the Arts Foundation of Cape Cod, which sponsors many events, including Pops by the Sea, and supports many arts events from museum exhibits to music festivals and dance performances.

Special events like these are part of what makes the Cape so special, but we don't lack for everyday offerings, either. Summer visitors can find big-name entertainment nightly at venues like the Cape Cod Melody Tent. Places like Christine's Restaurant and Show Club in West Dennis offer live performances year-round. And in addition to our famous summer theater, we have winter theater too.

If you're an artist yourself, be sure to check out the opportunities for work-

shops and classes here on the Cape, which we offer in our Education and Child Care chapter. But first, for you and for everyone else who loves art, we offer a broad overview of the Cape's cultural offerings. We start by taking a look at the theater scene. Then we move on to music, dance, art galleries and art museums, and movie theaters that show more than box-office hits. There's plenty here to lure you off the beach—take a break from the sun and bathe in creativity instead.

THEATER

Theater has played a starring role in the Cape's history since the summer of 1915, when a group of "wash-ashores," including writers John Reed and Susan Glaspell, gathered in Provincetown to write, produce, and stage plays. A year later an aspiring playwright named Eugene O'Neill arrived in town, determined to make his mark on theatrical history. On July 28, 1916, his first play, *Bound East for Cardiff,* was staged in a waterfront fish house to tremendous acclaim. Two years later the group named themselves the Provincetown Players and moved to New York City to continue their work, where the theater bearing their name still remains.

Provincetown continues its theatrical tradition with several theater groups, but the rest of the Cape has much to offer at other theatrical venues, and many of them perform year-round. Kim Crocker, a local actress/director, put it best when she told us, "The reason the theater is so good here is because it's being done by people who do it for love, not money." And she is right. The theater offerings on the Cape are amazing. In any given season you can see musicals, comedy, original works, and reworked classics, performed by the likes of the Harwich Junior Theater, the Monomoy Theatre in cooperation with the Ohio University School of Theatre, and WHAT—Wellfleet Harbor Actors' Theatre. Ticket prices are a fraction of what you might pay in Boston or New York to see a production of equal caliber.

Here, the curtain goes up on a town-by-town stage sampling.

Upper Cape

The Cape Cod Theatre Project
Various venues
(508) 457-4242
www.capecodtheatreproject.org
Since the introduction of Jeff Daniels's play *The Vast Difference* in 1995, this professional group has staged readings of new plays in July only, usually at the Woods Hole Community Hall or Falmouth Academy. Some of the works originally read here have gone on to Broadway.

Falmouth Theatre Guild
Depot Avenue, Falmouth
(508) 548-0668, (508) 548-0400
www.falmouththeatrecompany.org
The Falmouth Theatre Guild puts on three or four shows a year at Highfield Theater. Favored as one of the best local theater companies, they perform two stage productions in the spring and usually a drama in the winter.

During the summer the College Light Opera Company (www.collegelightopera .com) moves in and stages nine musicals, each running a week. The shows begin the last week of June and run through the last week of August. Expect some Gilbert and Sullivan and plenty of Broadway classics.

Woods Hole Theater Company
68 Water Street, Woods Hole (Falmouth)
(508) 540-6525
www.woodsholetheatercompany.org
Established in 1974, this company presents six or seven shows a year at the Woods Hole Community Hall and sponsors occasional productions by other theatrical troupes. The company aims to provide a wide variety of theater for the community. Included in each season are comedy, drama, and musicals.

Mid-Cape

Cotuit Center for the Arts
4404 Route 28, Cotuit
(508) 428-0669
www.cotuitcenterforthearts.org
This busy arts organization broke ground on a new performance center in June 2002, and at press time, they were nearing completion. In the meantime the center is hosting numerous staged readings and small productions of new plays. When the new center opens completely, you can anticipate fully staged productions. Check their Web site for a schedule of performances. In addition to performances the Cotuit Center for the Arts offers drama and arts classes for children, teens, and adults (see our Education and Child Care chapter).

Barnstable Comedy Club
3171 Route 6A, Barnstable
(508) 362-6333
www.barnstablecomedyclub.org
The nation's third-oldest continuously operating theater, the Barnstable Comedy Club has been offering audiences the best in comedy, drama, and music since 1922. The group stages six major productions every year, with 10 performances of each show, beginning in June and running through Labor Day. The club's motto is "Let's produce good plays and remain amateurs," and that's a formula that works well here. And though the performers are all volunteers and nonprofessionals, remember their names: Past "nobodies" have included Geena Davis and Kurt Vonnegut.

Cape Playhouse
820 Route 6A, Dennis
(508) 385-3911, (877) 385-3911
www.capeplayhouse.com

For more than seventy years, the legendary Cape Playhouse has been bringing Broadway actors to Cape Cod. The Cape Playhouse has attracted so many stars since it opened in 1927 that it is often referred to as the "Birthplace of the Stars." The list of actors who appeared here reads like a *Who's Who?* of stage and screen. Young unknown Bette Davis first worked as an usher before returning the following summer to act. Humphrey Bogart, Shirley Booth, Robert Montgomery, and Gregory Peck made their early appearances at the Cape Playhouse before going on to win Academy Awards. As a student young Jane Fonda even appeared one summer with her father, Henry!

America's oldest professional summer theater, the Cape Playhouse offers first-rate theater each summer. Evening performances are offered Monday through Saturday, and matinees are on Wednesday and Thursday afternoons. On Friday mornings the Cape Playhouse Children's Theatre is a terrific way to introduce young people to the wonder and magic of live theater designed especially for them. Tickets are sold via subscription, though good-location single seats are usually available. The season begins in June and runs to September, with two-week runs of six plays, ranging from musicals and comedies to mysteries. In addition to the Cape Playhouse, the 26-acre complex is home to the Cape Cinema (see the Cinema section later in this chapter), the Cape Museum of Fine Arts (see the Art

Museums section later in this chapter), and the Playhouse Bistro.

Lower Cape

Cape Cod Repertory Theater Company
3379 Route 6A, Brewster
(508) 896-1888
www.caperep.org

Cape Rep operates the Cape's only outdoor theater, a beautiful venue among the pines across from Nickerson State Park in East Brewster, just off Route 6A. The group has an indoor theater at the same site, and there's usually something going on at both venues from late spring to early fall. Cape Rep also presents dinner reviews at the Old Sea Pines Inn, 2553 Route 6A, Brewster (508-896-6114). The group's offerings include musicals, original plays, and, at the outdoor theater, family-oriented productions. The company stages children's theater on Tuesday and Friday mornings in July and August; reservations are a must, as these shows sell out fast. Tickets for the children's theater are $6.00 for both adults and children. The price for a play performance is $16 for adults and $10 for those 21 and younger. Musical performance tickets are $22 for those older than 21 and $10 for those ages 21 and younger.

Harwich Junior Theatre
Corner of Division and Willow Streets, West Harwich
(508) 432-2002
www.hjtcapecod.org

Founded in 1952, this year-round company stages delightful family shows including dramas, musicals, comedies—even Shakespeare. Although the plays staged here are always great for children—*The Masque of Beauty and the Beast, Tom Sawyer,* the rock 'n' roll musical *Leader of the Pack*—they can also be enjoyed by people of all ages. Performances are held Friday and Saturday evening at 8:00 P.M. and on Sunday at 2:00 P.M. Tickets are $16, $12 for ages 21 and younger. The Harwich Junior Theatre also offers a full curriculum of inspiring and fun classes taught by theater professionals (see our Kidstuff chapter).

Chatham Drama Guild
134 Crowell Road, Chatham
(508) 945-0510
www.chathamdramaguild.com
The guild does four major shows a year in fall, winter, and spring. Productions range from musicals to comedy and mystery. *Chathamania,* a brand-new old-fashioned variety show, as well as more traditional productions such as Ibsen's *A Doll's House,* were featured during past seasons. Over the years the guild has staged productions in conjunction with Chatham High School, making an educational experience for the students as well as a grand experience for the general audience. Tickets cost $15.

Monomoy Theatre
776 Main Street, Chatham
(508) 945-1589
www.monomoytheatre.org
Monomoy Theatre's annual season kicks off in June with a delightful mix of musicals, comedies, dramas, and thrillers, and closes, as it traditionally does, with a Shakespeare play. Since 1957 the theater, operated by the Ohio University School of Theater Arts, has combined talented students with visiting professors, faculty, and professional guest artists. Many Monomoy graduates continue on to be successful actors, set or costume designers, directors, and stage managers. The season usually begins with a two-week musical followed by seven one-week plays. Season subscriptions are available. Theater tickets are $20, except for Thursday matinees, which cost $15; tickets for musicals are $25, with Thursday and Saturday matinees costing $20.

Academy of Performing Arts
120 Main Street, Orleans
(508) 255-1963
www.apa1.org

Founded in 1975, the academy stages more than 12 productions throughout the year—musicals, dramas, comedies, and everything in between—many of them works by local and regional playwrights. The quality of performances is high. The building itself dates to 1873 and once served as the Orleans Town Hall; the academy is still raising funds to continue renovations and upgrades to the building. General admission tickets for a main performance are $16. A children's theater show is presented Fridays from July through August at 10:00 A.M. General admission to the children's show is $5.00. The academy also offers a plethora of courses in dance, music, and acting at its teaching facility on Giddah Hill Road (see our Education and Child Care and Kidstuff chapters).

Wellfleet Harbor Actors Theater (WHAT)
Town Pier, Wellfleet
(508) 349-6835
www.what.org
WHAT cofounders and directors Gip Hoppe and Jeff Zinn bring something different to the theater experience on Cape Cod, providing an alternative to more traditional theaters. Among the most daring companies around, WHAT is worth checking out for its quality, off-the-beaten-path productions. The theater only seats 90 people, so reserve your seats early. The group stages up to eight shows a year from May through October. There's a box office on Main Street in Wellfleet.

Provincetown Repertory Theatre
238 Bradford Street, Provincetown
(508) 487-7487, (800) 791-7487
www.provincetowntheater.org
This group stages performances of American plays and music May through October. In partnership with the Provincetown Theatre Company, the Provincetown Repertory Theatre is making strides toward a new playhouse for Provincetown. At press time construction of a new 180-seat building at 238 Bradford Street had begun, with completion anticipated just in

time for the 2004 summer season. In the interim productions of works such as Eugene O'Neill's *Long Day's Journey into Night* and Terrence McNally's *Master Class* are being produced in venues throughout town. They also host a Fall Playwright's Festival in mid-September and a Woman's Week New Play Festival in October.

MUSIC

From Big Band to Broadway, blues to bebop, reggae to rockabilly, there is music in the salt air on the Cape, especially during the summer when crowds gather in a celebratory atmosphere that just cries out for accompaniment. Many towns offer weekly free outdoor concerts during July and August that feature some of the best local musicians. Just bring your lawn chair and head toward the music! Some annual events are so popular that many visitors plan their vacations around them (such as Pops in the Park and Jazz by the Sea). The Cape Cod Melody Tent is the place to go for big-name entertainment in summer. It really is a seasonal outdoor tent—a huge one with stadium seating—and it's a terrific place to see a concert. If you are looking for alternative music, you've come to the right place—because the Cape is within a few hours driving time of Boston and Providence, Rhode Island, area nightclubs are able to draw some of the best national touring bands to their small ven-

ues. (Our Nightlife chapter will provide you with a sample of restaurants and bars that offer live entertainment.) Here's a listing of some of the best musical venues on the Cape. Check local newspapers for exact dates and concert schedules.

Upper Cape

**College Light Opera Company
Highfield Theater, off Depot Avenue, Falmouth
(508) 548-0668, (216) 774-8485 (winter number)
www.collegelightopera.com**
The College Light Opera Company stages nine musicals a summer, each running a week, from the last week of June through the last week of August. Shows include operettas by Gilbert and Sullivan and heaps of Broadway classics.

**Woods Hole Folk Music Society
Woods Hole Community Hall, Water Street, Woods Hole (Falmouth)
(508) 540-0320**
Here's something to liven up those quiet winter months. From October to May the Woods Hole Folk Music Society stages concerts on the first and third Sundays of the month. The programs often attract nationally known performers such as Bill Staines, Peggy Seeger, Roy Bookbinder, Oscar Brand, David Mallett, and Kim and Reggie Harris. Admission runs about $10 with discounts for members, seniors, and children.

**Boch Center for the Performing Arts
Various venues around Mashpee
(508) 477-2580
www.bochcenterarts.com**
This organization has ambitious plans for a 2,000-seat outdoor amphitheater (1,000 seats will be under a tent canopy and another 1,000 will be lawn seats) and for a 900 seat indoor theater. At press time groundbreaking was scheduled for spring

Music on the Green is a series of free concerts held Friday nights on the town green in Falmouth throughout the summer. These family-oriented concerts start at 6:00 P.M., and feature a variety of local professional musical talent from Irish folk music to swing. For more information contact the Arts Foundation of Cape Cod (508-362-0066), or visit www.artsfoundation.com.

2004, with an anticipated completion of the indoor theater in spring 2005.

Meanwhile the center has already added richness to the cultural mix on Cape Cod, with such treats as concerts by the Vienna Boys Choir, who return year after year to delight the local audiences. Various acclaimed jazz musicians and internationally recognized classical musicians, such as violinist Gil Shaham, make regular visits. Tickets vary with performance, but a classical performance ticket price is $38 for adults, $35 for seniors, and $18 for youth 18 and younger.

Mid-Cape

The New Driftwood Coffee House
2150 Main Street, Marstons Mills
(508) 771-9000
www.newdriftwood.com

The New Driftwood hearkens back to those 1960s coffeehouses featuring folk music and beat poets. It's the largest folk and acoustic venue on the Cape and features top local and national folk-singing talent. They have concerts the first Saturday of most months. Call for a schedule.

P.M. by the Sea
Sandy Neck Beach, Route 6A, West Barnstable
(508) 771-8298

Here's a true Cape Cod experience: Sit on the beach before a bonfire on a moonlit evening and listen to folk music, poetry, and other low-key entertainment. P.M. by the Sea stages these delightful events on the Friday night closest to each full moon in the summer. The fun begins at dusk, and it's a great family venue. Bring a beach chair and a piece of firewood. A donation is requested. Ages 12 and younger are admitted free.

Cape Cod Melody Tent
West Main Street and West End Rotary, Hyannis
(508) 775-9100
www.melodytent.com

The Cape's premier summer showcase, the Cape Cod Melody Tent is one of only 10 outdoor performance tents in the country. Many big names in show business have appeared here, including Willie Nelson, Aretha Franklin, and Tony Bennett, to name a few. The big tent is pitched at the end of May and is taken down mid-September. Shows sell out fast; check the box office for last-minute seat cancellations. Ticket prices vary from $25 to $50.

The Melody Tent also features popular children's theater and musical productions every Wednesday morning during the season; tickets are $6.50 to $13.50.

Cape Symphony Orchestra
BHS Performing Arts Center
Hyannis, and other venues
(508) 362-1111
www.capesymphony.org

The award-winning 90-member Cape Symphony Orchestra performs classical, pops, and educational concerts at the new Barnstable High School Performing Arts Center in Hyannis from September through May. Two hugely successful outdoor summer pops concerts are performed at the Mashpee Commons at the end of July and at Eldredge Park in Orleans in mid-August. Music Director Royston Nash conducts the Cape's only symphonic orchestra. Ticket prices range from $25 to $52.

Fleet Pops by the Sea
Village Green, Main Street, Hyannis
(508) 362-0066
www.artsfoundationcapecod.org

Fleet Pops by the Sea is a first-class evening of fun put on by the Arts Foundation of Cape Cod. In 2003 Boston Pops Conductor Keith Lockhart conducted the Boston Pops Esplanade Orchestra with Ed Asner as the event's celebrity guest conductor. Because it's a fund-raiser, tickets can run high (it's $2,500 for patron tables of 10 individuals). But don't worry: You can still afford to come. It's only $15 if you bring your own blanket or folding chair and $50 for open seating in chairs on the lawn. The Arts Foundation of Cape Cod,

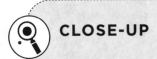
The Sounds of Summer

Just about every town on the Cape offers free outdoor summer concerts. Here's a list of our favorites.

Buzzards Bay

Bring your blanket or lawn chair to the Gazebo at the Buzzards Bay Park every Thursday in July and August. Sponsored by the Cape Cod Canal Region Chamber of Commerce (508-759-6000), the Concert in the Park series is a favorite with locals. There is plenty of free parking at the train depot and U.S. Army Corps of Engineers lot at the base of the railroad bridge. Concerts start at 7:00 P.M.

Falmouth

Join the crowds at the Town Band Shell on the west side of Inner Harbor, Marina Park, on Scranton Avenue for concerts by the Falmouth Town Band. They're held every Thursday evening from 8:00 to 9:30 P.M. during July and August.

The Falmouth Village Association also presents a concert series on Friday nights in Peg Noonan Park on Main Street starting at 6:00 P.M. Call (508) 548-8500 for a schedule of both series of concerts.

Sandwich

The Sandwich Town Band performs free concerts on Thursday evenings from 7:30 to 9:00 P.M. at the Henry T. Wing School Bandstand, Route 130. It features Broadway favorites, light classical music, marches, and special segments for children. Bring your picnic dinner, lawn chair, blankets, and insect repellant. If it rains, the concert is moved inside to the school auditorium.

Mashpee

Mashpee Commons, which is just off the rotary at Routes 28 and 151, offers an extensive free concert series. The sessions, held under the festival tent, feature everything from R&B favorites to ragtime, Bourbon Street blues, and Big Band. Call (508) 477-5400 for a complete schedule.

Yarmouth

Enjoy a wonderful evening of entertainment at the Monday Night Concert Series sponsored by the Yarmouth Area Chamber of Commerce (508-778-1008). The music ranges from classical to Irish to jazz and Big Band. The location is the Mattacheese Middle School, Higgins Crowell Road, West Yarmouth, at the outdoor band shell. The concerts begin at 7:00 P.M.

Dennis

Dennis comes alive with music in the summer as both town greens host free concerts. Every other Monday night in July and August at 7:00 P.M., you can hear a free outdoor concert at the gazebo at the Dennis Town Green, Route 6A. This one is sponsored by the Village Improvement Society. Every Wednesday night in July and August at 7:00 P.M. the Town Green on Route 28 in Dennisport is the location of a free concert sponsored by the Southside Civic Association.

Brewster
You can enjoy a concert in a Norman Rockwell setting at Drummer Boy Park on Route 6A in West Brewster. The 45-piece Brewster Town Band performs on a bandstand set on a large rolling field overlooking Cape Cod Bay. The concerts take place each Sunday in July and August, weather permitting, at 6:00 P.M. Admission is free, although donations are accepted, and there is ample parking at the park. Picnic suppers are encouraged. There is also a children's playground in the park. Bring your own chairs or blankets. For more information call (508) 896-7770.

Harwich
Brooks Park, Oak Street, is the setting for concerts every Tuesday evening in July and August at 7:30 P.M. There is plenty of parking. Bring a lawn chair or blanket.

Chatham
Up to 6,000 music lovers pack Kate Gould Park every Friday night from July through Labor Day to hear the town's brass band perform. A summer tradition for the past 60-plus years, the weekly concerts start at 8:00 P.M. and are extremely popular, so get into town early to grab a parking space! The park is next door to the Chatham Wayside Inn, 512 Main Street.

On Sunday nights you can enjoy the Music for a Summer's Night series held at the First United Methodist Church, 16 Cross Street (508-945-0474). These start on Independence Day weekend and continue through Labor Day. Though admission is free, a free-will offering is taken before each performance. The music begins at 8:00 P.M.

Orleans
Every Monday evening from 7:00 to 9:00 P.M. in July and August, the gazebo at Nauset Beach is the site of wonderful free concerts. Bring a blanket and someone to dance with; this is an evening the whole family will enjoy.

an arts agency in Barnstable County, serves to support, promote, and celebrate art and culture on the Cape.

Lower Cape

Cape Cod Chamber Music Festival
Various venues
(800) 229-5739
www.capecodchambermusic.org
Now in its 24th season, the Cape Cod Chamber Music Festival hold concerts in various venues for three weeks in August, with special events other times. The roster includes chamber music concerts, programs for young people, evenings of jazz, and the annual screening of a music-themed film. Concert tickets average $20.

Pops in the Park—Cape Symphony Orchestra
Eldredge Park, Orleans
(508) 255-1386, (800) 865-1386
www.popsinthepark.com
This annual outdoor concert is a popular summertime tradition featuring the Cape Symphony Orchestra (see our Annual Events chapter). The concert benefits the Pops in the Park Scholarship Fund, which supports Nauset Regional High School students. More than $10,000 is raised annually through this event, which usually takes place in late August. Table seats are $55 per person. Lawn seating is between $5.00 and $28.00 per person, and the concert starts at 5:00 P.M.

First Encounter Coffeehouse
Samoset Road, Eastham
(508) 255-5438
www.firstencounter.org
The coffeehouse boasts some of the biggest names in acoustic and folk music, including Wellfleet's own Patty Larkin, Deb Pasternak, Boston City Limits, and Livingston Taylor. Admission is about $12 (see our Nightlife chapter), and seating is limited. Performances are on the second and fourth Saturday of each month.

The Beachcomber
Cahoon Hollow Road, Wellfleet
(508) 349-6055
www.thebeachcomber.com
Once an 1897 lifesaving station, the Beachcomber is the place to go on the Lower Cape for the best in roots, rock, and reggae. Admission varies per performance; expect to pay between $5.00 for regional bands on up to $20.00 for nationally acclaimed bands. Toots and the Maytals, Weezer, Ween, the Samples, Jonathan Richman, and NRBQ have all played there. Shows are staged throughout the summer with performances Friday, Saturday, and Sunday evenings. The Beachcomber is open weekends only from the end of May until mid-June, and then seven days a week noon to 1:00 A.M. from late June through Labor Day (see our Nightlife chapter).

The Great Music Series at the Meeting House
Universalist Meeting House,
236 Commercial Street, Provincetown
(508) 487-9344
www.ptownmusic.com
Entering its fifth year, this series is organized by the Meeting House Instrument Trust, a group working toward restoring the historic Universalist Meeting House organ housed in this 1851 Greek Revival gem. Concerts are varied programs of classical music from all periods and feature high-caliber vocalists and instrumentalists. Concerts are held in May (Memorial Day weekend kicks off the series) through October on Sundays at 5:00 P.M. Tickets are $10; the group also welcomes donations.

DANCE
Mid-Cape

Cape Cod Ballet Company
49 John Maki Road, West Barnstable
(508) 362-3111
www.capecodballetsociety.org

This company produces a *Nutcracker* gala each December; recently the production was a joint venture with the Cape Cod Symphony Orchestra at the new performing arts center at Barnstable High School in Hyannis. A second major performance of each year is staged in the spring. Ticket prices begin at $20 and go up. A ballet school is also associated with the company and gives lessons to students of all ages.

Cape Dance Theater of Cape Cod
Community College
Route 132, West Barnstable
(508) 375-4044
Made up of faculty, students, and area residents, this 16-member dance troupe mainly focuses on modern dance, though it has broadened its scope in recent years to include such traditional fare as ballroom dancing. The troupe usually stages three annual shows at the college's Tilden Arts Center.

Lower Cape

Studio 878
878 Main Street, Chatham
(508) 945-8780
Studio 878 is a nonprofit educational organization directed by Naomi Turner. It offers professional training in dance from beginning through professional levels. Through performance opportunities Studio 878 nurtures the dancer through innovative technique and creative exploration.

ART GALLERIES

The Cape is home to a diverse selection of world-class art galleries, so it's easy to paint a glowing portrait of the art world on the Cape, which is one of the most sophisticated in the country.

Museum-quality installations grace the walls of art galleries like Jan Collins Selman's Fine Art Gallery in Falmouth, Three's Place in Orleans, and the Left Bank Gallery in Wellfleet. Much of the art is generated by local artists, but not always—many of these galleries represent nationally and internationally known artists, as well as New York artists who summer on the Cape. Cape Cod attracts extraordinarily talented artists whose work ranges from contemporary forms of realism and impressionism to postmodernism. Much of the art created is inspired by the stunning natural beauty of the Cape, rendered in many different styles, from realistic to impressionistic and abstract. Because the Cape Cod lifestyle is largely unassuming, the art is too—in many cases, it is inspired by the solitude of the outer beaches, sunrise over a salt marsh, and, yes, fishing boats in quaint harbors.

Ask any artist why he or she prefers Cape Cod and almost each of them says the same thing: the light. The Cape's unique light and natural beauty was drawing artists here even before Charles Hawthorne founded the Cape Cod School of Art in Provincetown in 1899. And it continues to attract painters, sculptors, and other artists. Is it any wonder Edward Hopper summered in Truro from 1920 to 1967? The profusion of galleries here, particularly in the Lower Cape towns of Wellfleet and Provincetown, attest to our high population of visual artists. Many galleries are run by these artists, and you can often catch a glimpse of them at work while you're browsing in galleries with attached studios.

Here are some of our favorite galleries. Remember that hours vary greatly during the off-season, so it's best to call in advance.

Upper Cape

Gallery 333
333 Old Main Road, North Falmouth
(508) 564-4467, (617) 332-5459
(off-season)
Housed in an 1800 home, this gallery has three rooms of paintings, sculpture, ceramics, and photography, representing a

range of styles from about 40 artists. The gallery, which celebrated its 15th anniversary in 2003, focuses on distinguished local and New England artists. Open Wednesday through Sunday from June to late September and by appointment in the off-season by calling the number above, Gallery 333 offers five or six shows each summer, with Saturday evening receptions opening each show.

Jan Collins Selman Fine Art
317 Main Street, Falmouth
(508) 457-5533
www.jancollinsselman.com
Jan Collins Selman is an award-winning artist best known for her pastels and oils of Cape Cod, Martha's Vineyard, and Nantucket. Here you can purchase her work in oil, pastel, monotype, woodcuts, etchings, and prints, as well as the work of 20 other award-winning artists. The gallery also displays lovely works in ceramics and sculpture. The gallery is open year-round.

Woods Hole Gallery
14 School Street, Woods Hole (Falmouth)
(508) 548-7594
www.arts-cape.com/whgallery
Since 1963 Edith Bruce, owner of the Woods Hole Gallery, has been cultivating the newest and freshest talent in the world of art. The collections here are superb, representing only New England artists in a range of media including pastels, watercolors, oils, and acrylics. Bruce, an artist herself, also restores paintings and teaches art. The gallery is open daily during July, August, and September; call for off-season hours.

Woodruff's Art Center
Mashpee Commons, Routes 28 and 151, Mashpee
(508) 477-5767
Here you'll find watercolors, acrylics, oils, and pastels by John Richardson Woodruff and his wife, Amy Rice Woodruff, along

with aerial photographs by two photographers. The Woodruffs also offer custom framing and a wide range of art supplies. The gallery is open daily year-round.

Mid-Cape

Cotuit Center for the Arts
4404 Route 28, Cotuit
(508) 428-0669
www.cotuitcenterforthearts.org
As stated previously in this chapter, the Cotuit Center for the Arts broke ground on a new performance center in June 2002, and, at press time, they were nearing completion. In addition to staging performances and offering art and drama classes, the center features frequent exhibits of artwork by students, teachers, and others year-round.

Birdsey Gallery
12 Wianno Avenue, Osterville
(508) 428-4969
This friendly gallery, housed in an old building with lots of character, represents more than 40 artists. You can pick up a framed print here for a mere $35, or you could spend as much as $3,500 for an original painting. Some of the popular artists whose work graces Birdsey's three rooms include Jane Shelly Pierce, Vern Broe, Susie McLean, and Neil McAuliffe. This is a gallery that actually welcomes children, and while you browse, your little ones can pet the two friendly English cocker spaniels and receive their own helium balloon. The gallery is open daily except Sunday May through December, and Saturday by appointment in winter.

Cape Cod Art Association
3480 Route 6A, Barnstable
(508) 362-2090
www.capecodartassoc.org
The nonprofit Cape Cod Art Association was established in 1948 and offers year-

---

[Facing page] *The light and landscapes of the Outer Cape have inspired countless artists and keep many galleries in business.* SUSAN BLOOD AND THE LEFT BANK GALLERY

round art exhibitions, five for members only, and four open to area residents. Exhibitions change every three weeks. Some shows are juried, and artists are always present at openings. The CCAA also hosts classes and workshops year-round.

Cummaquid Fine Arts
4275 Route 6A, Cummaquid (Barnstable)
(508) 362-2593
www.cfa-ltd.com
Cummaquid Fine Arts is itself a work of art: an 18th-century home set on more than four acres of lush green. Inside are works by Cape and New England artists. The gallery is open Tuesday through Sunday in summer, Wednesday through Sunday in late spring and early fall, Thursday through Sunday in late fall, and most weekends or by appointment in winter.

Higgins Art Gallery
Cape Cod Community College, Route 132, West Barnstable
(508) 362-2131
Housed in the Tilden Arts Center of Cape Cod Community College, the Higgins Art Gallery features a variety of works. It is open to the public daily September through May, with several special shows a year.

Guyer Barn
250 South Street, Hyannis
(508) 790-6370
This restored 1865 barn, owned by the town of Barnstable and adjacent to the town hall complex and the library, shows the work of local artists, both recognized and new. Here you can see both rotating and permanent displays of art in a variety of media from April through October. The nonprofit gallery, sponsored by the Barnstable Cultural Council, hosts two special holiday craft show fairs in November and December.

The Gallery at the Cape Cod Community Media Center
307 Whites Path, South Yarmouth
(508) 394-2388
www.c3tv.org

The Gallery at C3TV, housed within the offices of the Cape's community access TV station, mounts 10 exhibits a year, each running about a month and featuring Cape artists. Admission is free, and the gallery is open daily.

Worden Hall Art Gallery
1841 Route 6A, East Dennis
(508) 385-9289
www.devitaart.com
Behind the majestic door of Worden Hall lies artwork that since 1965 has awed its audiences. The works of owner Donn DeVita and his late wife, Nancy—landscapes and seascapes, mostly in oils—compete for attention. Donn also creates what he calls "unusual art," for example, drawing with a knife instead of a pencil, then filling the broken surface with color. The gallery is open seven days a week, year-round.

Lower Cape

Art House Gallery
Thad Ellis Road, Brewster
(508) 896-5557
www.arthousecapecod.com
Visiting this gallery, on a little street off Route 6A (right near the entrance to Ocean Edge), is an especially nice experience because the gallery is so homey. There's a couch in the main room where you can sit and view featured works by some 15 artists from the Cape and beyond, including some from Europe. Cape artists featured here include printmaker Liz Perry and pastel artist Joan Ledwith. The gallery is open Wednesday through Sunday.

Maddocks Gallery
1283 Route 6A, Brewster
(508) 896-6223
Working primarily in acrylics, Jim Maddocks creates beautiful Cape Cod scenes, often offering a glimpse of old Cape Cod.

Filled with flowers, sandy lanes, and views of the bay, his paintings have a dreamy quality that lulls and charms the viewer. A bonus: Very often you can catch the artist at work in his studio/gallery located in a carriage house adjacent to his historic home. It's open most days in season; call for off-season hours.

Ruddeforth Gallery
3753 Route 6A, Brewster
(508) 255–1056
Debra Ruddeforth's oils and watercolors are soft, lush, and inviting; they include many Cape landscapes as well as florals and still lifes. A full selection of limited-edition reproductions is available as well. Open daily year-round 10:00 A.M. to 5:00 P.M., the gallery also displays the still-life and fine-arts landscape photography of Tom Ruddeforth.

Struna Galleries
3873 Route 6A, Brewster
(508) 255–6618
www.strunagalleries.com
Timothy Struna's pen-and-ink renderings are so distinctive you'll know them anywhere. They feature Cape landscapes and old houses and perfectly capture the essence of the Cape. He also works in watercolors and acrylics, and we highly recommend a visit to his cozy gallery, near the Orleans line. It's open daily all year. There is another location of Struna Galleries on Main Street in Chatham.

Underground Gallery
673 Satucket Road, Brewster
(508) 896–3757
www.karennorthwells.com
The Underground Gallery is an architectural wonder supported by tree trunks and nestled under 250 tons of earth. But the real attractions are the vivid, distinctive watercolors by Karen North Wells. The works of her husband, architect and artist Malcolm Wells (who designed the gallery), are also on display, as are a sampling of books and a collection of greeting cards reproduced

from Ms. Wells' paintings. It's open year-round, Wednesday through Sunday.

Winstanley-Roark Fine Arts
601 Route 6A, Brewster
(508) 385–4713, (866) 385–4713
www.masterfulart.com
This newly renovated gallery features the luminous oils and pastels—portraits, landscapes, and still lifes—by Robert K. Roark and the fine art photography of Anita Winstanley-Roark. They also host the work of a dozen other artists. Open daily in summer, the gallery is open Monday through Saturday in spring and fall, and by chance or appointment in the winter months.

Creative Arts Center
154 Crowell Road, Chatham
(508) 945–3583
www.capecodcreativearts.org
The nonprofit Creative Arts Center has two galleries hosting several members-only shows a year. The center, open daily year-round, also offers a wide range of classes.

Addison Holmes Gallery
43 Route 28, Orleans
(508) 255–6200, (877) 291–5400
www.addisonart.com
The Addison Holmes Gallery represents a number of acclaimed fine artists, including Lois Griffel, Peter Quidley, and Garry Gilmartin. The two-level gallery, in a former home on Town Cove, is bright and inviting. It's open year-round, with shorter hours in winter.

Left Bank Gallery
8 Cove Road, Orleans
(508) 247–9172
www.leftbankgallery.com
For many years an institution in Wellfleet, the Left Bank's opening of an Orleans location was welcomed by local art-lovers. The gallery lives up to Left Bank's consistently high standards, offering works in a variety of media. In addition to paintings, sculpture, textiles, and ceramics by local, regional, and nationally known artists,

you'll find gorgeous handcrafted jewelry. The gallery also has a third room, which is filled with the works of a new slate of artists. During the summer months the gallery is open seven days a week from 1:00 to 6:00 P.M. The rest of the year the gallery is open Monday through Saturday; call for hours.

Rock Harbor Art Gallery
104 Rock Harbor Road, Orleans
(508) 255-3747

This beautiful barn, just a few doors down from Rock Harbor, houses the works of talented husband-and-wife artists Kely and David Knowles. Kely Knowles exhibits her luminous, shimmering watercolors along with pen-and-ink renderings and greeting cards. Her husband carves unique wood sculptures, including unusual fish wall hangings. The gallery is open most of the time in summer and often in spring and fall—if the barn doors are open, stop in—or by appointment any time of year.

Star Gallery
76 Route 6A, Orleans
(508) 240-7827

This gallery has a contemporary flair, displaying a mix of abstract and impressionist works along with some more traditional work. Owner Doug Johnson, whose paintings and "surrealographs" are on display here, likes to show exciting, adventurous works. The gallery is open daily May through October, with a full schedule of shows in summer, and on weekends or by appointment the rest of the year.

Tree's Place
Routes 6A and 28, Orleans
(508) 255-1330
www.treesplace.com

The collection of paintings in the gallery space at Tree's Place couldn't have been better coordinated. Several rooms house pieces of art, many oversized, and all beautifully hung; the effect is a museumlike ambience. Featured artists include Sam Barber, Robert Vickrey, Robert Douglas Hunter, and Sam Vokey. You'll also find delightful, rich folk art of Elizabeth Mumford; the soft, graceful realism of Betsy Bennett; the vibrant, powerful compositions of Pamela Pindell; and American luminist works by Joseph McGurl. Tree's Place presents weekly exhibitions throughout July and August, including exhibitions during the first few weeks of September. Opening nights are usually Saturday evenings from 5:00 to 7:00 P.M. Don't forget to go upstairs, where a beautiful assortment of gifts awaits, and stop in at the Tilery, which has an array of tile works from around the world. Tree's Place is open daily year-round except in the quietest winter months, when it is closed on Sunday.

Blue Heron Gallery
20 Bank Street, Wellfleet
(508) 349-6724
www.blueheronfineart.com

The Blue Heron has one of the largest collections around, featuring representational contemporary art in a range of mediums, including oil, egg tempera, watercolor, pastel, acrylic, photography, etchings, sculpture, and limited-edition prints. The gallery's roster of artists from around the United States is impressive, and many have been displaying their work here for years. Among them is Sybil D'Orsi, whose large canvases often depict window views of the Cape. There's also Robert Huntoon, whose intricately detailed Cape landscapes are created using an oil-glazing technique derived from Flemish painting. With rooms on two floors, this gallery has a light, clean look and a relaxed atmosphere that makes viewing art here a particular pleasure. Open daily Mother's Day through Columbus Day weekend, Blue

[Facing page] *The Left Bank Gallery, a Wellfleet institution, has been in business for more than 30 years.* SUSAN BLOOD AND THE LEFT BANK GALLERY

Heron hosts artist receptions on most Saturday evenings in July and August, offering new art and the opportunity to meet the artists.

Cove Gallery
15 Commercial Street, Wellfleet
(508) 349-2530
www.covegallery.com
Cove Gallery displays works by such internationally recognized artists as Leonard Baskin and children's book illustrator Tomie de Paolo. Also look for the bold, semi-representational paintings of John Grillo. The rooms are airy and uncluttered and include one room devoted to illustrated children's books, where you may also purchase children's illustrations, including works by Barry Moser. Out back is a peaceful garden overlooking Duck Creek. The Cove also does custom framing. It's open year-round, daily in summer with reduced hours in the off-season, so call ahead.

Jacob Fanning Gallery
25 Bank Street, Wellfleet
(508) 349-9546
This bright gallery in an 1865 building displays the work of some 30 artists, including environmental sculptor Stephen Thomas, who creates whimsical creatures such as cockroaches and crickets using recycled metal painted bright colors. He even makes potted flower arrangements using outdoor faucets and other materials to charming effect. You'll also find painted furniture by Jean Nelson and color etchings by Lynn Shaler. The gallery is open daily May through Columbus Day, then weekends only until Christmas.

Kendall Art Gallery
40 Main Street, Wellfleet
(508) 349-2482
This gallery represents 30 contemporary artists including Harry Marinsky, whose massive bronze sculpture, *Made for Each Other,* greets visitors outside the gallery. Artist-in-residence Walter Dorrell creates his Wellfleet watercolors in his "floating"

studio, a canoe he takes into the town's kettle ponds. The gallery is open May through October, daily in summer and Wednesday through Saturday in fall.

Left Bank Gallery
25 Commercial Street, Wellfleet
(508) 349-9451
www.leftbankgallery.com
Left Bank represents more than 50 local and nationally known artists, such as Rosalie Nadeau, Jim Holland, and Gail Bessette. It also hosts changing exhibitions. Check out the Potter's Room, filled with American crafts, and the outdoor sculpture garden. The gallery is open year-round, daily in summer and early fall, Thursday through Monday during the winter. Also check out the gallery's second location, Left Bank Small Works and Jewelry at 3 West Main Street in Wellfleet, and its newest location in Orleans (see listing above).

DNA Gallery
288 Bradford Street, Provincetown
(508) 487-7700
www.dnagallery.com
Ever since the DNA (for Definitive New Art) opened in 1994, it has been a welcome artistic refuge for those seeking the latest in environmental art. DNA, which represents some 30 emerging and established artists, also ties in its openings with various readings, films, and musical events, usually held on weekends. It's open daily May through October.

Rice/Polak Gallery
430 Commercial Street, Provincetown
(508) 487-1052
www.ricepolakgallery.com
Also in the East End is the Rice/Polak Gallery, where you'll find contemporary artworks in various media by local and other artists. It's open May through December, daily in season and weekends in fall.

Wohlfarth Galleries
234 Commercial Street, Provincetown
(508) 487-6569

Wohlfarth Galleries features both photography and fine art, and represents past and present students of the Cape Cod School of Arts (see our Education and Child Care chapter) established by Charles Hawthorne. The gallery is open May through December.

ART MUSEUMS

The Cape's three art museums are treasures not only for their wonderful collections but also for their very existence, as they preserve much of what is important to Cape Codders. In addition to making art accessible to the public, these institutions hold keys to both the past and the future, showing the legacy left by early artists and encouraging a new generation. The cultural events they sponsor sustain and nurture the community's passion for the arts.

Mid-Cape

Cahoon Museum of American Art
4676 Route 28, Cotuit
(508) 428-7581
www.cahoonmuseum.org
Housed in a 1775 Georgian colonial farmhouse, the Cahoon Museum is best known for its collection of fanciful primitive paintings by the late Ralph and Martha Cahoon. The building, worth a visit in itself, was actually the Cahoons' home and studio for 37 years. In addition to the Cahoon paintings, the permanent collection features 19th- and early 20th-century American marine paintings, landscapes, and still lifes. Founded in 1984, the museum also holds six special exhibits each year and houses a shop where you can purchase Cahoon prints, custom Cahoon items, and mermaid gifts of every description. Talks, demonstrations, and classes are held throughout the year. Admission is $3.00. The museum is open Tuesday through Saturday from February through December.

Cape Museum of Fine Arts
Route 6A, on the grounds of the Cape Playhouse, Dennis
(508) 385-4477
www.cmfa.org
The Cape Museum of Fine Arts conveys the important role that Cape Cod and the islands have played in American art. Founded in 1981 by a group of artists, educators, and community activists, CMFA focuses on the works of artists who have been influenced by the Cape environment, its people, and the interactive exchange of artistic ideas. The museum houses a collection that ranges from the late 1800s to the modern era, with more than 800 works by such icons as Charles Hawthorne, Paul Resika, Martha Cahoon, and Chiam Gross.

The museum sponsors frequent classes, trips, a winter lecture series, and a film series. Admission is $7.00 for adults, free for those 16 and younger. The museum is open daily year-round.

Lower Cape

Provincetown Art Association and Museum
460 Commercial Street, Provincetown
(508) 487-1750
www.paam.org
PAAM was established in 1914 to "promote education of the public in the arts and social intercourse between artists and laymen." Since then its permanent collection has grown to 2,000 pieces, all by artists associated in some way with Provincetown. PAAM has grown so much, in fact, that major renovations are planned. At press time construction on phase 1 had begun. The expansion will eventually include new gallery space, as well as a new bookstore, rest room, four new classrooms, and an outdoor terrace. It is scheduled to stay open throughout. The museum is open daily in summer; off-season hours fluctuate, so call ahead. A small admission is charged.

CINEMA

Moviegoers have some unique options on the Cape. Although multiplex movie theaters are sprinkled throughout the Cape (in Mashpee, Hyannis, Dennis, Falmouth, Wellfleet, and Harwich), there are a few theaters that offer alternatives to the current box-office hits. If you prefer art and foreign films to the latest thriller or you like the idea of watching a movie in an unconventional setting, check out these unique venues. Also, join in the fun at the annual Provincetown Film Festival, which takes place each June and brings stars to town.

Launched in June of 1999, the Provincetown International Film Festival is a mid-June, five-day festival showing more than 50 movies that reflect the tradition of diversity and commitment to creativity for which Provincetown is known. A Filmmaker on the Edge award is also given to honor filmmakers who have consistently pushed the boundaries of filmmaking. Recent award-winners have been Todd Haynes (Far From Heaven) and Gus Van Sant (Good Will Hunting). For more information on the festival, visit www.ptownfilmfest.com.

Mid-Cape

Cape Cinema
Cape Playhouse grounds, Route 6A, Dennis
(508) 385-2503

Insiders know that the Cape Cinema, built in 1930, is the place for serious movie watching. The theater shows the finest in foreign, independent, and art films from April through October.

Getting there early will not only guarantee you a seat but also give you time to bask in the cinema's beauty. The exterior was designed in the style of the Congregational Church in Centerville, and the interior ceiling is covered with a 6,400-square-foot mural of heavenly skies designed by Rockwell Kent and executed by Jo Mielziner. (Kent also designed the stage's golden sunburst curtain.)

Lower Cape

Wellfleet Cinemas
Route 6 at the Eastham-Wellfleet line
(508) 349-7176
www.wellfleetcinemas.com

Wellfleet Cinemas, built in 1986, is independently owned and operated. The cinemas have four screens equipped with Dolby Stereo and offer weekly first-run moves. Looking for something to do with the kids? Bring them to a matinee. The cinemas are open for matinees every day all summer long. The Wellfleet Cinemas is open 365 days a year.

Wellfleet Drive-in
U.S. Route 6, Wellfleet
(508) 349-7176
www.wellfleetdrivein.com

It's the only one of its kind left on the Cape—and one of a few left in the country. Ever since it opened in 1957, the Wellfleet Drive-in has been one of the most popular after-dark spots. But it's not all nostalgia here. The drive-in has a state-of-the-art FM stereo system and a huge screen (100 feet by 44 feet). Enjoy first-run double features most every night. Admission is $7.00 for adults, $4.00 for children ages 5 through 11 and senior citizens age 62 and older. Children younger than 4 are admitted free. The huge parking lot is also home to the Cape's largest flea market (see our Shopping chapter).

HIKING AND BIKING TRAILS

Though most people tend to associate Cape Cod with its spectacular beaches, many visitors do not realize the Cape is also graced with inland beauty from Bourne to Provincetown. We encourage you to explore the uplands and byways of Cape Cod and discover areas that locals consider some of its most beautiful hideaways.

There's a good reason why Cape Cod is paradise for people who love the outdoors, and that reason is the miles of maintained hiking and biking trails that meander throughout our meadows and uplands and through Cape Cod's many public areas.

One of the most impressive trails is the Cape Cod Rail Trail, 21 miles of paved surface running parallel to U.S. Route 6 beginning just south of Patriot Square Mall in Dennis on Route 134, through Nickerson State Park, and ending in Wellfleet behind the South Wellfleet General Store. The rail trail, the former route of the Cape Cod railroad, is a smooth and mostly flat surface providing bicyclists with a private universe where they can roll along merrily at whatever speed they choose.

Hiking through Cape Cod's conservation and parklands is still the best way to see some of the Cape's most spectacular sights, such as a pristine kettle pond or perhaps a great blue heron perched by the shoreline. The many walking trails of Cape Cod reward the outdoor enthusiast with a wealth of scenery and the blessing of solitude. These trails lead nature lovers and the casual stroller to every corner of the Cape, through woodlands, over cedar swamps, into open salt marsh, and onto open shorelines. In this chapter you'll find information on 48 of these trails.

If you want to discover what it's like to walk the whole Cape from end to end, try Elliot Carr's *Walking Cape Cod;* it's a good source and a good read. The Cape Cod National Seashore also offers invaluable trail information. There you can find maps, updates on trail status and condition, and information about which of the trails in the National Seashore are best suited to your particular interests and experience.

On the trail you'll want extra water, a good pair of shoes, and most importantly, common sense. Tell someone where you are going and when you expect to be back. Now, grab your camera, and if you travel quietly enough, maybe you'll see an otter swimming in the salt marsh, seals basking on the seashore, or a deer feeding under a crabapple tree, and you will be able to catch on film a wonderful memory of your Cape Cod adventure.

HIKING TRAILS

Upper Cape

There are a variety of stunning walking trails in the Upper Cape area, such as the trail along the Cape Cod Canal between Bourne and Sandwich. The 7-mile paved path runs along both sides of the canal and is relatively level. You'll see cormorants diving for fish while elegant sailboats and tugs towing gigantic tankers pass by within a few hundred yards. Or for something completely different, journey into the woodlands of Beebe Woods in Falmouth in search of glacier boulders and kettle ponds that dot the grounds.

DeNormandie Woods Conservation Area and Broyer and Robinson Conservation Area
Red Brook Road, Bourne
(508) 563-2884

The DeNormandie Woods Conservation Area comprises 9 acres of wooded upland with a connecting two-thirds of a mile trail to the 30-acre Broyer and Robinson Conservation Area. This is one of our favorite walks because you rarely see anyone here. Watch out for lady slipper orchids and rhododendrons, which bloom spectacularly in the late spring and early summer. Enter either by Shore Road between Red Brook Harbor Road and County Road or along Red Brook Road between Scraggy Neck Road and Parker's Boat Yard.

The historic character of Olde Kings Highway, also known as Route 6A, makes it a unique experience for bicyclists and walkers. Once a Native American trail, the road between Plymouth and Provincetown is America's largest designated historic district. It is suited to experienced bicyclists because it is heavily traveled by cars. If you like shopping and fine dining as well as biking, you'll want to travel this route, which is brimming with art galleries, dining establishments, antiques and gifts shops, and boutiques.

Four Ponds Park and Town Forest
Barlows Landing Road, Bourne
(508) 759-6025

Trails around Freeman Pond, Upper Pond, the Basin, and Shop Pond, and then through the Town Forest comprise this roughly 300-acre conservation area maintained by the Bourne Conservation Department. Laced with marked hiking trails, the area also has marked points for pickerel and trout fishing. Although no prominent structure remains, the area used to be part of the Pocasset Iron Works. You can park in the lot on the right of Barlows Landing Road about a mile from MacArthur Boulevard. This is a nice area for bird-watching, and you might see deer, too.

Nivling-Alexander Reserve
Shore and Thaxter Roads, Bourne
(508) 563-2884

Also known as the Red Brook Pond Conservation Area, the Nivling-Alexander trail is a half-mile circular wooded trail through pitch pine and hardwoods (vibrant in the fall), passing through 40 acres of land along Red Brook Pond and working cranberry bogs. There are birds aplenty, and you may see animal tracks along the trail. The entrance is at Shore Road and Thaxter Road.

Boyden Farm Conservation Lands
Cotuit Road, Sandwich
(508) 888-4200

Boyden Farm is a 48-acre conservation area that fronts Peter's Pond and features walking trails and a wildlife management area. Bring your binoculars to the wildlife field where you may spot deer, hawks, and wild turkeys, which have been successfully released through the management program of the Sandwich Conservation Commission. Parking is west of Cotuit Road and just south of Farmersville Road.

Maple Swamp Conservation Area
Service Road, Sandwich
(508) 888-4200

Maple Swamp Conservation Area is a network of dirt roads and paths spreading out over 500 acres along a service road parallel to U.S. Route 6 between exits 3 and 4. It is closed to vehicles and has numerous trails and roads for walking (no biking). Here you can find all types of wildlife, including white-tailed deer. The kettle-hole ponds and irregular terrain are typical of the topography that glaciers created thousands of years ago. The elevation at Maple Swamp ranges from 40 feet above sea level to 250 feet at one of the highest points of land on the Cape.

Ryder Conservation Area
Cotuit and South Sandwich Roads, Sandwich
(508) 888-4200

The lovely 243-acre Ryder Conservation Area is accessible from Cotuit and South Sandwich Roads and offers about 5 miles of walking trails. Wakeby Pond has fishing areas and a boat ramp and is an excellent area for canoeing and swimming. Nature lovers will appreciate the large holly trees (some more than 100 years old), the beech/pine tree groves, and the old abandoned cranberry bogs. Lifeguards are on-site during the summer months (Ryder Conservation Area is open May to October). A local beach sticker is required during the summer months between 9:00 A.M. and 4:00 P.M. A daily pass may be purchased for $10 at the Sandwich Town Hall (508-888-4910). There are several parking areas and entrances off the west side of Cotuit Road between Harlow Road and Boardly Road.

Scusset Beach State Reservation
Scusset Beach Road, Sandwich
(508) 888-0859

Scusset Beach Reservation, on the north side of the canal (see our Campgrounds and State Parks chapter), is a large state-run park that is mostly used for camping, but hiking and fishing are permitted. A 1-mile trail through Scusset leads to Sagamore Hill, which offers a panoramic overlook of Cape Cod Bay. Take Meetinghouse Road east off the Sagamore Rotary to Scusset Beach Road to the trail entrance opposite the pier. A daily parking fee of $7.00 is charged.

Shawme-Crowell State Forest
Route 130, Sandwich
(508) 888-0351

This large 742-acre state-run park is used mostly for camping and offers an abundance of wildlife, flora, and fauna. This quiet campground at the beginning of Cape Cod has 285 campsites, and toilets and hot water are available for a nightly fee of $12 (see our Campgrounds and State Parks chapter). The park also has 15 miles of roads and trails that provide excellent hiking and biking access to the pitch pine and scrub oak forests. A hike to Mt. Perry, within the park, is well worth the trip—you can view all of Cape Cod Bay from the summit. A camping permit allows campers to use Scusset Beach.

Talbot's Point Conservation Lands
Old County Road, Sandwich
(508) 888-4200

Talbot's Point Conservation Lands on Old County Road has a relatively level trail system through a red pine forest planted for soil control by the Conservation Corps during the Great Depression. Its 112 acres abut a saltwater and freshwater marsh, and walkers may see shore and upland game birds as well as osprey. The area features a freshwater bubbling spring. Park on the wide sandy road north from Old County Road, about 1 mile east of Hoxie Pond.

The Briar Patch
Route 6A, East Sandwich
(508) 888-6870

The Briar Patch is a 166-acre conservation area off Route 6A in East Sandwich. This pleasant area of white pine, black locust trees, and meandering trails was a source of inspiration to Thornton W. Burgess, who wrote *Old Mother West Wind* and many other popular children's books in the early 20th century. Two trails loop through the abandoned pastures and groves of black locust and white pine. Enter the trailheads on Discovery Hill Road off Route 6A behind the Green Briar Nature Center.

Murkwood Conservation Area
Route 6A, East Sandwich
(508) 888-4200

To explore the 79-acre Murkwood Conservation Area, park at the East Sandwich Fire Station on Route 6A and walk across the street. A peninsula, this former farmland abuts Scorton Creek, and you might be fortunate enough to see eagles, osprey, shorebirds, and white-tailed deer. The area's several miles of trails pass through swampy areas and pinewoods, and the view of Scorton Marsh, especially at sunset is breathtaking.

You've come to the right place if you want to walk. Cape Cod Pathways is our ever-expanding network of trails that link open space with all 15 towns. Pick up a map of trails from the Cape Cod Chamber (508–862–0700), or most town chambers. You may also call Cape Cod Pathways at (508) 362–3828.

Ashumet Holly Wildlife Sanctuary
Ashumet Road, East Falmouth
(508) 362–1426

Owned by the Massachusetts Audubon Society, the Ashumet Holly Reservation and Wildlife Sanctuary, off Route 151 (signs are posted) on Currier Road and Ashumet Road, is a popular 45-acre preserve that is open from sunrise to sunset all year. Along the trails you can see flowering magnolias, dogwood, rhododendron, and rare wildflower such as Plymouth gentian. The grounds include 65 varieties of holly trees, as well as Franklinia trees, which are actually a type of tea plant named in honor of Benjamin Franklin. In the spring swallows nest in the Ashumet barn. The sanctuary offers workshops, bird walks, and field trips throughout the year. Admission to the Ashumet Holly Reserve is $4.00 for adults and $3.00 for seniors and those 12 and younger. Maps are available at the visitor center at the sanctuary.

Beebe Woods
Off Depot Avenue, Falmouth
(508) 457–2536

Beebe Woods was a generous gift to the town of Falmouth from benefactor Josiah K. Lilly in 1966. Located at the end of Depot Avenue, the wooded grounds of the nearly 400-acre estate have extensive trails and are open to the public for walking, cross-country skiing, horseback riding, and bird-watching. Four large kettle ponds dot the woodlands, as do glacier boulders and wetlands. If you are looking for a serene outing, a 1.6-mile walk to Ice House Pond at the end of the trail is as peaceful as it gets on Cape Cod.

Bourne Farm
Route 28A and Thomas Flanders Road, West Falmouth
(508) 548–8484

The 49-acre Bourne Farm is owned and operated by Salt Pond Area Bird Sanctuary, Inc. In July and August you can take an afternoon tour (by appointment—call the number above) of the 1775 farmhouse and a barn with an old cattle tunnel. This former working farm has hiking paths and a parking area. A free nature program geared to children is given every Tuesday afternoon during July and August at 3:00 P.M. The trails are open year-round.

Frances A. Crane Wildlife Management Area
Ashumet Road, Falmouth
(508) 759–3406

The Frances A. Crane Wildlife Management Area is a 1,700-acre reserve regulated by the Massachusetts Division of Fisheries and Wildlife. The land is an extensive sand plain with mostly pitch pine and little deciduous growth. It is stocked with game during the fall hunting season and should not be considered safe for recreational activities at that time. At other times of the year, it is a popular place for walking and horseback riding.

Goodwill Park
Palmer Avenue, Falmouth
(508) 457–2543

The 85-acre Goodwill Park is a spacious wooded area with a lovely pond. The park is open daily from 8:00 A.M. to 4:00 P.M. for hiking, swimming, Frisbee-playing, and canoeing. With a lovely freshwater beach, restrooms, barbecue grills and play equipment, this is a good place for families and picnickers. To bring a large group call the parks department at the above number to reserve the pavilion area.

Washburn Island
Waquoit Bay, East Falmouth
(508) 457-0495

Washburn Island is a 334-acre wooded island in Waquoit Bay managed by the state Department of Conservation and Recreation. It is only accessible by boat and has no fresh water. If you wish to camp on the island, you must purchase a permit (see our Campgrounds and State Parks chapter). Call the Waquoit Bay National Estuarine Research Reserve at the number above for more information.

John's Pond Park
Hooppole Road, Mashpee
(508) 539-1400

John's Pond Park is a 258-acre park with a trail system and a 1,200-foot sandy beach. Nature lovers can watch herring swim up the Quashnet River in the spring and fall and explore an extensive area of cranberry bogs. As you head toward North Falmouth, you'll find the park off Route 151 past the Barnstable County Fairgrounds; turn right onto Currier Road, then right on Hooppole Road and right again onto Back Road. John's Pond Park is just beyond the trailer park.

Lowell Holly Reservation
South Sandwich Road, Mashpee
(508) 670-2115

At the Lowell Holly Reservation, marked by a small sign on Sandwich Road (the entrance is opposite a sign that says Carpe Diem), you'll find a delightful 1½-mile trail among American beech, huge holly, white pine trees, and rhododendron. There's a perfect little swimming beach with a picnic table on the Cape's largest (and arguably most beautiful) lake. Birders have spotted eagles, ospreys, and hawks here. Once owned by James Lowell, the former president of Harvard University,

this 135-acre property is maintained by the Trustees of Reservations. The parking fee on summer weekends is $6.00.

Mashpee River Woodlands
Quinaquisset Road, Mashpee
(508) 539-1400

The 400-acre Mashpee River Woodlands has 8 miles of hiking trails along the Mashpee River, a protected waterway that is perfect for canoeing, bird-watching, and walking. This location is a good place to see the natural transition between freshwater and saltwater habitats. Coming from the Mashpee Rotary, follow Route 28 toward Hyannis to the first right, Quinaquisset Road.

Pine Barrens
Great Neck Road South, Mashpee
(508) 539-1400

The Pine Barrens is a 300-acre reserve that has about 4 miles of marked walking trails and sandy roads. To get there turn right off Great Neck Road onto the dirt road opposite Punkhorn Point Road.

South Cape Beach State Park
Great Neck Road, Mashpee
(508) 457-0495

At the end of Great Neck Road is South Cape Beach, where the state maintains a public beach, parking lot, and conservation land with 3 miles of sandy roadways suitable for hiking. Here you can explore both freshwater and saltwater wetlands. There is a $7.00 fee for parking. For more information about South Cape, contact the Waquoit Bay National Estuarine Research Reserve at the above number.

Mid-Cape

Crocker Neck Conservation Area
Santuit Road, Cotuit
(508) 862-4093

The 97-acre Crocker Neck Conservation Area in Cotuit is a peninsula created by

Shoestring Bay, Popponesset Bay, and Pinquickset Cove. It is wooded and has an interpretive trail with permanent numbered markers and an observation deck overlooking tidal pools. The area also has saltwater marshes. You can park in a lot off Santuit Road.

Long Pond Conservation Area
Santuit-Newtown Road, Cotuit
(508) 862-4093
A community garden with two observation decks overlooking the 37-acre Long Pond are features of Long Pond Conservation Area. An interpretive network of trails totaling 2 miles passes through fields and woodlands. A parking entrance on Newtown Road is about 2½ miles from Route 28.

Burgess Park
Route 149, Marstons Mills
(508) 790-6345
Burgess Park is a 17-acre park with an 18 "hole" Frisbee golf course, walking trails, a playground, volleyball court, croquet area, horseshoe pits, and barbecue grills. The park overlooks Hamblin Pond, and it's an easy walk to the pond's beach.

Bridge Creek Conservation Area
Route 149, West Barnstable
(508) 862-4093
To reach Bridge Creek Conservation Area you can park at either the fire station on Route 149 or at Church Street (which can be found off Route 6A). This large 246-acre conservation area has 2½ miles of well-cleared trails for you to explore. Maps are available at the trailhead.

Hathaway's Pond Recreation Area
Old Phinney's Lane, Barnstable
(508) 862-4093
The Hathaway's Pond Recreation Area in Barnstable has oak and pine forests, two ponds, an interpretive trail, and a picnic

area within its 94 acres. The entrance is on Phinney's Lane off Route 132.

Sandy Neck Recreation Area
Off Route 6A, West Barnstable
(508) 862-4093
The Sandy Neck Recreation Area has about 5 miles of sandy trails bordered by wildflowers and cranberries. It's a nice place to canoe and fish. You can plan your hike from a trail map at the beach guard station. Parking is available, and a small fee is charged during the summer.

West Barnstable Conservation Area
Route 149, West Barnstable
(508) 862-4093
West Barnstable Conservation Area is an extensive 1,114-acre area with 15 miles of trails. A good number of the trails are geared toward mountain biking. You'll find limited parking at the intersection of Popple Bottom Road and Route 149 or off the service road.

Horse Pond Conservation Area
Higgins Crowell Road, West Yarmouth
(508) 398-2231
Located near the Mattacheese School, this ¾-mile hilly trail is marked by pitch pines, white oaks, sassafras, and blueberry and huckleberry bushes. Though the trail is joined by side trails that lead off toward longer journeys, the main trail keeps Horse Pond within sight.

Meadowbrook Road Conservation Area
Meadowbrook Road, West Yarmouth
(508) 398-2231
Meadowbrook Road Conservation Area is a pretty walking area with a short boardwalk over a freshwater marsh that leads to a scenic overlook of Swan Pond. Benches provide a good place for a reflective moment or to examine the beautiful salt marsh vegetation that grows so abundantly here.

[Facing page] *A tree stands sentinel during the off-season at Lowell Holly Reservation.*
RICHARD CHEEK AND THE TRUSTEES OF RESERVATIONS

CLOSE-UP

Birding on Cape Cod

One of the best spots along the North-eastern seaboard to view birds is Cape Cod. During the migration seasons more than 260 different species of birds may make a stop on Cape Cod to feed on marine worms, insects, crustaceans, and mollusks before continuing their long journey, which may have started in the Arctic Circle to end in South America, 12,000 miles away. Cape Cod lies about halfway along this busy flyway, and places like Monomoy Island and Nauset Marsh are regular stopovers for these birds, perfect areas to feed and rest before flying either north or south in the spring and fall.

Birds can, for the sake of simplicity, be divided into three main categories: back-yard birds, shorebirds, and raptors. Local naturalist Peter Trull states, "One of the most exciting times to watch backyard birds on Cape Cod is during their spring migration. They are in their breeding plumage, the weather is pleasantly warm, and the birds often move through in 'waves,' providing great looks at number of species, including warblers, sparrows, bluebirds, chickadees, and finches."

It's no surprise that shorebirds top the list of birds on Cape Cod. Among the many varieties of shorebirds found around these shores are dunlins, sander-lings, gulls, ducks, mergansers, sand-pipers, and Canada geese.

Birding is terrific on Cape Cod no matter what the season, though spring is the best time to view migrating birds, and August is best for observing shore-birds. Many gulls and terns, having bred in June and fledged their young in July, become roving flocks in August. From mid-July to Labor Day, great concentra-tions of shorebirds can build up around feeding grounds. September is a good month for birding because of the possi-bility of a rare sighting. If a Nor'easter hits the Cape, sometimes migrating birds such as shearwaters, northern gannets, loons, and petrels become trapped near land and instinctively turn eastward to the Cape. If you set up watch in the morning after a storm at a beach such as First Encounter Beach in Eastham, you'll have an excellent chance of observing some rare birds. September is also a wonderful month when many migrating birds linger on these shores, delaying their flights south for as long as possible. These birds tend to concentrate near their favorite food source before continu-ing on their journey.

Raymond J. Syrjala Conservation Area
Winslow Gray Road, West Yarmouth
(508) 398-2231
The Raymond J. Syrjala Conservation Area is about a half-mile from Route 28. The 3,540-foot trail encircles a kettle-hole pond that serves as a great frog pond. The trail itself is spongy because it's made up of decaying leaves and pine needles. Many species of vegetation, such as red maple, pitch pine, and blueberries, are marked.

Winter birds are plentiful, too. Herons, egrets, and sandpipers, all birds associated with wetland habitats, are abundant this time of year. A variety of waterfowl—including buffleheads, common eiders, canvasbacks, and goldeneyes—make the Cape their home during different months in the winter. A winter walk along a salt marsh, beach, or tidal flat will give food opportunities to observe these birds feeding and resting.

Here are a few pointers offered by Peter Trull to make identifying these birds easier: Use binoculars to scan the horizon, the marshes, and tidal flats. When trying to locate a bird in a tree, first orient yourself by focusing on its trunk, or a branch; then look for the bird. Judge the size to determine what type of bird it is. Several good field guides illustrated with drawings or photos are available, including Peter Trull's own book, *A Guide to Common Birds of Cape Cod,* which makes life a little easier for the novice birder by including only birds that are commonly found in this area.

Depending on what season it is, you may observe the following birds in these locations:

The Crane Reservation in Mashpee and Beech Forest in Provincetown offer wooded areas for locating:

- pine warblers
- rufous-sided towhees

- common yellowthroats
- Carolina wrens
- gray catbirds
- northern orioles
- black-capped chickadees
- tree swallows

The Wellfleet Bay/Audubon Sanctuary and the Cape Cod Museum of Natural History in Brewster provide short hikes that take you through upland areas, marshlands, and areas fronting Cape Cod Bay. These multiple habitats offer great opportunities to view:

- ospreys
- red-tailed hawks
- red-winged blackbirds
- willets
- sparrows

Sandy Neck Recreation Area in Barnstable and Monomoy Wildlife Refuge in Chatham offer a beach and wetlands habitat that is perfect for viewing:

- common terns
- common grackles
- least terns
- kingfishers
- oystercatchers
- great blue herons
- laughing gulls

Bass Hole (Gray's Beach)
Center Street, Yarmouthport
(508) 398-2231

Bass Hole, also called Gray's Beach, at the end of Center Street, is the place to stroll along the boardwalk, put your toes in the water, and enjoy the beach, playground, and barbecue facilities. Many consider this the best place to watch a sunset on Cape Cod.

Callery-Darling Conservation Area
Center Street, Yarmouthport
(508) 398–2231

The Callery-Darling Conservation Area is a great place to spot woodland and water birds, such as the great blue heron, the largest heron in North America, which fishes in both fresh and salt water. There is a trail system here comprising some 2.4 miles wandering through lands where foxes, rabbits, and deer make their home.

Crab Creek Conservation Area
North Dennis Road, Yarmouthport
(508) 398–2231

Blue crabs (*Callinectes sapidus*) are abundant here, and their presence gave this conservation area its name. A 500-foot trail follows a creek that joins Follins Pond with Mill Pond; it is a prime fishing spot and features a dock just for that purpose. Besides the creek and the crabs, there is also an old bog and plenty of red maple, cranberry, pitch pine, blueberry, and poison ivy.

Dennis Pond Conservation Area
Willow Street, Yarmouthport
(508) 398–2231

As its name suggests this conservation area is adjacent to Dennis Pont and features a 1,325-foot trail that leads through woodlands of red maple, white pine, and sweet pepperbush. Your walk will take you through many faces of Cape Cod woodlands, including an old bog, pine forests, and a small swamp. Moss is plentiful in some spots, fallen pine needles in others. There's a small parking area out on Willow Street where you begin your journey.

Nature Trails
Route 6A, Yarmouthport
(508) 362–3021

The Nature Trails behind the Yarmouthport Post Office on Route 6A are owned by the town and maintained by the Historical Society of Old Yarmouth. The area has a little herb garden and a 150-year-old weeping beech tree. There is a gatehouse at the beginning of the trail where you can pick up a trail map and where a donation is requested (50 cents for adults, 25 cents for children). The main trail is approximately 1 mile long, and the pond trail around Millers Pond adds another half-mile to the trek.

Simpkins Neck Romig-Jacquinet Conservation Area
New Boston Road, Dennis
(508) 760–6123

Simpkins Neck and the Romig-Jacquinet Conservation Area are two connected parcels of land that are largely surrounded by marshlands. Once you find the entrance (off New Boston Road, two houses past Berrien Studios on your left), you can follow the trail to the edge of the marsh. It's 1.5 miles round-trip. Bird-watchers will be in heaven, as will wildlife lovers, because Simpkins Neck is also refuge to raccoons and deer.

Crowe's Pasture
South Street, East Dennis
(508) 760–6123

Nature lovers will relish Crowe's Pasture, a bayfront site of more than 50 acres off South Street at the end of Quivet Cemetery. Follow the dirt road (about 2½ miles round-trip), and revel in an oasis barrier beach with marsh hawks and wild apple and cherry groves.

Fresh Pond Conservation Area
Route 134, South Dennis
(508) 760–6123

Fresh Pond Conservation Area, right on Route 134, is 27 unspoiled acres of blueberries and wild cranberries. You can occasionally spot ducks and red-tailed hawks here while you walk one of four informal trails ranging from a 15-minute loop to a leisurely 45-minute walk.

[Facing page] *Lowell Holly Reservation offers great birding opportunities.* THE TRUSTEES OF RESERVATIONS AND RICHARD HEATH

Indian Lands Conservation Area
Main Street, South Dennis
(508) 760-6123
Some of the Cape's most awesome flora and fauna abound in Indian Lands Conservation Area, a 2-mile walk that hugs the banks of Bass River. Birders can easily spot kingfishers and blue herons in the winter. You know summer is around the corner when the lady's slipper orchids start sprouting in May. We know of a hiking aficionado who found, on three separate occasions, artifacts of the Native Americans who lived here in centuries past.

Lower Cape

The Lower Cape is dominated by the expansive Cape Cod National Seashore, one of America's most beautiful recreational shorelines (see our Cape Cod National Seashore chapter). Adding to this bounty of natural areas are other excellent parks and wildlife refuges, including Nickerson State Park in Brewster, the Massachusetts Audubon Society's Wellfleet Bay Wildlife Sanctuary, and the magnificent Monomoy National Wildlife Refuge.

Nickerson State Park
Route 6A, Brewster
(508) 896-3491
This 1,779-acre wonderland has 8 miles of bike trails that link with the Cape Cod Rail Trail as well as miles of hiking trails that meander through the woods. Some wind past the park's two main attractions, Flax Pond and Cliff Pond. The trails are also great for cross-country skiing in winter, if the Cape is blessed with a real snowfall (yes, it does happen!). Hike out to Higgins Pond, a major migration stop for endangered birds such as ospreys and peregrine falcons. You'll also see cormorants, wrens, hawks, owls, warblers, thrushes, great blue herons, Canada geese, and the common loon—it's a birder's heaven. Nickerson also has bayfront land on the north side of

Route 6A (an easy walk from the park's entrance on the south side of the road) and offers ranger-guided interpretive programs and informative walks explaining plant and wildlife in a variety of habitats. Call for program schedules, or check the big board in the main parking lot.

Punkhorn Parklands
Run Hill Road, Brewster
(508) 896-3701
Here you'll find a maze of 45 scenic trails throughout more than 800 acres of rugged parkland made up of marshes and meadows, quarries and woodland, pine and oak—a tranquil paradise interrupted only by warbling birds, howling coyotes, and the occasional mountain bike. Along the paths you'll spot old pumps once used by cranberry grower to flood these former bogs.

Spruce Hill Conservation Area
3341 Route 6A, Brewster
(508) 896-3701
This 25-acre parcel, hidden behind the Brewster Historical Society Museum on the eastern end of town, features a half-mile-long former carriage road leading to Cape Cod Bay and an expansive beach. Rumor has it that bootleggers used the trail during the time of Prohibition. Fragile plant life is abundant here, so please, as always, stay on the official path.

Bell's Neck Road Conservation Area
Off Bell's Neck Road, Harwich
(508) 430-7506
One of the finest bird-watching sports on the Lower Cape, this is a magnificent 245-acre utopia of marshlands, herring runs, reservoirs, and tidal creeks.

Monomoy National Wildlife Refuge
Monomoy Island, Chatham
(508) 945-0594
monomoy.fws.gov
Accessible from Chatham only by boat in good weather conditions, Monomoy is a 7,600-acre, two-island wilderness area, one of only four remaining between Maine

Hiking and biking trails crisscross the most beautiful areas of the Cape and islands—which are also the habitat of the deer tick. These ticks are known to carry Lyme disease and should obviously be avoided. They are at their most plentiful May through July. Some helpful hints for a worry-free walk: Wear light clothing, tuck your pant legs into your socks, and use insect repellant containing DEET (though not on infants!). Inspect yourself, your children, and your pets after the walk just to be sure. If you find a tick, remove it within 24 hours. Use tweezers to dislodge the tick. Pull straight out with steady pressure, save the tick, and contact the Cape Cod Cooperative Extension at (508) 375-6617 or the Barnstable County Department of Health and the Environment at (508) 375-6617 so they can identify the tick for you and let you know if you should seek treatment.

and New Jersey. Acquired by the federal government in 1944 and now under the administration of the U.S. Fish and Wildlife Service, Monomoy has no electricity, no human residents, no vehicles, no paved roads—and more than 285 species of birds inhabiting saltwater and tidal flats, bayberry and beach plum thickets, freshwater ponds, and a 9-mile-long barrier beach. There is also a nonworking lighthouse (built in 1823, restored in 1988). Beach areas are closed from April to mid-August so that the nesting areas of piping plovers and terns won't be disturbed.

Quiet is the best word to describe Monomoy. In the winter thousands of seals take harbor here. Monomoy is an important stop along the North Atlantic flyway, and in May and late July migrating waterfowl and shorebirds stop here for a rest. Monomoy was once attached to the mainland; a 1958 storm severed the relationship. Twenty years later another storm divided the island in two. The Cape Cod Museum of Natural History (508-896-3867), and Wellfleet Bay Wildlife Sanctuary (508-349-2615), offer regular guided tours; see our Tours and Excursions chapter. Morris Island, a 40-acre island accessible by car and foot, is home to migrating warblers, and tidal flats provide food for oyster-shucking birds. Check your tide chart before visiting—the interpretive walking trail closes during high tide.

**The Cape Cod National Seashore
Salt Pond Visitor Center, U.S. Route 6, Eastham
(508) 255-3421
Province Lands Visitor Center, Race Point Road, Provincetown
(508) 487-1256
Park Headquarters, Marconi Station, off U.S. Route 6
(508) 349-3785
www.nps.gov/caco**

With some 27,700 acres of federally protected undeveloped uplands, bogs, pitch pine forests, sand dunes, and ponds in the six towns (Chatham, Orleans, Eastham, Wellfleet, Truro, and Provincetown), the National Seashore takes up almost half of the town of Wellfleet and about 70 percent of Truro. In addition to six glorious ocean beaches, comprising nearly 40 miles of the finest seashore on the Atlantic coast (see our Beaches chapter), the Cape Cod National Seashore boasts nine hiking trails that meander through varied terrain. You can get free hike and bike maps at the Salt Pond Visitor Center in Eastham, which is open all year (daily except January and February, when it's open on weekends only) and shows free interpretive videos in addition to hosting a variety of interpretive programs.

Right behind the Salt Pond Visitor Center are several trails, including the quarter-mile Buttonbush Trail, which has a

Many Eastern coyotes now call the Cape home. A young male coyote is known to wander up to 300 miles. Sightings on the Cape have been reported since the late 1970s, and coyotes have been spotted in each Cape town at this point. There's little to fear from them: They are evasive creatures who are not interested in you (though they may cast an eye toward small pets). Absolutely do not try to feed them, though!

guide rope and Braille map interpretations along the way. It's a good trail not only for the sight impaired, but for people who want to experience what life is like without the sense that most of us take for granted. Close your eyes and try it. Another nearby trail takes a wooded route out to the 1.2 mile Salt Pond trail, which passes by the Salt Pond, along Nauset Marsh, and circles back to the visitor center; you can also walk or bike on the 2-mile bike trail that leads out to Coast Guard Beach, past Doane Rock—a good place to stop and picnic (see our Cape Cod National Seashore chapter for more information regarding trails).

One of our favorite walking spots is the National Seashore's Fort Hill in Eastham, where 1½ miles of trails meander through fields with stunning water and marsh views, through woods and a cedar swamp. You're likely to spot rabbits, birds, and other wildlife, but watch out for monster poison ivy plants on the edge of the trail! We're also partial to the Seashore's longest and most difficult trail, Great Island in Wellfleet. Accessible by driving out past the harbor to the parking area, the trail is a hilly 8 miles (round-trip) through soft sand, pitch pines, and marshes that offers breathtaking views of Wellfleet Bay. Look for fiddler crabs—fast-moving, harmless little black creatures so named because the males have one oversized claw that's reminiscent of someone playing a fiddle. Be sure to check the tides, because much of

the trail is flooded at high tide. In Provincetown check out the 1-mile-long Beech Forest Trail, where you'll circle a freshwater pond as you walk among American beech trees, sheep laurel, yellow and gray birch, and swamp azaleas.

Wellfleet Bay Wildlife Sanctuary
U.S. Route 6, Wellfleet
(508) 349–2615
www.wellfleetbay.org

The Massachusetts Audubon Society operates this 1,000-acre-plus tract of salt marsh, woodland, beach, tidal flats, and moorland. What was once a turnip and asparagus farm is now a haven of self-guided nature trails and superb bird-watching, along with a natural history day camp for children and weeklong field trips for older folk. Guided walks, canoe cruises through Nauset Marsh, Monomoy cruises, and seal and whale-watching trips are regularly sponsored. The excursions are extremely popular and book up fast. The 1½-mile Goose Pond Trail, part of the 5 miles of trails, offers a look at a diversity of habitats and leads to the shore. It's an excellent place for viewing shorebirds, hawks, and herons. If you're still getting to know Mother Nature, borrow or purchase a copy of the 32-page Goose Pond Trail plant identification booklet at the visitor center. In keeping with the theme of preservation, the visitor center uses passive solar heating and composting toilets. It's open year-round. A donation is requested: $5.00 from adults and $3.00 from seniors and children younger than 12. Of course if you are a member of the Massachusetts Audubon Society, the donation is waived.

BIKING

Whether you're seeking a new challenge or simply an escape from the madding crowd, you can find it on Cape Cod. Whatever your biking abilities you can choose among an abundance of trails throughout the Cape. It's easy to get deep into the Cape Cod National Seashore wilderness on bike, or pedal the miles upon miles of asphalt that roll parallel to the world's widest canal, or experience the spectacular sand dunes of the Province Lands bordering the Atlantic Ocean. In this section we highlight paved trails, though we mention some dirt trails, and also let you know about bike shops that provide maintenance and rentals.

Biking Trails

UPPER CAPE

Cape Cod Canal Area
Buzzards Bay to Cape Cod Bay
(508) 759-4431

Owned and operated by the U.S. Army Corps of Engineers, this 8-mile-long paved surface rolls gently along both sides of the Cape Cod Canal area in Bourne and Sandwich. The path is used every day in every season by bikers—from newcomers to experienced bicyclists—and by in-line skaters, walkers, and dog owners. The views are appealing—cormorants dive for fish while towering tankers and elegant sailboats pass by within a few yards. As sunsets are usually spectacular along the Cape Cod Canal, you might want to plan your ride along the canal at sundown.

The path can be accessed at many points along its length. Those access points along the north side of the canal are northeast of Bourne Bridge, Herring Brook Fishway in Bournedale, Scusset State Park, and at the east side of Sagamore Bridge. South side accesses are along Pleasant Street in Sagamore, the southeast side of the Bourne Bridge, and the Boat Basin off Freezer Road in Sandwich. The access roads are marked, so you should be able to find your way.

Shining Sea Bike Path
Woods Hole to Falmouth
(508) 548-7611

A favorite with bikers, walkers, and in-line skaters is the Shining Sea Bike Path,

named in honor of Katherine Lee Bates, who wrote the lyrics of *America the Beautiful* and was born in Falmouth in 1859 in a house that still stands today at 16 Main Street. The bikeway is a level, 3-mile paved path and was built over the old Penn Central Railroad tracks. It overlooks Vineyard Sound as it passes alongside marshland and then gently winds by Nobska Point Lighthouse, on its way from Falmouth to Woods Hole. As the route follows the shore, it provides a great opportunity to take a swim, so bring your bathing suits.

We suggest that you use the parking lot on Locust Street (at Mill Pond) in Falmouth and ride toward Woods Hole. As you start your pedal, you'll see the Salt Pond Bird Sanctuary on your right. If you look carefully, chances are you will catch a glimpse of a nesting osprey. Farther down the path, and still to your right, is Oyster Pond; Vineyard Sound is on your left. Benches have been placed along the path, so do make the effort to take a breather and absorb the beauty this path offers. As you pass Nobska Point, you can get a good view of the island of Martha's Vineyard, just 5 miles off the coast. Here you'll be about as close as you can get to the island without sailing toward it. Cross a few vintage wooden bridges, travel past the Coast Guard Station, and you're gliding into the quaint seaside town of Woods Hole. The trail also connects with paths that take you to other beautiful areas, such as Quisset Harbor.

LOWER CAPE

Cape Cod Rail Trail
Dennis to Wellfleet
(508) 896-3491

Here is a great ride for bike enthusiasts who want to sample all the fun biking can offer. This 25-mile paved trail offers you a glimpse of the heartland of Cape Cod as it runs from Dennis to Wellfleet, following an old railroad bed. The trail is fairly straight and sweeps by sweet-smelling cedar and pine forests and includes long straight stretches between roadway intersections; they are all well marked with a post situated in the middle of the path separating bike and car traffic.

The trail enters Nickerson State Park in Brewster where you will find just the right mix of pathway and off-road biking if you are looking for more of a bicycling challenge. There are not many rest rooms along the route, but there are facilities at Nickerson State Park in Brewster and a composting toilet in Eastham.

Parking areas for trail access are in Dennis on Route 134; in Harwich on Headwaters Road near Route 124; in Brewster on Route 137 at Nickerson State Park off Route 6A; in Orleans Center; in Eastham at the Cape Cod National Seashore Visitor Center; and at the National Seashore trailhead on LeCount Hollow Road in South Wellfleet.

Rubel Bike Maps publish great detailed maps for trails on the Cape and islands. Check www.bikemaps.com.

Nickerson State Park
Route 6A, Brewster
(508) 896-3491

If you are in search of new terrain for off-roading, you'll find that Nickerson State Park is practically the only place on the Lower Cape to ride a mountain bike. Service roads wind along the perimeter of the park, offering some fun dirt paths to play on; weave in and out of pine forests, and suddenly you've left the paved world behind. And once you do that at Nickerson, the possibilities are endless.

The park has 8 miles of paved biking trails that connect to numerous freshwater ponds and picnic areas. If you want the park to yourself, come here in late fall, winter, or early summer before the campers arrive. A map of the park is available at the entrance.

Cape Cod National Seashore
U.S. Route 6, Eastham
(508) 255-3421
www.nps.gov/caco

The Cape Cod National Seashore maintains three bicycle trails ranging from 1½ miles to just over 7 miles long. The trails are relatively flat with only a few hills in the dune areas where you might need to walk. Bike maps of the National Seashore are available at the visitor center in Eastham.

At the visitor center right near the Cape Cod Rail Trail (exit the trail at Locust Road, and cross U.S. Route 6 at the traffic light, if you are on a bike) is the Nauset Trail, a lovely 2-mile trail that goes out to Coast Guard Beach on the Atlantic Ocean. The highlight of the ride comes when the trail opens to a wide vista of Nauset Marsh with the Atlantic Ocean in the distance. Although it's only a 15-minute ride to the beach from the visitor center, you parallel Nauset Marsh the entire way, through groves of cedar and locust trees. We recommend that you stop at the scenic-view benches along the way. You'll love crossing the wooden bridge over the salt marsh just before you reach Coast Guard Beach.

The Head of the Meadow Trail is 2 miles long and wanders straight through the marshlands and dunes of the North Truro highlands. You can access the trail at High Head Road or at the Head of the Meadow Beach parking area. During July and August there is a nominal fee to park in the Head of the Meadow lot. We recommend you start at High Head Road and bike south toward Head of the Meadow. If you wish to venture further than just the 2-mile trail, it's easy. From Head of the Meadow head by bike to U.S. Route 6, and head south a short distance to Highland Road and up the paved road through the dunes to a vista that takes in both the Atlantic Ocean and Cape Cod Bay. To head back retrace your path, or stay on U.S. Route 6 to High Head Road. This is another one of those trails that should be explored at sunrise or sunset in order to catch a glimpse of a Monet moment.

In Provincetown the Seashore has miles of trails—you could ride around all day! In fact biking around Provincetown is one of the best ways to spend a day on Cape Cod. Our favorite, the Province Lands Trail, is a 7-mile loop that winds up and down dune hills, past lily ponds and bogs, through woods and sand dunes to the beaches at Race Point and Herring Cove. The trail starts at either Beech Forest at one end or Herring Cove at the other. Again there is a parking fee in season. The trail may also be picked up at the Province Lands Visitor Center, where there is no parking fee.

Bike Rentals

The Cape has plenty of shops that rent and sell bicycles and cycling equipment. Below we list a few that are close to the major bike routes.

UPPER CAPE

P&M Cycles
29 Main Street, Buzzards Bay
(508) 759-2830
This bike rental outfit is right on the Cape Cod Canal bike trail. It rents bikes by the hour, day, week, or month and has the largest selection of used bicycles to choose from on the Cape.

Holiday Cycles
465 Grand Avenue, Falmouth Heights
(508) 540-3549
If you're vacationing in Falmouth, you'll want to spend some time on the Shining Sea Bike Path. Stop by Holiday Cycles for bike rentals and any equipment you might need.

MID-CAPE

Barbara's Bike and Sport Equipment
430 Route 134, South Dennis
(508) 760-4723

If you're a beginner or riding with a family with younger members, the wide, flat fire roads throughout Cape Cod National Seashore are a great place to start. Check with the National Park Service for a map.

Barbara's is right at the parking lot at the beginning of the Cape Cod Rail Trail. It rents bicycles by the hour, day, or week for all members of the family, from toddlers to teenagers to grandparents.

LOWER CAPE

Rail Trail Bike & Blade
302 Underpass Road, Brewster
(508) 896-8200
With direct access to the Rail Trail and only minutes from Nickerson State Park, Rail Trail Bike & Blade may be one of the most convenient locations to enter the Rail Trail. There is plenty of all-day parking available at Bike & Blade, so you can hop on one of their rental bikes and spend the whole day exploring Nickerson State Park and the Lower Cape.

Little Capistrano Bike Shop
Salt Pond Road, Eastham
(508) 255-6515
This friendly shop is just across U.S. Route 6 from the Cape Cod National Seashore Visitor Center, right near the Cape Cod Rail Trail and the Seashore bike trails. It offers rentals, sales, accessories, and repairs. It's open April through December, and by appointment only January through March.

Idle Times Bike Shop
Town Center Plaza, U.S. Route 6, North Eastham
(508) 255-8281
www.idletimesbike.com
With shops here, in Wellfleet, and on Bracket Road in North Eastham, Idle Times boasts the largest fleet of rental bikes on the Cape. They also sell bikes and acces-

Mountain bike enthusiasts may want to take on the "Trail of Tears" off Race Lane in Marstons Mills. It's an 18-mile loop, appropriate for those with experience. Pick up a map of the area at Barnstable Town Hall in Hyannis.

sories. The Town Center Plaza shop is open year-round, and the other two are seasonal.

Arnold's
329 Commercial Street, Provincetown
(508) 487–0844
Located in the center of Provincetown, Arnold's is known as the place "where you rent any kind of bike." From children's 20-inch coaster brake bikes to Fuji and Speed Royce bikes, you can rent by the hour, half-day, day, or week. They also specialize in bike repairs, tires, tubes, and accessories. Arnold's is open seasonally.

Nelson's
43 Race Point Road, Provincetown
(508) 487–8849
Whether you are looking for some exercise or a carefree outing for the family, the bike trails to the Province Lands start just 100 yards from Nelson's. They offer a large selection of mountain bikes in a wide range of sizes. They also offer families Trail-a-Bikes, kiddie carts, and a large selection of youth bikes. Parking is free for all their customers. Nelson's is open seasonally.

TOURS AND EXCURSIONS

The Cape is beautiful from any perspective, whether it's riding in a car or walking on a beach. But to truly experience its many charms, try switching viewpoints. Get out on the water in a cruise ship or sailboat; take a train that chugs through country farms and hidden fields; or get a bird's-eye view from plane or glider. See villages and towns from the comfortable seat of a tall-windowed trolley, or clip-clop down streets in a horse-drawn carriage. Or combine exercise with education by taking a walking tour. Make the most of your visit by including a few of these tours, and you'll take home memories to treasure forever.

Here are some of our favorite tour and excursion companies, arranged by mode of transportation: boat, train, trolley, and plane. Keep in mind that most of these tours are only offered in season, and reservations may be required. We've given times wherever possible, but keep in mind they are subject to change. It's best to call ahead to check.

BOAT CRUISES

Upper Cape

Patriot Party Boats
Scranton Avenue, Falmouth
(508) 548-2626, (800) 734-0088
www.patriotpartyboats.com
Patriot Party Boats is a family-owned and operated business started more than 40 years ago. Docked at the entrance of scenic Falmouth Harbor, Patriot Boats operates fishing and charter boats, scenic sunset cruises, and operates the *Liberté*, a 74-foot schooner.

Liberté makes three cruises a day at 10:30 A.M., 2:00 P.M., and 6:30 P.M. The fare for an adult is $20 to $25 ($15 to $25 for children 12 and younger). This two-hour sail on the *Liberté* is only offered during July and August.

You can also enjoy a relaxing cruise along Falmouth's shoreline during a Lighthouse Sunset Cruise. See six lighthouses, four harbors, two islands, the village of Woods Hole, wildlife, and the sunset. The cost is only $15 for adults and $10 for children 12 and younger. Tours run daily in July from 6:30 to 8:30 P.M. and in August, 6:00 to 8:00 P.M. Snacks and soda are available, but this cruise is a great opportunity to pack a picnic or some wine and share the beautiful scenery of Cape Cod from the water.

Last but not least are the deep-sea fishing charters, which offer a great time and the possibility of catching sea bass, flounder, tautog, and scup. You can get detailed information about these in our Fishing chapter. Patriot Boats offers free parking for those boarding their boats. They also operate private charter fishing excursions; contact the number above for more information.

Cape Cod Canal Cruises
Onset Pier, Onset
(508) 295-3883
www.hy-linecruises.com
Many people pass over the Cape Cod Canal by car and wonder what it would be like to be on one of those boats down there. Find out! This is a great way to explore Buzzards Bay and the Cape Cod Canal. As you travel the length of the 7-mile canal, you may pass tankers, sailing yachts, fishing boats, or plush cruise ships.

When down at any one of the many harbors on Cape Cod, look for a catboat—a broad, shallow sailboat with a large sail mast stepped near the bow. These sailboats are excellent for use in the shallow waters around the Cape, which is why many of the sailboat charters are catboats.

A division of Hy-Line, Cape Cod Canal Cruises offers trips daily in summer, departing from Onset Pier in Onset at 10:00 A.M. and 1:30 P.M. A two-hour cruise costs $10.00 for adults and $5.00 for ages 5 to 12. A three-hour cruise costs $12.00 for adults and $6.00 for ages 5 to 12. Children younger than 5 ride free. There's a sunset cruise on Tuesday, Wednesday, and Thursday evenings in June through August from 7:00 to 9:00 P.M.; it costs $10.00 for adults and $5.00 for children. A great bargain is the Family Cruise, offered at 4:00 P.M. Monday through Saturday in season: Kids 12 and younger ride free with a parent! The fare is $10. If you want to enjoy some live music, take the TGIF cruise, which has a cash bar and free popcorn, or the Saturday Moonlight and Music cruise. Both are from 8:00 to 11:00 P.M., are for passengers 21 and older, and cost $14 per person. Enjoy live Dixieland jazz on the Jazz Cruise on Sunday afternoons at 1:30 P.M.; the cost is $14.00 for adults and $8.00 for children ages 5 to 12.

The *Island Queen*
75 Falmouth Heights Road, Falmouth
(508) 548–4800
www.islandqueen.com
For $12.00 round-trip ($6.00 for children under 13 and free for those younger than age 3), you can take the 500-passenger *Island Queen* from Falmouth Harbor to Martha's Vineyard. The trip, which is available from Memorial Day weekend to Columbus Day, is a leisurely 35 minutes each way, and food service is available on board, along with a full bar. The passenger-only vessel makes seven trips each day in summer, and reservations are not needed. Take your bicycle for an additional $6.00. The *Island Queen*'s summer schedule has trips from Falmouth at 9:00 and 10:30 A.M., noon, and 1:30, 3:00, 4:30, and 6:00 P.M. The *Island Queen* is also available for charters.

OceanQuest Waterfront Park
100 Water Street, Woods Hole
(508) 385-7656, (800) 376-2326
www.oceanquestonline.org
Here's a great opportunity to learn and have fun, with an information-packed cruise that includes a hands-on science lesson for all ages. "It is geared to the general public—the nonscientist," says OceanQuest founder and director Kathy Mullin, a marine biologist who has worked on whale-watch boats for 10 years. "We take a sample of the ocean, and with that we look at temperature, depth, salinity, density, the pH, and we talk about the greenhouse effect and global warming." Passengers also get a chance to practice with a plankton tow, a trawl, microscope, and lobster trap. Cruises are offered weekdays July through August. The cost is $20 per adult ($15 for kids 3 to 12 and free for those younger than 3). Group rates are also available.

The Steamship Authority
Woods Hole
(508) 477-8600
www.islandferry.com
Although no commentary is provided, taking an island ferry (see our Getting here, Getting Around chapter) is another excellent way to see the Cape from offshore.

[Facing page] *The Sea Star is certified by the U.S. Coast Guard, and can carry 66 passengers. Her primary use is for OceanQuest cruises during the spring, summer, and fall. In addition, she is available for private charters.* OCEANQUEST

Steamship vessels depart from Woods Hole in Falmouth, offering scenic views of the Elizabeth Islands and the southeastern end of Buzzards Bay on the way to Martha's Vineyard. (In Hyannis the Steamship Authority, 508–771–4000, provides service to Nantucket only.)

Mid-Cape

Eventide
165 Ocean Street Dock, Hyannis
(508) 775–0222
www.catboat.com
This classic Cape Cod catboat makes about six trips daily out of Hyannis Harbor from mid-April through October. You have your choice of harbor cruises, a starlight cruise, and a nature cruise to the Pine Cove Wildlife Sanctuary in Lewis Bay that departs at 10:15 A.M. Other cruises include a Hyannisport cruise at 12:15 P.M. and 2:15 P.M.; a 4:00 P.M. blue-water cruise; a 6:00 P.M. sunset cocktail cruise, and an 8:00 P.M. starlight cruise. The 34-foot *Eventide,* which has a 38-foot sloop-rigged mast, carries up to 22 people and is available for private parties. It can sail in only 30 inches of water, allowing it to get vary close to the shore and attractions such as the Kennedy Compound and local light-houses. Cruise prices are $25 for adults, $20 for senior citizens, and $10 for children less than 90 pounds (Captain Marcus Sherman explained that he goes by weight rather than age because Coast Guard regulations use 90 pounds as the cutoff for wearing a child's lifejacket). Call ahead for reservations. When you arrive look for the sign of the cat.

Hyannisport Harbor Cruises
Ocean Street Dock, Hyannis
(508) 778–2600
www.hy-linecruises.com
Hy-Line offers cruises of Hyannisport Harbor on board the *Patience* or the *Prudence,* 1930s Maine coastal steamer replicas. You'll see the Kennedy Compound in Hyannisport as well as Squaw

Island, Great Island, the Hyannis Yacht Club, and Point Gammon Lighthouse. Depending on the season, the schedule includes four to 17 trips a day between April and October. The cost for a one-hour cruise is $12.00 for an adult, $6.00 for ages 3 to 11, and free for children 2 and younger. In summer there are also 2 evening blues-and-cocktail cruises for $15 and a Sunday ice cream cruise for families, which costs $12.75 for adults and $7.00 for children 3 to 11. In summer cruises are offered from 9:00 A.M. to 7:00 P.M.; in spring and fall the last cruise is usually around 4:15 P.M. One-hour Family Cruises depart daily before noon, and cost $12 per adult, and children under 12 are free with a parent.

Hy-Line also has special excursions and regular ferry service from May to October to Nantucket and Martha's Vineyard. The company also offers an Around the Sound full-day cruise ($40.50 for an adult, $20.25 for ages 4 to 12) that includes stops on both Martha's Vineyard and Nantucket, and offers a bus tour of each island. The ferry returns to Hyannis between 9:00 and 9:30 P.M. We wouldn't recommend this tour to the elderly or families with young children, as it can be exhausting; but if you absolutely must squeeze in a visit to both islands in one day, this is the way to do it.

Starfish Bass River Cruises
Waterfront Park, Route 28, West Dennis
(508) 362–5555
www.capecodrivercruise.com
The only river cruise on Cape Cod, Bass River Cruises takes you over the gentle waters of the Bass River, Grand Cove, and Weir Creek on the *Starfish,* a custom-built, flat-bottomed vessel. You'll see Cape wildlife such as egrets, herons, and terns, along with gorgeous riverfront estates, windmills, and a lighthouse, with commentary by the knowledgeable Captain Cliff Smith. Cruises run from Memorial Day weekend through Columbus Day, with four trips a day from late June through Labor Day (11:00 A.M., 1:00 P.M., 4:00 P.M.,

and 6:00 P.M.) and three trips a day in spring and fall (11:00 A.M., 1:00 P.M., and 4:00 P.M.). Refreshments are available on board, including a full bar. The cost for a 90-minute cruise is $14.00 for adults and $7.00 for children. Group rates are available. Reservations are strongly recommended, and you should plan on arriving 20 minutes before the boat is scheduled to depart to claim your tickets.

Lower Cape

Cape Cod Museum of Natural History
Route 6A, Brewster
(508) 896-3867
www.ccmnh.org

During the summer months the museum offers day and overnight trips to Monomoy National Wildlife Refuge, a 2,750-acre wilderness area off the coast of Chatham. The refuge is a birder's paradise and home to a year-round population of seals. Beginning each May the museum offers a two-hour tour of the smaller of the two islands making up Monomoy Refuge. This tour focuses on the many rare, endangered species in our area and costs $30 per adult and $25 per child.

The museum also offers naturalist-escorted overnight cruises to Monomoy Island. Participants get to sleep in the keeper's cottage attached to the 1820 lighthouse. Because the island has no electricity, lighting is provided by gas lanterns. What could be more rustic? The cost for this unforgettable experience is $200 per person.

If it's seals you want to see, the museum offers summer seal cruises off Chatham Harbor and around Monomoy Island, where thousands of gray seals and harbor seals winter and linger during the summer months. Call for a schedule and rates.

If you'd like a tour where you do some of the work yourself, sign up for one of the Museum of Natural History's guided canoe or kayak trips. The trips are offered several times a week in season at a number of different sites, including rivers,

ponds, inlets, and bays, many of which are not accessible by any other means (see also the entry in our Boating and Water Sports chapter). All equipment (canoes, paddles, life jackets) and a snack are included. The cost is $55 for adults and $40 for children ages 8 to 12. All tours and cruises require pre-registration.

Cape Sail
Saquatucket Harbor Marina, Route 28, Harwichport
(508) 896-2730
www.capesail.com

Captain Bob Rice offers half-day, full-day, and overnight charters aboard the 35-food Southern Cross Cutter *Sabbatical* along with sunset and moonlight cruises, from May to October. He also offers overnight trips to Nantucket. Exclusively for private charters, this lovely boat can accommodate up to six passenger; call for rates. If being out on the water makes you yearn to pilot your own boat, talk to the patient and experienced captain about private lessons—he offers both basic and advanced courses.

Remember, all water cruises and tours are dependent on the weather. If in doubt, call ahead to make sure your trip hasn't been canceled.

Catboat Charters
Saquatucket Harbor Marina, Route 28, Harwichport
(508) 432-3416

From May to October Captain Jack Bradley sails his 22-foot traditional catboat *Jubilee* in Nantucket Sound on half-day, full-day, and two- to three-hour sunset cruises. He also does overnight cruises to Nantucket. The *Jubilee* offers a smooth, comfortable ride to the six passengers it can accommodate, courtesy of her catboat design with a beam half as long as her length. Captain Jack does not mix groups and will take a minimum of two people for a sail. The vessel is

equipped with an auxiliary diesel engine. Troll fishing for blues and bass can be made part of the charter. Call for rates.

Beachcomber Boat Tours
Stage Harbor or Ryder's Cove, Chatham
(508) 945-5265
www.sealwatch.com
Chatham's surrounding islands are home to numerous species of shorebirds, and Beachcomber's exciting two-hour cruise is a perfect way to see them. An onboard naturalist will fill you in on these and other creatures living in or near the beautiful Stage Harbor and the Monomoy Island Wildlife Refuge. The list of creatures includes seals too. Once out on the harbor, you're likely to see them, frolicking in the water or sunbathing on the barrier beach sandbar—truly a sight to behold. Tickets are $18 for adults and $12 for children 3 to 12 years old. Children younger than 3 ride for free. Reservations are recommended. Parking is limited at Stage Harbor, so the Beachcomber offers a shuttle from Crowell Road, Chatham.

Beachcomber Boats also offers a boat-to-the-beach, a shuttle service between the town fish pier on Shore Drive and Chatham's outer beach on the Atlantic Ocean. Shuttles leave from the fish pier docks regularly every 15 minutes throughout the day in July and August. A round trip shuttle costs $10.

Outermost Harbor Marine
83 Seagull Road, Chatham
(508) 945-5858
www.outermostharbor.com
This is the place to go for seal cruises and shuttles to South Beach from late June through mid-September. The beach shuttle, which runs on demand from 8:00 A.M. to 5:00 P.M. daily, costs $10. Seal cruises, by reservation, are $16 for adults and $12 for children younger than 12.

Bay Lady II
MacMillan Wharf, Provincetown
(508) 487-9308
www.sailcapecod.com
This 73-foot vessel, which boasts 2,230 square feet of sail, will take you on a two-hour sail across Provincetown Harbor and into Cape Cod Bay. Choose from morning, afternoon and sunset sails, priced at $12, $14, and $16 respectively. Sailing times are 10:00 A.M., 12:30 P.M., 3:30 P.M., and sunset. If you fall in love with the experience ask about the frequent sailing discount and come back for more! Children younger than 12 sail for $7.00. The schooner sails daily from mid-May to late October; reservations are recommended.

Flyer's Boat Rentals, Inc.
131A Commercial Street, Provincetown
(508) 487-0898, (800) 750-0898
www.sailnortheast.com/flyers
In business more than 50 years, this boatyard offers hourly shuttles between town and Long Point, the very tip of the Cape (see our Beaches chapter) on a 24-foot float boat. The cost is $12.00 round-trip or $8.00 one-way. Shuttles run daily in summer.

Schooner *Hindu*
MacMillan Wharf, Provincetown
(508) 487-0659
www.schoonerhindu.com
A replica of the seaworthy schooners that sailed out of Provincetown during the 19th and early 20th centuries, the *Hindu* offers four two-hour sails a day in summer on Cape Cod Bay, at 10:00 A.M., 1:00 P.M., 4:00 P.M., and sunset, plus romantic moonlight cruises during full-moon periods May through October. Sails are $20.00 for adults and $10 for children 12 and younger.

[Facing page] *A horseshoe crab walks up the arm of a young visitor. Learn the natural history of species captured during one of the OceanQuest's Hands-On Discovery Cruises.* OCEANQUEST

Erin-H
Wellfleet Harbor Marina, Wellfleet
(508) 349-9663, (508) 349-1999
www.virtualcapecod.com/erinh
Captain Robert Hussey runs five- and eight-hour and all-day charters on his 36-foot *Erin-H* from mid-May through the end of September. Up to six passengers are taken at a time; call for rates.

Naviator
Wellfleet Harbor, Wellfleet
(508) 349-6003
www.naviator.com
In addition to fishing charters (see our Fishing chapter), Captain Rick Merrill offers seasonal hour-long evening harbor cruises and a weekly marine-life cruise in conjunction with the Wellfleet Bay Wildlife Sanctuary (see below) on his 49-passenger vessel. Call for the schedule.

Wellfleet Bay Wildlife Sanctuary
U.S. Route 6, Wellfleet
(508) 349-2615
www.wellfleetbay.org
In the summer the sanctuary offers three-hour naturalist-led marine-life cruises aboard the *Naviator.* Cruise from Wellfleet Harbor into Cape Cod Bay to look at some of the marine creatures that live in the sea. The cost is $30 for Massachusetts Audubon members and $35 for nonmembers; there is a $10 discount for children younger than 12.

Three-hour tours of Nauset Marsh are offered from May through October. For hand-on fun, take the kids on the family cruise around Nauset Marsh. This two-hour trip, offered several times a week, is done at low tide, so you can get out of the boat and explore tidal pools, dig for shellfish, and see other sea life. The family cruise is $35 per person and $30 for members. You can also take seal and seabird cruises around Wellfleet Bay on weekends in November.

Wellfleet Bay also offers tours of North Monomoy Island from May through November for $35 for nonmembers and $30 for members; travel time is 20 minutes round-trip, with two-and-a-half hours spent walking around the island. From April through November the sanctuary offers frequent seal cruises off Chatham, during which you can explore the coasts of South Beach and the Monomoy Islands for harbor seals and gray seals (the latter are more common in summer). The cost is $40 ($35 for members) for a 90-minute cruise. Seal cruises are also available all year long; call for details. Also call for specific times for any of the above-mentioned cruises, as schedules vary according to the day of the week.

TRAIN TOURS

Mid-Cape

Cape Cod Central Railroad
Main Street, Hyannis
(508) 771-3800, (888) 797-RAIL
www.capetrain.com
Climb aboard the Cape Cod Central and feel the thrill as the whistle blows and you begin your fun-filled adventure from Hyannis to Sandwich and back. You'll pass cranberry bogs, natural woodlands, lush marshes, and more as you make your way to the Cape Cod Canal. The scenic trains operate daily from the end of May through October, except on Mondays and holiday weekends. The ride takes about 50 minutes to get to the canal, with a 10-minutes stopover to gather passengers, and another 50 minutes back to Hyannis. The fare is $15 per adult; $13 for seniors 62 and over; and $11 for children 3 to 11 years of age. The train leaves three times a day from the Hyannis station at Main and Center Streets and can also be picked up in Sandwich at the Jarves Street station.

The railroad is also bringing back the dinner train, a three-hour gourmet excursion. Recapture the romance of a bygone era on the Cape Cod Central while you enjoy a five-course gourmet meal served on crisp white linen. The three-hour trip departs at 6:30 P.M. from the Hyannis Station. The fare is $58 per person and is an adults-only excursion. Proper dress and reservations are required.

If you're bringing the kids, however, you can still have a dining-train experience: Cape Cod Central offers a fun and affordable dining experience for the whole family too. While the kids dine on hot dogs, hamburgers, and pizza, parents enjoy a menu of their own for a more refined dining experience. This two-hour dinner trip departs from the Hyannis Station at 6:30 P.M. each Tuesday evening in July, and Monday and Tuesday in August. The cost is $38.95 for adults and $24.95 for children younger than 12.

SIGHTSEEING TROLLEY

Lower Cape

Provincetown Trolley
37 C Court Street, Provincetown
(508) 487-9483
www.provincetowntrolley.com
Take a ride on an old-fashioned open-air trolley for a 40-minute narrated tour through picturesque Provincetown. The trolley runs along Commercial Street's waterfront and out to the Province Lands Visitor Center and National Seashore. The fare is $9.00 for adults, $8.00 for senior citizens, and $5.00 for those ages 12 and younger. Trolleys departs daily from in front of the town hall every half-hour from 10:00 A.M. to 4:00 P.M. as well as hourly between 5:00 and 7:00 P.M. from mid-May through late October. All aboard!

AIR TOURS

Mid-Cape

Cape Cod Soaring Adventures
Martsons Mills Airport, Race Lane and Route 149, Barnstable
(508) 540-4201
www.capecodsoaring.com
Owner/operator Randy Charlton says that on a clear day you can see Mt. Monadnock in New Hampshire from the cockpit of his glider floating 5,000 feet above the Cape. Fly with hawks and eagles during one of three different aerial tours of varying lengths up to 40 minutes. A 20-minute flight costs $75, a 25- to 35-minute flight is $100, and a 30- to 40-minute flight is $125. Tours are available year-round and can be tailored to your tastes. Instruction and rentals are also available.

Lower Cape

Cape Aerial Tours
Chatham Municipal Airport, 240 George Ryder Road, Chatham
(508) 945-2363, (508) 945-9000
Cape Aerial Tours offers two tours, a 25-minute sightseeing flight for $85 for three people, and a 55-minute flight for $155 for three people. Trips take you over Chatham, the Monomoy Islands, and Pleasant Bay as you fly along the shores of Cape Cod. Cape Aerial Tours operates year-round except for Christmas.

Willie Sightseeing Tours
Provincetown Airport, Race Point Road, Provincetown
(508) 487-0240
Take a 15-minute flight over the tip of the Cape in a lemon yellow 1930 Stinson SM-8A Detroiter dubbed *Willie*. Not an acrobatic plane by any stretch, slow and stately *Willie* gives a calm, lovely ride.

These unique tours are offered from the end of May through Columbus Day. The plane doesn't take reservations and only makes flights on nice days. The cost for a 15-minute ride is $25 per person and $60 for three people, which is the maximum the plane can carry.

UNIQUE LAND TOURS

Lower Cape

Back Road Scenic Tours
Corsair Motel, Chase Avenue, Dennisport
(508) 398-6886
www.back-road-scenic-tours.com
Want to explore the back roads of the mid- and lower Cape, but aren't sure exactly where to go? Join Back Road Scenic Tours in six- or eight-passenger vans for a two-hour tour of Chatham, Dennis, or Yarmouth, or a five-hour tour of Eastham, Wellfleet, and Truro. The two-hour tour includes scenic overlooks of Cape Cod Bay, marshes, and sand dunes, whereas the five-hour tour wends its way between the ocean, lakes, ponds, and dunes. The tours run in July and August. The two-hour tour runs Monday through Saturday from 10:00 A.M. to noon and 6:00 to 8:00 P.M. (for the sunset tour). The cost is $20 per adult, $10 for children age 13 and younger. The five-hour tour runs from 10:00 A.M. to 3:00 P.M. on Sunday. The cost is $40 per adult, $20 for children age 13 and younger. You may purchase your tickets at the vans, but be sure to call ahead to reserve a space at least 45 minutes in advance.

Art's Dune Tours
Corner of Commercial and Standish Streets, Provincetown
(508) 487-1950, (800) 894-1951
www.artsdunetours.com
Since 1946 Art Costa has piled people of all ages into his four-wheel-drive vehicles for an hour-long journey to the outer reaches of the Cape Cod National Seashore, through fragrant pine woods, fields of beach grass and beach plum, and, of course, sand dunes. You'll get to see the beach shacks of yesteryear, where many famous writers and artists lived, and have a chance to get out and stretch and snap some photos. The most popular tours are the sunset ones; reservations are a must for these. Ask about Art's clambake and barbecue dinner tours—you'll enjoy a delicious meal *and* a sunset. Tours are given from April through October and depart throughout the day. Tours start at $16.00 for adults and at $9.00 for children ages 7 to 11. Reservations are required for the 60- and 90-minute special sunset tours. Children younger than 6 usually ride for free. Children requiring a car seat may be subject to a child's price during peak season.

Pilgrim Monument and Provincetown Museum
High Pole Road, Provincetown
(508) 487-1310
www.pilgrim-monument.org
In conjunction with the Cape Cod National Seashore, the museum offers weekly walking tours through Provincetown in summer. Led by a National Seashore ranger and a museum staffer—both of whom are very knowledgeable about the area and its history—the tours are very educational and really great fun. It's a good way to get your bearing geographically, and you'll pick up all sorts of interesting bits of history and trivia. Tours, which begin at the monument at 9:00 A.M. sharp on Tuesday mornings, cost $5.00 and require preregistration. The walks last about two hours, usually a little longer; wear comfortable shoes, as you'll cover a lot of ground!

TOUR RESERVATION SERVICE

Explore Cape Cod
P.O. Box 651, South Orleans, MA 02662
(508) 240-2620
www.explorecapecod.com

If this chapter has left you slightly overwhelmed, you may want to put your plans in the hands of the professionals. Explore Cape Cod will arrange land or sea tours tailored to your interests, from ecotours on Nauset Marsh aboard a 17-seat catamaran to seal-watching along Monomoy Island. This friendly, accommodating reservation service represents a variety of outdoor fishing charters, fishing guides, canoe and kayak adventure tours, tours of Pleasant Bay—even driving tours through Cape Cod's quaint seaside villages. Whether you want to charter a sailboat for two, ride the rail trail with a biking guide, or take a guided nature walk in the hidden hollows of the outer beaches, Explore Cape Cod can make it happen. Choose from

In southeast Massachusetts some 11,000 acres of cranberry bogs thrive in the area primarily because of the sandy, acidic soil and good supply of clean water. The bogs lie amidst extensive forestland. Besides being home to cranberries, these lands shelter wildlife. They also lie near reservoirs filled with many varieties of fish.

30 outdoor adventures—half-day, full-day, and overnight adventure tours are available in the Upper, Mid-, and Lower Cape. Call for a schedule of activities, and then relax and let the experienced outdoors people of Explore Cape Cod take care of the rest.

BEACHES ☀

Cape Cod has some of the most unspoiled beaches in the world, in part because of the foresight of President John F. Kennedy, who signed a bill on August 7, 1961, making the Cape Cod National Seashore a reality. Stretching the entire length of Cape Cod's Atlantic shoreline from Chatham to Provincetown, the National Seashore (see our chapter on Cape Cod National Seashore for more information) operates ocean beaches through six towns along this coast. Called the "outer beach" by locals, the surf-washed sands and ocean rollers are bordered by a continuous sweep of sandy cliffs and windswept dunes.

Of course the National Seashore isn't the only place to enjoy a beautiful beach. The Cape has more than 150 saltwater and freshwater beaches, offering something for everyone. Some Cape beaches have rough-and-tumble waves great for surfing, such as Coast Guard Beach in Eastham or LeCounts in Wellfleet; others are gentle and quiet, like Corporation Beach in Dennis or Old Silver Beach in North Falmouth. Some are broad, like Nauset Beach in Orleans; and others are narrow, such as Nobska in Falmouth. Some are rocky, like Town Beach in Sandwich; and some are all sand, like Craigville Beach.

The beaches of Cape Cod Bay, crooked in the inner curve of Cape Cod's bent arm from Dennisport to South Wellfleet, are fast tidal flats that can be up to a mile wide at low tide. A long walk on the flats out to the water's edge will afford you the opportunity to view and gently handle many creatures of sea and shore life in the intertidal zone such as moon snails, hermit crabs, starfish, and horseshoe crabs. One of the best starting points for a walk along the flats is from Paine's Creek in Brewster, but be sure to check the tide charts before you leave or you might get caught too far out on the flats when the tide starts coming in (we provide more information on tides under the section on Beach Safety, below).

Cape Cod's bay beaches are naturally calmer and safer for young children, and to the south of the Cape, the warm waters of Nantucket Sound play host to families with kids and the younger adults who gather at Craigville Beach in Centerville and along the Falmouth Heights Beach. The bays and sounds are relatively shallow bodies of water and warm up faster than the Atlantic Ocean, which reflects rather than absorbs light and heat. In the height of the summer, average temperatures in Cape Cod Bay on the north side are in the high 60s, whereas the beaches on the south side in Nantucket Sound reach the high 60s and mid-70s. Ocean temperatures on the east side linger in the high 50s, rarely getting higher than the low 60s.

There are also many freshwater lakes and ponds that have calm waters and small sandy beaches, many with picnic facilities. The 700-acre Mashpee-Wakeby Pond is the Cape's largest freshwater body. Swimming in the pristine waters of a brilliant blue Cape Cod kettle pond on a hot summer's day is a unique.

BEACH SAFETY

As you venture into the water, here are some things you should know to make your days at the beach safe and serene. Lifeguard are posted at many beaches from mid-June through Labor Day to oversee hundreds of swimmers, but their watchfulness should not be a replacement for adult supervision of children. Be aware of the waves, the currents, the undertow, and the tide.

Waves

The ocean surf provides an experience completely different from the conditions found in Cape Cod Bay, Nantucket Sounds, or any nearby pond or lake. At sea powerful forces generated by water movements are continuously at work. Ocean waves crest and become more rounded as they move in from the open ocean and before they break on shore.

When a wave breaks in shallow water, a vigorous suction is caused both by the breaking wave and by the backwash of the previous wave. Those unfamiliar with this ocean action should know that a person can be swept off his or her feet and actually be pulled into the oncoming wave. If this should happen to you, don't panic. Push under the water and toward the oncoming wave, and curl your body to form a smaller mass; this will allow you to withstand the force of the wave. Once the wave has passed, you will pop up on the other side.

Currents

A lateral current, also known as a long-shore current, runs parallel to the beach and perpendicular to the direction at which waves approach the shore. This current is usually strong enough to move you sideways along the shoreline. Again, don't be alarmed if after an extended period of time swimming in the ocean you notice that you don't recognize any of the beach umbrellas or landscape on shore. You have probably moved with the current and are in a new position relative to shore. Those who pay no attention can be swept sideways into a rip current and beyond the breaking waves.

Rip currents occur when waves breaking over an offshore sandbar spill into a trough on the shoreward side of the sandbar, pile up, and then exit quickly through

any break in the mound of the sandbar that had trapped the water. Water rushing out to sea from the trough seeking a seaward outlet may move faster than a swimmer can swim, sweeping him or her out with it. Although rip currents can vary greatly in appearance, as a general rule they look especially rough or choppy, may have the dark color of deeper water, and may or may not have foam. Considering the seriousness of a rip current, it is clear that any swimmer caught in one should stop, look, and study a rip before making his or her next move. There is usually no suction, so remain calm. If you feel you can swim across the current, parallel to the shore, you can work yourself back to the beach at an angle. A rip current can also be escaped when you relax and allow it to carry you to the outermost limit, which is usually not far beyond the breakers. After judging the width of the rip current, you can swim parallel to the beach in the relative calm water outside the breakers, reenter the surf at the end of a set, and the swim safely to shore and your beach blanket.

Undertow

At surf beaches, we were told, the greatest percentage of drownings result from persons exhausting themselves fighting currents and waves. By understanding how a wave works, you will understand how to react to certain circumstances when they occur. For instance when a wave breaks on the beach and returns back to sea, it gains momentum and can knock individuals off their feet and sweep them swiftly into the surf. If you are carried out, don't resist. The undertow will subside once it hits the surf line. Swimmers get in trouble in the undertow when they panic. The ocean is a great place to be if you know what to look for and how to react if caught off guard.

Tides

Most visitors to the Cape today have little reason to pay attention to the ebb and flow of the ocean's tide. A hundred years ago the lives of the people of Cape Cod were inseparably connected to the sea. They relied on the ocean-going vessels for their food, travel, and trade, so an understanding of the tides was essential for their survival. Today, though the tides play a smaller part in daily life, they are still an important factor to bear in mind when living at or visiting the coast.

The tides are an essential consideration when planning your day in or around the bay, sound, or ocean. Visiting a bayside beach during low tide when the flats extend out for more than a mile can be a dangerous situation as the tide can sometimes rush in over the flats quicker than you could walk back to the shoreline. Cape Cod, like most places on the coast, experiences semidiurnal tides, meaning that two high and two low tides occur daily. Each tide, controlled by lunar movements, takes place fifty minutes later than the previous day. The moon completes a full circle around the earth every 24 hours and 50 minutes, causing the variation of tidal timing from day to day. Translated, this means that if high tide is at 10:00 A.M. on Tuesday, it will be high at 10:50 A.M. on Wednesday. To make matters more confusing, because Cape Cod is surrounded by the Atlantic Ocean, the canal, the bay, and the sound, the tides vary in time difference by as much as two hours between the Upper and Lower Cape. Ask for a tide chart when you arrive for your visit—all the area newspapers publish a tide chart.

Child Safety

Children should not take water toys such as boogie boards, flotation rings, or rafts into the ocean because they can quickly be carried out to a depth that's over their heads, or even be swept far away by off-shore breezes. And though many of us remember digging in the sand to "bury" each other as children, that activity can be dangerous as well, which is why notices at the Cape Cod National Seashore warn against it. The sand can easily collapse and trap a child. Each year we hear of a child being buried while digging in the sand and having to endure a life-threatening experience that could have easily been avoided. Also, don't forget sunscreen. And while you're protecting your child with it, don't forget yourself. The cool salty air may make it seem as if you aren't getting too much sun when in fact you are.

Tips for the Disabled

Most towns now have beaches that are wheelchair accessible; several have purchased special beach wheelchairs that are available for those who request their use, and many beaches are equipped with heavy rubber mat planks that make it easy to bring a wheelchair out onto a sandy expanse. The individual beach entries later in this chapter give phone numbers that you can call for more information.

PARKING

Parking is a big consideration when you're planning a day at the beach. Many beach lots fill quickly on nice summer days (Nauset Light Beach in Eastham, for instance, is often full by about 10:00 A.M. in July and August). Most beaches either charge admission or require a parking sticker, generally available at town halls or, in some cases, at certain beaches. Requirements differ from town to town and, within towns, from beach to beach, with some beaches offering parking by sticker only and others staffed with attendants who sell daily passes. We've detailed the procedure in each town in this chapter's listings. A note of caution: If you park illegally, you will be ticketed and fined. Sometimes public transportation is an option—Hyannis, for instance, offers a beach trolley. Or ride a bike—admission to most beaches is free for those who walk or bike in. Also keep in mind that the rates printed here are subject to change; when towns decide to raise their beach parking rates, they usually do so in the spring at annual town meetings.

Some towns have beaches that are designated for residents only. This means the beach is town-owned but supposed to be reserved for the use of resident taxpayers. In most cases this designation is made because these beaches are small and have very limited parking. Generally "resident only" means you must have a resident/taxpayer sticker on your car to park in these areas, but there's nothing to stop you from walking or biking there. So we have included these beaches in the listings for each town with the caveat that they are intended for residents only— please, don't try parking at such beaches without a resident sticker—you will be ticketed and in some cases towed! And respect the rules at all beaches.

PRIVATE BEACHES

Yes, there is such a thing, though this issue has been and will continue to be debated, particularly in reference to shellfishing rights. Unlike most other states, in Massachusetts, waterfront property owners may own the beach in front of their home to mean low tide—an imaginary line between high tide and low tide. This line obviously varies with the moon, season, and atmospheric conditions. (See our section on tides in this chapter.) What it boils down to is an archaic law we have all learned to live within. It actually dates back to colonial times, when the king granted waterfront deeds that specified the owner had ownership of the beach to high tide rather than low tide. Someone then came up with the phrase "mean low tide," and it's impossible to generalize with

any certainty how close you should hug the waterline when passing in front of private property. The law reads that access across beaches is allowed for "fishing, boating, and waterfowling," so you might want to carry a fishing pole just in case. What you need to know is that many of the public beaches are alongside private beaches, and as inviting as that nearly empty beach past the public beach may appear, you don't have the right to spread your blanket on it. These private beach areas are usually marked with small NO TRESPASSING or PRIVATE PROPERTY signs. Most waterfront property owners understand the lure of the open beach, and they certainly relish a beach walk. If you pass with respect, they won't get upset—some of our best walks are across miles of bay beach, both public and private.

PETS ON THE BEACH

Cape beaches operate a dog ban generally between mid-May and mid-September, though the length of the ban can vary by town. It doesn't matter if your dog is on a leash or under control of your command: Taking a dog on the beach during these months is punishable by a fine of up to $50. Some beaches like Nauset Beach in Orleans and Craigville in Centerville will not permit you entrance to the parking area if a dog is in your vehicle. At the smaller beaches signs are posted at the entrance path to the beach area.

If you bring your dog during the off-season when the crowds have gone and the rules are more relaxed, be sure your dog is under your control at all times. Remember, it's not just humans your pet can disturb—it's nesting birds or stranded seals. The Endangered Species Act provides penalties for taking, harassing, or harming the piping plover, for example, and we take the law seriously here: It's likely that if your dog disturbs a plover's nest or otherwise disturbs one of the protected species, someone will be waiting for you in the parking lot upon your return.

Also, please remove your dog's waste from the beach. It's a form of pollution that contaminates our shellfish beds, as well as the wetlands. Most trails and beaches offer some sort of doggie "dispoza-scoop." The Cape Cod Canal Bike Path offers a pooper-scooper bag at the end of the trailhead that is convenient to use. Other mittlike contraptions are available.

CAPE COD BEACHES

Below we introduce you to some of our most beautiful Cape Cod beaches. Those included have lifeguards during the summer unless otherwise noted. Many have restrooms and changing facilities, whereas some only have portable toilets; we've noted available facilities in each entry.

So pack up your picnic basket (though you'll want to leave glass containers at home—they're not allowed on National Seashore and many town beaches). If you chance to forget it, though, all is not lost. Some beaches have snack bars, and virtually all are included in routes of local ice cream trucks, whose bells call children in from the water faster than you can say Creamsicle.

Ready for a day at the beach? Grab your sunscreen, shades, a blanket or beach chair, and come along!

Upper Cape

The Upper Cape towns have coastlines along the waters of Cape Cod Bay, Buzzards Bay, Vineyard Sound, Nantucket Sound, and the Cape Cod Canal. The waters of the south side are generally calm and warm, with water temperatures in some spots reaching the 70s during the summer, whereas the bay beaches in Sandwich are influenced by a different tidal system and are colder. Another influence on Sandwich beaches is the Cape Cod Canal, a structure that since it was dug has interrupted the natural sweep of wind-carried sands along the curve of the shore. As a result Sandwich beaches tend to be rockier than others, but they are distinctly charming. On a clear day you can see the Pilgrim Monument in Provincetown, 26 miles across the bay.

BOURNE

Bourne is home to a number of fine salt-water beaches stretching across its more than 50 miles of coastline along Buzzards Bay. The town also has about 2 miles of frontage on Cape Cod Bay to the north as well as a couple ponds available for fresh-water swimming. Like many Cape towns Bourne holds a tight guard on parking at its beaches. The only beach with public parking is Monument Beach, near the southern mouth of the Cape Cod Canal. There is also the state-owned Scusset Beach, which straddles the Bourne-Sandwich line to the north. You can park here for $7.00 a day. To park at any other beach in Bourne you need a sticker, given only to residents or those who can prove they are staying in Bourne, such as those staying at a campground or renting property. Beach parking stickers are required if you want to park at a town beach and can be picked up for $30 at the Natural Resources Office, Bourne Town Hall, 24 Perry Avenue, Buzzards Bay, (508) 759-0623. Bourne does not have a daily parking fee.

Electric Avenue Beach on Buzzards Bay rests at the entrance to Buttermilk Bay near the Buzzards Bay rotary at the west end of the Cape Cod Canal. Lifeguards are on duty at this beach.

Monument Beach along Shore and Emmons Roads has public parking and looks out upon the Bourne entrance to the Cape Cod Canal and the Monument Beach Marina. Situated at a small harbor, it is a pleasant place to spend the day in the sun and water. Lifeguards are on duty.

To the southwest of the entrance to the Cape Cod Canal you will find **Gray Gables Beach** in the village of Gray Gables. It is here that President Grover

Cleveland spent his summer vacations when he was president during the 1880s and 1890s. Gray Gables has lifeguards, portable toilets, and concessions.

A popular north side option is **Scusset Beach** on Cape Cod Bay. This large, clean, state-run beach is predominantly in the town of Sandwich, yet you approach it by taking Meetinghouse Road off the Sagamore Rotary just before the Sagamore Bridge. From Meetinghouse take Scusset Beach Road into Sandwich to the beach parking area where you'll pay a $7.00 fee (or $35.00 for a Massachusetts resident season pass, $45.00 for a nonresident season pass). This beach has a snack bar and bathhouse available.

Sagamore Beach at the Sagamore Highlands is really three interconnected beaches on the mainland side of the Cape Cod Canal. These north-side beaches can be found off Samoset Road. Though there are no concession stands at these beaches, there are lifeguards on duty and portable toilets available.

Off Barlows Landing Road in Pocasset is the appropriately named **Barlows Landing Beach.** Overlooking beautiful Pocasset Harbor, this beach has lifeguards and portable toilets but no concession stands.

Hen Cove Beach, also known as Pocasset Town Beach, is on Hen Cove in Pocasset, which empties into Red Brook Harbor. The beach is well protected by both the cove and harbor, making it a nice place for the kids. There are lifeguards on duty and portable toilets but no concession stands.

Another well-protected beach is **Squeteague Beach** at Cataumet's Squeteague Harbor. There are no lifeguards or concessions at this beach, though there is one portable toilet.

Freshwater swimming can be found at **Queen Sewell Pond** in Buzzards Bay, just south of Little Buttermilk Bay. There are lifeguards and portable toilets at this beach, but you'll need a sticker to park.

Another freshwater pond open to swimmers is **Picture Lake,** located off

Williams Avenue between County Road and Route 28 in Pocasset. This beach has lifeguards but no bathroom facilities. You'll need a sticker to park.

SANDWICH

Sandwich has saltwater access along the north side of the town that borders Cape Cod Bay. A portion of this north shore lies on the other side of the Canal (the mainland side). Although deprived of the large harbors, coves, and bays present in may of the other Cape towns, Sandwich features a number of fine freshwater ponds in the southern portion of the town, including Peters Pond and Snake Pond. Sandwich also has frontage on a portion of Mashpee's Wakeby Pond, just enough to sneak in a beach.

You need a sticker to park at all beaches in Sandwich. The resident sticker costs $20. The nonresidents must pay $75 and the sticker will not get you to the resident-only Snake Pond area, but will get you everywhere else. All stickers are sold at the Sandwich Town Hall Annex (508–888–4910). One-day parking passes are also available at the beaches, except Snake Pond, for $10.

Town Neck Beach, at the end of Town Neck Road, offers the perfect place to watch boat traffic pass on the Cape Cod Canal. Though there are no lifeguards on duty, there are rest rooms and a concession stand.

Town Beach rests at the entrance to Sandwich Harbor. This Sandwich beach can be reached by taking Town Neck Road to Freeman Avenue. Nearby is the famous Sandwich boardwalk crossing Mill

Creek, which winds through the picturesque marshes long the north side of Sandwich. Town Beach offers concession stands and rest room facilities but no lifeguards.

East Sandwich Beach, also known as Springhill Beach, is off Route 6A at the end of Ploughed Neck Road where it empties into North Shore Boulevard. Just to the east is Scorton Harbor and beautiful Scorton Creek. The parking area accepts permits only. The beach has no lifeguards, concession stands, or toilet facilities.

Sandy Neck Beach is a beautiful beach with high sand dune that stretches for miles along Cape Cod Bay off Route 6A at the extreme eastern boundaries of the town. This beach lies within both Sandwich and Barnstable and offers lifeguards, concession stands, and bathroom facilities. Many people enjoy taking a four-wheel-drive vehicle onto Sandy Neck Beach for a day of fishing and swimming; this requires buying a permit through the Town of Barnstable. Your four-wheel-drive vehicle must undergo an inspection at the gatehouse for proper emergency equipment such as a tow rope, shovel, and spare tire. For weekly or monthly parking passes for the public beach, call the Recreation Department at (508) 790–6345. For four-wheel-drive permits, call the Sandy Neck Gatehouse (in season) at (508) 362–8300. The beach is open year-round.

Sandwich has a beach on the Wakeby portion of the beautiful Mashpee-Wakeby Pond. The beach, which can be found off Sandwich-Cotuit Road, has a large parking area, rest rooms, and a big gazebo for grilling and picnics. Lifeguards are on duty.

FALMOUTH

Falmouth offers more miles of coastline than any other Cape town. This coastline is blessed with many fine harbors as well as a number of wonderful beaches. The southern shoreline borders Vineyard Sound and the western side overlooks Buzzards Bay.

If you plan to park at any but three of these beaches, you need a sticker, given only to residents or guests who can show they are staying in Falmouth. Stickers are available at the Surf Drive bathhouse. Guest stickers cost $125 per year, $50 for one week, $60 for two weeks, $70 for three weeks, and $80 for four weeks. Residents pay $20 for a two-year beach parking sticker. Three beaches—Surf Drive, Old Silver, and Menauhant—have daily passes available for anyone. For more information about Falmouth beaches, call the Falmouth Beach Committee at (508) 548–8623. Wheelchairs are available for all beaches.

Along Vineyard sound **Surf Drive Beach** is the closest beach to Falmouth village center. This beach offers lifeguards, a bathhouse with showers, and a concession stand. The waters here are warm and calm with wonderful views of Martha's Vineyard across the sound and Nobska Light nearby. A small inlet to the north of the beach is popular with families who have little kids. Surf Drive is one of the three beaches in town where you can park without a sticker for $10 a day.

Old Silver Beach in North Falmouth is as popular as it is beautiful. The Buzzards Bay waters here are warm and ideal for youngsters. A creek splits the beach in two; one side is for residents and the other side is for visitors to the town. Lifeguards watch over the swimmers, and a concession stand keeps hunger at bay. Portable toilets and showers are available. You don't need a sticker to park here, but you do need to buy a $15 pass.

Another North Falmouth beach is **Megansett Beach** on Buzzards Bay. Like

---

[Facing page] *The Sandwich boardwalk meanders through the marshes along Sandwich's north side.* MASSACHUSETTS OFFICE OF TRAVEL AND TOURISM

If you can't get to the beach before 10:30 A.M., most likely you'll have to wait in line to get a parking space. If you go after 4:00 P.M., you won't have to pay.

Old Silver Beach the waters here are warm. The beach has lifeguards but no concession stands or bathhouses. Parking is by resident sticker only.

Chapoquoit Beach rests along Buzzards Bay just south of West Falmouth Harbor off Chapoquoit Road. This residents-only beach has lifeguards and toilet facilities.

Wood Neck Beach can be found at the mouth of the saltwater Little Sippewisset Lake in West Falmouth. Its waters are warmed by Buzzards Bay. Wood Neck has portable toilets on-site as well as lifeguards. Parking is by sticker only.

Falmouth Heights Beach overlooks Vineyard Sound and Martha's Vineyard, and the waters are warm and inviting. There are lifeguards on duty and portable toilets available, and though there are no concession stands, there are a number of places nearby to go get something to eat.

Two other wonderful Vineyard Sound beaches are **Menauhant** and **Bristol.** Both south-side beaches have lifeguards, concession stands, and portable toilets. Menauhant also has showers. Bristol Beach is accessible by sticker only. There is a $10-per-day parking fee at Menauhant for those without a sticker.

Grews Pond is a wonderful little freshwater pond in Goodwill Park off Gifford Street just north of Falmouth center. The pond has lifeguards on duty, and toilet facilities are available.

MASHPEE

The southernmost portion of Mashpee touches Nantucket South, Waquoit Bay, and Popponesset Bay. Within the town are a number of large ponds: Ashumet and John's Ponds in the west, Santuit Pond in the east, and the connected Mashpee and Wakeby Ponds along the northern border with Sandwich. Parking at all but one beach requires a Mashpee resident sticker obtained at the town hall on Great Neck Road; call the Mashpee Town Hall at (508) 539-1446 for more information. If you're not a resident, or more appropriately, do not have a resident parking sticker, South Cape Beach at the southern tip of Mashpee is run by the state and allows anyone to park for a fee.

South Cape Beach on Nantucket Sound is a great, unspoiled place to enjoy sand, sea, and sun. About 3½ miles from the Mashpee Rotary at the end of Great Neck Road South, the beach is operated by both the town, which has a parking lot and requires a resident sticker, and by the state Department of Environmental Management, which has a large parking lot and charges nonresidents of Mashpee $7.00 per day. Lifeguards are on duty, and toilet facilities are available.

For freshwater swimming go to **Attaquin Park** on the 700-plus-acre Mashpee-Wakeby Pond, the Cape's largest freshwater body. The park, off Route 130 at the southern end of the pond, has a swimming area, lifeguards, toilet facilities, and a state boat ramp with parking available.

Another popular freshwater spot is **John's Pond** at Hooppole Road off Route 151 and Currier Road. It has a public beach complete with lifeguards and toilet facilities.

Mid-Cape

The beaches of the Mid-Cape can be found on two separate bodies of salt water—Nantucket Sound to the south and Cape Cod Bay to the north. These have the Cape's warmest waters. Nantucket Sound is fed by warm southern waters, and its relatively shallow depth of about 40 feet—sandbars stretch as far as Nantucket—allows it to hold its warmth. On the bay side the tidal flats of the Mid-Cape heat up the north-side waters as they ebb and flow over the sand, which has been baking in the sun. The best time to swim in these waters is when high tide occurs late in the day and the sun has had all day to warm the sands. On the whole beaches in this long middle area of the peninsula are not as affected by currents and rips as the Lower Cape. There are also a number of beautiful lakes and ponds offering freshwater options.

BARNSTABLE

Cotuit has three fine beaches, all requiring resident stickers to park. Beach stickers are available at the Kennedy Rink in Hyannis on a seasonal basis. Resident stickers are $20 per season, nonresident stickers are $40 per week. Parking is $10 per weekday and $12 on weekends and holidays. **Oregon Beach** off Main Street has no lifeguards or rest rooms, nor does **Ropes Beach,** located in the protected Cotuit Bay. Cotuit's **Loop Beach,** also off Main Street does have lifeguards and bathroom facilities. Neighboring Osterville has a fine saltwater residents-only beach on Vineyard Sound at the end of Wianno Avenue called **Dowses Beach.** Lifeguards oversee Dowses Beach, and toilet facilities and concessions are available

The often-crowded **Craigville Beach** off Craigville Beach Road in Centerville is a favorite with sunbathers and swimmers. On Nantucket Sound, this beach has a large parking lot and a bathhouse with outdoor showers. There are lifeguards on duty.

Two nearby residents-only parking beaches in Centerville are **Covells Beach** along Craigville Beach Road to the east of Craigville Beach and **Long Beach** on Long Beach Road to the west. Covells has lifeguards and rest rooms; Long Beach has neither.

Hyannis has four beaches—East Beach, Kalmus Beach, Sea Street Beach, and Veterans Beach. **East Beach,** just west of Hyannis Harbor, has residents-only parking with no food or bathroom facilities and no lifeguards on duty.

As a windsurfing beach **Kalmus Beach**

at the end of Ocean Street in Hyannis is considered by some to be the best on the Cape. One of two beaches in Hyannis Harbor, Kalmus has a windsurfing area, snack bar, bathroom facilities, and a picnic area; and the beach is protected by lifeguards.

Sea Street Beach at the end of Sea Street is the second public beach in Hyannis Harbor and is within walking distance of many accommodations in Hyannis. This beach has a bathhouse, snack bar, and picnic area; lifeguards are on duty in season.

With a delightful view of Lewis Bay, **Veterans Beach** on Ocean Street in Hyannis is a popular place where families enjoy picnics and cookouts shaded by a pine grove. The facilities include a bathhouse, snack bar, picnic area and playground, and lifeguards. The Kennedy Memorial (see our Attractions chapter) is adjacent to Veterans Beach.

Six-mile-long **Sandy Neck Beach,** north of Route 6A in West Barnstable, is the town's longest beach. The road that leads to the beach, Sandy Neck Road, actually connects with Route 6A just over the town line in East Sandwich. Sandy Neck Road then works its way north into West Barnstable before reaching the beach parking lot. This beach offers swimming, fishing, camping, and hiking. Facilities include indoor rest rooms, showers, and a snack bar; lifeguards work this beach.

Next to picturesque Barnstable Harbor at the end of Millway along the north shore of town is **Millway Beach.** This beach offers a great view of the boat traffic entering and leaving the harbor, but parking is for residents only. Millway

"Shark sightings" are common during summers on the Cape. They are nearly always harmless sharks, of the brown, thresher, or basking varieties. If you're worried about encountering sharks, stay near shore, and swim with groups.

Beach has lifeguards and rest rooms. Across the waters is Sandy Neck with its decommissioned lighthouse at the point.

For freshwater swimming there is the residents-only **Hamblin Pond** of Route 149 in Marstons Mills with lifeguards, restrooms, and a picnic area. Another Marstons Mills pond is **Lovells Pond** off Newtown Road, with lifeguards and rest rooms. **Joshua's Pond** on Tower Hill Road in neighboring Osterville has bathroom facilities and a playground for the kids, as well as lifeguards.

Lake Wequaquet, also residents-only, on Shoot Flying Hill Road in Centerville, is a freshwater playground. The lake is almost 2 miles long and roughly a mile wide. Bathroom facilities are on-site, as are lifeguards.

Hathaway's Pond off Phinney's Lane in Barnstable has rest rooms and a picnic and playground area. Lifeguards are on duty. Parking is $5.00 weekdays, $6.00 on weekends.

YARMOUTH

Yarmouth has coastlines to the north on Cape Cod Bay and to the south on Nantucket Sound and Lewis Bay. The east side of the town borders Bass River to the south and Garden Creek to the north. The north side of the town on Cape Cod Bay is only about 1½ miles long and is largely marshland, save for a small beach at Bass Hole on the east end. The south side has many fine beaches, and all but four require a parking sticker. Sea Gull, Sea View, Parker's River, and Bass River beaches all allow daily parking for an $8.00 fee if you do not have a sticker. Two beaches in Yarmouth—Dennis Pond and South Middle Beach—require a resident parking sticker. Nonresidents can obtain a sticker for $45 a week or $125 a season. Stickers are available at beach entrances

only. Call the Park Department (508-775-7910) from 7:00 A.M. to 3:30 P.M. for more information.

Off Sea Gull Road, which is off South Sea Avenue in West Yarmouth, is where you'll find **Sea Gull Beach.** Offering plenty of parking spaces, this is Yarmouth's largest and most popular beach, especially with high school and college students. Sitting just west of Parker's River, it has lifeguards, toilet facilities, a few picnic tables, and concessions. There is a daily parking fee at Sea Gull Beach of $8.00.

From **Bay View Beach,** at the end of Bay View Street in West Yarmouth near the town line with Barnstable, you have a good view of Lewis Bay and the thousands of boats that enter Hyannis Inner Harbor every year. Bay View Beach has lifeguards on duty (on weekends only) and bathroom facilities.

Colonial Acres Beach at Lewis Bay is at the end of Standish Way in West Yarmouth. It has portable toilets and a bridge to the beach.

Englewood Beach, also in West Yarmouth on Lewis Bay, is at the end of Berry Avenue. Englewood has rest rooms and lifeguards.

On the east side of the mouth of Parker's River is **Sea View Beach** off South Shore Road in South Yarmouth. This south-side beach is protected by lifeguards, it has a picnic area and portable toilets, and the $8.00 parking fee is well worth it—it's a lovely beach.

To the east of Sea View Beach along the Cape's southern shore is **Parker's River Beach,** which lies along the warm waters of Nantucket Sound. The beach has rest rooms, a concession stand, outdoor showers, swings, good parking, and lifeguards. It costs $8.00 a day to park.

South Middle Beach on South Shore Drive in South Yarmouth is a residents-only beach offering a large

---

[Facing page] *An empty stretch of beach in Hyannisport.* HYANNIS AREA CHAMBER OF COMMERCE

parking lot and rest rooms. Lifeguards keep an eye on the activities out on Nantucket Sound.

Smugglers Beach (also known as Bass River Beach) is a good family beach with a fishing pier, a large parking area, and a snack bar. This beach, located at the mouth of the Bass River in South Yarmouth, also has lifeguards and bathroom facilities. A daily parking fee of $8.00 is required.

About a half-mile up Bass River is where you'll find **Windmill Beach** off River Street. It is a small beach with no lifeguards or toilet facilities, but the views of the river are spectacular. Nearby is the Judah Baker windmill, built in 1791.

Wilbur Park and its beach area are about 4 miles up Bass River where Highbank Road bridge connects South Yarmouth with the village of South Dennis. Though there are no lifeguards or bathroom facilities, Wilbur park has a picnic area and a boat ramp.

The only beach on the north side is **Bass Hole,** also known as Gray's Beach. It is at the end of Center Street off Route 6A in Yarmouthport and is considered by many to be one of the great spots on the Cape to watch the sun going down. Bass Hole is at the mouth of Garden Creek and has a long boardwalk that extends over the salt marsh and offers an excellent view of coastal plant and marine life. Across the river is Dennis's Chapin Beach. Bass Hole Beach is rather small and, at low tide, has very little water, which makes it perfect for small children (just pay attention to the tidal current in the creek). Bass Hole Beach has a large picnic area complete with a pavilion and bathroom

ℹ️ *Lose your wedding ring on the beach? Hoping to find buried treasure? Rent a metal detector from J & E Metal Detectors, located at Old Main Street and Forest Road in South Yarmouth. Call (508) 760–2100 for more information.*

facilities. There are lifeguards on duty.

In addition to its wealth of saltwater beaches, Yarmouth also has four public beaches at freshwater ponds. **Sandy Pond** off Buck Island Road in West Yarmouth offers not only a beach for swimming but also playing fields for softball, basketball, and soccer; tennis courts; and a playground. The beach has lifeguards on duty and a comfort station.

Long Pond is off Indian Memorial Drive in South Yarmouth. Lifeguards are on duty on weekends, and portable toilets are available. The beach also has a playground on-site and free parking.

Also in South Yarmouth **Flax Pond Recreation Area** has picnic areas, tennis and volleyball courts, and softball fields. Toilet facilities are provided, and lifeguards are on duty on weekends.

Dennis Pond off Summer Street in Yarmouthport requires a town beach parking sticker. You'll find lifeguards and toilet facilities at this pretty pond located just a stroll from Yarmouthport village.

DENNIS

With fine beaches on both the north and south sides of town, it's no wonder that so many tourists make Dennis their vacation destination. There are eight beaches on Cape Cod Bay and another eight on Nantucket Sound. If you prefer freshwater swimming, Scargo Lake offers two beaches. Residents pay $20 for a parking permit, whereas nonresidents pay $155 for the season. A seasonal pass can be acquired for $115 for those who can produce a rental lease for four or more weeks. Weekly stickers run $40, and daily parking fees cost $10. Stickers can be obtained at the Dennis Town offices on Main Street in South Dennis at (508) 394-8300.

Chapin Memorial Beach on Chapin Beach Road at the northwest corner of Dennis is a favorite among owners of four-wheel-drive vehicles. At low tide those looking for shellfish will delight in being able to walk more than a mile out on the tidal flats of Cape Cod Bay. The beach has no lifeguards and no restrooms, but portable toilets are available. Across the water are Yarmouth's Bass Hole and Gray's Beach.

Also on Cape Cod Bay is **Mayflower Beach** at the end of Beach Street. In addition to rest rooms and concessions, this beach features a boardwalk that stretches from the large parking lot over the dunes to the beach below. Mayflower Beach is staffed with lifeguards.

Bayview Beach at the end of Bayview Road is a residents-only beach. Though there is a boardwalk leading to the beach, there are no rest rooms or concession stands, but lifeguards are on duty.

Crescent-shaped **Corporation Beach,** off Corporation Road and hugging Cape Cod Bay, is a popular spot on hot summer days. The curve of the beach forms a tidal pool that's perfect for children. Corporation Beach has lifeguards, a concession stand, rest rooms, and even a swing set for children set on a bluff overlooking the bay.

Howes Beach is a small public beach off Howes Street, just east of Corporation Beach. Howes has a boardwalk and lifeguards, but no rest rooms.

Two East Dennis residents-only beaches are on each side of Sesuit Harbor. On the west side is **Harborview Beach,** which has no facilities, although a lifeguard is present. **Cold Storage Beach** on the east side of the harbor has rest rooms and lifeguards.

The last public beach on the north side is **Sea Street Beach** at the end of Sea Street in Quivet (East Dennis). There is a boardwalk leading to the beach, as well as lifeguards and portable toilets.

There is perhaps no more popular Mid-Cape beach than **West Dennis Beach,** off Davis Beach Road in West Dennis. Situated on a narrow patch of sand on Nantucket Sound just east of the mouth of Bass River, the beach stretches for more than a mile. Beachgoers begin to arrive here by 10:00 A.M., but because the parking lot has room for more than 1,000 cars, you'll rarely have to worry about finding a space. The eastern end of the beach is reserved for Dennis residents; the western

Russian immigrants have begun buying vacation cottages on the Cape in greater numbers over the last few years, especially in the Dennis area. They fondly refer to it as Dennisovka. In fact one of their favored beaches—Glendon— is now locally known as Russian Beach.

end, however, is less crowded and open to everyone. A well-equipped snack bar concession, rest rooms, and showers provide all the comforts, and 10 lifeguard stations make this a safe, secure haven. At the beach is the Old Bass River lighthouse (see our Attractions chapter).

About three-quarters of a mile east of West Dennis Beach is **South Village Beach,** a residents-only beach, by the mouth of Swan River. Toilet facilities and lifeguards are on-site, but there are no concession stands.

A number of Dennisport beaches are available for the visitors who rent cottages in this south-side village. **Haigis Beach** lies where Ocean Drive meets Old Wharf Road. Lifeguards are on duty, toilet facilities are available, and there are concession stands.

Further down Old Wharf Road is **Glendon Beach,** opposite Glendon Road. Like Haigis Glendon has lifeguards, toilet facilities, and a concession stand.

Sea Street Beach at the end of Sea Street in Dennisport is perhaps a half-mile east of Glendon Beach. Like Glendon and Haigis the Nantucket Sound waters here are warm, and the beaches are marked with rock jetties. Sea Street Beach has rest room facilities, concessions, and lifeguards on duty.

The next two beaches do not have lifeguards, rest rooms, or concessions. **Raycroft Beach** is at the end of the short Raycroft Parkway off Old Wharf Road. To the east about a couple hundred yards is **Depot Street Beach** at the end of (you guessed it) Depot Street.

At the end of Inman Street off Chase Avenue is the final saltwater beach in

CLOSE-UP

Letting the Sun Set
on Your Cape Excursion

As visitors from over the bridge often remind those of us who live here, we sometimes take a lot for granted in this little corner of New England. While we Cape Codders often poke fun at the stressed and high-strung mannerisms of our city brethren, we often pass over the spectacles and mysteries that inhabit our own backyard.

Though summer traffic might sometimes make us forget, we year-round residents are thankful for the friends and family who stop by and remind us how special Cape Cod really is. It's the sight of a half-dozen visitors scattered on the beach, silent as their faces glow in the gold and red hue of a sunset, that reawakens locals' appreciation for their beloved home. There is no place on earth like Cape Cod.

The truth is that almost any point on the Cape is a fine vantage for a gorgeous sunset. Even when you move north along the east-facing beaches of the Lower Cape, you still are not far away from awe-inspiring sunsets. Perhaps one of the best venues to observe the phenomenon of sun meeting sea, though, is Skaket Beach in Orleans.

Witness the beauty for yourself at this and some of our other favorite spots.

Gray's Beach, Yarmouthport
Many also call this Bass Hole. Perhaps this less-complimentary-sounding name is just a clever way of disguising one of the Cape's great sunset spots. A long boardwalk, lots of sand, and a picnic area give Gray's Beach a wonderful bit of charm, but it's the sight of the sun disappearing into the horizon of Cape Cod Bay and the Upper Cape that makes this a special spot.

Chapin Memorial Beach, Dennis
Right across the town line from Gray's Beach, Chapin Memorial Beach also offers a great venue to admire the sunset. You have to bring your own blanket or beach chairs, as there are no picnic tables here.

Wychmere Harbor, Harwichport
Considered one of the prettiest harbors on the Cape, Wychmere can be a superb place for sunset watchers. The beach next

Dennisport. Flanked by motels with private beaches on either side up and down the popular Chase Avenue, **Inman** is a public beach that offers toilet facilities and concessions. Lifeguards keep tabs on what's going on out in the water.

Scargo Lake is a 50-plus-acre freshwater sandy-bottomed kettle hole—nearly 50 feet deep—nestled at the bottom of Scargo Hill. The lake is home to two popu-

to the harbor is part of the private Wychmere Harbor Beach Club, but the real view can be taken from a little observation area off Route 28. This pulloff is so popular, parking is limited to 15 minutes. That's OK. Nick and Dick's ice cream parlor is just down the street. Now what could be better than grabbing an ice cream and crossing the street to witness a lovely Cape sunset?

Skaket Beach, Orleans

Right in the crook of the Cape's elbow, Skaket offers a view that is distinctly Cape Cod. On a clear day you can glimpse most of both the Upper and Lower Cape coastlines. In the evening the sun dips into Cape Cod Bay, offering you that rare East Coast treat of seeing the sun set on water.

Great Island, Wellfleet

This secluded section of the National Seashore overlooks Cape Cod Bay to its west and Wellfleet Harbor to the east. This rather secluded area is a hiker's delight and an artist's dream at sunset.

Cape Cod Light, Truro

Take advantage of the boardwalk and benches that were built when the lighthouse was moved back from the cliff. Even though you are on the ocean side of the Cape, you are high enough to see the water and much of the setting sun on the bay side. It's simply a spectacular view from these Truro cliffs, where you have dunes, ocean, bay, Pilgrim Monument, and Cape Cod Light to frame your sunset.

Race Point, Provincetown

At any time of day, Race Point is a scene stealer. The knuckles on the fist of Cape Cod, Race Point sits on the very tip of the Cape, surrounding you with water on three sides.

At Sea

We've saved the best for last on this list. Nantucket and Martha's Vineyard are great vantage points for a sunset, but for a truly memorable sight, book your return trip from either island to catch the setting sun from the back of the ferry. How lovely is a Cape sunset from there? Well, on at least a few occasions after the sun, sky, sea, and horizon have worked their magic, the crowd of 40 or so at the back of the ferry has been known to applaud spontaneously. Now that's tough to beat.

lar beaches: Princess Beach, off Scargo Hill Road, and Scargo Beach, off Route 6A. **Princess Beach** has rest rooms and a picnic area as well as lifeguards. **Scargo Beach,** narrow and tree lined, also has toilet facilities and a lifeguard.

Lower Cape

Beaches in this area are on Cape Cod Bay, Nantucket Sound, and the Atlantic, plus numerous freshwater ponds. The Cape Cod National Seashore (CCNS,

508–349–3785) has great beaches in Eastham, Wellfleet, Truro, and Provincetown. Admission to any CCNS beach from late June to Labor Day is $10.00 per car; admission is $3.00 for walkers or bikers. For $30 you can get a season pass good at all CCNS beaches—a wise investment if you'll be staying a while or visiting often over the course of the summer. Those older than age 62 can get a Golden Age Passport, good at all national parks. And anyone, regardless of age, can get a Golden Eagle pass for a fee, good at all national parks for one year. Lower Cape beaches, as a rule, are relatively undeveloped; most have no real rest room facilities but usually have portable toilets. National Seashore beaches, however, do have restrooms and shower facilities. Most Lower Cape beaches do not have concession stands; we've noted the exceptions.

BREWSTER

Brewster has eight public beaches on Cape Cod Bay, plus a couple of beaches on freshwater ponds, the largest being Long Pond, which lies half in Brewster and half in Harwich. Parking permits for town beaches are available in the lower level of Town Hall on Route 6A, at the rear entrance, (508) 896–4511, from 9:00 A.M. to 3:00 P.M. daily. The cost is $10 for residents, and for nonresidents its $10 a day, $30 a week, $25 for each subsequent week, or $100 for the season—very reasonable rates. Facilities are limited at Brewster beaches. There are no snack bars, though the ice cream truck cruises the beach parking lots on summer days. Portable toilets are the best you'll do for bathrooms. The only lifeguarded beach is at **Long Pond,** where the town holds its swimming instruction program.

Going from west to east, **Paine's Creek** is the first town beach on the bay. As its name implies it is fed by a creek and is perfect for children. Parking, however, is limited. Off Lower Road, **Robbins**

Hill Beach and **Saint's Landing Beach** are both pretty and quiet, and, like all Brewster beaches, are incredible at low tide when the flats seem to go on forever. **Breakwater Beach** is a popular spot for families. At the end of charming Breakwater Road off Route 6A by the Unitarian Church, the beach is bordered by grassy dunes, and there is plenty of parking. **Point of Rocks Landing** is nice and quiet, but has virtually no parking. **Ellis Landing** and **Crosby Landing** are both great beaches; Crosby is larger and has more parking and is walkable from **Nickerson State Park** across Route 6A. Within Nickerson State Park you'll find **Flax Pond** and **Cliff Pond,** both great for swimming and picnicking.

HARWICH

Harwich has many beautiful beaches on Nantucket Sound, plus four on freshwater ponds. Stickers are required for parking and are available at Town Hall on Route 39 (508–432–7638). Residents get stickers for $5.00 a season. The cost for nonresidents, who must show proof of renting in Harwich, is $25 for a week, $40 for two weeks, and $50 for a season. The exception is Red River Beach, off Depot Road in South Harwich, where you can park daily for $5.00 on weekdays, $10.00 on weekends and holidays. The town's larger beaches—**Red River** and **Bank Street**—have lifeguards and rest rooms; a few of the smaller ones like **Earle Road** are equipped with portable toilets. Other small beaches on Nantucket Sound in Harwich are **Jenkins Beach,** right next to Saquatucket Harbor, and **Merkel Beach,** tucked next to Wychmere Harbor.

Harwich also has five freshwater beaches: **Bucks Pond,** off Route 39; **Sand Pond,** off Great Western Road; **Hinckleys Pond** and **Seymour Pond,** both off Route 124; and **Long Pond,** off Long Pond Drive. Sand Pond, the site of the town's recreation program's swimming lessons, does have restrooms.

Cape Cod Bay is considered the normal northern extent of the Kemp's Ridley turtle, the world's most endangered sea turtle. Following warm-water currents, the Ridley and other sea turtles move north from feeding grounds along the eastern seaboard to Cape Cod Bay, where they feed during the summer and early fall. Normally the cooling temperatures of fall signal the turtles to head south for the winter. Each fall about a dozen Kemp's Ridley turtles are found stunned by cold water and air temperatures, having floated helplessly on the surface, carried ashore by the tides and winds. If you find a sea turtle on the Cape Cod Bay beaches in the fall, do not remove the turtle. Rather cover it with seaweed or some blankets, and call the local town authorities.

CHATHAM

Parking permits are required at most of Chatham's nine beaches; the exceptions are Jackknife Harbor and Oyster Pond beaches, which have limited but free parking. Stickers good at the other beaches can be obtained at the Permits Department at 283 George Ryder Road. Daily parking is $8.00, a one-week sticker is $36.00, and a season sticker is $60.00. Residents and property owners can get season stickers for $20 at the Permits Department on George Ryder Road (508–945–5180). Only five beaches have lifeguards: **Hardings, Cockle Cove, Ridgevale, Oyster Pond,** and **Schoolhouse Pond.** Those beaches also have rest rooms; other town beaches have portable toilets. Jackknife Harbor Beach is located on Pleasant Bay, off Route 28 on the Harwich/Chatham line. It's a popular beach, but there are no rest rooms. **Cockle Cove Beach,** off Cockle Cove Road, is the best choice for families with little ones, because it has lifeguards. It also has rest rooms, and parents will appreciate the calm waves and long stretches of soft sand. **Hardings Beach,** off Hardings Beach Road, has a concession stand for snacks, rest rooms, and quietly pounding surf. **Ridgevale Beach,** between Hardings and Cockle Cove (at the end of Ridgevale Road), also has lifeguards, rest rooms, and a concession stand in summer. Also on Nantucket Sound are **Pleasant Street Beach** (where you don't need a sticker to park) and **Forest Beach Road Beach.** Those seeking solitude should head over to Atlantic Ocean–fronted **North Beach.** Located at the southern end of Orleans's Nauset Beach, it's accessible only by boat. Area water taxis will take you there (and bring you back) for a small round-trip fee per adult.

The remote **South Beach,** off Morris Island Road just beyond the Chatham Light, and also on the Atlantic, provides solitude without requiring a boat. It has no parking lot, so you'll have to walk or bike there. The most desolate stretches take quite a hike, but the quiet and grandeur cannot be beat.

Oyster Pond, an inland saltwater pond off Stage Harbor Road that's connected to Nantucket Sound via Stage Harbor and Oyster Creek, is calm and relatively warm and has a lifeguard in season; it also has rest rooms. Schoolhouse Pond, situated on Schoolhouse Road in West Chatham, is also worth a visit for its tranquility, but note that parking is limited to Chatham residents.

ORLEANS

Orleans has only a few public beaches, but when one of them is beautiful Nauset Beach, famous for its wide expanse, big Atlantic Ocean surf, and lovely dunes, and the other is Skaket Beach on Cape Cod Bay, one of the best places to watch a sunset, who could ask for more? Residents get beach stickers for free; renters (who must show proof of renting in Orleans, such as a lease or rent receipt) can get stickers for $40 a week, or $100 for the season. People who are renting in nearby towns can get a season sticker for $135. Call (508) 240-3780 for beach sticker information. A $10 fee is charged for parking at Skaket and Nauset beaches, paid at the tollbooth upon entering. The one-day permit entitles you to go to either beach—or both—during that day.

Nauset Beach, at the end of Beach Road in East Orleans (just follow Main Street east), has lifeguards, a snack bar, and restrooms. You can rent beach chairs and umbrellas, too. Four-wheel-drive vehicles are permitted on one section of the beach, except when plovers and other birds are nesting, but you must have a permit from the Orleans Parks and Beaches Department, 18 Bay Ridge Lane, (508) 240-3775.

Over on the bay side, **Skaket Beach** (508-255-0572), off Skaket Beach Road, is just as popular as Nauset and also has rest rooms. Parking is limited, and the lot fills up fast. At low tide people flock here for the chance to walk a mile or so through the beach grass and onto the flats. At high tide it's great for frolicking in the calm water.

If you don't want to swim but just want to get your feet wet, stop at the little beach at **Rock Harbor,** another great place for sunsets. One secret gem is the tiny beach that is reachable by walking down the trail at Paw Wah Point Conservation Area, off Namequoit Road. You'll

even find a few picnic tables scattered here and there.

Orleans has a freshwater pond worth visiting: **Pilgrim Lake,** off Kescayogansett Road, features a lifeguard in season as well as changing rooms, picnic areas, a small beach, and even a dock should you decide to moor your boat while taking a dip.

EASTHAM

Parking at Eastham town beaches requires a sticker, available at the Natural Resources building on Old Orchard Road (508-240-5972). Stickers are $5.00 for residents; for nonresident renters the cost is $40.00 for one week and $125.00 for the season. Visitors can park for $10 a day. But note that although Eastham resident stickers are good for both town and National Seashore beaches, visitor stickers purchased from the town are good only at town beaches and not Seashore beaches.

The National Seashore beaches have lifeguards in season, but Eastham town beaches do not, with the exception of **Great Pond Beach,** on Great Pond Road, and **Wiley Park,** on the other side of Great Pond off Herringbrook Road. Wiley Park also has a small playground and rest rooms and is great for families. Eastham beaches have no concession stands, but the ice cream truck visits each one periodically all day long. Town beaches that dot the bay side include First Encounter, which is beautiful but can get crowded. To get away from it all, drive beyond the main parking lot and find a spot down by the river, where the beach is lovely and the water is calm. First Encounter is one of the few beaches in Eastham with real rest rooms, the other two being Wiley Park and Cook's Brook; the others have portable toilets.

Moving up the bay coast, you'll find **Thumpertown Beach,** which is nice but has limited parking and a stairway down to the beach. Just north of Thumpertown is **Campground Beach,** which has a larger parking lot and easier access to the beach but can get cramped at high tide. **Cook's**

Brook is quiet and pretty, as is **Sunken Meadow;** both have limited parking and are frequented largely by the occupants of nearby cottages.

On the ocean side are two popular Cape Cod National Seashore beaches. They're easy to find—just turn east at the Visitors Center off Route 6, and keep driving. **Coast Guard Beach** has virtually no parking at the beach, but there is a large lot just a half-mile away that is serviced by a frequent shuttle bus. Or park at the Doane Rock picnic area, and hike through the woods and over the boardwalk—a pretty walk, but long if you're carrying much gear or have young children. Just to the north is Nauset Light Beach, whose namesake lighthouse was moved back from an eroding cliff in 1996. The lot here fills up fast. If you're really desperate, you can park at the high school on Cable Road, but it's a hearty walk from there. You may want to note that **Nauset Light Beach** features a towering stairway that leads down to the beach, so if your party includes someone who has difficulty with stairs, choose Coast Guard Beach instead, as it has a gentle ramp leading down to the sands.

WELLFLEET

Many of the beaches in Wellfleet require a town sticker; renters can buy one at the town marina for $50 a week, $95 for two weeks, and $200 for the season. These include the bayside **Duck Harbor,** at the very end of Chequessett Neck Road; **Indian Neck Beach,** off Pilgrim Spring Road; nearby **Burton Baker Beach; Powers Landing,** off Chequessett Neck Road; and, on the Atlantic side, **Newcomb Hollow Beach** and **LeCount's Hollow Beach** (also called Maguire Landing).

With the exception of Duck Harbor, all the bayside beaches are really on the harbor, with views of Great Island, which juts into the bay. Great Island is National Seashore territory and more for hiking than beaching (see our Hiking and Biking Trails chapter), but if you really want to get away from it all, put on your backpack and hiking shoes and trek out to Great Island's remote shores. Indian Neck Beach is perhaps the nicest of all, with its soft, sandy stretch looking out over the harbor and the bay beyond. Adjacent Burton Baker Beach is the only town beach that allows windsurfing, but only at certain times of the day. Sailboarders should pick up a copy of the regulations at the beach sticker booth at Wellfleet Harbor.

Beach stickers are also needed to park at **Great Pond** (off Cahoon Hollow Road), **Gull Pond** (off Gull Pond Road), and **Long Pond** (off Long Pond Road). Just past the harbor on Kendrick Avenue is **Mayo Beach,** perfect for families with children. Here you can see boats heading in and out of the harbor, and you can actually park for free here if you can get a space. Right across the street is a terrific playground, so even if the kids get restless and bored with the beach (and they sometimes do), you can take them over to Baker's Field for some swinging, climbing, and sliding. Parking is free, and you'll also find full rest rooms there. Other town beaches have portable toilets.

On the Atlantic side **Cahoon Hollow Beach** attracts a big college crowd, who later in the day flock to the beach-side Beachcomber bar and restaurant (see our Nightlife chapter). The lot fills up quickly, and you can opt to use a beach sticker or pay a daily parking fee of $15. The same goes for **White Crest Beach,** just to the south. The waters at White Crest Beach (also called Four Mile Beach and Surfer's Beach) are rougher, making it ideal for the surfers who flock here. Please note that White Crest is not a place to bring young children, senior citizens, or the disabled,

Public nudity is considered indecent exposure by the Commonwealth. Nude sunbathing could net you a $200 fine or six months in jail.

as a steep dune path with no staircase leads down to the beach.

The National Seashore's **Marconi Beach** will take your breath away with its beauty. Parents will appreciate the easy access from the parking lot to the beach itself. In season facilities here include full restrooms and outdoor showers.

TRURO

You'll need a sticker, available to renters in the Beach office in Truro Center, to gain access to just about all of the beaches in Truro. The cost is $10 a year for residents; for nonresidents it's $20 a week or $100 for the season. All the town beaches are equipped with portable toilets. If you want the real facilities, go to the National Seashore portion of **Head of the Meadow Beach** on the ocean side—Head of the Meadow Beach is owned half by the town and half by the Seashore. Both side have lifeguards in season, so this is a good choice for families with children. Another plus is that the ice-cream truck cruises this lot. If you don't have a beach sticker, you can park at the town portion of Head of the Meadow for a fee. The same goes for **Corn Hill Beach** on the bayside; all other Truro beaches require stickers to park.

Also on the ocean side, **Ballston Beach** and **Long Nook Beach** are very popular, so you must get there early to get a parking space. Long Nook is quiet and banked by dune cliffs; Ballston requires some walking to get out to the beach, so, if you have lots of gear, carrying it can be awkward. Another Truro beach on the ocean side is **Coast Guard Beach** (not to be confused with the National Seashore beach by the same name in Eastham). On the bay side Corn Hill (also on the ice-cream truck's route) has plenty of parking and is popular with families. This picturesque beach is right at the mouth of the Pamet River, and you'll see boats heading in and out of the harbor.

At the southern end of town, also on the bay side, is **Ryder Beach,** which as been something of a well-kept secret. It's a lovely beach but not heavily frequented, so it's a nice choice for those who want to get away from crowds. Just north of that is **Fisher Beach,** which is nice but has only a tiny parking lot. North of Corn Hill is **Great Hollow Beach,** which is lovely and quiet, and then **Cold Storage Beach,** also called Pond Village, which is very popular, so get there early in the day.

PROVINCETOWN

Provincetown is unique in that it has no real town beaches—and thus, there is no such thing as a Provincetown beach sticker. The two main beaches here are both part of the National Seashore: **Herring Cove** and **Race Point.** The waters are warmer and calmer at Herring Cove, but sun worshippers often prefer Race Point because it faces north and gets sun all day long. Still everyone agrees that the sunsets at Herring Cove are unparalleled on the entire Cape, because the sun actually seems to set into the ocean, unusual for the East Coast. National Seashore beaches have lifeguards, full restrooms, and outdoor showers. It's $10.00 to park, $3.00 to walk or bike in. Season passes are available for $30.

The **Harbor Beach,** running parallel to Commercial Street alongside the bay, is ideal for those more interested in a walk at water's edge than a swim. There's no beach lot per se, but the closest parking is in the town lot at MacMillan Wharf, which has hourly rates. There are also various town landings along the entire length of Commercial Street that give beach access.

If you really want to get away from it all, head for the very tip of Cape Cod: **Long Point,** where Long Point Lighthouse signals the entrance to Provincetown's busy harbor. You can get there by

Piping plovers and least terns are threatened species under Massachusetts State Law. Pay special attention to signs posted around beaches and beach parking lots. Sometimes plovers decide to nest there, necessitating the closure of parts of beaches and parking lots. Rules about staying away from nesting areas are enforced.

two routes, one by land, the other by sea. Walk across the breakwater at the western end of Commercial Street adjacent to the Provincetown Inn. It's a delightful walk, about two hours—but it seems like a longer walk back. Or hop aboard a water shuttle from Flyer's Boat Yard at 131A Commercial Street

(508–487–0518). The shuttle leaves every hour or so, with the last return around 5:00 P.M., and costs $8.00 one-way, $12.00 round-trip.

Hatches Harbor, off Herring Cove, is a natural harbor reachable only two ways: either by a long walk along Herring Cove Beach or by a short drive with a four-wheel-drive vehicle over the sand. Its remoteness makes Hatches a perfect spot for those seeking solitude. On any given day there's usually just a handful of visitors, most of them townies picnicking or fishing from their four-wheel-drive vehicles. The area surrounding Hatches Harbor was once home to early fishing settlements. Race Point Lighthouse is nearby, adjacent to the newly renovated light-keeper's house, which you can rent for a weekend, a week, or more.

CAPE COD NATIONAL SEASHORE

On August 7, 1961, President John F. Kennedy signed legislation establishing Cape Cod National Seashore (CCNS) and in doing so, founded the first park of its kind in the nation—a park situated on both a residential and commercial area.

As someone who spent much time on Cape Cod, JFK was well aware of the urgency to protect the natural beauty of the Cape from development. His vision "to provide enjoyment and an understanding of the unique natural, historic, and scientific features of Cape Cod" has surely been realized. Other parks have been created since then, but the Cape Cod National Seashore remains one of the most popular of the nation's public parks, with nearly 5 million visits made to its beaches, ponds, and pathways every year.

The CCNS is made up of 44,000 acres. The federal government maintains 27,700 acres of that land—mostly undeveloped upland, woodland, bogs, pitch pine forests, moorland, and many freshwater ponds, plus 40 miles of coastline along the Cape's outer arm in the towns of Chatham, Orleans, Eastham, Wellfleet, Truro, and Provincetown.

Here, amidst a rare scenic beauty, is a place that allows you to commune with nature and revitalize your soul. Thoreau walked it, birds migrate to it, and the Atlantic Ocean continues to pound it, and now we may enjoy it, whether we prefer a relaxing day at the beach or a solitary hike.

The Seashore encircles half of the town of Wellfleet and about 70 percent of Truro, and more than 80 percent of Provincetown's total area is within the National Seashore. Hundreds of families still live within its boundaries. These local inhabitants exhibit a fierce independence,

yet the park is a place where the people of Cape Cod are interdependent—they all use resources preserved by the Seashore: fresh water, scenic beauty, fish and shellfish, and yes, unpolluted air.

Join us as we take you to some off-the-beaten-path walking trails that traverse Cape Cod, tracks that seek out hidden hollows and take you to the tops of gigantic dunes towering over beaches far from anywhere. Follow us as we explore the Cape Cod National Seashore from an Insider's perspective. A complete up-to-date listing of all programs offered through the Cape Cod National Seashore can be found on their Web site at www.nps.gov/caco.

VISITOR CENTERS

Salt Pond Visitor Center

We suggest that before setting out for a day at the National Seashore you stop first at the CCNS Salt Pond Visitor Center (508-255-3421) off U.S. Route 6 in Eastham. Traveling north you'll see it on your right: a hexagon-shaped pavilion, which is sometimes called the "Gateway to the Seashore."

Besides providing you with free hiking and biking maps and a host of other information, the visitor center will help you to get oriented to Cape Cod. As you enter the building, the large three-dimensional map of Cape Cod is a perfect place to start. Even to locals the geography and geology of Cape Cod can be confusing. This contoured map allows you to view the formation of this curving arm of land called Cape Cod in relationship to its off-shore shoals and surrounding islands, and to note the many kettle ponds that dot our terrain.

From the lobby of the center you can enjoy a spectacular panoramic view of Salt Pond, Nauset Marsh, and, in the distance, the barrier beach and Atlantic Ocean, and witness an encapsulation of our most precious ecosystems—pond, marsh, beach, and ocean.

We recommend that you see the short interpretive films offered in the visitor center auditorium. These movies, which run continuously throughout the day, orient you to the area and allow you to see into the geological past, understand why there were so many offshore shipwrecks, and take a step back in time to our local heritage.

The Province Lands of the Cape Cod National Seashore are a naturalist's paradise. Here within the flora and fauna of the dunes you will find beach plum, bayberry, salt-spray roses, and beach heather.

There is also a first-rate museum featuring early Cape Cod artifacts, including mementos belonging to sea captains. The museum has a little of everything, with exhibits on topics from *Shipwrecks and Sea Rescue* and *Whaling* to *Plants of Cape Cod* and *Cranberries*.

Marconi Area/National Seashore Headquarters

Though smaller in size than the visitor center at Salt Pond, the Marconi Area (508-349-3785) is the Cape Cod National Seashore Headquarters. Located just off U.S. Route 6 in Wellfleet, the Marconi building is not really a visitor center, but rather houses the administrative offices of

the National Seashore. There isn't a lot to do in the building, though the lobby has a few exhibits, and you can talk to a park historian and naturalist.

Province Lands Visitor Center

A second visitor center, the Province Lands Visitor Center (508–487–1256) on Race Point Road in Provincetown, provides many of the same offerings found at the Salt Pond Visitor Center. It features exhibits on native flora and fauna, plus information on the history of the fishing industry. A park ranger is always on hand to answer your questions and offer guidance. A small theater shows orientation films, and there are outdoor programs similar to those at Salt Pond.

As mentioned one of the highlights at the Salt Pond Visitor Center is the spectacular view of Nauset Marsh from the lobby. At the Province Lands Visitor Center, the highlight is an upper viewing deck that gives you an extended view of the rolling moors, dunes, and ocean to the east, and views of Cape Cod Bay with its fabulous sunsets to the west.

NATURE WALKS

Before you hit the beaches, take a walk along any one of the 11 self-guiding trails at the Cape Cod National Seashore. The Nauset Marsh Trail along the Salt Pond is a good place to start. Adjacent to the Salt Pond Visitor Center, this trail winds along the edge of Salt Pond and Nauset Marsh, crosses fields, and returns to the visitor center. There are spectacular views along the way. The area is a full-scale nursery for oceanic fish, shellfish, and microscopic plankton. Because of this it serves as an important habitat along the Atlantic flyways for shorebirds, wading birds, and waterfowl. Traveling inland along this mile-long path from the marsh, the landscape

CLOSE-UP

Rescue at Sea

Rescue! Perhaps no other word conjures up the courage and selflessness of brave men at the peak of heroics. But the idea of launching a large, wooden rescue boat through pounding surf during a fierce winter storm is more than most of us wish to imagine. Before the opening of the Cape Cod Canal in 1914, it was the job of men in the U.S. Lifesaving Service to man the 13 lifesaving stations found along the Cape Cod coastline and rescue mariners who had fallen victim to the Atlantic Ocean.

More than 3,000 shipwrecks occurred off Cape Cod before the opening of the Cape Cod Canal (see our Close-up on the canal in the Historic Cape Cod chapter). Enough was enough: In 1872 Congress created the U.S. Lifesaving Service.

From 1872 to 1915 this agency rescued shipwreck victims. Sometimes the wind and surf were too strong to allow them to launch their double-ended rescue boats. In such circumstances they shot a "breeches buoy line" from a Lyle Gun (a small cannon) out over the helpless vessel and hauled the crew ashore in a basket.

The U.S. Lifesaving Service played an integral role in easing the hardships faced by Cape Codders who depended on the sea for their livelihood. Historically towns-

folk often attended the surfmen's drills, making them a popular local activity.

For 24 years the Cape Cod National Seashore has been staging a reenactment of the Beach Apparatus Drill at Old Harbor Life-Saving Station in Provincetown. Held at 6:00 P.M. Thursdays in July and August, the reenactment is the same drill the U.S. Lifesaving Service performed at the turn of the century. Park Rangers take on the role of the turn-of-the-20th-century surfmen and demonstrate the firing of the Lyle Gun and use of the breeches buoy. Though there is no ship to be rescued in the demonstration, you will leave with a better understanding of how the breeches buoy allowed the Lifesaving Service to rescue shipwreck victims when the surf or weather made rescue boats unsafe. Cape Cod National Seashore currently is the only unit of the National Park system that provides this visually powerful demonstration.

Old Harbor Life-Saving Station is located at Race Point Beach. Cost to view the demonstration is $4.00 for adults and $2.00 for seniors age 62 and over. Children age 16 and younger are admitted free. For more information contact the Province Lands Visitor Center (508–487–1256).

changes rapidly into an area of red cedar, low-lying juniper, and aromatic bayberry. The red cedars (actually junipers) are sun-loving trees, quick to take over the plowed fields and barren grounds of the Cape. Until the late 1930s a private golf course was in this area, complete with sand traps,

open fairways, and putting greens. Some evidence of the golf course can still be seen amid the changing landscape.

The CCNS has done an exemplary job when it comes to having wheelchair-accessible facilities. Several of its nature paths are wheelchair accessible, and the

Buttonbush Trail, also at the visitor center in Eastham, is one of them. An easy quarter-mile loop path that connects to the Nauset Trail, it has a guide rope and text panels in both Braille and large lettering along its route. As you walk along a wooded boardwalk that takes you through a freshwater environment, listen to the sounds of the many bird species that call this habitat home. Because the Buttonbush Trail has been designed to encourage multiple sensory experience, it has become popular with a wide variety of park users. It is used routinely by full-sighted educational and family groups, who often follow the guide rope in pairs of two—with one person blindfolded and the other reading the text on the panels out loud.

The Seashore has a number of other short, self-guiding nature trails. One of our favorite walking paths is at Fort Hill in Eastham. The **Fort Hill Trail** is a 1½-mile series of connected pathways that lead through cedar and oak forests, along the edge of Nauset Marsh, and then across fields that lead back to the starting point opposite the Penniman House, named for Captain and Mrs. Edward Penniman, a prominent whaling family in the 19th century, whose house is now a museum. You can start your walk at the entrance to the half-mile **Red Maple Swamp Trail,** which adjoins the Fort Hill Trail located across from the Penniman House. Walk down the path and loop through the heart of the swamp on a boardwalk, which is wheelchair accessible. Continue on to the Skiff Hill shelter, where an interpretive sign will tell the story of Indian Rock, which the Wampanoag Indians supposedly used to sharpen their tools. Here stretching out before you is Nauset Marsh, a large salt marsh, important because it produces food for ocean fish, birds, and other wildlife. Directly below you aquaculture flats are marked by buoys in the channel. Proceed along the path overlooking the marsh, through fields that once produced crops, to the Fort Hill overlook. Again Nauset Marsh lies before you, and beyond that, the barrier beach protecting the shoreline from the Atlantic Ocean.

To the right is the entrance to Orleans Town Cove. Orleans is that spit of land across the water to the right. Coast Guard Beach and the old Coast Guard Headquarters are to the left in the distance high on a bluff overlooking the ocean.

Another favorite ramble, as you head up the coast, is the **Atlantic White Cedar Swamp Trail** in Wellfleet, just north of Marconi Beach. When you arrive at the entrance to the Marconi area, follow the trailhead north to the Marconi Station Site and not south toward the Marconi Beach parking lot. The 1¼-mile trail is heaven for naturalists as it takes you through varying environments of scrubland, mixed oaks, and pitch pine perfect for birding. For diversity, there is nothing like this trail anywhere on Cape Cod as it descends through woodland and leads to a boardwalk that loops through the Atlantic White Cedar Swamp. The trail returns via the historic "Wireless Road" to the starting location.

Farther up the coast is the **Pilgrim Spring Trail,** an easy ¾-mile walk that provides yet another rewarding outdoor experience through bayberry and blueberry woodlands to a hillside with scenic views across the moors and dunes to the sea. Pilgrim Spring Trail is a short distance off U.S. Route 6 in the Pilgrim Heights area of North Truro and is well marked. There is an interpretive site that features illustrations and maps detailing the story of the Pilgrim Spring, which you will be able to find on the trail—the water is clear

[Facing page] *Nauset Light is located in Eastham, within the Cape Cod National Seashore. In 1996 it had to be moved farther inland to protect it from encroaching beach erosion.* PAULINE WONG, COURTESY OF THE NATIONAL PARK SERVICE

Join National Park Service rangers on a Cape Cod National Seashore interpretive program and learn more about the nature and history of Cape Cod. Ranger-led activities range from guided canoe trips to historic house tours and backcountry nature hikes. The nature walks and house tours are free; there is a small fee for canoe and surf-casting lessons and trips. For more information call (508) 255–3421, or visit www.nps .gov/caco.

and pristine, and you can cup your hand and take a drink, just as the Pilgrims did 380 or so years ago.

The 1-mile **Beech Forest Trail** in Provincetown circles a freshwater pond laden with water lilies and waterfowl, through American beech trees, sheep laurel, yellow and gray birch, and swamp azalea. A loop to this trail takes walkers through the heart of a beautiful beech forest, which is particularly beautiful in the fall, but you can walk this trail any time of the year and have a wonderful experience. The trail is located just off Route 6 on Race Point Road in the Province Lands.

HIKING TRAILS

So what's the difference between walking and hiking? For our purposes any trail that demands some physical conditioning and lasts more than an hour is considered a hike. We also recommend that on a hike you remember to wear a hat and bring a backpack containing sunscreen, drinking water, snacks, binoculars—and don't forget the camera. Now we are ready—let's go hiking!

The Great Island Trail, about a 6-mile hike on the bay side, is perhaps our favorite because it gives the greatest feeling of remoteness within the Cape Cod National Seashore. Kayaking is the ideal way to get to Great Island, but because it's not really an island anymore, you can

access the trailhead easily by car off Chequesset Neck Road in Wellfleet. The trail begins just after the Herring River Dike and the Sunset Hill Lookout. It winds through the middle of the island with beautiful views of Wellfleet Harbor on one side and Cape Cod Bay on the other. The island is a mix of shaded pitch-pine forests, marshes, and sandy stretches along deserted beach. It is home to fiddler crabs and blue herons, beach plum, and bay berry. It is also an island steeped in history and mystery—whalers often retreated to the island to a tavern site and a clearing that overlooks Wellfleet Harbor and the lower half of the island. Allow three to five hours to explore Great Island. It's well worth it!

On the ocean side the unofficial Truro Hills Trail winds through wooded hollows, down dirt paths, through open fields, and along dune trails, occasionally following CCNS trails. This is an all-day hike and requires planning. You should obtain a map from the Seashore before setting out. This trail takes you from Ballston Beach to Highland Light (approximately 10 miles), through bearberry coverings, across a cranberry bog on a boardwalk, through overgrown woods, across hillsides and dunes, and gives you sweeping views of the Seashore's finest beaches along the way. To enjoy this day thoroughly, you might consider forming a shuttle between the two trailheads. Also, when you pass the entrance to Long Nook Beach along the way, walk down the high dune path to the beach below—it's a beautiful stretch of sand.

BEACHES

During your visit to Cape Cod National Seashore, a trip to the beach is a must. The CCNS boasts six protected beaches, comprising nearly 40 miles of the finest seashore on the Atlantic coast. For us an early-morning walk in the solitude of a deserted beach is a perfect way to enjoy the beach, but if you prefer to visit later in

Forty miles of coastline lie within the protective boundaries of Cape Cod National Seashore.
THE NATIONAL PARK SERVICE

the day, be prepared for company, especially in summer months.

Coast Guard Beach and the adjacent Nauset Light Beach in Eastham, Marconi Beach in South Wellfleet, Head of the Meadow in North Truro, and Herring Cove and Race Point in Provincetown are all operated by the Seashore. All beaches have lifeguards, rest rooms, and showers except Head of the Meadow. A food stand is available only at Herring Cove Beach in Provincetown. A daily pass for CCNS beaches costs around $10 per day, and a season pass costs $30. It's a good idea to get one if you are planning on spending lots of time at various Seashore beaches during your stay. (Check our Beaches chapter for more details.)

BIKE TRAILS

The National Seashore offers visitors three trails. The Nauset Trail, 1.6 miles long,

starts at the Salt Pond Visitor Center and winds along the upland woodlands above Nauset Marsh to a boardwalk that traverses the marsh and connects the trail to Coast Guard Beach overlooking the Atlantic Ocean. It is an idyllic trail and perfect for families, with no steep hills or dangerous curves. If you don't have bikes with you, you can rent them at the Little Capistrano Bike Shop across U.S. Route 6 opposite the entrance to the Salt Pond Visitor Center.

The Head of the Meadow Trail runs for 2 miles between High Head Road and Head of the Meadow Beach parking lot in Truro. Flat and curvy, the trail takes you through a dune area past low-lying vegetation.

Looking to experience more excitement on a bike trail? Then the Province Lands Bicycle Trail is for you! The trail is very hilly and features hairpin curves and few straight stretches. The 5½-mile loop traverses several formidable dune ridges and takes riders around cranberry bogs, lily ponds, and scenic wetlands. The variety of topography is truly breathtaking. For us it's exhilarating to bike through the dunes in brilliant sunshine on a clear summer's day and then race through a cool, scented pine wood. Along the way you can leave the main loop and access Race Point and Herring Cove Beaches for a dip in the ocean. A word of caution: Be on the lookout for loose sand on the trail, especially at corners, and stay to the right. Slow down on curves and going downhill, and please wear a helmet.

FISHING

Saltwater fishing is one of the most popular recreational activities on the Cape and certainly at the Seashore. Surf fishermen line up on the more accessible beaches to cast their lines into the Atlantic hoping for a bite from striped bass, bluefish, and flounder.

No license is required for saltwater sport fishing, but there are size and number limits. We recommend that you check at one of the visitor centers for exact regulations—they do have a tendency to change from year to year (for more information refer to our Fishing chapter).

WHALE WATCHING

Cape Cod provides visitors with the opportunity to observe the largest creatures on earth in their natural habitat. Nothing is quite as thrilling as seeing these enormous mammals gliding smoothly through the water. Often you'll see whales in pairs or threesomes, either a mother and her calf or these two accompanied by another adult whale acting as guardian. Ironically the whales are visitors here too: they come to the area annually to feed on Stellwagen Bank, which lies roughly 6 miles northeast of Provincetown. Predictably this city on the tip of the Cape offers some of the most appealing excursions, because trips from this location offer more time to look at whales and less time getting there and back.

"There" of course is Stellwagen Bank, an 842-square-mile section of the shallows in the open ocean lying in the Gulf of Maine just off the mouth of Cape Cod Bay. Long a prime fishing area, Stellwagen's unique conditions and topography enable it to support a tremendous diversity of marine life, from single-cell organisms to great whales. But it wasn't always that way. The shallow platform known as Stellwagen Bank was once dry land where mastodon and mammals roamed. It is believed that about 12,000 years ago, the bank stood well above sea level and may have been connected to Lower Cape Cod. Early humans arrived in New England about 11,000 years ago, and they may have witnessed the beginning of the final chapter in the history of Stellwagen Bank. By then, as waters from the melting glaciers continued to raise the level of the sea, Stellwagen Bank slipped beneath the waves. Today it is covered by at least 65 feet of water and attracts a wide variety of sea life, including huge quantities of plankton (tiny single-celled plants that float in the water) and many species of fish and marine mammals who feed on them.

A protected National Marine Sanctuary since 1992—the first area in the Northeast to receive that designation—Stellwagen Bank attracts the whales that migrate here because of its abundant food supplies. Many types of whales are found here, including finback (the largest), humpback (the most playful), right (the most endangered), sei, minke, killer (also known as Orca), and pilot whales (also known as black fish). Each species has its own distinct habits, but generally the whales begin arriving in this area in early spring and leave for warmer waters in early winter.

Although the whales may be busy feeding underwater at Stellwagen Bank, they'll take time out to flirt with the whale-watching boats and will often voluntarily approach the boats and swim alongside and underneath them for hours. Humpback whales are the most popular species to watch because they are inquisitive enough to come close to the boats and have an engaging tendency to perform. Humpbacks feed for about six or seven months in the waters of Stellwagen Bank, which is rich with plankton, squid, herring, sand lance, and other sea life, and then leave the area, fasting until they return the following year from their wintering ground in the West Indies, where they breed and give birth.

Different species of whales feed on different types of sea life. Right whales, for instance, feed mostly on plankton. Whales follow the food sources, and whale-watching boats follow the whales, so when you're out on one of these boats, you'll often find yourself zipping around a bit until the boat operators get a handle on exactly where the whales happen to be. If you leave from either Barnstable or Provincetown, you'll generally see whale-watch boats from Plymouth and Boston approaching from the other direction.

Only after seeing a live whale dive and splash its mighty tail against the ocean water can one truly comprehend the majesty and size of these mammals. HYANNIS AREA CHAMBER OF COMMERCE

Despite the fact that whaling was for centuries an important New England industry (see our Historic Cape Cod chapter), it was the 20th century that brought some species close to extinction. Between 1910 and 1963 140,000 humpback whales were killed; today only a few thousand survive. The right whale, so named because it is relatively slow-moving and floats when killed—therefore the "right" whale to take—is practically extinct; researchers estimate there are fewer than 300 northern right whales left in the Atlantic Ocean today.

In 1975 a group of schoolchildren took the first whale-watching tour on the East Coast, conducted by Captain Al Avellar of the Dolphin Fleet out of Provincetown. More than 25 years later, the concept of peacefully watching whales, rather than killing them, has caught on, and now tens of thousands of people leave every summer from Plymouth, Barnstable, and Provincetown to visit the summer homes of the whales. During whale-watching trips staff members, often naturalists or marine biologists, provide commentary about the natural history of the area, especially the whales and their habitat. When the scientists spot whales, the excitement in their voices is genuine; for many it's like encountering old friends. Those who have worked around whales for a long time can identify individual whales by distinctive markings on the flukes of the whale's tail, underside, body, or head, and often know specific details of their lives, from their offspring to their travel patterns.

The most exciting moment during a whale watch comes—if you are lucky, that is—when one of the whales shoots straight up out of the water and splashes down again into the sea in a move known as "breaching." A collective "Ooh" rises from the boat and all is quiet for a

No matter how hot the weather, don't forget to bring a jacket on a whale watch. The temperatures at sea are always cooler.

moment as viewers take in the awesome scene. After that you'll be hooked, finding yourself telling your friends that they absolutely must experience a whale watch and offering to accompany them so you can experience it again!

The issues and restrictions that accompany whale-watching tours are far more complex than those for other types of tours. State and federal agencies have developed guidelines for the whale-watching industry that are probably based as much on safety for the marine mammals as for the humans. For example boats are prohibited from coming within more than 300 yards of most whales and 500 yards of the endangered right whale. In 1999 environmentalists and whale-watching concerns met to discuss ways to ensure that whale watching would be as safe as possible for these huge, trusting mammals. This fostered a spirit of comradeship between whale-watch captains, who now stay in constant contact monitoring whale-pod movement. The days have gone when whale-watch boats would try to outmaneuver another boat for position. Instead boats today approach an area where whales might be and cut the engines so all is quiet except for the lapping of the ocean's surf on the side of the boat. There is an incredible feeling that will come over you—you know they are out there, you closely watch the surface of the water, not knowing which direction to look in, and then suddenly, dark dorsal fins rise above the waves in graceful synchronization just feet away from the boat.

CLOSE-UP

Seal Sightings

Seals are carnivorous aquatic mammals with front and hind feet modifies as flippers, or fin-feet. The name *seal* is applied broadly to any of the fin-footed mammals, or pinnipeds. The two species of seal predominantly found along the Cape and islands' shorelines are the harbor and gray seal. These are sometimes joined in these waters by other species of seals—harp, hooded, and, most rarely, ringed seals.

It is believed that seals evolved from animals that once lived exclusively on land. Some 30 million years ago, as the climate gradually changed and the water cooled, the ancestors of the animals that would become seals abandoned the land for the sea. Though their true ancestry ties them to bears, harbor seals are most commonly compared with dogs. Gray seals have also been compared with horses, because their head is horselike and massive compared with the head of

the harbor seal. In fact they're sometimes called horsehead seals. A male gray seal can reach 8 feet in length and weigh as much as 800 pounds; while the female is smaller, reaching only 7 feet in length and weighing 550 pounds.

Cape Cod is a great spot to see seals. It is estimated that as many as 3,000 to 5,000 seals inhabit the waters of Cape Cod year-round, and because these waters surround our peninsula, there are lots of places where you can see them without ever leaving land. The best time to spot them is November through April. Chatham is a popular viewing spot, because the majority of our seals spend time along South Monomoy Island and most recently have been moving to nearby North Beach, Tern Island, and Aunt Lydia's Cove, which is across from the Chatham Fish Pier. You can also see seals around Wellfleet, Provincetown, and

Whale watching is now a $100 million industry in New England—an important part of the Cape's tourist economy, having extended off-season business in areas such as Provincetown. Because whale watching begins in April many seasonal shops, restaurants, and other businesses in Provincetown open then rather than waiting for Memorial Day. If you decide to take a whale watch out of Provincetown, make a day of it and include some shopping, lunch, or dinner—but be prepared to

sleep well that night; a few hours on a whale-watching boat can tire you out!

In this chapter we acquaint you with several of the organizations that conduct whale-watching excursions. Always call ahead to make sure the trips haven't been canceled because of adverse weather or rough sea conditions. Reservations are a must in summer, and a good idea even in spring and fall—both great times to experience the Cape. Whale-watch tours run from mid-April through the end of Octo-

Woods Hole. Nantucket Sound and Vineyard Sound have been seeing more seal activity too.

The best time to view seals is at low tide. When the tide goes out and the sandbars are left exposed, seals generally haul themselves out on land to rest, conserving energy and gaining body heat from the sun. Generally between September and October the large population of gray seals begins to arrive in the waters of Cape Cod. The breeding season, especially for gray seals, runs from late September through early March. During this time the pups are born on the barrier beaches or the Monomoy Island shore.

Of course you can also been them in the water too. A seal cruise is a great way to view these elusive marine mammals. A trained naturalist will be on board and will instruct you to keep your eyes open as the boat approaches a seal population. At first they will appear way off in the distance as black dots bobbing in the surf or like dark rocks protruding from the water.

But as the boat draws closer, you'll see that these dark spots are seals, and that they are everywhere—and what a thrilling sight it is. There's nothing quite like hearing the bark and chatter of seals as they frolic in the water, and you'll certainly have a better appreciation for these sleek mammals after seeing their big brown eyes inquisitively looking your way.

If a seal cruise interests you, there are a number of tours that leave from Stage Harbor in Chatham during the summer months and out of Ryder's Cove in North Chatham from October through May. You can inquire at Beachcomber Boat Tours, (508) 945-5265, www.sealwatch.com; Chatham Water Tours, (508) 432-5895, www.chathamwatertours.net; or the Monomoy Island Ferry, (508) 945-5450.

ber and usually last between three and four hours. Most companies offer three trips a day: The morning boat ride is ideal for families with small children, the afternoon trip is usually the most crowded, and the sunset trip is most romantic and beautiful, though it can be tough to see the whales at dusk.

All charters guarantee sightings; in the rare chance no whales are spotted, you'll be given a rain check to use at another time.

CHARTERS

Mid-Cape

Hyannis Whale Watcher Cruises
Barnstable Harbor
(508) 362-6088, (888) WHALEWATCH
www.whales.net
About 3 miles north of Hyannis in Barnstable Harbor, next door to Mattakeese Wharf Restaurant, the Hyannis Whale

Watcher Cruises run excursions across Cape Cod Bay to the Stellwagen Bank area. The company's 120-foot jet-powered cruiser has open upper and lower deck viewing areas and two-enclosed cabins. Travel time to reach the whales is often less than an hour, and trips last three to four hours. Naturalists provide the commentary and also point out landmarks on the shore, including the 100-year-old cottage colony on Sandy Neck, a barrier beach at the entrance of Barnstable Harbor. The boat has a full galley serving food and beverages.

The cost is $29 for adults, $25 for adults 62 and older, $16 for children ages 4 to 12, and free for children 3 and younger. Trips run May through October.

Group rates for 20 or more are available. The boats are wheelchair accessible. For educational groups, Hyannis Whale Watcher Cruises also offers a two-hour floating classroom trip for students that makes nature trips into Cape Cod Bay.

Lower Cape

Dolphin Fleet
MacMillan Wharf, Provincetown
(508) 349-1900, (800) 826-9300
www.whalewatch.com
Originator of the whale-watching industry on the Eastern Seaboard, the Dolphin Fleet always has a naturalist on board to provide informative and entertaining commentary about the whales, many of which they know by name. We like the fact that whale watches on this line are small; although the boats can hold more, the number of passengers is limited to 145. It

Humpback whales measure from 40 to 60 feet in length and weigh as much as 40 tons. On your excursion you may see them breaching—that is, rising from the ocean's depths and leaping straight out of the water into the air. Scientists don't know what it means or why they do it, but for those who witness a breach, it's truly a memorable experience.

also helps that the vessels were designed with stability in mind. The central cabin is heated, and the galley serves breakfast, lunch items, and snacks. During peak season the Dolphin Fleet offers nine trips a day, and it offers trips April through October. The cost is $22 for adults and $19 for children ages 6 to 12. Children 5 and younger ride free.

Portuguese Princess
MacMillan Wharf, Provincetown
(508) 487-2651, (800) 442-3188
www.princesswhalewatch.com
With two 100-foot vessels the Portuguese Princess makes six trips a day April through October. Naturalists provide commentary and information and offer hands-on activities for children and adults. Full galley and bar service are available on board, offering snacks, bagels, pizza, chowder, beer, wine, and cocktails. The boats have heated cabins. Peak-season rates are $22 for adults, $19 for children ages 5 to 12, and free for children ages 4 and younger. (The 1:00 and 2:00 P.M. trips charge full price.) If you're looking for the best rates, try the 9:30 A.M. cruise—$19 for adults and $16 for children.

[Facing page] *The whale-watching industry is dedicated to protecting the environment and educating the public to save these majestic mammals.* HYANNIS AREA CHAMBER OF COMMERCE

BOATING AND WATER SPORTS

The silhouette of a small boat outlined against the distant horizon evokes thoughts of a life filled with romance and adventure. Escaping the routines of daily life by sailing away on a boat is a common fantasy. Here on Cape Cod such fantasies may be realized.

In this chapter we explore the different ways you can safely get out on the water for an enjoyable day of power boating, sailing, kayaking, surfing, Jet-Skiing, or diving.

Boating for pleasure is well suited for relaxing get-togethers, family celebrations, or a carefree day out on the water with a friend. With the advent of summer, present-day Cape Cod sailors in pleasure boats follow in the watery wake of their earlier ancestors who went to sea to earn a living.

Whether you're bringing your own boat, or plan on renting one here, you'll be happy to know that each town here has numerous boat ramps, marinas, and boatyards, as one would expect in a land surrounded by water. If you are renting a boat, be sure you are qualified to handle it. Boat rentals are dwindling, primarily because of increased insurance costs; that should serve as warning enough that handling a sail or powerboat is no simple matter. Not to worry though—the Cape still has plenty of rentals available and a number of instructors to help you find the boating experience that best suits you. Another delightful way to explore the Cape's many inlets and creeks is by kayak or canoe. Paddling is an increasingly popular sport on Cape Cod, and there are many guides and rental opportunities from which to choose—or bring your own

kayak or canoe and launch it from one of the Cape's many boat ramps.

Water sports have become the rage for those who like to push the edge of the watery envelope. The Cape has some of the best windsurfing beaches on the East Coast, and the surfing is superb on the Outer Cape's Oceanside beaches. For an unusual water sport adventure, how about diving for shipwrecks in the untamed Atlantic?

Jet-Skiing is another popular sport—and also a red-hot topic here. Personal watercraft are being prohibited from certain areas to protect sensitive marine life and its habitats. If you plan to bring a Jet-Ski or other personal watercraft on your vacation, remember that you are considered a boater and are required to follow boating regulations. We can't tell you here what you can and cannot do on a personal watercraft, so we recommend that you check with the local authorities before launching yours. You'll want to avoid areas that are habitats for shorebirds and marine mammals.

Also, whether you're in a small personal watercraft or large boat, remember to keep lifejackets and first-aid supplies on hand. Carry emergency supplies, and make sure they're in working order. If you're cruising the coast, carry an accurate navigation chart, because the Cape's sandy coastline can change with just one storm. Keep an eye on the weather, and don't take any chances if you see fog rolling in. The waters around the Cape, especially along the Outer Cape and the Buzzards Bay and canal areas, can be a little tricky.

But most of all, have fun! That's what it's all about, folks. Enjoy!

BOATING

If your vision of a Cape Cod vacation includes a ride on a sailboat tacking across a gleaming bay, you'll be glad to know that sail cruises, boat rentals, and sailing lessons are readily available. If you are a seasoned boater or cruising the coastal waterways in your own boat, the following will help you find a marina for refueling, pumping out, or simply getting ice.

Sailing Instruction

There are more than 40 yacht clubs and sailing associations around the Cape and islands that offer sailing lessons to members and nonmembers. The instructors at many of these places are seasoned locals, many of them having learned to sail at the clubs where they now teach.

Because junior sailing programs are very popular here, early registration is recommended. After an initial instructional period and sailing with an instructor, you'll soon be sailing around in a dinghy. Instructors may then move you up to the bigger 16-foot day sailors, boats specifically designed for a day of sailing in local bays and coves. In no time you'll be a master of terminology and seamanship, helming and crewing, rigging and docking. In short you'll have mastered the basic fundamentals of navigations, and even more importantly, you'll know about safety on the sea.

A number of towns offer instruction, including Barnstable (508-790-6345), Falmouth (508-457-2567), Harwich (to residents), (508-430-7553), Sandwich (508-888-4361), and Yarmouth (508-398-2231). Here are a few other possibilities to get you out on the water.

UPPER CAPE

Buzzards Sailing School
99 South Road on Wings Neck, Pocasset
(508) 563-6731
The Buzzards Sailing School is a 35-year-old nonprofit instructional sailing program for young people ages 8 to 18. All classes, which run from late June through mid-August, emphasize fun and enjoyment of the water as well as water safety and the learning of sailing skills. All groups are taught in Widgeons, 420s, and Optimist dinghies. Those who enroll for the four-week minimum or take the full eight-week program will benefit most. Four classes per week cost $120.

MID-CAPE

South East Sailing School
115 Walnut Avenue, West Barnstable
(508) 420-1144
Rather than a vacation on Cape Cod, why not have an adventure and learn to sail on beautiful Lewis Bay and in Hyannisport Harbor? South East Sailing School will teach you the basics that every sailor should know. Group and individual lessons are available. Call the number listed above for more information.

Wianno Yacht Club
101 Bridge Street, Osterville
(508) 428-2232
www.vsb.cape.com/~wianno
The Wianno Yacht Club has a junior sailing program dedicated to teaching kids how to sail in a fun and encouraging environment. From the Seamen level (ages 7 to 9), to Mates (ages 8 to 10), Ensigns (ages 10 to 13), to Advanced Sailing for non-racers and the Racing Team, which practice skills in 420s, Wianno Yacht Club offers a program for everyone. The summer is divided into two four-week sessions, and you may register for one or both of them. The full eight-week program is $750; each of the two four-week

sessions costs $400. For adults who want to join a sailing program, the Wianno Yacht Club offers private sailing instruction to adults by appointment.

LOWER CAPE

Cape Sail
Saquatucket Harbor, Route 28, Harwich
(508) 896–2730
www.capesail.com

Bob Rice shares his more than 20 years of sailing experience in an extensive, hands-on six-hour course. His "classrooms" are either a small boat (in Brewster's Punkhorn Parklands) or large boat (Saquatucket Harbor in Harwichport). He promises to have the patience of a saint with novices; intermediate sailors will love his overnight learning excursions on Nantucket Sound. Lessons are held from Memorial Day to early October. For more information on charters see the entry in our Tours and Excursions chapter.

Arey's Pond Boat Yard Sailing School
Arey's Lane, South Orleans
(508) 255–0994
www.by-the-sea.com/areyspondboat yard

APBY operates on beautiful Pleasant Bay all summer long. Under the guidance of experienced instructors, APBY Sailing School specializes in teaching folks of all ages, from those just starting out to those brushing up to those interested in learning racing techniques. If you're a beginner, you'll take the tiller and sail a boat during your first lesson. They offer one- and two-week group lessons for students age 8 to 18 for $186 per week, and private lessons for the individual, couple, family, or group. Private lessons start at $65 per hour for one person with a two-hour minimum.

Chequessett Yacht & Country Club
Chequesset Neck Road, Wellfleet
(508) 349–0198
www.cycc.net

In season from early July through the end of August, Chequessett Yacht & Country Club offers eight weeks of junior sailing clinics at a cost of $120 per week for six hours of instruction. Private instruction for adults is also available at $75 per hour.

Marinas and Boatyards

When it comes to boating, there isn't much that you can't get with one stop to a local marina or boatyard. You'll find the necessities like fuel, launch services, repair workshops, and, in most cases, a retail store that carries marine essentials. If you have a specific question, harbormasters are a good source of general information, but they certainly have enough on their hands and can be hard to track down. We recommend relying on the numerous personnel you'll find at the various town piers, marinas, and boatyards around the Cape to provide an overview of boating activities, along with places to go and people to see to help make your boating experience memorable.

Cape Cod boasts more than 40 marinas, nestled in protected harbors and coves in some of the most picturesque parts of the peninsula. Most have repair service and an extensive array of full-service conveniences. You'll also find boatyards and boat builders not only right on the water but scattered about in such unlikely locations as industrial parks and along major roadways miles from the nearest waters. Take advantage of their knowledge. Marina personnel and boat builders understand the demands the sea makes on a boat. Many can incorporate the best designs and techniques into restorations, modifications, and repairs, whereas others offer new construction and sales of new boats, to which they often add their name. For instance Nauset Marine, with a location in Orleans (508–255–0777) is one of the largest Boston Whaler distributors in the country. Arey's Pond Boat Yard (see entry below), builder for the world-renowned APBY catboats, is a wooden boat center. Crosby

Yacht Yard in Osterville (see entry below), in business since 1850, builds a classic gaffed rigged sloop, the Wianno Senior. Function, quality, and durability—what else would you expect from Cape Codders?

UPPER CAPE

Bourne Marina
One Academy Drive, Buzzards Bay
(508) 759-2512
In town within easy walking distance of shops, restaurants, and family recreational facilities, Bourne Marina has 144 slips and can accommodate 60-foot boats with a 6-foot draft. It has fuel, water, 30- and 50-amp electrical service, and pump-out facilities, as well as rest rooms, showers, lockers, and a laundry area. You'll have use of a community lounge, a pressure washer, and pump-out, and a marine and grocery store. The marina is open from May through October.

Kingman Yacht Center
One Shipyard Lane, Cataumet (Bourne)
(508) 463-7136
www.kingmanmarine.com
The 235 dock slips here can accommodate vessels up to 100 feet long. The marina offers water, 110- and 220-volt outlets, and fuel. There are also rest rooms, a laundry, shops, and a marina store. The marina is open year-round.

Parker's Boatyard
Red Brook Harbor, 68 Red Brook Harbor Road, Cataumet (Bourne)
(508) 563-9366
www.parkersboatyard.com
Located in picturesque Red Brook Harbor, Parker's Boatyard carries both gas and diesel fuel and has 130 seasonal and transient moorings and slips with launch service and limited overnight dock space. The facilities include bathrooms, showers, and a picnic area with grills. A complete boatyard that specializes in sailing yachts, Parker's does repairs, repowering, awl-grip work, rigging and spar work, hauling, launching, and winter storage. Though the

boatyard is open year-round, the marina is closed for the winter months.

Wondering about the waves? Call the WQRC forecast phone at (508) 771-5522. The recording provides a weather forecast and tells you what to expect on the water.

The Sandwich Marina
Ed Moffitt Drive, Sandwich
(508) 833-0808
www.sandwichmarina.com
This marina on the Cape Cod Canal has 200 commercial and recreational slips and offers water, electricity, and diesel fuel as well as showers, parking, a playground area, a boat ramp, and winter storage. Stores are within walking distance. Open year-round, the marina can accommodate boats as long as 80 feet.

Brewer Fiddler's Cove Marina
42 Fiddler's Cove Road, North Falmouth
(508) 564-6327
www.byy.com
Well located for access to the Cape Cod Canal, Fiddler's Cove is a marina and boatyard with complete marine service. The facility has no moorings, but it has 105 seasonal slips and offers power, fuel, water, and cable. It can accommodate boats up to 80 feet in length and up to a 7-foot draft. The marina has a 35-ton travel lift for launching or hauling. It also has a laundry, showers, clubhouse, and a picnic area with grill. The marina is open year-round.

Edwards Boatyard
Route 28, East Falmouth
(508) 248-2216
www.edwardsboatyard.com
Edwards Boatyard has slip and mooring rentals with showers and rest rooms, gas and diesel fuel, ice, pump-out facilities, a marine store, a boat-launching ramp, and storage. This is a full-service yard that does

safety and environmental inspections, has a factory-trained staff for repairs, and sells new and used power- and sailboats. Edwards is open year-round.

Falmouth Harbor Marine
53 Falmouth Height Road, Falmouth
(508) 457-7000
www.falmouthharbormarine.com
Falmouth Harbor Marine offers gas and diesel fuel and repair service for inboard and outboard motors, including Yamaha and Mercruisers, as well as hauling services.

Keep our waters as clean as possible. If you come across the discharge of oil or oily waste, or notice a film or sheen upon the surface of the water, call the local harbormaster's office or the U.S. Coast Guard. In Sandwich the number is (508) 888-0020; in Woods Hole it's (508) 457-3253; and in Chatham it's (508) 945-3830.

Falmouth Marine
Falmouth Inner Harbor, 278 Scranton Avenue, Falmouth
(508) 548-4600
Falmouth Marine has 30 slips and 16 moorings. It can accommodate boats up to 90 feet with an 11-foot draft and haul boats weighing up to 70 tons. A full-service yacht yard with stock room, gas and diesel fuel, electrical hookups, and pump-out service, Falmouth Marine also offers passenger ferry service to Edgartown. The year-round facility is within walking distance of restaurants and shops.

Falmouth Town Marina
Scranton Avenue, Falmouth
(508) 457-2550
This marina has seasonal and transient slips, but there is a waiting list for seasonal slots. The marina accepts boats up to 100 feet. It offers water, electricity, and shower facilities, and you can get fuel

nearby. The marina is open from the beginning of April to the end of October.

MacDougalls' Cape Cod Marine Service
145 Falmouth Heights Road, Falmouth
(508) 548-3146
www.macdougalls.com
MacDougalls' is a full-service boatyard with a sail loft and an engine shop. It rents 70 slips and 20 moorings, has electrical service, gas, ice, and a marine store, as well as a railway and a 50-ton travel lift. The facility is open year-round and offers storage, laundry, and showers.

Quissett Harbor Boatyard
Quissett Harbor, 36 Quissett Harbor Road, Falmouth
(508) 548-0506
Set in a small harbor in a wooded area, this boatyard is a lovely place to tie up for the night. It has 86 moorings and offers repairs, water, electric hookups, and ice, but no fuel. Quissett Harbor Boatyard is open year-round with limited hours during the winter months.

Woods Hole Marine
91A Water Street, Woods Hole
(508) 540-2402
www.woodsholemarine.com
Woods Hole Marine has a full-time mechanic available and can handle boats up to 65 feet long with about 37 moorings and 28 slips. Facilities include dinghy docks, showers, toilets, and a pump-out boat that services five harbors in the area. The facility has water and 15-amp electrical service and is within walking distance of a convenience store, shops, and restaurants. It's open from early spring to the end of October.

The Half Tide Marina
Frog Pond Close Road, Mashpee
(508) 477-2681
www.halftide.com
This full-service marina has 60 slips and 15 moorings. There are rest rooms and some supplies available, along with boat sales, storage, and all types of repairs.

Little River Boatyard
15 Riverside Road, Waquoit (Mashpee)
(508) 548-2005
www.littleriverboatyard.com
Little River Boatyard is a full-service marina that does repairs, sells gas and ice, and rents ice eaters (things that keep ice from forming around docks). It is open year-round.

New Seabury Marina
Rock Landing Road, New Seabury
(Mashpee)
(508) 477-9197
New Seabury has five transient slips and gas, water, and electrical service, as well as a marina store. It can accommodate boats up to 39 feet in length. The marina is close to tennis, golf, and restaurants. is open from May to October.

MID-CAPE

Crosby Yacht Yard
72 Crosby Circle, Osterville
(508) 428-6900
www.crosbyyacht.com
A popular rendezvous place for yacht clubs and boating groups, Crosby Yacht Yard can accommodate power- and sailboats up to 120 feet. It has both slips and moorings, shower and laundry facilities, fuel, water, ice, electricity, and a marine store. Repair service is available seven days a week. The facility has travel lifts, marine railways, inside and outside storage, and launch service. The home of the Cape Cod catboat, Crosby's is also a boat builder and an authorized dealer for Scout, Sealine, and Uniesse Marine Boats, and offers full brokerage services. There is a restaurant on the premises. Crosby Yacht Yard is open year-round.

Nauticus Marina
West Bay Road, Osterville
(508) 428-4537
This marina is open from May to November and can accommodate boats up to 120 feet with a 6-foot draft. It has 100 feet of transient dockage and 15 slips for sea-

sonal use. Electrical, water, and cable service are available, but the marina has no gas, nor does it offer repair service. The marina is within walking distance of village shops and restaurants.

Oyster Harbors Marine
122 Bridge Street, Osterville
(508) 428-2017
www.oysterharborsmarine.com
Oyster Harbors Marine has 110 slips and 30 moorings; it can accommodate boats from 8 to 100 feet long and has gas and diesel fuel, pump-out facilities, a 55-ton travel lift, and storage. This full-service boatyard offers a marine store, rest rooms, showers, carpentry, and mechanical and electronic repairs, as well as sales for yachts and outboard motors. It is open year-round.

Barnstable Marine Service
Barnstable Harbor, Off Mill Way,
Barnstable
(508) 362-3811
Barnstable Marine, on Cape Cod Bay, has 45 slips. It sells diesel fuel and gasoline, has showers and rest rooms, bait and tackle, ice and snacks, haul-out facilities with a 20-ton travel lift, and full mechanical, carpentry, finishing, and repair services. It is open year-round and is a short walk from village shops and stores.

Hyannis Marina
1 Willow Street, Hyannis
(508) 790-4000
www.hyannismarina.com
Offering a calm, sheltered refuge, Hyannis Marina has 180 slips, diesel fuel and gasoline, water and electrical hookups, and a complete parts and service department. The marina can accommodate everything from motor boats to mega-yachts up to 200 feet. It has a full restaurant and bar, swimming pool, cabana bar, courtesy and rental cars, showers, dockside telephone, Internet, and TV service, a coin-operated laundry, and game room. The facility also includes an electronics and canvas shop, valet rack service, a marine store, and emergency service. It is open year-round.

Ship Shops
Pleasant Street, South Yarmouth
(508) 398–2256
www.shipshops.com
Ship Shops is a full-service boatyard in South Yarmouth with a limited number of transient slips and moorings. It sells gas and diesel fuel and has a marine shop. Ship Shops is open year-round.

Bass River Marina
Route 28, West Dennis
(508) 394–8341
www.seachain.com
Bass River Marina is open year-round and offers 158 slips. This Mid-Cape marina on the beautiful Bass River has gas and pump-out facilities, showers, a restaurant, and ice. It is open May through October.

Northside Marina
Sesuit Harbor, 357 Sesuit Neck Road,
East Dennis
(508) 385–3936
www.northsidemarina.com
This northside marina on Sesuit Harbor offers 120 slips, storage, gas, diesel, pump-out facilities, showers, and a restaurant. The marina is open year-round.

LOWER CAPE

Allen Harbor Marine Service
335 Lower County Road, Harwichport
(508) 432–0353
www.allenharbor.com
This year-round facility on picturesque, protected Allen Harbor was founded in 1927 and is another full-service yard, offering slips and moorings, a gas dock, repairs, sales, and storage (they'll shrink-wrap your boat for the winter). Next to Allen Harbor Marine is a town-owned docking ramp.

Harwichport Boat Works Inc.
4 Harbor Road, Harwichport
(508) 432–1322
A year-round facility, Harwichport Boat Works offers a handful of guest mooring spots both here and in the inner harbor. This is a full-service marina, offering storage, gas and diesel fuel, boat and engine sales, and repairs. The yard is renowned for its restoration work; wood and glass are its specialties. Tie-ups are short-term only.

Saquatucket Harbor
Municipal Marina, 715 Main Street (Route 28), Harwichport
(508) 430–7532
The marina, a quarter-mile from the village, has 192 slips and a dozen visitor slips, making it the largest municipal marina on the Cape. Services and amenities include washers, dryers, rest rooms, showers, pump-out service, and 20/30-amp/110-volt electrical service. The marina is open from early May to mid-November.

Chatham Yacht Basin
Barn Hill Lane, Chatham
(508) 945–0728
Open year-round, Chatham Yacht Basin has 30 moorings and 70 slips on pretty Oyster River. Chatham Yacht Basin is a full-service marina.

Outermost Harbor Marine
83 Seagull Road, Chatham
(508) 945–2030
www.outermostharbor.com
Outermost Harbor Marine offers slips and moorings. It has a gas facility, hauling and launch service, storage facilities, and a marine hardware and supplies shop. It also specializes in fiberglass repairs. The facility is closed January and February.

[Facing page] *The Crosby Yacht Yard in Osterville is a year-round, full-service marina that also builds and sells boats.* HYANNIS AREA CHAMBER OF COMMERCE

Oyster River Boatyard
Barn Hill Lane, Chatham
(508) 945-0736
Instead of moorings Oyster River Boat-yard offers 20 floating docks. It also has 22 slips, but don't count on getting one anytime soon as there is a long waiting list. The year-round boatyard also has a gas facility and repair service.

Ryder's Cove Boatyard
Town Landing, 46 Ryder's Cove Road, Chatham
(508) 945-1064
Ryder's Cove, in Pleasant Bay, has 36 slips and 73 moorings. The marina offers gas and seasonal rack storage. Ryder's Cove is open throughout the year.

Stage Harbor Marine
Bridge Street, Chatham
(508) 945-1860
www.stageharbormarine.com
Stage Harbor Marine has 33 slips and 33 moorings, gas, hauling and storage facili-ties, and a first-rate repair shop. Stage Harbor is open year-round.

Arey's Pond Boat Yard
Arey's Lane, Orleans
(508) 255-0994
www.by-the-sea.com/areyspondboat yard
This year-round boatyard has 60 pro-tected moorings off Pleasant Bay that can accommodate boats up to 30 feet. It also offers custom wooden boat building and repairing, and sells new and used boats and skiffs. Arey's Pond Boat Yard offers a sailing school in the summer.

Nauset Marine
Off Barley Neck Road, Orleans
(508) 255-3045
www.nausetmarine.com

Open year-round, this marina has 55 slips, 45 moorings, and 40 dry-rack storage spaces. Gas and pump-out facilities are available.

Rock Harbor
Rock Harbor Road, Eastham
(508) 240-5972
There are nearly 40 municipal town slips at Rock Harbor, but the waiting list is more than a decade long! There are a few transient slips available through the East-ham Natural Resource Office on a reserva-tion basis.

Wellfleet Marine
Town Pier, Wellfleet
(508) 349-2233
This year-round marina offers seasonal mooring by the night, week, and month on a first-come, first-served basis. It has a gas facility as well as diesel; pump-out is done via the harbormaster's boat. Several slips are available through the harbormaster.

Provincetown Marina
Fisherman's Wharf, Provincetown
(508) 487-0571
Smack in the middle of town, Province-town Marina has more than 200 berths and 100 moorings, with launch service from 7:00 A.M. until midnight (later on weekends in season). Three launches operate from Memorial Day through Columbus Day weekend. The marina also has a pump-out station, trash Dumpster, and gas dock, as well as showers, tele-phones, soda machines, and a coin-oper-ated laundry. Information is provided 24 hours a day on Channel 9. The marina is open from Memorial Day through Colum-bus Day weekend.

[Facing page] *Experience the charm and elegance of the Cape's many harbor marinas.*
HYANNIS AREA CHAMBER OF COMMERCE

Provincetown Yacht and Marine Marina
MacMillan Pier, Provincetown
(508) 487-9256
This newer marina has 22 slips, available by the night, week, or month. The marina also offers water and electrical hookups, showers, and a pump-out station. Though this is one of the smallest marinas in New England, it can accommodate large boats because there is 10 feet of water even at low tide.

Boat Rentals

If you're in the mood to do a little sailing or motoring upon the waves and you've got some prior experience, you may want to consider renting a boat. There are several rental outfits across the Cape to help you out, and some of them are listed below. Those people looking for charters and cruises, where you can sit back and enjoy the sights while someone else does the sailing, should refer to the Tours and Excursions chapter. Or, if you wish to mix in a little fishing, see the Fishing chapter.

The hurricane season coincides with prime boating time. To prepare your boat for bad weather, seal hatches, portholes, windows, doors, and vents with duct tape. At a slip or tie-up, make the lines as long as possible, set extra anchors, and add extra fenders and chafe protection. Most importantly do not stay on board during a hurricane.

MID-CAPE

Cape Cod Waterway Boat Rentals
Route 28, Dennisport
(508) 398-0080
You can rent manually powered and electric paddleboats, canoes, and kayaks here, and because it is located right on Swan River, between Swan Pond and Nantucket

Sound, renters can enjoy a variety of nearby Cape waters. The shop is open from May through October, and rentals are flexible in terms of hours, days, or weeks.

LOWER CAPE

Cape Sail
Saquatucket Harbor, Route 28, Harwich
(508) 896-2730
www.capesail.com
Looking for a great Cape sailing experience? Cape Sail offers a range of opportunities from congenial captained charters to hands-on learning expeditions. Experience offshore Cape Cod on a three-hour private charter or a more adventurous overnight trip to Nantucket. Trips of other durations can be arranged. Captain Bob Rice shares his nearly 40 years of sailing and teaching experience on his boat, the *Sabbatical*, or in smaller day sailers. Charters are available for a three-hour trip. Lessons are also available as a six-hour course for two people. Reservations are needed for all charters, trips, and lessons.

Jack's Boat Rental
Nickerson State Park, Route 6A, Brewster
(508) 896-8556
www.jacksboatrental.com
Almost nothing beats sailing on Flax Pond on a warm summer day, and Jack's Boat Rental is the place for one-stop shopping. It's all here: Sunfish, sailboards, seacycles, pedal boats, canoes, and kayaks. Jack's also offers windsurfing and sailing lessons. Jack's has other locations at Gull Pond in Wellfleet and a retail shop on U.S. Route 6 in Wellfleet (508-349-9808). They are open late June through Labor Day.

Wellfleet Marine
Town Pier, Wellfleet
(508) 349-2233
From mid-June to mid-October Wellfleet Marine rents (by the hour or day) Stur-Dee Cat 14-foot sailboats, 14-foot skiffs (with 6-horsepower motors), 19-foot Rhodes sloops, and 21-foot MacGregor sloops for use in Wellfleet Harbor.

Flyer's Boat Yard
131A Commercial Street, Provincetown
(508) 487-0898, (800) 750-0898
www.flyersrentals.com

Since opening its doors in 1965, Flyer's has satisfied the needs of all kinds of boaters because it has one of the largest rental fleets on the Cape. Here they offer power-boats (ranging from 8- to 50-horsepower) and sailboats from a Sunfish to a 19-foot Rhodes. There is a two-hour minimum on rentals, with options for renting by the day or week.

Waterway Access

Cape Cod boat ramps come in a variety of forms: sand, gravel, and asphalt. Some town landings provide free use, whereas others require a sticker, so you'll want to inquire at the local town hall (phone numbers are listed in our Area Overview chapter). You'll find public boat ramps are very busy during the summer. Try to arrive before 10:00 A.M.; otherwise you may not find a place to park your vehicle and trailer.

KAYAKING AND CANOEING

As you glide through the water in a kayak or canoe, you'll find a peace and stillness most of us rarely experience. On Cape Cod you'll find beauty too, whether you're in a river inlet full of colorful sponges that reflect off the bottom or in the mooring fields of some boatyard. You'll be seeing Cape Cod's natural beauty from a different angle, too.

Getting Started

To kayak or canoe? That is the question. You may want to try both, preferably on the protected waters of a pond, lake, or bay. Here are a couple things to consider as you make your decision. In a kayak you sit closer to the water, where you're snug

Red Brook Harbor in Buzzards Bay offers great variety to a paddler. Open, calm water, island vistas, and jagged shoreline highlight your trip. Start at the boat landing at Barlow's Landing off Red Brook Road in Cataumet. Gliding in and out of a mooring field, head north toward Bassett Island. You'll see a variety of nesting birds and might get a glimpse of a fox, coyote, or osprey. Shoreline rocks make the paddling more challenging. Turn around at the abandoned lighthouse and head back to Red Brook Harbor. The return distance is about 2 miles.

in the cockpit and not as easily disturbed by wind and rolling waves. In a canoe you sit higher up, on a bench, so this kind of craft can be less stable, especially in choppy waters. You propel a canoe by a single-ended paddle that you stroke first on one side of the craft and then the other. The high gunnels catch the wind, the upcurved bow pounds the surf, and all this translates into more work over less distance traveled. In a kayak, on the other hand, you use a two-ended kayak paddle, and you'll move through the water much more efficiently than in a canoe, so you can travel greater distances. Still, canoes provide advantages that kayaks don't, and one of them is space. This isn't so much a factor for those into solo canoeing, but it is an attraction for people who want to bring along fishing gear, a cooler, and definitely the dog. And although some people think of a kayak's easy maneuverability as an advantage over canoes, others are attracted to the challenge of successfully maneuvering a canoe. They say canoeing is more "interesting."

Whatever you decide don't rent a fancy watercraft just because it looks cool. You may want to talk to enthusiasts of both sports, and then try out crafts based on where and how you intend to pursue your sport of choice.

Kayaking Nauset Marsh

Much of Cape Cod's allure comes from its natural beauty and its unique location, jutting out into the Atlantic Ocean. A large number of migrating birds and marine mammals visit these shores at specific times each year to feed and breed, and kayakers who want to see some of this wildlife have the perfect opportunity. Nauset Marsh is one of the most productive salt marsh habitats in the world. A vast secret world of marshy grassland, it's crisscrossed by meandering streams and tidal creeks of seawater, which flow in and out with the tide and are ideal for kayaking. These marsh areas are also a birder's paradise; depending on the season, you will see many species of nesting and shorebirds, including the blue heron and osprey, and you may see otters as well. Farther out toward the Nauset Inlet at the outer barrier beach section of Nauset Marsh, you may even encounter basking seals.

Access to Nauset Marsh is quite easy, with plenty of parking available at two Eastham town landings. We recommend that your first choice be the landing at Hemenway Road off U.S. Route 6 in Eastham, directly after the Fort Hill entrance and the right after the Eastham Visitor Center. Once in the water head in any direction for a wonderful day of exploration. Heading south and east you will pass acres of sedge islands, known locally as hummocks, separated by channels of water that all connect the salt marsh to the greater ocean ecosystem. Paddling into coming currents on a moderately calm day is pleasant for novice and experts alike. The beginner gets the feeling of open space, and seasoned paddlers have the chance to travel into oncoming seas at the spit to the Atlantic Ocean. Navigational charts are not necessary even at low tide.

You can also enter Nauset Marsh at the Salt Pond town landing off U.S. Route 6—after the stoplight in Eastham Center, it's the next right after the police and fire stations. As you make your way out from

Canoes, like kayaks, come in solo and tandem versions and in various weights and sizes, so make your decision based on where you'd like to go, how seriously you intend to pursue the sport, and whether you'll be going alone or with a friend.

If you're renting a kayak, look for a relatively flat bottom for stability. It should be shorter than 15 feet and be between 2 and 2½ feet wide. In this size kayak you can go just about anywhere on Cape Cod comfortably. In addition you may want to consider getting a spray skirt, which covers the cockpit and prevents water from dripping off your paddle onto your clothing.

You'll also need a personal flotation device (PFD). A whistle is a good idea too; it might prove useful if you run into a creeping fog. Also consider purchasing a Loran map of the area you are paddling; these mark channels and depth of water.

Many people enjoy kayaking in the quiet waters of Waquoit Bay, where they can explore Washburn Island. Other good

Salt Pond and into Nauset Marsh, you'll be entering the marsh a half-mile north of the Hemenway Landing (just so you have your bearings). Once past the cedar trees and the Salt Pond inlet flow, follow the shoreline east to the great expanse of barrier beach, which protects the marsh from the surf of the Atlantic. As you approach the beach, past the boardwalk on your right, you will see a perfect place to beach your boat to take a walk along the barrier beach and collect some shells.

Back in your boat, as you make your way south down the outer beach, conditions will change. The currents get stronger the nearer you get to the Nauset Inlet. For those experienced paddlers prepared with the proper gear and skills, it is a short run through the inlets and into the Atlantic Ocean and playtime in the surf. It can be dangerous for the beginner, even an intermediate paddler, and it does require specialized gear, including spray-skirt, wetsuit, and helmet. If you are not ready for the surf riding, no problem; continuing south you can skirt the inlet and enter the sheltered waters of Nauset Harbor.

Nauset Harbor has lots of spots to stop for a swim or picnic. Paddling the shoreline you will pass Nauset Heights, with its beautiful homes overlooking the Atlantic Ocean. From there it's across the entrance to Town Cove and a paddle in front of historic Fort Hill. You have almost completed the full circumference of Nauset Marsh and are less than a mile from the Salt Pond landing where you started your paddle. The Cape Cod National Seashore Visitor Center will act as your beacon, as it sits overlooking Salt Pond.

If you wish to take this tour with a guided interpreter, several of the tour companies mentioned in this chapter offer tours of Nauset Marsh, including the Cape Cod National Seashore, Wellfleet Bay Audubon, Cape Cod Museum of Natural History, and Cape Cod Coastal Canoe and Kayak.

spots to start include Barnstable Harbor and Little Pleasant Bay in Orleans. Once in the water cruise the shoreline and enjoy the sense of freedom you will experience in your kayak. Once you've gotten the hang of the sport, you may move up to a more seaworthy vessel that is usually 16 to 20 feet in length, but narrower, from 22 to 24 inches wide. These longer kayaks move through the choppy waters with more ease.

Before you begin any outings, be sure to check the tides and wind conditions, and take these into account when deciding how far you'll venture. Kayaks are capable of covering 1 to 2 miles in a couple of hours with a steady "touring" stroke. With the tide and wind at your back, you could increase that distance to 3 miles quite easily, but when you have to turn around and paddle against the tide and wind, you'll be going much slower and you'll be testing your stamina.

First-time canoeists will find excellent opportunities in the Cape's many marshes and tidal inlets. The Herring River in Harwich is a perfect place to start a canoe adventure. There is easy access to the river from the parking area on the east side of the Herring River Bridge on Route 28 in West Harwich. Once on the water, head upriver, where the water winds gently for miles past the salty scent of marsh peat. You may see egrets, great blue herons, and ospreys. To get the most out of your excursions, the best time to paddle the Herring River is at high tide. This will assure that you'll be able to see above the lush green marsh grasses that line the waterway.

Nickerson State Park's Cliff Pond also offers the first-time paddler a way to explore coves and hidden beaches in the shelter of lake surroundings. From Route 6A in Brewster, go through the park entrance, drive on the main road approximately 1.6 miles, and take a left onto the dirt road at the FISHERMAN'S LANDING sign. The sandy beach launching area makes getting in and out of your canoe in water easy. Be sure to pack a picnic—Cliff Pond has many deserted pond beaches easily accessed by canoe, where you may find yourself in the company of red-tailed hawks and Canada geese.

Canoe and Kayak Tours and Rentals

Whether you choose a guide interpretive paddling tour or rent a boat, the Cape has more than 60 paddling routes to explore. We recommend that you contact any one of the paddling tour companies listed below for professional instruction led by a trained guide. Tour guides offer a different tour every day through a different habitat. Be sure to call ahead for reservations, and ask specifically what you might see on the tour. In cases when a street address is not listed, assume the truck and boat trailer is the company's office during the summer

months as they travel from location to location. Have fun! Kayaking and canoeing are sports that will grow with you.

UPPER CAPE

Cape Cod Kayak
Route 28A, Cataumet (Bourne)
(508) 540-9377
www.capecodkayak.com
Cape Cod Kayak provides a full range of activities for the kayak enthusiast out of various locations in the Upper Cape area. They offer tours that range from two to three hours. The cost is $25 to $75 for the kayak, paddle, spray-skirt, PFD, and brief, basic instruction. Though they will deliver kayaks to most locations throughout the Cape, they primarily run kayak tours in the Upper Cape area, such as along the Mashpee River, in Wild Harbor and West Falmouth Harbor, and Scorton Creek in Sandwich, to name a few. Besides offering a different tour each day during the summer months, Cape Cod Kayak also offers daily, weekend, and weekly rental options on kayaks, and they don't charge for delivery. Rental prices start at $35 for up to 24 hours for a solo kayak. Kayaks with rudders rent for $50 for the day.

Waquoit Kayak Company
Edwards Boatyard, Route 28, East Falmouth
(508) 548-9722
www.waquoitkayak.com
Waquoit Kayak Company sells and rents canoes and kayaks, and also specializes in guided tours of the Waquoit Bay estuary, one of the largest bays and most beautiful areas on the Cape. The tours take advantage of their location right on the tranquil, picturesque Childs River, which provides paddlers with a protected starting point where they can become familiar with their kayak or canoe. After a 20-minute paddle on the river, you will enter Waquoit Bay, which has shallow, clear water with an average depth of 5 feet, allowing for interesting

bottom viewing. Here, too, you get to explore Washburn Island, which is great for walking or a picnic. Paddlers with all levels of experience should enjoy this tour, which includes your choice of kayak or canoe, a PFD, and instruction on basic paddling techniques and water safety for $50. Private kayaking or canoe lessons are also available by the hour starting at $25. Kayak and canoe rentals are available for $35 for a half-day and $49 for a full day. There's convenient parking at Edwards Boatyard.

MID-CAPE

Eastern Mountain Sports
1513 Route 132, Centerville
(508) 362-8690
www.ems.com
Open year-round on Route 132, this store has access to sit-on-top kayaks, which have no cockpit and are often used by scuba divers. The store also carries flat-water kayaks, which are shorter, and sea kayaks, which range in length from 15 to 22 feet and are used for touring, because they have a lot of storage capacity. Eastern Mountain Sports also has a full range of paddles, flotation vests, safety equipment, maps and charts, camping and backpacking equipment, and clothing for sale in their retail store. EMS recently started to offer an occasional basic kayak tour for beginners to intermediates. Call for a schedule and rates.

Cape Cod Waterway Boat Rentals
Route 28, Dennisport
(508) 398-0080
This company rents canoes and kayaks for use on Swan River, Swan Pond, and Nantucket Sound. A solo kayak rents for $18 per 90 minutes; a tandem is $29. Canoes rent for $20 for 90 minutes. Daily rentals are $40 for a solo and $50 for a tandem kayak or canoe. Safety equipment is included with the rental price. The shop is open from the beginning of May through September.

Keeping beaches sanitary is hugely important on the Cape, where beaches are a major summer attraction. The Barnstable County Department of Health and the Environment conducts weekly surveillance of the water quality at more than 250 beaches on Cape Cod during the summer bathing season. To check the status of your favorite bathing spot, access the town directory of public marine and freshwater beaches at their Web site: www.barnstablecounty health.org/beachsampling.htm.

LOWER CAPE

Cape Cod Museum of Natural History
Route 6A, Brewster
(5080 896-3867
www.ccmnh.org
The Cape Cod Museum of Natural History offers guided natural history tours of Cape waterways. You can explore different locales all over Cape Cod—in ponds, rivers, and marshes—and learn the basics of paddling and water safety. Trips include rest stops and drinking water, and some include a short hike. Tours run daily from April through October, and reservations are necessary. Call the museum for times and details. The cost is $55 per adult and $40 for children ages 8 to 12. The trips range from three to four hours, and the time of day that tours are offered depends on the tide.

Goose Hummock Shop
Town Cove, Route 6A, Orleans
(508) 255-2620
www.goose.com
The Goose Hummock Outdoor Center is a great place to start your Cape kayaking experience. Located on the sheltered waters of Town Cove in Orleans, just off the U.S. Route 6 Rotary on the Orleans/Eastham town line, this outdoor center is

the Lower Cape's number-one resource for paddling. Staffed by local sports enthusiasts, the Goose Hummock is also a great source for Cape Cod sporting goods and has been for more than 50 years. The Goose offers the largest selection of kayaks and accessories for sale on Cape Cod. There's also a large selection of canoes and kayaks for rent, from $25 for four hours and $45 for full days up to $175 a week. The store is open year-round but only offers rentals during the summer months.

The Goose Guides offer instruction and guided tours during the summer as well. Basic coastal kayaking instruction is $50 per person for two-and-a-half hours. Tours range from $50 to $65 depending on length of tour.

Audubon Society Wellfleet Bay Wildlife Sanctuary
U.S. Route 6, Wellfleet
(508) 349-2615
www.wellfleetbay.org
Audubon Society Wellfleet Bay Wildlife Sanctuary offers guided canoe and kayak trips with an environmental slant from the beginning of April through the end of October. Trips through marshes and ponds, from Chatham to Provincetown, are the specialty here, and you won't find more knowledgeable guides anywhere else on the Cape. Learn about the natural history of this area, and practice your canoeing skills. The fee is $25 for non-members and $20 for members, and reservations are necessary.

Jack's Boat Rental
U.S. Route 6, Wellfleet
(508) 349-9808
www.jacksboatrental.com
You can explore the Outer Cape's hidden ponds, inlets, and marshes on guided kayak tours from this location. Tours are given from Memorial Day through Columbus Day weekend. Because no experience

is needed, beginners and children are especially welcome. Note that times vary because of the fluctuating tides. Jack's, which also has locations at Nickerson State Park in Brewster (508-896-8556) and Gull Pond in Wellfleet (508-349-7553), also rents single and double kayaks and canoes for $15 to $18 per hour.

Venture Athletics Kayak Shop
Whaler's Wharf, 237 Commercial Street, Provincetown
(508) 487-9442
www.ventureathletics.com
This company has operated an outdoor gear shop on Commercial Street for several years, and started offering kayak rentals in 2003. Explore the coastline of Provincetown in an ocean kayak: One-person kayaks are available for $25 for up to four hours, and two-person kayaks for $35 for up to four hours. Guided tours of the Provincetown area are available too, including one to Long Point, which culminates with a catered lunch. You must be 18 or older to rent. They recommend you arrive early to familiarize yourself with the equipment. The shop is open mid-May through mid-October, weather permitting. Reservations are accepted year-round.

WATER SPORTS
Surfing and Windsurfing

The oceanside beaches of the Lower Cape cater to the surfing crowd, but, for the most part, the waters of Nantucket and Vineyard Sounds are too calm even for a boogie board. Primarily surfers tend to gather at Nauset Beach in Orleans and the Wellfleet beach triumvirate of LeCount Hollow, Cahoon Hollow, and Newcomb Hollow. The waves along this coast will

[Facing page] *Windsurfing off Kalmus Beach, Hyannis.*
HYANNIS AREA CHAMBER OF COMMERCE

never rival those of Hawaii and Southern California, but surfers travel from all over New England to surf the waves of a good nor'easter wave surge. The surf travels for miles across an unbroken stretch of ocean, stumbling only slightly over the shoals as they approach the shore. Yet the shoals only seem to heighten the oncoming waves' power and resolve. The waves build, sprout whitecaps atop their peaks, curl, build some more, and then race toward shore.

Don't be frightened if you are a beginner, for on most days the seas are relatively calm and ideal for getting caught up in the sport or for sampling the surfer lifestyle. There are a number of shops around the Cape that cater to the surfing crowd, and these can tell you where the surf is best and set you up with good equipment. Beware of a nasty undertow present at many of the outer beaches, and no matter the time of year, you'll want to pack a wet suit. The waters of the ocean-side of the Lower Cape can be quite chilly, even in mid-August, especially if you are in the surf bobbing on your board for hours on end.

Windsurfing, sometimes called sail-boarding, requires you to maneuver a sail that pivots 360 degrees on top of a rudderless board. It's more related to sailing than surfing and was accepted as an official Olympic sport in 1992. Several years ago the largest sailboarding regatta in the country was hosted by the Hyannis Yacht Club in coordination with the U.S. Windsurfing Organization and the International Mistral Class Organization. The calm waters that make the southern waters off Cape Cod poor for surfing combine, however, with steady winds to make for great windsurfing. Still the water can get choppy enough at times for experienced windsurfers to try some aerial maneuvers.

Considered to be one of the best places for sailboarding in the United States, and a past host of the national competitions, Kalmus Beach is well protected and has steady winds that usually blow 10 to 20 knots. Chapoquoit Beach on Buzzards Bay in Falmouth has also been the site of national competitions and is popular with advanced-intermediate to advanced windsurfers. Old Silver Beach on Buzzards Bay in North Falmouth and most of the Vineyard Sound shore are well suited to basic sailboarding skills. Other popular beaches where you can ply the waters include Chapin and Corporation Beaches in Dennis on Cape Cod Bay, and West Dennis Beach on Nantucket Sound. Pleasant Bay, with beach access in both Orleans and Chatham, provides a good mix of calm water and stiff breezes.

The following establishments sell and rent equipment or make repairs.

UPPER CAPE

Cape Cod Windsurfing
350 Quaker Road, North Falmouth
(508) 801-3329, (508) 457-7806
On beautiful Vineyard Sound this outfit rents watercraft such as kayaks, pedal boats, Sunfish, and sailboats. It also has windsurfing and sailboarding equipment and instruction available. The shop is located on Old Silver Beach at the Sea Crest Hotel.

MID-CAPE

Boarding House Surf Shop
302 Main Street, Hyannis
(508) 778-4080
This year-round Hyannis shop sells everything to do with the three sports of surfing, skateboarding, and snowboarding. They offer all the clothing and accessories you'll need as well as videos to help you learn the techniques, and also a repair service.

Sound Sailboards
223 Barnstable Road, Hyannis
(508) 771-3388
In business since 1988 Sound Sailboards sells boards and sails, masks, wet suits and hoods, and offers lessons and rentals. It is open from April through December, seven days a week.

LOWER CAPE

Monomoy Sail and Cycle
275 Route 28, Chatham
(508) 945-0811
Monomoy Sail and Cycle rents sailboards for use on Nantucket Sound and Pleasant Bay. Remember that although Pleasant Bay offers calm, delightful waters, Southern Pleasant Bay, in Chatham, is much rougher—and potentially dangerous.

Nauset Sports
Route 6A, Orleans
(508) 255-4742
www.nausetsports.com
This year-round shop rents and sells the latest in wet suits, boards (sail, surf, skim, and body), and essential windsurfing and surfing equipment.

The Pump House Surf Company
9 Cranberry Highway (Route 6A), Orleans
(508) 240-2226
Offering a complete line of surfboards as well as clothing, swimwear, and eyewear, the Pump House is an ideally located Lower Cape surf shop convenient to the Atlantic-side beaches. It provides a repair service, a surf report, and rentals, and also offers lessons. The Pump House is open weekends from early April to the end of May, stays open seven days a week from the end of May until October, and then reverts to weekend hours from October to December. It's closed January through March.

Jasper's Surf Shop
U.S. Route 6, Eastham
(508) 255-2662
Jasper's has a large selection of surf-boards and equipment and sells some sailboards, swimsuits, wet suits, and life-guard equipment. Repairs are done in the summer only. In the off-season, the shop takes mail orders via telephone.

Diving

Beach diving is popular on the Cape, especially at Corporation Beach in Dennis and Sandwich's Town Beach, which is considered safe and easy for divers because the current is light and the rocky bottom is interesting. Divers see plenty of striped bass, bluefish, tautog, flounder, sea robins, sea urchins, and starfish.

Several books about underwater exploration in the area are available, including three by Donald L. Ferris and Bill Dubiel: *Beneath the Waters of Cape Cod, Beneath the Waters of Massachusetts Bay,* and *Exploring the Waters of Cape Cod: Shipwrecks and Dive Sites,* which has information on 94 dive sites, complete with maps, photos, and Loran numbers.

The ocean beaches of the Lower Cape have more currents and shoals than the bay. This is the untamed Atlantic, and you have to exercise caution, especially when near the shore. The waters of the bayside Cape are calmer and warmer, and the warmest waters tend to be those of Nantucket and Vineyard Sounds. The visibility also tends to be better in Cape Cod Bay and on the southern sounds than in Buzzards Bay. Just as winds alter the landscape, currents cause underwater changes, so you should consult the staff at local dive shops for suitable areas and current conditions for diving.

Check with one of the following dive shops for instruction, information, or gear before entering the water.

UPPER CAPE

Aqua Center
2 Freezer Road, Sandwich
(508) 888-3444
www.aquacenter.com
Aqua Center is open year-round and has diving equipment, masks, snorkels, and fins. It also offers instruction and equipment rental.

There are around 365 freshwater ponds on Cape Cod. Most of them are kettle ponds. They were formed when ice blocks from glaciers created depressions in the land. These depressions were deep enough to reach the groundwater. Several fine kettle ponds are located within Cape Cod National Seashore.

MID-CAPE

Cape Cod Bay Charters
Barnstable Harbor, Mill Way (off Route 6A), Barnstable
(888) 488-3483
www.ccbcharters.com
Charter the *Lucky Lady* for an ocean dive out of Barnstable Harbor, where you can choose wreck or reef dives. Scallop and lobster dives are also popular (you must have a Massachusetts lobster license in order to take a lobster). Six certified divers are needed for each charter. Four-hour charters are $75 per diver, and up to eight-hour charters can be accommodated.

The Dive Locker
237 Falmouth Road, Hyannis
(508) 775-1185
www.capedivelocker.com
This store offers full scuba and snorkel gear rentals, swimming supplies, and scuba instruction classes and leads local dives and charters. Call ahead to reserve equipment or schedule a dive during the summer months. Open daily year-round.

Sea Sports
195 Ridgewood Avenue, Hyannis
(508) 790-1217
A full-service scuba-diving shop, Sea Sports caters to snorkeling and has "everything you need to go diving." Sea Sports organizes an informal dive club and night dives, and also has a full-service surf shop. The shop is open year-round.

FISHING 🎣

Cape Cod is one of the best places to fish along the East Coast. And it's no secret why: It has more than 360 freshwater ponds and sports a coastline loaded with jetties, inlets, tidal rivers, and flats. It lies just west of the very fertile Stellwagen Bank and is along the migratory route for stripers and blues moving from southern waters to the Gulf of Maine. In short it's a great place to catch fish.

Fishing has a rich history on the Cape, literally. The majority of the large homes and estates that line the main roads of the Cape almost certainly belonged at one time to fishing or whaling captains who prospered greatly from the sea. Of course it wasn't always an ocean of opportunity. Remember, the folks who arrived here in 1620 had crossed the ocean with the thought that they'd be farmers in what we now call Virginia. The crops yielded by the Cape's sandy soil were not as bountiful as these settlers has hoped, so they had to explore other ways to supplement their diet and provide a means of support. They soon realized that money could be made by venturing offshore to harvest fish from the sea.

Centuries later the Portuguese arrived here and added another layer to the Cape's fishing heritage. Provincetown, where many of the Portuguese settled, became a major fishing port during the 19th and early 20th centuries.

Though commercial fishing still exists, recreational fishing has grown to a point that it now rivals its commercial cousin, mainly because of the many restrictions placed on commercial fishing these days.

In this chapter we give you an overview of the sport, along with places to go and people to see to help make your fishing experiences memorable. A word of advice: Familiarize yourself with the many local regulations. The Massachusetts Division of Marine Fisheries (508-563–1779) can be reached Monday through Friday from 7:00 A.M. to 4:30 P.M. It can provide current information about species availability and regulatory restrictions, which often change.

Whether bait fishing or fly-fishing, you'll be in heaven on the Cape. Fly-fishing is especially attractive here, because of the Cape's geography. Saltwater anglers go after striped bass, blues, bonito, false albacore, Spanish mackerel, cod, and fluke, whereas freshwater anglers find trout, small- and large-mouth bass, and yellow perch.

Experienced fly-fishers head out at night to hook the big fish. This is because the bright shadows produced during the daylight spook the fish, heading them into deeper water. Casting at night is a bit tricky, but once you gather confidence and find the quiet solitude of the darkness comforting, you'll find that nighttime fishing increases your odds of landing the big one, heightens your awareness of your surroundings, and improves your daytime successes. No license is required for saltwater fishing. However, in order to fish in the freshwater ponds and lakes on Cape Cod, you'll need to purchase a license, which can be obtained from any town clerk and at many tackle shops around the Cape.

Shellfishing for mussels, clams, and quahogs is also quite popular around the Cape. Get a license and a clam rake or just a trowel and dig for your chowder. Types of shellfish available, regulations, and licensing fees vary from town to town. Contact the individual town for more information. Also, eels for family use or for bait, or seaworms for bait, are covered by local regulations, and permits are required.

To land the right fish, or any fish for that matter, you have to use the right bait. That's just one more reason to start your Cape fishing at a bait and tackle shop.

Local experts recommend that if you're fishing in waders, you should wear a personal flotation device and tell someone where you're going and when you expect to be back. When in the water shuffle and slide your feet to move your body. But always keep both feet on the ground. If your waders fill with water and you're wearing a personal flotation device, roll onto your back and paddle toward shore. Also carry a knife so that if you aren't wearing a personal flotation device, you can cut off the waders.

You may also want to consider a local guide. The sandy shores of the Cape change constantly, especially after a rough winter or during the later summer hurricane season, and an experienced guide will get you into the right place. See our recommendations later in this chapter.

FRESHWATER FISHING

The most popular freshwater fish on the Cape are trout and small- and large-mouth bass. More than 50 of our 360-plus ponds and lakes and a dozen streams give Cape Cod the reputation for top-notch freshwater angling. Bass, pickerel, white and yellow perch, brook, rainbow and brown trout, as well as other species, such as sunfish, catfish, and crappie, all grace our inland waters. Additionally about four dozen streams and ponds are stocked with trout each year. Stocking usually takes place in March, though ice fishers have been known to land some large leftovers from the previous year.

You can often get some good tips from the local bait and tackle shack. Even a friendly "hello!" to a fellow fisher on the shore will yield you some good Insiders' tips. Here's one that many take as doctrine: Fish near a herring run. As one old-timer puts it, "Where there's herring, there's bass," and probably a good deal of other

fish as well. Herring travel along herring runs from the ocean to lakes and ponds where they spawn, creating a fertile supply for the freshwater food chain. In early spring the fish start hopping as the water warms up. When it reaches 60 degrees or so, trout head for the deeper, cooler water, whereas bass like to stay in the warmer waters of our shallow estuaries. If you're fishing for trout at this time of year, you may find success with shiny lures and spinners, but live bait is often your best bet. Fly-fishers usually stick with dark muddlers and woolly buggers. During the summer you have to go deeper, and may find success with bait or imitation minnows. Trout are usually caught on cloudy days and prefer clear, moving water.

Bass, on the other hand, like to hide among the weedy sections of the waterways and like to stay in the warmer waters of our shallow estuaries. They do not travel in schools, so even when the water warms by late June, you'll find them a challenge to catch. You will probably have the most luck catching bass on overcast days. Your best bet is to fish with shiners, but bass have been known to go for a variety of lures. We mentioned that muddlers and woolly buggers are popular flies for trout fishing, and they are also popular with anglers fishing for bass as well. Smallmouth bass fishing is known to be great on the Cape. The best bets for bait are minnows, nightcrawlers, or even crayfish. The best time to catch smallmouth bass tends to be early morning. They don't feed much at night. Fly-fishers should consider sinking or weighted lines for these deep fish. Other popular freshwater species include perch, panfish, pike, and catfish. Generally these species lurk near weeds and rocks and go for live bait, such as nightcrawlers and minnows.

Remember, a license is required to fish the Cape's freshwater ponds, lakes, streams, and rivers. State fishing licenses may be obtained at town halls or at certain bait and tackle shops. Typically licenses are not required for children younger than 15. If you are a Massachusetts resident, the adult fee is $27.50; for residents 15 to 17, it's $11.50. The annual fee for nonresidents is $37.50; you can buy a three-day license for $23.50.

Freshwater Fishing Spots

UPPER CAPE

Flax Pond in Bourne is a good place to catch both bass and pickerel. This shallow pond with a maximum depth of 6 feet can be accessed from the northwest off Old County Road.

Lawrence Pond is Sandwich's largest pond at nearly 140 acres. It has a maximum depth of 27 feet and a boat ramp at the southeastern corner off Great Hill Road. Here you can fish for white perch, pickerel, and bass.

Peters Pond, Sandwich's second-largest body of water, is stocked with trout, though pickerel and white perch can also be found here. A boat ramp is at the extreme eastern shore off John Ewer Road. The depths of this pond exceed 50 feet.

Snake Pond in Sandwich is more than 30 feet deep. Bass and pickerel can be caught here. Access is from the south off Snake Pond Road.

Spectacle Pond in Sandwich is stocked with trout and is also home to numerous white perch, bass, and pickerel. Access can be made from the southwest shore off Pinkham Road. Two other Sandwich ponds stocked with trout are Pimlico Pond and Hoxie Pond. Scorton Creek is also stocked with trout, and you may also find some good-sized bass in it as well.

Deep Pond in Falmouth is a bit misleading as there are several deeper ponds in town. At a maximum depth of nearly 30 feet, the pond is stocked with trout. You can access the pond from the southwest off Sam Turner Road.

Grews Pond is another trout-stocked Falmouth pond. A boat ramp south of the pond provides access. Maximum depth is

35 feet. Childs River in Falmouth has been known to yield big trout.

Jenkins Pond, between Goodwill Park Road and Pumping Station Road in Falmouth, has a maximum depth of more than 50 feet and is home to bass, white perch, and pickerel. Much of this nearly 90-acre pond is more than 20 feet deep.

Ashumet Pond in Mashpee is stocked with trout and is also full of bass and pickerel. The pond has a maximum depth of 65 feet. Access can be found along the western shore off Currier Road in Falmouth.

Johns Pond in Mashpee achieves a maximum depth of 60 feet where stocked trout, pickerel, white perch, and bass swim. There is a boat ramp to the east off Hooppole Road providing access to this large body of water, more than 300 acres.

Mashpee Pond and Wakeby Pond in Mashpee are connected and, when combined, create a body of water of more than 700 acres. Mashpee Pond is the deeper of the two at nearly 90 feet. Both ponds are stocked with trout and also harbor bass, pickerel, and perch. Access Mashpee Pond at a boat ramp on its southern shoreline just north of Route 130.

MID-CAPE

Hamblin Pond in Marstons Mills is stocked with trout and also provides good bass and pickerel fishing. There is easy access from Route 149 by taking the road adjacent to the small cemetery.

Hathaway Pond in Barnstable is stocked with trout and has a maximum depth of nearly 60 feet. A boat ramp can be found on the southern shore off Phinney's Lane near the intersection of Route 132.

Lovells Pond in Marstons Mills is larger than 50 acres and is stocked with trout, as well as bass and pickerel. Access can be found along the southern shoreline off Newtown Road.

Shallow Pond in Barnstable lives up to its name—the maximum depth is less than 8 feet over its nearly 70 acres. This is mainly a pickerel pond. It sits between Route 132 and Huckins Neck Road.

i

Barnstable's 3,400-acre Great Marsh is home to snowy egrets, mute swans, oystercatchers, hawks, eider ducks, and much more. It's an excellent place for exploring by kayak. The guides at Great Marsh Kayak Tours will take you on a tour. Stop for a picnic, stake out prime bird-watching areas, or learn to fly-fish—by kayak. For more information call (508) 375-9000, or visit www.great marshkayaktours.com.

Wequaquet Lake, between Centerville and West Barnstable, is a huge lake by Cape Cod standards—650 acres—though its depth rarely exceeds 25 feet. This lake is stocked with northern pike and is also home to many bass, white perch, and plenty of pickerel. Access can be found along the northern shore off Shootflying Hill Road.

Dennis Pond in Yarmouthport is a great place to fish for pickerel and bass because it is a shallow pond that averages a depth of 10 feet. Access is along the east side off Summer Street.

Long Pond in South Yarmouth is stocked with trout. You can also catch bass, white perch and pickerel in this largely shallow pond with a maximum depth of 30 feet. There is a boat ramp on the south side of the pond north of the point where Route 28 and Wood Road intersect.

Fresh Pond in South Dennis is a shallow pond—about 5 feet deep—with access on its east side off Route 134. Pickerel can be caught here.

Scargo Lake in East Dennis achieves a maximum depth of about 50 feet over its 50-plus acres. The lake, which is stocked with trout, also has white perch and bass. Two access points can be found, one along the north side off Route 6A and another at the northeast corner off Scargo Hill Road.

LOWER CAPE

Cliff Pond in East Brewster is stocked with trout to swim in its nearly 200 acres. Access can be gained from the east off Nook Road and the west off Pond Road, both within Nickerson State Park. Nearby Little Cliff Pond is also trout-stocked.

Flax Pond in East Brewster is trout-stocked. It is more than 70 feet at its deepest point, and its waters are home to bass and pickerel. Access is from the northwest off Deer Park Road within Nickerson State Park.

Long Pond on the Brewster Harwich town line is very large, spanning nearly 750 acres. In some spots the waters exceed 50 feet in depth, with just more than 60 feet being its greatest depth. Here you'll find plenty of bass fishing, along with white perch and pickerel. Access is from the east off Route 137 and south off Long Pond Drive as well as from the north off Crowells Bog Road (east of Route 124).

Sheep Pond is a 150-acre Brewster pond stocked with trout. Bass and pickerel also swim in its depths, which exceed 60 feet. Access is from the southwest off Route 124 (take Fisherman's Landing Road).

Seymour Pond on the Brewster/ Harwich line has pickerel, bass, and white perch. It is about 180 acres in area and about 40 feet at its deepest point. It can be accessed from the east off Route 124.

Goose Pond in Chatham is trout-stocked. Access to this 50-foot-plus pond is gained from the north off Old Queen Anne Road to Carriage Drive.

Schoolhouse Pond in Chatham is a small 20-acre pond stocked with trout. Maximum depth is about 50 feet. Access can be gained from the northwest off Old Queen Anne Road.

Baker's Pond in Orleans is trout-stocked. A small pond at 28 acres, its maximum depth approaches 50 feet. Access is from the east off Bakers Pond Road.

Crystal Lake in Orleans has bass and pickerel along with stocked trout.

Access points can be found along the northwest off Route 28 and southeast off Monument Road.

Great Pond is Eastham's largest pond at 110 acres. Bass and pickerel can be caught here. Access is off Great Pond Road.

Herring Pond of Eastham reaches a maximum depth of about 35 feet. Its 40-plus acres are trout-stocked, and bass, white perch, and pickerel can also be found here. Access to the pond is from the southwest off Crosby Village Road.

Gull Pond in Wellfleet is stocked with trout, though you'll also catch bass, pickerel, and perch here. There is a boat ramp along the west side of the 100-plus-acre pond off Schoolhouse Hill Road. Maximum depth here exceeds 60 feet.

Long Pond in Wellfleet is like two ponds, the east side dropping to more than 30 feet and the west side going a bit deeper, more than 50 feet. Access to this bass and pickerel pond can be found along the northwest side off Long Pond Road.

Great Pond in Truro is a small trout-stocked pond that drops to greater than 35 feet in its center. There is access at the southwest tip just off U.S. Route 6.

Gull Pond, just off Gull Pond Road in Truro, has been known to yield some good-size trout and bass. The Pamet River is also stocked with trout each year.

Pilgrim Lake in North Truro, on the right of U.S. Route 6 just before entering Provincetown, is a bit deceiving for its size. Its total area is 350 acres, but its deepest waters are scarcely 6 or 7 feet. White perch and pickerel can be found here. Access is from the south off High Head Road.

SALTWATER FISHING

The entire Cape coastline is potential fishing ground. At any given hour on any given day during spring, summer, and fall, you are bound to find somebody casting from a jetty or dropping a line off a bridge. When the blues are running, the beaches are lined with surf casters hoping to snag a big one.

Today the most popular saltwater fish on the Cape is the striped bass, followed figuratively and literally by the bluefish. The bass usually first appear near Martha's Vineyard in mid-spring. A week or two later, they start showing up in the waters off the shores of the southern Upper Cape. The bluefish usually follow a week or two behind them. If you unroll a map of the East Coast, it becomes clear why the Cape shores are so fertile. Stripers follow the Gulf Stream as it pushes its way north in the spring. (The Gulf Stream is one reason the water on the southern side of the Cape seems like bathwater in mid-August and the water on the east side feels like ice water.) The stripers, the blues, and others traveling north for the summer come by Martha's Vineyard first and then head along the southern shore of the Upper Cape.

Once the water temperature reaches into the 70s, around July, the stripers head for cooler water, right up the eastern forearm of Cape Cod. Monomoy Island off Chatham proves to be a nice block for the stripers and blues trying to navigate the Cape's elbow. But beware: Fish aren't the only ones caught by Monomoy. The shifting sands in the area and shallow flats have been known to strand a few boaters as well. Once past Monomoy, it's a clear run up the Cape to Provincetown and then onto the Gulf of Maine. During the late summer and early fall, Cape Cod's National Seashore becomes one of the best places anywhere for a surf caster to land a large striped bass as they return after a summer of good feeding in northern waters.

Massachusetts does not require a license for recreational saltwater angling, which is considered to include fishing in all tidal waters of Cape Cod Bay, Nantucket Sound, and the Atlantic Ocean. There are limitations and restrictions on

Except for bluefin tuna, which require going to sea, striped bass, bluefish, flounder, and mackerel are all available from shoreline locations just about everywhere on Cape Cod. If you are looking for surf-casting locations in the Falmouth area, try Chapoquoit Beach off Chapoquoit Road in West Falmouth, or Nobska Point off Church Street in Woods Hole.

certain saltwater fish: minimum size, number of fish you can take in a day, and, in some cases, what month of the year you can take them. There are also rules on how you can catch a particular species.

For example there's a 30-inch minimum size for striped bass, and you can only take one a day. If you are after cod and haddock, you can only take a combination of 10 fish. On the other hand, bluefish have no minimum size requirement, and the possession limit is 10. (By the way, bluefish have very sharp teeth and literally attack when out of the water, so watch your fingers.) Regulations are known to change from year to year, so it's best to contact the Massachusetts Division of Marine Fisheries at (508) 563-1779 for the latest rules and regulations. Or visit a bait and tackle shop—they should be able to help out.

Below is a quick listing of some of the more popular coastal fishing locations from Bourne to Provincetown.

Saltwater Fishing Spots

UPPER CAPE

If you're in Bourne, try the pier at Shore Road in Pocasset or anywhere along the Cape Cod Canal.

In Sandwich the jetty at the Sandwich basin is a good spot, or else the jetty or pier at Scusset Beach, the jetty at Sand-

wich Beach, or along Scorton Creek off Route 6A.

Falmouth, with its long coastline and many finger inlets, has a lot of great locations, including the bridge at Green Pond and the jetties at Falmouth Harbor, Woods Hole, and Great Pond.

Mashpee Neck Road and South Cape Beach in Mashpee are also great spots, as is the jetty at Dead Neck.

MID-CAPE

In Barnstable, give Barnstable Harbor, Craigville Beach, and Sandy Neck Beach a try.

Bass Hole (Gray's Beach) in Yarmouthport is a wonderful spot to kill a couple of hours (even if the fish aren't biting). Other spots in the town of Yarmouth are Sea Gull Beach, the jetty at Bass River Beach, and the Bass River Bridge linking Yarmouth with neighboring Dennis.

Dennis has a number of hot spots, including jetties at Corporation Beach, Davis Beach, Cold Storage Beach, and Sesuit Neck Beach. Chapin Memorial Beach is also a good spot.

LOWER CAPE

Cast your line at Paine Creek and Point of Rocks in Brewster, or at Bridge Street, Harding Beach, or Nauset Beach in Chatham. Monomoy Island off Chatham is great for boat fishing or even wading in the flats, and another good spot nearby is South Beach near the Chatham break— both these areas are right on the path of stripers and blues. The mouth of Pleasant Bay has been known to be a hot spot to catch a variety of saltwater species, including an occasional flounder.

Rock Harbor in Orleans is a nice spot, and so is Nauset Beach.

When in Eastham take your rod over to Sunken Meadow Beach and First Encounter Beach on the bayside, and Coast Guard Beach and Nauset Light Beach on the oceanside.

Wellfleet's town pier is a popular fishing spot. Also in Wellfleet are Cahoon Hollow, Duck Harbor Road, and the jetty at Indian Neck.

Head of the Meadow Beach, Highland Light Beach, and the jetty at Corn Hill Beach in Truro are all spectacular spots.

In the fishing port of Provincetown, you can cast your line off historic MacMillan Wharf or at various spots along Provincetown's 3-mile long harbor beach.

SHELLFISHING

There's perhaps nothing more relaxing than an early morning's jaunt to the local shellfish beds to dig for tasty critters hiding in the mud flats. Oysters, quahogs, clams—the very thought of them makes our lips smack with images of a steaming bowl of chowder or a nice stuffed quahog. Yum!

Regarding all shellfish: You need to consult the local town hall for restrictions and permits. Regulations and minimum-size requirements can be a little confusing at first. The minimum size of a good oyster is one with a certain shell diameter (currently 3 inches), whereas a minimum quahog size is measured in shell thickness (1 inch). Conch is measured in shell width (2 inches), and sea scallops must meet a certain shell height (3 inches).

Each town has its own restrictions in terms of possession limits. You'll also want to find out which beds are open and which are closed and what types of shellfish are available for the taking. Contact the local town hall for local regulations and limits. (See the list of town halls in our Area Overview chapter.) We find that when the rules are followed, the chowder tastes a whole lot better!

SPORTFISHING CHARTERS

While shore fishing is a big attraction on Cape Cod, to get a shot at some of the bigger fish, namely tuna, you need to head to sea. It also helps to heed the guidance of someone that knows the area and current regulations.

Wellfleet is the top aquaculture town in the state, with more than 100 aquaculture operations in the harbor. They rent half-acre or larger plots of ocean bottom from the town to grow oysters, clams, and mussels. These plots are marked with yellow buoys and are not to be disturbed. Wellfleet also stocks and maintains an area for shellfishing by visitors. Ask for information when you buy your beach sticker.

That's why a fishing charter is a great idea—whether you're looking for a family activity or an afternoon of competitive fishing among friends, you'll be able to find a boat and captain to accommodate you and your party.

Most charters include bait and equipment and provide some kind of instruction for beginners. Some will also rent you a rod and reel for a nominal fee. However, most are not staffed to provide supervision for children, so if you're coming as a family, you'll need to be the one to help your young anglers handle their rods and reels (especially when the big ones start biting!).

You will also find that boats vary greatly in size. Most small-group charters take a maximum of six guests, and in several cases the captain will charge you the full rate even if there are less than six in your party, or he will at least try to pair you with other folks so that he has a full boat. The larger-party boats vary greatly in the number of people they can take. Larger boats generally are less expensive per person, but you don't get the individual attention you receive on a small charter. Depending on the boat's size, the number of passengers is set by Coast Guard regulations, and boat captains cannot bend the rules for you.

Most of the common game fish are found within an hour's ride from a Cape port. Many are found considerably closer, and, of these, some can be taken from skiff or shore. But whatever fish you wish

to chase, there are experienced charter skippers who can guide you. Below is a list of recommendations.

UPPER CAPE

Cool Running Charters
Falmouth Inner Harbor, Falmouth
(508) 457-9445
www.coolrunningcharters.com
Captain Dan Junker of the *Relentless II* is fully insured and U.S. Coast Guard licensed. From May to October, this 30-foot Blackwatch sportfisherman, fully equipped to handle any type of fishing, takes day trips to the waters off Nantucket, Martha's Vineyard, and the Elizabeth Islands. The catch usually ranges from tuna, marlin, bass, blues, bonito, and shark. The crew instructs new anglers in the fundamentals, and the per-hour charter price includes use of fishing gear for up to a maximum of six people. Passengers bring their own lunch.

Eastwind Sportfishing Charters
Falmouth Inner Harbor, Falmouth
(508) 420-3934
www.capecodstripers.com
Catching stripers is the *Eastwind's* specialty. According to Captain Mike Doak, "They are the most exciting and sought-after game fish in New England." The *Eastwind* is a 35-foot Sportfisherman and is fully equipped with Coast Guard–approved safety devices, state-of-the-art electronics, and top-of-the-line fishing tackle. Four-, six-, and eight-hour charters are available for up to six passengers at $100 per hour.

Lee Marie Sport Fishing
Falmouth Inner Harbor, Falmouth
(508) 548-9498
www.lee-marie.com
Do you enjoy sportfishing but not the cramped quarters on small boat charters? Try Lee Marie Sport Fishing. For the past 20 years, Don Oliver has been bringing fishing enthusiasts to the bass, blues, and bonito in the waters off the South Cape and islands. His 31-foot boat,

complete with living quarters, won't leave you feeling confined. Don can take a maximum of six people on four- or six-hour charters, depending on how much fishing you want to do.

Patriot Boats
Falmouth Inner Harbor, Falmouth
(508) 548-2626, (800) 734-0088
www.patriotpartyboats.com
These family-owned and -operated boats depart from the entrance of Falmouth Harbor for half- or full-day deep-sea fishing trips with bait and tackle included. The fleet includes three party boats, the *Minuteman,* the *Doughboy,* and the *Patriot II.* These boats take anywhere from 36 to 49 passengers. There is plenty of room, outside seating, and a snack bar. The fare for adults is $30 per half-day, $45 all day. The fare for children 12 and younger is $20 per half-day and $30 all day. Or you may want to book a Patriot Boats charter, which takes up to six people. Services include water-taxi service and excursions on board the *Liberté,* a replica of a 1750s pinky schooner.

MID-CAPE

Barnstable Harbor Charter Fleet
Barnstable Harbor, Barnstable
(508) 362-3908
The Barnstable Harbor Charter Fleet offers four-, six-, and eight-hour fishing trips. The charter captains are U.S. Coast Guard licensed and will take groups of six on tours for tuna, bass, blues, and shark. The fleet also pairs smaller groups into groups of six to help spread the cost. All bait and equipment are provided, and the fleet runs charters for roughly $100 per hour from the end of April to mid-October.

Hy-Line Fishing Trips
Ocean Street Docks, Hyannis
(508) 778-2600
www.hy-linecruises.com
Hy-Line offers a variety of fishing trips that leave throughout the day. Within a 45-minute cruise into Nantucket Sound,

Returning to port after a day of fishing on Nantucket Sound. ERICA BOLLERUD

you will find yourself in one of the best areas on the East Coast for bottom fishing. This is your chance at the scup (porgy), fluke, and tautog found in these waters. Vessels are equipped with fish-finding electronics, and though they can't guarantee you a catch, we will assure you that it's fun for the whole family. Half-day trips leave three times a day and cost $23 for adults and $18 for children 12 and younger. A rod-rental fee is $2.00. All-day trips cost $40 for adults and $30 for children.

Hy-Line also offers blue fishing with each trip 4½ hours in length. This is the most-talked-about fishing trip on the docks, probably because bluefish are the strongest fighting fish found in these waters. The trip costs $30 per person.

Bluefish Sportfishing Charter
Sesuit Harbor, Dennis
(508) 385-7265
www.sunsol.com/bluefish

Sailing aboard the 37-foot custom-built sportfisherman *Bluefish* provides you plenty of room, especially in the larger comfortable salon. This makes it ideal for family fishing trips. Captain George Mabee is a Coast Guard licensed captain, with more than 25 years experience on these waters. He provides all the fishing equipment, some foul-weather gear, and will clean and package all the fish you catch. The rate for one to six persons for four hours is $410. Each additional hour is $40 per hour.

LOWER CAPE

Golden Eagle
Wychmere Harbor, Harbor Road, Harwich
(508) 432-5611
Once a day during weekdays and twice on weekends, Captain Paul Donovan takes the *Golden Eagle* into the waters of Nantucket Sound on expeditions for scup, sea bass, and tautog. The 42-foot boat holds 33 anglers and leaves at 8:00 A.M. and

returns at 2:00 P.M. weekdays. The cost of this six-hour charter is $35 for adults and $25 for those younger than 12 year. On the weekends Captain Paul runs two four-hour charters at 8:00 A.M. and again at 12:30 P.M. The cost is $26 for adults and $22 for children. Cash and traveler's checks are accepted, no credit cards. Fish-cleaning service is available, and the Golden Hook Award is given for the largest fish caught each trip. The *Golden Eagle* operates from mid-May to mid-October.

The *Banshee*
Stage Harbor Marina, Bridge Street, Chatham
(508) 945-0403

The *Banshee* is owned and operated by Captain Ron McVickar, who has more than 40 years of fishing experience, 30 of them doing charters. The 32-foot *Banshee* takes groups of six after striped bass, bluefish, and the occasional bonito. A four- to five-hour charter costs $500, a six-hour charter costs $600, and an eight-hour charter costs $675. McVickar specializes in light tackle, with no line heavier than 30-pound test. The *Banshee* operates from May to early November.

The *Booby Hatch* Fishing Charter
Stage Harbor Marina, Chatham
(508) 430-2312
www.capecodfishingcharters.com

Captain Bob Miller has more than 20 years experience fishing the waters around Chatham and Nantucket. He is very patient with novice anglers and can challenge the expert. He fishes all year round, so he knows what is happening and where to go. His boat, *The Booby Hatch*, is a fully-equipped and comfortable sportfishing boat. It is able to accommodate a six-person charter easily.

Rock Harbor Charter Fleet
Rock Harbor, Rock Harbor Road, Orleans
(508) 255-9757, (800) 287-1771
(Massachusetts only)

With its 18 boats, Rock Harbor is home to one of the Cape's largest charter fleets. Ranging in size from 35 to 42 feet, each boat can take parties of six. They will also pair smaller groups into six to help spread the cost. From mid-May through mid-October, U.S. Coast Guard–licensed captains offer four- and eight-hour bluefish and striped bass fishing expeditions.

The *Naviator*
Town Pier, Wellfleet
(508) 349-6003
www.naviator.com

Some say the star of the *Naviator* is its captain, Rick Merrill, a 32-year veteran of Cape Cod waters. Others say it's the 60-foot, 49-passenger boat herself. Four-hour fishing trips leave Wellfleet from late June through Labor Day twice a day at 8:00 A.M. and 1:30 P.M. The *Naviator* departs on weekends only in May and offers one trip daily during June and September. In conjunction with the Massachusetts Audubon Society, the *Naviator* also hosts cruises to view seals and seabirds from Columbus Day until December. Call Wellfleet Bay Audubon at (508) 349-6003 for reservations on a Marine Life Cruise.

FISHING GUIDES

For a true Cape Cod fishing experience, enlist an expert to show you how it's done. Inquire at local bait and tackle shops for the names and numbers of guides who know the waters well. Guides provide the expertise and the equipment needed for fly- or spin-fishing for striped bass and bluefish, as well as other species such as tautog, fluke, mackerel, scup, cod, shark, and tuna. Call ahead to schedule your outing. Prices depend on the length of the season. Most guides will take only one or two people, and often it is the same price regardless of whether you are alone or with a friend. It's great fun. A guide will certainly increase the odds of your getting a fish—and a few good fish tales to take back home.

Fishing the Cape
Harwich Commons, Routes 137 and 39, East Harwich
(508) 432-1200, (800) 235-9763
www.fishingthecape.com
Learn saltwater fly-fishing from Orvis-trained guides. Two-and-a-half-day courses are offered May through August for $490 per person (including lunch, bait, and the use of equipment). Lessons include distance casting, saltwater fly selection, big-game knots, leader rigging, fish feeding habits, "reading the surf," and safe wading practices. This outfit also employs ten Orvis-endorsed fishing guides who lead flats-fishing, rip-fishing, and wading trips mostly in the Monomoy Flats area.

BAIT AND TACKLE SHOPS

If you're ready to go after the big ones, you'll want to first stop at one of the following bait and tackle shops to stock up on the tools of the trade. From rods and crawlers to lures and reels, you're certain to find what you need. Besides, there's nothing like a bucket of slippery eels to get your fishing day off to a good start! You'll also want to get your hands on a current tide chart, and these are generally available free or for a nominal price at bait and tackle shops.

UPPER CAPE

Red Top Sporting Goods
265 Main Street, Buzzards Bay
(508) 759-3371
With the Cape Cod Canal at its doorstep, this shop is just a few steps from one of the richest sources of saltwater fish—striped bass, bluefish, flounder, tautog, and mackerel—in the region. This year-round shop (hours are limited in winter)

sells fishing tackle and other outdoor gear. It also handles fishing licenses and has tide charts. Ask for the staff's advice on what's biting.

Sandwich Ship Supply
68 Tupper Road, Sandwich
(508) 888-0200
This shop carries an extensive line of equipment, bait and tackle, safety gear, flags, clothing, maps, anchors, chains, ropes, and other nautical necessities.

Eastman's Sport & Tackle
387 Main Street, Falmouth
(508) 548-6900
www.eastmanstackle.com
Open year-round, this large Upper Cape shop carries all types of fresh- and saltwater fishing tackle, including extensive fly-fishing gear. At Eastman's you can obtain Massachusetts, New Hampshire, and Maine fishing licenses, as well as clamming equipment and tide charts.

MID-CAPE

Sports Port
149 West Main Street, Hyannis
(508) 775-3096
One of the Cape's oldest tackle shops still run by its original owners, Sports Port sells all salt- and freshwater tackle as well as shell-fishing gear and fly-tying equipment. Along with live bait for both fresh and salt water, the Sports Port will also offer you fishing information so you'll know what's biting where. This shop is open year-round.

Riverview Bait & Tackle
1273 Route 28, South Yarmouth
(508) 394-1036
This store, just a half-mile west of Bass River, sells offshore tackle, bait, custom rods and reels, nautical charts, and fly-fishing supplies. It also rents equipment and offers rod and reel repair. It's open year-round.

Truman's
608 Main Street, West Yarmouth
(508) 771-3470

Open year-round, Truman's supplies fishing tackle, fly-fishing equipment, shellfishing gear, and provides rod and reel repair. Also available are live bait, tide charts, and fishing licenses.

Bass River Bait & Tackle
42 Route 28, West Dennis
(508) 394-8666

Bass River sells rods and reels, bait, fishing licenses, and a full line of supplies for freshwater and saltwater fishing. It also rents rods and reels. The shop is open year-round.

LOWER CAPE

Fishing the Cape
Harwich Commons, Routes 137 and 39, East Harwich
(508) 432-1200, (800) 235-9763
www.fishingthecape.com

An Orvis fly-fishing shop that is open year-round, Fishing the Cape has all the accessories for both saltwater and freshwater fly-fishing and is a complete outfitter, providing local fishing guides and arranging freshwater and saltwater fishing trips. Tide charts are also available.

The big feature here is the Orvis Fly Fishing School, which offers two-day sessions every weekend between May and August. Class size averages about 16 students for each session. Call for more information.

Goose Hummock Shop
Route 6A, Orleans
(508) 255-0455
www.goose.com

For almost 60 years, Goose Hummock has been catering to the needs of Lower Cape anglers. This shop carries a full line of fishing equipment, including a newly expanded line of major brands of fly-fishing equipment, outdoor clothing, hunting and hiking gear, canoes, and kayaks. Goose Hummock is open year-round, offer fishing licenses, and has an extensive inventory in both sales and rentals. The tide charts and advice are free. Goose Hummock fishing guides conduct trips of three hours and longer.

GOLF 🏌

Cape Cod's top-rated golf courses attract many visitors. Long recognized for its quaint charm, glorious beaches, and superb dining, the Cape today is also known as a golfer's paradise, offering some of the most scenic and diverse layouts found anywhere in the United States. *Golf Digest* magazine ranks Cape Cod as one of the top 10 areas in the country for good, affordable public golf courses. And this is no wonder, considering that there are no less than 46 courses scattered around this scenic peninsula and its neighboring islands.

A marvelous blend of championship courses, rugged links, and beginner-friendly layouts makes the Cape a great golf destination. In fact only Florida, California, and Myrtle Beach, South Carolina, have more golf courses per capita than Cape Cod. Additionally golfers on the Cape can enjoy their sport in any season. The weather here—warm ocean temperatures moderate the climate—keeps many golf courses open all year.

The majority of the Cape's courses are located between the Cape Cod Canal and Brewster. Once you venture past Brewster, you will find only nine-hole offerings. These are on the Cape's elbow: Chatham's Seaside Links, the course at Wellfleet's Chequessett Yacht and Country Club, and Truro's Highland Links. These short courses are great stops for families and beginners searching more for scenery than forced carries over water hazards, and all three of these nine-hole courses offer spectacular ocean views, especially Highland Links.

You'll encounter a full variety of conditions and hazards on the Cape. From the wide fairways of Falmouth Country Club to the tree-lined routing of Dennis Pines, and from the 64 pot bunkers of Ocean

Edge to the postage stamp greens of Bass River Golf Course, golf course architects seem to have thrown a bit of everything at the golfer. Water hazards may include Vineyard Sound, Bass River, or even the Atlantic Ocean. A hook may land you in a conservation area; a slice may send you into a pine forest. Of course the most prevalent hazard on the Cape is the wind. What might play as a seven-iron one day turns into a two-iron with a shift of the wind.

On paper the back tees at Falmouth's Ballymeade Country Club appear to be the toughest public layout on the cape, but most local players consider New Seabury's Ocean Course the Cape's best challenge, in part because of the ocean wind on its back nine. Other courses that will satisfy golf masochists include Bayberry Hills, Quashnet Valley Country Club, Cranberry Valley, Dennis Pines, Ocean Edges, and the Captains' Course. All these tracts have USGA slopes of about 130 from the back tees. (The slope system reflects a course's difficulty, measuring from 55 for the easiest to 155 for the hardest, with a course of average difficulty scoring 113.) Most beginners and casual players won't want to venture too far into the 120s. But that's the beauty of Cape courses—they all offer tees of varying lengths and slope ratings. In many cases there are more than 1,200 yards (not to mention several slope rating points) difference between the front and back tees at these top-ranked tracts. No matter what your ability might be, both you and your playing partners can enjoy the same course.

The Cape's golf landscape varies greatly from course to course. From the manicured look of Ocean Edge to the unkempt and unirrigated cliff-top venue of Truro's Highland Links, the Cape golfer can experience a wide spectrum of conditions. You can play a different course every day and never face the same shot twice.

The best season for Cape golf is the fall when the crowds have cleared, leaving open tee times and uncrowded courses. Many layouts drop their rates after the summer season, and the temperatures dip to a more comfortable 60- to 70-degree range after the heat of summer. New England golfers also recognize that fall is the prime time for course conditions as the turf springs back from the summer traffic. And don't forget the foliage, too—inland courses, such as the Quashnet Valley Country Club, burst into color in mid- to late October.

Several golf course architects, including the renowned Donald Ross, have left their marks on the Cape, but Geoffrey Cornish and his partner Brian Silva dominate the list of designers. Even though this duo, as individuals or as a team, are responsible for eight of the Cape's layouts—including that of the exclusive Cape Cod National Golf Club (find out how to get a tee time in our golf vacation Close-up)—there has been no cookie-cutter approach here.

State and national amateur and professional championships, as well as regional tournaments, are held on Cape Cod. Mashpee's Willowbend Country Club, a private course, sponsors the annual Children's Charity Pro-Am, attracting such pros as Greg Norman, Tom Watson, Brad Faxon, Nick Faldo, and Annika Sorenstam (see our Annual Events and Sports and Recreation chapters for more details on the event).

Although the Cape might not enjoy the same reputation as the West Coast or the South, it nonetheless has made its mark on the golf world. Cape Codders Paul Harney, Carri Wood, Sally Quinlan, Jim Hallet, and John Curley have all played on the professional tours. The Cape is also home to some great local golf schools. The best time to take advantage of these packages is in the shoulder season, especially in the spring, when the courses and resorts are looking for business and you'll be looking to get your game in shape.

Driving ranges can be found at about half the Cape's courses and at dedicated facilities such as the Longest Drive in Dennis or T-Time in Eastham (see individual Driving Range listings in this chapter). Town-owned courses such as Cranberry Valley in Harwich and Bass River and Bayberry Hills in Yarmouth offer relatively inexpensive memberships to town residents, and many courses feature free or inexpensive golf clinics during the summer. Nearly all of the courses charge reduced greens fees if you sign up for a "twilight" tee time (after 2:00, 3:00, or 4:00 P.M., depending on the course).

And if you yearn for a view of the first tee from your own backyard, the Cape is home to several golfing communities where luxury homes and condominiums line the fairways and greens (see our Relocation chapter).

Since its beginnings more than a century ago on the oceanside links of Truro, the game of golf on Cape Cod and the islands has become a way of life for most Cape Codders. No longer a game just for the country-club wealthy, golf is for everyone and the nearest thing on the Cape to a year-round sport. In the sections that follow, we describe some of the cape's best golf courses open to the public. Most of the courses are available for year-round play, and each offers full pro shops and lessons. Make sure that you plan ahead, though. In-season tee times can be a rare commodity, and many golf courses only take tee times a few days in advance. But if you are willing to prepay, several courses will take tee times many months ahead.

One thing we can't overlook: Though we have done our best to give you the most up-to-date greens fees for 18 holes, 9 holes, and the charge for a cart, fees are subject to change. We advise you to confirm the fee when making the reservation.

Enjoy yourself, and never forget the fundamental rule of a golf vacation—a lousy day of golf is always better than a great day at work!

COURSES

Upper Cape

Holly Ridge Golf Club
121 Country Club Road, South Sandwich
(508) 428-5577
www.hollyridgegolf.com

Set within a residential community on some 90 acres, Holly Ridge is an 18-hole, 2,952-yard, par 54 public course designed by Geoffrey Cornish. The signature hole here is the seventh, which has a pond to avoid on your tee shot. The course has a driving range, practice green, carts, and pro shop as well as a restaurant and lounge (the Holly Ridge Grille). Holly Ridge is open year-round and offers an extensive lessons program. Reservations are accepted up to seven days in advance for tee times. Greens fees are $29 for 18 holes, $28 for 9. After 3:30 P.M. the fee drops to $18 for 18 holes. Carts are $10.00 per person per 18 holes, $6.00 per person per 9 holes, and $3.50 for pull carts.

Sandwich Hollows Golf Club
One Round Hill Road, East Sandwich
(508) 888-3384
www.sandwichhollows.com

Owned and operated by the town of Sandwich, the club offers an 18-hole, par 71 course that reaches 6,190 yards and a slope of 124 from the back tees. The 120-acre setting features views of Cape Cod Bay, and facilities also include a new driving range with more than an acre's worth of teeing area, two practice greens, a clubhouse, and pro shop. The 420-yard, par 4 ninth hole forces you to hit into the prevailing wind to an elevated green. It's not such a bad idea to ride rather than walk around this hilly course (formed of hollows left by the receding glacier). You can reserve a tee time by calling in advance. The course is open year-round.

Off-season weekday greens fees are $30 (including cart) for 18 holes. On weekdays in season residents pay $30, and nonresidents pay $35. Off-season weekend fees are $30 (including cart) for 18 holes. On weekends in season residents pay $38, and nonresidents pay $44. Golf-cart fees, when not included, are $15 for 18 holes.

Ballymeade Country Club & Estates
125 Falmouth Woods Road, North Falmouth
(508) 540-4005
www.ballymeade.com

Ballymeade opened in 1987 and immediately became known as one of the toughest layouts on the Cape. This semiprivate 18-hole course plays to a 139 slope of more than 6,900 yards from its back tees. Ballymeade is obviously not a beginner's course, but the front tees do knock the course down to size for most high- and mid-handicappers. Ballymeade has hilly, rocky terrain, and narrow, tree-lined fairways. The panoramic views are stunning, especially from the par 3 11th hole, which is one of the highest points on Cape Cod and offers fantastic views of Buzzards Bay.

Ballymeade is a spikeless course. Reservations for tee times can be made up to seven days in advance, and groups of 16 or more can book up to a year in advance. Greens fees in the summer, including mandatory carts, are $85 weekends and $70 weekdays. Off-season fees drop. The course is open year-round and has a driving range and a putting green complete with a bunker so you can practice those pesky sand shots. Ballymeade also has PGA teaching pros and a fully stocked pro shop.

CLOSE-UP

Planning Your Cape Crusade

So how do you get the best Cape golf for your buck? First, plan ahead. Whether you are on a tight budget or you're looking to pamper your golf ego, in-season tee times are a tough commodity. As such many courses only take tee times a few days in advance, but if you are willing to prepay, several courses will take tee times many months ahead

To help you plan your Cape vacation, we've constructed a sample itinerary for every budget.

The Deluxe Package: You can spend as much on greens fees at you would on a weeklong rental with this package. There are three golf resorts on Cape Cod: New Seabury, Ocean Edge, and Cape Cod National Golf Club at the Wequassett Inn. All three offer great golf. New Seabury could be a two-nighter for you. As Mashpee is one of the first stops on the Cape, it only makes sense to play here first. Open your vacation with the Dunes Course, a rigorous layout that will help you shake off the rust. The next day attack the Ocean Course, one of the toughest on the Cape. That night move to the Ocean Edge Resort in Brewster. The following morning play on one of the best-maintained courses on the Cape and have fun trying to avoid the 64 treacherous pot bunkers throughout the course. Next move into your accommodations at the Wequassett Inn.

Now, even Cape regulars will be a little baffled to hear Wequassett has a course. Well, it does: The exclusive Cape Cod National Golf Club offers what is expected to become a landmark layout. Let's put it this way: The cart paths here put Boston's central artery project to shame; you can just imagine the quality of the rest of the course. Here's the Insider scoop: Wequassett has access to a limited number of tee times at Cape Cod National for its guests. This may be the most expensive greens fee you'll face on the Cape, but this club is first class all the way. While in the Brewster-Harwich area, be sure to tag on a trip to the Captains' in Brewster. For a casual cool-down, make the drive to Wellfleet and Truro to play Chequessett and Highland Links. These are expensive nine-hole courses, but they offer a view and charm that make Cape golf unique.

Cape Cod Country Club
Theatre Drive and Route 151, North Falmouth
(508) 563-9842
www.capecodcountryclub.com
The big question at Cape Cod Country Club is: Who actually designed this beautiful course? Originally designed by Devereaux

Emmet and Al Tull, designers of the posh Wee Burn Country Club in Connecticut, as well as the Congressional Country Club outside Washington, D.C., the course is rumored to have been redesigned by noted architect Donald Ross; however, no one can prove this rumor. Meanwhile this course sets up for everyone, good players and begin-

The Priced-Right Package: Most Cape golf vacations are built around one of six public courses: Ballymeade, Bayberry Hills, Quashnet Valley, Cranberry Valley, Dennis Pines, and Captains'. These are some of the most challenging courses on the Cape, and they don't require the expense of a resort stay to guarantee a tee time. Still, they aren't cheap; expect to spend $45 to $100 on greens fees alone. However, you can't go wrong at any of these courses. Beginners will want to avoid Ballymeade, and Quashnet Valley is a water-hazard haven. A good supporting cast for this package includes Hyannis Golf Club, Dennis Highlands, Falmouth Country Club, and Cape Cod Country Club. To balance the load on your wallet, try a few late-afternoon rounds, as many of these courses offer a discount after 3:00 or 4:00 P.M. If you play in the shoulder season of spring or fall, you can squeeze in an affordable round at New Seabury's Ocean Course, too. For an inexpensive warm-up or cool-down, pencil in Cotuit High Ground Golf Course, right around the corner from New Seabury.

On the Cheap: Some of the best deals going are the weekday twilight rates at Holly Ridge ($18 after 3:30 P.M. for 18 holes) and Twin Brooks ($20 after 4:00 P.M. for 18 holes). With a little luck you can make 18 holes. If you seek a kinder course that is gentler on your wallet, the smaller venues offer some great deals. At $17 for 9 and $28 for 18, Chatham Seaside Links is one of the most affordable deals around. Make Chatham your weekend warm-up and then hit the afternoon deals during the weekdays. Cotuit High Ground is also priced right, making it a great stop for those who just want to take a few swings in a relaxed Cape atmosphere. If you hope to play a lot of golf, consider staying in the Mid-Cape area. Past Brewster courses are hard to come by, and the traffic may be too much if you try to make it out to Brewster from Falmouth. Tee times are difficult to come by; you wouldn't want to miss one.

The beauty of a Cape golf vacation is its diversity. Off-season rates make most courses affordable for any budget, and in season, you can always find something that will fit your wallet and your golf ego. Enjoy yourself, and never forget the fundamental rule of a golf vacation: A lousy day of golf is always better than a great day at work!

ners alike. From the tips this par 71 course measures a moderate 6,400 yards with a slope of 120. There are several elevated greens on this layout, including the par 4 14th hole, where you'll feel like you're trying to land your approach on a mountaintop. A few feet left or right turns into several yards with a kick off the side of the hill. Cape Cod Country Club offers rental carts and equipment, a pro shop, and lunch counter. There is a practice green, and lessons are available. Fees are $41 on weekdays and $55 on weekends for 18 holes. After 3:00 P.M. rates go down. Carts are $14 per person. Tee times are taken up to a week in advance. The course is open year-round.

Falmouth Country Club
630 Carriage Shop Road, East Falmouth
(508) 548-3211
www.falmouthcountryclub.com
Falmouth Country Club is a 6,535-yard, par 72, 18-hole course. It is open year-round and features a beautiful par 4 fourth hole with a pond guarding the front of the green. The course itself is wide open without many trees and is relatively flat, making it perfect for walkers and beginners, who may want to start on the separate nine-hole, par 37 course. It also has a nice practice range, putting green, and pro shop and offers rental equipment and carts. Greens fees are $35 Monday to Friday, and $50 on weekends for 18 holes. Golf carts rent for $15. Greens fees for nine holes is $25.00 daily and $8.00 per person per cart. Tee time reservations can be made up to seven days in advance.

Paul Harney's Golf Club
74 Club Valley Drive (off Route 151),
East Falmouth
(508) 563-3454
www.paulharneysgolfcourse.homestead.com
Owned and operated by former PGA pro Paul Harney, this 18-hole executive course offers outstanding play with five par 4 holes and 13 par 3s, totaling some 3,600 yards (par 59 if you're counting). The 16th hole is a par 3 with an elevated tee and a pond protecting the green about 230 yards from the tee. Those who frequently play this course note that if you stray, you'll end up in the trees. There are plenty of ways to get into trouble here, so you'll want to hit your shots long and straight. Greens fees are $30, possibly up to $35 on Saturday and Sunday. Carts are $12. Weekends are busy, and the course does not take reservations; still, it's a good idea to call ahead to see how long the wait might be. This course is open year-round and has a practice green to putt on while you wait for your tee time.

Woodbriar Golf Club
339 Gifford Street, Falmouth
(508) 495-5500
Woodbriar is an attractive nine-hole public course that is open year-round and features lots of water. For 18 the course plays to a par 56 of about 2,600 yards. The longest hole, and only par 4 , is the 215-yard fifth hole, which has a stream to cross. Greens fees are very reasonable at $20 for 18 holes in season, $15 for 18 holes in the off-season. It has a practice green and offers food and drink inside the clubhouse. The scenic course is situated right next to the Coonamesset Inn (see our Restaurants chapter). Tee times are on a first-come, first-served basis.

Quashnet Valley Country Club
309 Old Barnstable Road, Mashpee
(800) 433-8633
www.quashnetvalley.com
Be sure to pack plenty of golf balls when you play Quashnet Valley. Water hazards in the way of rivers, cranberry bogs, and even wetlands come into play on 15 of Quashnet Valley's 18 holes. Set among picturesque bogs, this semiprivate par 72 plays 6,600 yards from the back tees to a slope of 132. The course is a nature-lover's bounty but can be a hacker's nightmare. If you play conservatively around the water hazards, you'll find smooth sailing on large greens and wide fairways. The sixth is a particularly demanding, 430-yard par 4 that calls for your best drive and approach to a two-tiered elevated green with water on the right and woods on the left. The facilities include a pro shop, driving range, carts, and a practice green. Carts are $15 for 18 holes and required on weekends from 9:30 A.M. to 2:30 P.M. Greens fees are $35 Monday through Thursday for 18 holes, $18 for 9 holes; and on Friday $45 for 18 and $23 for 9 holes. Saturday, Sunday, and holidays it's $60 for 18 holes and $30 for 9 holes. There is also a twilight fee. The course is open year-round. Tee times are taken up to a week in advance.

New Seabury Cape Cod
Off Great Neck Road South, New
Seabury (Mashpee)
(508) 539–8322
www.newseabury.com

New Seabury is distinguished by its two top-notch courses: the renowned Ocean Course overlooking Vineyard Sound and the recently revamped Dunes Course. The Ocean Course (formerly known as the Blue Course) has long been considered one of the top 100 golf courses in the United States, earning the nickname "Pebble Beach of the East." Why? Let's look at the numbers: 7,131 yards from the tips, a slope of 133, and a course rating of 75.7 for the par 72. And many think that the course plays even harder than those numbers. Not content to rest on past accolades, the course recently received a tweaking at the hands of architect Marvin Armstrong. The gorgeous front nine treats golfers to increasingly beautiful ocean views—and an invigorating ocean wind—as they play.

The Ocean's sister course, the Dunes, was entirely redesigned in 2001 by Mr. Armstrong. Thanks to its 18 revamped holes, it can no longer be regarded as the Ocean's more boring sister. Once known as the Green Course, 300 yards have been added, making this par 70 course 6,340 yards from the tips. It also gained two additional ponds, numerous strategically placed bunkers, and more waste areas than you will find on any other New England course.

New Seabury charges different greens fees per course, so we recommend that you check greens fees when making your reservation. The Dunes Course is open to the general public year-round, whereas the Ocean Course is only open to the general public from mid-October through mid-June (though guests staying at the New Seabury Resort may play there at any time during their stay). In season at the Dunes Course, greens fees are $70 on weekdays and $80 on weekends (Friday through Sunday), which includes the cart rental fee.

The twilight rate is $50, which starts after 3:00 P.M. during the summer season. Tee-time reservations are taken two days in advance from the general public.

Mid-Cape

Cotuit High Ground Golf Course
Crockers Neck Road, Cotuit
(508) 428–9863

If you're looking for an inexpensive round of golf, then throw your clubs in the car and head for then Cotuit High Grounds. It's been owned and operated by the same family for 50 years and is a great place to introduce kids to the game. Greens fees are $15 (and just $10 after 4:00 P.M.). Seniors and juniors pay less than $10. This is a semiprivate, nine-hole, par 28 course. The 2,580-yard layout is known for its small greens and narrow fairways. On the par 3 fifth hole, you'll need to make sure your drive clears the swamp, otherwise you'll be knee-deep in trouble. Open year-round, reservations are not required during the week; for a weekend tee time, plan on calling ahead during the week. A putting green and small pro shop are available, as well as pull carts and three or four riding carts. Individual memberships are available for $350.

Olde Barnstable Fairgrounds Golf Course
1460 Route 149, Marstons Mills
(508) 420–1141, (508) 420–1143
www.obfgolf.com

Opened in 1992, this par 71 plays to 6,503 yards and a slope of 123 from the tips. This is a generally flat course with difficult par 5s and tricky contoured greens. The 18th hole is a par 5 with a big holly tree in the middle that comes into play as you consider your second shot. Facilities include a fully stocked pro shop, a huge practice ranges, and putting green. Pull and motorized carts and rental clubs are available. Another nice feature is a full-service restaurant (Fairways Restaurant)

The game of golf has become a way of life for many Cape Codders. HYANNIS AREA CHAMBER OF
COMMERCE

where you can sit on the deck and watch biplanes and gliders take off and land at the small Cape Cod Airport across the street. The in-season fees are $40 for residents, $50 for nonresidents Monday through Thursday; $60 Friday through Sunday. Twilight play is $30. Carts are $15 per person for 18 holes, $10 per person for 9 holes. Olde Barnstable Fairgrounds is open year-round, and reservations can be made anytime after January 1 for the calendar year if you plan on paying in advance; otherwise, you can call up to two days in advance.

Hyannis Golf Club
Route 132, Hyannis
(508) 362-2606
www.hyannisgc.com

Hyannis Golf club plays to a 6,700-yard par 71 from its back tees, but wide fairways keep this course from turning into a monster. The second hole, a 420-yard par 4, is a local favorite that features a marsh before the elevated tee. (The marsh is particularly beautiful in autumn.) This fine course hosts the Cape Cod Open and the Cape Cod Senior Open, two of the major golfing events on the Cape. Amenities include a golf school, full pro shop, driving range, two putting greens, rental carts, and equipment. In-season greens fees range from $50 on weekdays to $60 on weekends, and carts are $16 for 18 holes. Reservations, which are accepted anytime, are recommended in the summer. On-site is the Iyanough Hills Food and Spirits restaurant.

Twin Brooks Golf Course
West End Rotary, Hyannis
(508) 862-6980
www.twinbrooksgolf.net

Golf Digest rated this course, located on the grounds of the Sheraton Hyannis Resort, as the toughest par 54 on the Cape. The resort offers a picturesque 2,621-yard,

18-hole course with five water holes. Play is excellent year-round. The third hole is considered the toughest on the course—the only way you'll ever make par is to hit straight as an arrow. The resort has two putting greens and a fully equipped pro shop with equipment and cart rentals. Greens fees are $38 daily. After 4:00 P.M. rates drop to $20. Cart rentals are $22. Tee time reservations are advisable. Various memberships are available.

Bayberry Hills Golf Course & The Links 9
West Yarmouth Road, West Yarmouth
(508) 394-5597
www.golfyarmouthcapecod.com

Known as an excellent public course, this challenging par 72 course has 18 holes, two practice greens, and a large driving range. Designed by Geoff Cornish and Brian Silva, Bayberry Hills goes from almost 7,200 yards from the back "professional" tees to about 5,300 yards from the front. Most players opt for the middle sets of tees, which feature a 125 slope and 119. Beware the par 4 fourth hole. Not only did Cornish and Silva hide the green below a hill, they also hid a water hazard! This course hosts about 45,000 rounds a year, even though it's closed January through February. It also has a separate nine-hole links-style course. Peak-season fees are $55 before noon, $45 between 2:00 and 4:00 P.M., and $30 after 4:00 P.M. Carts cost $15 and are mandatory until 2:00 P.M. Friday through Sunday. Bayberry Hills accepts tee times no more than four days in advance unless you prepay, and you are strongly encouraged to prepay if you want a weekend morning time in the summer. Call (508) 398-4112 to reserve a time.

Bass River Golf Course
62 Highbank Road, South Yarmouth
(508) 398-9079
www.golfyarmouthcapecod.com

The signature hole on this appropriately named golf course is the sixth, a par 3 right on the tidal Bass River. In fact if you are going west over the Bass River Bridge, look to your right, and you can see the hole across the water. Views of scenic Bass River are just one of the nice things about this course, one of the busiest in Massachusetts. Playing to 6,129 yards and a slope of 124 from the back, this par 72 hosts more than 65,000 rounds of golf a year. A fully stocked pro shop, snack bar, and practice green are additional amenities at this Donald Ross layout. This is a year-round course with summer rates of $50 before noon, $40 after 2:00 P.M., and $25 after 4:00 P.M. Carts are $15. Call (508) 398-4112 to reserve a time. It is strongly recommended to call well in advance.

Blue Rock Golf Course
Off Highbank Road, South Yarmouth
(508) 398-9295
www.bluerockgolfcourse.com
A favorite of longtime Cape golfers, Blue Rock is rated one of the best par 3 golf courses in the Northeast. In fact *Sports Illustrated* just called Blue Rock the top par 3 course in the country. Well designed and beautifully maintained, this public 18-hole, 3,000-yard course is open year-round and has holes that range from 103 yards to 255 yards. There are a number of beautiful holes, many crossing a river that runs through the course. Both the 9th and 18th require you to drive over the river to an elevated green. Facilities include two practice greens and a golf school run by PGA pro Patrick Fannon. The on-site Blue Rock Resort (see our Hotels, Motels, and Resorts chapter) offers a number of play-and-stay packages. Summer greens fees are $45. Only pull carts are available here, and tee times can be booked starting seven days in advance. You can book them further out if you pay a 50 percent deposit.

Dennis Highlands
825 Old Bass River Road, Dennis
(508) 385-8347
www.dennisgolf.com
Opened in mid-1984, Dennis Highlands has become a favorite among locals and tourists. Besides a solid 6,464-yard layout from the back tees, this 18-hole par 71 offers a large two-tier practice range, a putting green, and a full pro shop. The 175 rolling acres are dotted with stands of pine and oak. The sixth hole, a tricky par 4, has a very difficult two-tiered green. Reservations are suggested during the summer/fall season; they are accepted up to four days in advance, or up to six months in advance if you are prepaying. In the summer greens fees are $55. In the spring fees for Monday through Thursday dip to $35; $45 on the weekend. Carts are $14.00 per person per 18 holes and $9.50 per person per 9 holes. Dennis Pines (see previous entry) and Dennis Highlands are both owned and run by the town of Dennis. Both are open year-round, weather permitting.

Dennis Pines
Off Route 134, East Dennis
(508) 385-8347
www.dennisgolf.com
From the back tees Dennis Pines is a tournament-caliber 7,100 yards with a slope of 127. Don't fret though; the front tees chop off more than 1,200 yards, making this par 72 suitable for many tastes. The narrow fairways at this year-round course emphasize accuracy off the tee. The 12th is a devilish par 5 dogleg left that can be tamed with a precise tee shot. Expect to use every club in your bag here, as the holes are a good mix of lengths. Water only comes into play on four holes. A giant pond sits between holes 10 and 11, and most would be advised to play a conservative iron off the tee on those holes. As Dennis Pines is one of the busiest Cape courses, you'll need to reserve tee times in season: The

course takes them four days in advance, or six months in advance with prepayment. In the summer season greens fees are $55. In the spring fees Monday through Thursday dip to $35; $45 on the weekend. The fees drop further to $30 during the fall. Cart rentals are $14.00 per person per 18 holes and $9.50 per person per 9 holes.

Lower Cape

Cranberry Valley Golf Course
183 Oak Street, Harwich
(508) 430-5234
www.cranberrygolfcourse.com

After 17 holes you are faced with an interesting 18th at Cranberry Valley: a par 5 double dogleg right that looks like a bent-open horseshoe. This 18-hole championship layout, spread over rolling fairways fringed with pines and cranberry bogs, is the centerpiece of many golf vacations. The first three holes on the back side have water. Cranberry Valley features 6,745 yards and a 129 slope from the back tees. But, like Dennis Pines, this course loses more than 1,200 yards when you move to the front tees, making it suitable for many skill levels. On-site are a driving range, putting green, and pro shop, and a new 6,000-square-foot clubhouse just opened up last year. Tee times are required in season and can be made up to 10 days in advance. Those who prepay can reserve a tee time after March 1 for the rest of the year. Clubs and cart rentals are available. Greens fees are $60 in season and $14 per person per 18 holes for a cart. Off-season greens fees for 18 holes drop to $35 weekdays and $45 weekends. The course is open year-round, but temporary greens are in effect from December through the beginning of March.

Harwichport Golf Club
South and Forest Streets, Harwichport
(508) 432-0250

This pocket-size course is a real charmer. Two laps around these nine holes will get you about 5,076 yards and a par 68. It may be small, but it's not easy. There's plenty here to challenge you. For instance the eighth hole is a par 4 dogleg left to a small green. Harwichport offers relatively flat terrain, and a flat greens fee structure as well.

Fees are $28 for 18 holes and $18 for 9 during both summer and fall. This public course is open year-round, "as long as there's no snow on the ground." Reservations are not needed; it's first come, first served. There are no riding carts here (they're not necessary), but there are plenty of pull carts available. There's a putting green and the most quaint clubhouse you'll ever lace up your golf shoes in. A membership costs $350.

The Captains' Golf Course
1000 Freeman's Way, Brewster
(508) 896-5100, (877) 843-9081
www.captainsgolfcourse.com

The Captains' two 18-hole courses—Port and Starboard—regularly draw praise for being two of the state's finest public golf courses. The par 72 Port Course features 6,724 yards and a slope of 131 from the back tees. This challenging but accommodating course has a well-bunkered layout, and all the holes are named for Brewster sea captains. The 14th hole is a very difficult par 5 and is the only hole on the course with water, which must make its namesake Captain Myrick very happy. The par 72 Starboard Course is only a few years old but has already become a Cape favorite. It features 6,776 yards and has a slope of 122. There is also an expansive driving range featuring bunkers and rolling terrain and a fully stocked pro shop. PGA professionals are on hand for lessons and clinics. In-season greens fees are $55 daily for 18 holes, $45 after 2:00 P.M. on weekdays, and $30 after 4:00 P.M. Cart rentals are $15.00 per person per 18 holes or

$4.00 for a pull cart. Call to reserve a tee time, or book one on-line at their Web site.

Ocean Edge Golf Club
Route 6A, Brewster
(508) 896-5911
www.oceanedge.com

Avid golfers will relish the Ocean Edge Golf Club, which features a championship-style, 18-hole course sporting five ponds and 64 pot bunkers. Open all year long the par 72 boasts 6,665 yards and a slope of 129 from the back tees. The eighth is a 601-yard monster par 5 (don't leave anything in the bag off the tee on this one!). Ocean Edge is a spikeless course. Guests of Ocean Edge Resort can book a tee time when they confirm room reservations; otherwise, Ocean Edge takes reservations a week in advance. The spectacular Ocean Edge Resort (see our Hotels, Motels, and Resorts chapter), which spans both the north and south sides of Route 6A in Brewster, features a driving range, two putting greens, and a fully stocked pro shop. Although the course is open to the public, resort guests receive preferred tee times. Greens fees are $50 on weekdays and $64 on weekends May through June; $64 daily June through September; $50 weekdays and $64 weekends September through mid-October. Their four-day golf school is a great way to stay here and learn to play.

Chatham Seaside Links
209 Seaview Street, Chatham
(508) 945-4774

Nestled among Chatham's beautiful oceanside community of historic houses and summer homes, the nine-hole Chatham Seaside Links offers an intimate golfing experience, as well as a great view of the Atlantic Ocean from the seventh green. At about 4,800 yards for 18 holes,

this par 34 hides its challenge in tiny greens and strong ocean wind. The course sits next door to the magnificent Chatham Bars Inn (see our Hotels, Motels, and Resorts chapter) and is often packed with guests. Greens fees are $17 for 9 holes, $28 for 18. Tee times are determined on a first-come, first-served basis. There is a practice green at the course.

Chequessett Yacht and Country Club
Chequessett Neck Road, Wellfleet
(508) 349-3704
www.cycc.net

Chequessett is a nine-hole gem hidden away in the charming town of Wellfleet on the Lower Cape. Bring a camera for the fourth tee's view of Wellfleet Harbor and Cape Cod Bay. The par 70 reaches 5,168 yards for 18 from its back set of tees. Over the past few years, the club has put a lot into the course by creating new tees for a more interesting back nine and installing irrigation. Chequessett is a short, pretty course. On-site are a pro shop, putting green, and a clubhouse with grill and snack bar. Greens fees during the summer season are $30 for 9 holes and $44 for 18. Off-season rates go as low as $22 for 9 ($16 after 3:00 P.M.) and $36 for 18 holes. Tee times can be reserved up to three days in advance by phone.

Highland Golf Links
Highland Light Road, North Truro
(508) 487-9201

This is the granddaddy of all Cape courses, where winds offer as much challenge as the wild rough that accents the fairways. Founded in 1892, Highland is the oldest course on the Cape and one of the oldest in America. It takes 5,299 yards to go around this nine-hole layout twice from the back set of tees. Highland has a modest difficulty rating with a slope of

[Facing page] *Due to the Cape's moderate climate, you can golf virtually year-round. Fall brings open tee times, lower prices, and comfortable temperatures to Cape courses.*
HYANNIS AREA CHAMBER OF COMMERCE

103. But it's not the challenge that has earned this course a spot on golf itineraries for more than a century—it's the appeal of playing one of the few courses in this country that mirrors the rustic charm of the great links of Great Britain. Perched high along windswept bluffs overlooking the Atlantic, Highland is as natural as golf gets on this side of the ocean. The open fairways, deep natural rough and moorlands, wild cranberry, beach plum, and thicket are reminiscent of the unkempt look of the Scottish links. At this truly special course, it is not uncommon to spot whales spouting in the Atlantic or fishing vessels fighting the waves as they make their way up and down the coast.

From the course you can also view Provincetown's Pilgrim Monument. Standing tall between the seventh and eighth holes is Cape Cod Lighthouse (see our Attractions chapter's Close-up for more information on these landmarks), further adding to the unique environment of Highland.

It's almost impossible to walk onto the course in the summer, so call to reserve a tee time up to a week in advance, Greens fees are $24 for 9 holes and $40 for 18 holes. Carts are $6.30 per person per nine holes. Highland is open year-round, weather permitting, and club rentals are available. Annual memberships are available for $500.

---

i *Cape Cod has more than 120,000 yards of public golf courses—about 68 miles. That's like golfing from the Cape Cod Canal to the tip of Provincetown.*

INSTRUCTION

Most of the courses on the Cape offer lessons from golf professionals who can help you work on all facets of your game. These pros can tell you why you're slicing and hooking or why you just can't seem to get the ball in the hole. Your best bet is to call any of the golf courses featured above and inquire about lessons. Or you can take a look at our short list below.

Upper Cape

Holly Ridge Golf Club
121 Country Club Road, South Sandwich
(508) 428-5577
The year-round Holly Ridge Golf Club offers three LPGA professionals who provide lessons. You can learn from former New England PGA teacher-of-the-year Jane Frost through her golf school or else take a private, one-hour lesson costing $225. Another pro, DeLayne Pascal, can also provide private lessons at a rate of $50 for a half-hour and $90 for an hour. And don't forget the free clinics every Saturday at 11:00 A.M. during the season.

Mid-Cape

Hyannis Golf Club
Route 132, Hyannis
(508) 362-2606
PGA pro Sue Kaffenburgh, along with instructors Mike Boden and David Porkka, offer individual and group lessons. Their instruction focuses on all skill levels. The club has a great practice facility as well as state-of-the-art video equipment to allow golfers to analyze their own swing and problem areas. Individual lessons cost $120 for an hour.

Olde Barnstable Fairgrounds Golf Course
1460 Route 149, Marstons Mills
(508) 420-1141
PGA professionals Gary Philbrick and Mike Haberl provide lessons year-round to

Driving Ranges

Upper Cape

Bourne Sports World
Route 18, Bourne
(508) 759-5500

Holly Ridge Golf Club
121 Country Club Road, South Sandwich
(508) 428-5577

Round Hill Country Club
1 Round Hill Road, East Sandwich
(508) 888-3384

Falmouth Country Club
630 Carriage Shop Road, East Falmouth
(508) 548-3211

Ballymeade Country Club & Estates
125 Falmouth Woods Road, North Falmouth
(508) 540-4005

Quashnet Valley Country Club
309 Old Barnstable Road, Mashpee
(508) 477-4412

New Seabury Cape Cod
off Great Neck Road South, New Seabury
(Mashpee)
(508) 539-8322

Mid-Cape

Olde Barnstable Fairgrounds Course
Route 149, Marstons Mills
(508) 420-1141

Hyannis Golf Club
Route 132, Hyannis
(508) 362-2606

Bayberry Hills Golf Course
West Yarmouth Road, West Yarmouth
(508) 394-5597

Bass River Sports World
Route 28, South Yarmouth
(508) 398-6070

Dennis Pines
Route 134, East Dennis
(508) 385-8347

Dennis Highlands
825 Old Bass River Road, Dennis
(508) 385-8347

The Longest Drive
131 Great Western Road, South Dennis
(508) 398-5555

Lower Cape

Captains' Golf Course
1000 Freeman's Way, Brewster
(508) 896-5100

Ocean Edge Golf Course
Route 6A, Brewster
(508) 396-5911

Cranberry Valley
183 Oak Street, Harwich
(508) 430-5234

T-Time Family Sports Center
U.S. Route 6, Eastham
(508) 255-5697

GOLF

improve all areas of your game, from driving to putting and all those tricky shots in between. Call for current rates.

Blue Rock Golf Course
Great Western Road at Todd Road,
South Yarmouth
(508) 398-9295
PGA professional Patrick Fannon, along with his assistant professionals, can help you correct that hook or show you how to make the perfect approach shot. Besides a golf school with extensive class offerings for different skill levels from late spring to early fall, they also provide very affordable clinics throughout the summer. Available year-round, there are indoor facilities available if the weather outside
is frightful.

Lower Cape

Ocean Edge Golf School
Ocean Edge Resort, Brewster
(508) 896-5911, (800) 343-6074
www.oceanedge.com
The three-day golf school at beautiful Ocean Edge is designed for golfers of all levels looking to build, improve, and refine their game. PGA instructors, headed by director Ron Hallett, cover full-swing techniques, including putting and chipping. The school offers a maximum 6-to-1 student/pro ratio and personalized video analysis. You can golf after school too. Deluxe accommodations (double occupancy) are $755 (April to May) or $895 to $975 for the rest of the summer. They also offer private lessons with pros: $80 for an hour, $40 for half an hour.

SPORTS AND RECREATION

Some visitors are surprised by the caliber of sports they find on Cape Cod. Yet Cape Cod is well known for its baseball, road races, golf and even soccer. If baseball is your game, then you'll have plenty to watch with the Cape Cod Baseball League, probably the best non-professional baseball league in the country, playing nightly from mid-June to mid-August. The Falmouth Road Race, along with other topnotch road races, attracts runners from around the world. Each June Willowhead Country Club in Mashpee hosts a children's charity golf Pro-Am that draws professional celebrities from golf, football, basketball, and hockey. Not to be outdone the Cape Cod Crusaders bring soccer to the peninsula throughout the summer. In this chapter we have listed some of the major spectator sports events in the area. For exact schedules and dates, check the sports section of the *Cape Cod Times*.

If you're in the mood to play yourself rather than watch someone else, we'll let you know where you can ride a horse, ice skate, or skateboard. If you're up for a game of tennis or bowling, we'll point you in the right direction. And if you'd just like to work out, we tell you all about fitness centers too. For those of you who prefer to play in the ocean or spend your time on the links, we offer separate chapters on Boating and Water Sports and on Golf.

SPECTATOR SPORTS

Baseball

Cape Cod Baseball League
449 Braggs Lane, Barnstable
(508) 432-6909
www.capecodbaseball.org

Often referred to as a college all-star league, the Cape Cod Baseball League delivers a quality of baseball that will satisfy the most demanding fan. Among the major league players who have graced our fields are Mo Vaughn, who played for the Wareham Gatemen; Jeff Bagwell, who was voted Most Valuable in the National League in 1994 and once played for the Chatham A's; Frank "the Big Hurt" Thomas, who played for the Orleans Cardinals; and Nomar Garciaparra, who also played for the Cardinals and lit up local baseball diamonds to all our delight before heading up to Boston.

Like much else on the Cape, the Cape Cod Baseball League is historic. The first game was played about 100 years ago between Barnstable and Sandwich. What began as a local sport is now considered one of the best amateur baseball organizations in the country. True baseball purists will appreciate the fact that the league only allows use of wooden bats. Imagine the late-afternoon summer sunlight filtering across the ball field, casting players' shadows upon the grass of the outfield. Here is where spectators fill wooden benches or throw a blanket on the side of a hill. You can buy a jumbo hot dog with heaps of mustard for the price a hot dog should be. You see future big leaguers play the game with the same enthusiasm, not to mention salary, of little leaguers. The quality of baseball is as good as you will find in many professional ballparks. In fact on any given night, there probably is a professional scout in the crowd looking to spot the next superstar.

Some 300 ballplayers from colleges and universities across the country are recruited each year to play on the 10 teams of the Cape league. They are hosted by local families, who often enjoy following the career of a young player who ate breakfast at their house for the summer and then made it into the major leagues. It's not all play for the players though. Being able to play in the Cape Cod League does carry some additional responsibilities. Each June, before our public schools let out for the summer, players visit our classrooms to talk to the kids and build team support, in some cases creating bonds that will never be forgotten by our kids. The Cape Cod Baseball League also sponsors baseball clinics each summer for aspiring youngsters.

The Cape League season runs from mid-June to mid-August. Each team plays a 44-game schedule—that's 220 games across the Cape each summer! An all-star game is held in mid- to late July, and playoffs are held around the second week of August.

You'll find games at Spillane Field in Wareham, Coady School Field in Bourne, Guv Fuller Field in Falmouth, Lowell Park in Cotuit, McKeon Field in Hyannis, Red Wilson Field at the Dennis-Yarmouth Regional High School in South Yarmouth, Cape Cod Regional Technical School in Harwich, Whitehouse Field at Harwich High School, Veterans Field in Chatham, and Eldredge Park in Orleans. Games are typically held at 1:00, 5:00, and 7:00 P.M. Printed schedules are available in many local stores and newspapers.

The Bourne Braves and Brewster Whitecaps joined the league in 1988. At that time it was decided to split the 10 teams into two divisions, East and West, thus setting the stage for playoffs at the end of the season. The top two teams in each division face off, with the winners going to the dramatic best-of-three championship series.

Many of the fields, if not all, offer concession stands, but no one will complain if you pack a meal and make a picnic out of it. Because the league's 10 fields are within a 50-mile radius of each other, it is possible to visit all of them throughout a summer. Admission is far more in keeping with the spirit of the sport than at pro ball-

parks: Donations are accepted, and a hat is passed during the game. So find a seat on the hillside, and let the cool summer evening settle in around you. As you watch a Cape Cod Baseball League game, you will remember something you had perhaps forgotten: pure sport.

Senior Babe Ruth League
Cape-wide
www.capecodbaberuth.com
Other baseball events, such as the Senior Babe Ruth League featuring 16-through-19-year-olds, are also on tap Cape-wide. Games are played during June and July at many fields across the Cape with playoffs held in mid-July. Here's a chance to perhaps see some future members of the Cape Cod Baseball League.

American Legion Baseball
Upper and Mid-Cape
www.post188.org/baseball
www.barnstableamerlegbb.org
During the summer months American Legion baseball games can be seen at fields in Sandwich and Falmouth. The Cape has two American Legion teams: Post 188, which plays their home games at the Sandwich High School field; and Post 206, which plays its games at the McKeon Field in Hyannis or Lowell Field in Cotuit. Both teams are zone 10, which includes a dozen American Legion teams from Southeastern Massachusetts. They play 26 regular season games from the first week of June to the last week of July. Playoffs begin during the first part of August, with the winners going to the championships in Massachusetts, then New England, and, eventually, the national world series. Players range in age from 16 to 18. The Cape teams recruit from the Bourne to Dennis-Yarmouth areas.

Golf

Cape Cod is synonymous with golf. Upon this sand trap of a peninsula are more than two dozen public golf courses. No matter where you are, somebody is teeing one up not too far away. (See our Golf chapter for a list of courses.) A number of tournaments are held on Cape Cod for amateurs and pros alike. We encourage you to check with local golf courses and watch the *Cape Cod Times* sports pages for upcoming matches.

Willowbend Children's Charity Pro-Am
**Willowbend Country Club,
100 Willowbend Road, Mashpee
(508) 539-5000
www.willowbendproam.com**
This is the premier golf tournament on Cape Cod, attracting some of the biggest names in golf, professional sports, and some 15,000 fans. It takes place during late June at Willowbend in Mashpee. Since the first tournament in 1992, it has raised about $1.2 million to benefit children's programs on Cape Cod.

Popular pro golfers have included Davis Love III, Nick Faldo, Greg Norman, Bruce Lietzke, and John Daly. On the amateur side were such great sports names as Hall of Fame Boston Bruins defenseman Bobby Orr, Dallas Cowboys running back Emmitt Smith, and Denver Broncos quarterback John Elway. This is a tournament not to be missed.

All the holes here are beautiful and offer you unrestricted views of the competition, but plan to set aside some time to watch the drives along the par 5 tenth hole.

Tickets are a very reasonable $15.00 for adults and $5.00 for ages 12 and younger for the one-day event, and it benefits a great cause.

Running

If you're a serious runner, then you already know all about Cape Cod's famous Falmouth Road Race. In running circles around the world, the word "Falmouth" means one thing: one of the best non-marathon events anywhere. Cape Cod plays host to many other races as well. Johnny Kelley has attached his name to an annual road race in Hyannis. The Cape

Even if you don't run yourself or enjoy watching others, you might want to check the schedule of road races anyway. As many cross the major traffic routes of the Cape, you may encounter a nasty traffic jam if you happen to be out on the day of a major race.

Cod Marathon is a qualifying event for the Boston Marathon. And then there's that special kind of race that involves running—and more. The New England Triathlon Series Sprint Race, starting in Centerville's Craigville Beach, puts its participants in Nantucket Sound first. After swimming the first leg of the triathlon, participants bike through the public roads of this Mid-Cape community, then finally run back to Craigville Beach.

Many of our races are known for their scenery and challenge, but a good many also have festive post race parties, giving all the more incentive for those of us more sedate to come out and support the runners along the way.

We begin with a detailed look at our most famous race, then give listings for annual road races across the Cape. Finally, we take a look at other kinds of races—biathlon, triathlon, and walking races.

Falmouth Road Race
**Falmouth
(508) 540-7000
www.falmouthroadrace.com**
For those who run or who like to watch other people run, Falmouth is a mecca. The streets here are painted with the race's proud history, and we don't only mean the start and finish lines painted on the asphalt or the mile markers that follow the flow of footfalls. even in the chill of winter you cannot escape the drama of the race as you walk or drive the fabled route. With the heat of August come the runners and the crowds to cheer them on.

Considered one of the country's best nonmarathons, the Falmouth Road Race began in 1973. Today the world-class annual event, which is held on the third Sunday in August, attracts more than 9,500 runners from around the world to challenge its demanding 7.1-mile course. Some great names in marathon running who have competed here include Alberto Salazar (he won this race in 1981 and 1982); U.S. gold medalist Frank Shorter; four-time winner of the Boston and New York marathons Bill Rodgers; and U.S. gold medalist Joan Benoit Samuelson. Others of note include Grete Waitz, Lorraine Moller, and Lynn Jennings.

Of course, the thing that sets Falmouth apart from other road races is the incredible Cape Cod scenery, from the course's Woods Hole start to its Falmouth Heights finish. Between those two points runners pass the refreshing waters of Vineyard Sound and the stoic white column of Nobska Light. The race attracts some 70,000 spectators who line the streets.

For that one day a year, Falmouth's population becomes that of a small city. If you wish to attend the event, we strongly advise that you make your accommodations reservations well in advance. If you are interested in participating in the Falmouth Road Race, call the number above or send a business size SASE to Box 732, Falmouth, MA 02541. Applications are mailed by May 1, and entries close May 9. Accepted runners are determined by lottery. Organizers strongly discourage unregistered runners.

Marathons and Other Footraces

UPPER CAPE

Paul E. White Memorial Road Race
North Falmouth
(800) 443-4990

Held annually in July since 1977, this 5K road race takes place in lovely North Falmouth. Wheelchairs are welcome, but no walkers please.

Falmouth Main Street Mile
Falmouth
(508) 540-1910
www.falmouthtrackclub.org

Sponsored by the Falmouth Track Club, this 1-mile race always takes place on the Sunday after Labor Day. The emphasis here is more on fun than competition.

Cape Cod Marathon
Falmouth
(508) 540-6959
www.capecodmarathon.com

In late October the Cape Cod Marathon attracts about 1,200 participants. It is a Boston Marathon qualifying event and also includes a team relay event. It begins and ends at the Falmouth Village Green and is sponsored by the Falmouth Track Club. Part of the race traces the Falmouth Road Race course. The men's and women's winners each receive $1,500.

Hyannis Marathon, Half Marathon, 10K, Relay
Hyannis
(508) 775-0143

This event, usually held in late February, starts and finishes at the Sheraton Hyannis Resort Hotel. Some 300 marathoners, 1,500 half marathoners, 500 10Kers, and 50 relay teams wend their way along a scenic course that passes Craigville Beach, Hyannis Harbor, Lewis Bay, the John F. Kennedy Memorial, and the Kennedy Family Compound. The marathon is a Boston Marathon–qualifying event.

Centerville Old Home Week 5K Road Race
Centerville
(508) 771-0650

This 3-mile race starts at the Centerville Elementary School and finished at Covell Beach along Craigville Beach Road to the east of Craigville Beach. It usually takes place the second or third week of August. More than 150 contestants participate in age groups ranging from 13 and younger to 69. A kids' race starts at 6:45 P.M.; a mile beach run starts at 7:15 P.M. The entry fee is $10.00, $12.00 on the race day; it's $2.00 for kids. There's even a special race for the kids afterward at the Craigville Elementary School.

Johnny Kelley Road Race
Hyannis
(508) 775-8877
www.johnnykelleyroadrace.com

This Memorial Day weekend race is for competitive and recreational runners. Named for the octogenarian who ran more Boston Marathons than anyone, Johnny Kelley is *Runner's World* "Runner of the Century." Choose the 5-mile course, or run the double loop for the 10-mile distance. Both are certified by the USATF. More than 100 awards are given, including those presented to the top three runners overall in male and female divisions in both distances and to the top three runners in the seven age divisions. Proceeds benefit the Cape Cod Hospital Foundations, a favorite charity of Kelley. The entry fee is $20.

Annual Dennis Road Race and Fun Run
Dennis
(508) 760-6162
www.dennisrecreation.com

The year 2004 marks the 27th running of the Dennis Recreation Road Race and Fun Run. Walkers and wheelchairs are welcome. Three hundred runners compete in this 5-mile road race. Held in late July or early August, it begins at Wixon School on Route 134 and winds through Dennis, utilizing the bike bath when possible. The entry fee is $10, but $12 on race day.

LOWER CAPE

Annual Brew Run
Brewster
(508) 896-6574

The Brew Run is a great warm-up for the Falmouth Road Race, for both runners and spectators. The 5.2-mile race is sponsored by the Wood Shed pub to benefit Brewster Rescue and Safety. The race is followed by an awards and raffle party at the Wood

Shed. To register send a SASE to the Wood Shed, Box 967, Brewster, MA 02631. It is held the second Saturday in August.

Irish Pub Road Race
West Harwich
(508) 432-8808
www.capecodsirishpub.com

Sponsored by the Irish Pub in West Harwich, this annual 5.25-mile road race, begun in 1976, takes place the first Saturday in August to raise money for the Harwich Ambulance Fund. It begins and ends at the Irish Pub on Route 28, West Harwich, where a post-race party is held with an awards ceremony and live entertainment. The entry fee is $10, $12 on race day.

Triathlons, Biathlons, and Walkathons

UPPER CAPE

Coast Guard Air Station Duathlon
Massachusetts Military Reservation
(508) 485-5855

Held at Camp Edwards Recreational Center, Massachusetts Military Reservation over Memorial Day weekend, this race features a 2-mile run, 12-mile bike race, and another 2-mile run.

NETT-Falmouth Sprint
Falmouth
(508) 477-6311
www.timeoutproductions.com

The annual Falmouth Sprint has been run since 1991. The race, staged alongside Vineyard Sound and run through Falmouth Heights, is a 33-mile swim, 9-mile bike, and 3.1-mile run. The first 4 miles of the bike stage hug the ocean, and the 3.1-mile run takes you along the prestigious Falmouth Road Race course. The event, part of the New England Triathlon Tour, takes place in late July. The entry fee is $40 for ages 10 to 17 and $55 for pros and those older than 18.

MID-CAPE

NETT–Hyannis Sprint I and II
Centerville/Osterville
(508) 477-6311
www.timeoutproductions.com

Start the season fast at Cape Cod's longest-established triathlon in early June. Staged from beautiful Craigville Beach, this is the ideal race for athletes of every ability. It begins with a 0.25-mile ocean swim in Nantucket sound, continues as a scenic 10-mile bike loop through Centerville and Osterville, and ends with a 3.5-mile run through the quiet neighborhoods of Centerville village. Spring I is held in mid-June, and Sprint II takes place in early September. The entry fee is $40 for those ages 10 to 17; the pro fee is $55; it's also $55 for those older than 18.

LOWER CAPE

Beach to Bridge Swim and Run
West Harwich
(508) 862-5606

This biathlon begins with a 0.8-mile swim from Pleasant Road Beach to the town dock. It is then followed by a 3.1-mile run from the town dock to Pleasant Road Beach. This event is usually held on a weekend in mid-July, but it depends largely on the tides. Proceeds benefit Cape Cod Hospital's Cancer Unit.

Soccer

Cape Cod Crusaders
143 Station Avenue, South Yarmouth
(508) 394-1171
www.capecodcrusaders.com

Soccer has come to Cape Cod with the Cape Cod Crusaders. All home games are played at Dennis-Yarmouth High School. (Take U.S. Route 6 to exit 8, take your first right off the ramp, then go straight for 1.5 miles; the stadium is on your left.)

The team plays two dozen games each summer season. There's usually at least one game held each weekend from April to mid-August. Game time is 7:30 P.M. For the other half of the games, they travel to New Jersey, New York, and as far south as North Carolina for matches. The season concludes with national championships on Labor Day weekend. The Crusaders, who compete in the Premier Development League, considered the top amateur league in the country, won back-to-back PDL championships in 2002 and 2003.

Players come from as far away as Ireland and England, and others hail from nearby New England colleges. Games can draw as many as 2,000 spectators. Ticket prices are $8.00 for adults and $5.00 for children younger than 12. Tickets are sold in packages if you know that you will be attending three or more games during the season. Call for ticket and schedule information.

Softball

Any spring or summer evening, or weekend morning for that matter, you can find a men's or coed softball game at a field nearby.

Cape Cod Senior Softball Classic
Eastham
(508) 255-8206

For a special treat check out the Cape Cod Old Timers League in the Mid- and Lower Cape towns. The season runs from early May to the Sunday before Labor Day. The league wraps up with the annual Cape Cod Senior Softball Classic, a three-day tournament in early September. This event features surprisingly entertaining softball from these players 55 years and older. Teams come from as far away as Connecticut and New Hampshire, and there are divisions for 65 and 70-plus.

Tennis

As with golf, it is impossible to list all the Cape's tennis tournaments. It is estimated that the Cape's many private and public tennis courts hold in excess of 100 tournaments, 30 of which are played at Mid-Cape Racquet Club in South Yarmouth. Imagine the number of serves we're talking about! Below is a sampling of the events.

MID-CAPE

Cape Cod Community College Open
Cape Cod Community College, Route 132, West Barnstable
(508) 375-4015
Held over a two-week period in early July, this tennis tournament at the college features men's and women's singles and doubles matches. Junior and adult divisions are based on age, not experience. Matches typically take place between Wednesday and Sunday over the two-week period.

Mid-Cape Open
Mid-Cape Racquet Club, 193 Whites Path, South Yarmouth
(508) 394-3511
www.midcaperacquet.com
These matches take place over a two-week period in late July and early August at various locations around the Cape and feature singles, doubles, and mixed doubles. Semifinals and finals are held at the Mid-Cape Racquet Club. The Open is great fun for competitive as well as club players. There are divisions for all ages and skill levels. The entry fee for adult singles is $24; for adult doubles it's $36.

LOWER CAPE

Lower Cape Open
Eldredge Park, Orleans
(508) 240-3785
In this August tournament players younger than 11 to older than 70 battle it out in junior, men's, women's, and seniors divisions at Eldredge Park in Orleans and on private courts located throughout Orleans. Highly competitive tennis buffs

come from all over New England representing college level through ranked adults. There are singles and doubles (men's, ladies, and mixed) competitions. The entry fee for singles is $20; for doubles teams it's $50.

Provincetown Tennis Club Year-Rounders Tournament
Provincetown Tennis Club, Bradford Street, Provincetown
(508) 487-9574
Started more than 20 years ago as a tournament for local year-rounders, the tournament has expanded to include seasonal residents as well as players from outside Provincetown. The fun begins in mid-June with men's and women's singles, doubles, and mixed doubles, culminating in the finals held on the July 4 weekend. The event sponsors singles, doubles, and mixed-doubles divisions. The entry fee is $17 for singles, $20 for doubles.

Get your ya-yas out at Adventure Isle on MacArthur Boulevard in Bourne. It has minigolf, a driving range, go-carts, bumper cars, bumper boats, batting cages, and a super slide, all at one place. Call (508) 759-2636, or visit www.adventureisle.com.

RECREATION

When you've had your fill of competing or watching the pros compete and want to get out there and practice some of those techniques you've admired—or maybe just get some exercise—you'll need to know where you can practice your sport of choice. Turn to our Boating and Water Sports chapter if you have the beach in mind, or to Golf if you're looking for a challenging (or easy) course. Here we provide information on bowling, horseback riding, indoor swimming, ice skating, tennis, and fitness clubs.

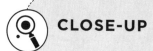

Public Tennis Courts

If you're looking to hit a ball and just get some exercise, the Cape has many public town courts locate in parks and on school grounds. The following list gives these courts, some of which are available on a first-come, first-served basis, and some of which require reservation. These courts are run by the town recreation departments. We provide phone numbers so you can call ahead to determine when the courts are open.

Upper Cape
Bourne Memorial Community Building
Main Street, Buzzards Bay
(508) 759-0650

Bourne Town Hall Park
Perry Avenue, Buzzards Bay
(508) 759-0621

Bourne High School
75 Waterhouse Road, Bourne
(508) 759-0670

Chester Park
Monument and Arthur Avenues,
Monument Beach
(508) 759-0600

Clark Field
Clark Road, North Sagamore
(508) 759-0600

Oak Ridge School
Quaker Meeting House Road, Sandwich
(508) 888-4900

Sandwich High School
Quaker Meeting House Road, Sandwich
(508) 888-4900

Forestdale Elementary School/Henry T.
Wing School
Route 130, Sandwich
(508) 888-4361

East Falmouth Elementary School
33 Davisville Road, East Falmouth
(508) 548-1052

Lawrence School
113 Lakeview Avenue, Falmouth
(508) 548-0606

Falmouth High School
Gifford Street Extension, Falmouth
(508) 540-2200

West Falmouth Park
Blacksmith Shop Road, West Falmouth
(508) 457-2567

Nye Park
County Road, North Falmouth
(508) 457-2567

Bell Tower Field
Bell Tower Lane, Woods Hole
(508) 457-2567

Mashpee Middle School/Coombs
Elementary School
150 Old Barnstable Road, Mashpee
(508) 539-1400

Mid-Cape

Grade Five School
Hyannis
(508) 790-6458

Hyannis Middle School
895 Falmouth Road (Route 28), Hyannis
(508) 790-6460

Osterville Bay School
West Bay Road, Osterville
(508) 428-8538

Cotuit Elementary School
140 Old Oyster Road, Cotuit
(508) 428-0268

Centerville Elementary School
Bay Lane, Centerville
(508) 790-9890

Barnstable-West Barnstable School
Route 6A, Barnstable
(508) 790-6345

Dennis-Yarmouth High School
Station Avenue, South Yarmouth
(508) 398-7630

Wixon Middle School
Route 134, South Dennis
(508) 398-7697

Lower Cape

Brewster, four courts are behind the
Brewster Police Department, near the Old
Town Hall on Route 6A, Brewster
(508) 896-9430

Brooks Park
Route 39 and Oak Street, Harwich
(508) 430-7553

Cape Cod Technical High School
Route 124, Harwich
(508) 430-7553

Depot Road near the Railroad Museum
Chatham
(508) 945-5175

Chatham High School
Crowell Road, Chatham
(508) 945-5175

Kitty Lane
South Chatham
(508) 945-5175

Eldredge Park
Route 28 and Eldredge Parkway, Orleans
(508) 240-3785

Nauset Regional High School
Cable Road, Eastham (Courts are available only from late June to Labor Day for
a small fee.)

Mayo Beach
Kendrick Street, Wellfleet
(508) 349-0330

Motta Field
near the Pilgrim Monument, Provincetown
(508) 487-7097

Prince Street
near the high school, Provincetown
(508) 487-7097

Bowling

Sometimes you just get the urge to bowl a few strings. The Cape can accommodate you with a number of fine alleys.

UPPER CAPE

Ryan Family Amusements Center Bowling & Miniature Golf
200 Main Street, Buzzards Bay
(508) 759-9892

This popular Upper Cape facility has candlepin bowling, a pro shop, and a game room; next door is an 18-hole miniature golf course (Bourne Bridge Adventure Golf). Ryan hosts leagues as well as good old recreational bowling and offers birthday party packages.

Leary Family Amusements Center
23 Town Hall Square, Falmouth
(508) 540-4877

Falmouth has plenty of fun spots to explore, and the Leary Family Amusements Center is one of them. It offers good candlepin bowling alleys for leagues as well as for nonleague recreational bowlers. There is a pro shop on-site, and the facility hosts birthday parties. The center is open year-round daily from 10:00 A.M. to 10:00 P.M. Monday through Friday, 10:00 A.M. to 11:00 P.M. on Saturday, and noon to 9:00 P.M. on Sunday.

Trade Center Bowl & Amusements
89 Spring Bars Road, Falmouth
(508) 548-7000

This bowling facility features tenpin with computer scoring. There are leagues for children and high school students as well as moonlight bowling and odyssey bowling where a light show adds to the challenges of the sport. Also on premises are pool tables, video games, a pro shop, and a snack bar.

MID-CAPE

Cape Bowling
441 Main Street, Hyannis
(508) 775-3411

Cape Bowling in the heart of downtown Hyannis features tenpin and hosts leagues for all ages. Some lanes have built-in bumpers for kids, and other lanes even glow in the dark. There's a pro shop, video games, and souvenir and gift shops on-site. Cape Bowling is open year-round and open until 11:00 P.M. in the summer.

Ryan Family Amusements Center
Route 28, South Yarmouth
(508) 394-5644

A very busy recreational hotspot, this Ryan Family Amusements Center has both tenpin and candlepin lanes, a pro shop, and a game room. Like the other Ryan Family Centers on the Cape, the Yarmouth facility hosts leagues and birthday parties. Ryan Family Amusements are open year-round daily until 11:00 P.M. (10:00 P.M. in the off-season).

LOWER CAPE

Orleans Bowling Center
Route 6A, Orleans
(508) 255-0636

With 14 lanes, this is an all-candlepin bowling center. Even during league events, there are lanes available for the public. Weekend nights are popular for families. The center is open year-round from 9:00 A.M. to 10:00 P.M. Monday through Saturday; on Sunday it opens at noon.

Horseback Riding

The Cape has a number of good stables for boarding, riding lessons, and trail rides. We will point out that beach riding has been restricted on most of our beaches over the last few years. The Cape Cod National Seashore and Sandy Neck Beach have both decided not to allow riding horses on the beach.

UPPER CAPE

Fieldcrest Farm
774 Palmer Avenue, Falmouth
(508) 540-0626

Fieldcrest Farm offers riding instruction, boarding, and training and has a large indoor ring and a complete tack shop with saddles, bridles, clothing, and supplies. Call for rates, which vary with experience levels.

Haland Stables
Route 28A, West Falmouth
(508) 540-2552
Located in West Falmouth, Haland Stables provides a guided trail ride through pine woods and cranberry bogs. Only walking and trotting are allowed on the trails, and all riding is English style. Appointments are required, and both private and group lessons are offered.

Maushop Equestrian Center
Sampson's Mill Road, Mashpee
(508) 477-1303
Mashpee's Maushop Equestrian Center focuses on riding lessons but will conduct trail rides by appointment. It also offers boarding services, a summer camp, and an indoor arena. Call for rates.

MID-CAPE

Holly Hill Farm
Flint Street, Martsons Mills
(508) 428-2621
www.hollyhillstable.com
Holly Hill offers lessons running from $25 to $50 per hour. This Marstons Mills establishment is a show stable of hunters and jumpers and provides such services as boarding and training. There are no trails on-site.

LOWER CAPE

Moby Dick Farm
Great Fields Road, Brewster
(508) 896-3544
This friendly, year-round equestrian center offers instruction and the opportunity to clip-clop through the miles of trails in the wooded Punkhorn Parklands. The staff is specially trained to handle beginners, and the horses here are reliable, steady types. For seasonal fun ask about hayrides,

sleigh rides, and carriage rides. Trail rides cost $40 and last more than an hour, sometimes closer to two. We highly recommend them. You'll learn a lot about the natural history of the area and come back to the stable as refreshed and invigorated as only a good trail ride can leave you.

Woodsong Farm
Lund Farm Way, Brewster
(508) 896-5800
www.woodsongcentral.com
Right next to Nickerson State Park, this facility offers riding lessons and boarding and boasts a lovely network of trails. Unfortunately the trails are only for use by those who board horses here. Woodsong Farm also hosts horse shows—terrific ones, we might add, that are great fun on a summer day.

Nickerson State Park
Route 6A, Brewster
(508) 896-3491
The park has one marked bridle trail and a network of other trails. There is no fee to ride.

Punkhorn Parklands
Run Hill Road, Brewster
(508) 896-3701
This maze of scenic trails lends itself perfectly to horseback riding, and there's no charge to ride here. Many of the trails are ancient cart paths still wide enough to ride two abreast, so you can chat with your riding buddies. On the narrower trails, though, watch out for uneven terrain.

Ice Skating and Hockey

Most people don't associate Cape Cod with ice skating, yet the Cape is a hot spot on ice. Perennial state high school hockey powers, our Cape high school teams have won the state championship at the Fleet Center in Boston (where the Bruins play) and practice at area rinks. Todd Eldredge, a world champion men's figure skater, hails from Chatham, and Olympic medalists Nancy Kerrigan and Paul Wylie have both trained at the Tony Kent Arena in South Dennis. Rentals are available at most rinks. Because times for public skating change frequently, your best bet is to call ahead for hours. Below are some of the Cape's rinks.

UPPER CAPE

Gallo Ice Arena
231 Sandwich Road, Bourne
(508) 759-8904

Located along the Cape Cod Canal, the Gallo Ice Arena plays host to hockey schools, camps, and clinics, as well as figure-skating camps and public skating. There is a pro shop on-site. The arena is open year-round with free skating September to June. There is no free skating during the summer months due to camps and league play.

Falmouth Ice Arena
9 Skating Lane, Falmouth
(508) 548-0275
www.falmouthicearena.com

Ice skating is offered on an 85-by-185-foot rink and includes youth and adult ice-hockey programs, figure-skating programs, and public skating. A pro shop and snack bar are on-site. It is open to the public daily from the end of September through March. It costs $4.00 per skater.

MID-CAPE

Joseph P. Kennedy Memorial Skating Rink
141 Bassett Lane, Hyannis
(508) 790-6345, (508) 862-4001

Named for the brother of John F. Kennedy who was lost during World War II, this rink in the center of Hyannis is used for local hockey games and figure skating as well as public skating. The rink is open October through March. They offer free skating throughout the week at different times, so it's best to call ahead. It costs $5.00 for adults and $3.00 for children 12 and

younger to skate. Skate rentals are available for $3.00.

Tony Kent Arena
8 South Gages Way, South Dennis
(508) 760-2400, (508) 760-2415
www.tonykentarena.com

Olympians Nancy Kerrigan and Paul Wylie have both practiced and performed here. The rink, off Route 134, is home to Dennis-Yarmouth youth hockey as well as figure skating and learn-to-skate programs. The rink also offers public skating Saturdays from 5:15 to 6:45 P.M.; the cost is $5.00 for adults and teens, $3.00 for children younger than 12, and $2.00 for seniors; skate rentals are $2.00. Their popular Rock Night, skating to rock music, is held each Friday for youngsters ages 9 to 13 and costs $6.00.

LOWER CAPE

Charles Moore Arena
O'Connor Way, Orleans
(508) 255-2971

This arena offers ice skating year-round. Rentals are available, and there is a snack bar.

Indoor Swimming and Fitness Clubs

With hundreds of miles of coastline, it seems redundant for the Cape to offer so many swimming pools. (It's just that we Cape Codders love the water so much!)

Most hotels and motels have a pool or two. The resorts around the Cape normally have a couple. And a number of health and fitness clubs also offer indoor swimming facilities. In fact indoor pools are an excellent resource for those who want instruction, physical therapy, and aerobic exercise as well as an opportunity to continue their favorite form of exercise all year.

Of course the Cape's health and fitness clubs offer more than just the opportunity to swim. You can continue your exercise routine at a club while you're on vacation or visit one for a round of racquetball. Fees and access to facilities vary, but generally fitness centers are open all year. Fees are in the range of $10 to $15 per day for a guest visit.

UPPER CAPE

RMA Nautilus Racquetball & Fitness Center
MacArthur Boulevard, Bourne
(508) 759-7111
www.rmafitness.com
This club has a full complement of Nautilus equipment and free weights plus cardiovascular equipment and racquetball courts. Soothe those aching muscles in the sauna, spa, and steam rooms.

Massachusetts Maritime Academy
Taylor's Point, Buzzards Bay
(508) 564-5690
www.capecodswimclub.com
Massachusetts Maritime Academy has beginner swimming lessons, lap swimming, competitive swimming, a masters group, and water polo for all ages. And a big plus: Their pool has a giant water slide.

Sandwich High School–Sandwich Community School
365 Quaker Meeting House Road, East Sandwich
(508) 888-5300
The Sandwich Community School coordinates public use of the constantly busy Sandwich High School swimming pool. The pool offers lessons, family and lap swims, water aerobics, and a masters program for those interested in improving their water lifesaving skills.

Sportsite
315 Cotuit Road, Sandwich
(508) 888-7900
Sportsite offers classes in aerobics, step, and body shaping, and has Nautilus and cardiovascular equipment.

Children's programs and child care are other features here.

The Woman's Workout Company
Route 130, Mashpee
(508) 477-4777
155 Attucks Lane, Hyannis
(508) 771-1600
www.womansworkoutco.com
The Woman's Workout Company offers a variety of creative alternatives to help members achieve their fitness goals with cross-training workouts. They offer more than 100 aerobics classes per week, a full cardiovascular room, swimming lessons, full dance programs, and a Nautilus and free-weight room. The center also offers babysitting, tanning, a hot tub, steam room, and a beauty shop. If you plan to use the facility often during your Cape Cod visit, you might consider their 10-visit punch card or their three-month membership.

Falmouth Health and Fitness Inc.
133 East Falmouth Highway, Falmouth
(508) 540-6180
Falmouth Health and Fitness Inc. has a StairMaster, treadmill, and NordicTrack equipment and offers boxing and slide, step and water aerobics in their pool. Monthly memberships are available.

Falmouth Sports Center Health Club
33 Highfield Drive, Falmouth
(508) 548-7433
The Falmouth Sports Center Health Club offers Nautilus, free weights, and cardiovascular equipment. The club also has a physical therapy department. Daily passes and monthly memberships are available.

MID-CAPE

YMCA
2245 Route 132, West Barnstable
(508) 362-6500
www.ymcacapecod.org
The Cape's only YMCA has water exercise, water jogging, lap swimming, and lessons as well as special arthritis exercise classes.

Bikes and rollerblades are everywhere on the Cape, especially the Shining Sea Bike Path, from Falmouth to Woods Hole, and the Cape Cod Rail Trail, from Dennis to Wellfleet. Another popular spot is along Ocean Drive in Wellfleet. Park your vehicle behind the Wellfleet General Store on U.S. Route 6, and skate or bike down to LeCount's Hollow Road until it turns into Ocean Drive. You can only turn north, and the paved road takes you along the dunes of the Atlantic Ocean, which are called Four Mile Beach and Surfer's Beach.

The club also has fitness equipment, saunas, and aerobic classes. You do not have to be a member to use the facility; the guest fee is $10 per day, but certain rules pertain. Children 9 year old and younger must swim with an adult. Those younger than 14 years of age must have an adult supervising.

The Fitness Club of Cape Cod
55 Attucks Lane, Hyannis
(508) 771-7734
The Fitness Club of Cape Cod offers whirlpool and sauna, fitness equipment, racquetball, a tanning salon, and basketball and wallyball courts. This club is open daily year-round.

R&R Fitness Center
12 Thornton Drive, Hyannis
(508) 778-6446
R&R has many bikes and treadmills available and offers more hammer-strength equipment than any other club on the Cape. There are men's and women's locker rooms as well as personal trainers.

Mid-Cape Racquet & Health Club
193 White's Path, South Yarmouth
(508) 394-3511
www.midcaperacquet.com
Mid-Cape is a complete fitness center with Nautilus and free weights and a personal training program. After your workout enjoy the sauna, steam room, and whirlpool. Daily passes are available. The club is a popular choice for private soccer or basketball parties for kids. Mid-Cape Racquet Club is open daily year-round.

David's Gym
50 Route 134, South Dennis
(508) 394-7199
Step- and cardio-aerobic classes, hi-tech Cybex equipment, Nautilus equipment, one-on-one training, whirlpool and sauna, professional and amateur boxing, and karate training, all offered in a super-clean, super-friendly environment. Guests can use the gym for a daily fee.

LOWER CAPE

Ocean Edge Resort
2660 Route 6A, Brewster
(508) 896-8671
www.oceanedge.com
The resort has two indoor pools (one Olympic-size lap pool is by the golf course on the south side of Route 6A and the other is behind the conference center on the north side) and two fitness centers (again, one on each side of the highway). Although these facilities are generally closed to the public, off-season pool use and classes are available. You can purchase a winter pool membership from the beginning of October until May 1. Prices are prorated if you join after October. If you're not staying long enough to purchase a membership, you can still use the pool for a daily fee. You can also buy two-day, three-day, or weekly passes.

Willy's Gym
21 Old Colony Way, Orleans
(508) 255-6826
www.willysgym.com
This well-established fitness facility offers a full slate of cardiovascular and toning equipment and an ever-expanding free

weight area. Willy's also offers some 60 different classes in spinning, step aerobics, dance, martial arts, kickboxing, and yoga. There are complete spa facilities, and child care is available. Guests can pay for a daily or weekly membership.

Willy's Gym
4730 U.S. Route 6, Eastham
(508) 255-6370
www.willysgym.com
Willy's recently opened this second location. It offers Nautilus and Cybex equipment, a 25-yard indoor swimming pool, racquetball and squash courts, six indoor asphalt tennis courts, a basketball court, and spa. Martial arts, aerobics, and yoga are among their class offerings. It also has the only climbing wall (30 feet tall) on the Cape. Clinics offered for both members and nonmembers.

Mussel Beach Health Club
35 Bradford Street, Provincetown
(508) 487-0001
www.musselbeach.net
This popular, coed fitness club offers cardio equipment—including rowing machines, treadmills, and stair climbers—step aerobics, yoga classes, dry saunas, showers, and free parking! Nonmembers can come and use all the facilities for daily, weekly, and monthly memberships.

Provincetown Gym
Shank Painter Road, 170 Commercial Street, Provincetown
(508) 487-2776
This club features complete free weights and cardiovascular equipment, classes, and some of the best trainers around. Nonmembers are welcome for a daily or weekly fee.

Skateboarding

Skateboarders have gained a few alternatives to parking lots and sidewalks. A number of towns have developed skateboard parks to give youngsters a safe place to skate, and others are planning to create skateboard parks shortly. Orleans was the first town to establish a park in the Lower Cape and now has a permanent location on Eldredge Parkway. It's called Finch Park, in honor of Jean Finch, whose tireless efforts on behalf of young skateboarders were inspired by her grandson. Wellfleet took the lead from Orleans and built a large skateboard park and ramp course down by the town pier at Wellfleet Harbor. Barnstable, Bourne, and Falmouth have facilities, and Chatham has a new park near the airport on George Ryder Road. Call local recreation departments to see what the current facilities are.

For those parks listed kids pay a nominal fee and must adhere to a roster of common-sense rules. Helmets are a must!

Tennis Clubs

This section lists tennis clubs whose facilities are open to the general public. These facilities can offer you more than just a place to play. We tell you about their amenities, which may include pro shops, snack bars, racquet repair, instruction, and league play.

UPPER CAPE

Falmouth Sports Center
33 Highland Drive, Falmouth
(508) 548-7433
Open daily, the Falmouth Sports Center has nine hard courts, six indoor and three outdoor. Membership is not required to play. The facility offers leagues, a pro shop, and a ball machine for rent by the hour.

Southcape Resort
Route 28, Mashpee
(508) 477-4700
www.southcaperesort.com
For an hourly fee ($15 to $30) you can

play on any one of their three hard out-door and two indoor clay courts. The Southcape Resort is open year-round.

MID-CAPE

Kings Grant Racquet Club
Main Street, Cotuit
(508) 428-5744
An expert professional staff maintains the six clay courts and one hard court. This club, which offers a pro shop and clinics, is open seasonally from late May through September.

Mid-Cape Racquet and Health Club
193 White's Path, South Yarmouth
(508) 394-3511
www.midcaperacquet.com
Centrally located on Cape Cod in South Yarmouth, the Mid-Cape Racquet and Health Club is easily accessed off the Mid-Cape Highway (U.S. Route 6). If you are looking for a game, the Mid-Cape offers nine well-lit hard indoor courts. Mid-Cape has a pro shop, and racquet stringing is available through their professional staff. Court fees are $28 per hour. The club here frequently hosts tournaments, the Mid-Cape Open among them (see the Tennis listings in the Spectator Sports section of this chapter).

Sesuit Tennis Centre
1389 Route 6A, East Dennis
(508) 385-2200
The small Centre boasts a pro shop, and is the place where the locals get their racquets strung. Three outdoor courts offer fine league play or instruction, and the staff will find you a match if you are looking for new competition while visiting the Cape. The courts and pro shop are open from sunrise to sunset in season and charge $10 per person per hour for singles.

LOWER CAPE

Bamburgh House Tennis Club
Route 6A, Brewster
(508) 896-5023
Set back off Route 6A, with a small wooden sign at the entrance to the drive-way, this club offers four asphalt courts that are available from sunrise to sunset. The tennis club offers court time and lessons and stringing is available.

Oliver Tennis Courts
U.S. Route 6, Wellfleet
(508) 349-3330
Clay court enthusiasts, this is your spot. Beautifully maintained red-clay courts highlight this family-owned club. Stop by, and the pros will arrange a match for you. Leagues, lessons, and a pro shop are all available at Oliver, which is open seven days a week, mid-May through October. Court time is $18 per person to play singles.

Provincetown Tennis Club
286 Bradford Street, Provincetown
(508) 487-9574
This private club offers five clay and two hard-surface courts for nonmembers. Daily and weekly memberships are available for nonmembers (in addition to court fees). Games can be arranged, and the club also restrings racquets. The club is open from May through Columbus Day.

RELOCATION

If you've often imagined yourself standing in the doorway of your own Cape or islands home, the sea gleaming in the distance, you're in good company. Thousands of prospective homebuyers pore over the real estate listings every week hoping to find the perfect saltbox, historic sea captain's home, or contemporary beach house. A fair number of them must have spotted it: Nantucket, Dukes (Martha's Vineyard), and Barnstable Counties are ranked numbers 1 through 3 respectively as the fastest-growing counties in the Massachusetts.

People find plenty of reasons to buy on the Cape. The temperate climate, beautiful environment, laid-back lifestyle, and congenial neighborhoods are just a few of those reasons. Odds are that if you are thinking of becoming a "wash-ashore," you already know all about these things. The chapters that follow this one also give you a more complete picture of the services available to year-rounders: Education and Child Care, Health Care, Retirement, Media, and Worship.

Because of high real estate prices on the Cape, many young homeowners with growing families who choose to stay are adding on to their homes rather than moving into larger ones. Those young families who choose to leave often get a hefty price for their homes. Even as the nation's economy slumped during the early years of the 21st century, the Cape and islands housing market barreled ahead full tilt. The average selling price of a single-family home on the Cape in 2002 was roughly $360,000. In 2003 it was $423,000. That's an increase of nearly 20 percent in one year. Seeing the median selling prices might make it a bit more bearable: 2002 values range from a low of roughly $200,000 in Hyannis to a high of $466,000 in Truro. Regardless of those variations the net effect is that smaller, inexpensive homes are a distant memory.

If you can foot the bill, however, there is a wide range of housing available on this desirable spit of land. Inland you'll find neighborhood communities just like those in any town across the country. Old sea captains' homes and other antiquities are available if you prefer historical dwellings. Additionally there are streets lined with iconic, indigenous "Cape" houses: full-Cape homes, three-quarter Capes, half-Capes, and even some quarter-Capes. There are saltboxes, colonials, Greek Revival houses, and Federal dwellings; there are condominiums, second homes, investment homes, and seasonal cottages.

You may also choose to build your dream house. Land is available in many of the Cape's towns, but check on building restrictions. The Cape is known for its restrictive zoning bylaws and ordinances, which are intended to help preserve its many charms. If you are seriously considering building, it would be well worth your time to call the town hall and have a conversation with a member of the local planning board.

Also be aware that a common Cape concern is that too much of its land has already been developed, to the detriment of its once-rural character. With Mashpee growing in population by 64 percent since the 1990 U.S. Census, Truro by 32 percent, and Sandwich by 30 percent—and with most other towns showing double-digit growth—some towns fear that they will reach "build out" (a point at which all available land within a town is developed with residential homes) by a year startling close at hand. Buildable land is finite on this sandy peninsula, so many towns have reacted by instituting growth-management measures. Barnstable, for instance, has put a cap on the number of building permits it approves each year.

An act of the state legislature formed the Cape Cod Commission, which studies land-use issues and serves as a regional planning body. Polls have affirmed that the majority of Cape residents value protecting their groundwater; encouraging only clean, light industry, cultural facilities, and neighborhood businesses; and restricting the development of new, large hotels, malls, and factory outlets. The commission tries to uphold these values as it reviews the merits of proposed projects. It's a challenge, however, to protect a fragile environment and preserve community character while also meeting the needs of an increasing population, and the commission's decisions often lead to heated debates about the changing face of the Cape.

In Massachusetts local government is funded primarily by property taxes. Historically Cape towns tended to come in below the state's average tax rate. As more people move to the peninsula, however, towns are facing the need to improve infrastructure and provide more local services, such as police, emergency services, and school facilities, by increasing tax levies and fees. Rest assured, however, that property on the Cape is a good investment: Property values have increased dramatically over the last several years. To highlight an extreme the Town of Eastham saw the average assessed value of a single-family home increase 94 percent in one year!

An Insiders' tip to purchasing on Cape Cod: Don't spend every cent you have on the purchase. Many homes built on the Cape were meant only as three-season cottages; be sure to budget enough to pay for any necessary all-season home improvements after you buy. Another expense potential residents should consider is less than glamorous: septic systems. The Cape is a single-source aquifer, meaning that all of its water comes from one source, and few Cape homes are connected to limited town sewer systems. Residents have recognized the seriousness of protecting their drinking water, so living on the Cape means investing in and maintaining the high standards set by

state septic regulations. The condition of a home's septic system is generally the seller's responsibility. Make sure enough time is left for required inspections and any necessary repairs to be made before you close on a property.

In the same vein many Cape homes have private wells, which run off electric pumps, and this adds to the monthly electric bill. Cape residents also pay a fee on their tax bills that goes into the Cape Cod Land Bank fund, which is used to finance the preservation of parcels of open space. It is intended to safeguard the Cape environment and therefore, down the line, your investment in real estate.

Besides primary homes and second homes, the Cape is also known for its rental properties. Many a future year-rounder started out on the Cape by renting a cottage during the summer. A summer rental property close to the beach can fetch $800 and more each week during the summer. Over the course of a ten-week season, this can add up to nearly enough to carry a mortgage on a similar property.

The Cape Cod & Islands Association of Realtors, 22 Mid Tech Drive in South Yarmouth (800-442-0006, www.cciaor .com), is a good year-round source of information. For those who are interested in building or remodeling, real estate agencies generally have ample information about local builders.

Another source of information is the Home Builders Association of Cape Cod, 25 Mid Tech Drive in South Yarmouth (508-778-2424, www.capecodbuilders .org). This association represents approximately 90 builders and 80 suppliers throughout the Cape who work on new homes and remodeling projects.

The sections that follow provide you with a good range of real estate professionals available on the Cape. At the end of the chapter, look for a listing of the Cape's exclusive golfing communities. No matter what you choose or where, you really can't go wrong on Cape Cod.

REAL ESTATE AGENCIES

Upper Cape

Cape Coast Realty
18-B MacArthur Boulevard, Bourne
(508) 759-9517
www.capecoastrealty.com
This year-round real estate office handles properties in Bourne, Sandwich, Falmouth, and Mashpee, and deals primarily with residential properties, many of which are waterfront.

Eagle Associates Real Estate
116 Route 6A, Sandwich
(508) 888-4366
This office has much to be proud of. Principals Frank Murphy and Betsy Warren have nearly 70 years of combined experience in Cape Cod real estate. Established in 1974, the office deals primarily with the sale of land and residential and commercial property. The company covers real estate in the Upper and Mid-Cape areas from Sandwich to Barnstable and stresses the importance of personalized service.

Jack Conway and Company Inc., Realtor
128 Route 6A, Sandwich
(508) 888-2300
www.jackconway.com
The four-decade-old Conway and Company has 36 offices and approximately 600 brokers and sales staff from Boston and the South Shore to the Cape. It deals with residential, commercial, and investment properties and has a financial service division that works with out-of-town buyers. The office has specialists in development, sales, and project making and remodeling. The relocation service provides information and introduction to the community at no extra cost. The company has an in-house insurance company and other offices in Falmouth, Mashpee, and Dennis.

Kinlin Grover GMAC Real Estate
95 Route 6A, Sandwich
(508) 888-3333, (800) 303-3288
www.kinlingrover.com

Kinlin Grover GMAC has 140 sales agents plus rental agents. The company's 11 strategically located offices—from Sandwich to Wellfleet—offer you the help of local experts who know their territory and can help you find just the right property. Also see the Kinlin Grover listings under Mid-Cape and Lower Cape.

Today Real Estate
233 Cotuit Road, Sandwich
(508) 888-8008, (800) 792-6456
www.todayrealestate.com
Today Real Estate enjoys the distinction of being one of the top locally owned real estate companies on the Cape. Besides being a full-service real estate agency with more than 90 full-time associates and four office locations (Centerville, South Yarmouth, and East Harwich being the others), it also offers its clients the services of Today Mortgage Services, a full-service mortgage brokerage. All offices are open seven days a week, year-round.

Vincent Associates
Town Hall Square, 159 Main Street, Falmouth
(508) 548-6500
www.vincentassociates.com
This real estate agency has been in business in Falmouth for nearly 40 years. It offers primarily residential land and dwellings but also deals with commercial transactions and conducts home appraisals. Most of the agency's property listings are in Falmouth, Bourne, and Mashpee, but the office does not restrict itself to sales and rentals only in this area. Vincent also offers summer rentals.

Ermine Lovell Real Estate
881 Palmer Avenue, Falmouth
(508) 548-0711
www.erminelovellre.com
The office of Ermine Lovell Real Estate has been providing complete real estate service since 1935. Francesca Parkinson took over the business for Ermine Lovell. Francesca emphasizes that they haven't changed: "We still know our neighborhood,

all its advantages, and we still provide the knowledgeable service that is required to make your decision a happy one."

The company deals primarily with properties in Falmouth, Woods Hole, and Pocasset and Cataumet in Bourne. Options include land, waterfront, and residential properties; the company also operates a busy summer rental business.

Nearly half of the homes on the Lower Cape are second homes for people who live elsewhere. This is especially true in Eastham (52 percent are second homes), Truro (61 percent are second homes), and Wellfleet (64 percent are second homes).

Harriet Dugan Realty
598 Main Street, Falmouth
(508) 548-4093
Harriet Dugan knows Falmouth real estate like the back of her hand. After all, she was born and brought up in Falmouth and has been in the real estate business for more than 40 years. the company handles a full range of properties and services, including commercial land sales and leases, and waterfront property. The office, which also handles summer rentals, specializes in properties in Mashpee and Falmouth.

Great Bay Associates
77 Cypress Street, East Falmouth
(508) 540-3775
The Realtors of Great Bay Associates have been handling the sale of property in Falmouth for more than 20 years. They specialize in water-view or near-the-water properties in the East Falmouth area, more specifically on the Maravista, Acapesket, and Davisville finger peninsulas on Little, Great, Green, and Bourne pond inlets, which border Vineyard Sound. Great Bay deals primarily with residential properties—

primary homes, second homes, and investment properties, as well as land.

Century 21 Regan Realtors
Mashpee Commons, 9 Steeple Street, Mashpee
(508) 477-5200, (877) 477-5200
www.realestatecapecod.com
Celebrating 21 years in the real estate business, Century 21 Regan Realtors is a large office that specializes in waterfront properties from Bourne to Hyannis. The office has a rental division and also deals with new construction, land sales, and condominiums, as well as commercial properties. Because of its affiliation with Century 21, the Mashpee office of Century 21 Regan Realtors is linked with listings, referrals, and relocation services and general information from 6,000 offices worldwide.

Mid-Cape

RE/MAX Liberty Real Estate
3860 Falmouth Road, Marstons Mills
(508) 428-2300, (888) 428-2300
www.capecodrealestate.com/remaxliberty
A national franchise, RE/MAX has a service approach to real estate and handles many of the details that usually fall to the client, such as scheduling the time for inspection of septic systems and smoke detectors. This office focuses on residential and commercial sales and rentals within their primary market area from Dennis to the Cape Cod Canal.

The Buyer Brokerage of Osterville
874 Main Street, Osterville
(508) 420-1804, (800) 290-1804
www.osterville.com
This ten-year-old company acts exclusively as a buyer's broker, counseling the buyer throughout the home-purchase process. Partners Jane Tardanico and Stephen Perry serve as advocates for the buyer. The six-broker Osterville office specializes in properties in the Mid-Cape area and relies heavily on their team approach. The

first real estate office in the Osterville area to offer exclusive buyer representation, this firm charges no additional fee for their service (beyond the sales commission).

Coldwell Banker/Murray Real Estate
2957 Falmouth Road, Osterville
(508) 420-9955, (800) 254-6701
osterville.capecodproperty.info
Murray Real Estate has been serving the towns from Falmouth to Chatham since 1974, both as an independent agency and Coldwell Banker affiliate. The company's listings encompass a wide range of residential and commercial properties, with a focus on the Osterville area.

Kinlin Grover GMAC Real Estate
4 Wiano Avenue, Osterville
(508) 420-1130
3321 Route 6A, Barnstable
(508) 362-2120, (800) 321-2120
www.kinlingrover.com
A dynamic leader in the real estate industry, Kinlin Grover GMAC Real Estate provides distinctive personal attention to all their customers and clients with local expertise and in-depth knowledge of the area. Committed to providing exceptional real estate services with care, uncompromising honesty, and integrity, Kinlin Grover's greatest asset is an energetic team of sales professionals located throughout Cape Cod (see other Kinlin Grover listings in Upper Cape and Lower Cape sections).

Prudential Premier Properties
1284B Main Street, Osterville
(508) 428-3320
www.prupremierproperties.com
This firm has been in business for nearly 40 years, and has been associated with Prudential for several of them. The company has 45 agents in four offices (other locations include 767 East Falmouth Highway in Falmouth [508-540-3810], and 17 Cove Road in Orleans [508-255-5555], and one off-Cape in Franklin, Massachusetts). Premier Properties can provide

appraisal, purchase, sale, and rental services for both residential and commercial properties. The office deals extensively with waterfront village and golf course properties, as well as new construction.

Today Real Estate
1533 Route 28, Centerville
(508) 790-2300, (800) 966-2448
www.todayrealestate.com
Established in 1985, this large and active real estate company has offices in Sandwich, South Yarmouth, East Harwich, and at the Centerville location listed above. Today's other Mid-Cape office is in South Yarmouth and located at 487 Station Avenue (508-398-0600 or 800-966-0369). Today boasts more than 90 full-time sales associates who specialize in residential property, both owner-occupied and investment properties. Today Real Estate also publishes and distributes its own listings catalog. The office is open seven days a week. (See the Upper and Lower Cape sections for other Today Real Estate offices.)

Bay Harbor Realty Inc.
3227 Route 6A, Barnstable
(508) 362-5505
www.capecodrealestate.com/bayharbor
Ruth Cutler and Marge Gibson are the principals of this office, which covers the Mid-Cape area from Sandwich to Orleans. Cutler has been active in real estate for more than 20 years, and her partner has close to 30 years of experience. This office has four full-time and four part-time Realtors, and deals with properties from starter to upper-end homes.

Strawberry Hill Real Estate
340 West Main Street, Hyannis
(508) 775-8000, (800) 882-8586
www.strawberryhillre.com
Principal Adrienne Siegel has been selling real estate on Cape Cod for more than 20 years. The agency deals primarily with Barnstable and its villages and with the Mid-Cape area in general. She and five

other brokers sell mostly residential real estate—single-family homes, condominiums, estate sales, and waterfront property.

Realty Executives
1330 Phinney's Lane, Hyannis
(508) 362-1300, (800) 244-1592
www.capecodschoice.com

A national firm, Realty Executives is generally credited with starting the concept of 100 percent commissions, a motivating factor that allows a broker to earn nearly the entire sales commission rather than splitting it with the agency. About 95 percent of calls to the office are generated by agent advertising. The Hyannis office, along with offices on Gifford Avenue in Falmouth (508-495-3222) and at the junction of Routes 137 and 39 in East Harwich (508-432-5100), have between 300 and 400 listings. For regional referrals Realty Executives has offices scattered throughout Massachusetts.

Bill Harrison, Realtors
Cape Realty Building, 299 Route 28, West Yarmouth
(508) 771-7974
www.harrisonre.com

A Realtor since 1958, Harrison and the nine other brokers in his office deal primarily with residential property in the Mid-Cape area in Barnstable, Yarmouth, and Dennis. The full-service real estate office deals with listing and selling property. Harrison has been named Realtor of the Year, is a certified residential specialist, and a graduate of the Realtor Institute in Washington, D.C.

Peter McDowell Associates
585 Route 6A, Dennis
(508) 385-9114, (888) 385-9114
11 Route 28, Dennisport
(508) 394-5400, (800) 870-5401
www.capecodproperties.com

Serving the Dennis, Yarmouth, Barnstable, Brewster, and Harwich areas for nearly 40 years, Peter McDowell Associate has two offices in the town of Dennis—one on the north side and the other on the south side. A well-respected real estate company, it offers many fine residential properties for sale in the five-town area, as well as hundreds of rental properties in the town of Dennis.

Steele Associates Real Estate
1372 Route 134, East Dennis
(508) 385-7311
www.steelerealty.com

Independently owned and operated by Joseph D. Steele, this full-service real estate agency has developed a specialty of handling beach-area property, particularly along the north section of Dennis. The agency also handles the sale of residential homes, condominiums, land, and commercial properties in the towns of Yarmouth, Brewster, and Harwich. Steele Associates has a staff of 9 agents offering the highest degree of personal service.

James E. Mischler Realtors
Intersection of Routes 28 and 134, West Dennis
(508) 394-3330, (800) 863-3330
www.capecodrealestate.com/mischler realtors

Established in 1979 by Jim and Rita Mischler, James E. Mischler Realtors specializes in the sale and rental of property on or near salt water. The company handles sales throughout the Cape from their central West Dennis location, as well as some 400 vacation rental properties near the water in the towns of Dennis, Harwich, and Brewster.

Reef Realty Ltd.
24 School Street, West Dennis
(508) 394-3090, (800) 346-4059
www.reefrealty.com

Since it was established in 1985, this firm has won numerous local and regional sales awards. The staff of Realtors handles an extensive number of sales properties, both residential and commercial, with a focus on Dennis and Yarmouth properties. Reef Realty Ltd. is also a residential custom-building company and developer with more than 100 years of combined experience. They are members of the Cape Cod Home Builders Association as well as the National Home Builders Association.

Lower Cape

Great Locations Real Estate
2660 Route 6A, Brewster
(800) 626-9984
www.greatlocationsre.com

This full-service real estate office specializes in vacation homes, golf course properties, and retirement properties in the Brewster, Dennis, and Orleans areas, and represents the Ocean Edge Resort properties. Great Locations Real Estate offers expert property management and rental management on the properties it sells, which range from beautiful condominiums to elegant waterfront homes.

Kinlin Grover GMAC Real Estate
1990 Main Street (Route 6A), Brewster
(508) 896-7000, (888) 316-8533
2548 U.S. Route 6, Wellfleet
(508) 349-9800, (888) 349-8800
www.kinlingrover.com

Whether you are looking for beachfront on Cape Cod Bay or high on the dunes overlooking the Atlantic Ocean, the Wellfleet office provides distinctive personal attention to your needs and lifestyle.

Today Real Estate
160 Route 137, East Harwich
(508) 430-8288, (800) 430-4848
www.todayrealestate.com

Established in 1985, this large and active real estate company has other offices in Sandwich, South Yarmouth, and Centerville. Today's 90-plus sales associates handle both residential and investment properties from the Cape Cod Canal to the Lower Cape. Other services include a full-service mortgage brokerages and educational services for Realtors. The office is open seven days a week. (See

Today's listings in the Mid-Cape and Upper Cape sections.)

Coldwell Banker/Murray Real Estate
587 Main Street, Harwichport
(508) 432-6600, (800) 775-9980
harwich.capecodproperty.info

Murray Real Estate has been serving the towns from Falmouth to Chatham since 1974, both as an independent agency and the Coldwell Banker affiliate. The company's listings encompass a wide range of residential and commercial properties, with a focus on the Harwich area.

Pine Acres Realty
9368 Route 28, Chatham
(508) 945-1186
www.pineacresrealty.com

One of the oldest real estate offices in Chatham (Pine Acres opened in 1948), this company has many exclusive properties along Chatham's waterfront as well as in the towns of Harwich and Orleans. It is an affiliate of Christie's Great Estates, which is a high-end referral network. Pine Acres Realty has 10 brokers. They also offer rentals.

Most homes on the Cape have septic systems. If you're thinking of buying here, you should know that state regulations require the seller to inspect the system and repair or replace it if necessary as part of the sale.

Sylvan Realty
Town Hall Square, 37 Cross Street, Chatham
(508) 945-7777
www.sylvanrealty.com

Sylvan is a full-service real estate company that specializes in Lower Cape properties, particularly in Chatham and Harwich. Exclusive listings include homes, cottages, condominiums, land, and commercial properties.

American Heritage Realty
414 Route 28, South Orleans
(508) 255-2202, (800) 420-1776
www.capecodforsale.com,
www.americanheritagerealty.com
American Heritage has been one of the leading real estate companies on the Lower Cape for nearly 40 years. They specialize in the sale of waterfront and water-view properties in the towns of Orleans, Chatham, Harwich, Eastham, Brewster, and Wellfleet.

The professional staff can also assist you with sales of vacation homes, ocean-front properties, condos, and land. You can view on-line their inventory of homes for sale and vacation rentals.

The Real Estate Company
207 Main Street, East Orleans
(508) 255-5100
www.capecodvacation.com
Owner/broker Trisha Daly-Karlson has thrived in the Lower Cape real estate community for 30 years. Located on the road to Nauset Beach in East Orleans, her sales department is staffed with 12 professional agents dedicated to providing you with the most up-to-date information available in the marketplace. Supported by some of the most progressive and technically advanced innovations in the industry, they are always striving to meet your ever-changing needs.

The Real Estate Company also manages more than 300 vacation rentals on the Lower Cape (check out their listing in the Vacation Rentals chapter). Their Web site allows you access to their entire inventory of homes.

Anchor Real Estate
U.S. Route 6, North Eastham
(508) 255-4949
www.anchor-realestate.net
Suzanne Goodrich opened this office in 1980. Anchor's staff includes seven brokers who live and work in Eastham. Their primary focus is sale of residential homes and vacant land throughout the Lower Cape, particularly in Orleans, Eastham,

Wellfleet, and Truro. The staff also offers more than 200 summer rental properties (see our Vacation Rentals chapter).

Outer Cape Realty
5150 U.S. Route 6, North Eastham
(508) 255-0505
www.outercaperealty.com
The oldest real estate company in Eastham, Outer Cape was established in 1956. This office features a friendly staff of four Realtors who offer single-family homes, cottages, and beautiful waterfront homes in the Eastham and South Wellfleet area.

Duarte/Downey Real Estate Agency
12 Truro Center Road, Truro
(508) 349-7588
www.ddre.com
This Truro real estate agency first opened its doors for business in 1937. A full-service brokerage with six Realtors, Duarte/Downey offers residential properties, including single-family homes, cottages, and condominiums in its primary market area of Truro and Wellfleet. The agency also features water-front homes and land as well as rentals in the Truro area.

Truro Real Estate
U.S. Route 6 at Fisherman's Road, Truro
(508) 487-4225
www.trurorealestate.com
Chuck Leigh founded this company more than 10 years ago and offers residential homes, condominiums, and cottages as well as land and commercial sale properties in its primary market area of Wellfleet, Truro, and Provincetown. Many of the properties are in and around the Cape Cod National Seashore. Truro Real Estate has three Realtors covering the Lower Cape.

Chequessett Village Real Estate
3 West Main Street, Wellfleet
(508) 349-3411, (800) 334-0909
www.chequessettvillage.com
Known as one of the first real estate offices in Wellfleet (and the oldest surviving one in town), Chequessett Village has

been privately owned and operated for more than 50 years. It handles Wellfleet properties, commercial and residential, in all price ranges.

Harborside Realty
162 Commercial Street, Provincetown
(508) 487-4005, (800) 838-4005
www.harborside-realty.com
This agency handles sales and rental properties in Provincetown—from residential homes and condominiums to guesthouses and commercial properties. Realtor Len Bowen has been in the business for more than 30 years.

GOLF COMMUNITIES

If your idea of living well is rolling out of bed and right onto the first tee, you may be interested in buying into one of the Cape's superlative golfing communities. These developments feature luxury home sites, some built right alongside the property owners' private course. Most of the communities have clubhouses and other recreational facilities—swimming pools and tennis courts, for example—to appease the nongolfing members of the family.

New Seabury Resort & Conference Center
12 Mallway, New Seabury (Mashpee)
(508) 477-8300
www.newseaburyre.com
New Seabury is a premier golfing and resort community with two championship courses (see our Golf chapter). The complex also boasts 16 outdoor tennis courts, walking and riding trails, 3 miles of beach front, and outstanding dining facilities in the area. The resort is about 3 miles from Mashpee Commons and abuts South Cape Beach and conservation land.

Condominiums here are referred to as villas, and numerous communities are available. Beautifully situated on the water, Maushop, for example, is styled after Nantucket village—crushed seashell paths and white picket fences—and consists of

The last hurricane to really batter Cape Cod was Hurricane Bob, back in 1991. Winds reached speeds of 110 mph. Given its geographic location, weather forecasters believe the Cape could someday be hit with a storm with winds up to 130 mph—not good news for all the new development along the shoreline. In case of a storm, the Massachusetts Military Reservation would be used as a shelter.

mostly two-bedroom villas. The Mews units have a contemporary New England style and are scattered among the golf courses. These villas on one or two floors are built on small lots that utilize the outdoor areas and maintain privacy. Tidewatch condominiums, in the original area of New Seabury developed on the water, are like a hotel with a common area. The units have two sometimes three bedrooms, and some are on three levels. Most are an easy walk to the country club. Beautiful oceanfront house lots are also available. Some properties here have a pool and two-car garage.

Ballymeade Country Club & Estates
Route 151, North Falmouth
(508) 457-4455
www.ballymeade.com
Situated on 1,045 acres of land, Ballymeade Country Club & Estates is a golf course residential community featuring New England colonial architecture with a contemporary Cape flair. It currently has 274 single-family homes and 30 townhouses. The property's rolling hills permit distant water views and gorgeous sunsets. Ballymeade offers a challenging 18-hole golf course (see our Golf chapter), a large clubhouse, 10 tennis courts, a swimming pool, and a restaurant.

A property includes duplex townhouses with wonderful views of Buzzards Bay and the golf course. Ballymeade is 6 miles from Falmouth and 7 miles from the

Bourne Bridge. Many residents here commute to work in Boston. Among the favorable features are spacious grounds, a limited number of residences, and conservation land. Ballymeade has a building division and works with buyers on designs.

Kings Way
Route 6A, Yarmouthport
(508) 362-8800

Situated off Route 6A in Yarmouthport near the Yarmouth-Dennis line, Kings Way is a condominium community with an 18-hole executive-style golf course, a clubhouse, tennis court, swimming pool, country store, and meeting house. The townhomes range in size from 1,300 square feet to 1,800 square feet. All units have a minimum of two bedrooms, two bathrooms, a two-car garage, and a full basement. Carriage homes range from 900 to 1,200 square feet and include two bedrooms, two baths, an attached one-car garage, a private courtyard entrance, and deck or patio overlooking the golf course. Out of the planned total of 450 units, more than two-thirds are presently occupied. Residents are predominantly retired.

EDUCATION AND CHILD CARE

Educational opportunities on the Cape abound. From Montessori preschools through colleges, the Cape matches its rich natural environment with an equal wealth of academic offerings. Excellent public schools prepare students for an academic career anywhere in the United States, including at Ivy League or top-ranked state and private colleges. Two private high schools, Cape Cod Academy and Falmouth Academy, also are known for preparing students for stellar academic careers in higher education. Our pair of technical schools offers excellent vocational education, and several colleges, including Cape Cod Community College in Barnstable—which has ties to the University of Massachusetts at Dartmouth—offer extension courses. The arts are highly valued on the Cape, and specialized schools offer both residents and short-term visitors exciting classes in the visual arts, theater, and creative writing.

Just about every town on the Cape offers continuing education enrichment classes for adults and stimulating nondegree programs for senior citizens. Community school programs in most towns provide all ages with academic and recreational opportunities, and, befitting the region's maritime tradition, two educational programs dedicated to the sea are located here: Massachusetts Maritime Academy in Buzzards Bay and the Sea Education Association Semester (SEAS) offered at Woods Hole.

For younger learners there are a number of preschool and child care centers available. We'll begin with a rundown of the Cape's public schools, them move on to private schools, preschools, and child care centers. The chapter concludes with a listing of local libraries.

EDUCATION
Public Schools

Each town on the Cape has its own school department with administration overseen by an elected school committee. The Cape's two regional school systems (Dennis-Yarmouth and Nauset) have both regional and local school committees, and all schools now have advisory councils. Many schools offer after-school programs. Some public schools, such as Barnstable, also offer preschool programs, but most preschools are operated privately; see the end of this chapter for information on preschools and child care.

UPPER CAPE

Bourne has six schools, including two high schools, one middle school, and three elementary schools, serving a student population of 2,612. Three of the schools are on the Massachusetts Military Reservation, one is in Sagamore, and the rest are in Bourne.

Falmouth serves 4,578 students in seven schools—four elementary, one middle (for grades 5 and 6), one junior high (grades 7 and 8), and one high school.

Mashpee has seen tremendous residential growth in recent years, and the town's total school enrollment of 1,960 is close to double the size it was in the mid-1990s. Mashpee has a state-of-the-art high school, a middle school, and two elementary schools: Coombs School, which offers preschool through grade 2, and the Quashnet school for students in grade 3 through grade 6.

Sandwich has a public high school built in 1975 and three schools for kindergarten through 8th grade in the village,

East Sandwich, and Forestdale. One of the fastest-growing towns in the Commonwealth during the 1990s, Sandwich has a school system serving 4,171 students. The high school is a focus for many activities in the community, including night classes and swimming programs; call (508) 888-5300 for information.

The Upper Cape is also home to a technical school that serves 610 students in grades 9 through 12 and those at the postsecondary level. Upper Cape Cod Regional Technical School (508-563-5515), located on Sandwich Road in Bourne, also accepts students from outside the Upper Cape area on a tuition basis. The LPN (licensed practical nurse) program graduates about 32 students a year. The high school offers instruction in subjects as diverse as carpentry, cosmetology, and culinary arts, among many others.

MID-CAPE

The Mid-Cape area has the largest school system on the Cape, located in the Cape's largest, most populated town of Barnstable. The Barnstable School System has about 6,229 students in 12 schools, including a large high school. There are also two middle schools and 9 elementary schools in town.

Barnstable now has a charter school, the Sturgis Charter School (508-778-1782), launched in the fall of 1998. The school, located on Main Street in Hyannis, serves 280 students in grades 9 through 12. Barnstable also has a charter middle school: The Barnstable Horace Mann Charter School serves 525 students in grade 5. Charter schools were created under the state's Education Reform Act of 1993 and are designed to be laboratories of experimental teaching; they offer an alternative to public schools and, at the same time, encourage public schools to become more inventive. Like the other charter schools scattered throughout the state (the first one on Cape Cod was the Lighthouse Charter School in Orleans, listed below), Sturgis is publicly funded, and, in

choosing its limited enrollment, the school gives priority to those who reside in the host district.

Serving both Dennis and Yarmouth is the Dennis-Yarmouth Regional School District with a total enrollment of 4,329 students in eight schools. The regional high school on Station Avenue in South Yarmouth has 1,214 students from both towns, each of which have their own middle and elementary schools. The high school is the site of most classes in the region's adult education program.

LOWER CAPE

Harwich schools serve 572 children in preschool through grade 4 at Harwich Elementary School, 509 students in grades 5 through 8 at Harwich Middle School, and 419 students in grades 9 through 12 at Harwich High School. Adult education courses are offered in the fall and winter; call (508) 430-2355 for more information. For updates on courses and activities, check out their Web site at www.harwich.edu.

Harwich is also home to Cape Cod Regional Technical School, which has an enrollment of 665 students, hailing from towns as far away as Mashpee and Provincetown. The students alternate between attending technical and academic classes, and earn both high school diplomas and certification in such fields as electrical engineering, plumbing, auto maintenance, computer technology, horticulture, cosmetology, and graphic arts. One of only two technical schools on the Cape, Cape Cod Tech has become so popular that it has had to turn students away in recent years.

Chatham operates three schools, an elementary school with 289 students in prekindergarten through grade 4, a new middle school with 217 students in grades 5 through 8, and a high school with 233 students in grades 9 through 12. The middle school was built adjacent to the high school on Crowell Road, so the two share some core facilities.

The Nauset Regional School District includes the towns of Brewster, Orleans, Eastham, and Wellfleet. Each has its own local elementary school. Brewster, which has seen tremendous growth in the last decade, now has two schools: Stony Brook Elementary School (formerly called Brewster Elementary School) and Eddy Elementary School, which opened in 1997. Stony Brook has an enrollment of 338 in kindergarten through grade 5. The Eddy School has 253 students in kindergarten through grade 5.

Orleans Elementary School has 229 students in kindergarten through grade 5. Eastham Elementary School has 258 students, and Wellfleet Elementary is the district's smallest school with 131 students. Students from all four towns attend Nauset Regional Middle School in Orleans, which has an enrollment of 819 students in 6th, 7th, and 8th grades, and Nauset Regional High School in Eastham, which serves a student population of 1,013 in grades 9 through 12. Adult continuing education courses are held at the middle school; for information call (508) 255-4300.

The Cape Cod Lighthouse Charter School (508-240-2800) in Orleans is an independent public school with open enrollment for grades 6 through 8. The first of its kind on the Cape, it was formed under the state's Education Reform Act and opened in 1994 as one of a handful of experimental public schools across the Commonwealth. The school has an enrollment of 180. Tuition is free; however, students must meet admission requirements. The majority of the students are from the Nauset District, and admission is by a lottery process.

Truro has no middle or high school of its own, but has an excellent elementary school, Truro Central School, which has 113 students in preschool through grade 6. Older students attend either Nauset Regional Middle School and then Nauset Regional High School or Provincetown Junior and Senior High School.

Provincetown's school system comprises two schools with a combined enrollment of about 300. Veteran's Memorial Elementary School serves 128 students from preschool through grade 6, and Provincetown Junior and Senior High School has 163 students in grades 7 through 12—some of whom, as explained above, come from neighboring Truro.

Private Schools

UPPER CAPE

Falmouth Academy
7 Highfield Drive, Falmouth
(508) 457-9696
www.falmouthacademy.org
A college preparatory school with roughly 200 students, the academy provides a core curriculum (science, math, English, history, and a foreign language) for grades 7 through 12, plus an inclusive athletic program and numerous elective courses, including chamber orchestra, volunteer work, and boating. Students come from as far away as Orleans, Martha's Vineyard, and Carver. Situated in the beautiful Beebe Woods property donated to the town by the late Josiah Lilly of Lilly Drug Company, the school has an aggressive financial-aid program; nearly 40 percent of the students receive some type of financial aid.

Heritage Christian Academy
655 Boxberry Hill Road, Falmouth
(508) 564-6341
This nondenominational Christian school offers a Bible-based curriculum and boasts small class sizes with a teacher-student ratio of about 1 to 10. It currently has an enrollment of 67 students in kindergarten though grade 8. Heritage is also proud of its standardized testing scores, which generally show its students are one to two years ahead of their public school counterparts here. Art, music, and gym are all standard offerings, and the school maintains a financial-aid program.

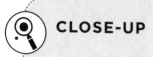

Libraries

Welcome to CLAMS—Cape Libraries Automated Materials Sharing. Twenty-six libraries from Falmouth to Provincetown, have joined together to share resources through a computerized system with terminals located in each library. Not only has it made it more convenient to borrow books, it has improved service by providing immediate information on the location of the 1.5 million items—including books, periodicals, and audiovisual resources—available through the system.

Your CLAMS card is easy to obtain; all you need to do is show the librarian a proof of identity and have a local phone number to give them, and you may borrow material from any CLAMS library. It also give you membership benefits, such as video borrowing or access to a variety of museum passes. These offer a free pass or discount to admissions to some of this region's finest museums, such as the Cape Cod Museum of Natural History, the Heritage Plantation in Sandwich, and the Boston Museum of Science.

Each library has a Friends organization, usually a very active group of community members who support the activities of each library with book sales, authors' luncheons, and lecture series.

Upper Cape

Sandwich Public Library
142 Main Street, Sandwich
(508) 888-0625

Jonathan Bourne Library
19 Sandwich Road, Bourne
(508) 759-0644

Falmouth Library
123 Katherine Lee Bates Road, Falmouth
(508) 457-2555

East Falmouth Library
310 East Falmouth Highway, East Falmouth
(508) 548-6340

North Falmouth Library
Chester Street, North Falmouth
(508) 563-2922

West Falmouth Library
575 West Falmouth Highway, West Falmouth
(508) 548-4709

Mashpee Public Library
Route 151, Mashpee
(508) 539-1435

Mid-Cape

Centerville Library
585 Main Street, Centerville
(508) 790-6220

Cotuit Library
871 Main Street, Cotuit
(508) 428-8141

Hyannis Public Library
401 Main Street, Hyannis
(508) 775-2280

Marstons Mills Public Library
2160 Main Street, Marstons Mills
(508) 428-5175

Osterville Free Library
43 Wianno Avenue, Osterville
(508) 428-5757

Sturgis Library
3090 Main Street, Barnstable
(508) 362-6636

Whelden Memorial Library
2501 Meetinghouse Way (Route 149),
West Barnstable
(508) 362-2262

Cape Cod Community College
Route 132, Barnstable
(508) 362-2131

South Yarmouth Library
312 Main Street, South Yarmouth
(508) 760-4820

West Yarmouth Library
391 Main Street, West Yarmouth
(508) 775-5206

Yarmouthport Library
297 Main Street, Yarmouthport
(508) 362-3717

Dennis Memorial Library
1021 Old Bass River Road, Dennis
(508) 385-2255

Dennis Public Library
673 Main Street, Dennis
(508) 760-6219

Jacob Sears Memorial Library
23 Center Street, East Dennis
(508) 385-8151

South Dennis Free Public Library
389 Main Street, South Dennis
(508) 394-8954

West Dennis Free Public Library
272 Main Street, West Dennis
(508) 398-2050

Lower Cape

Brewster Ladies' Library
1822 Main Street, Brewster
(508) 896-3913

Brooks Free Library
739 Main Street, Harwich
(508) 430-7562

Chase Library
5 Main Street, West Harwich
(508) 432-2610

Harwichport Library Association
47 Lower Bank Street, Harwichport
(508) 432-3320

Eldredge Public Library
564 Main Street, Chatham
(508) 945-5170

South Chatham Public Library
2559 Main Street, South Chatham
(508) 430-7898

Snow Library
67 Main Street, Orleans
(508) 240-3760

Wellfleet Public Library
55 West Main Street, Wellfleet
(508) 349-0310

Eastham Public Library
190 Samoset Road, Eastham
(508) 240-5950

Truro Public Library
5 Library Lane, Truro
(508) 487-1125

Provincetown Public Library
330 Commercial Street, Provincetown
(508) 487-7094

Brewster Ladies' Library, located on Route 6A, features a large children's area and sponsors frequent lectures and exhibits. ERICA BOLLERUD

MID-CAPE

Cape Cod Academy
50 Osterville-West Barnstable Road,
Osterville
(508) 428-5400
www.ccacademy.pvt.k12.ma.us
Now in its 27th year, this private school has an enrollment of about 400 students from kindergarten through 12th grade. Students come from as far away as Wellfleet and Duxbury. The student/teacher ratio is 8 to 1, and the average class size is 15 students. Athletics, the arts, foreign languages, advanced placement courses, and computer science for all grades are areas of emphasis. The school, which includes a student activity center with a gymnasium, has a strong financial-aid program.

LOWER CAPE

Trinity Christian Academy
10 Carter Road, South Yarmouth
(508) 394-4118
Opened in 1967, this interdenominational Christian school has about 55 students in preschool through grade 8. The curriculum is traditional and Bible based. French is taught in grades 1 through 8, and writing skills are emphasized in every grade. The school holds weekly chapel and has a bell choir.

Family School-Saltbox School
3571 Route 6A, Brewster
(508) 896-6555
Housed in two buildings in a pleasant wooded setting with outdoor play areas and a pool, the Family School offers programs for infants, toddlers, preschoolers, and elementary school students through grade 5, as well as an after-school program and summer camp. Accredited by the National Academy of Schools, the Family School emphasizes nurturing and the developmental stages of each child, and it accepts state-funded voucher programs for tuition.

The Laurel Day School
1436 Route 137, Brewster
(508) 896-4934
www.laurel-school.com
This private, state-certified school offers programs for preschool through grade 8, with a focus on individualized instruction that encourages children to develop into self-starters and perpetual learners. With an enrollment of about 130 students, Laurel stresses environmental studies, language arts (including French), and creative and artistic expression. The school also offers a series of after-school arts classes.

Higher Education

Cape Cod Community College
Route 132, West Barnstable
(508) 362-2131
www.capecod.mass.edu
Set on 116 acres a few miles from Hyannis, Cape Cod Community College offers both day and evening classes to its 4,000 students. Two-year programs lead to associate degrees in several areas, including the arts, humanities, and sciences, as well as in nursing, hotel and restaurant management, dental hygiene, and criminal justice. The academic programs are organized into two divisions with seven departments: business, health, social sciences, arts and communications, natural sciences and life fitness, mathematics, and languages and

Get your bachelor's or master's degree on the Cape. Cape Cod Community College (known as 4Cs) has an office of extended studies. It coordinates BA and MA programs being offered on campus by participating colleges and universities such as Suffolk, Lesley, Wheelock, and U-Mass Dartmouth. Call (508) 375-4082 for more information.

The Academy for Lifelong Learning is a program offered through Cape Cod Community College. Open to all residents age 50 and older, for $75 in tuition you can take two classes per semester in subjects such as literature, history, language, music, religion, and more. Call (508) 362-2131, ext. 4400, or visit www.allcapecod.org for more information.

literature. The college has a particularly strong communications program.

Opened in 1961 in the building that is now the Barnstable Town Hall, Cape Cod Community College was established as part of the community college system in Massachusetts. One hundred and sixty-three students from 33 communities enrolled during its first year. Outgrowing space quickly, the college moved in 1970 to its current location in West Barnstable, making it the first community college in the state to build a new campus.

Massachusetts Maritime Academy
101 Academy Drive, Buzzards Bay
(508) 830-5000, (800) 544-3411
www.maritime.edu
The Massachusetts Maritime Academy is the oldest continually operating maritime academy in the country. Bachelor of Science degrees are awarded in marine engineering, marine transportation, facilities and environmental engineering, and marine safety and environmental protection. Some students use their time to earn a Merchant Marine officer's license or a Naval officer's commission. The four-year coed course of study includes practical experience on the training ship *Patriot State*, which gives students an opportunity to visit numerous countries during their semester-at-sea. Eight hundred and fifty students come from across the nation and participate in a full range of activities and athletics. The academic year includes two academic semesters of approximately 15 weeks and a sea term or internship.

Sea Education Association
171 Woods Hole Road, Woods Hole
(800) 885-3633
www.seaeducation.org
This unusual college program offers the academic equivalent of a full college semester on board the *Robert C. Seamens* or the *Corwith Cramer,* both 134-foot brigantines. The *Cramer* is named for the founder of SEA, who designed a program for college students that enables them to spend 12 weeks on shore studying oceanography, nautical science, and maritime studies, followed by six weeks at sea practicing oceanography. Each student is also expected to complete an academic project. Students do not need any prior sailing experience, nor do they have to be science majors. The academic complex, a ca. 1889 estate, is located on a scenic hilltop site, it includes a lecture hall, classrooms, a laboratory, student library, computer room, study areas, and faculty and staff offices.

Arts Education

UPPER CAPE

Falmouth Artists' Guild
744 Main Street, Falmouth
(508) 540-3304
www.arts-cape.com/falag
The guild offers classes and workshops year-round in drawing, painting, pottery, silversmithing, and weaving for very reasonable prices (members get a discount). Class offerings vary from season to season, but run the gamut of media from watercolors to colored pencils. There are also classes for children.

MID-CAPE

Cape Cod Conservatory
Route 132, West Barnstable and
Beebe Woods Highfield Drive, Falmouth
(508) 362-2772, (408) 540-0611
www.capecodconservatory.org
The conservatory's main facility is in its

47th season of teaching music, art, dance, and drama, and also offers classes at the Beebe Woods Center. The conservatory has about 1,200 students, mostly from the Cape. Dance classes for adults and children include ballet, tap, and jazz. Drama and art are also offered. Adults may take courses in oil painting, monotype, and music instruction in all instruments. High school students make for about 60 percent of the music classes, which are open to all ages.

Cotuit Center for the Arts
4404 Route 28, Cotuit
(508) 428-0669
www.cotuitcenterforthearts.org

This thriving arts center offers a wide range of arts classes for all ages. Children as young as 4 can sign up for combined arts and music classes, and teens and adults can sign up for drama, individual or group instruction in drawing and painting, photography, and painting en plein air. There are also computer graphics classes, writing workshops, life-drawing sessions, and more.

LOWER CAPE

Academy of Performing Arts
5 Giddish Hill Road, Orleans
(508) 255-5510
www.apa1.org

Associated with the Academy Playhouse (see our Arts chapter), this school offers a variety of performance classes, including dance, acting, voice, and music lesson. Classes are for the young and the young-at-heart and are given in two 18-week sessions. The academy also offers a summer camp. (See the reference in our Kidstuff chapter.)

Cape Cod Photo Workshops
135 Oak Leaf Road, North Eastham
(508) 255-6808
www.capecodphotoworkshops.com

Cape Cod Photo Workshops is dedicated to teaching all facets of photography.

With more than 20 separate weekend and weeklong workshops scheduled from May through September, you can study everything from light meters to photo collage. There are about 18 instructors who have distinguished themselves in the world of photography, and there are classes to suit every level, from beginner to advanced. On photo-taking excursions you'll visit some of the most beautiful nature spots in the area.

Truro Center for the Arts at Castle Hill
Castle and Meetinghouse Roads, Truro
(508) 349-7511
www.castlehill.org

One of the Lower Cape's most respected nonprofit educational institutions, Castle Hill has for 30 years offered classes with instructors who are both talented and distinguished. Housed in an 1880s barn with and adjacent windmill that contains the school's administrative offices, this unusual school offers a full range of courses in painting, sculpture, printmaking, pottery, poetry, playwriting, and fiction. Course offerings vary from year to year, but are always interesting and challenging. There are classes for children, a lecture series, and artist receptions. Classes are held in July and August, and it's a good idea to register as early as possible, because many of them fill up fast.

The Cape Cod School of Art
48 Pearl Street, Provincetown
(508) 487-0101
www.capecodschoolofart.com

Founded in 1899 by Charles Hawthorne, the painter who is credited with transforming Provincetown into an important art colony, the Cape Cod School of Art is now run by noted impressionist painter Lois Griffel. The studio itself is a large rustic barn, but most of the teaching is done outdoors—something Hawthorne encouraged his students to do. Griffel herself teaches workshops in "Painting the Impressionist Landscape," one of the school's most popular classes. Other well-known local and nationally known artists teach weeklong workshops in pastels, figure painting, and watercolor. The school operates in the summer and early fall. It was closed at press time for expansion and renovation and is expected to open again for the summer of 2004.

Hawthorne School of Art
29 Miller Hill Road, Provincetown
(508) 487-1236
www.hawthorneacademy.org
Charles Hawthorne built this studio (not to be confused with the Cape Cod School of Art he also founded; see above) in 1899 high upon a sand dune. In 1989 Olga Opsahl-Gee and her husband, painter Peter Gee, reopened the studio with the hopes of "creating new artists on Cape Cod." In the summer they offer weeklong classes and workshops taught by local and world-renowned instructors in such areas as raku pottery, experimental painting, fiber craft, and photographic imaging. The school also has children's workshops, a perfect (and creative) way for parents to have a little time to themselves while their children have fun in a bucolic setting!

Fine Arts Work Center
24 Pearl Street, Provincetown
(508) 487-9960
www.fawc.org
Founded in 1968 by a group of visionary artists and writers (including poet Stanley Kunitz and artist Robert Motherwell) as a place where emerging artists are given an uninterrupted seven months to hone their work, this former lumberyard has since become one of the world's leading artistic retreats, nurturing such creative artists as Portia Munson, Jayne Anne Phillips, Dennis Johnson, Tama Janowitz, and Michael Cunningham. More than 1,000 people apply for the competitive Winter Program each year, but only 20 (10 creative writers and 10 visual artists) are accepted. Residencies, which run from October through April, include room and board plus monthly stipends. The application deadline for writers is December 1; for visual artists it's February 1.

The open-enrollment summer program is a series of weeklong and weekend workshops in creative writing and visual arts. These workshops run from late June through August, and a distinguished faculty, including Robert Pinsky, Paula Vogel, and Grace Paley, conduct the workshops.

The Fine Arts Work Center also hosts scores of readings and exhibitions throughout the year, as well as occasional benefits, including the much-anticipated fund-raising auction, held each August (see our Annual Events chapter). A free catalog for the summer program is available each January from the address above.

CHILD CARE

One of the top priorities for the local communities on Cape Cod is providing adequate child care for the local workforce. Although the Cape has a large retirement population, it is also filled with young families who live here year-round. As in other areas of the country, working parents sometimes find good day care hard to come by. A number of family day-care providers have sprung up in response to that need, along with a growing number of pre-schools. This region still lags behind urban areas in responding adequately to the demand, but new centers are being proposed, and state agencies are attempting to find solutions.

In some cases preschools also offer infant care and toddler programs, but finding the right care often requires an extensive search. A few local businesses now offer on-site day care, and this number continues to grow, so you might want to check into that option.

Preschools and child-care centers must be licensed by the state or show that they are exempt from licensing. You can check the compliance record of any Cape childcare center by calling the Massachusetts

Office of Childcare Services at its Lakeville office at (508) 947-1133.

One important resource for referrals is the Child Care Network of Cape Cod, 115 Enterprise Road, Hyannis (508-778-9470, 888-530-2430), a nonprofit agency that maintains a list of all preschools and day-care facilities in the area. They know where vacancies are and which centers are licensed to take drop-in students; the agency can also refer families to other services children may need. On the Lower Cape check with the Cape Cod Children's Place, 995 Nauset Road, Eastham (508-240-3310), a regional family resource center that not only offers child care but also has information about local child-care providers and preschools, and other services that families may require.

Despite the number of preschool and day-care centers that have opened on the Cape, gaps still remain; many Cape residents work at night and rely on family members and babysitters to take care of their youngsters. There are no "tot-drop" places or 24-hour child-care services on the Cape, and no babysitting services, but on Nantucket, there's Nantucket Babysitters Service (508-228-4970). The Children's Place in Eastham (see above) maintains a list of referrals for babysitters on the Lower Cape. You might also check the bulletin boards at libraries for local babysitters, who often advertise their services there.

HEALTH CARE Ⓗ

Health care is of primary importance to Cape Codders. Many of us have chosen to live here because of life-quality issues, and good health is one of them. We are blessed with a number of facilities that help us stay healthy; more and more of those facilities have been able to offer us sophisticated health-care services that once required a trip to Boston. Those who live and work here are also concerned with being able to meet the health-care needs of visitors. And the Cape has a relatively high percentage of elderly residents who need access to health care. For those reasons rescue units in every town are well equipped and well prepared, with extra staff on hand or on call in the busy summer months. Medical clinics as well as many family practices accept walk-in patients.

Cape Cod is also a place where venerable traditions and promising innovations have met in the formation and growth of a new health care system: Cape Cod Healthcare.

Cape Cod Healthcare began in 1996 with the merger of Falmouth Hospital and Cape Cod Hospital and Cape Cod Hospital. This health system serves all 15 towns along the 70-mile peninsula that is the Cape. Cape Cod Healthcare, more than an administrative structure or just a new name, embodies a new philosophy of how health-related services should be delivered to the community.

Before the merge, health care on the Cape was defined traditionally: treatment of the ill and injured. Cape Cod Healthcare now offers a comprehensive range of health services, including those that maintain health. In addition the Cape has a number of specialized and general health care clinics, many with 24-hour emergency service. Look for listing in this chapter.

If you have a major medical emergency, dial 911 to reach a rescue unit. Another valuable resource offered here is Cape Cod Ask-A-Nurse, (800) 544-2424, which is available 24 hours a day and provides accurate answers to health-care questions. You can utilize this number also to listen to audiotapes that discuss in length specific health-care questions. For home visits, screenings, and a variety of other services, the Visiting Nurse Association (VNA) is a great resource. VNAs on the Cape, which are all affiliated with Cape Cod Healthcare may be reached at (800) 631-3900.

CAPE COD HEALTHCARE

Cape Cod Healthcare comprises the following services:

Primary-care physicians: With more than 500 physicians practicing throughout the area, Cape Cod Healthcare has made it easier for Cape Cod residents to get the health care they need, when they need it. Call Cape Cod Healthcare's information line for a referral to a qualified doctor or specialist: (877) 227-3263.

Emergency care: Two hospital-based emergency departments operate around the clock and treat more than 90,000 emergencies each year. These department are complemented by urgent-care facilities within each hospital and at locations in Harwich and Sandwich.

Outpatient services: Diagnosis testing facilities and services include mammography services, MRI, CAT scans, and community-based outpatient lab sites around the Cape.

Hospital care: Two acute-care hospitals—Cape Cod Hospital and Falmouth Hospital—offer more than 300 inpatient beds and admit more than 20,000 people per year.

Surgical care: Specialized surgeons conduct more than 12,000 surgeries annually.

Specialty care: Hospital and community-based facilities offer treatment for cancer, arthritis, rheumatic disease, wound care, behavioral health services, physical therapy, speech and occupational therapy, and infectious disease consulting, among other specialized services.

Home care and support services: The Visiting Nurse Associate of Cape Cod specializes in community and home health care. They provide a comprehensive range of services to patients in their own homes. Along with specialized nursing care, they offer personal care, dressing, feeding, shopping, homemaker services that include light cleaning and cooking and companionship. VNA also supervises volunteer from hospice care.

HOSPITALS

Upper Cape

Falmouth Hospital
100 Ter Heun Drive, Falmouth
(508) 548-5300
www.capecodhealth.org
Falmouth Hospital, located 45 minutes west of Hyannis, serves the Upper Cape towns of Falmouth, Sandwich, Bourne, and Mashpee. The 83-bed facility offers an excellent full-time emergency room and intensive-care unit, maternity and pediatric units, occupational and physical therapy, catheterization lab, older adult health care services, and a full range of diagnostic testing, including MRI, CAT scan, ultrasound, mammography, and nuclear medicine. The hospital is at the center of a large medical complex that includes the JML Care Center, a 56-bed assisted-living facility known as Heritage at Falmouth, and private medical offices. The hospital includes a new wing, the Faxon Center, featuring an outpatient surgery center, a maternity center, diagnostic imaging, and a Women's Health Resource Center, which offers educational services and a library.

Falmouth Hospital has more than 200 affiliated physicians (62 primary-care physicians and 140 specialist physicians).

Affiliated with the hospital, the Visiting Nurse Association of Upper Cape Cod offers a private-duty nursing service, two adult day health-care centers, and maternal and child home health care. For information on any of the VNA's services, call (800) 631-3900, ext. 7476. For a courtesy bus ride to the hospital, call (800) 352-7155. Also affiliated with the hospital, and operated by Cape Cod Healthcare Inc., is the JML Care Center, which offers nursing home care, short-term rehabilitation service, and an adult day health program.

Mid-Cape

Cape Cod Hospital
27 Park Street, Hyannis
(508) 771-1800
www.capecodhealth.org
Cape Cod Hospital, located in Hyannis serves 11 towns of the Mid-, Lower, and Outer Cape. A large medical complex of more than 12 buildings, the hospital offers 24-hour medical care with on-call specialty consultation. The hospital has 218 beds and nearly 250 affiliated physicians. It is the largest surgical center on the Cape and islands and the only one with an inpatient/outpatient psychiatric center. It is a regional center for cancer and radiation treatment and features an emergency wing, a maternity unit, and a lab that offers cardiac catheterization—a service that patients previously had to travel to Boston to obtain.

The family-care assisted-living program allows senior citizens and HIV patients to stay at home during treatment. The hospital also has short- and long-term rehabilitative care; two nursing homes, the JML Care Center and the Pavilion, for extended care; and the Heritage at Falmouth, an assisted-living facility.

The Spaulding Cape Cod Hospital Rehabilitation Center and Sports Medicine

Falmouth Hospital is an 83-bed facility with one of the busiest emergency centers in Massachusetts during the summer months. ERICA BOLLERUD

Complex is an outpatient facility for physical and occupational rehabilitation. An extensive radiation department provides MRI testing. The hospital has numerous support groups for bereavement, cancer, maternity bereavement, smoking cessation, and domestic violence.

CLINICS

Upper Cape

Bourne Health Center
1 Trowbridge Place, Bourne
(508) 743-0322

Affiliated with Falmouth Hospital, this year-round, walk-in clinic has a physician on call at all times. Medical services include primary care, physical therapy, lab and X-ray, immunizations, and allergy injections. Major insurance and Medicare are accepted. Call for walk-in hours.

Sandwich Health Center
Route 28, Sandwich
(508) 833-4950

This year-round walk-in clinic is affiliated with Falmouth Hospital. They can lend a hand with stitches, X-rays, infections, insect bites, rashes, sprains, and the like. Referrals are made to the Falmouth Hospital Emergency Room or specialists if more treatment is required. Open daily 10:30 A.M. to 7:30 P.M.

The Rehabilitation Hospital for the Cape and Islands
Off U.S. Route 6, exit 3, East Sandwich
(508) 833-4000
www.rhci.org

An independently owned rehabilitation hospital, the Rehabilitation Hospital offers comprehensive rehab treatment for adult inpatients and adult and child outpatients. With 60 beds and a staff of 200, its resources include a therapeutic pool, a home-activities apartment, specialized evaluations (including hearing), state-of-the-art exercise equipment, and orthotics and prosthetics clinics. The hospital provides treatment for a variety of conditions, including stroke, joint replacement, neurological conditions, complex medical conditions, back and neck injuries, amputation, chronic pain, and work-related and sports injuries. The hospital has a branch in Orleans, which provides comprehensive outpatient therapy for children and adults (see subsequent listing).

Mashpee Family Medicine
Mashpee Health Center,
Route 28, Mashpee
(508) 477–4282

This family practice sees patients of all ages, from infants to centenarians. The practice offers daily walk-in care. Mashpee Family Medicine offers both family and urgent care. The office prides itself on offering same-day care.

Mid-Cape

Cape Cod Breast Evaluation Center
40 Quinlan Way, Hyannis
(508) 771–0688

Right next to Cape Cod Hospital, this year-round facility provides on-site mammograms and ultrasounds, as well as physical examinations. Although appointments are generally scheduled well in advance, there are usually a few open slots at short notice. The office is open from Monday through Friday from 9:00 A.M. to 5:00 P.M.

Mid-Upper Cape Community Health Center
30 Elm Avenue, Hyannis
(508) 778–4299
www.mucchc.cc

This new clinic opened in February 2003. It offers family medicine, disease prevention, lab and radiology services, and dental care. It is geared toward serving

Health care is the second-largest employment sector on the Cape, second only to the hospitality industry.

people with little or no insurance, as well as all community members in need of treatment.

Mid-Cape Medical Center
489 Bearses Way, Hyannis
(508) 771–4092

Open since 1981 for daily year-round health care, this walk-in center has on-duty physicians and provides medical, lab, and X-ray service. It does immunizations for patients age 12 and older, Pap tests and gynecological exams, and routine physicals. The center also treats minor injuries, such as cuts, abrasions, lacerations, and simple fractures. The center, which is about a mile from Cape Cod Hospital, accepts most types of insurance. It opens at 8:00 A.M. every day and stays open until 7:45 P.M. Monday through Thursday, 4:45 P.M. Friday and Saturday, and 1:00 P.M. Sunday. In most cases you do not need an appointment.

Cape Cod Artificial Kidney Center
241 Willow Street, Yarmouthport
(508) 362–4535

This is a year-round, outpatient hemodialysis unit. It does not usually have a waiting list. Hours vary but are generally Monday through Saturday 8:00 A.M. to 4:30 P.M. with longer hours in summer.

Cape Cod Medical Center
65 Route 134, Dennis
(508) 394–7113

This full-service facility, with one attending physician and a physician's assistant, welcomes walk-in patients. The center accepts most insurance and credit cards. In the winter the center is open Monday, Tuesday, Thursday, and Friday 8:00 A.M. to 4:00 P.M. and Wednesday 8:00 A.M. to noon.

Many medical offices are located in the Cape Cod Medical Center. ERICA BOLLERUD

Lower Cape

Long Pond Medical Center
525 Long Pond Drive, Harwich
(508) 432-4100

This medical center provides comprehensive care for everything from fractures to hives. Hours vary seasonally. The center accepts most insurance and major credit cards.

Orleans Medical Center
Bayberry Square, 225 Route 6A, Orleans
(508) 255-9577

Established in 1984, this center offers walk-in attention for urgent medical needs. It is open all year Monday through Friday from 8:00 A.M. to 4:00 P.M. In July and August the center is also open Saturday from 8:00 to 11:30 A.M. It accepts some insurance plans and MasterCard and VISA.

RHCI-Orleans
Orleans Marketplace, 21 Old Colony Way, Orleans
(508) 240-7203, (888) 234-3220

This branch of the Rehabilitation Hospital for the Cape and islands (see our listing in the Upper Cape section) provides comprehensive outpatient therapy for children and adults including physical, occupational, speech, and language therapy. It also offers physician services with board-certified rehabilitation physicians, a gym, and specialized services such as electro-diagnostic testing.

Outer Cape Health Services
81 Old Colony Way, Orleans
(508) 255-9700
www.outercape.org

Outer Cape Health Services is affiliated with Beth Israel Deaconess Medical Center in Boston. The Orleans office is much smaller than the Wellfleet or Provincetown sites (see following entries). Call ahead for an appointment.

Outer Cape Health Services
U.S. Route 6 at Briar Lane, Wellfleet
(508) 349-3131
www.outercape.org

Outer Cape Health Services offers a full range of services for acute and chronic medical conditions. It has a lab and X-ray facility, and a team of physicians, nurse practitioners, physician assistants, and nurses. Walk-in care is available on a first-come, first-served basis. The center accepts most insurance plans and credit cards, and also offers a sliding-scale payment plan for low-income patients. Winter hours are 8:00 A.M. to 5:00 P.M. Monday through Friday, plus extended evening hours until 8:00 P.M. on Wednesday and Friday. In summer it is also open Saturday and Sunday from 9:00 A.M. to 5:00 P.M.

Outer Cape Health Services
49 Harry Kemp Way, Provincetown
(508) 487-9395
www.outercape.org

The services offered here are the same as at the Wellfleet center (previous listing). Winter hours are 8:00 A.M. to 5:00 P.M. Monday through Friday, with evening hours until 8:00 P.M. on Tuesday and Thursday, and 9:30 A.M. to noon on Saturday. Summer hours are the same except Saturday, when the facility stays open until 1:00 P.M. Call for an appointment.

ALTERNATIVE HEALTH-CARE PRACTITIONERS

The Cape is home to a large number of chiropractors as well as other alternative health-care practitioners, including naturopaths, acupuncturists, massage therapists, and nutritionists. What draws many people to these practitioners is their focus on health and prevention, rather than the treatment of illness (though they do that

Elder Services of Cape Cod & the Islands offers information and referral services. They'll help seniors and their families research resources, provide information customized to callers' needs, and can help with questions about housing, home health aids, recreation, and meal programs. Call (800) 244-4630 for more information.

too). We've listed just a few; check your local phone book for more.

Upper Cape

Holistic Health Associates
58 Tupper Road, Sandwich
(508) 833-0822

This center offers chiropractic treatment, massage, Reiki, nutritional counseling, hypnotherapy, acupuncture, acupressure, and vibrational sound therapy (music designed for certain energy centers of the body). Holistic Health Associates is open 9:00 A.M. to 5:00 P.M. Monday through Friday, and 9:00 A.M. to noon on Saturday. Appointments are needed.

Mid-Cape

Complete Wellness
10 Main Street, Cotuit
(508) 428-1969

This center combines conventional and alternative medicine, offering treatment by an MD—Dr. Patricia Fater—as well as nutrition, herbology, energy healing, stress management, massage, myotherapy, and psychotherapy. The center also has its own on-site lab. Appointments are necessary.

Great Marsh Chiropractic
1049 Route 6A, West Barnstable
(508) 362-4533

Great Marsh has two staff chiropractors, Dr. Christian Smith and Dr. John Dorris,

CLOSE-UP

Who to Call in an Emergency

Emergency	911
Battering/Physical Abuse of Women:	
Independence House	(800) 439-6507,
	(508) 428-4720
Child Abuse (Department of Social Services)	(800) 792-5200
Disabled Persons Abuse	(800) 426-9009
Drug Abuse/Crisis Intervention	(800) 234-0420
Drug/Alcohol Abuse Hotline	(800) 234-0246
Elder Abuse Hotline	(800) 922-2275
Emergency Mental Health Services	(508) 778-4627,
	778-4628
Helping Our Women (HOW)	(508) 487-4357
Missing Children Hotline	(800) 843-5678
Parental Stress Hotline	(800) 632-8188
Poison Hotline	(800) 682-9211
Rape Crisis Line	(508) 428-4720
Runaway Hotline	(800) 231-6946
Samaritans Suicide Prevention:	
Cape-wide	(800) 893-9900
Falmouth	(508) 548-8900
Buzzards Bay	(508) 759-2828

along with a massage therapist who is on hand during office hours. The center is open Monday to Friday, with evening hours on Thursday.

Lower Cape

Sperry Chiropractic
855 U.S. Route 6, Eastham
(508) 240-0700

"Don't let a bad back spoil your vacation," says Dr. Paula Sperry, who has been treating residents and visitors on the Lower Cape for more than a decade. And she treats more than bad backs: Bring your neck aches and headaches to her office, just north of the Orleans-Eastham rotary. Doctor Sperry uses various high- and low-force techniques to suit your needs. The office is open Monday, Tuesday, Wednesday, and Friday, with evening hours and other times by appointment.

[Facing page] *Located on the Cape Cod Healthcare campus in downtown Hyannis, the Davenport-Mugar Cancer Center boasts the most advanced technology and treatment alternatives.*

ERICA BOLLERUD

RETIREMENT 🌴

The dream of retiring to Cape Cod, for many, dates back to their youth, when they would come here to vacation. They remember this peninsula for its serene quality of life, beautiful scenery, and pristine beaches. Others come because the Cape has so much to offer.

Beginning with golf: The climate here allows for many golf courses to stay open all year long. With nearly 50 public, semi-private, and resort courses, the Cape and islands boast both quality and quantity. Water sports, such as canoeing, kayaking, and sailing, are appealing too.

The Cape also attracts history aficionados—those who appreciate the fact that Pilgrims helped settle much of the Cape and that three of its important towns (Sandwich, Barnstable, and Yarmouth) date back to 1639. Those who love the sea and who love nature are drawn here too—to the Cape Cod National Seashore and other gorgeous Cape beaches, the National Audubon bird sanctuaries, and resources such as the Thornton Burgess Society and the Cape Cod Museum of Natural History. Artists and art lovers can enjoy numerous fine galleries, museums, and theaters sprinkled throughout the Cape towns, not to mention the Cape Cod Symphony. Cape Cod truly has something to offer everyone.

Another attractive feature of the Cape is its proximity to Boston. The Cape is a refuge from the hustle and bustle of the hub and its suburbs, but it's just a short bus ride away from the cultural facilities of the country's largest and most historic cities. Many, in fact, choose to experience the best of both worlds before they fully retire, moving here early and commute until their formal retirement.

Still, if city life isn't for you, you could go years without ever finding a reason to cross the bridge to the mainland. In terms of health care, Cape Cod Healthcare Inc.—Cape Cod Hospital and Falmouth Hospital—provides full health care for area residents. And in terms of finances, a number of major brokerage houses and Boston banks have set up shop on the Cape.

You'll also find that our businesses and town governments seriously consider the needs of the aging population—an important segment of the population here (almost half of all Cape Codders are older than 50). We've mentioned the senior centers: Every town on the Cape has an active organization run by each town's Council on Aging. These centers provide interesting activities and the chance to make new friendships.

The many nonprofit organizations also offer a great opportunity to share, with visitors and locals alike, your past life experience through volunteer programs. Imagine this for a moment: In one year volunteers (most of them retired) donated 30,000 hours of volunteer time to the Cape Cod Museum of Natural History. Whether a museum, nature center, or town organization, volunteerism is alive and well on Cape Cod, providing a great way to meet others and get involved with the community.

And that's not all. The Cape also offers you a comfortable, safe place to call home. Besides the many options we outline in our Relocation chapter, the Cape also offers you a number of assisted-living communities that provide the very best of both worlds—independent-living options coupled with on-site health care and supportive services.

In this chapter we offer information about these resources and services for retirees as well as descriptions of retirement villages.

SENIOR CENTERS

You certainly won't ever be bored with all that the Cape's senior centers have to offer. Run by the various Cape Cod Councils on Aging, these offer a full roster of activities designed to keep older adults on the move.

You can learn a new hobby—perhaps how to knit, quilt, sew, paint, or even carve wood. You can learn good health management and have regular medical screenings for high blood pressure, diabetes, hearing and visual impairment, other physical conditions, and mental health concerns. You can take yoga classes; you can participate in good nutrition programs through home-delivered or on-site meals; or you can join in any of the councils' fun-packed activities such as dining clubs, cribbage matches, choral groups, bingo games, birthday parties, film festivals, and day trips.

The senior centers are open year-round. Below is a brief summary of each agency, but we urge you to telephone centers to see if they provide the services you require. We have found that the majority of the centers have their own newsletters, and you may want to ask them to send you one so you can see what the center near you is all about. Most councils on aging have Web sites. You may link to them through www.cape andislandscoas.org.

Upper Cape

Bourne Council on Aging
239 Main Street, Buzzards Bay
(508) 759-0654

The Bourne council operates a food pantry and nutrition center and provides counseling, social support, exercise clubs, art classes, and health and fitness clinics. The council runs bingo, cribbage, Scrabble, and whist games and also offers a number of services from knife sharpening to outreach programs. Transportation via minibus for shopping and medical appointments is also provided.

> Prime Time, *a free publication put out by the* Cape Cod Times, *is geared specifically for the 50-plus crowd. You may pick up a copy at local libraries or grocery stores throughout the area.*

Sandwich Council on Aging
270 Quaker Meetinghouse Road,
East Sandwich
(508) 888-4737

The Sandwich Council on Aging offers a variety of classes and activities, including yoga, Reiki, tai ji, scrabble, poker, bridge, Weight Watchers, computer classes, regular trip offerings throughout New England, movie screenings, and a handyman program that provides affordable help for work around the house. Other services include legal, financial, medical, and recreational assistance, as well as outreach counseling, elder services, lunches, hearing tests, transportation to local stores, flu clinics, and even foot-care programs. Each New Year's Day the center hosts a community breakfast.

Falmouth Council on Aging
300 Dillingham Avenue, Falmouth
(508) 540-0196

At the active Senior Center, activities include exercise classes, oil painting, quilting, bridge, chess, and much more. Health clinics, health information, and education are also provided. Eligible seniors receive home-delivered meals via the Meals on Wheels program, and elder transportation is available within the town of Falmouth.

Mashpee Council on Aging
500 Great Neck Road North, Mashpee
(508) 539-1440

This council, located at the Carol H. Jacobson Senior Center, offers a busy schedule of arts and crafts as well as physical activities. Seniors benefit from blood pressure clinics, flu shots, smoking cessation classes, chiropractic wellness workshops, outreach programs, and ses-

The Carol H. Jacobson Senior Center is the home of the Mashpee Council on Aging, which coordinates human service, educational, social, and recreation services for local seniors.
ERICA BOLLERUD

sions by support groups such as AA and Al-Anon. The center also offers insurance counseling and has a program that provides transportation to medical appointments and shopping.

Mid-Cape

Barnstable Senior Center
825 Route 28, Hyannis
(508) 862-4750
Seniors in the town of Barnstable can benefit from the wide array of services available to them at the Barnstable Senior Center. Legal and financial consultation as well as tax assistance are provided. Seniors may receive Meals on Wheels, borrow medical equipment, and receive flu shots, blood pressure consultation, foot-care advice, and overall medical counseling. There are recreational and cul-

tural programs and even a potluck luncheon each month.

Yarmouth Council on Aging
528 Forest Road, South Yarmouth
(508) 394-7606
The Yarmouth Council offers health-related programs including breast cancer screening and diabetic screening, foot care, and the services of a psychotherapist. Their educational programs range from bank statement balancing to computer classes. Recreational activities include duplicate bridge, Scrabble, beano, and pool. Other services include legal assistance, the telephone lifeline, and insurance advice.

Dennis Council on Aging
1045 Route 134, South Dennis
(508) 385-5067
The Dennis Senior Citizens' Center offers a host of benefits, including programs on

financial management and income tax preparation, Meals on Wheels, and lunch on weekdays (reservations are necessary). The council sponsors programs and workshops on various topics such as medical issues. It also provides transportation for shopping and makes telephone calls to seniors who live alone. This center is networked with several illness-related support groups.

Lower Cape

Brewster Council on Aging
1673 Route 6A, Brewster
(508) 896-2737

The council in Brewster offers an array of programs and services including home support, legal and financial aid, an out-reach program, a sight-loss program, a senior dining program, and support groups for arthritis sufferers and those mourning the death of a loved one. Seniors can have their blood pressure checked and receive flu shots. Recreation includes bridge, poker, Scrabble, chess, swimming, art classes, and a men's coffee club. Beach wheelchairs are available.

Harwich Council on Aging
100 Oak Street, Harwich
(508) 430-7550

The list of services offered by the Harwich council seems endless: blood pressure clinics, hearing clinics, outreach programs health-insurance counseling, legal advice, and support groups for alcohol abuse, and sight loss. Equipment (walkers, wheelchairs, etc.) is loaned free of charge. Volunteers provide seniors with rides to medical appointments. Fitness, cooking, and craft classes are offered, and day-trip and other travel opportunities are available.

Chatham Council on Aging
193 Stony Hill Road, Chatham
(508) 945-5190

The Chatham council's outreach program provides a mobile book service, health-insurance counseling, tax preparation services, medical transportation, shut-in telephone reassurance services, flu and pneumonia clinics, and free medical equipment. It also has an air-conditioned library, offers trips and tours, exercise classes, and caregiver support groups. Special events include cooking classes and beginners' bridge, and weekly activities include exercise classes and a walking club. Meal service is provided on weekdays through senior center volunteers; reservations are required.

Orleans Council on Aging
150 Rock Harbor Road, Orleans
(508) 255-6333

This center offers classes in bowling, bridge, yoga, watercolor painting, tennis, and fitness. Bingo, chess, knitting, quilting, a monthly birthday party, and an amateur radio club are offered. Lunch is served at the center Monday through Thursday; reservations for lunch must be made by calling the Nutrition Center at (508) 255-9871 at least 24 hours in advance.

Eastham Council on Aging
1405 Nauset Road, Eastham
(508) 255-6164

Ongoing services at the Eastham center include computer classes, painting and craft classes, beano, and open bridge. The travel club's day and overnight trips keep the seniors on the move. A noon meal is provided every Monday and Wednesday; reservations are required. The center also is home to the

Elder Services of Cape Cod & the Islands coordinates many national volunteer programs for seniors, such as Retired and Senior Volunteer Program (RSVP), the Senior Environment Corps, and America Reads. Interested seniors can join community service projects to address serious local needs. Call (800) 244-4630.

Lower Cape Adult Day Care Center, which includes a full day's worth of programs.

Wellfleet Senior Center
715 Old Kings Highway, Wellfleet
(508) 349-2800
At the Wellfleet Senior Center you can play cribbage, bridge, and beano; take an art class; or receive answers to your legal, insurance, and tax questions. The council also provides personal and fire safety programs as well as support groups for people with cancer, heart problems, stroke, and sight loss. Senior meals are served on Tuesdays; reservations must be made by calling (508) 349-6325.

Truro Council on Aging
346 U.S. Route 6, Truro
(508) 349-9525
This center offers many workshops and services including blood pressure, food-care and flu shot clinics, insurance and tax counseling, fitness classes, financial assistance referrals, and a course designed to teach safe driving habits to seniors. Outreach touches on such topics as fuel assistance, emergency food distribution, health proxy services, transportation to medical appointments, and services for the homebound. Meals on Wheels and emergency food distribution are also provided.

Provincetown Council on Aging
26 Alden Street, Provincetown
(508) 487-7080
The Provincetown Council keeps seniors busy with yoga, oil painting, swimming, chair caning, bingo, Scrabble, aerobics, and strength training. Hearing tests, massages, and smoking cessation programs are also provided. Van transportation takes seniors on shopping trips to Hyannis on Monday, to Orleans on Tuesday, to the local A&P on Wednesday, and to Wellfleet on Thursday. Senior dining provided on Wednesday at noon; reservations are required.

RETIREMENT COMMUNITIES

Retirement communities include three basic types—independent living, assisted living, and independent living with some assistance.

Independent living is aptly named because senior citizens enjoy all the independence of living on their own but with the added advantages of being part of a community. Assisted living is a housing alternative that combines independent living with personalized support service. Health-care needs are also included, and programs are designed to cater to the individual. Independent living with some assistance is somewhere between the two. It is for someone who is largely self-sufficient, but requires assistance from time to time. Below we've listed the retirement community options on Cape Cod.

Upper Cape

Pocasset Place
Country Road, Bourne
(617) 268-9140
www.seniorlivingresidences.com
Newly opened in the spring of 2004, Pocasset Place offers both independent and assisted living. The 24 independent-living apartments include 20 one-bedroom and 4 two-bedroom units. All apartments include private baths and kitchenettes. A beauty parlor, exercise room, country kitchen, dining room, and general store are all located on this campuslike setting.

Atria Woodbriar
339 Gifford Street, Falmouth
(508) 540-1600
Woodbriar, opened in 1976, has the distinction of being Cape Cod's first retirement community. Today Woodbriar is an assisted-living and retirement community

[Facing page] *The lovely Brewster Council on Aging building is located on historic Route 6A.* ERICA BOLLERUD

that includes a nine-hole golf course and indoor heated pool, both of which are available to residents' families at reduced fees or free of charge. Their philosophy is to help individuals remain as independent as possible by providing eight levels of personalized, supportive services, ranging from fully independent to those suffering from memory loss. Located in the heart of Falmouth, Atria Woodbriar also has an entertainment room, four dining rooms, and a sun-filled pond side common room. Their modern one-bedroom studio apartments overlook John's Pond and colorful gardens. Upon request a van is available to transport residents to shopping centers, medical appointments, and cultural events. The special excursions are very popular.

Heritage at Falmouth
140 Ter Heun Drive, Falmouth
(508) 457-6400
www.heritageatfalmouth.org

Located on the grounds of Falmouth Hospital, Heritage is an assisted-living community offering 56 apartments, including studios and one- and two-bedroom units compete with a private bath and kitchenette. All utilities and maintenance are provided, as are three daily meals, housekeeping, personal care, transportation, and activities including social events, wellness classes, and lectures. Heritage is owned by the Falmouth Hospital Foundation.

Mid-Cape

Harbor Point at Centerville
22 Richardson Road, Centerville
(508) 778-2311
www.benchmarkquality.com
Harbor Point is Cape Cod's assisted-living community for the memory impaired. Specially trained staff understand that memory loss is a disorder of the memory,

not of the spirit, and this is most evident in the cheerfulness of the care given. Private apartments are available for this safe, homelike setting.

Whitehall Estate
790 Falmouth Road, Hyannis
(508) 790-7666
www.parksidesenior.com
One of the newest facilities on the Cape, Whitehall Estates opened in the spring of 1999. It is an assisted-living home with 80 units with just the right amount of support so residents can do as they please. What's more, it seems their wishes are respected as the staff works with them to develop a flexible personal service plan that suits their lifestyle and honors their privacy. It's warm and friendly in every detail, from the cozy fireplace to the inviting pub—perfect for socializing. Choose from a private studio and a one- or two-bedroom apartment.

Heatherwood at Kings Way
100 Heatherwood Drive, Yarmouthport
(508) 362-4400, (800) 352-0365
Located at the beautiful condominium community Kings Way off Route 6A, Heatherwood is one of the Cape's premier retirement communities. It offers 183 one- and two-bedroom independent-living units as well as 14 assisted-living units. Amenities include a meal plan, housekeeping, maintenance, transportation, social activities, and arts and crafts activities. The facilities include a greenhouse and resident storage areas. A doctor visits once a week.

Heatherwood also shares numerous amenities with Kings Way, including walking trails, tennis courts, swimming pool, and, of course, the Kings Way golf course (see our Golf chapter). Surface and underground parking is plentiful, and each resident has a security and emergency response system.

Mayflower Place
579 Buck Island Road, West Yarmouth
(508) 790-0200

This retirement community has 126 full apartment units as well as an on-site 72-bed skilled-nursing facility. The smallest unit (called the Chilton) has a kitchen, living room, one bedroom, and one-and-one-half baths; the largest (the Allerton) also has a dining room, one bedroom, and two full baths. totaling 884 square feet. The facility offers support services and a medical clinic staffed 24 hours a day by RNs and certified nurse's aides.

Mayflower Place has a on-site library, post office, chapel, theater, dining room, two craft rooms, pub, greenhouse, beauty parlor, bank, game room, indoor swimming pool, and a complete senior-focused fitness center.

---

i

Nearly 25 percent of the population in Barnstable County (most of the Cape) is age 65 or older—twice the national average. The median age on the Lower Cape is 49, with Chatham and Orleans claiming the oldest populations in Massachusetts.

Thirwood Place
237 North Main Street, South Yarmouth
(508) 398-8006, (800) 248-5023
www.thirwoodplace.com
With a total of 214 units, this facility, situated on 45 acres overlooking Flax Pond, offers both assisted and independent living. The amenities at this impressive retirement community include an auditorium, swimming pool, dining room, arts and crafts room, post office, greenhouse, and billiards room. The Village at Thirwood Place is new and features 28 graciously appointed apartments. Many services are provided, including activities programs, transportation, a nurse who is available daily, and emergency-trained personnel who are on hand around the clock. All meals, utilities, housekeeping, and laundering are included in the monthly fee. Pets are welcome.

The spacious Barnstable Senior Center building is located just outside of downtown Hyannis.
ERICA BOLLERUD

Lower Cape

EPOCH Assisted Living of Brewster
855 Route 124, Brewster
(508) 896-3252
www.epochsl.com
This assisted-living community provides 68 apartments, each with a kitchenette and private bath. Opened in November 1996, it offers independence supported by 24-hour assistance and plenty of personal touches, including a staff nurse. The monthly charge includes three meals a day, housekeeping, personal care needs, utilities, and health programs. Transportation is also provided for local errands. Laundry facilities are on each floor. Brewster Place is next to the Brewster Manor nursing home. Pets are welcome.

Harwich House
26 Pleasant Lake Avenue, Harwich
(508) 432-5291, (800) 529-5291
www.wiselivingchoices.com

This retirement community, located near the junction of Routes 124 and 39, offers 18 one- and two-bedroom condominium units. The facility provides a dining room where dinner is served for a nominal fee. Staff nurses are available 24 hours a day. Each unit is privately owned. There is a common room with laundry facilities for those who still enjoy doing their own laundry. For a monthly fee you can choose what additional services you need, such as housekeeping, personalized health care, concierge services, and more.

The Melrose
601 Route 28, Harwichport
(508) 430-4796, (800) 529-5291
www.wiselivingchoices.com
The Melrose is built on the same site as the old Melrose Supper Club, which served as a hotel before being converted into a 29-unit housing complex. The building's appearance remains much the same, but inside you will find modern conven-

iences. All two-bedroom apartments feature full kitchens and private laundry rooms. Meals are provided at a nominal charge in the common dining room. The monthly service fee includes 24-hour assistance.

Chatham House
33 Cross Street, Chatham
(508) 945–2239, (800) 529–5291
www.wiselivingchoices.com
Chatham House is a 10-unit cooperative apartment complex set in bustling yet beautiful downtown Chatham. Within walking distance are many shops, restaurants, churches, and the impressive Eldredge Library. The one-bedroom apartments share laundry facilities. Meals are served in a common dining room.

Orleans Convalescent and Retirement Center
60 Daley Terrace, Orleans
(508) 255-2328
The Orleans Retirement Center, built in 1969, was one of the early pioneer provid-

Boardwalks are popular paths for seniors because they provide even footing and have rails for balance. The Cape has many boardwalks that stretch across tidal marshlands. The 860-foot Bass Hole boardwalk in Yarmouthport passes alongside an osprey nest. Sandwich's famous boardwalk connects to the town beach on Cape Cod Bay, and Uncle Tom's Bridge in Wellfleet leads to a small harbor island and conservation area.

ing supportive living concepts for older adults. It has 19 apartments (with garages and security systems) ranging in size from studio to two-bedroom units. The evening meal, which can be served either in the common dining room or in the privacy of the individual apartments, is included in the monthly fee, as are housekeeping and laundry services. This facility also offers a 33-bed private skilled-nursing facility with 24-hour medical coverage.

MEDIA 📺

Cape Codders, as a rule, like to stay informed, especially when it comes to local news. And that's not hard to do here. The Cape has a daily newspaper, several weekly newspapers, special-interest magazines, a public-access television station, and a range of radio listening choices to keep residents and visitors informed and entertained. This chapter is a composite of our media choices—newspapers, magazines, TV services, and radio and television stations.

NEWSPAPERS

Cape Cod Times
319 Main Street, Hyannis
(508) 775-1200
www.capecodonline.com
The Cape's only daily paper, the *Cape Cod Times*, covers news throughout the area, including Martha's Vineyard and Nantucket, as well as state, national, and world news. It is delivered to subscribers in the morning. It has a daily circulation of approximately 53,000 and Sunday circulation of 65,000.

The *Cape Cod Times* started in 1936 as part of the *New Bedford Standard Times* (some old-timers still refer to the paper as the *Standard Times*), and its offices in downtown Hyannis date to 1938. In 1966 the paper was acquired by Ottaway Newspapers Inc. (a Dow Jones subsidiary), which has more than 20 daily newspapers.

ℹ *The* Cape Cod Times *publishes a special insert each weekend during the summer, filled with entertainment and activity listings.*

In addition to the daily newspaper, the *Cape Cod Times* also publishes *Prime Time,* a free monthly magazine with an age 50-plus target audience; *CapeWeek,* a weekly events supplement to the Saturday edition; and special seasonal and topical editions.

Barnstable Patriot
326 Main Street, Hyannis
(508) 771-1427
www.barnstablepatriot.com
The oldest newspaper on Cape Cod, the *Barnstable Patriot* was launched in 1830. Published by Rob Sennott and his wife, Toni, who took over the paper in 1994, the *Patriot* is published every Thursday and covers the town of Barnstable and its seven villages. The paper focuses on county government and local news and is widely respected for its investigative reporting. Weekly sections deal with such topics as senior citizens, sports, and entertainment. In early summer the paper publishes the well-regarded annual *Summerscape* supplement, which focuses on Cape Cod history.

Bound volumes of the *Barnstable Patriot* dating back to 1926 are available at the newspaper office; bound and microfilm copies in the Sturgis Library in Barnstable go back to the first issue.

The Falmouth Enterprise
Depot Avenue, Falmouth
(508) 548-4700
This biweekly paper has been published since 1895 and has been owned by the Hough family of Falmouth since 1929. Today they publish not only the *Falmouth Enterprise,* but also the *Bourne Enterprise,* the *Mashpee Enterprise,* the *Sandwich Enterprise,* and the *Upper Cape Local,* covering local news through the Upper Cape. The Falmouth and Mashpee papers

are distributed on Tuesday and Friday; the *Upper Cape Local* is mailed on Thursday. The *Bourne Enterprise* comes out on Friday, as does the *Sandwich Enterprise*. These papers include calendars of events, arts and entertainment, and weddings and births. The papers have a total circulation of about 45,000 and are sold at newsstands and by subscription. Home delivery is available.

Cape Cod Community Newspapers
923-G Route 6A, Yarmouthport
(508) 375-4900
www.townonline.com
Owned by the Boston Herald, this large newspaper group publishes local weekly newspapers, including the *Register,* the *Harwich Oracle,* and the *Cape Codder.* It also publishes *The Upper Cape Codder,* which in 1999 replaced the *Sandwich Broadsider, Bourne Courier,* and *Mashpee Messenger.* The combined weekly circulation of the Cape Cod Community Newspapers is about 47,000.

All the papers are sold on newsstands and by subscription. The *Cape Codder* covers the eight Lower Cape towns from Brewster to Provincetown and comes out on Tuesday and Friday. The *Register,* which comes out on Thursday covers Dennis, Yarmouth, and Barnstable. The newspapers are community-oriented, general interest papers that report on news and events along with local features and columns.

Cape Cod Chronicle
60 Munson Meeting Way, Chatham
(508) 945-2220
www.capecodchronicle.com
Established in 1965, the *Chronicle* is the Lower Cape's only independent weekly newspaper. Published on Thursday, it focuses on Chatham and Harwich and is chock-full of news, features, sports, community-service listings, and entertainment news.

Provincetown Banner
167 Commercial Street, Provincetown
(508) 487-7400
www.provincetownbanner.com
The independently-owned *Banner* debuted in May 1995, and although some residents wondered if there was room for a second local paper, it is the weekly paper that survived the newspaper war. Published on Thursday, it's a particularly well-designed paper with bold graphics, and it covers Provincetown, Truro, and Wellfleet.

Begin your visit to Cape Cod by picking up a free issue of the Best Read Guide *or* Kids on the Cape *publications. Each vacation guide is distributed widely throughout Cape Cod and packed with tons of suggestions for vacation activities. They are also full of coupons that come in handy during a fun-filled day.*

MAGAZINES

Cape Cod Life
4 Barlows Landing Road, Unit 14, Pocasset
(508) 564-4466, (800) 645-4482
www.capecodlife.com
Launched in 1979 by local publisher Brian Shortsleeve, this glossy, attractive magazine comes out six times a year and is sold by subscription and on newsstands. The full-color magazine concentrates on local people, historic and current topics, events, and activities. Topics include art, cooking, nature, shopping, dining, and lodging on Cape Cod, Nantucket, and Martha's Vineyard. Noted for its beautiful photography, *Cape Cod Life* runs an annual photo contest.

Cape Cod Life also publishes articles covering gardening, interior decorating, house styles, retirement, and a complete list of all the art galleries on Cape Cod, Nantucket, and Martha's Vineyard in their annual *Cape Cod & Islands Home* and *Cape Cod Arts* magazines.

On the Water
Depot Avenue, Falmouth
(508) 548-4705, (800) 614-3000
www.onthewater.com
Published monthly by the *Falmouth Enterprise, On the Water* covers fishing and boating with a focus on the Cape and islands. With a large format, it's filled with photographs and articles by Cape fishermen, among others.

Cape Cod Magazine
P.O. Box 208, Yarmouthport, MA 02675
(508) 771-3769
www.capecodmagazine.com
Cape Cod Magazine is a free full-color quarterly that prints features on Cape Cod real estate, shopping, and dining. Topical and relevant recent stories have covered topics such as the state of Cape Cod health care, the Land Bank, health and fitness, entertainment, and chefs of Cape Cod. Widely distributed on Cape Cod, the magazine offers subscriptions as well as home delivery.

The Cape Cod Voice
56 Main Street, Orleans
(508) 247-8900
www.capecodvoice.com
Started in 2001, this well-designed, colorful newsmagazine delivers in-depth reporting and news about the Cape from Dennis to Provincetown. It includes columns from local writers, profiles of local fixtures both past and present, and entertainment listings and reviews. Issues tend to be organized around major cover stories, such as the Cape's rich art scene, its long history of enterprising smugglers, its little-known coastal islands, as well as issues devoted to the Cape's literary and humor offerings. As they put it: "We're local, and proud of it. But we're

not parochial, and we're proud of that too." It's published every two weeks and available by subscription or on local newsstands.

Golf on Cape Cod
143A Upper Country Road, Dennisport
(508) 398-6101
www.golfoncapecod.com
Golf on Cape Cod is a publication written for and about the Cape Cod golf community. Feature articles are illustrated by full-color photography and cover a wide range of topics such as golf course development, Donald Ross's Cape Cod gems, the best of the best par 3s, and private and public courses. The magazine is published three times a year and is available for purchase at most local bookstores, magazine racks, or by subscription.

TELEVISION

Although the Cape has only one station of its own, we get lots of others. Most are from Boston; a few are from Providence.

In addition there's a plethora of cable stations available, depending on the cable package you (or the place where you are staying) pay for.

Cape Cod Community Media Center
307 Whites Path, South Yarmouth
(508) 394-2388
www.c3tv.org
Formerly known as C3TV, Cape Cod's Community Media Center is a versatile community resource that airs social, political, and cultural programs from 9:30 A.M. until midnight. It also has conference and workshop space and a gallery that hosts 10 community art exhibits a year. The station is funded by the towns of Barnstable, Yarmouth, Dennis, Harwich, and Chatham.

Its two studios are used to produce such programs as *Books and the World, The Gadfly, Tales of Cape Cod,* and others. Programming covers local sports, selectmen's meetings, and committee meetings.

RADIO

CLASSICAL

WFCC 107.5 FM

COMMUNITY

WQMR 92.1 FM (Provincetown)
WFPB 91.9 FM (folk, jazz, and NPR)

CONTEMPORARY/ADULT/EASY LISTENING

WCOD 1060 FM (adult contemporary)
WQRC 99.9 FM (easy listening, jazz)
WRZE 96.3 FM (Top 40)
WOCN 103.9 FM ("memory music" from 1930s to '80s)
WUMB 91.9 FM (folk)

ROCK

WPXC 103 FM (classic rock)
WMVY 92.7 FM (adult rock)
WCIB 102 FM (classic rock)

TALK

WBUR 1240 AM (NPR)
WCAI 90.1 FM (NPR)
WNAN 91.1 FM (NPR)
WCCT 90.3 FM (NPR)
WKKL 90.7 FM (Cape Cod Community College)
WSDH 91.5 FM (Sandwich High School)
WXTK 95.1 FM (news talk)

WORSHIP 🙏

Religion has long played a role in the lives of Cape Codders, beginning with the American Indian thanking their Great Spirit for all the life-giving gifts they received each day. The religion of the Wampanoag Indians was the only religion of the area for 10,000 years, until European settlers came at the beginning of the 17th century.

OUR RELIGIOUS ROOTS

This migration commenced with the landing of the Pilgrims in 1620. These 102 hearty souls braved the Atlantic and hardships of the New World so that they could be free to live and worship as they pleased. Half of them did not survive the first winter. The Pilgrims were certainly devout to begin with, the New World adversity only caused the Pilgrims to turn more deeply toward their faith. It is against this backdrop that the settlements of the area were built and laws formed.

England's established church of the time was the Church of England. In opposition to this establishment were the Pilgrims, separatists seeking to forge their own church. Their pilgrimage to Plymouth brought more settlers in the following years. These settlers brought a Congregational church with them with more conservative ideas. They established settlements all along the northeast coast, including the Cape, as early as 1637.

As soon as enough Congregationalists gathered and built a meetinghouse (and encouraged a minister to relocate to their corner of the wilderness to preach to them), they were in line for incorporation. Incorporation brought more settlers to add to the flock. As the flock grew and people began to settle in the outlying areas, east and west parishes and north and south parishes were established. Many of these local parishes would lead to the incorporation of completely separate townships in years to follow. (See our Historic Cape Cod chapter.)

In those days religion and community meant the same thing. The meetinghouse served as both the religious and political center of the community. Church and state were one and the same (and would be until 1692 when a charter provided religious freedom). All members were expected to contribute to the church that had earned their township incorporation.

Congregationalists were not the only ones settling down during the 17th century. By the mid-1600s Quakers began to settle in Sandwich, Falmouth, Barnstable, and, later, Harwich. These Quakers, whose religion taught them to tremble or quake at the fear of God's wrath, attempted to gain converts from the Congregationalist flock and in some cases succeeded. Despite their efforts the Quakers were singled out as heretics. Many were forced through repeated persecutions to flee town for other parts. Some, such as John Wing of Falmouth, relocated to a remote wilderness lying between Yarmouth and Eastham to begin the settlement of what would become the town of Harwich. Quakers tended to settle in sparsely populated areas, such as in South Yarmouth, which became a Quaker village. The Quakers were followed by Baptists, who settled at Harwich during the mid-18th century and later spread outward across the Cape.

By the late 18th century a new religious group arrived on Cape Cod. In Eng-

[Facing page] *The First Congregational Church of Yarmouth was built in 1870.*

ERICA BOLLERUD

land Methodism has grown from a spiritual awakening of John Wesley in 1738. Great Britain and Ireland saw the spread of this new religion, and by the latter quarter of the 18th century, Methodism made its way across the Atlantic. The first Methodist meetinghouse on the Cape was erected in Harwich in 1792, followed by another in Bourne in 1794. By the early to mid-19th century, Methodism had rattled the Congregational spires, and the latter began to see many divisions and splinter groups emerge.

The middle of the 19th century saw a religious revolution on Cape Cod as small religious sects began to form from factions of the more established churches of the day. During this period the town of Dennis saw its church separate into a half-dozen groups; in neighboring Harwich no less than 15 divisions formed from the church in that town. Each group had its own issues, its own agenda, and its own particular belief system that set it apart from the others. It was during this time that the Unitarian Universalists came into being. By the end of the century, though, many of these groups were able to resolve their differences, and they came back together.

Meanwhile Catholicism began to emerge with the coming of Irish immigrants during the 1830s and throughout the 19th century. The first Catholic parish was established in Sandwich 1830 as Irish immigrants were settling there to work in the factories. A second parish was erected in 1869 at Harwich. Portuguese fishermen in Provincetown had already brought their Catholic church along with them. Cape Verde Islanders, who settled in Falmouth as farmers, did the same. As the 20th century arrived and people began to migrate southward from around Boston, the Catholic population of the Cape began to grow. Today this once predominantly Protestant peninsula, settled initially by Congregationalists, is largely Roman Catholic.

WORSHIP TODAY

Despite more than three centuries of change and growth, religion continues to play a major role on this sandy peninsula, as is evidenced by the many churches here—150 in total! Some of the best examples of the Cape's ability to blend its religious tradition with secular festivity are the blessing of the fleet celebrations at the beginning of each summer season.

Recent trends on the Cape reflect the national growth of many conservative congregations. Here on the Cape you also see many interfaith efforts to address social issues, such as homelessness, domestic abuse, and poverty. By most accounts religious attendance is on the rise. It might not seem unusual to see the older generation religiously active, but many young families living on or visiting the Cape take part in regular worship as well. As a matter of fact, during the summer, several parishes host vacation Bible schools in August.

Some of the Cape's private religious schools have significant waiting lists—further indication that young families, like so many Cape Codders before them, place a high value on religion.

The Cape remains largely Christian, but there are two Jewish synagogues and other groups such as Baha'i spiritual assemblies. For a listing of all church locations, consult the Yellow Pages of the local phone book. Most Cape Cod newspapers have information on services. The *Cape Cod Times* prints a listing on Saturday. Also, the Cape Cod Council of Churches at 320 Main street in Hyannis (508-775-5073) is an excellent source of

[Facing page] *The Trinity Lutheran Church in Brewster is shingled in the quintessential Cape style.* ERICA BOLLERUD

information on places of worship. The council operates a food and clothing service center at 355 Main Street in Dennisport (508–394–6361) and encourages the various religious societies to work together in an effort to provide for the Cape community.

United Church of Christ churches, which grew from the old Congregational parishes, are the largest Protestant sect on the Cape. Three UCC churches can be found on the Upper Cape, seven in the Mid-Cape area and six along the Lower Cape. Among them are a number that lie along Main Street in the following towns and villages: Sandwich, Falmouth, Centerville, South Dennis, Harwich, Harwichport, East Orleans, Chatham, and Wellfleet. Other UCC churches are in North Falmouth, Waquoit, Cotuit, West Barnstable, West Yarmouth, Dennis, and Truro. The First Congregational Church of Yarmouthport is not a member of the United Church of Christ, retaining its original congregational charter as a member of the National Association of Congregational Christian Churches.

There are some 16 Baptist churches on the Cape—American Baptists, National, and Independent. Five of these churches are in the Upper Cape, seven are in the Mid-Cape, and four are along the Lower Cape. Baptist Churches can be found in the towns of Bourne, Sandwich, Falmouth, Mashpee, Barnstable, Yarmouth, Brewster, Chatham, and Eastham.

United Methodists have 14 churches, five in the Upper Cape towns of Bourne and Falmouth, two in the Mid-Cape towns of Barnstable and Yarmouth, and seven in the Lower Cape towns of Harwich, Orleans, Chatham, Eastham, Wellfleet, and Provincetown.

Roman Catholic churches account for 21 of the Cape's more than 150 places of worship. Adding seasonal parishes brings the total number of Catholic churches closer to 30. There is at least one Roman Catholic church in each of the Cape's 15 towns. The town of Falmouth has four Catholic churches, as does Barnstable. Although the Protestants on the Cape have more church buildings, the average membership of a Catholic parish is much larger than that of a Protestant congregation. As a result the Cape is predominantly Catholic by a ratio of nearly 2-to-1. President John F. Kennedy was a member of the St. Francis Xavier Church in Hyannis, where he and his brothers, Joe, Bobby, and Ted, served as altar boys.

Episcopalians arrived in Woods Hole in 1852 and at Sandwich in 1854. Today they are well represented on the Cape. There are 12 Episcopal churches in Buzzards Bay, Sandwich, Woods Hole, Falmouth, Osterville, Barnstable, South Yarmouth, Harwichport, Orleans, Chatham, Wellfleet, and Provincetown. Three Assembly of God churches can be found in Hyannis, Dennisport, and Wellfleet.

Lutheran churches are in Falmouth, West Barnstable, East Harwich, and Brewster. Pentecostal churches are in Mashpee and Dennisport. Two Church of Jesus Christ of Latter Day Saints congregations are on Cape Cod, one in Cataumet and the other in Brewster.

Community Churches can be found in Marstons Mills, East and West Dennis, as well as in South Chatham. For Unitarian Universalist parishes, you'll want to look in the towns of East Falmouth, Barnstable, Brewster, and Provincetown. The Society of Friends has meetings in West Falmouth and South Yarmouth (once known as Quaker Town and Friends Village). In Falmouth and South Dennis, you can find a Church of the Nazarene, whereas Buzzards Bay, Falmouth, Hyannis, Brewster, Harwichport, Chatham, and Orleans all have Christian Science churches. Jehovah's Witnesses

[Facing page] *The current Unitarian Universalist Church of Barnstable was built in 1907 and was designed by Guy Lowell, the architect of the Boston Museum of Fine Arts.*
ERICA BOLLERUD

can be found in three locations across the Cape: Hatchville, Hyannis, and East Harwich. West Barnstable has a Presbyterian church, and Centerville is home to a Greek Orthodox church with its Byzantine building erected in 1949.

Rounding out the Christian places of worship are two Christian Missionary churches in Buzzards Bay and Brewster, and two Federated Churches in Cotuit and Hyannis. Seventh Day Adventists are in Osterville, Full Gospel churches are in Sandwich, Mashpee, West Barnstable, and Dennisport, and the Church of New Jerusalem (Swedenborgian) was established in 1870 in Yarmouthport. Orleans is home to the chapel of the community of Jesus and Hyannis is home to the Salvation Army, which holds services.

Hyannis has a Zion Union church that caters to the black members of the community. Interdenominational parishes are in Centerville and Hyannis; nondenominational parishes are in Sandwich, Mashpee, and Marstons Mills; a Christadelphian Ecclesia parish is in Cataumet; and an Evangelical Covenant church is in Brewster. A Unity church is located in Centerville.

Cape Cod also hosts the Falmouth Jewish Congregation in Hatchville (East Falmouth). It is housed in what was once the East End Meetinghouse of the United Church of Christ, founded in 1797. The Cape Cod Synagogue in Hyannis was erected in 1949. There is also a Lubavitch Chabad Jewish Center in Hyannis.

Last, but by no means least, the Wampanoag Indians of Mashpee hold services at the Old Indian Meeting House on Route 28 in Mashpee. Built in 1684, this meetinghouse is the oldest church on Cape Cod.

NANTUCKET

The name, of Native American origin, means "faraway island," and so it is. Perhaps that's why Nantucketers have always been a particularly independent breed and why the community here is so close-knit.

Nantucket is the only place in the United States that is a town, a county, and an island, and in its entirety, both a State Historic District and a National Historic Landmark. It is a place where nearly half the land is held in conservation, and there are no stoplights, shopping malls, or fast-food franchises. Instead, in the cobblestone streets and along the brick sidewalks of Nantucket Village, friends call out greetings and stop to chat, and everyone seems to know each other. It doesn't take long to feel at home here.

Nantucket may indeed be far away, but the island is readily accessible, so visitors feel that although it's nice to stay for a few days or more, even a day trip here is worthwhile. The trip from Hyannis is a little more than two hours by boat or just an hour by high-speed ferry) and only 15 minutes by air. We especially enjoy arriving by ferry and seeing the whole town come into view as the vessel rounds the lighthouse at Brant Point and enters the harbor. The first thing you'll notice is the uniformity of the buildings, which are built almost exclusively of gray weathered shingle with white trim, one of the indications that construction and alterations are strictly monitored. In 1970 the entire island was established as a Historic District, which means that all construction must be accepted by the Historic District Commission, the Nantucket Building Department, and the Planning Board. Residents may grumble or joke about the stringent regulations, but there's no arguing with the result: Nantucket has an incredibly unspoiled appearance.

Islanders have also taken care to preserve the land here. More than 12,000 acres—40 percent of the island—are protected from development, much of that through the Nantucket Conservation Foundation, which owns and manages more than 8,700 acres. History, of course, has also been carefully and lovingly preserved. This community, which has a year-round population of nearly 12,000 (which swells to 55,000 during the summer and contributes roughly 70 percent of the economic base), maintains more than a dozen museums. Make sure you fit in at least one or two of these to get a real taste of the island's history, which is really its essence.

The island is 47.8 square miles—3.5 miles deep and 14 miles wide—a bit larger than Manhattan, which is 2.5 by 12 miles.

As islanders, Nantucketers are keenly sensitive to the environment and their quality of life. They are generally friendly and good-humored, but if you sense that your car is not exactly welcome on Nantucket, you are right. Islanders are happier to see visitors arrive without an automobile, largely because traffic has become a real problem here in summer. The truth is you don't really need a car for a visit. It is very expensive to bring a vehicle to the island, and you can walk or bike just about anywhere. There are also taxis and bus service. Even if you are staying for an extended time, you can rent a car when you need one. You'll find it's actually quite liberating not to have to worry about parking, gas, and navigating the narrow roads. Nantucket forces you to forsake some aspects of modern life, and that is part of its charm.

Don't mistake being physically remote for being culturally isolated or provincial, however. Nantucket has more than just its stretches of beach and bogs and the natural beauty of its moors to offer. Its uniqueness comes from its inhabitants as much as from its geography, and Nantucketers both past and present have been known for their individuality, creativity, and practicality. Nantucket has enough sophisticated shops and great restaurants to please the most demanding urbanite.

AREA OVERVIEW

Nantucket Village, the most concentrated part of the island, is situated around the harbor. Most businesses and accommodations are here, so if there is no town named in an address for any of the following listings, assume it is in Nantucket Village. We'll tell you if a business or accommodation is found in any of the outlying villages, which are less populated and more seasonal. The village of Madaket, to the west, consists of residences and a few businesses. The residential village of Cisco is on the island's southern shore. The village of Siasconset, more commonly referred to as Sconset, is a bustling summertime resort on the eastern end of the island known for its excellent restaurants and rose-covered cottages with sweet names such as Little House and Auld Lang Syne, the oldest cottage on the islands. Look for the images of spouting whales cut into privet hedges. The old schoolhouse, now a fire station, was used until 1957.

If you're an artist, bring your sketchpad. Nantucket's air is full of moisture, and it is warmer in winter and cooler in summer than the rest of the area, which results in beautiful flowers and gardens. You'll want to take lots of photographs or at least pick up one of several good pictorial books on Nantucket.

Wildlife you may see on Nantucket include deer, pheasants, rabbits, and squirrels, Forty years ago squirrels were nonexistent on the island because they had been hunted out. They recently reappeared, and it is believed they arrived as stowaways on logging trucks. Today the island is host to several grassland-nesting bird species, including short-eared owls and northern harriers, which are scarce on the mainland but thrive here because there are fewer natural predators. Nantucket is a popular spot for birders, and it's easy to see why: Some 354 bird species have been recorder here. The island abounds with wild blueberries, blackberries, beach plum, and elderberries. The 260-acre Milestone Cranberry Bog is one of the largest in the United States. The highest point of land is Folger Hill, which at 109 feet is a foot higher than Altar Rock.

It's true that much of Nantucket shuts down in the off-season, but even in the quiet months, it's a beautiful place. Nantucketers, however may be less than eager to share that. "Don't tell anyone how great it is in the off-season," said one resident. "We like it quiet then."

HISTORY

Indian legend has it that the giant Maushop created Nantucket and Martha's Vineyard from the sand in his moccasins. The scientific version, though less romantic, is consistent with what we know about the formation of Cape Cod. Prehistoric glaciers deposited sand, rock, and rubble in the area. As the glaciers melted the water level rose. About 6,000 years ago Nantucket Sound was flooded, separating the Cape from the islands. By roughly 2,000 years ago, Nantucket and Martha's Vineyard had taken the general form they have today.

In the mid-1500s the island was home to about 1,500 native inhabitants. European explorers first laid food on Nantucket sand around that time but did not explore it. Credit for the island's "discovery" generally goes to Bartholomew Gosnold, a sailor who in 1602 noted the island in the log of his ship, the *Concord,* even though he did not land. In October 1641 William, Earl of Sterling, a representative of Charles I of England, executed the deed of sale of Nantucket granting Thomas Mayhew of Watertown, a merchant who had never visited the island, and his son, Thomas Mayhew Jr., the right to "plant and inhabit upon Nantucket and two other small islands adjacent," meaning Muskeget and Tuckernuck. William also granted Martha's Vineyard and the Elizabeth Islands to the Mayhews in a second transaction. The two Mayhews shortly thereafter settled on Martha's Vineyard, limiting their Nantucket activities to Christianizing the Wampanoags.

In the fall of 1659, Thomas Macy, Tristram Coffin, and Edward Starbuck arrived on Martha's Vineyard from England to escape religious bigotry and persecution. Learning that the Mayhews were willing to dispose of most of Nantucket, these men formed a partnership with the Mayhews and settled the island of Nantucket. Like the Mayhews on Martha's Vineyard, they too raised sheep on Nantucket, taking advantage of the island's lack of predators and the fact that livestock here could not just disappear into the wilderness. As the population on the island grew, sheep raising, spinning, and weaving became the main occupations, and the settlers prospered. In 1671 the town of Nantucket was incorporated, and it became a very important town, very much in the mainstream of colonial America's economy. (Nantucket's physical isolation was not then such a barrier; most mainland communities were isolated too—for lack of roads. Also, rivers and oceans were widely used then as highways for travel and commerce.)

More settlers would arrive over the next quarter century. By 1700 the island population consisted of approximately 800 Native Americans and 300 European settlers, who lived together in relative harmony. During this time Tristram Coffin was considered the patriarch of the island. Benjamin Franklin's grandfather, Peter Foulger, lived on Nantucket, and like his grandson was a versatile person, respected as a preacher, poet, artisan, Native American interpreter, and Clerk of

Sturdy, utilitarian Nantucket lightship baskets originated, not surprisingly, on Nantucket. They were made and used by men stationed on the lightships off the coast. Gradually these baskets, made of rattan woven around wooden ribs, became more ornate. They were fitted with hinged tops, embellished with ornamental carvings, and more. They're still a popular, if pricey, souvenir from Nantucket.

the Works. Three ships involved in the Boston Tea Party were out of Nantucket.

In addition to raising sheep—at one time, there were 10,000 sheep on the island—and farming, Nantucketers also began whaling, first from offshore and then from whaling boats, and this activity in time became the mainstay of the island's economy. By 1774 150 Nantucket vessels were plying the Atlantic, producing two-thirds of the whale oil in New England. The island's original town, called Sherborn, was renamed in 1795 and moved to the "Great Harbor," a change reflecting the island's transformation from a farming community to the center of America's whaling industry.

Though Quaker influences kept the island neutral during the American Revolution and the War of 1812, the wars with England were devastating to Nantucket. With enemy blockades and control of the seas, Nantucket was, for the first time, truly isolated from the mainland. Eighty percent of the whaling fleet was destroyed, and many seamen died in prison ships.

After the War of 1812, Nantucket regained its prosperity and once again thrived as a whaling port. New technologies allowed ships to store blubber and remain at sea longer. The economy flourished. Nearly four decades of growth and prosperity produced fine homes and a cosmopolitan atmosphere unique to such a small island. By 1840 the population increased 600 percent to 9,712 year-round residents, and Nantucket became an important source of capital for a growing nation. However, the whaling era was soon to end—this time for good.

Although each year more oil was produced than before the Revolution, 1830 was the last year Nantucket would lead the American whaling industry. In 1846 a fire destroyed Nantucket Village center and, despite a quick rebuilding, the decline in whaling activity had begun. In addition a sandbar across the mouth of the harbor made it increasingly difficult for large whaleships to enter. The railroad connected New Bedford's flourishing whaling industry to a growing American market, and the demand for oil in Europe declined as more people began to use less expensive gaslight. Nine years after the fire, Nantucket's whaling activity was cut in half. The last whaling ship, the *Oak*, left in 1869, and with its departure the whaling industry closed on Nantucket.

By 1875 two-thirds of the population had left Nantucket; only 3,200 remained. With railroads connecting the mainland cities, Nantucket was increasingly isolated. It was decidedly not a practical location for the Industrial Revolution with its factories and jobs. The failing island economy did, however, protect Nantucket's buildings from the dramatic changes that were sweeping the country.

As steam and electric power began making life easier, "vacation mania" sent people in search of places to enjoy their new freedom. Nantucket, with an overabundance of houses and a pleasant summer climate, became a favorite place for increasing numbers of visitors.

Once again economic growth and prosperity returned to Nantucket. At first a mere trickle of wealthy summer people came to Nantucket to enjoy boating and saltwater bathing. But with the introduction of steamboat service from New Bedford and the construction of its first airport in 1920, vacation travel to Nantucket boomed. Today 40,000 to 50,000 people visit Nantucket on a busy weekend.

GETTING HERE

Nantucket maybe an offshore island, but it's not hard to get here. You may reach it by regularly scheduled air service, aircraft charters, private aircraft, ferry, or private boat. Many visitors love to fly in because the aerial views are spectacular. And the speedy flights give you added time to enjoy the island. Bear in mind, however, that it costs roughly two-thirds more to fly to Nantucket than to take the ferry. If you're flying in, you'll arrive at Nantucket Memorial Airport.

By Air

Nantucket Memorial Airport
30 Macy Lane, Nantucket
(508) 325-5300
www.nantucketairport.com
Off Old South Road Nantucket Memorial Airport is the second most active commercial airport in Massachusetts. Shuttle service is available from Logan Airport in Boston, Hyannis, Martha's Vineyard, and New Bedford, all in Massachusetts, as well as from T. F. Green Airport in Providence, Rhode Island, La Guardia in New York City, and Newark International Airport in New Jersey. The facility is open year-round.

Surprisingly, for a small island, the airport terminal is quite accommodating with an information desk, a restaurant, ATM machine, gift shop, and car rental agencies. Taxi service is available, but if you call ahead to make arrangements, most of the resorts offer shuttle service. The Nantucket Regional Transit Authority shuttle service runs from late May through late September and goes from one end of the island to the other.

Nantucket Memorial Airport accommodates anything from twin-engine Cessnas to 19-seat Beechwoods and jets. For private planes, the airport offers servicing and repair facilities; fuel is available 24 hours a day.

The following charter and commercial airlines are at Nantucket Memorial Airport.

Cape Air
(508) 771-6944, (800) 352-0714
www.flycapeair.com
Cape Air offers hourly flights, with year-round shuttle service between Hyannis and Nantucket, and regular service from New Bedford, Boston, Providence, and Martha's Vineyard. Seasonal service from Province-town is available as well. In the peak season the company offers more than seven flights daily from Boston. Fights from Hyannis leave every hour on the half-hour; these are approximately 15-minute flights. Flights from Boston leave at hour intervals at 15 minutes past the hour. These are approximately 50-minute flights. Joint fares with Delta service from New York's La Guardia and Washington's Ronald Reagan National Airport to Boston are available. Charter service is also available.

Continental Express
(800) 525-0280
www.continental.com
This carrier offers nonjet regular seasonal service from Newark, New Jersey, Boston, or Martha's Vineyard to Nantucket.

Island Airlines
(508) 228-7575, (800) 248-7779
www.nantucket.net/trans/islandair
Island Airlines, a Nantucket-owned business, offers more than 21 scheduled flight daily year-round between Hyannis and Nantucket.

Nantucket Airlines
(508) 228-6234, (800) 635-8787
www.nantucketairlines.com
Nantucket Airlines, affiliated with Cape Air, flies between Nantucket and Hyannis. Fights leave from Hyannis on the half hour and Nantucket on the hour every day.

Ocean Wings Air Charter
(800) 253-5039
www.capecodweb.com/wings
Ocean Wings offers 24-hour year-round service to any New England, U.S., or Canadian destination. This company has a pri-vate hangar and offers flight instruction. Ocean Wings also has winter service based in Puerto Rico and the Caribbean.

US Airways Express
(800) 428-4322
This carrier provides five daily flights in season to Boston, with connecting flights to La Guardia and also to Martha's Vineyard.

By Sea

FERRYBOATS

If you'd prefer to spend a few hours enjoying a ride on Nantucket Sound—sunshine, sea breezes, and perhaps a glass of wine on the upper deck of a pas-senger ferry—you can take advantage of regular ferry service throughout the year from Hyannis. The standard ferry ride takes about two-and-a-quarter hours. The *Grey Lady,* Hy-Line's speedy catamaran (named for the island's longtime nick-name, a reference to the fog that sur-rounds Nantucket at times), makes the trip from Hyannis in a hour.

Ferryboats departing from Hyannis provide daily transportation to Nantucket year-round. (Note: Falmouth's ferry serv-ice only goes to Martha's Vineyard, not Nantucket.)

Freedom Cruise Line
Saquatucket Harbor, Route 28,
Harwichport
(508) 432-8999
www.nantucketislandferry.com
Sailing from Saquatucket Harbor in Har-wichport, this line is a real boon to Lower Cape–based residents and visitors. It pro-vides seasonal (mid-May through mid-October) passenger-only service to Nantucket and offers private charters too. Travel time is 90 minutes. The 66-foot boat has a bar and snack bar. The round-trip cost is $46 for adults and $37 for chil-dren 12 and younger. Parking is free for day-trippers.

Hy-Line Cruises
Ocean Street Dock, Hyannis
(508) 778-2600, (800) 492-8082
www.hy-linecruises.com

Hy-Line offers seasonal (May through October) passenger-only ferry service between Nantucket and Hyannis. Reservations are not required, and the trip takes about two hours. The cost is $13.50 one-way and $27.00 round-trip for adults, and $6.75 one-way, $13.50 round-trip for children ages 5 to 12 (children 4 and younger ride free). First-class tickets cost $23 each way. The number of daily departures ranges from three in season to one in late spring and fall. Hy-Line also offers seasonal ferry service between Martha's Vineyard and Nantucket.

Hy-Line also operates a luxurious high-speed catamaran that makes trips to Nantucket year-round. The *Grey Lady* makes six round-trips daily to Nantucket. Travel time is now less than one hour. One-way for adults is $33 ($58 round-trip), and tickets for children 12 and younger are $25 ($41 round-trip). Reservations are strongly recommended on the *Grey Lady* because of its limited seating capacity; call (508) 778-0404. You can bring your bicycle on any of Hy-Line's boats for an additional charge of $5.00 one-way or $10 round-trip.

The Steamship Authority
South Street Dock, Hyannis
(508) 477-8600 (reservations),
(508) 495-3278 (fast ferry)
www.islandferry.com

The Steamship Authority provides year-round transportation to Nantucket from Hyannis for passengers, vehicles, bicycles, and pets. Reservations are required for vehicles but not for passengers. With indoor and outdoor seating, the ferries can accommodate about 1,000 passengers. Each vessel has a full concession stand and a bar that serves beer and wine. If you decide to leave your car behind, parking costs $10 per day.

The trip take about two-and-one-quarter hours. The fare is $13.00 one-way,
$26.00 round-trip for adults; and $6.50 one-way or $13.00 round-trip for children ages 5 to 12. Children younger than 5 ride free. Bring your bicycle along for an additional $5.00 each way. In season the ferries make six daily departures from Hyannis (three in the off-season), with additional ferries scheduled at major holidays, when the island draws larger-than-normal crowds for such events as the Christmas Stroll and Daffodil Festival. (See our Annual Events section in this chapter.)

Reservations for an automobile cost $165 one-way from May through October. The fare is reduced in winter. If you are bringing a car, you must make your reservations several months in advance. The Steamship Authority recommends that you (1) have several alternatives for departure dates and (2) arrive at least 30 minutes before departure to avoid having your space released. Be aware that the penalty for canceling an auto reservation can be as high as the full-ticket price. Refunds will be given only if the reservation is canceled at least 14 days in advance; after that it is possible to reschedule without a refund.

The Steamship Authority also operates a year-round high-speed catamaran, whose travel time between Hyannis and Nantucket is just one hour. Fares are $26.00 one-way, or $42.00 round-trip, for adults; and $19.50 one-way, or $39.00 round-trip for children ages 5 to 12; children younger than 5 ride free.

PRIVATE BOAT

The boating crowd will find superb facilities within Nantucket harbor, which has moorings, tie-ups, fuel, and food service. Most of the island's restaurants, accommodations, and attractions are within easy walking distance. For more information call the Town Pier at (508) 228-7261; the Nantucket Boat Basin at (508) 228-1333 or (800) NAN-BOAT; or Nantucket Moorings at (508) 228-4472.

Marine supplies are available at Nantucket Marine, (508) 228-5510; Madaket

Nantucket— the town and the county—are one and the same. It was incorporated in 1671.
ERICA BOLLERUD

Marine, (508) 228-1163; and Nantucket Ship Chandlery, (508) 228-2300, at the harbor.

GETTING AROUND

Nantucket Town is the main part of the nearly 50-square-mile island, which has only a few paved roads. Madaket Road leads to the community of Madaket, about 5.5 miles from town. Hummock Road leads to Cisco Beach, about 4.5 miles away; Surfside Road leads to Surfside Beach, about 2.5 miles from town; and Siasconset is about 9 miles from town along Milestone Road. Take Polpis and then Wauwinet Road to get to Wauwinet, an area roughly 5.5 miles from town. Past Wauwinet is conservation land on Great Point. Nantucket Memorial Airport is about 2.5 miles from town.

By Shuttle Bus

A highly successful means of coping with traffic and transportation has been the use of shuttle buses, which run seasonally. It may even bring romance: a few years ago, a couple who met on the shuttle were married on Nantucket!

Nantucket Regional Transit Authority (508) 228-7025, (508) 325-7516 (TDD) www.nantucket-ma.gov/departments/ nrta
Nantucket Regional Transit Authority has expanded its seasonal shuttle service to serve the entire island, with routes to Sconset and Madaket and loops out to Surfside Beach and Jetties Beach. Downtown shuttle stops are on Washington Street and Salem Street; other stops are on the routes. The Mid-Island Loop bus

costs $1.00, as does the Miacomet Loop bus. Two different routes run regularly to Sconset (one via Polpis Road and one via Old South Road/Nobadeer Farm Road) and cost $2.00. Service to Madaket costs $2.00. One-, three-, and seven-day, as well as weekly, monthly, and season passes are available. Senior citizens older than 65 and children 6 and younger ride free. Buses are wheelchair accessible and have bicycle racks. Service runs from late May to late September, seven days a week from 7:00 A.M. to 11:30 P.M. Park-and-ride lots are at the elementary school, the Muse, the Chicken Box, Faregrounds Restaurant, and Odd Fellows Lodge parking lot.

There is also a summer beach shuttle service to Surfside and Jetties Beaches from downtown. Fares are $2.00 each way to Surfside Beach and $1.00 each way to Jetties Beach.

By Car

One important piece of advice concerning cars: Leave your vehicle behind. Nantucket Town, was designed in the 1700s, and its cobblestone streets and narrow lanes are not conductive to high-volume traffic. Streets become congested with traffic, especially during the summer months, and parking can be difficult, if not impossible. Simplify your stay by leaving your car behind. You really don't need a car here, particularly for day trips; you can walk to just about anyplace in town and get out of town by bike, bus, and taxi. We actually welcome the freedom of not having a car during our stays; it seems to immerse us more completely in the far-away-from-the-world feeling that being on Nantucket brings.

If you won't part with your car, be prepared to part with your money, because it is expensive to bring a car to the island (see the Ferry Service section); consider renting a car instead. You'll need a $100 beach vehicle permit to drive on beaches; contact Nantucket Police Department (508-228-1212). A special permit is also required for driving on property managed by the Nantucket Conservation Foundation (508-228-2884).

There are no in-town parking lots, only street parking: it's free, but the one-hour limit is enforced. A final note: Nantucket has many one-way streets, so watch for signs.

Car Rentals and Taxis

Once on the island transportation is not difficult to arrange. Taxis meet incoming flights at the airport and incoming ferries downtown. Car rental agencies are at the airport and in town.

Many rental agencies offer four-wheel-drive vehicles. You'll want to call Nantucket Windmill Auto (508-228-1227, 800-228-1227) at the airport. This year-round, full-service agency has a fleet of Jeeps, Wranglers, and Explorers, along with the more traditional sedans, vans, and station wagons, complete with beach vehicle permits. They also provide free pickup service at your hotel or guesthouse or at the Steamship Authority

Some of the other rental services on the island include Affordable Rentals, 6 South Beach Street, (508) 228-3501; Budget Rent A Car, (508) 228-5666 or (800) 486-5666; and Hertz Car Rental, (508) 228-9421 or (800) 654-3131. The latter two are at the airport.

By Bicycle or Moped

Bicycles are an excellent way to get around because the island is relatively flat, and there are more than 24 miles of paved bike paths that stretch from Nantucket Town to Siasconset to the ease, Surfside to the south, and Madaket to the west (but the wind can sometimes make biking a challenge!). Mopeds are faster, but inexperienced drivers can get in trouble with sand on the roads. To avoid getting ticketed (or hurt), please familiarize yourself with local regulations and observe them. Rental agencies can inform you of the regulations.

Do not ride bikes on sidewalks or moped on bike paths, and heed one-way street signs and other street signs. Front and rear reflectors are required.

The following shops have bike and moped rentals (Young's also repairs bikes). All are within walking distance of the ferry dock.

Cook's Cycle Shop Inc.
6 South Beach Street
(508) 228-0800

Holiday Cycle
4 Chester Street
(508) 228-3644

Nantucket Bike Shops
Steamboat Wharf and Straight Wharf
(508) 228-1999, (800) 770-3088
www.nantucketbikeshop.com

Young's Bicycle Shop
Steamboat Wharf
(508) 228-1151
www.youngsbicycleshop.com

ACCOMMODATIONS

Nantucket has outstanding accommodations of all types. Ask someone about their trip to the island, and the first thing they'll tell you is how much they loved where they stayed. With nearly 1,400 rooms to choose from, you can stay in a single cottage on the inner harbor or in a small guesthouse nestled amongst rose gardens. Or perhaps you'd rather be centrally located in one of the many fine bed-and-breakfasts or inns situated in the center of town. Nantucket has no private campgrounds, and public camping is prohibited. The closest you'll get to camping is the hostel, which offers dormitory-style accommodations.

Most places have lower rates in the off-season, which is a nice time to visit anyway. Many of the smaller inns do not allow children, whereas some allow children older than a certain age. One

innkeeper hedged, "It depends on the child." Families with children might be better off renting a cottage or staying at a larger resort that accommodates children.

It is always wise to inquire about the specific policies of any facility concerning children, pets, cancellations, and refunds. Most places accept major credit cards, we tell you of those that do not.

Reservation and Information Services

If you're planning a vacation on Nantucket, reserve your accommodations well in advance—many places are booked months ahead of time. One innkeeper we talked to said summer guests often reserve rooms before they leave for the October Cranberry Festival and the Christmas Stroll (see our Annual Events section of this chapter), and then reserve their summer vacation slot while here for the holidays.

However, people's plans do change, and cancellations can easily create the opportunity for you to get a room in a first-rate inn without reserving far in advance. That's when reservation services come in especially handy. Here are a few resources to try.

Accommodations
11 India Street
(508) 588-0078
www.robertshouseinn.com
This year-round reservation service represents a group of historic inns, bed-and-breakfasts, and cottages distinguished by fireplaces, harbor views, and antique furnishings.

Nantucket Accommodations
4 Dennis Drive
(508) 228-9559
www.nantucketaccommodations.com
This well-established year-round reservation service represents about 95 percent of the licensed accommodations on the island,

including hotels, inns, bed-and-breakfasts, rental homes, and cottages. They will book rooms for you. They also have private house rental listings and cottages.

Nantucket Chamber of Commerce
48 Main Street, Nantucket
(508) 228-1700
www.nantucketchamber.org

Call or write for an extensive brochure that covers everything you could want in the way of accommodations. The office is open year-round.

The Nantucket Concierge
P.O. Box 1257, Nantucket, MA 02554
(508) 228-8400
www.nantucketconcierge.com

You name it, Carolyn Hills will arrange it. She books accommodations; makes reservations for airline tickets, dinner, and entertainment; arranges the delivery of everything from flowers to birthday cakes; and can get tickets for anything on the island. She can fix you up with swimming or sailing lessons and tennis court time too, as well as golf lessons and tee times. Need a babysitter while you're out on the town? She can arrange that as well.

Nantucket Vacation Rentals
15 North Beach Street
(508) 228-3131, (800) 228-4070
www.nantucketrealestate.com

If you have questions about rental houses, cottages, and apartments, give Nantucket Vacation Rentals a call. The office, at Nantucket Real Estate Co., is open all year.

Nantucket Visitors Services and Information Bureau
25 Federal Street
(508) 228-0925
www.nantucketlodging.org

This town-run bureau, along with the Chamber of Commerce, has compiled a detailed list of accommodations on a day-by-day basis where vacancies exist, but they do not make bookings. The office is open daily year-round.

PRICE CODE

The following key is based on the average cost of a night's stay in a double-occupancy room in the busy season, minus tax and special charges. State and local taxes add about 9.7% to a bill.

$	Less than $75
$$	$75 to $110
$$$	$111 to $175
$$$$	$176 or more

Inns, Bed-and-Breakfasts, and Guesthouses

Anchor Inn $$$
66 Centre Street
(508) 228-0072
www.anchor-inn.net

Next door to the historic Old North Church just outside of town, this old sea captain's home retains its original antique paneling and random-width floorboards. The comfortable common room has a fireplace, and guests enjoy home-baked muffins, coffee, and other goodies each morning on the bright, enclosed breakfast porch. Each of the 11 guest rooms is named for a Nantucket whale ship and has a private bath; most have queen canopy beds.

Brass Lantern Inn $$$-$$$$
11 North Water Street
(508) 228-4064, (800) 377-6609
www.brasslanternnantucket.com

The inn is charming but you'll especially love the outdoor gardens in the backyard. The setting is in a very quiet neighborhood within a few minutes' walk of town. Some rooms have a fireplace and a canopy bed, and you can order room service for breakfast if you wish, but that means you'd have to turn down having breakfast outdoors in the Shakespearean herb garden.

Centerboard Guest House $$$-$$$$
8 Chester Street
(508) 228-9696
www.centerboardguesthouse.com
This immaculate Victorian-style guesthouse has six rooms, beautifully decorated with fresh flowers and lace; some have lovely painted murals in pale pastels. One suite has a private Jacuzzi and fireplace, and there is also a cottage available with a whirlpool bath and private garden. Rooms offer a private bath, telephone, refrigerator, and television. Your hosts serve a continental breakfast. The facility is nonsmoking.

Centre Street Inn $$$
78 Centre Street
(508) 228-0199
www.centrestreetinn.com
Built in 1742, this was originally the residence of Peter Foulger, a whale-oil trader. It became a boarding house in 1875. A close walk from both town and beaches, it offers 13 guest rooms with antique brass or canopy beds and private or shared baths. The large common room, where a continental breakfast is served each morning, is especially inviting, and guests can enjoy a cup of coffee or tea there any time of day. The inn, which is a nonsmoking facility and welcomes children older than 8, is open April to mid-December.

The Century House $$$
10 Cliff Road
(508) 228-0530
www.centuryhouse.com
Nestled partway up the hill between Cliff Road and Centre Street, this is the oldest operating guesthouse on the island. Built in 1833 by Capt. Robert Calder, it became a rooming house in 1870. It was purchased in 1984 by its present owners, Gerry Connick and Jean Ellen Heron, a husband-and-wife team who loving restored the old building. Guests are treated to a veritable feast each morning, including "Gerry's famous granola," homemade coffeecake, bagels, and breads. Guests can relax anytime in the comfortable common room.

An interesting touch: all 14 rooms feature lovely and varied paintings by artists who have stayed here. The Century House is open from mid-May through mid-October.

Hawthorn House $$$
2 Chestnut Street
(508) 228-1468
www.hawthorn-house.com
Right in town, this homey, 1849 historic house offers nine guest rooms decorated with antique furnishings, original artwork by local artists, and, in many cases, handmade quilts. A separate cottage is also available. Coffee is offered in the cozy upstairs common room, and guests receive a coupon good for a full breakfast at one of several restaurants in town. Innkeepers Diane and Mitchell have also devoted the past 20 years to acquiring art from Nantucket's finest artists and craftspeople, and their beautiful collection is placed throughout the house, which is open year-round.

Martin House Inn $$$
61 Centre Street
(508) 228-0678
www.martinhouseinn.net
Polished mahogany, classic paintings, and Oriental rugs characterize this elegant 1803 mariner's home, which became an inn in the 1920s. A piano graces the common room, where window seats beckon, and a continental breakfast is served at a large, beautifully appointed table. Many of the 13 guest rooms have four-poster beds, fireplaces, and private baths. Guests can sit on the veranda in summer or curl up in front of the fire in cooler months. The inn, open year-round, is just a short walk from town.

The Nesbitt Inn $$
21 Broad Street
(508) 228-0156
If you don't mind sharing a bathroom, this historic inn is a great value. Innkeepers Dolly and Nobby Noblit are two of the friendliest hosts you'll ever meet, which is no doubt part of the reason guests come

back year after year. It must be genetic: Dolly is a third-generation innkeeper, part of the same family that has had the Nesbitt Inn since 1914. Built in 1872, this is the oldest inn built for that purpose on the island. The regal staircase, wide hallways, and comfortable rooms seem to take you back in time—as does the claw-foot tub in one of the bathrooms. Guests can lounge in the common room or on the wide front porch. Children are welcome—there's even a play yard for them—but not pets. A continental breakfast is included in season; the inn is open year-round.

Weddings are huge on Nantucket. Inns and hotels fill up with wedding parties, especially during September and October.

The Pineapple Inn $$$–$$$$
10 Hussey Street
(508) 228-9992
www.pineappleinn.com

Built for Capt. Uriah Russell in 1938, this elegant old home was completely renovated in 1997 by owners Bob and Caroline Taylor. They spared no expense here, managing to not only maintain the inn's historic ambience but to include modern amenities such as air-conditioning, telephones with voice mail, cable televisions (tastefully concealed in reproduction wardrobes), and even computer hookups in the 12 guest rooms, which feature marble bathrooms. One room is wheelchair accessible, as is the beautiful brick garden patio, compete with a pineapple fountain. Just outside the busy center of town, the inn is quiet, yet close to shops and restaurants. The Taylors brought along some remnants of their restaurant days, including a juicer and cappuccino machine, not to mention culinary skills and recipes that make the hearty continental breakfasts here a real treat, whether served in the formal dining room or on the patio. Open

May through Christmas, the inn is non-smoking and designed for adults.

Sherburne Inn $$$–$$$$
10 Gay Street
(508) 228-4425
www.sherburneinn.com

Named for the original settlement on Nantucket, this eight-room inn was originally a silk factory and later converted to a lodging house. Today it is a beautifully appointed inn with real character. Its quirky layout includes front and back stairways, so you can get to your room either way, and the floors slope charmingly in places. The rooms are nicely furnished in elegant, yet warm, old-fashioned style, with antiques, lace canopies, and fresh flowers. Each guest room has central air-conditioning, phone, cable TV, and a private bathroom. Guests are served a continental breakfast in the common room or out in the garden, and there is also a second-floor sitting room with a television. Tucked just outside of town in a quiet neighborhood, it is still close to attractions, shops, and restaurants.

Ships Inn $$$–$$$$
13 Fair Street
(508) 228-0040
www.nantucket.net/lodging/shipsinn

Open seasonally, this inn began as the home of Capt. Obed Starbuck, who built it in 1812; many of its rooms are named for the ships he commanded. The antiques-filled home is also distinguished as the birthplace of Lucretia Coffin Mott, the first female abolitionist and advocate of women's suffrage. The inn has a romantic downstairs restaurant and bar that is open to the public for dinner; continental breakfast is available for guests.

The Woodbox $$$$
29 Fair Street
(508) 228-0587
www.woodboxinn.com

Built in 1709, this is known as the oldest inn on the island, and the original, unpainted wood paneling, hand-hewn beams, low ceilings, and huge old fire-places bear witness to its history. Period antiques and reproductions are used throughout. The Woodbox has nine units, which include six suites with one or two bedrooms and three double-bed guest rooms. All rooms have private baths, and some have working fireplaces. It is open from May through mid-October. The inn's restaurant serves breakfast from 8:30 A.M. to 10:30 P.M. and dinner in their romantic restaurant is open to the public and served from 6:30 to 9:00 P.M. No credit cards.

Hotels and Resorts

Cliffside Beach Club $$$$
Jefferson Avenue
(508) 288-0618
www.cliffsidebeach.com

This luxury hotel was built on the site of a prestigious beach club, where members once gathered to be assured of having a private stretch of beach with the same umbrella and chairs each day. Today guests come for the private beach, waterfront rooms, daily maid service, exercise facility, and fine restaurant. Open mid-May to mid-October, Cliffside offers hotel units, suites, studio apartments, and a cottage; some rooms have private decks; most rooms have an ocean view, both a queen-size bed and sleeper sofa, and air-conditioning. All rooms have refrigerators, cable television, and phones. Guests get a continental breakfast and have use of beach umbrellas, chairs, and beach towels. NOTE: The hotel does not accept all credit cards.

Harbor House Village $$$$
South Beach Street
(508) 228-1500, (866) 325-9300
www.harborhousevillage.com

This outstanding resort hotel complex has 104 fine rooms (many of them in town-houses), one cottage, a lovely dining room, tennis courts, nightly entertainment in season, an outdoor heated pool, concierge, and, well, just about anything a person could want in a hotel. The decor is traditional Nantucket; the brick sidewalks and street lighting are all part of the historic ambience here. Business conferences and tour groups are notably well handled at the Harbor House. This facility, which does not allow pets, is open April through December. NOTE: Whether you stay here or not, make a point of enjoying the buffet Sunday brunch at the Harbor House's restaurant, the Hearth Bar.

Jared Coffin House $$$-$$$$
29 Broad Street
(508) 228-2400, (800) 248-2405
www.jaredcoffinhouse.com

Jared Coffin, a successful Nantucket merchant, built a handsome brick house for his wife, but she complained that it was too far from town (8 blocks). So he built this fine three-story brick house, which also apparently failed to please her. Eventually the Coffins moved to Boston, and the house has been an inn ever since.

The inn is now one of the best-loved accommodations on the island, not to mention famous throughout New England. The elegant Jared Coffin House is one of four buildings that make up the year-round inn. Sixty guest rooms and suites have single, double, or queen-size beds and private baths and telephones. Furnishings are colonial and Victorian, highlighted by lace curtains, parquet floors, canopy beds, and Oriental rugs.

Breakfast at Jared's is such a treat that people who are not staying at the inn often go there for their first meal of the day. One local resident confided she breakfasts there once or twice a week just to experience a truly civilized morning repast. Jared's also serves dinner, and the rustic Tap Room downstairs is great for a more casual lunch, dinner, or snack.

Wauwinet Inn $$$$
120 Wauwinet Road
(508) 228-0145, (800) 426-8718
www.wauwinet.com

If you want an ocean view, privacy, natural beauty, country tranquility, and premier service and accommodation, you'll find it here. This ultraromantic deluxe country inn is 8 miles from town between the bay and the ocean. It offers a 35-bedroom inn and cottages. Toppers, the elite restaurant is open to guests for three meals and open to the public for lunch and dinner. The picnic-basket menu is fantastic.

The Wauwinet is open from May through October. Rates include a full breakfast; recreational activities such as tennis, bicycling (bikes provided by the inn), sailing, kayaking, and cruising the bay; a daily wine-and-cheese tasting; nature excursions; and four-wheel-drive trips along the 20 miles of nearby beach. The Wauwinet is a nonsmoking inn and does not allow pets.

Nantucket has something most parents really appreciate: a babysitting service. Nantucket Babysitters' Service (508-228-4970 or www.nantucketbabysitters. com), sends sitters to you—to your home, cottage, hotel, even your boat. Sitters are experienced, carefully screened, and do everything from caring for infants to supervising teens, so you can enjoy some adult time during your stay.

The White Elephant $$$$
Easton Street
(508) 228-2500, (800) 445-6574
www.whiteelephanthotel.com
One of the island's premier facilities, the White Elephant is an expansive harborfront complex that offers everything from regular hotel rooms and deluxe suites to cottages. If you want truly luxurious accommodations, book into the Breakers, a separate and more contemporary section with water-view rooms and suites with private patios.

The White Elephant has 68 guest rooms and 32 one-, two-, and three-bedroom cottages, some with full kitchens. Outdoor facilities include a swimming pool and a private dock for smaller boats. You can eat breakfast, lunch, and dinner in the dining room, the Brant Point Grill, which has an outstanding view of the harbor and is open to the public. A full-time concierge can assist you with your plans. The White Elephant is air-conditioned and does not allow pets. It is open from mid-May until the end of October.

Cottages

Bartlett's Beach Cottages $$$$
Hummock Pond Road, Cisco
(508) 228-3906
www.bartlettsoceanviewfarm.com
If you've always dreamed of waking up in a rustic cabin on Nantucket Island, throwing on your bathing suit, and heading down to the ocean for an early morning swim, call and reserve one of these quaint year-round cottages. Four miles from town, the cottages can accommodate 1 to 10 people. Pond boats are provided.

The Cottages at the
Boat Basin $$$-$$$$
Old South and Swain's Wharves
(866) 838-9253
www.harborviewcottages.com
These 33 newly renovated waterfront cottages each feature full eat-in kitchens, radio/CD players, cable television, polished pines floors, and classic Nantucket decorations; many have balconies or terraces. The one-, two-, and three-bedroom cottages are available from mid-May through mid-October. A few of the cottages are specially outfitted for families traveling with pets.

The Summer House $$$$
South Bluff, Siasconset
(508) 257-4577
www.thesummerhouse.com
Eight rose-covered cottages are beautifully situated on a bluff overlooking the ocean. Five of the cottages have one bedroom, two have two bedrooms, and one is a suite. All have bathrooms; two have kitchenettes. Guests have beach access,

and there is also a top-notch restaurant. The Summer House is open from late April through October.

Wade Cottages $$$$
Siasconset
(508) 257-6308
The grounds of this former estate are delightful, and you'll enjoy the solitude of the private beach. The accommodations include guest rooms with private or shared bathrooms, apartments with one to four bedrooms, and cottages with three, four, or five bedrooms. The facility is open from late May to October.

Hostel

Hostelling International-Nantucket $
31 Western Avenue
(508) 228-0433, (800) 909-4773, ext. 29
Those who enjoy roughing it can make this their base for biking or backpacking getaways. This hostel, once a historic lifesaving station, has 49 beds, cooking facilities, and beautiful sunset views from its location just across from Surfside Beach. Reservations are required in season (you can call for reservations beginning December 1), and the cost is $18 to $24. It's open from April 25 through mid-October.

Vacation Rentals and Real Estate

More and more visitors to Nantucket are choosing the relaxing vacation lifestyle that is best enjoyed in the quiet seclusion of a lovely private home or cottage. Despite the fact that Nantucket has strict building regulations, it has an active and extremely pricey real estate and new-construction market. In 2000 the average new inventory was about 350 homes, which was considered low, but then builders weren't constructing as many speculation houses.

The low end of the market is high here. A basic home or handyman's special can go for $250,000 or more, and three-bedroom or four-bedroom homes can start at $700,000. That's understandable when you realize that the cost of land—which is limited on an island—is very high here. The price of most available lots is as much as most people would expect to pay for a house and lot elsewhere. If you can afford it, there are some great listings in the higher end of the market. You can get a classic antique in the heart of the historic district for anywhere from upward of $1 million to $8 million, and a waterfront estate may go for $10 million or more.

Nantucket's land bank tax plays an integral role in the real estate scene, with 2 percent of the price from the sale of land or a building going into the fund, which is used to buy and retain land for preservation.

Some of Nantucket's larger real estate offices have a rental department, in case the price of buying is out of the question or you're here strictly for R&R.

The Nantucket Listing Service is another resource for prospective buyers.

The following agencies represent the best sources on the island for real estate purchases and rentals.

Coffin-'Sconset Real Estate
40 Centre Street
(508) 228-1138
www.coffinrealestate.com
Open year-round, since 1963 this long-standing and experienced real estate office of nine brokers and agents offers seasonal and vacation rentals, and residential and commercial sales.

Congdon & Coleman Real Estate Inc.
57 Main Street
(508) 325-5000
www.congdonandcoleman.com
Established in 1981, Congdon & Coleman is one of Nantucket's oldest firms. The full-service company offers sales, appraisals, year-round rentals, and summer rentals by

month or season. The office is open year-round and has about 14 brokers.

Denby Real Estate Inc.
5 North Water Street
(508) 228-2522
www.denby.com

Established in 1987, Denby Real Estate, Inc. has been providing expert service to Nantucket for more than 30 years. With 10 brokers and sales representatives, their knowledge and experience can help you arrange a summer rental from a selection of more than 800 homes. Rentals range widely from weekly rates of $1,500 to $4,000. The office also does appraisals and subscribes to the Nantucket Listing Services.

Island Properties Real Estate
35 Old South Road
(508) 228-6999
www.islandpropertiesre.com

Island Properties offers both sales and rentals (long- and short-term). Home sale prices are seldom less than $1 million and often much, much more. The experienced rental agents here pride themselves on finding just what you are looking for. Rental rates will vary depending on location, size of the house, and proximity to the water. The firm has a staff of 11 and is open year-round.

The Maury People Inc., A Resort Quest Company, Exclusive Affiliate of Sotheby's International
35 and 37 Main Street
(508) 228-1881
www.maurypeople.com

One of the largest and most active real estate and rental offices on Nantucket the Maury People, a Resort Quest Company, has extensive sales listings throughout the island and approximately 1,500 rental listings. Open daily year-round (the Sconset office is open June through September), the Main Street office has 20 Realtors on staff and has been doing business on Nantucket for more than 30 years. The specialties here are historic and beach homes.

RESTAURANTS

The caliber of dining facilities on Nantucket makes this an island you wouldn't mind being stranded on. It could take all summer, or possibly longer, to sample all the great restaurants here, and there is plenty of variety. It is not, however, what you would call cheap.

Dinner for two at some restaurants can easily cost $120. (At one place the inexpensive wine by the glass is $12.) But there are less expensive options. One idea: Go out for lunch instead of dinner at your favorite elegant restaurant. And look into more casual places for dinner, or restaurants that offer bistro or tavern menus in addition to full dinners.

For a quick bite duck into one of the two Main Street drugstores, Congdon's Pharmacy or Nantucket Pharmacy, which both have sit-down counters and friendly atmospheres. They're side by side, so if one counter is crowded (as is often the case), try the other. And you thought soda fountains had gone out of style!

Although we have given you a great head start on finding your own special place among Nantucket's long list of restaurants, consider yourself morally and gastronomically obliged to do your own research. Most of the places we have included are open year-round, but they may take a much-needed break sometime after New Year's; it's best to inquire about winter hours at any facility.

As a general rule, you don't have to dress up for dinner here; we signal restaurants that require specific dress. Most restaurants accept major credit cards; we'll tell you the ones that do not.

PRICE CODE

We've included the following pricing codes as guidelines in helping you decide where to dine. The key is based on the average price of dinner for two, excluding appetizers, alcoholic beverages, dessert, tax, and tip.

$	Less than $20
$$	$20 to $50
$$$	$51 to $80
$$$$	$81 and more

Arno's Restaurant $$
41 Main Street
(508) 228-7001

A popular, reasonably priced meeting place for working folk, families, and hungry tourists, Arno's serves a big breakfast (until 2:00 P.M.), lunch, and dinner. Get a window table and people-watch while you enjoy your food. We suggest you try the surf 'n' turf. Children have their own menu. Arno's is open April through December.

The Atlantic Cafe $$
15 South Water Street
(508) 228-0570
www.atlanticcafe.com

We find ourselves coming back to this casual, congenial place time and again whenever we're on Nantucket because we know we'll always get a great meal at a reasonable price. The waiters and waitresses are super friendly, and children are welcomed here with high chairs and a children's menu. Popular menu items include seafood dishes such as scallops, swordfish, and fried clams, and hearty appetizers such as nachos and fried zucchini sticks. In operation since 1978, the cafe serves lunch and dinner daily year-round; the full menu is available from mid-morning to late night.

The Boarding House $$$
12 Federal Street
(508) 228-9622

In Nancy Thayer's novel *Belonging*, which is set on Nantucket, the sophisticated, affluent heroine Joanna Jones dines twice at the Boarding House. The lady, however fictional, knows her restaurants. Chef-proprietor Seth Carter Raynor's innovative cuisine has both Mediterranean and Asian influences; yellowfin tuna with wasabi aioli and soy ginger glaze and grilled Szechwan quail are two examples

of dishes that appear on the ever-changing menu. Choose from a lighter bistro menu or more formal fare, and sit in the romantic, smoke-free lower dining room with low-beamed ceilings and fresco walls; in the comfortable bar area; or, in summer, outside on the patio. The Boarding House serves lunch and dinner and is open year-round.

The Brotherhood of Thieves $
23 Broad Street
no phone

Low, oak-beamed ceilings, wood paneling, and lots of candlelight create a wonderfully warm and cozy atmosphere. The food is terrific, and there's lots of it. The corkscrew fries served with burgers and sandwiches are great, and the chowder is hard to beat. It is casual, offers pub fare, and is open daily year-round for lunch and dinner, with evening entertainment. The Brotherhood does not take reservations, so you may have to wait for a table outside in a line. But it's worth it! No credit cards.

Caffe Bella Vita $$
2 Bayberry Court, Nantucket Commons
(508) 228-8766

If the urge for authentic Italian food hits when you are surrounded quite literally by seafood, stop in here for some linguini alla carbonara or ziti con salsa. Or try the *tonna griglia* (grilled tuna) if you feel obligated to have fresh fish while on Nantucket. The chef makes delicious sauces! You'll love the outdoor patio, perfect for a candlelit dinner. The year-round cafe is just outside of town, providing the perfect opportunity to work off dinner by walking.

Cap'n Tobey's Chowder House $
Straight Wharf
(508) 228-0836

This moderately priced tavern-style restaurant offers a menu and prices that families can appreciate. The clam chowder is widely and highly recommended. It is open daily for lunch and dinner May through October.

The Chanticleer $$$$
9 New Street, Siasconset
(508) 257-6231
www.thechanticleerinn.com

The Chanticleer has perhaps the best wine list on the island, as *Wine Spectator* has duly and consistently noted, and the classical French cuisine is legendary. Chef-proprietor Jean-Charles Berruet has been at the Chanticleer for more than three decades.

The restaurant's annual opening on Mother's Day is an anxiously anticipated event; it closes in October. In June, when the roses are out and hanging baskets of pink fuchsias are everywhere, go for lunch in the rose garden—and don't plan anything for the rest of the afternoon. Quintessential Nantucket! Unlike most other restaurants on the island there is a dress code here: Men must wear jackets.

For prime sunset views over dinner, visit the Westender at 326 Madaket Road. This two-story restaurant has a bar serving "Madaket Mysteries" on the first floor and a cathedral-ceilinged second floor that showcases the evening show over the water.

Cioppino's $$
20 Broad Street
(508) 228-4622
www.cioppinos.com

An intimate atmosphere adds to the dining experience here, where you'll find a friendly maitre d' and sophisticated fare, including the restaurant's signature dish, made with fresh local shellfish, lobster, and shrimp over linguini. The menu, which changes seasonally, may include hazelnut-crusted salmon or tournedos of beef and vegetarian pasta, to name just a few compelling entrees. There's also a refreshing array of salads and tempting desserts. Cioppino's is open for dinner from May to October and has a small bar as well.

The Club Car $$$
1 Main Street
(508) 228-1101
www.theclubcar.com

Near the waterfront with a ringside seat on Main Street, this well-regarded restaurant skillfully combines casual dining and elegant eating. The menu is rich and varied—you may find anything from rabbit to octopus—and the food is consistently excellent. If your budget is tight, have lunch at the bar in season. If, however, rack of lamb is a favorite of yours, just remember that you only live once.

The lounge is the last-known existing railroad car from the Nantucket Railroad Company. For more than 20 years, the Club Car has opened seasonally, from May through the Christmas Stroll, serving lunch and dinner.

DeMarco $$$$
9 India Street
(508) 228-1836
www.nantucket.net/food/demarco

This restaurant has outstanding Northern Italian food, an absolutely superb wine list (more than 100 Italian selections!), and a wonderful atmosphere. We once dined at a window-side table where the moon peeked in from above, adding to the romance. If the menu offers swordfish, don't pass it up. Owner Don DeMarco has operated the restaurant for many years. The menu changes regularly, and breads and desserts are made on the premises. DeMarco is open from April to December. Reservations are advised.

Le Languedoc $$
24 Broad Street
(508) 228-2552
www.lelanguedoc.com

This family-owned restaurant is known and loved by an appreciative following for its warm, intimate, and comfortable atmosphere; excellent service; and wonderful wine—it's one of the few places you can get superior wines by the glass. You can choose between a more elaborate and pricey menu upstairs and a more casual and affordable but equally fine cafe menu downstairs or on the outdoor terrace in summer. The restaurant is open for dinner daily in season. Lunch and dinner are available in the fall from September through Christmas Stroll (the first weekend in December; see the Annual Events section), and then it closes until April.

Provisions $
3 Harbor Square
(508) 228-3258

This gourmet deli is a popular place among both locals and visitors, who come for hearty soups, salads, and terrific sandwiches. Or you can opt for pâtés or cheese with French bread, and treat yourself to a cappuccino. In fine weather the benches outside are filled with people enjoying lunch. Provisions is open for breakfast, too, and they'll pack picnic lunches for you to take along. It's open April through November.

RopeWalk $$
1 Straight Wharf
(508) 228-8886
www.theropewalk.com

Nantucket is surrounded by water, yet this is one of the few eating places with a water view. Situated near the wharves, RopeWalk is a convenient place to eat lunch or dinner before or after your ferry ride. You'll find ample indoor seating, or you can eat outdoors at the raw bar. It's very casual, the food is good (especially the crab cakes), and some say the calamari is the best on the island. RopeWalk is open seasonally from mid-May through Columbus Day.

The SeaGrille Restaurant $$
45 Sparks Avenue
(508) 325-5700
www.theseagrille.com

The creative and well-prepared seafood, especially the lobster bisque served with dill pastry crust topping, makes the Sea-Grille popular with locals, but you can find most any other kind of entree here too. In fact they specialize in local and regional fresh seafood, prepared both traditionally and creatively, as well as the standards—filet mignon, grilled tenderloin of baby lamb, and chicken Provençal. The SeaGrille wine list has earned the prestigious *Wine Spectator* award of excellence three years in a row. And the hand-painted murals set a nautical tone. A reasonably priced array of seasonal specials are also offered and include bouillabaisse and quesadilla salad (which challenges even big eaters). The SeaGrille serves dinner nightly and lunch Monday through Saturday year-round.

Something Natural $
50 Cliff Road
(508) 228-0504
www.somethingnatural.com

This is a great place to stop on your way out to Madaket. Pack one of their incredible, healthy sandwiches in your bike pack, and you'll have something to look forward to when you stop—if you can wait that long. You might just want to stay and eat at one of the shaded picnic tables, where you're likely to see a number of locals filling up on their lunch break. The homemade breads alone are wonderful, and if you really want to indulge, try one of their fresh-baked chocolate chip cookies. It's open from April to October.

The Summer House Restaurant $$$$
17 Ocean Avenue, Siasconset
(508) 257-9976
www.spiceoflifeonnantucket.com/summer house.html

Set on an ocean bluff overlooking the Atlantic Ocean with a dark green interior and white wicker furniture, the Summer House conjures up the very image of, well, summer. One of the loveliest restaurants on the island (and one of the few that is actually on the water), this is the place people come to for special occasions as well as for the excellent food. The Summer House Restaurant is open from the Nantucket Wine Festival Weekend in May (see the Annual Events section in this chapter) to Columbus Day weekend from 6:00 to 10:30 P.M., though the bar stays open until 1:00 A.M. Reservations are recommended. The casual Oceanside Restaurant, on the grounds, is open from late June until Labor Day serving lunch from noon until 3:30 P.M. in a comfortable beachfront Caribbean atmosphere just feet from the Atlantic Ocean.

21 Federal $$$
21 Federal Street
(508) 228-2121
With polished wood, linen, and candlelight, this place is quietly sophisticated—and the food has the same quality. Entrees such as braised lamb shank and sautéed breast of duck are simply and elegantly prepared, and first courses include some unusual appetizers, such as tuna tartare. Do not skip dessert, which might be hazelnut and raspberry Dacquoise with coffee butter cream or warm berry compote. They are open for lunch and dinner April to December.

Vincent's $$
21 South Water Street
(508) 228-0189
This bright, friendly little restaurant has been serving up generous helpings of Italian dishes since 1954, including seafood specialties and all sorts of pastas, at great prices. Open from May to late fall, serving lunch, dinner, and a late-night menu, Vincent's is housed in the only surviving Humane Society building on Nantucket, one of the houses of refuge that preceded the U.S. Lifesaving Service. Now it's a lifesaver for hungry visitors and residents.

SHOPPING

If you love small shops with fine merchandise, you'll find paradise in Nantucket Town. Just as the island's old-time sea captains traveled the world and brought home exotic wares of distant ports, today's shopkeepers import the best from all over, without neglecting the quality items produced right here on the island. You'll find everything from gold jewelry and pearls to beautiful hand-woven shawls and the lightship baskets for which Nantucket is famous.

Most of the shops listed below are open all year; we'll let you know when hours are seasonal.

Claire Murray
11 South Water Street
(508) 228-1913
www.clairemurray.com
Claire Murray's handmade rugs, both finished pieces and kits, fall into a unique class of artwork. Beautiful, colorful, and cheerful, some patters are simple enough for beginners, others are a challenge to accomplished rug makers, but all are visually exquisite. You can buy a finished rug for $70 to $3,000, and kits average about $130 each. Needlepoint and counted cross-stitch kits, gift items, and cotton throws are also available. Classes are offered with a purchase. Also check out Claire Murray's beautifully illustrated book; it's a wonderful gift.

Cold Noses
1 Courtyard, Straight Wharf
(508) 228-5477
www.coldnoses.net
How many shops get letters from dogs? Owners Barbara and Ralph Maffei readily comply with orders from pooches all over the country requesting mail-order doggy snacks. This shop has everything for the canines in your life and gifts for felines too! Those much-in-demand homemade dog biscuits come in an assortment of flavors, shapes, and sizes and contain no salt, sugar, or soy. The shop stocks other healthy pet foods as well. The Maffeis, who also have a shop in Boston, cram a lot into this small shop, including dog clothing, greeting cards, pillows, and collars with matching human belts. Cold Noses will definitely warm your heart.

Cross Rip Outfitters
24 Easy Street
(508) 228-4900
www.crossrip.com

If there's an angler on your gift list, be sure to stop here. In addition to rods and reels, this shop has a great collection of fishing-related gifts, including beautiful painted mugs, ties, jewelry, hats, shirts, sunglasses, and even stationery. Cross Rip also offers fly-fishing instruction, equipment rentals, and guide service.

Diana Kim England, Goldsmiths
56 Main Street
(508) 228-3766
www.dianakimengland.com

Seven goldsmiths contribute to the elegant handmade jewelry sold here, all of which is produced in the studio upstairs, including earrings, pendants, and bracelets in ivory and 14- to 18-karat gold. Among the most popular pieces are the gold lightship basket pendants with scrimshaw. Prices here range from about $70 to $2,400. The shop is open year-round.

Erica Wilson Needle Works
25 Main Street
(508) 228-9881

This store has lovely original gifts, including quilts and hand-knit sweaters from England and Ireland, contemporary women's petite and children's clothing, and European specialty silk shoes. Erica Wilson Needle Works also displays locally crafted jewelry, Nantucket baskets, and special Nantucket china. Unique needlepoint kits range in price from $20 to $1,200 (for a rug) work into patterns adapted from famous tapestries and original designs.

Handblock
42 Main Street
(508) 228-2358
www.handblock.com

This visually enticing boutique carries unique clothing for women and children, plus some wonderful gift items including gorgeous pottery, jewelry, and lifelike stuffed cats and dogs. In the rear of the shop are shelves and shelves of colorful linens, woven pillows and blankets, and beautiful hatboxes.

The Hub
31 Main Street
(508) 228-3868

This is the place to go to buy a newspaper—just about any newspaper. The Hub also sells magazines, books, lottery tickets, postcards, and sundries, and offers photocopy and fax service. As its name implies, it's generally a lively place, great for chatting with perfect strangers.

The Kiteman
14 South Water Street
(508) 228-7089

While you're in the childlike, carefree mood that Nantucket inevitably inspires, why not pick up a great kite and head for a sandy beach? The Kiteman sells a huge selection of Valkyrie and Ace kites to a high-flying clientele.

The Lion's Paw
0 Main Street
(508) 228-3837

Baskets, pillows, hooked rugs, linens, and boldly colorful ceramics make up the bulk of inventory in this delightful, spacious store. There is a terrific selection of tablecloths, beautiful hand-painted furniture, accessories, and unique gift items.

Mitchell's Book Corner
54 Main Street
(508) 228-1080
www.mitchellsbookcorner.com

If you love books, you won't be able to resist this corner shop. The Nantucket Room is especially engrossing, with the island's more complete offering of books about Nantucket, whaling, marine history, boating, and nature. Choose from such titles as Nathaniel Philbrick's *Away Off*

Shore, deservedly touted as one of the most readable Nantucket histories; *Death in Rough Water* by Francine Matthews; Martha Lawrence's *Lightship Basket,* and John McCalley's *Nantucket Then and Now.* Mitchell's also has a great general inventory and a large selection of quality children's books.

Murray's Toggery
62 Main Street
(508) 228-0437
www.murraystoggeryshop.com
Family owned and operated, Murray's opened in 1945. There is a reason for its longevity: It's got everything. You'll find shoes, sweaters, hats, and Estee Lauder products, and it is the largest men's clothing store on Main Street. Started by Philip Murray, the popular Nantucket Red menswear line originated here from a type of slacks made in France. It has now expanded to Oxford shirts, coats, jackets, sweatshirts, and caps—even some caps for women.

Nantucket Bookworks
25 Broad Street
(508) 228-4000
www.nantucketbookworks.com
This year-round store not only has a wonderful collection of books and plenty of room to browse, but a fun assortment of greeting cards stationery, blank books, and other gifts for writers. It has a great children's section, and gifts for all ages are scattered throughout the store. Even the cash register receipts are fun, each with an interesting quote from notable literary figures. In business more than 25 years, Nantucket Bookworks keeps long hours, so you can browse after dinner!

Nantucket Country Antiques
38 Centre Street
(508) 228-8868
"I only buy things I would put in my own home," says Cam Dutton, who opened this two-story antiques shop in April 1996. Chock-full of one-of-a-kind pieces, the shop specializes in old quilts and folk antiques. It has a few new items as well, such as hooked rugs and country accent pieces. It's open year-round, but weekends only in the quiet off-season.

Nantucket Gourmet
4 India Street
(508) 228-4353, (866) 626-2665
www.nantucketgourmet.com
This store has everything for the true or aspiring gourmet, from Nantucket-made jams and jellies to mustards, cranberry marmalade, vinegars, and teas. The pepper gun, an unusual one-handed grinder invented by Tom David of Nantucket, is particularly popular. The shop also has a full deli with more than 40 types of cheeses and other edibles for party platters and picnic lunches.

Nantucket Lightship Baskets
112 Washington Street Extension
(508) 228-8976
Beautiful, practical, versatile—and undeniably expensive—the traditional Nantucket lightship baskets that are exquisitely handmade by Bill and Judy Sayle range in size from miniatures as small as a thimble to ones as big as a baby's cradle. Woven with fine caning material, the baskets are made with a cherry wood bottom, oak stays, oak handles, and leather hinges, and the lids are decorated with carved ivory or scrimshaw scenes. Both Bill and Judy create the baskets, and Bill hand carves the decorative whales, shells, or birds in ivory. (It was Bill's mother, Mickey, who first suggested putting a lid on the traditional lightship basket and his father, Charlie, who carved the first decoration on a basket made in 1948 by Jose Reyes.)

The prices vary according to the size, the type of wood used for the tops, and the type of decoration. Miniature baskets can range in price from $195 to $525, and

medium-sized covered baskets with a carved sperm whale on the lid can start at around $775. The Sayles' shop is open weekdays from 10:00 A.M. to 3:00 P.M. and weekends by appointment year-round (unless they take a winter break after the holidays).

Nantucket Looms
16 Main Street
(508) 228-1908
www.nantucketlooms.com
Nantucket Looms displays beautiful hand-woven throws, mufflers, and shirts and small elegant toiletries, jewelry, and over-size mugs. Local and international crafts-men have contributed to this rich assortment of clothing and gift items, including decorative birdhouses and dog doorstops, handmade sweaters, and hand-painted furniture. Their cotton fishermen's sweaters are classics.

Nantucket Natural Oils
5 Centre Street
(508) 325-4740, (800) 223-8660
www.nantucketnaturaloils.com
Perfumer John Harding has any name-brand scent you can think of, but with an important difference: There is no alcohol or other additives. These are essential oils, so they have amazing staying power and can even be used by most people who find conventional perfumes give them a headache or make them sneeze. And these oils last and last—we can tell you from per-sonal experience that a tiny bottle can eas-ily last a year. The shop also carries lotions, bath gels, shampoos, and soaps that can be scented, along with lovely perfume bot-tles and other accessories.

The Nantucket Sleigh Ride
3 India Street
(508) 325-4980, (888) 626-8858
With ivy growing across the front of the building, this shop is as pretty outside as

in. It carries Christopher Radko Christmas ornaments, which collectors consider the ultimate in glass, as well as other Christ-mas collectibles by Miriam Mandell and Ginny Moore and copies of 19th-century candle molds. Although the Nutcracker is usually a male figure (had you ever thought about that?), here you can get a female Christmas Nutcracker.

Nina Hellman Marine Antiques & Americana
48 Centre Street
(508) 228-4677
www.nauticalnantucket.com
Her is a wonderful collection of marine antiques—everything from old anchors, tools, and ship lanterns to intricate ship models and ships in bottles. The shop also has a great collection of old books on whal-ing, sailing, and other nautical topics. It's open from Daffodil Weekend to Christmas.

Sweet Inspirations
26 Centre Street
(508) 228-5814, (888) 225-4843
www.nantucketclipper.com
Chocolate, chocolate, chocolate. Those who love the stuff will find a haven in Sweet Inspirations, where the glass-front display cases are filled with plates of all sorts of positively inspired creations. Try one of their heavenly truffles, chocolate buttercrunch, chocolate-covered cranber-ries, or, our perennial favorite, a simple square of dark chocolate wrapped in foil embossed with a tiny Nantucket Island. Sweet Inspirations has lovely collectible tins to fill with the chocolates of your choice, and they do mail order too.

Weeds
14 Centre Street
(508) 228-5200
www.weeds-nantucket.com
A beautiful take on the Nantucket Light-ship basket is a line of porcelain baskets

---

[Facing page] *Murray's Toggery is the place to get your Nantucket Red pants.*
ERICA BOLLERUD

designed by George Davis, manufactured by Bennington Potters, and sold exclusively through Weeds on Nantucket. Davis, founder and owner of Weeds, also has a beautiful collection of fine bone china, which he designed for Wedgwood, that is still sold worldwide and is available exclusively on Nantucket at his shop. Of course there's a lot more to see than dinnerware in this year-round shop, which sells antique and reproduction furniture, hatboxes, tins, garden items, and gifts to fit every price range.

ENTERTAINMENT AND NIGHTLIFE

The streets of Nantucket are wonderfully quiet when the stars come out, but if you're a night owl, there are some lively spots. Also consider taking in some of the cultural arts offerings of Nantucket. During the summer season, theater is performed on the island.

Theater

Actors Theatre
Methodist Church, 2 Centre Street
(508) 228-6325
www.nantuckettheatre.com
Nantucket's only professional theater company, this company, which stages productions in the basement of the Methodist Church, combines professional and amateur talent in new productions in the summer. The small stage lends an intimate flavor to the plays performed by this talented ensemble, who stage six to eight

i *The Nantucket police and the Parks and Recreation Commission show free movies every Friday evening from early July through August at Children's Beach. Movies start at dusk. Call (508) 228-7213 for more information.*

performances each summer. Shows begin at 8:30 P.M. and tickets cost between $12 and $30.

The Theatre Workshop of Nantucket
Bennett Hall at the Congregational Church, 62 Centre Street
(508) 228-4305
www.theatreworkshop.com
If you're a fan of community theater, attend a production by the island's year-round community theater company, which has showcased local talent for enthusiastic audiences for more than 40 years. Performances are staged Wednesday through Saturday evenings at 7:00 P.M. Tickets can be reserved by calling the number listed above.

Movies

Check out the Dreamland Theater on South Water Street (508-228-5356) and the Siasconset Casino in Siasconset (508-257-6585). Both are open seasonally. The Gaslight Theatre on North Union Street (508-228-4435) is open year-round.

Live Entertainment

The Brotherhood of Thieves
23 Broad Street
no phone
This is a cozy eatery that has great food, good drinks, and often performances by solo guitarists or folk duos.

Chicken Box
14 Dave Street
(508) 228-9717
www.thechickenbox.com
Heading toward Surfside Beach, you can find this super-casual, year-round bar, better known as the Box. The Box has live bands seven nights a week from Memorial Day to Labor Day and every weekend the rest of the year.

Cross Rip Coffee House
Methodist Church, 2 Centre Street
(508) 228-4352
The Cross Rip Coffee House has cut back its schedule of entertainment over the last couple of years, but during the fall and winter months look for the Coffee House to open every other week with a variety of entertainment from comedy to folk music.

The Muse
44 Surfside Drive
(508) 228-6873
The Muse is Nantucket's hottest nightclub and concert venue. Here you will find everything from pizza to cool tunes. You might even find yourself competing in the air band competition. The Muse has live entertainment on weekends, usually bands but occasionally DJs. It also offers keno and video trivia games.

Rose & Crown
South Water Street
(508) 228-2595
www.theroseandcrown.com
In town the Rose & Crown is a perennial favorite of islanders and visitors, offering traditional pub atmosphere. They serve lunch and dinner and offer lively entertainment on their stage, varying nightly from rock 'n' roll to karaoke. It is closed in winter.

The Tap Room at the Jared Coffin House
29 Broad Street
(508) 228-2400
www.jaredcoffinhouse.com
You won't find hard rock here, but often this downstairs respite will feature folk music with a guitarist adding to the homey, old-fashioned atmosphere. Have a bite to eat, and then linger over conversation and drinks to hear the music.

HISTORICAL BUILDINGS AND MUSEUMS

Nantucket's place in history is richly illustrated in the island's museums and historic buildings. You can visit them for an Insiders' view of the past, including the whaling period that shaped Nantucket's salty character. Be sure to allow plenty of time to see everything, including the three picturesque lighthouses that dot the shoreline.

The African Meeting House
Five Corners
(508) 228-4058
This small post-and-beam building was built around 1827 by African American island residents, who used it as a school, church, and meetinghouse. The building, which is the only remaining public African-American landmark, is owned by Boston's Museum of Afro-American History, and was restored in 1999. It is open June through September. Tours are available by appointment.

The Coffin School
4 Winter Street
(508) 228-2505
www.eganinstitute.com
Completed in 1854, this Greek Revival building succeeded the island's first school on Fair Street after the Great Fire of 1846. Around the turn of the 20th century, the school became a center for nautical training and home economics for the Nantucket Public Schools. It now houses the Egan Institute of Maritime Studies and is open from 1:00 to 5:00 P.M. to the public from June to October, offering lectures, exhibits, and history videotapes. Lectures cost $5.00 to attend, and the school is free to walk through.

Peter Foulger Museum
Broad Street
(508) 228-1655
This facility hosts changing exhibits on Nantucket history. Admission is $10.00 for adults and $6.00 for children 5 to 14.

The Hinchman House
7 Milk Street
(508) 228-0898
Wildlife enthusiasts will appreciate the natural history collection of living and pre-

served varieties of wildlife here. The staff conducts children's nature classes and bird and nature walks. The Hinchman House is open for self-guided tours June through August, Tuesday through Saturday, 10:00 A.M. to 4:00 P.M. Admission is $4.00 for adults and $3.00 for children.

The Life Saving Museum
158 Polpis Road
(508) 228-1885
www.nantucketlifesaving.org

This is an authentic re-creation of the original 1874 station built in Surfside to assist mariners. It is open daily from mid-June through Columbus Day weekend, 9:30 A.M. to 4:00 P.M. Admission is $5.00 for visitors ages 16 and older and $2.00 for children older than 5.

Macy-Christian House
Liberty Street and Walnut Lane
(508) 228-1894
www.nha.org

Built in 1723 and restored in the late 19th century, this house has furnishings and architecture representative of the colonial and colonial Revival periods. Daily tours are available and admission is covered by the Nantucket Historical Association general admission tickets (see entry below).

Maria Mitchell Birthplace
1 Vestal Street
(508) 228-2896
www.mmo.org

America's first female astronomer, who taught at Vassar College in 1865, is memorialized in her preserved home. The Maria Mitchell Society (508-228-9198) works to preserve her contributions. You can tour the home from June through August, Tuesday through Saturday, 10:00 A.M. to 4:00 P.M. The admission fee for nonmembers is $4.00 for adults, $3.00 for children.

The society also operates the Maria Mitchell Observatory, next door at 3 Vestal Street (508-228-9273), and the Marine Aquarium at 28 Washington Street (508-228-5387).

Nantucket Atheneum
Lower India Street
(508) 228-1110

The recently renovated handsome Greek Revival library is one of the oldest continuously operating libraries in the country; Maria Mitchell was the first librarian. It contains some 40,000 volumes as well as paintings, ship models, scrimshaw, and sculpture, and also has a wonderful children's room. Be sure to visit the Upper Hall, where such figures as Daniel Webster, Ralph Waldo Emerson, Henry David Thoreau, and Frederick Douglass once spoke.

Nantucket Historical Association Sites
2 Whalers Lane
(508) 228-1894
www.nha.org

The association maintains and operates 24 historic sites, locations, and buildings all over Nantucket. Among them are the Quaker Meeting House; the Old Mill, Mill and Prospect Streets, which has original mechanisms and stones; the Old Gaol, Vestal Street, which is nearly 200 years old and is one of the oldest jails in the United States; and the Hadwen House, 96 Main Street, which contains architectural detail and furnishing characteristic of the 19th century. Other sites maintained by the association are the Oldest House and Hose Cart House.

These facilities are open to the public daily from mid-June to Labor Day from 10:00 A.M. to 5:00 P.M. and from September 5 through October 9 daily from 11:00 A.M. to 3:00 P.M. A general pass, good for entry into all the association-maintained sites, is $15.00 for adults (those older than 14) and $8.00 for children. The association's gift shop (508-228-5785) is next to the Whaling Museum.

The Oldest House
Sunset Hill
(508) 228-1894

This colonial saltbox was built in 1686, nearly 100 yeas before the American Revolution. It was built for Jethro and Mary

Gardner Coffin, as a wedding present from their parents, ending a notorious feud between the two families. Admission is $3.00 for adults and $2.00 for children 5 to 14. A Historical Association general pass is also good for admission (see entry above) It is open from late May through Columbus Day.

The Whaling Museum
Broad Street
(508) 228-1894
www.nha.org
Originally a candle factory, this superb museum offers displays of whaling equipment, scrimshaw, early records, and the skeleton of a 43-foot finback whale. Don't miss the lively lecture on the history of whaling, presented three times a day. The museum is open Thursday through Monday starting in May and daily late May through September from 10:00 A.M. to 5:00 P.M. Admission is $10.00 for adults and $6.00 for children 5 to 14. A Historical Association general pass is also good for admission.

LIGHTHOUSES

Brant Point Lighthouse
Harbor entrance
Built in 1746, Brant Point Light is the second-oldest lighthouse in the United States. Photographs of its Christmas wreath have graced numerous magazine pages. This is the lighthouse you see when entering the harbor on the ferry.

Great Point Light
Great Point
Destroyed by a storm in 1984 and rebuilt, Great Point Light sits at the northern tip of the island in an area frequented by bird-watchers and picnickers. (See the Natural Areas section of this chapter).

Sankaty Head Lighthouse
Sankaty Bluff
Picturesque red-and-white Sankaty Head Lighthouse is perched on Sankaty Bluff at

the eastern end of the island. It overlooks the sea and a golf course.

ART SCHOOLS AND GALLERIES

Art Instruction

Nantucket Island School of Design and the Arts
23 Wauwinet Road
(508) 228-4487
www.nisda.org
If the visual arts are your love, contact the school and take some classes. The school offers courses for academic credit and enrichment to both children and adults in such subjects as drawing, painting, photography, clay, textiles, and crafts. The school has accommodations on Washington Street on the harbor.

Shredder's Studio
Salros Road off Appleton Road
(508) 228-4487
www.madeonnantucket.com
Shredder's offers oil painting, watercolor, jewelry making, and stained glass classes to adults and young adults and watercolor, ceramics, and other classes for children. It even has a preschool creative workshop for little budding artists.

Galleries

Artists' Association of Nantucket
19 Washington Street
(508) 228-0294
www.nantucketarts.org
This small gallery near Straight Wharf features paintings, photography, sculpture, jewelry, and drawings by established island artists and emerging local talent. It hosts a year-round schedule of changing member exhibitions, featured artist shows, juried shows, auctions, fund-raisers, and community-oriented arts events. New

Just a short walk from the bustle of Main Street, you'll find a historic section of Nantucket. Stroll up and down Union and East York Streets while visiting galleries and shops selling antiques, fine arts, and more.

And you may have guessed already that when you're visiting a spot in the middle of the ocean, local tours aren't limited to land. You can choose from among sunset cruises, children's cruises, and—not surprisingly, as Nantucket was once the center of America's whaling industry—cruises that search for whales—just for the joy of sighting them of course.

shows are usually unveiled at Friday evening opening receptions.

The Gallery at Four India Street
4 India Street
(508) 228-8509
www.galleryatfourindia.com
This gallery is open year-round. It has 19th- and 20th-century oils, pastels, watercolors, sculpture, and bronze work, 80 percent of which is the work of local and regional artists.

The Nantucket Gallery & Frame Shop
23 Federal Street
(508) 228-1943
This gallery is owned by artist Marshall DuBock, who sells Nantucket scenes.

Robert Wilson Galleries
34 Main Street
(508) 228-2096
While in Nantucket be sure to visit this gallery, which has exquisite landscape and still-life renderings in oils and watercolors.

TOURS AND EXCURSIONS

Nantucket's experienced tour guides show off their island with the love and pride of a gardener showing off a bed of roses. You'll get a history lesson, personal insights, and priceless anecdotes. You'll also witness the easy camaraderie of the islanders, who are likely to roll down the car window and give the traffic cop—probably a friend—a hard time.

Most tours will meet you at a central location or pick you up. The cost is generally about $14 per person.

Land Tours of Nantucket

Ara's Tours
P.O. Box 734, Nantucket, MA 02554
(508) 221-6852
www.arastours.com
Ara's offers a 90-minute tour that covers 30 miles of this unique and beautiful island. Listen to guided commentary in an air-conditioned van. See historic Main Street, the rose-covered cottages of Sconset, and the lighthouses of Nantucket. Tours leave at 11:15 A.M., 1:30 P.M., and 3:30 P.M. and cost $14 per person. You can be picked up at your in-town accommodations, boat, or a convenient location in-town. Advance bookings for tours are highly recommended. Tours are available on a daily basis from mid-April thorough mid-November. Naturalist and photographer Ara Charger provides the commentary and always stops for photos. The van tour can accommodate 14 people, and private tours are also available.

Barrett's Tours
20 Federal Street
(508) 228-5455
Barrett's provides narrated one-and-one-half-hour bus tours of Nantucket daily April through November, and also offers shuttle-bus service to Jetties, Surfside, and Madaket Beaches and to Siasconset. A family-owned and -operated business for more than 5 years, Barrett's also offers tours and transportation for special groups, such as wedding parties, with group rates for 20 or more people. Tours depart 11:30 A.M. from the steamship

wharf, and 1:45 P.M. from the Federal Street offices. Call for prices.

Gail's Tours Inc.
(508) 257-6557
www.nantucket.net/tours/gails

A sixth-generation native, Gail Nickerson Johnson has a wealth of knowledge and a great sense of humor, which she shares generously on her tours. Her two air-conditioned vans can accommodate a total of 13 people. She offers sightseeing and private tours, including sunset, picnic, or beach excursions. Regular tours depart at 10:00 A.M., 1:00 P.M., and 3:00 P.M. Call for prices.

Great Point Natural History Tours
(508) 228-6799

Run by the nonprofit group the Trustees of the Reservations, these three-hour, naturalist-led tours offer a rare opportunity to explore the Coskata-Coatue Wildlife Refuge. Get close-up looks at migrant and nesting shorebirds, learn about wildflowers, see deer tracks crossing coastal heathlands, and visit historic Great Point Lighthouse—you even get to climb to the top! Tours meet at the gatehouse just before the Wauwinet Inn parking lot and are limited to seven people. Only two trips are scheduled a day, and reservations are required. Tours are offered from June to October. Adults pay $40 and children 12 and younger pay $15.

Cruises and Whale Watching

Endeavor
Straight Wharf
(508) 228-5585
www.endeavorsailing.com

Since 1982 this Friendship sloop, owned and operated by Jim and Sue Genthner, has been offering three daily sails around Nantucket Sound plus a sunset cruise. The longest operating sailing charter on the island, the *Endeavor* was built by Captain

Jim, and if you wish, he will share his knowledge of traditional boat building with you. The sail cruises leave at 10:00 A.M., 1:00 P.M., 4:00 P.M., and sunset. The 90-minute sail costs $25 per person regardless of age. The sunset cruises are $35.

For the children the *Endeavor* offers a one-hour special sail each day at 11:30 A.M. for $15 per person. Or ask about the Songs and Stories of the Sea trip, which is fun for children ages 4 to 8, and the Fiddlin' on the Sea trip, which provides whaling-era instrumental music for families with older children. Both of the latter sails are also one hour and cost $15 per person.

Nantucket Harbor Cruises
Straight Wharf
(508) 228-1444

Nantucket Harbor Cruises offers several trips daily in season aboard the *Anna W II*, starting with a 90-minute morning marine cruise in which you pull lobster traps and learn about what's in the boat's touch tank. The cost is $27 per person regardless of age, but you must be at least 4 years old to come aboard. Captain Bruce Cowan is a naturalist and very knowledgeable about marine life as well as boats. We especially enjoy the evening sunset cruises which are both romantic and relaxing. Bring you own beverages and sit at the boat's comfortable tables as you watch the boats come in through the fading light. The sunset cruise, also a 90-minute cruise, costs $25 per person.

Nantucket Harbor Cruises also offers an afternoon Ice Cream Cruise at 1:30 and 3:30 P.M. for $17. Children get complimentary ice cream.

Shearwater Excursions
Town Pier
(508) 228-7037
www.explorenantucket.com

On Sundays from mid-June through September, take the catamaran *Shearwater* on a six-hour whale-watching trip 15 to 30 miles southeast of Nantucket. Out on the open Atlantic, you are guaranteed to spot humpback, minke, and finback whales—

and maybe dolphins and sea turtles—or you get a free ticket for another whale watch. Shearwater Excursions also offers two-hour seal cruises and one-hour lobster cruises. The cost for whale watches is $100 per adult and $75 per child age 12 and younger.

BEACHES

When you're on a relatively small island, it's hard to get away from the beach. Aw, what a pity. Whether you go to an ocean beach with crashing surf or a harbor beach with gently lapping waves, don't miss the opportunity to savor the Nantucket seaside.

Take time to learn the existing swimming conditions before you head for the beach. Currents can be very strong along the entire south side of Nantucket, including Cisco, Madaket, and Surfside Beaches. The Parks and Recreation Department (508-228-7213) recommends that people swim only at beaches with lifeguards; beaches are closed when conditions warrant it. Free parking is available at all beaches, and you can usually find a space even in the busy summer months. All of

---

Nantucket is justifiably proud of its beaches, especially the fact that 80 miles or so of them are largely open to the public, regardless of public or private ownership. Lately, however, the increasing number of SUVs on the island has led to some conflict. More and more people are arriving with SUVs, buying beach permits, and going four-wheeling or holding loud parties on the beach, to the chagrin of many beach owners. To help allay tensions between these owners and vacationing four-wheelers, a town beach manager has been appointed to maintain friendships . . . and open beaches.

Nantucket's beaches are lovely; here are some of our favorites.

North Shore and In-Town

Brant Point
Easton Street
This beach right by the lighthouse has no lifeguards or facilities, but the view of the harbor is always entrancing. An easy walk from town, it's a great place to just sit and watch the boats rounding the point.

Children's Beach
Harbor View Way
Families naturally gravitate toward this pleasant beach; It's on the harbor, an easy walk from town, a lifeguard is on duty, rest-room facilities are available, and there is a snack bar. And as you might expect, it has a nice play area for children, as well as picnic tables and a bandstand.

Dionis Beach
North Beach Street
This large, popular beach is a long walk from town or an easy bike ride of about 3 miles. Shuttle service is also available. It has lifeguards, rest rooms, bathhouses, a restaurant, tennis courts, and towels and chairs for rent. The town's Park and Recreation Commission (508-228-7213) offers swimming lessons here for children ages 6 and older from July 4 through Labor Day, 9:30 A.M. to noon.

Francis Street Beach
Francis Street and Washington Street
A five-minute walk from Main Street, Francis Street Beach is on the calm waters of the harbor and ideal for swimming. There is no lifeguard.

Jetties Beach
North Beach Street
An easy bike or shuttle ride from town, this beach is great for families. It has lifeguards, rest rooms, concessions, a play-

ground, and volleyball nets. Sailboard, sailboat, and kayak rentals are available, and swimming lessons are offered by the Parks and Recreation Commission for children age 6 and older. Call (508) 228–7213 for dates and times.

South Shore and Out of Town

Cisco Beach
Off Hummock Pond Road
Travel southwest about 4 miles out of town to reach this stretch of shore, which is a popular place for surf casting. A lifeguard is on duty. You can also take the 4-mile bike path to the end of Hummock Pond Road.

Madaket Beach
Madaket Road
As far west on the island as you can go. There is a regular bus shuttle, or you can take the 6-mile paved scenic bike path from town. The surf and currents here are strong and can be dangerous depending on weather conditions. Still, it's a popular spot for surf swimming, and lifeguards are on duty. Rest rooms are available at the beach. Madakeet is known for its spectacular sunsets.

Miacomet Beach
Miacomet Road
This beach, located at the end of Miacomet Road, has no facilities or lifeguards on duty. The surf is also very heavy and strong. But if you want to get away from it all and find a deserted spot on the beach, this is the place to go.

Surfside Beach
Surfside Road
Located at the end of Surfside Road, this is one of the most popular Nantucket beaches. The beach is wide—perfect for kite flying—and has a bathhouse, rest rooms, and lifeguards. You can also get food nearby at a number of restaurants

For the last dozen years, the Nantucket Parks and Recreation Commission has sponsored popular tie-dye clinics on Fridays throughout the summer at Children's Beach. They're free and open to the public from noon to 1:30 P.M. Bring your own white cotton shirt, or buy one when you get there.

and convenience stores. It's accessible by shuttle bus, or you can take the 3-mile paved bike path from town.

Eastern Shore and Out of Town

Siasconset Beach
Sconset Village
A regular shuttle bus gets you to this popular area, which is the only public beach on the east shore of the island. There is also a 7-mile paved bike path that you can take. Surf and currents can be heavy. There is a lifeguard, and food is available in nearby 'Sconset.

NATURAL AREAS

Nantucket's unique natural resources can be shared by all. The Nantucket Conservation Foundation owns many properties that can be used by the public for recreation such as hiking. Other properties are owned by the Nantucket Land Bank or other conservation organizations. The Conservation Foundation owns and manages more than 8,452 acres, about 40 percent of all the land on Nantucket. We've listed a few of our favorite properties; for others, look for their maroon concrete posts decorated with the Foundation's gull and waves logo. For a complete map of all Foundation properties and regulations, visit the Foundation office at 118 Cliff Road, or call (508) 228–2884. Remember: Vehicles on these properties are strictly regulated or prohibited.

The Sanford Farm, Ram Pasture, and the Woods

These properties total 767 acres of wetlands, grasslands, and forests in the southwest portion of the island. With more than 6.6 miles of roadways and trails to explore, the area includes a panoramic view of Nantucket's south shore from the barn in Ram Pasture. Ambitious hikers can follow a 6-mile round-trip trail that leads to the ocean and travels alongside Hummock Pond. You'll find a variety of wildflowers and may spot such wildlife as ring-necked pheasant, ospreys, red-tailed hawks, rabbits, and deer. the land is accessible from a parking area off Madaket Road, near the intersection of Cliff Road.

Guides from the Maria Mitchell Association know where the most productive birding sites are on the island. They run bird field trips Tuesday and Saturday during the summer at 6:30 A.M. and Thursday at 8:00 A.M. Trips start at the picnic tables at the Hinchman House Natural Science Museum, 7 Milk Street. Adults cost $10.00, children cost $6.00. You can also call the Maria Mitchell Association/Massachusetts Audubon Society Birding Hotline at (888) 224–6444 to learn about recent on-island bird activity.

Long Pond

Owned by the Nantucket Land Bank, this 64-acre property is especially good for bird-watching. It features a 1-mile walking path that runs along the pond, past meadows and a natural cranberry bog. To reach the area take Madaket Road and look for a dirt road on the left across the sign to Hither Creek, near Madaket. Cross the bridge to reach a parking area and the entrance to the trail.

Eel Point

A spit of sand on the western end of the island, just north of and bordering Madaket Harbor, Eel Point is a Nantucket Conservation Foundation property that attracts great numbers of birds. The 100-plus acre property abounds in goldenrod, roses, wild grapes, bayberries, and other vegetation. To get there take Eel Point Road off Cliff Road and park on the dirt road. If you're biking, take a right off the Madaket bike path onto Eel Point Road.

Coskata-Coatue Wildlife Refuge

This barrier beach that stretches across Nantucket Harbor is actually several protected areas in one: Coatue Wildlife Refuge and the Haulover, 476 acres owned by the Nantucket Conservation foundation; Coskata-Coatue Wildlife Refuge, 792 acres owned by the Trustees of Reservations; and Nantucket National Wildlife Refuge at Great Point, owned by the U.S. Fish and Wildlife Service. Great Point, which is home to the lighthouse of the same name that's a replica of the one lost in a severe storm in 1984, is the island's northernmost point, slicing up between Nantucket Sound and the Atlantic Ocean. Remote and wild, the barrier beach offers breathtaking views and the opportunity to observe nature first-hand. In spring it's a nesting place for piping plovers, least terns, northern harriers, and other shorebirds.

The area as a whole includes not just beaches and sand dunes, but salt marshes and wind sheared oak and cedar forests. Vehicles are strictly controlled here; a pass is required for four-wheel-drive vehicles, and officials advise inexperienced beach drivers not to drive in the very soft sand. This is a place for serious nature lovers who don't care about frills or modern amenities. There are no lifeguards, and some of the beaches are particularly dangerous for swimming. There are no rest rooms, concessions or public buildings within the refuge; come here only if you want to be one with nature and are willing to respect her.

The Trustees of Reservations offers guided natural history tours of the refuge that take you all the way out to Great Point Lighthouse and back. Call (508) 228-6799 to make reservations (they're required). These tours are very popular, so be sure to plan for your trip in advance. Tours leave at 9:30 A.M. and 1:30 P.M. daily from the Wauwinet Gatehouse on Wauwinet Road. Cost is $40 per adult; children age 12 and younger are $15.

RECREATION

Boating and Water Sports

Water sports are big here, and it's a great place to finally learn how to sail or sailboard or try kayaking. Whether you're an old hand or just starting out, look to the following places for equipment and sales.

Nantucket Boat Rental
Slip 1, Straight Wharf
(508) 325-1001

If the sight of all those beautiful boats in the harbor makes you want to take one out yourself, contact Nantucket Boat Rental. They rent a good selection of well-maintained powerboats (13-foot, 17-foot, 20-foot, or 22-foot) that you can rent by the hour, half-day, day, week, or month.

Nantucket Community Sailing
Jetties Beach and Polpis Harbor
(508) 228-6600
www.nantucketsailing.com

Community Sailing offers popular youth and adult sailing instruction at levels from beginner to advanced sailor, as well as to those interested in racing, at their Polpis Harbor and Jetties Beach locations. Adult programs include women's sailing clinics, private and group lessons, and racing clinics. NCS also offers sailboat rentals of

Rhodes 19s and Marshall Cat 15s. They also have an open sailing program, which allows experienced sailors to "borrow" the NCS sailboats for two-hour periods for sailing within Nantucket Harbor.

Nantucket Harbor Sail
Swain's Wharf
(508) 228-0424

This operation rents sailboats during the season.

Sea Nantucket Family Boat Rental & Sales
Washington Street Ext.
(508) 228-7499

This seasonal shop offer rentals, lessons, and guided trips. It can deliver kayak, sailboat, and powerboat rentals anywhere around the island.

Fishing

Fishing has been a way of life for Nantucketers for generations and still provides a healthy and popular form of recreation, not to mention a delicious meal. If you want to go for bluefish or striped bass, you can pick up equipment, bait, and a guide with a four-wheel-drive and head for Great Point, Smith Point, or Surfside Beach.

A four-wheel-drive vehicle is needed for access to Great Point and Smith Point, but you can walk onto Dionis, Surfside, and Pebbles Beaches. These are perhaps the best-known beaches, but keep in mind that Nantucket is rimmed by beaches, so finding a fishing spot is not difficult. Of course, as any angler knows, finding fish is another matter. We highly recommend that you contact the local tackle shops for current information about fishing (we suggests several below), because obviously the location of fish and conditions at sea change from day to day.

The Nantucket Anglers Club (508-228-2299) sponsors the Annual Billfish Tournament for offshore fishing. Open to the public, this weeklong tournament takes place around the last week in July and the first week in August.

If you don't own a boat, you can go fishing in a head boat (charges by the person) or a charter boat (charges for the boat). Head boats always provide fishing equipment, and you generally do not need reservations, but it is always best to check ahead. The cost is in the vicinity of $25 per person. There are not many big-game fish charters out of Nantucket. Ask at local tackle shops for recommendations on big-game fishing charters.

If your kids want to do a little bottom fishing off the wharves, they might catch some scup or flounder, but most people head to the beaches. Nine- to 11-foot spinning rods are prevalent for surf fishing. According to Bill Pew at Bill Fisher Tackle, 90 percent of fishing here is done with artificial lures rather than live bait, and he sees growing interest in fly-fishing.

TACKLE SHOPS

Barry Thurston Fishing Tackle
Harbor Square at Nantucket Marina
(508) 228-9595
www.nantucket.net/sports/thurston
With more than 25 years of experience, this fishing shop outfits for deep-sea fishing, surf casting, freshwater fishing, and shellfishing. It's a licensed Orvis dealer and sells equipment and clothing, offers daily or weekly equipment rentals, and does repairs.

Nantucket's six bicycle paths range in length from 2.5 miles to 8 miles. The paved paths offer scenic routes along Cliff Road, Milestone Road, Surfside Road, Madaket Road, and Polpis Road. Plan a day of exploration—pack a picnic, take your swimsuits, and keep your eyes open for the wild blueberries, blackberries, and beach plums that grow near some of the paths.

Bill Fisher Tackle
14 New Lane
(508) 228-2261
Open year-round, this shop has a full line of conventional freshwater and saltwater tackle, spinning tackle, and fly-fishing tackle. It also offers freshwater bait, rental equipment, referrals for guide service, and maintenance and repairs.

Golf

Miacomet Golf Club
Off Somerset Road
(508) 325-0333
Owned by the Nantucket Land Bank since 1985, this is the island's only publicly owned course. It has 18 holes, a par of 74, a driving range, pro shop, and both pull and electric carts. Reservations for tee times are required at least a week in advance; the course turns away about 100 people a day in summer. Call for current greens fees.

Sankaty Head Golf Club
Sankaty Road, Siasconset
(508) 257-6391
This year-round private course is open to the public only from October 1 until the first Friday in June, excluding Memorial Day weekend when, as in summer, it's reserved for members. The 18-hole, par 72 course, developed in 1920 and still recognized as one of the country's finest links courses, enjoys water views from just about every hole. Carts are available, and an on-site pro shop offers everything a golfer may need. Call for greens fees.

Siasconset Golf Course
Milestone Road
(508) 257-6596
Founded in 1894, this is one of the oldest golf courses in the United States. It's a nine-hole, par 34 public golf course surrounded by conservation land. No tee

times are required, and club and pull cart rentals are available. Open late-May through mid-October from 8:00 A.M. until the last tee time at 6:00 P.M. Call for current greens fees.

Tennis

Brant Point Racquet Club
48 North Beach Street
(508) 228-3700
This club has nine clay courts open to the public. You can pay hourly for court time or opt for instruction to improve your game. It also has a fully equipped pro shop, rental racquets, and equipment.

Jetties Beach Public Tennis Courts
North Beach Street, Jetties Beach
(508) 325-5334
These courts are free and open to the public.

Tristram's Landing Tennis Center
440 Arkansas Avenue, Madaket
(508) 228-4588
This center has five hard-surface courts available for play.

ANNUAL EVENTS

There's a lot going on here, and not just in summer. Besides the annual events, there are dozens of concerts, craft fairs, and other events to watch for when you come to the island. Check with the chamber of commerce (508-228-1700) for a current guide.

April

The Daffodil Festival
(508) 228-1700
In its 30th year in 2004, the Daffodil Festival heralds spring as the island's millions of yellow daffodils come to life in late April. The road to Sconset is lined with thousands of the brilliant blooms, which the Garden Club and townspeople started planting in 1974. The highlight of the festivities is the gathering of 100 or so antique and classical cars on Main Street and the parade and giant tailgate party at Sconset.

May

The Nantucket Wine Festival
(508) 228-1128, (508) 228-1700
www.nantucketwinefestival.com
Launched in 1997, the annual weeklong Nantucket Wine Festival has become a huge success. More than 135 wineries of international acclaim are represented, and chefs vie to produce the class of cuisine that best enhances fine wines. Participants get to sip wine in private mansions and dine on world-class cuisine. It culminates with a charity gala at the White Elephant Hotel. Call ahead for a program so you can make reservations. Ticket prices vary per event, with such events like the Grand Tasting costing $60 per person and the charity gala costing $125 per person.

Figawi Race
Hyannis to Nantucket
(508) 4HYANNIS, (508) 778-6100
www.figawi.com
Now in its 33rd year, this sailboat race from Hyannis to Nantucket and back generates as much excitement here as it does on the Cape. It takes place on Memorial Day weekend (see our Cape Cod Annual Events chapter for details).

June

The Nantucket Film Festival
(508) 228-1700, (212) 708-1278
www.nantucketfilmfestival.org
An inspiring inside look at screenwriting for film authorities and fans alike, the four-day film festival is in its ninth year and attracts more than a few celebrities as

---

 The best place to get a bird's-eye view of Nantucket is from the tower of the First Congregational Church on 62 Centre Street. It's a climb, but well worth it, and the 94-step journey to the top is interrupted by a display of old photographs and history of the Old North Church, as it is known. Tours begin in mid-June and continue through mid-October.

---

well as film buffs and fans. It's held around the middle of the month.

July

Independence Day
Nantucketers do it up on the Fourth, with a riotous fire-hose contest on Main Street, pie-eating contests, face painting, and more. In the evening, a gala celebration with music and children's games takes place at Jetties Beach. The grand finale, of course, is a fireworks display.

August

Sandcastle and Sculpture Day
Jetties Beach
Nantucket
In its 31st year this popular event, cosponsored by the Nantucket Chamber of Commerce and the Nantucket Island School of Design and the Arts, attracts residents and visitors of all ages who vie for honors sculpting the most creative sandcastle and sand sculptures. The event, held on Jetties Beach, is always held the third Saturday in August. Entries are judged in five divisions, ranging from Family to Under 10; preregistration is required. You can use tools, but you cannot add any supporting

or form devices to the sculpture. It costs $5.00 per person to register.

September

Nantucket Island Fair
Tom Nevers Navy Base
(508) 228-7213
Set for the third weekend in September, this is a real old-fashioned tradition started in 1992. Baked goods, jams, and jellies vie for ribbons, and an animal tent, hayrides, pet show, and square dancing are some of the lively activities.

October

Nantucket Arts Festival
(508) 325-8588
This weeklong festival is held in early October. Island musicians, authors, actors, artists, and dancers come together to celebrate the arts on Nantucket through roughly 80 events. You'll find everything from chamber music concerts and readings to puppet shows.

November

Festival of Wreaths and Silent Auction
Preservation Institute, 11 Centre Street
(508) 228-1894
Nearly 100 wreaths decorated by merchants, local artists, and community members adorn the walls of the Preservation Institute during this festival. The wreaths are auctioned off at the end of the festival, for prices ranging from $45 to $1,000. Held the weekend after Thanksgiving, the auction proceeds go to the Nantucket Whaling Museum's School Program, which enables students to visit the museum free of charge.

Important Numbers

Medical, fire, or police emergencies	911
A Safe Place, 24-hour hotline	(508) 228-2111
Alcoholics Anonymous	(800) ALCOHOL
Children at Risk	(800) 792-5200
Missing Persons	(800) 622-5999
Alzheimer's Information	(800) 351-2299
Cancer Information	(800) 422-6237

December

Nantucket Christmas Stroll
(508) 228-1700

During the first weekend in December, the Christmas Stroll draws tens of thousands of people to Nantucket for the townwide celebration of Christmas. Christmas trees are placed throughout the town and decorated by local businesses, services, and students in a decorating contest. At noon on Saturday a U.S. Coast Guard cutter (not Rudolph and company) delivers Santa, who is then transported to the stroll in a horse-drawn carriage. Schoolchildren, carolers, and bell ringers in period costume create a joyful atmosphere with holiday song. And everywhere you look you'll find wonderful food, hot chocolate, and beautiful decorations—even a talking Christmas tree!

NOTE: Make your holiday hotel reservations way in advance—a year ahead is strongly advised. And bring those Christmas lists (and wallets); Nantucket shops have the most exquisite gifts!

HEALTH CARE

Nantucket Cottage Hospital
57 Prospect Street, Nantucket
(508) 228-1200
www.nantuckethospital.org

The only medical facility on the island, this hospital offers 24-hour emergency care, home health care, chemotherapy, X-rays, mammography, physical therapy, dialysis, and laboratory service.

MEDIA

Newspapers

The Inquirer & Mirror
Old South Road
(508) 228-0001
www.ack.net/IM

The Inquirer & Mirror is Nantucket's oldest newspaper, established in 1821. The publication started as *The Inquirer* and merged with the competing paper, *The Mirror,* in 1865. This newspaper operated as an independent until 1990 when it was sold to Ottaway Newspapers Inc., a subsidiary of Dow Jones. Marianne Giffin Stanton, whose parents once owned the paper, is the editor and publisher.

The *Inquirer & Mirror,* affectionately known on the island as the Inky, is published every Thursday and has a circulation of about 10,000. It has the largest classified section on the island and also publishes the *Nantucket Holiday* and a monthly vacation guide. Mailed subscriptions reach far and wide, including towns and cities in every state.

The *Nantucket Independent*
119B Pleasant Street
(508) 228–1654
www.nantucketindependent.com
Second newspapers on the island have come and gone over the years. The latest contender is this locally owned upstart, which published its first issue in the summer of 2003. It bills itself as the island's "weekly newspaper for businesses and entrepre-neurs." Reporting focuses on island-related economic news, local business profiles, analysis of town contracts, and listings of property transactions. Reporting also explores standard-of-living and quality-of-life issues that have particular relevance on this isolated isle, such as the economics of environmental preservation, beach erosion, and the eternal complaint that groceries are cheaper on the mainland.

MARTHA'S VINEYARD

There's something about the feel of being on an island. You are in a special world where time slows, the sun brightens, and the salt air refreshes. When in Massachusetts there is no easier way of experiencing this phenomenon than with a trip to Martha's Vineyard.

Depending on the point from which you measure, the Vineyard, as we Cape Codders call it, lies only 7 to 9 miles from the mainland. If you are riding on the Falmouth ferries on a clear day, you never lose full sight of either the Cape or the Vineyard. Martha's Vineyard is a convenient respite full of spectacular views, quaint villages, charming gingerbread cottages, and elegant sea captains' homes.

While the island certainly embraces the visitor, it has not fallen victim to the tourist traps that have infested many seasonal communities, reaching and grabbing for that fleeting tourist dollar. Like the Cape and its island neighbor Nantucket, Martha's Vineyard represents a unique balance between active commerce and peaceful conservation.

Perhaps that is one reason why this unique island has attracted famous stars of stage and screen for years. Some of the more popular islanders include Carly Simon, political humorist Art Buchwald, actress Patricia Neal, retired news anchor Walter Cronkite, and actors Dan Ackroyd and Jim Belushi (his late brother John is buried on the island).

While you might come to the island in search of the rich and famous, your gaze will likely be diverted very quickly by the striking charm each town possesses. You may find yourself replacing your search for the stars with a tour of the island's real celebrities: its five unique lighthouses.

If you are wedded to your automobile, you had better do some planning. Only a limited number of vehicles can make it over on the Steamship Authority ferry.

You have to make a reservation several months in advance if you hope to take a car over in the summer season. Sometimes you can get a spot at the last minute on one of the first ferries out in the morning, but don't bet your vacation on it. Also, once driving on the island, you'll have to practice a lot of patience as intersections are crowded with pedestrians and bicyclists.

Even though Martha's Vineyard is New England's largest island at 10 miles long and 9 miles wide, you'll find it easy to negotiate on foot or pedal. The island consists of six towns, each with its own personality. Some 16,000 year-round residents call the island home, but, during the busy summer months, that population swells to nearly 100,000. Together with the town of Gosnold on Cuttyhunk Island (the only public island of the Elizabeth Island chain just west of the Vineyard) and No Man's Island (and uninhabited island off Aquinnah, the island's westernmost community), the six towns of Martha's Vineyard are part of Dukes County. FYI: You can get to Cuttyhunk Island from the Vineyard (see the Excursions section of this chapter).

The island's northernmost town is incorporated as Tisbury, but most call it by the name of its very busy harbor Vineyard Haven. The gateway to Vineyard Haven is marked by two spits of land, West Chop, the northern tip of Tisbury, and directly across the harbor, East Chop, the northern tip of the town of Oak Bluffs. Southeast of Oak Bluffs is the town of Edgartown, which includes the island of Chappaquiddick, known locally by its nickname, Chappy. "Up island" (or sometimes "outer island") refers to the more rural towns of West Tisbury, Chilmark, and Aquinnah. Chilmark includes the fishing village of Menemsha. The term "up island" can be confusing to visitors. Up, in this case refers to longitude. The farther west one travels, the higher the longitude—it's a nautical thing.

You'd expect prices to be a little higher because Martha's Vineyard is a resort, but because it's an island, most of the goods have to be shipped over by ferry or plane, which increases the prices a bit, too. Do you essential shopping on the mainland to help you save money for mementos and entertainment.

As far as the weather goes, don't be caught off guard at night. A cool ocean breeze and dropping temperatures can demand an evening sweater, even in mid-summer.

HISTORY

Though the legend of Moshaup creating Martha's Vineyard with the sand from his moccasin is fun to relate, Martha's Vineyard was in fact created during the last ice age when the Laurentide ice sheet deposited the boulders and gravel it had carried along on its slow journey southward. As the ice sheet receded, the southernmost deposits became the islands of Nantucket and Martha's Vineyard. The oceans began to rise with the melting ice, thus forming Nantucket Sound between these lovely islands and the equally lovely peninsula to the north known as Cape Cod.

As the climate warmed, American Indians began to migrate to the island, settling here some 5,000 years ago.

Legend has it that Viking explorers discovered the island back around A.D. 1000, but that story is very hard to prove—or disprove for that mater. What is known for sure is that in March 1602, English navigator Bartholomew Gosnold set off in his vessel *Concord* across the Atlantic to arrive months later along the coast of Maine. Farther south he discovered Cape Cod and, on May 22, he arrived at Martha's Vineyard (Edgartown to be more exact—Cape Pogue, Chappaquiddick to be even more exact), which he named for his daughter, Martha. Gosnold later

attempted to establish a settlement on nearby Cuttyhunk Island but abandoned the attempt, citing unfavorable living conditions.

Though there is a story of white settlers arriving as early as 1632, the official settlement of Martha's Vineyard by Thomas Mayhew Jr. would not occur until 1642. During the previous year, in October 1641, his father, also named Thomas Mayhew, a merchant of Watertown, and Thomas Jr. were deeded rights "to plant and inhabit" the islands of Martha's Vineyard, Nantucket, and the neighboring Elizabeth Islands by William, Earl of Sterling, a representative of Charles I. Thomas Mayhew Jr. brought a group of 80 to settle at Great Harbor, which later incorporated as Edgartown in 1671. The settlement was named by New York Governor Lovelace to honor Edgar, the son of the Duke of York, and was no doubt done to earn the favor of the royal family. Edgar was the 3-year-old nephew of King Charles, and because the King did not have any children of his own, Edgar appeared to be heir to the throne. Unbeknownst to Lovelace, poor little Edgar died a month before the town's incorporation.

White settlers and American Indians quickly learned to live together in this island paradise. As they had at the Plymouth colony, the American Indians shared their farming and fishing skills with the settlers. Hostilities between the two groups were nonexistent, and even during the King Philip War of 1676–77 (which saw white settlers and Indians battling on the mainland), relations on the island remained friendly. Yet this paradise turned into disaster for the American Indians as they began to fall in great numbers to the diseases brought by the white settlers. Around 3,000 Indians lived on Martha's Vineyard when Mayhew and his group first arrived. Within 30 years, the Indian population has been cut in half as a result of disease. Many of the surviving American Indians converted to Christianity because they believed the English settlers' god was protecting the settlers from the diseases that swept through the Native American community.

Very soon the settlers outnumbered the dwindling American Indians. By the middle of the 18th century, there were perhaps only 500 American Indians remaining. Fortunately pockets of them survive, and today half the population of the town of Aquinnah are Wampanoag Indians.

The Towns

The history of each of the Vineyard's towns is as varied as their differing personalities. Though settlement began in Edgartown, people began to settle in different parts of the island. Farming and fishing provided the staples of life early on, but soon each town developed based on its unique characteristics.

Edgartown prospered as a whaling port during the early to mid-1800s. More than 100 whaling captains hailed from this town, and today their stately homes, a majority of them built between 1830 and 1845, line the main road as remainders of the fortunes made harvesting whale oil. The last half of the 19th century saw a rapid decline in whaling when the discovery of petroleum made the pursuit of the leviathan an obsolete profession. Edgartown's prosperity stagnated until tourism restored the town and its many beautiful buildings to their 18th- and 19th-century splendor.

Vineyard Haven, known early as Holmes Hole, is the island's second-oldest town, incorporated in 1671 as Tisbury. Its excellent harbor made it an important port town where the wares of the Vineyard could be readily sold to off-islanders. Oceangoing traffic was so busy in the area that Nantucket and Vineyard Sounds were considered second only to the English Channel for the number of vessels passing through. The sea played a large part in the town's development—locals would serve as sailors and fishermen on local and foreign vessels. Today Vineyard

Haven maintains its port status, providing a busy harbor connecting the island to the mainland—and to the rest of the world for that matter.

The town of Oak Bluffs, incorporated in 1907, was once part of Edgartown. Its development as a seasonal community began in 1835 when an Edgartown man, Jeremiah Pease, selected the area of Oak Bluffs to hold a Methodist camp meeting. The idea caught on, and each summer the camp meeting grounds were visited by religious folk who pitched tents to spend time worshiping and relaxing beneath the oaks, which grew abundantly in the area. Very soon the tents were replaced by cottages. So many cottages were built when Oak Bluffs broke away from the town of Edgartown in 1880 it was named Cottage Town (until 1907 when it was renamed). Residents decorated the cottages with ornate woodwork, and today their gingerbread flavor dictates the personality of this quaint resort town.

Up island lie the towns of West Tisbury, Chilmark, and Aquinnah (formerly known as Gay Head). West Tisbury was largely a farming community and maintains its rural personality. It was formally a part of the town of Tisbury until it broke away as a separate town in 1892. Meanwhile Chilmark, with its fishing village of Menemsha, earned its living from both the sea and the land. Chilmark was incorporated in 1694. Aquinnah, which became an independent town in 1870, is a geological wonder, with its cliffs of clay displaying the fingerprint of the last ice age. The town's roots stem from a Native American settlement, and today Aquinnah is home to more than 100 members of the Wampanoag tribe.

At present Martha's Vineyard's economy is largely driven by tourism. Tourism began in the mid-19th century at Oak Bluffs. In fact the tourism prevalent in Oak Bluffs and then in neighboring Vineyard Haven helped resurrect Edgartown years after the whaling boom of the mid-1800s had gone bust. Islanders seized this new industry by renovating the old

sea captains' houses, turning them into inns, bed-and-breakfasts, shops, and restaurants. In the process they also preserved magnificent architecture, and irreplaceable history. Today Edgartown is an upscale vacation town where you can stay and dine in buildings that speak volumes about a century when men went to sea to hunt whales.

GETTING HERE

From Woods Hole Martha's Vineyard appears to be just a good swim away—it seems that close! Well, not quite. It takes a bit more than a brisk breaststroke to get to the islands.

More than once we've heard a visitor to Cape Cod asking a native of the peninsula for directions to "the bridge to Martha's Vineyard," and more than once we've heard the story of how a wisecracking local directed them to it. There's no bridge, or tunnel for that matter. There are only two ways of getting to the island: by air and by sea.

By Sea

Journeying to the island by water, you get a feel for what Gosnold saw and felt upon that May day in 1602 when he first made his discovery. Yet, for a singular treat, make the journey after nightfall and watch as Nobska Light of Woods Hole, West Chop Lighthouse of Vineyard Haven, and East Chop Lighthouse of Oak Bluffs beam across the waves to one another like a triangle of lovers.

Once you've decided that you're going to travel to the island via water, you then have to decide how. Here are your options.

FERRIES

Falmouth Ferry Service
278 Scranton Avenue, Falmouth
(508) 548-9400
www.falmouthferry.com
This ferry service is unique in that it runs from Falmouth directly to Edgartown (most other ferry services dock at either Vineyard Haven or Oak Bluffs, from which you must take a shuttle or other transportation to Edgartown). Round-trip fares run $30 for those older than 12 and $24 for children 12 and younger; children 5 and younger sail for free. Bicycle rates are $8.00 each way. Falmouth Ferry Service runs daily from Memorial Day to Columbus Day. The trip takes exactly one hour. Parking costs $14 per calendar day. Reservations are required.

Hy-Line Cruises
Ocean Street, Hyannis
(508) 778-2600
www.hy-linecruises.com
Hy-Line is the only line that provides daily service from downtown Hyannis to Oak Bluffs from early May through late October. The crossing takes about one and three-quarters hours, and round-trip tickets cost $27 for those 13 and older and $13 for children ages 5 to 12. Children 4 and younger travel free with boarding pass. Your bicycle travels for $5.00 each way. From June to mid-September the line also offers the only daily interisland service between Martha's Vineyard (Oak Bluffs) and Nantucket. This sojourn takes a little more than two hours; the round-trip fare is $27; $13.50 for children ages 5 to 12. Ages 4 and younger ride free.

Island Queen
Falmouth Heights Road, Falmouth
(508) 548-4800
www.islandqueen.com

[Facing page] *The tightly-knit Methodist Campground community of Oak Bluffs is composed of hundreds of colorfully painted cottages.* MASSACHUSETTS OFFICE OF TRAVEL AND TOURISM

The *Island Queen* departs from Falmouth Inner Harbor daily from Memorial Day through Columbus Day and arrives at Oak Bluffs Harbor 35 minutes later. Round-trip fares are $10.00 for adults, $5.00 for children younger than 13, and no charge for children younger than 3. You can bring a bicycle for $6.00 round-trip. A great thing about the *Island Queen* is that its parking lot is only a few yards from the harbor, making it very convenient, especially if you are running late. Parking costs $10 per calendar day in the main lot and $15 per calendar day in the lot adjacent to the dock.

Thousands upon thousands of people visit the Vineyard every summer. Most of the summer population visits between July 4 weekend and Labor Day weekend. You can usually find accommodations—it's the car you have to worry about. You'll need to reserve a space for your car on the Steamship Authority ferry months in advance or rent one on the island.

The Steamship Authority
Railroad Avenue, Woods Hole
(508) 548-3488, (800) 352-7144
(Massachusetts only)
Vehicle reservations: (508) 477-8600,
(508) 477-7447 (same day)
www.islandferry.com
The lifeline to the Vineyard, the Steamship Authority has been making the run between Woods Hole and Martha's Vineyard for more than three decades. The line's large ships provide daily, year-round service to the ports of Oak Bluffs and Vineyard Haven. The trip across takes about 45 minutes. Passenger tickets can be purchased at all Steamship Authority terminals, the Plymouth and Brockton Bus Lines terminals, and Bonanza Bus Line terminals. Passengers never need a reservation, but we recommend arriving one hour ahead of sailing time, as the Steamship

Authority sometimes has cutoff times on busy weekends and holidays. The ride for passengers (no cars) costs $11 round-trip for adults and half that for children. Children younger than 5 travel for free. It costs $6.00 to transport a bicycle round-trip.

The Steamship Authority is the only ferry service that can transport your car to the island, but make your reservations as early as possible by calling the numbers above. Space fills up quickly, especially in summer. The price for a round-trip car reservation depends on the time of year. From May through October it's $110, dropping to $68 in the dead of winter.

If you decide to leave your car behind, which is actually a pretty good idea as the island has an outstanding shuttle service, the Steamship Authority has a number of parking lots available. Beware that those near the docks fill quickly. The authority is good about posting notices on the major routes into Falmouth as to what lots are open. Believe the signs, and allow for a little extra time to unload your gear and load up on a shuttle bus to the docks. Daily parking fees depend on the lot in which you park. Expect to pay $10.

PRIVATE BOATS

For those of you who captain your own vessel, the island offers four harbors where you can dock. Menemsha offers slips with electricity; the harbormaster (508-645-2846) can provide more details. Edgartown Harbor has moorings available by the day, week, or season. None have plug-in facilities. One pump-out station and one pump-out boat are available. You can reach the Edgartown harbormaster at (508) 627-4746.

Vineyard Haven offers moorings, launch service, and dockage. The harbormaster's number is (508) 696-4249. Oak Bluffs has plug-in slips for sail and motorboats; a small number of moorings are available in the harbor. The Oak Bluffs harbormaster's number is (508) 693-4355. As you can imagine there is a high demand for slips in season. Be sure to plan ahead.

By Air

If you cross by sea you'll notice the seagulls of Woods Hole following along in hopes of grabbing a morsel of food from the passengers. Large, powerful engines move the ferry forward, yet the gulls seem to coast along at the same speed with very little effort, their God-given aerodynamics accomplishing with ease what it takes man's mighty machines to do.

The gull's graceful aerial passage reminds us that we too can fly to the island and causes us to consider what wondrous sights can be seen along the way. Several airlines service the island and can provide those incredible sights.

The island has two airports: Martha's Vineyard Airport (508-693-7022) near the center of the island, and the smaller Katama Airfield in Edgartown (508-627-9018) offering runways of grass (how quaint!). Katama is one of the original Curtiss-Wright fields from back in the early airmail days and is one of the largest turf fields of its type remaining in the Northeast. The following airlines serve the Martha's Vineyard Airport.

Cape Air
(800) 352-0714
www.flycapeair.com
Cape Air makes regularly daily flights between the Vineyard and Hyannis, Boston, Nantucket, Providence, and New Bedford. In fact their summer schedule offers more than a dozen flights a day from Boston to the Vineyard. The airline has an interline baggage agreement for joint ticketing and interline baggage handling for connecting flights with more airlines. Cape Air also has joint fares for discounted travel with America West, Continental, Delta, and USAirways Express.

Ocean Wings Air Charter
(800) 253-5039
www.capecodweb.com/wings
For those folks who don't look forward to spending several hours in a car followed or preceded by a ferry ride, you may want to look into Ocean Wings Air Charter. Ocean Wings is an air taxi from areas in Connecticut, New York, and Washington, D.C., to Martha's Vineyard and Nantucket. It's a great mode of transportation for a family—they accommodate up to seven passengers per flight. Price varies depending on location. You might pay a little more than you would for a scheduled flight into Boston or Hyannis, but the convenience it well worth it.

Pan Am Clipper Connections
(800) FLY-PANAM
www.flypanam.com
Pan Am offers flights during the summer months to Martha's Vineyard from Baltimore, Maryland; Manchester and Portsmouth, New Hampshire; White Plains, New York; and Groton, Connecticut.

US Airways Express
(800) 428-4322
www.usairways.com
If you are from the Boston Area, you can take the direct route to the island onboard USAirways.

Getting Around by Car (or Bike or Moped)

Arriving at the island without your car? No problem. The island is prepared for your arrival in a big way. There are cars, mopeds, scooters, and bicycles for rent. Buses run every 15 minutes during peak season. For less than $5.00 the buses will shuttle you to the three towns of Vineyard Haven, Oak Bluffs, and Edgartown and back again! Sightseeing tours and taxis are available as well.

Depending on your visit, you may not even need any of the above. For instance if you arrive at Oak Bluffs or Vineyard Haven via ferry for a day trip and don't plan to leave the town at all, your legs alone can get you to nearly all the hot spots. Or a shuttle can take you to an adjoining town for a couple of bucks and your legs can take care of the rest.

This is probably as good a point as any to give you an idea of the distance between the island towns. Vineyard Haven and Oak Bluffs are side by side, straddling the Harbor of Vineyard Haven; it's a 10-minute car ride (if that) from the ferry dock of one, around the harbor, to the ferry dock of the other. Southeast of Oak Bluffs is Edgartown, a good 15-minute car ride along Beach Road. Southwest of Vineyard Haven, lies West Tisbury, maybe 10 minutes from Vineyard Haven and about 20 minutes from Edgartown via the Edgartown-West Tisbury Road. From that point in West Tisbury to Beetlebung Corner in Chilmark is about 4 or 5 miles, about 10 minutes of driving. Another 6 miles (10 minutes, perhaps 12) along State Road brings you to Aquinnah. Then to get from Aquinnah back up north to Vineyard Haven, allow perhaps 35 to 40 minutes for the 18-mile trip. There, you just traveled the island of Martha's Vineyard in one paragraph's time!

The basic rule of thumb in driving between towns is fairly easy. Once you get in town, traffic slows down considerably, especially when ferries are arriving or departing. The towns of Edgartown, Oak Bluffs, and Vineyard Haven are far more active than West Tisbury, Chilmark, and Aquinnah.

RENTALS

Auto rentals during peak season are offered at, of course, peak prices. Call around—and in advance—for the best prices. Larger cars, of course, are more expensive. Jeeps and off-road vehicles cost even more. In Vineyard Haven is Thrifty Rent-a-Car (508-693-8143). Budget Rent A Car (508-693-1911) is located near the harbors at Vineyard Haven and Oak Bluffs in Edgartown and at the main terminal at Martha's Vineyard Airport. AAA Island Auto Rentals is in Edgartown (508-627-6800 or 800-627-6333).

For about $30 to $80 you can rent a moped for the day. Daily bicycle rates run from about $15 to $30 for a three-speed and $20 to $25 for a mountain bike. As you come off the boat at either Vineyard Haven or Oak Bluffs, these rental outfits are everywhere. In fact we challenge you to swing a striped bass without hitting a bike rental shop.

By Shuttle Bus

The island's bus service is superb. The drivers, who each probably answer the same dozen questions a couple hundred times a day, do so in such a courteous way that you'd think you were the first person ever to ask, "Does this bus go to Edgartown?"

**Martha's Vineyard Regional Transit Authority
(508) 627-7448, (508) 693-9440
www.vineyardtransit.com**
The VTA offers 13 scheduled routes around the island. A one-day pass costs $6.00; a three-day pass is $11.00.

In Edgartown nothing can beat the Edgartown Shuttle, which you can ride for the cost of the change you might find buried under your sofa at home. From May

Oak Bluffs and Tisbury are the only towns on Martha's Vineyard that currently offer moped rentals. If you opt to rent one, be careful on the Vineyard's narrow, winding—and during summers, quite crowded—roads. Mopeds are not allowed on bike paths or sidewalks and must follow the same traffic rules as automobiles.

to September the shuttle runs throughout the historic streets of Edgartown. Edgartown also has an open-air trolley that carries passengers from the center of town to the very popular South Beach every 30 minutes, June to September.

ACCOMMODATIONS

From the moment you step off the ferry, you will feel welcome at Martha's Vineyard. The excitement that only an island can offer greets you, whether you are here for a day trip, a night, or an extended vacation.

If you are here for an overnight stay or for several nights you'll need to know your different options in the way of accommodations. By the way, if you happen to be glancing at this section on the boat ride over to the island, we hope you've already made reservations. Even in September and October it is common to see the NO VACANCY signs posted.

If your choice is to stay at an inn or bed-and-breakfast, you'll be happy to learn that there are many sprinkled throughout the island. Some are quaint places; others are majestic showplaces. All are beautiful in their own distinct way. Many of them are old sea captains' houses, or in the case of Edgartown, the former abodes of whaling captains. The history in these houses is omnipresent; it lulls you to sleep each tranquil evening amid dreams centuries old and gently awakens you again each morning with sunlight anew.

For those not in with the inn crowd, there are a number of fine hotels, some with spectacular views. More frugal travelers might opt for the hostel with rates starting around $15 a night. Also there is a campground starting at around $38 per night for those who seek oneness with nature.

The peak season generally runs from late May (Memorial Day) to late September—in some cases until Columbus Day in mid-October. During this peak season hotels, inns, bed-and-breakfasts, and guesthouses charge peak prices. During the off-season room rates are lowered, in some cases substantially. It is not uncommon to see rates cut in half after Columbus Day, and with the crowds gone, you feel like you own the island!

Unless otherwise noted, all accommodations are nonsmoking and welcome well-behaved children with prior approval. We'll let you know which places accept pets. Most accept major credit cards; we'll let you know those that don't.

Reservation Services

Martha's Vineyard and Nantucket Reservations
Box 1322, Vineyard Haven
(508) 693-7200, (800) 649-5671
(Massachusetts only)
www.mvreservations.com
For more than 15 years this company, the islands' oldest reservation service, has been booking rooms in inns, hotels, cottages, bed-and-breakfast, and guesthouses. The service does not handle vacation rentals, but if you are looking for a room on the island, this is the number to call. About 95 percent of the islands' inns and hotels work with this service. Although the sooner you book the better, especially for a room in season, the inns and hotels on the island regularly notify the service of cancellations, making this one of the first numbers to call if you are throwing together plans at the last minute. You pay no fee for the service.

PRICE CODE

Our price code is based on the average cost of a night's stay in a double-occupancy room during peak season, minus tax and special charges. (State and local taxes add up to about 10 percent of the bill.) Because this is an average, rooms may be had in some places for more or less than what's reflected in our code.

$	Less than $75
$$	$75 to $110
$$$	$111 to $175
$$$$	$176 and more

Bed-and-Breakfasts and Country Inns

VINEYARD HAVEN

The Hanover House $$$$
28 Edgartown Road
(508) 693-1066, (800) 339-1066
www.hanoverhouse.com

Behind a row of large hedges hides the Hanover House, a cozy, quiet bed-and-breakfast inn located just steps from the harbor. This village inn offers 16 impeccably maintained rooms, each with private bath, two double beds or a queen-size bed, air-conditioning, and cable TV. Many of the rooms feature entrances that open onto one of two spacious sundecks. In a separate carriage house are three suites, two of which have kitchenettes. Each suite has a private deck or patio. Complimentary breakfast includes homemade breads and muffins and fresh-ground gourmet coffee. Hanover House is open year-round.

Mansion House $$$$
9 Main Street
(508) 693-2200, (800) 332-4112
www.mvmansionhouse.com

Located at the foot of historic Main Street and just a few blocks from the ferry, the Mansion House rose from the ashes of the Tisbury Inn, destroyed by fire in late 2001. Construction finished on the new building during the summer of 2003. Its 32 rooms feature air-conditioning, cable television, telephone, high-speed Internet connections, and refrigerators. Deluxe rooms and suites offer soaking tubs, flat-screen plasma TVs, fireplaces, and balconies with views of Vineyard Sound. Rooms can be converted into suites complete with kitchen to accommodate larger groups. Guests of the Mansion House enjoy a complimentary breakfast at the on-site restaurant, Zephrus. For everyone else it's open daily for lunch and dinner (remember to BYOB). The Mansion House also has the Vineyard's only 75-foot indoor pool, as well as its largest health club.

Thorncroft Inn $$$$
460 Main Street
(508) 693-3333
www.thorncroftinn.com

The Thorncroft is one of the island's premier inns offering 15 guest rooms in two antique-appointed houses on three and a half acres of beautiful land. Each room features a private bath and central air-conditioning. Many have canopied four-poster beds, and 10 have wood-burning fireplaces. Three rooms offer two-person Jacuzzis, and two have 300-gallon hot tubs.

A full country breakfast and afternoon tea and pastries are served daily in the dining rooms. This has been cited as one of the ten best wheelchair-accessible inns in the country, as its private cottage was built keeping in mind the needs of the disabled. The entire inn and grounds are smoke-free. Special services include a fire-ready fireplace upon your arrival, a *New York Times* at your door in the morning, and turndown service. Thorncroft Inn is open year-round.

OAK BLUFFS

Beach House Bed and Breakfast $$$
Corner of Pennacook and Seaview Avenues
(508) 693-3955
www.beachhousemv.com

You couldn't ask for a better location: right across the street from the town beach on Vineyard Sound and within easy walking distance of all the sites in Oak Bluffs, including the community of gaily colored gingerbread cottages. It is also within a 5- to 10-minute walk of the ferry dock. This wonderful bed-and-breakfast, owned by Calvin and Pamela Zaiko, was converted to a year-round inn back in 1975 and has been owned by the Zaiko family since the 1940s. All nine rooms at the Beach House have private bathrooms. A complimentary continental breakfast buffet is served in the dining hall and on the front porch with magnificent views of the ocean. Children 10 and older are welcome at the Beach House.

Dockside Inn $$$
Circuit Avenue Extension
(508) 693-2966, (800) 245-5979
The outside of this gaily colored inn is surely a feast for the eyes. A simply beautiful building to look at, it is painted a combination of cream, pink, and soft pastel blue, as are the chairs that line its front porch. With its second-floor wrap-around balcony and its proximity to the harbor, the place has a riverboat feel to it. It's hard to believe that this beauty, with architecture pointing to the mid- to late-19th century, was actually built in 1989. All 22 of the Dockside Inn's rooms have air-conditioning, private baths, and cable TV; most rooms have queen-size beds. Five full kitchen suites are also available. The Dockside, convenient to all that Oak Bluffs has to offer, is open from April to November.

The Oak House $$$-$$$$
Seaview Avenue at Pequot Avenue
(508) 693-4187
The Oak House truly lives up to its name. Throughout most of the guest and common rooms, oak is the rule. It's everywhere: rich, warm, and inviting. This 1840s governor's mansion, overlooking Nantucket Sound, has 10 rooms (2 of which are suites), nearly all resembling oak-paneled ship cabins. All but three of the rooms offer water views; all have private baths. Some rooms have private balconies and some air-conditioning. You can relax on the sunporch or in a rocker on the wrap-around veranda while you watch the waves chase each other toward shore. Or you can settle down with a book in the elegant oak parlor. Innkeeper Betsi C. Luce, a professional pastry chef, serves a homemade continental breakfast and Victorian afternoon

tea. Children older than the age of 10 are welcome. The Oak House is open from May through October.

The Ship's Inn $$-$$$
14 Kennebec Avenue
(508) 693-2760, (800) 564-2760
(Eastern Massachusetts only)
www.shipsinn.com
The Ship's Inn is just a short five-minute walk from the island ferry and an even shorter two-minute stroll to Oak Bluffs Town Beach. All of Oak Bluffs, from her fanciful gingerbread cottages to her Flying Horses Carousel, is just around the corner. Each of the inn's 15 rooms is brightly decorated and include a private bath, air-conditioning in some rooms, and color TV. Several of the rooms also feature private entrances. The outdoor patio is a great place to socialize after a day of touring the island. The inn is open from March to the end of November.

EDGARTOWN

Ashley Inn $$$$
129 Main Street
(508) 627-9655
www.ashleyinn.net
This 19th-century sea captain's home features a spacious lawn with rose gardens and apple trees. Converted to an inn during the spring of 1983, it is convenient to the many shops of Edgartown. You can stroll the historic streets of the old whaling port, or simply kick up your feet and relax in a hammock out in the lawn. Each of the inn's 10 bedrooms are beautifully decorated with period antiques and has a private bath, cable TV, phones, and air-conditioning. Innkeepers Fred and Janet Hurley invite you to enjoy a continental breakfast in the English tea room. Children 10 and older are welcome at this year-round inn; younger children are welcome in the suites.

The Charlotte Inn $$$$
27 South Summer Street
(508) 627-4751
Like many of Edgartown's inns, the Charlotte Inn began life as a sea captain's

home. Built in 1860, it is today one of the premier inns in Edgartown and on the island. Brick courtyards and flower beds accent the grounds. Inside English antiques, fine furnishings, and high ceilings convince you that you're in a very special place.

Each of the inn's 25 rooms is different and was individually decorated by innkeepers Gerret and Paula Conover, who pride themselves on their meticulous attention to detail. Located within the Charlotte Inn is L'Etoile Restaurant, featuring French cuisine (see the Restaurants section of this chapter). The Charlotte Inn welcomes children older than 14. It is open throughout the year.

The Edgartown Inn $$-$$$
56 North Water Street
(508) 627-4794
www.edgartowninn.com
You don't have to be a lover of history to stay at the Edgartown Inn, but it helps. Built in 1798 by Capt. Thomas Worth (Ft. Worth, Texas, is named for his son, William, a hero of the Mexican War), this colonial inn has had many distinguished guests over the past two centuries. Daniel Webster, Nathaniel Hawthorne, abolitionist Senator Charles Sumner, and John F. Kennedy (while a senator from Massachusetts) have all stayed here. In fact Hawthorne was writing his *Twice Told Tales* while a guest at the inn.

The inn is small, with 12 rooms in the main inn all with private baths; some have balconies offering harbor views. The Garden House has two spacious rooms with king-size beds, private baths, and balconies overlooking the gardens below; a smaller room shares a bath. Two of the barn's five rooms have private baths; three share a bath and shower. The inn is open April through October. No credit cards.

The Hob Knob Inn $$$$
128 Main Street
(508) 627-9510, (800) 696-2723
www.hobknob.com

The Hob Knob Inn features great accommodations just on the outside of the hustle and bustle of Edgartown's center. In other words you're convenient to everything, but not in the middle of everything. Begin your day with a full farm breakfast of freshly baked muffins, scones, breads, juice and coffee in the sunlit tearoom. In the afternoon enjoy a cup of tea and sample some tasty treats or else relax in the parlor or on the porch sipping complimentary sherry. The Hob Know Inn's 16 rooms feature private baths, ceiling fans, and king-size brass or four-poster beds. This wonderful Victorian is elegant yet comfy all at the same time. Its convenient location along historic Main Street makes for a short stroll to the shops along Edgartown's waterfront. The inn welcomes children age 7 and older and is open year-round.

Point Way Inn $$$$
104 Main Street
(508) 627-8633, (888) 711-6633
www.pointwayinn.com
Beautiful high hedges, flower gardens, a vine-covered gazebo, and a manicured lawn welcome you to this very special inn. Each of the inn's 12 rooms are luxurious yet comfortable. Most have double or queen-size beds, private baths, and ceiling fans, and many have four-poster beds and fireplaces. All rooms are air-conditioned. A full breakfast is served daily, and you may choose your breakfast site according to your preference (and the weather)—in the breakfast room, in the sculpture garden, or in the comfort of your own room. Afternoon refreshments are served on the stately grounds. Children are welcome. The inn is open 12 months of the year.

Shiverick Inn $$$$
5 Peases Point Way
(508) 627-3797, (800) 723-4292
www.shiverickinn.com
This lovely inn was built in 1840 for the town physician Dr. Clement Francis Shiverick. It offers 11 guest rooms, many with fireplaces, two of which are suites. Through

painstaking attention to detail, the inn has preserved the graceful formalities of this distinctive period, blending American and English 18th- and 19th-century antiques with rich fabrics, fine wallpapers, Oriental rugs, and vivid colors borrowed from the New England landscape.

Enjoy a breakfast of breads, cakes, and freshly baked muffins in the garden room. Afterward stroll the grounds or lounge on the terrace. The Shiverick Inn, which is open year-round, welcomes children age 12 and older.

Tuscany Inn $$$$
22 North Water Street
(508) 627-5999
www.tuscanyinn.com
Innkeeper Laura Sbrana, a native of Tuscany, has succeeded in bringing a taste of Italy to Victorian Edgartown. She has combined her skills in art, interior design, and culinary arts, and transformed the Captain Fisher House into one of Edgartown's most unique lodging and dining experiences. Located in the very heart of the old whaling port, the inn's eight air-conditioned guest rooms are open year-round. (During the off-season Laura offers cooking classes at the inn.)

In the morning you will awaken to the aroma of one of Laura's Italian breakfasts. In the afternoon sample Laura's homemade biscotti while you sip a warm cappuccino in this unique blending of Italian and Victorian settings. The Tuscany Inn welcomes children older than 7.

The Victorian Inn $$$$
24 South Water Street
(508) 627-4784
www.thevic.com
Directly across the street from the famous Edgartown Pagoda Tree is the Victorian Inn, built ca. 1820 and listed in the National Register of Historic Places. Innkeepers Stephen and Karyn Caliri have carefully restored this whaling captain's home to its original elegance, and they cordially invite you to be their guest. All 14 guest rooms have private baths and are decorated with antiques and flowers. A number of rooms have four-poster beds, and some have balconies. Some rooms overlook the historic harbor, whereas others overlook the English garden below, where a complimentary gourmet breakfast is served from 8:00 to 10:00 A.M. An informal tea is also served in the afternoon. Children 8 and older are welcome at the inn, and from November to April pets are allowed. The Victorian Inn is open year-round.

UP ISLAND

Duck Inn $$-$$$
State Road, Aquinnah
(508) 645-9018
At nearly land's end lies the Duck Inn, with incredible views of the Aquinnah Cliffs and Lighthouse. To get to this cozy five-room, 200-year-old farmhouse, you must take a dirt road. The decor varies from Southwest to Japanese. The Southwest room has pink stucco walls, and the Japanese room is filled with silks. Only one room has a private bath, as well as a fireplace; all others share bathrooms. There's a hot tub and a licensed masseuse available for facials and bodywork. Oh, and we almost forgot to tell you: Miles and miles of the most secluded beaches lie outside the door. Duck Inn is open all year long, and children are welcome. Pets are welcome during the summer.

Lambert's Cove Country Inn $$$
Lambert's Cove Road, West Tisbury
(508) 693-2298, (866) 526-2466
www.lambertscoveinn.com
If you really want to get away from it all, this is the spot. Once a horticulturist's estate, Lambert's Cove is the kind of country inn you dream about. Off Lambert's Cove Road you take an unpaved path through wooded wilderness to this place hidden amid towering pines, 150-year-old vine-covered stone walls, gardens, and an old-fashioned apple orchard. The inn comprises sixteen rooms, with eight in the original 1790 main building

and the remainder in the restored carriage house and converted barn. Perhaps the most unique room is the Greenhouse Room, which features a greenhouse sitting room complete with white wicker furniture. All rooms have private baths, air-conditioning, and some have private sun decks. A gazebo rests in the yard beyond the inn, and a tennis court awaits you just past that. They provide a full breakfast. The inn is also home to one of the island's finest dining rooms (see the subsequent Restaurants section of this chapter). Though Lambert's Cove is in a country setting away from the shoreline, guests are entitled to passes to the two private West Tisbury beaches.

Menemsha Inn and Cottages $$$
North Road, Menemsha
(508) 645-2521
www.menemshainn.com
This complex of 17 shingled buildings is set in the pretty fishing village of Menemsha. The Carriage House features six suites. The Inn has nine rooms, six with a view of the water and all with private bath and deck. If you are more in the mood for the independence of a housekeeping cottage, try one of the 11 cottages spread out on more than 14 acres of land. They have kitchens, fireplaces, Internet access, and outdoor showers. The Menemsha Inn and Cottages is open year-round.

Hotels

OAK BLUFFS

Island Inn $$$-$$$$
Beach Road
(508) 693-2002, (800) 462-0269
www.islandinn.com
Along the road that connects Oak Bluffs and Edgartown lies the Island Inn. Overlooking the Farm Neck Golf Club, the Island Inn is a short walk to two of Oak Bluffs' best beaches, Oak Bluffs Town Beach and Joseph Sylvia State Beach. The inn offers an assortment of 51 rooms,

suites, and even a cottage—all sporting fully furnished kitchens, private baths, and cable TV. If you're into tennis, you'll be happy to learn that there are three Har-Tru tennis courts on-site. A full-time tennis pro is available to give you lessons. Families can take advantage of the 7 acres of grounds, including a barbecue area, an outdoor pool, and a playground for the kiddies. The Island Inn is open from late March to late November and has one wheelchair-accessible unit.

Wesley Hotel $$$
70 Lake Avenue
(508) 693-6611, (800) 638-9027
www.wesleyhotel.vineyard.net
The Wesley Hotel, built in 1879, is the last of the grand hotels of Oak Bluffs—and what a grande dame she is. Open from May to October, she seems to watch over the town from her knoll facing the harbor, where you can relax and enjoy the views from one of the rocking chairs on the spacious front porch.

Renovations over the years have restored the Wesley to her former greatness. You will feel yourself being transported back in time as you climb the steps to the veranda, enter the dark oak lobby, and walk up to the old-fashioned registration desk. The main building contains 62 rooms, many with outstanding views of the harbor. These rooms include private baths. Twenty more rooms with shared baths are in the Wesley Arms Building behind the main building. There are wheelchair-accessible rooms located on the first floor of the main building.

EDGARTOWN

Clarion Martha's Vineyard—Edgartown Heritage Hotel $$$
227 Upper Main Street
(508) 627-5161, (800) 922-3009
www.clarionmv.com
Those looking for a modern hotel just a 10- to 15-minute walk from Edgartown's historic waterfront will want to look into the Edgartown Heritage Hotel, built in

1985 as part of the Clarion chain. Each of the hotel's 34 rooms offer queen- or king-size beds, a private bath, cable TV, a radio, air-conditioning, and a telephone. A complimentary continental breakfast is provided. The Heritage can accommodate groups of up to 50 people for business meetings, social functions and private parties. This year-round hotel has two wheelchair-accessible rooms available. Children younger than 18 stay free with an adult.

Edgartown Lodge $$-$$$
67 Winter Street (corner of Church and Winter Streets)
(508) 627-9444
www.edgartownlodge.com
Like to get away but not feel isolated? Try the Edgartown Lodge and one of its six two-room suites. Each suite is set up like its own apartment with a bedroom and a living room and a separate entrance. Each suite sleeps four or five comfortably, and you're just a block off Main Street and a few blocks away from the beaches.

The Harborside Inn $$$-$$$$
3 South Water Street
(508) 627-4321, (800) 627-4009
www.theharborsideinn.com
A complete waterfront resort located right at Edgartown's historic harbor, the Harborside Inn offers seven buildings (some are former 19th-century whaling captains' homes) housing 89 rooms. About half of these rooms have exceptional views of the harbor, and some have huge private balconies. A large heated outdoor pool is just steps from the waters of the harbor. You can relax in the whirlpool or in the sauna after a busy day of shopping, swimming, or bike riding. Rooms include color TV, a refrigerator, a private bath, and air-conditioning. The resort is open April through early November and provides full service banquet facilities. If you have children, you'll be happy to learn that children younger than 12 stay at the Harborside Inn free with an adult.

The Harbor View Hotel $$$$
131 North Water Street
(508) 627-7000, (800) 225-6005
www.harbor-view.com
The windows command incredible views of Edgartown Lighthouse, Edgartown Harbor, and Chappaquiddick Island beyond. Dating to 1891 as two separate buildings, today the Harbor View Hotel is one large gem of a grand hotel, accented by a magnificent 300-foot veranda. A multimillion-dollar renovation a few years ago restored all her 124 rooms and suites to their former Victorian splendor

Guests are pampered by the accommodating staff. Concierge, room service, and the daily newspaper are just some of the extras that set this hotel apart. Seven townhouses on-site feature cathedral ceilings, kitchens, and outside decks. The 12-acre complex includes a swimming pool, a private beach, and all-weather tennis courts. The Coach House and Carlos Fuente Club House restaurants are on-site.

Kelley House $$$$
23 Kelley Street
(508) 627-7900, (800) 225-6005
www.kelley-house.com
Over the past two-and-a-half centuries, since 1742 to be exact, the Kelley House has been open for travelers and vacationers alike. It was formerly a tavern where whalers and sea captains raised their pints, and today all of the inn's 53 rooms maintain the colonial charm that guests a century ago would have enjoyed. Of course today's guests also enjoy modern-day amenities.

Period antiques, quilts, and an overall early-American personality will make you think you're staying back in 19th-century Edgartown. Some rooms have kitchens and private balconies. A complimentary breakfast awaits you, as does afternoon tea. Bedtime arrives with homemade cookies and milk. A refreshing outdoor pool offers views of Edgartown Harbor. After a swim you can wander into the

Newes from America, an American pub at the Kelley House that offers causal fare (see the Restaurants section in this chapter). Kelley House is open from May through October.

Hostel

Hostelling International—Martha's Vineyard $
Edgartown-West Tisbury Road, West Tisbury
(508) 693-2665
If you weren't paying just $15 to $19 a night, you'd think you were staying at the quaintest of country inns. This cedar-shake saltbox, which celebrated its 45th year as a hostel in 2000, sits at the edge of the Manuel E. Correllus Forest. The hostel has a fireplace in the common room, a volleyball court, a sheltered bike rack out back, and a spacious kitchen that awaits budding gourmets. Five dorms house 78 bunk beds; check-in is between 5:00 and 10:00 P.M. daily. The hostel fills up quickly; we suggest you make reservations (especially during the season) at least two weeks in advance. The hostel is open from April through November.

Condominiums

VINEYARD HAVEN

Harbor Landing Condo Trust $$
15 Beach Road
(508) 693-2600, (800) 545-4272
www.harbor-landing.com
For families who want to spend an extended period of time on the island, Harbor Landing offers 39 very affordable condo units with a full, private bath, color TV, air-conditioning and heating, refrigerator, and a common kitchen for guests to share. The efficiency units have a fully equipped kitchen. A large sundeck on the third floor offers great views of the harbor, and a five-acre park borders the rear of

the building. Complimentary coffee is served each morning. If you're interested in visiting the island during the off-season, check out Harbor Landing's incredibly low $60 rates. High season rates range from $120 for a budget unit to $195 for a double suite. Harbor Landing is open year-round.

Campgrounds

Martha's Vineyard Family Campground $
Edgartown-Vineyard Haven Road, Vineyard Haven
(508) 693-3772
www.campmvfc.com
Families who enjoy camping will love the time they'll have at the Martha's Vineyard Family Campground, located just a mile or so away from Vineyard Haven center. Each campsite is allowed one motor vehicle and either one large tent or two small tents. Trailer sites are also available. Both types of sites include electric and water hookups; the trailer sites also include sewer. Rates are $38 per night for a campsite and $42 for a trailer site. These rates are for two adults and any children younger than 18. Additional adults are charged $10 per night. Also, there are one- and two-room cabins and even tent trailers available. The grounds include plenty to keep the family busy: table tennis, billiards, biking, baseball, a store, and a playground. Cable TV is available. There are some 180 sites; it's open mid-May through mid-October. No dogs and no motorcycles are allowed in the campground.

VACATION RENTALS AND REAL ESTATE

There are a number of real estate companies on the island; unfortunately, space does not permit listing them all. Besides selling properties many of these companies also handle vacation rentals. Below are a handful that do handle rentals. We encourage you to shop around, but don't wait too long to decide, as it's best to reserve a rental at least 10 months in advance. Otherwise there may be nothing left.

Vineyard Haven

Island Real Estate
107 Beach Road, Suite 203
508) 693-4800, (800) 287-4801
www.mvrealestate.com
Living up to its name, Island Real Estate offers rentals throughout the island. Island Real Estate offers more than 400 properties from which to choose. The six agents can show you every land, home, and condo listing on the island.

Martha's Vineyard Vacation Rentals
107 Beach Road
(800) 556-4225
www.mvvacationrentals.com
The agents at Martha's Vineyard Vacation Rentals personally inspect each of the 500 privately owned homes they offer for rent. Their varied inventory includes vacation homes and waterfront properties in every price range. They also offer linen and baby-equipment rental services.

Edgartown

Conover Real Estate
19 South Summer Street
(508) 627-3757
www.conovermv.com
Conover Real Estate only represents waterfront properties and in-town historical homes for rent. The properties they handle are worth the price.

Linda R. Bassett Real Estate Sales and Rentals
201 Upper Main Street,
(508) 627-9201, (800) 338-1855
P.O. Box 968, West Tisbury
(508) 693-9655
www.mvinfo.com

Located in Edgartown, this company handles both the sale of properties and vacation rentals throughout Martha's Vineyard. In the area of sales, it deals primarily in private year-round homes, cottages, condominiums, and estates with many of its properties being either waterfront or water view. On the rental side Linda R. Bassett offers more than 800 properties from around the Vineyard. With 20 real estate agents, Linda R. Bassett is one of the largest outfits on the island.

Heading "up-island" means traveling in a southwesterly direction toward Aquinnah. "Down-island" refers to the easterly towns of Tisbury, Oak Bluffs, and Edgartown. These terms are nautical in origin: Sailing west means crossing increasingly higher degrees of longitude, hence going "up," and sailing east means going "down" in longitude.

Martha's Management Real Estate Rentals
P.O. Box 2866
(508) 627-5005, (888) 481-9504
www.marthasmgmt.com
On a cozy island like Martha's Vineyard, you may want to try a smaller rental agency like Martha's Management Real Estate Rentals. Martha's covers about 150 properties around the island, and the owners and employees are very familiar with each property, many of which they also maintain. In most cases they will also escort you to your rental, which is a great service if you happen to be unfamiliar with the island.

Sandcastle Vacation Home Rentals
256 Edgartown-Vineyard Haven Road
(508) 627-5665
www.sandcastlemv.com
This agency deals in rentals only. They offer more than 500 homes all over the island that range from simple cottages to elegant estates. Prices range from $1,000 to $10,000 per week, to $100,000 per month.

Sandpiper Rentals
60 Winter Street
(508) 627–3757
www.sandpiperrealty.com
Whether you're in the market for a small seaside cottage or a sprawling 200-acre waterfront estate, Sandpiper Rentals can fulfill your order from their list of more than 600 rental properties.

RESTAURANTS

If you're hungry, you're in luck. Martha's Vineyard offers a variety of excellent restaurants to satisfy your every culinary desire.

As you might expect, the Vineyard offers the fare one would expect from an island—plenty of seafood. But the offering does not end there . . . no, no, no! Man and woman do not live by lobster alone, but it might be fun trying! Across the island there are a number of specialty restaurants preparing the finest in Italian, French, Indian, Chinese, and Mexican dishes. There are also plenty of casual dining establishments serving your basic chow. Yet even basic chow tastes so much better when you have an ocean view. Heck, even a cheeseburger takes on a whole new meaning when Vineyard Sound is staring back at you.

Half the fun of vacationing is trying out different eateries, and not just because someone else has to clean up the dishes. Below is a listing of some of the restaurants located throughout the towns, but we encourage you to be like Bartholomew Gosnold and explore. You'll be fascinated at the wonderful discoveries you'll make. For instance, there are a number of fine dining establishments in Edgartown but sometimes there is nothing better than wandering into a local pub and ordering the special off the chalkboard along with a pint of beer to wash it down. What these places lack in cloth napkins and unpronounceable entrees they make up for in honest, down-home Yankee cooking and atmosphere.

Something to keep in mind: Only restaurants in the towns of Edgartown and Oak Bluffs are allowed to serve liquor. The other island towns are termed "dry," but you can bring your own bottle.

PRICE CODE

The price code used here is intended as a guide in helping you decide where to dine. It is based on the average price of dinner entrees for two, excluding appetizers, alcoholic beverages, dessert, tax, and tip. Most restaurants accept major credit cards; we note the ones that do not.

$	Less than $20
$	$20 to $35
$$$	$36 to $50
$$$$	$51 and more

Vineyard Haven

The Black Dog Tavern $$$
33 Beach Street Extension
(508) 693–9223
www.theblackdog.com
After seeing all the T-shirts and hats, you have to be at least a little curious about the Black Dog Tavern. While the Black Dog's Labrador silhouette logo has ventured well beyond New England, the menu at this landmark is down-home seafood with plenty of dishes for landlubbers as well. Just yards from the waters of Vineyard Haven Harbor during low tide and just a few feet away when the tide is high, rusted iron chains and anchors, weathered wooden barrels, a TAVERN sign swaying in the salty breeze all provide a wharf atmosphere. As for the Black Dog itself, it's a rustic wooden building decorated with quarter boards and other nautical items and windows providing spectacular views of the harbor.

There are no reservations here and, considering its renown, arrive very early if you want to even have a shot at a window table. The Black Dog is also BYOB (Bring

Your Own Booze) if you want a drink with dinner. Also on the ground are the Black Dog General Store and the Black Dog Bakery (see the subsequent Shopping section of this chapter). The Black Dog Tavern is open year-round and serves breakfast, lunch, dinner, and Sunday brunch.

Le Grenier $$$$
96 Main Street
(508) 693-4906
www.legrenierrestaurant.com

If you're going to open a French restaurant on Martha's Vineyard, it helps to hail from France. Le Grenier chef/owner Jean Dupon is a native of Lyon who excels at keeping his menu steeped in such traditional French cuisine as shrimp Pernod, Dover sole almondine, herb-crusted swordfish with an aioli, and lobster Nomande flambé with Calvados apples. Le Grenier is open for dinner nightly year-round. Reservations are suggested.

Oak Bluffs

Giordano's Restaurant Clam Bar and Pizza $$
Lake Avenue and Circuit Avenue
(508) 693-0184
www.giosmv.com

On summer weekend evenings patrons line up to get into Giordano's. It is worth the wait, for inside will be found an Italian dinner like your grandma used to make—that is, if your grandma was Italian. People have been waiting in line to get in ever since the Giordano family opened the Italian restaurant in 1930. The food here is hearty and wholesome; expect heaping plates of cutlets and cacciatore, pizza, pasta, fried clams, and seafood. There is a noisy ambience about the place, but it's all part of the charm of this family dining experience. Children's meals are offered at substantially lower prices. Lunch and dinner are served daily from mid-May through mid-September. Reservations are not accepted. No credit cards.

Jimmy Seas Pan Pasta $$
32 Kennebec Avenue
(508) 696-8550

Expect to receive your food in large portions, and expect to receive it served right in the pan in which it was cooked. The restaurant has a comfortable atmosphere, and the staff is very friendly. Jimmy Seas is a favorite spot of President Clinton when the former First Family is on the island. The restaurant does not accept reservations (although, for some reason, we can't see the Clintons waiting in line for a table). Dinner is served nightly except Tuesday mid-April through mid-December. No credit cards.

Linda Jean's $
25 Circuit Avenue
(508) 693-0493

If breakfast is your bag, then you'll definitely want to check out Linda Jean's on Circuit Avenue. Fluffy pancakes made from scratch are as good a way as any to start the day on the island. A year-round family-owned restaurant, it is a favorite spot for locals and visitors alike. Linda Jean's also serves lunch and dinner—check out the seafood platter with a full plate of clams, scallops, shrimp, haddock, fries and cole slaw. Good stuff! Open year-round, it has been an Oak Bluffs fixture for more than 20 years. No credit cards.

Lola's Restaurant $-$$
Beach Road
(508) 693-5007
www.lolassouthernseafood.com

There's something to be said for the fact that when the locals and island regulars go out to eat, most of them hit Lola's. It has some of the best food on the island, not to mention a selection that will satisfy even the most picky eater. Open year-round, Lola's is a wonderful, family-style restaurant where the emphasis is on seafood prepared in Southern style, including some great New Orleans dishes in its pub and main dining room. The pub offers a more moderately priced menu and live entertainment four nights a week.

You can also catch an occasional gospel brunch on Sundays during the summer. Lola's is open for lunch and dinner.

Mad Martha's $
Circuit Avenue
(508) 693-9151
This is the place for ice cream on the island. As a matter of fact, some Cape Codders have been known to make the day trip just to taste the creamy delights here. With more than two dozen flavors from which to choose, there's something here for even the most picky tastes. Established in 1971, Mad Martha's can be found at several other locations throughout the island: Dockside Market Place in Oak Bluffs, Lake Avenue in Oak Bluffs, Union Street in Tisbury, and North Water Street in Edgartown. Besides serving ice cream, Mad Martha's also offers burgers and grinders (sandwiches made with hard rolls) from early June to Columbus Day.

Ocean View $$
Chapman Avenue
(508) 693-2207
As its name suggests, the Ocean View restaurant serves up peeks of the ocean, or rather, Oak Bluffs Harbor, from its front-facing windows. The Ocean View serves great tasting food at very reasonable prices. Its menu features everything from pizza to prime rib and lobster. Shrimp is a local favorite, and you'll definitely want to try the fillet of sole Français. The lounge has a large hearth with a fire crackling on cooler days with a popcorn maker built into the hearth. There are two dining rooms complete with a mural of the harbor and a large fish tank. The clientele is a mix of locals and visitors. Lunch and dinner are served daily year-round.

Offshore Ale $$
0 Kennebec Avenue
(508) 693-2626
www.offshoreale.com
Offshore Ale is a favorite Vineyard establishment as an upscale brewpub with good food. There is live entertainment

five nights a week during the summer months and three nights a week during the slower months. The menu features a mix of seafood and typical fare such as pizza and burgers. Offshore Ale is open year-round.

Season's Eatery and Pub $$
19 Circuit Avenue
(508) 693-7129
www.seasonseatery.com
Located halfway down the much-happening Circuit Avenue and right next to the rocking Atlantic Connection is Season's. The menu contains some 70 moderately priced items, such as scallop and shrimp plates for seafood eaters, and chicken or shrimp stir-fry for those who can't make up their minds. During the summer there is acoustic entertainment, or for something a bit louder, you can slip next door to the Atlantic Connection. Season's takes part in the local chili fest in January. Season's is open year-round for breakfast, lunch, dinner, and brunch.

Edgartown

Coach House $$$
131 North Water Street
(508) 627-7000
www.harbor-view.com/coach_house
At the sprawling Harbor View Hotel (see the previous Accommodations section of this chapter), the Coach House is open year-round for breakfast, lunch, and dinner. Situated at land's end, across from the picturesque Edgartown Lighthouse, it is the ideal location for a bite to eat after you've shopped in Edgartown. The atmosphere here is relaxed, and the lunch prices are rather relaxed as well. You'll find many tasty sandwiches and salads to stave off those hunger pangs so you can get right back out there hitting the shops. At dinner time, Coach House is known for having one of the largest selections of seafood entrees on the Vineyard with a nightly dinner menu that offers main dishes made with scallops, tuna, soft-shell crab, salmon, or lobster.

David Ryan's Restaurant Cafe   **$$$**
11 North Water Street
(508) 627-4100
www.davidryans.com
As you're hitting all the shops along North Water Street in Edgartown, you may want to hit the brakes and stop for a bite at David Ryan's. How about Menemsha swordfish, blackened or grilled with citrus herb butter? Or perhaps Vineyard crab cakes with Jonah crab serve with remoulade? Nothing like native seafood to give you a real feel for the island. David Ryan's also serves innovative pasta dishes, choice meats, and has a full liquor license. After dinner you can either continue shopping or mosey on down to the wharf and just take in the sights. David Ryan's is open every day serving lunch and dinner.

Espresso Love   **$**
17 Church Street
(508) 627-9211
After a night out on the ol' whaling town, you'll want to step into Edgartown's own Espresso Love for a cup of espresso, a cup of coffee, or a late-night dessert before returning to your inn. It also serves breakfast and lunch. Espresso Love is open 11 months of the year; it's closed during February. Espresso Love specializes in satisfying your sweet tooth. The scones alone are worth a visit. Don't let the crowds deter you—good things truly come to those who wait.

L'Etoile   **$$$$**
27 South Summer Street
(508) 627-5187
Located at the elegant Charlotte Inn, L'Etoile is an exquisite French restaurant featuring the culinary artistry of chef/owner Michael Brisson. Begin with an appetizer of bacon-and-leek mashed potatoes with cognac cream sauce or perhaps sautéed fresh duck foie gras on sugar-pea tendrils with seared plums and green ginger muscat and ginger sauce.

Your choice of entrees includes sauteed fresh Dover sole fillets with fried green tomatoes and saffron-poached potato batons, or perhaps roasted spice-rubbed Australian lamb with artichoke, goat cheese, sunflower seed, couscous melange. The incredible desserts are sure to break even the most determined diet. Dinner is served nightly from June through September; Wednesday through Sunday for the remainder of the year. L'Etoile is closed in January. Smoking is prohibited, and reservations are required.

Main Street Diner   **$**
65 Main Street
(508) 627-9337
This is your classic—right out of a Norman Rockwell print—diner. It's a bit hard to find, but the journey is well worth it. You approach from Main Street by following a long, well-lit, flower-wallpapered walkway. Just keep going—the diner is down there, believe us! Along the way you'll pass American memorabilia. On the wall at the end is an American flag with 36 states. Turn left, and then take a quick right, and there you are. Open the door, and you enter a museum of early 20th-century stuff. What a place! The food is the good old-fashioned American variety, and the smells are delicious. The entrees are about $7.00. As you look at some of the pictures on the walls, you'll be amazed at who else has found this spot: Kevin Costner, Patricia Neal, Bill Pullman, even a Kennedy or two. Main Street Diner serves breakfast, lunch, and dinner year-round.

The Navigator   **$$$**
2 Main Street
(508) 627-4320
If your idea of island dining is fresh lobster while enjoying the views of Edgartown Harbor, this is the place for you. Besides offering plenty of seating inside, the Navigator also offers outside tables complete with umbrellas and, of course, the harbor waters just yards away. This is a perfect place to enjoy a late-afternoon cocktail and a spectacular view. Open for lunch and dinner from mid-May through Columbus Day, it is located at the very foot of

Main Street. The Navigator is a nonsmoking establishment.

Newes from America $-$$
23 Kelley Street
(508) 627-4397
www.kelley-house.com/newes_from_
america

You almost expect to see Captain Ahab limp through the door into this classic whaling port pub. Brick walls and rustic wood planking on the walls and ceiling provide its character. Housed in an 18th-century building, the Newes is a famous gathering place for visitors and locals in search of good food at a good price. The beers served here have become legendary. If you can't make up your mind which beer to have, why not order the Rack of Beers, which allows you to sample five different brews. Regulars who consume in the neighborhood of 1,000 short drafts, or 500 talls, receive their own personal bar stool for a full year! (Now there's something to put on your resume!)

The food served here is good old American pub chow—hamburgers, grilled sandwiches, and hot soups to burn away the thickest fog. (We had the veggie piago sandwich.) It's the kind of food that tastes great with a pint of beer and a salty sea tale. The Newes is open for lunch and dinner year-round and is beside the Kelley House (see the previous Accommodations section of this chapter).

For more than 50 years, Humphrey's on State Road in North Tisbury has been the place for your morning coffee and breakfast. Nothing's fancy here, but everything is good. They're known for their belly bombs—huge, perfect jelly-filled doughnuts. Enjoy your apple or cherry turnovers, huge cinnamon rolls, lemon cookies, bagels, and pies at the picnic tables outside. They also offer sandwiches and quiche for lunch.

Up Island

The Aquinnah $$
Cliffs of Aquinnah, Aquinnah
(508) 645-3142

The views from the restaurant's open porch are incredible, courtesy of the Cliffs of Aquinnah and the ancient glaciers that created them. An Aquinnah landmark since 1949, the Aquinnah features plenty of great seafood and plenty of crowds. Patrons are offered both inside and outside seating with take-out windows catering to those sitting outdoors to enjoy the awesome views. You can also buy clams and scallops by the pint and quart. The Aquinnah serves breakfast, lunch, and dinner while it's open from May to October.

Home Port Restaurant $$-$$$
512 North Road, Menemsha
(508) 645-2679

Since 1931 the Home Port Restaurant has been offering spectacular views along with great seafood. It is at the Menemsha fishing port with its weathered shanties lining the harbor, the very fishing port used as Quint's homeport in the movie *Jaws*. In fact as you dine on lobster here, you can look out across the water and see the remains of Quint's boat *ORCA* on the opposite shore. The Home Port is open for dinner starting at 5:00 P.M. from mid-April to mid-October.

Lambert's Cove Country Inn $$$$
Lambert's Cove Road, West Tisbury
(508) 693-2298, (866) 526-2466
www.lambertscoveinn.com

Housed in a 1790 building, this restaurant offers a romantic country setting featuring beautiful pastoral views far removed from the hustle and bustle of the more populated town centers. Located at the end of a magical path through enchanted woodlands, this restaurant is contained within the beautiful Lambert's Cove Country Inn (see the previous Accommodations section in this chapter). Besides offering an elegant dining room, an outside deck is also available if you wish to look out over the apple orchard. Seafood lovers will want to try the salmon. Landlubbers may wish to sample the smoked duck breast or the walnut-crusted rack of lamb. The restaurant is open year-round: seven days a week during the summer months for dinner only; during the off-season you should call ahead for days and hours of operation. Reservations are suggested, though walk-ins are always welcome. Lambert's is a nonsmoking establishment.

Shindig's $
Cliffs of Aquinnah, Aquinnah
(508) 645-3443

Open from May to the end of October, Shindigs offers fried seafood for those hungry tourists who have to come to view the Cliffs of Aquinnah. Though small and unassuming, the view from Shindig's three or four window seats is absolutely incredible. Only in Aquinnah can you eat a clam roll for less than $10 and enjoy a million-dollar view for free.

SHOPPING

Can a Martha's Vineyard vacation truly be called a vacation without a little shopping along the way? How will you be able to prove to your friends back home that you were on the island without purchasing a Black Dog T-shirt before you leave? Ours is not to question why, ours is to do the tourist thing and shop.

There are many fine shops dotting the main roads of Vineyard Haven, Oak Bluffs, and especially Edgartown, where you can kill an entire day browsing and buying. The offerings are varied and the treasures you'll find are many. Like most things in life, the pursuit is half the fun, and on Martha's Vineyard you are afforded many opportunities to enter the pursuit.

Besides individual shops you'll also find a handful of what can best be called minimalls (very mini, and "mall" isn't even the proper term). Tisbury Marketplace on Beach Road in Vineyard Haven is such a place. Another spot is Dockside Market

The West Tisbury Farmer's Market is a lovely Vineyard tradition. It's held at the historic Grange Hall on State Road on Saturday from 9:00 A.M. to noon. This is where many island farmers sell their produce, great greens, flowers, jams, herbs, and more.

Place on Oak Bluffs Harbor along Circuit Avenue Extension, which is a superb spot to do a little gift shopping, have a bite to eat, or just grab a beer or glass of wine and watch the boats go by. Not to be out-done, Edgartown has a number of shops clustered at the Colonial Inn on North Water Street, just across from the harbor.

What follows is a smattering of the island's shops—our short list of what we consider required stops. You'll find that many of these shopping locations, as well as many more not listed here, are a short walking distance from each other. For instance Circuit Avenue in Oak Bluffs provides an easy walking tour of what we estimate at 75 percent of the shops in that town, and Main and North Water Streets contain perhaps well over half (if not three quarters) of all the shops in Edgartown.

Unless otherwise noted, all shops listed accept major credit cards.

Vineyard Haven

All Things Oriental
123 Beach Road
(508) 693-8375

You'll think you've left the island for the Far East when you visit All Things Oriental, located right down there in the old Yankee port of Vineyard Haven. This store is brimming with a stunning collection of Oriental antiques for the serious collector, as well as furniture and porcelain, hand-carved fans, rugs, jewelry, lamps, and a host of other things too numerous to name. Whether you go home with a single pearl earring or a magnificent 19th-century armoire or rare hutch—or nothing at all—you'll probably be glad you stopped in just to look over a fascinating inventory. The name of the place says it all. All Things Oriental is open mid-May through Christmas.

The Black Dog General Store
Water Street
(508) 696-8182, (800) 626-1991
www.theblackdog.com/store

This is the place—the place where all those Black Dog T-shirts, sweatshirts, and caps come from. You've seen them everywhere. All the Black Dog souvenirs you could ever think of are here, even some for your own pooch at home. Sweaters, coffee mugs, key chains, even mouse pads emblazoned with that famous black lab. There are some sweets here too: brownies, espresso-bean brittle, and human shaped dog biscuits. Whatever you can't find at the store, you may find in their 26-page oversize catalog. Also on the grounds is the Black Dog Baker and the Black Dog Tavern (see our Restaurants section in this chapter). The store is open year-round.

Bowl & Board
35 Main Street
(508) 693-9441
www.bowlandboard.com

Wind chimes fill your ears with the sounds of invisible island breezes as you enter this airy building. It's filled with a premium selection of housewares, home furnishings, and wooden items. Wooden baskets abound. And if you ever need a candle, there are plenty here. You will also find an array of rugs, picture frames, and pottery, just to name a few items from the constantly changing inventory.

Bramhall & Dunn
19 Main Street
(508) 693-6437

This store, just up the road from the ferry, is a shoppers delight. Here you'll find things that are folkish—from women's clothing to hand-knit wool caps and

sweaters, hand-hooked and woven rugs, elegant picture frames, English pine antiques, beautifully crafted ceramic bowls, and so many other perfect gifts. Interestingly all the furniture in the store is for sale. Owners Emily Bramhall and Tharon Dunn personally choose the items they sell, and, in fact, they travel to England once a year to make their selections. Bramhall & Dunn also have a store on the island of Nantucket. Both stores are open year-round.

Bunch of Grapes Bookstore
44 Main Street
(508) 693-2291, (800) 693-0221
www.bunchofgrapes.com

Bunch of Grapes? This place should have been called Bunch of Books. Lots and lots of books are arranged on two floors in this rustic barn. As you go up the stairs there is a stained-glass window of yellow and red and orange—mesmerizing. With an endless array of best sellers and island-related titles (more than 38,000 titles spread throughout 5,000 square feet), it is one of the premier bookstores on the island, as well as being in the top 20 of independent booksellers in the nation. We're told that the late Jackie O shopped here! Browsers are especially welcome.

C. B. Stark
126 Main Street
(508) 693-2284, (888) 227-8275
www.cbstark.com

The artists here create jewelry in the form of familiar island sites, such as the Chappaquiddick Ferry; the Flying Horse Carousel; town and village signs; the Aquinnah, West Chop, East Chop, and Edgartown Lighthouses; a Chilmark scallop; Menemsha lobster; the island ferries; the Black Dog; and just about any other Vineyard thing that comes to mind. C. B. Stark is best known for its grapes design. All charms are available in sterling or 14-karat gold. C. B. Stark also sells six lines of watches with, of course, Martha's Vineyard on its face.

Midnight Farm
18 Water-Cromwell Lane
(508) 693-1997
www.midnightfarm.net
The great thing about being on an island is that even the shops have a view of the water. Such is the case with Midnight Farm, which has windows overlooking Vineyard Haven Harbor. Inside the store you'll find a wide assortment of items, from clothing to old-fashioned leather photo albums; to books, toys, candles, and antique furniture; to shampoos and bath oils. This is the store to visit if you're looking for that unique gift item. How about antique Victorian beach boxes, pottery, cashmere throws, baskets, or a CD or book autographed by Carly Simon (one of the owners of Midnight Farm)? It's open year-round.

Oak Bluffs

Laughing Bear
Circuit Avenue
(508) 693-9342
There's nothing like a bear with a sense of humor, but we still can't figure out the name. Regardless the Laughing Bear specializes in clothing—bright, colorful clothing. You'll find chenille and cotton fashions, velvet scarves, and satin gowns. The store also sells plenty of interesting jewelry. Laughing Bear is open from the beginning of May through mid-January.

The Secret Garden of Martha's Vineyard
41 Circuit Avenue
(508) 693-4759
This delightful store is full of great ideas for gifts, or better yet, for yourself. There are plenty of Crabtree & Evelyn products, Vera Bradley bags, a selection of books (many island-related), as well as jewelry and Vineyard-related items. We particularly enjoyed the miniature wooden gingerbread cottages. The Secret Garden is open year-round.

Edgartown

Bowl & Board
55 Main Street
(508) 627-8989
www.bowlandboard.com
What was once a former supermarket now houses a collection of impressive handmade wooden gadgets, everything from wooden kitchen utensils to wooden kids' toys to wooden bowls and wooden doodads with mysterious purposes. Did we mention the wood? Then there are the rugs, ornaments, and birch birdhouses.

Edgartown Books
44 Main Street
(508) 627-8463
This independent outfit is certainly the bookstore of Edgartown. A wide variety of titles, from classics to best sellers, line two floors of this bright and airy place. It also features a special section on the Cape and islands, and a deep selection of satisfying beach reads.

Edgartown Hardware
47 Main Street
(508) 627-4338
Built in 1946, this place personifies small-town Americana: a super-friendly staff, shelves overflowing with things you may need, and an ambience right off a *Saturday Evening Post* cover. It's worth a stop. Edgartown Hardware is open year-round.

The Chilmark Flea Market offers some of the best shopping bargains on the Vineyard. There's a nice selection of antiques, attic finds, books, crafts, and jewelry—much of it sold at half the prices you'll find in island shops. It's held weekly during the summer on Wednesday and Saturday from 8:30 A.M. to 2:00 P.M. off Middle Road in Chilmark, 1 mile east of Beetlebung Corner.

The Golden Door
18 North Summer Street
(508) 627-7740

This gallery features an extensive collection of sculpture, jewelry, coins, and furniture from throughout the Far East. Pieces from Indonesia, Papua New Guinea, and Thailand populate every corner, from tribal masks and pipes to ornate puppets, knives, and scabbards.

Island Pursuit
Main Street
(508) 627-8185

Stop by the Island Pursuit to pursue Vineyard sweatshirts and hats. Or to really prove that you were on the island, get one of those cool oval MV stickers for your car. Full of comfortable, high-quality, casual clothing, Island Pursuit also has some waterproof jackets to repel the most foul weather the island can dish up. Besides the Edgartown store, there is also an Island Pursuit in Vineyard Haven and on Nantucket.

Murdick's Fudge
21 North Water Street
(508) 627-8047
Corner of Union and Main Streets, Vineyard Haven
(508) 693-7344
5 Circuit Avenue, Oak Bluffs
(508) 693-2335
www.murdicks.com

This island fudge factory has locations in Edgartown, Vineyard Haven, and Oak Bluffs, so you'll know you're never very far from your next chocolate fix. Peanut butter fudge, double-chocolate fudge, butter-pecan fudge, Cape Cod cranberry fudge... it's just fudge, fudge, fudge everywhere you turn! Murdick's ships daily to 48 states, so now all your friends and relatives can join in too. Don't wait too long to order, though, as Vineyard Haven and Oak Bluffs stores (on Main Street and Circuit Avenue, respectively) close around Columbus Day. The Edgartown store is open from April 1 through December.

Willow
4 Kelley Street
(508) 627-6674

This jewelry shop showcases an incredible display of sterling silver, semiprecious stones, and pieces from Mexico, Africa, and Indonesia. Willow also has museum-quality geodes, amethysts, and crystals. The shop is open from the beginning of May through the end of October and on weekends only through the second week of December.

Up Island

Allen Farm
South Road, Chilmark
(508) 645-9064

Once a year the 70 or so resident sheep are shorn at Allen Farm, and the Allens use the wool to knit the most beautiful shawls, sweaters, scarves, and hats. This is a different kind of shopping experience out in the pastures of Chilmark, far removed from most everything else. The scenery is truly spectacular: Each direction offers a different picture with green rolling hills or the big blue sky pressing down the distant sea. The operating hours are sporadic or by appointment; it's best to call ahead, although it appears to be open every afternoon from Memorial Day through October.

Alley's General Store
State Road, West Tisbury
(508) 693-0088

The sign hanging out front says, in true Yankee form, "dealers in almost every-

Alley's General Store on State Road in West Tisbury has everything you need to keep kids happy. Ouija boards, kites, Mad Libs, table tennis sets, sand buckets, vintage tin toys, smoke bombs, and more line the walls. They also carry more workaday items, like hardware, produce, cookware, magazines, and videos.

thing." Believe it. You can buy most every-thing from fresh fruit and cookware to native jams and hiking boots. The West Tisbury post office used to be here, but moved out years ago although it left behind a good many post office boxes that are still in use. The antique scale out on the front porch will tell your weight for a penny; for 50 more cents you can get your horoscope as well. A few years back it looked as if this landmark was going to be forced to close its doors, but the Martha's Vineyard Preservation Trust stepped forward to save this treasure, which dates to 1858. Today you can still come here to get your mail or a gallon of milk, or to simply sit on the bench out front and watch the world go by.

The Granary Gallery
636 Old County Road, West Tisbury
(508) 693-0455, (800) 472-6279
www.granarygallery.com
Established in 1954, the Granary is one of the premier galleries on the island. It fea-tures the photographs of illustrious *Life* photographer and Vineyarder, the late Alfred Eisenstaedt, as well as island favorite Alison Shaw. Also on display is a varied range of original art representing more than 75 Martha's Vineyard-affiliated artists in oil, pastel, and acrylic, comple-mented by antiques and sculpture.

ENTERTAINMENT AND NIGHTLIFE

The Vineyard can kick up its heels as well as any resort destination. However, the island also is a haven for artists and per-formers, lending more than just a touch of culture to this island paradise.

For those in the 21-plus crowd, bars close at 1:00 A.M. (except in the dry town of Vineyard Haven where there are no bars). Many places have live entertainment in season. You'll find most of the action in Oak Bluffs and Edgartown. Unlike the Cape mainland you'll generally find a good

For the latest cinematic releases, check out the Capawock Theatre on Main Street in Vineyard Haven, which is open year-round. Seasonal theaters are the Island Theatre at Circuit Avenue in Oak Bluffs and the Strand across the street (and across the street from the Flying Horses Carousel). There's also Edgar-town Cinemas on Main Street in Edgar-town. Several island theaters can be accessed by calling the Martha's Vine-yard Moviehouses number at (508) 627-6689.

supply of public transportation and cabs to help you plan a fun and safe evening.

Here's a list of island spots where you can enjoy a well-rounded assortment of entertainment and nightlife.

Vineyard Haven

Island Theatre Workshop
(508) 693-5290, (508) 693-2769
itwmv.org
This is the island's oldest year-round the-ater company presenting original plays as well as musicals and dramas. The group presents several shows a year at various venues. They also offer classes for children and adults. It is associated with the Young Director's Studio, Apprentice Players, the Theatre Guild, and Children's Theatre.

Owen Park
Off Main Street, Vineyard Haven
Ocean Park
Seaview Avenue, Oak Bluffs
Music fans will appreciate the free Sunday night summer concerts alternately given at Owen Park off Main Street in Vineyard Haven and at the gazebo in Ocean Park on Seaview Avenue in Oak Bluffs. The events are quite festive, and as you lie back on your blanket, the music provides the starry night sky with a soundtrack.

While on-island call 311 for non-emergencies. All calls will be directed automatically to police stations in the town where the call originated. This is the line to call if your car gets stuck in the sand, to report noise complaints, graffiti, illegally parked cars, and the like. If it's an immediate emergency, call 911.

Tashmoo Overlook
Tisbury Amphitheater, State Road
(508) 693-6450
Summer Shakespeare takes the stage at the natural Tisbury amphitheater every Saturday at 10:00 A.M. from early July through August. Tickets cost $15 for adults; children 3 to 18 are $10 and ages 2 and under are free. Tickets are sold at the amphitheater before shows, and they accept cash only. A helpful hint: It's Shakespeare outdoors, so you may want to bring along a blanket, breakfast, and some mosquito repellent.

The Vineyard Playhouse
24 Church Street
(508) 693-6450
www.vineyardplayhouse.org
The Vineyard Playhouse is a nonprofit community center professional theater that puts on shows throughout the year. Tickets cost anywhere from $20 to $30 during the summer season. The Playhouse offers educational programs for both adults and children as well as children's shows with tickets around $6.00. The Playhouse stages four different presentations each summer, between June 15 and September 10, and during the summer of 2003 presented the Tony-award-winning play *Proof*.

Oak Bluffs

The Atlantic Connection
19 Circuit Avenue
(508) 693-7129
www.atlanticconnection.com
This is the dance place on the island for the under-30, younger crowd. When there isn't a live band performing, the music is provided via a DJ who hosts a dance party. The dance floor here is quite large and is usually packed. It is open seven nights a week from Memorial Day to Labor Day and Wednesday through Saturday nights in the off-season.

Lampost
111 Circuit Avenue
(508) 696-9352
This is a club for the under-30 crowd. Local bands and DJs perform here two nights a week until midnight or so, April to October. The Lampost is open from noon to 12:30 A.M. nightly.

Lola's
Beach Road
(508) 693-5007
www.lolassouthernseafood.com
This hot spot is next to the Island Inn on the Beach Road on your way to Edgartown (or if you're coming from Edgartown, it's on your way to Oak Bluffs). It's jazz and blues each night in July and August and Wednesday through Saturday night during the rest of the year. Look to their Web site for a calendar of entertainment. Lola's is open year-round.

Rare Duck
111 Circuit Avenue
(508) 696-9352
Another hot spot on Circuit Avenue is the Rare Duck, located beneath the Lampost. The Rare Duck attracts the under-30 crowd, offering an assortment of local entertainment April through October.

Season's Eatery & Pub
19 Circuit Avenue
(508) 693-7129
www.seasonseatery.com
Right next to (and adjoining) the Atlantic Connection is its more mellow companion, the Season's Eatery & Pub. This busy pub offers acoustic guitar, rock, and karaoke most evenings. There is a Sunday afternoon happy hour.

Tabernacle
Campgrounds
(508) 693-0525

The Tabernacle on the campgrounds in Oak Bluffs often hosts free band concerts and shows by big-name performers. Also, if you like sing-alongs, tune up your vocal chords and set aside an evening or two for communal music making. Every Wednesday at 8:00 P.M. in season, the Tabernacle hosts a community sing-along. A songbook is provided for a small donation.

Edgartown

The Old Whaling Church
89 Main street
(508) 627-4442

The Old Whaling Church is often used for live performances. The day we stopped by, there was an organ recital and high tea to benefit the restoration of the 1855 Simmons & Fisher organ. Performers such as Livingston Taylor visit regularly.

Up Island

Chilmark Community Center
Beetlebung Corner, Chilmark
(508) 645-9484

Beetlebung Corner's Chilmark Community Center is often a spot where outside concerts take place. The center also holds dances and other social events for all ages, including a family folk dance.

Hot Tin Roof
Martha's Vineyard Airport, West Tisbury
(508) 693-1137
www.mvhottinroof.com

Blues and rock are served in large portions here in this hot club located on the road leading to the airport. Local and nationally known artists perform here. The Hot Tin Roof was built in 1974 and was repurchased in 1996 by original owner Carly Simon.

Martha's Vineyard Chamber Music Society
Chilmark, Edgartown
(508) 696-8055
www.mvcms.vineyard.net

The MVCMS has been committed to bringing outstanding music to islanders year-round for 30 years. Winter concerts fill the cultural yearning of year-round residents, and the 12-concert summer series is always a highlight for vacationing music lovers. Call for a schedule; tickets are $20. Monday concerts are held at Edgartown's Old Whaling Church, and Tuesday concerts at the Chilmark Community Center.

The Yard
Middle Road, Chilmark
(508) 645-9662
www.dancetheyard.org

This is a 100-seat theater in a renovated barn off in the woods of Chilmark. A professional dance troupe, the Yard stages various theatrical events and dance previews throughout the summer season. Designed to sharpen the skills of professional artists, the Yard supports original works. Located near Beetlebung Corner, it is culture out amongst the trees. Tickets are $15 for adults and $12 for students.

ATTRACTIONS

Martha's Vineyard is an island rich in history. Settled just decades after the Pilgrims arrived in Plymouth, the island has grown, prospered, and suffered over the years.

The Vineyard is a natural playground with its miles and miles of beaches and beautiful country settings, which might make you forget that colonists, patriots, whaling ship captains, and Civil War soldiers once called this sandy island home. Today their homes and churches and even gingerbread cottages stand as reminders of the grand lives they lived, lives that helped put Martha's Vineyard on the map as an important American port.

Many of the attractions listed below are historical sites that have, over the years, played a role in the island's development. We feel strongly that you would miss out if you left these shores without first learning a bit about the history behind the beauty. The island's five lighthouses are listed according to location.

Vineyard Haven

Association Hall and Cemetery
Spring Street
Originally a Congregational and Baptist Church built in 1844, this building is now the town hall and is also home to the Katherine Cornell Memorial Theater. Behind the building is an old cemetery with stones dating back to the 18th century.

Old Schoolhouse
110 Main Street
(508) 693-9317
Owned by the Martha's Vineyard Preservation Trust, the island's first schoolhouse dates back to 1829. In 1776 a Liberty Pole stood in front of this building. When the British decided they would take it down for use as a spar on one of their vessels, three Vineyard Haven women blew up the pole with gunpowder rather than let the patriotic symbol fall into enemy hands. To commemorate their patriotism, a new pole was erected in 1898.

Seamen's Bethel
15 Beach Street
Bethels are chapels used by seamen. This one has been catering to the needs of visiting sailors since 1893 and houses a display of maritime artifacts, including carved ivory and old photographs—gifts of seafarers in appreciation of the bethel's work and hospitality.

Sea Captains' Houses
William Street
The largely residential William Street boasts many sea captains' houses, some of them now inns. Spared by the great fire of 1883 that engulfed much of the waterfront, William Street is now part of the official Historic District in which buildings are protected from alteration.

West Chop Lighthouse
Main Street
Follow Main Street westward to its end, and there you will discover West Chop Lighthouse, the island's first lighthouse site. The light was initially constructed of wood in 1817. This was replaced, in 1838, by the present brick structure. In 1848 it was moved back from the eroding 60-foot cliff, only to be moved again in 1891. It stands 84 feet tall and emits a white light that can appear either red or pinkish depending on your vantage point. This is due to red-tinted glass on one side of the tower.

Oak Bluffs

Civil War Memorial Statue
Seaview, Lake, and Ocean Avenues
At the busy intersection across the street from the Oak Bluffs ferry stop is a peculiar monument, and like most things in Oak Bluffs, it's the color scheme that is its peculiar attribute. This Civil War memorial dating to 1892 reads: "Erected in honor of Grand Army of the Republic by Charles Strahan, Co. B. 21st Virginia Reg." Yes, you read correctly, it was erected by a Confederate soldier—way up here in Yankee territory! In 1980 the town of Oak Bluffs repainted the Union soldier atop the memorial in Confederate gray colors to pay homage to Strahan.

The Cottage Museum & Shop
One Trinity Park
(508) 693-7784
This museum allows you a rare glimpse at the inside of a gingerbread cottage. It is representative of the more than 300 fancifully designed and painted cottages that line the narrow streets of the 30-acre-plus campground community. The architecture

CLOSE-UP

Tourist Information

To learn more about all that Martha's Vineyard has to offer, stop by, call, or write to Martha's Vineyard Chamber of Commerce, Beach Road, Vineyard Haven, MA 02568, (508) 693–0085. The chamber is open Monday through Friday, 9:00 A.M. to 5:00 P.M. year-round.

If you are interested in visiting Edgartown, you can contact the Edgartown Visitors Center at 29 Church Street, Edgartown, MA 02539 (no phone). The center is open seven days a week from Memorial Day through Labor Day.

of these cottages was modeled after the Newport, Rhode Island, Victorian style, but these have special (could we say, revolutionary) touches and colors that helped create a style unique to Oak Bluffs. Plan to take a better part of an hour just to stroll through the cottage community and examine the architecture and the many colors. The whole place is a 30-acre museum in itself!

East Chop Lighthouse
Tall atop the bluff it stands, some 80 feet above the sea, casting its lonely beam across the waves of Nantucket Sound below. This cast-iron lighthouse was built in 1876, replacing a wooden light erected in 1828 that burned down. Originally brown-red in color, it was known as the Chocolate Lighthouse until it was painted white in 1988. It emits a green light, marking the port side of Vineyard Haven Harbor and balancing West Chop's red beam marking the starboard side.

Flying Horses Carousel
Circuit Avenue
(508) 693-9481
This is the oldest operating platform carousel in the United States. It features 20 wooden horses sporting real horse hair and glass eyes. It was constructed in New York City in 1876 and arrived at Oak Bluffs

in 1884. Open from mid-April through mid-October, it is listed as a National Historic Landmark. Rides are only $1.00. It's great entertainment for the kids, and yes, you do get to grab for the brass ring!

Tabernacle
Trinity Park
At 100 feet high, 130 feet wide, and with seating for more than 3,000, this open-air auditorium is considered one of the largest wrought-iron structures in the United States. A uniquely beautiful piece of architecture combining the seemingly unlikely mixture of stained-glass windows and corrugated metal, it was built in 1879 amidst the Oak Bluffs campground community. It replaced a one-ton tent used by the Methodists, who congregated at this spot for their religious summer gatherings. The Martha's Vineyard Camp Meeting Association, (508) 693–0525, offers a free schedule of events open to the public, including concerts (James Taylor has played here), flea markets, and interdenominational services.

Union Chapel
Kennebec Avenue
(508) 693-5350, (508) 627-4440
When it was built in 1872, this was a nondenominational church. The octagonal-shaped

building is now used for summer concerts and a jazz series as its acoustics are quite good. The church building, owned by the Martha's Vineyard Preservation Society, features some interesting architecture, including a three-tiered roof.

Edgartown

Cape Pogue Lighthouse
Chappaquiddick Island

By far the toughest of the island's lighthouses to visit, the Cape Pogue Lighthouse is a the northernmost tip of Cape Pogue on the island of Chappaquiddick. Built as a wooden lighthouse in 1801, it was destroyed by the sea and replaced in 1838. The second light lasted for about 50 years until it too was destroyed and was replaced by a third light, which was replaced by a fourth in 1892 (do you see a trend developing here?). This fourth lighthouse, which stood 33 feet high, was replaced by the present structure in 1922. This present lighthouse has earned its place in the Lighthouse Hall of Fame by being the only one ever moved in one piece by helicopter. The feat took place in 1985 when the structure was moved 300 feet back from the water because—you guessed it—it was in danger of being destroyed by the ocean. It stands 555 feet tall. Located at the farthest reaches of Chappaquiddick, the lighthouse is not accessible by road. For information on touring the lighthouse, see the Cape Pogue Wildlife Refuge listing later in this chapter.

Edgartown Lighthouse
Off North Water Street

Originally constructed on an artificial island in Edgartown Harbor in 1828, sands have since built up to connect the site with the beach. But before the sands filled in, there was a long wooden walk that led out to the lighthouse. This was called the Bridge of Sighs because it was a popular place for young whalers to bring their girlfriends or wives before heading out on a long journey. In 1938 the lighthouse was replaced by another that was floated to this spot from Ipswich (a town on Massachusetts's North Shore).

Ferry to Chappaquiddick
Edgartown Harbor
(508) 627-9427

We don't know if you would actually consider this a point of interest, but it does meet the criteria for a must-see when visiting Edgartown. Two simple ferries, *On Time II* and *On Time III,* make the daily runs between downtown Edgartown and Chappy, transporting you, your car, bicycle, or moped in the process. By the way, the ferries have never been late, this earning their names. Of course there is no schedule, they just transport people and vehicles as they arrive, but regardless, they have never missed a deadline. Round-trip fares are $5.00 for a car and driver, $1.00 for each passenger, $3.00 for a bicycle and rider, and $4.00 for a moped.

Dr. Daniel Fisher House
99 Main Street
(508) 627-4440
www.mvpreservation.org

This fine example of Federal period architecture was built in 1840 as the home of town physician and whaling mogul Dr. Daniel Fisher. Fisher was also the founder of the Martha's Vineyard National Bank. The building was recently restored by the Martha's Vineyard Preservation Trust. For more information or to arrange a guided tour, call (508) 627-8619. Combination tours are offered, including the Old Whaling Church and the Vincent House; the cost is $7.00. The Dr. Daniel Fisher House is also available for weddings and receptions; call (508) 627-8017.

Old Whaling Church
89 Main Street
(508) 627-8017

This is an absolutely massive structure, with six gigantic wooden columns supporting the weight of the centuries and a 92-foot clock tower whose four-pointed spires seem to challenge the heavens. Since 1843 this soaring tower has been a landmark for sailors approaching Edgartown by sea. Built as sturdy as the old whaling ships, with 50-foot hand-hewn pine beams joined with wooden pegs, today the church is a 500-seat performing arts center. Summer church service is still held here on Sundays, as are weddings and receptions.

Pagoda Tree
South Water Street

A visit to Edgartown would not be complete without a visit to the famous Pagoda tree along South Water Street. The tree was planted during the mid-19th century by Capt. Thomas Milton, who carried it as a seedling from China. As you stand beneath its reaching branches, just imagine the sailors who, upon a hot summer's day, dodged the sun within the shade of her spreading limbs. It is considered perhaps the oldest and largest specimen of its kind in America.

The Vincent House Museum
Off Main Street
(508) 627-8619

This gem of a full Cape was build in 1672 and is considered to be Martha's Vineyard's oldest residence. It is behind the Old Whaling Church and the Fisher House. Interestingly sections of the interior walls of this museum have been left open and unfinished so you can observe its original colonial construction. The cost to tour the museum alone is $3.00, so you may as well pay the additional $4.00 to tour the Old Whaling Church and Dr. Daniel Fisher House (see the combined-tour information under the Dr. Daniel Fisher House entry above). Tours are held from 10:30 A.M. to 3:00 P.M. Monday through Saturday.

Vineyard Museum
8 Cooke Street
(508) 627-4441
www.marthasvineyardhistory.org

This museum complex consists of four buildings that form 1 square block. The 1765 Thomas Cook House was once a customs house and now houses antiquities of the island, including tools and folk art. Exhibits to honor the whaling industry, such as scrimshaw and ship models, can be found in the Foster Gallery, and Native American and island geophysical exhibits can be found in the Pease Galleries. The Gale Huntington Library is a must for those interested in genealogy. The carriage shed houses a whaleboat and a fire engine dating back to 1854. If you're a lighthouse enthusiast, be sure to get a look at the original Fresnel lens from the Gay Head Lighthouse. The lens, now resting on the museum's front lawn, was installed in 1856 and removed from the lighthouse in 1952. It is illuminated a few hours each evening during the summer months. The museum is open from 10:00 A.M. to 5:00 P.M. Tuesday through Saturday. Admission for adults is $7.00 and $4.00 for children younger than 15.

Whale Memorial
Across from Memorial Wharf

A fitting memorial to the whales and the whalers is the Whale Memorial located down near the harbor in Edgartown. The memorial features a sculptured whale diving into the ground with its flukes raised and a whaleboat in pursuit. It was erected in 1995 and says it is "Dedicated to the whales and the whalers who pursued them."

Up Island

Clay Cliffs of Aquinnah
State Road, Aquinnah

Travel up to Aquinnah and you'll think you've landed on an entirely different island. Aquinnah Cliffs, at the westernmost reaches of Martha's Vineyard, are the island's most popular and most photographed tourist attraction. Its clay cliffs cause you to catch your breath in awe of that which only nature herself could possibly create.

These 150-foot-high clay cliffs were originally named Dover Cliffs by explorer Bartholomew Gosnold, who first discovered the island in 1602. The Wampanoag Indians of the area have their own name for this place unlike any other—Aquinnah. Gay Head, the cliffs' other name, came from British soldiers who sailed past this distinctive geological formation in the 17th century.

Today the cliffs are owned by the Wampanoag Indians of the area. Formed during the ice age, the cliffs are a geological treasure chest as well as a paleontologic gold mine with the numerous fossils unearthed here. The cliffs also had some practical uses. For instance early islanders used the cliffs' clay to make paint and bricks. The high cliffs were also a prime vantage point—a high ground, you might say—and a perfect place to put a lighthouse (see below). The cliffs, now a national landmark, are protected in an attempt to reduce erosion. Only the Aquinnah Wampanoag Indians are allowed to remove clay from them.

Aquinnah Lighthouse
Aquinnah
High atop the Aquinnah Cliffs is the red brick Aquinnah Lighthouse, built in 1844 to replace its wooden sister. The original lighthouse was built by order of President John Adams. Due to a mingling of two tides, one from the north and one from the west, this stretch of ocean is considered to be very treacherous. Devil's Bridge off Aquinnah has wrecked many a ship over

Nestled back in the woods, the Chicama Vineyards (pronounced Chi-cay-ma) are located on Stoney Hill Road, off State Road in West Tisbury. Started in the early 1970s, these vineyards produce chardonnay, cabernet, merlot, and more. Visit for a tasting or a tour. They also offer mustards, vinegars, jams, and salad dressings.

the centuries, including the *City of Columbus* in 1884, with the loss of 120 lives. The Fresnel lens of the second lighthouse, which for the better part of a century warned sea captains of the hazardous cliffs, was removed in 1952 and is now on display at the Vineyard Museum in Edgartown.

Mayhew Chapel and Indian Burial Ground
Off Indian Hill Road, West Tisbury
This area known as Christiantown, known to the Wampanoag Indians as Manitouwattotan, can be found off Indian Hill Road in West Tisbury. You follow a dirt road to this historic site hidden in the woods (just keep going—it's up there, believe us!). Here stands the small Mayhew Chapel, built in 1829, and the adjoining Indian Burial Ground. The chapel is scarcely 20 feet by 15 feet, and yet it contains a dozen pews and a small altar! Early settler and minister Thomas Mayhew Jr. preached here, converting many native inhabitants in this area to Christianity. In the nearby cemetery nameless stones, perhaps as many as a hundred following the hilly terrain, mark Indian graves. It is a unique historical location, moving in its simplicity.

Menemsha Fishing Village
North Street, Menemsha
A classic fishermen's harbor, Menemsha was the site chosen to represent Quint's home port in the movie *Jaws*. There are some unforgettable shots of the harbor in the movie, notably as Quint's vessel *ORCA* is chugging out of the fishing port to hunt down the 25-foot great white shark. In fact a local told us that until recently one of the fishermen's shacks still had the name "Quint" painted on the door from the days when the movie was shot here. Furthermore, another local told us that the *ORCA* itself lies wrecked across the harbor at the mercy of the elements two decades after the mechanical beast staved her.

Beyond this bit of Hollywood, Menemsha is everything you expect from a salty fishing port: piles of lobster traps, heaps of discarded quahog shells, men wearing yellow waders bathed in fish blood, their faces aged by years at sea. Along the docks are little weather-beaten fishing shacks with shingles either warped with salt breezes, painted with gull droppings, or else missing altogether.

Menemsha also is home to one of the best sunset venues anywhere. From Menemsha Public Beach you're facing due west, giving you a great opportunity to watch the golden sun melt into the Atlantic.

TOURS AND EXCURSIONS

Boating excursions are popular throughout the island. We'll let you in on a few of our favorites.

There are a number of companies presenting narrated tours. Gay Head Sightseeing (508-693-1555), Island Transport (508-693-0058), and Martha's Vineyard Sightseeing (508-627-8687) all have buses waiting as you come off the ferries at Oak Bluff and Vineyard Haven. Tours run from mid-May through mid-October. All three tour companies offer two-and-a-half-hour tours of the six island towns; the cost is about $13.50.

The Arabella
Menemsha Harbor
(508) 645-3511
This 50-foot catamaran sails out of Menemsha Harbor twice a day in season. Captain Hugh Taylor will take you to Cuttyhunk (or the town of Gosnold)—the only public island in the isolated Elizabeth Islands chain. Or you can take a sunset cruise to the Aquinnah Cliffs. The day sail to Cuttyhunk leaves at 10:30 A.M. and returns by 4:00 P.M. It costs $60 per adult or teen, half that for children younger than 12. The sunset sail leaves at 6:00 P.M. (or thereabouts) and returns after the sun has totally set. The sunset cruise costs $50.

Ayuthia
Coastwise Harbor, Vineyard Haven
(508) 693-7245
www.mvy.com/ayuthia
This truly classic 48-foot Gaff Ketch yacht sails out of Coastwise Harbor offering half- and full-day sails and overnight trips to Nantucket and the Elizabeth Islands. Master Captain Tom Grew offers on e trip a day from 1:00 to 4:00 P.M. It's well worth packing a picnic, perhaps a bottle, and joining him as the experienced captain takes you on a traditional sailing experience.

Mad Max
Edgartown
(508) 627-7500
www.madmaxmarina.com
Mad Max leaves Edgartown to cruise along Chappaquiddick and past Oak Bluffs. A 60-foot-long by 25-foot-wide catamaran, it departs twice a day at 2:00 P.M. and 6:00 P.M. daily. Rates are $50, with children under 10 paying $40. An Insiders' tip: You get $5.00 off per person with a cash payment.

Shenandoah
Vineyard Haven
(508) 693-1699
www.coastwisepacket.com
If you really want to spurge, consider a six-day cruise aboard this square topsail schooner or ex-pilot schooner. If you have the time and money, you'll really enjoy life in various ports, including Newport, Rhode Island; Block Island, Rhode Island; and Nantucket. Meals are included, as are the memories. The fare depends on the trip, but average is $850 per person per trip and $650 for kids younger than 14. Or

Important Numbers

Emergency	911	Elder Abuse Hotline	(800) 922-2275
Alcoholics Anonymous	(508) 693-2150	Rape Hotline	(508) 696-SAFE
Narcotics Anonymous	(866) 642-3578	Child Abuse/Teen Crisis	
Overeaters Anonymous	(508) 693-9610	Hotline	(800) 231-6946
AIDS Alliance	(508) 693-8868		

opt for a day sail: $75 for a four-hour sail, including lunch.

BEACHES

We hope you brought along your bathing suit, because Martha's Vineyard has 125 miles of coastline offering some of the most memorable beaches you'll ever encounter. And we hope you wear your swimsuit because sunbathing in your birthday suit, or swimming in it for that matter, is against the law in all six Vineyard towns, even if you do happen to be the only bather for miles and miles and miles.

That having been said, to avoid surprises, visitors should know there are a few private beaches near the base of the Aquinnah cliffs that have built a reputation for their relaxed views toward bathing suits or the lack thereof.

Many of the beaches on Martha's Vineyard are private. In fact we only count a little more than a dozen public beaches out of all those 125 miles. The rest belong to the privileged few whose rights go down as far as the low-water mark, so you can't even swim by at high tide without trespassing!

Below we've listed our favorite public beaches. To park at some of these beaches, you'll need to get a parking and/or beach permit, which can be obtained by contacting the local town hall. (Vineyard Haven/Tisbury, 508-696-4200; West Tisbury, 508-696-0100; Chilmark, 508-645-2107; Oak Bluffs, 508-693-5511; Aquinnah, 508-645-2300; Edgartown, 508-627-6110.) Of the beaches below all but Aquinnah and East Beaches are free. For current fees for these two beaches, call the Aquinnah Town Hall.

So get your permit, pack a lunch, bring along a book, and head off to the beach.

Vineyard Haven

Lake Tashmoo Beach
Herring Creek Road
Sunbathers, swimmers, surf casters, and shellfish seekers flock to this beach on the island's north shore, where the lake meets the ocean. This teeny stretch of sand is also known as Herring Creek Beach. You'll find lifeguards here, but no bathhouses or concessions.

Owen Park Beach
Off Main Street
Here you'll discover a small, sandy, quiet harbor beach that offers great sunbathing, swimming, boat-watching, and lifeguards. It even has a separate kiddie play area. Bathhouses and concessions are nearby.

South Beach
Off Edgartown-West Tisbury Road

The 633-acre Long Point Wildlife Refuge Center preserve boasts this half-mile-long deserted beach where swimming and surf fishing are allowed in freshwater and salt-water ponds. Better get there early; there are only 55 parking spaces available. South Beach has bathhouses but no concessions or lifeguards.

Tisbury Town Beach
Owen Little Way

Sitting on the sand at Town Beach is the closest thing to being on a yacht as this beach is right next to the Vineyard Yacht Club. Lifeguards are on duty here, and concessions and bathhouses are close at hand.

Edgartown

Fuller Street Beach
Fuller Street

This section of beach, not far from Lighthouse Beach, is a popular hangout for the younger crowd. It looks out across the water at Cape Pogue and Cape Pogue Lighthouse. There are no lifeguards, concessions, or bathhouses at the Fuller Street Beach.

Joseph Sylvia State Beach
Beach Road, Edgartown and Oak Bluffs

This lovely beach is framed with grassy dunes and wild roses and marked by calm, shallow waters. It is also known as the Edgartown-Oak Bluffs State Beach because it stretches along 2 miles of those towns. (The Edgartown section of the beach is known as Bend-in-the-Road Beach because of its unusual shape.) The beach, which has lifeguards and nearby concessions but no rest rooms, is quite popular. It was along this stretch that some of the beach scenes from *Jaws* were filmed.

Katama Beach
Katama Road, Katama

Also known as South Beach, this 3-mile long barrier strand is the island's largest public beach. It's a favorite among surfers, who challenge heavy wave action of the mighty Atlantic pounding at its doorstep. (Watch for riptides, and check for swimming conditions!) In contrast to the Atlantic waves is a calm salt pond to the north of the beach. A shuttle bus runs between the beach and the center of Edgartown. Lifeguards are on patrol and bathhouses are available, but there are no concessions.

Lighthouse Beach
Starbuck's Neck

Lighthouse Beach is a perfect place to watch boats entering and leaving the harbor. From here you get a nice view of Chappy and Cape Pogue. At night it's an ideal spot for sunsets and stargazing. There are lifeguards at this beach, but no bathhouses or concessions. By the way, it's called Lighthouse Beach because it's right there beside the Edgartown Lighthouse.

Oak Bluffs

Eastville Beach
Beach Road

If you're looking for a quiet stretch of shoreline along the harbor, you've found it. You can find Eastville Beach at the bridge between Oak Bluffs and Vineyard Haven. When you're not being lulled by the gently lapping surf, you can watch the sails billowing in the breeze as the boats go tacking by. There are no lifeguards, rest rooms, or concession stands.

Oak Bluffs Town Beach
Seaview Avenue

Oak Bluffs Town Beach straddles both sides of the ferry wharf, and its calm surf makes it ideal for families with small kids. It's also a great spot to sit and wait for the ferry to come in. This beach has lifeguards on duty. Public rest rooms are available nearby on the ferry dock, and various concessions are close by as well.

Pristine beaches are a major draw on Martha's Vineyard. Many of them require resident's stickers to enjoy, however. MASSACHUSETTS OFFICE OF TRAVEL AND TOURISM

Up Island

Aquinnah Beach
Off Moshup Trail, Aquinnah

A wooden boardwalk winds alongside the famous cliffs, through cranberry bogs and beach plum bushes, down to the surf. Below is Aquinnah Beach, a 5-mile-long stretch that is actually four beaches in one. From north to south they are Aquinnah, Moshup, Philbin, and Zack's Cliffs. The last two beaches are private. The farther south you walk, the more isolated you find yourself. This truly feels like the ends of the earth. Fortunately, these ends of the earth have rest rooms and concessions located at the head of the cliffs, though you won't find any lifeguards out here. Be careful in the tricky surf. *NOTE:* the parking out here is a bit expensive—up to $15 a day!

Menemsha Public Beach
Menemsha Harbor, Chilmark

Resting right beside the stone jetty at the entrance to Ditcher's Dock, Menemsha Public Beach is a quiet place with a gentle surf and surprisingly few people. Sit and watch the fishing boats go in and out, or just kick back and catch some rays. Lifeguards, rest rooms, and nearby concessions provide all the comforts.

Chappaquiddick

East Beach
Chappaquiddick Road

Wasque Reservation and Cape Pogue Wildlife Refuge are adjoining beaches, known as East Beach, that run along the eastern coast of the island of Chappaquiddick. Even on the hottest day, you may find yourself the only one basking in the unspoiled glory. Because the beach sits at the end of a bumpy dirt road, it's accessible only by boat or four-wheel-drive vehicle. There are no bathhouses, concessions, or lifeguards. To get to Chappaquiddick Island, you'll need to take your car across on the *On Time* ferry. You will also have to pay a nominal fee to the Trustees of Reservations, which maintains and preserves the area. The beautiful beach is worth it, though.

NATURAL AREAS AND TRAILS

In a sense Martha's Vineyard is one big natural area brimming with beauty at every town and down every road. Each part of the island offers wonders so varied and so vast that you'll doubt if heaven could ever be an improvement.

The island offers a delicious mixture of settings, and as you travel through say, Chilmark, you will see a number of her settings all in the same eyeful. Turn a corner, and you get a vista of rolling fields dampened by small ponds and ending in a vast sweep of ocean blue. Look the other way, and you see painstakingly erected stone walls vanishing off into the distance, beyond a swaying marshland carrying the island to sea. Such natural beauty is hard to sufficiently appreciate in such generous doses.

Nature and humanity share the island, although in the Up Island area it seems that nature has the upper hand. Wildlife is ever apparent. Up on an autumn lane in Chilmark we had to stop our vehicle to allow a quorum of turkeys to cross. They gobbled as turkeys do and continued on their way, not the least bit deterred by our car or the fact that Thanksgiving was just a short month away!

More than a fifth of the island is protected from development, and there are several sanctuaries and parks you can explore. You may have to pay a nominal parking fee.

Cape Pogue Wildlife Refuge and Wasque Reservation
Chappaquiddick Island
(508) 693-7662

These two adjoining parcels of land (516 acres and 200 acres, respectively) bordering Katama Bay on the southeastern corner of Chappaquiddick Island form the perfect escape from crowds. Even on the hottest summer day, you'll find few people here.

Salt marshes, tidal flats, ponds, cedars, barrier beaches, and sand dunes are everywhere. A myriad of shorebirds such as ospreys, snowy egrets, kestrels, great blue herons, and the endangered least terns and piping plovers populate this haven. Swimming, fishing, and picnicking are permitted. The Trustees of Reservation own and manage this property, and offer several guided tours during the summer season. The Natural History Tour is a two-and-a-half-hour trip across Chappaquiddick to the Cape Pogue Lighthouse. The Lighthouse Tour focuses, not surprisingly, on the lighthouse. Explore it while learning about its history and the families who lived there on this one-and-a-half-hour tour. On the Wildlife Canoe Tour, you'll paddle through Poucha Pond, learn about salt marshes and tidewater environments, and see some of their inhabitants, like ospreys and cormorants. The Fishing Discovery Tour takes you to the prime fishing beaches of Wasque Point and Cape Pogue. A fishing guide teaches surf-fishing skills and fish and bird identification. All tours depart from the Mytoi parking area and run from Memorial Day through Columbus Day weekend. Reservations are recommended. Call (508) 627-3599 for ticket prices and reservations. The areas are open year-round.

Cedar Tree Neck Wildlife Sanctuary
Off Indian Hill Road
(508) 693-5207

This 300-acre natural habitat and living museum is tucked among the unspoiled woods of West Tisbury. It's a varied environment where freshwater ponds, brooks,

Many of the Vineyard's great ponds are occasionally opened (naturally, or with help from a backhoe) to the sea. This allows herring to return to freshwater to spawn, and improves pond conditions for growing oysters. Predators—osprey, stripers, and bluefish—gather for an easy meal. Fishermen show up to this rich fishing opportunity too, as soon as they catch word of an opening. These openings typically happen in the spring and fall, and there is no set schedule. Local tackle shops are the best place to pick up word of these fishing bonanzas.

scrub oaks, beech trees, bayberry bushes, rocky bluffs, and bogs all compete for your attention. The wooded color-coded trails offer many a delight: One leads to secluded North Shore Beach, another to a bird refuge, still another (the one starting at the parking lot) to the sanctuary's summit and breathtaking views of the Aquinnah Cliffs. It is open year-round.

Felix Neck Wildlife Sanctuary
Off Edgartown-Vineyard Haven Road
(508) 627-4850

Situated 3 miles outside of Edgartown and run by the Massachusetts Audubon Society, Felix Neck is a nature lover's dream come true—350 acres of open fields, woods, beaches, and marshlands inhabited by reptiles and other wildlife. In the summer visitors can hike 6 miles of meandering, marked trails; be sure to look for the osprey nesting platforms. Throughout the year professional naturalists offer various demonstrations and expeditions, including snake and bird walks, and stargazing and snorkeling sessions.

An exhibition center features displays of fish, snakes, and turtles and also has a library and gift shop. Felix Neck also offers summer camps for kids during the season.

Long Point Wildlife Refuge
Off Waldron's Bottom Road, West Tisbury
(508) 693-7662

Long Point is the best spot for bird- and duck watchers, provided, that is, you can deal with the very bumpy roads that get you here. This 633-acre area of open grassland and heath is bounded on the sides by salt and fresh water. The trails here wind their way through pine and oak forests and will take you to either idyllic Long Cove Pond (look for the river otters) or the lovely, but crowded, South Beach, where you can swim.

Manuel E. Correllus State Forest
Airport Road
(508) 692-2540

This forest sits smack-dab in the middle of the island. It's a 5,145-acre spread of scrub oak and pine laced with paved bike, nature, horse, and hiking trails. You can pack a picnic basket and bask in the cool shade of majestic trees. A hostel is located at the southwest corner of the forest (see the previous Accommodations section of this chapter). There is no parking fee.

Mytoi
Off Dike Road, Chappaquiddick
(508) 693-7662

This 14-acre Japanese garden is an astounding profusion of azalea, dogwood, iris, daffodils, rhododendron, wild rose, Japanese maple, holly, and sweet gum. We could sit all day and stare at the koi and goldfish, innocently swimming in their picturesque creek-fed pool beneath an ornamental bridge. Mytoi is open year-round.

Menemsha Hills Reservation
North Road, Chilmark
(508) 693-7662
www.thetrustees.org

This 211-acre Trustees of Reservations property includes trails that meander through distinct coastal ecosystems and offers stunning views. The Harris Trail

Sometimes the walk to the beach can be just as lovely as the beach itself; these beachgoers wend their way through beach plum and cranberry bushes to the sands below.
MASSACHUSETTS OFFICE OF TRAVEL AND TOURISM

curves through wetlands where red maples, cinquefoil, beech, and black cherry trees grow. Eventually you'll climb to the top of Prospect Hill, one of the highest points on Martha's Vineyard, with views of Menemsha village, the Elizabeth Islands, and Aquinnah Light. Turn around there, or follow the Upper or Lower Trails down to the rocky coast. At the overlook along the bluffs, you should be able to spy the remains of a 19th-century brickyard, a tall brick chimney.

Waskosim's Rock Reservation
North Road, Chilmark
(508) 627-7141
The Martha's Vineyard Land Bank Commission acquired this unique 185-acre property in 1990 from a developer who planned on building scores of houses on

it. Now it remains an unspoiled preserve of rolling hills, wetlands, oak, and beetlebung woods; it even has the ruins of an 18th-century homestead. As for Waskosim's Rock, it was deposited by a retreating glacier and, some say, looks like a breaching whale (which it does, sort of). The rock sits on a ridge from which you can soak in panoramic views of the Vineyard Sound foothills and the Mill Brook Valley.

RECREATION

The island is really one big playground. Surrounded as it is by the sea and the sounds, water sports and fishing abound. Meanwhile on land there is plenty to do and discover.

Bicycling

Perhaps the best way to explore Martha's Vineyard is by bicycle. Just waiting to be explored are several superb bike paths that transverse the island. The island terrain is not known for its smoothness. The east side of the island is flatter than the west side, which rises well above sea level in some places. The more level bike paths are those connecting Vineyard Haven to Oak Bluffs, Oak Bluffs to Edgartown and to South Beach, and State Road between North Tisbury and Vineyard Haven. Middle Road in Chilmark has little traffic and is a wonderful country jaunt.

If you do enjoy scaling hills, follow the circular trail that begins at the Aquinnah Lighthouse. The views are incredible. There are also several paved bike paths in the Manuel E. Correllus State Forest, off Edgartown-West Tisbury Road, and in Oak Bluffs, West Tisbury, and Edgartown.

Many people bring their own bikes across from the mainland on the ferry, but you can lease bikes and riding equipment at a number of rental shops throughout the island.

Beach Road Rentals
Vineyard Haven
(508) 693-3793

Martha's Bike Rentals
Vineyard Haven
(508) 693-6593, (866) 306-5351
www.marthasvineyardbikes.com

Anderson Bike Rentals
Oak Bluffs
(508) 693-9346

DeBettencourt's Bike Shop
Oak Bluffs
(508) 693-0011

Edgartown Bicycles
Edgartown
(508) 627-9008
www.edgartownbicycles.com

R.W. Cutler Bikes/Edgartown Bike Rentals
Edgartown
(508) 627-4052
www.edgartownbikerentals.com

Fishing

Perhaps one of the most popular recreational activities on the island is fishing, especially in the fall when the Vineyard hosts its annual fishing derby. Swimming along the coastline of the Vineyard are fish just looking to be caught. You don't have to be Quint, or Ahab for that matter, to catch the big one. You just have to be at the right place at the right time with the right equipment.

Fishing is superb at any of the beaches, so you'll notice plenty of surf casters. You'll also spot anglers casting their lines over the island's various bridges and stone jetties.

Insiders head to the Chappaquiddick shore at Cape Pogue and Wasque and to Lobsterville Beach in Aquinnah to reel in bluefish and bonito. Scup is common in the waters almost everywhere. Cod and striped bass are best caught during the spring and fall; head over to the entrance of Menemsha Harbor to find them.

If you're into surf casting, try the beaches at Aquinnah or any beach facing south. Remember the tides in the Atlantic Ocean can be tricky; for instance there is an eight-hour difference between high tides at Cape Pogue and Aquinnah. The *Vineyard Gazette* prints a tide chart each Friday on the Fishing page.

EQUIPMENT AND GUIDES

Several stores offer fishing rod, tackle, bait, and other equipment. Many stores also offer guide services. Tackle shops and guides also are the best places to find out about local limits on size and numbers of fish you can keep. Here are some of our favorites:

Dick's Bait and Tackle
New York Avenue, Oak Bluffs
(508) 693-7669

Captain Porky's
Dock Street, Edgartown
(508) 627-7117

Coop's Bait and Tackle
147 West Tisbury Road, Edgartown
(508) 627-3909

Larry's Tackle Shop
258 Upper Main Street, Edgartown
(508) 627-5008
www.larrystackle.com

CHARTER FISHING

Looking for tuna, shark, and white marlin? Consider taking a fishing expedition; you'll find them offered at all of the island's harbors. Here are several of the local tried-and-true charter services.

Banjo's Captain Robert Plante (508–693-3154, www.banjocharters.com) offers half- and full-day charters out of Oak Bluffs.

The party boat *Skipper* (508–693-1238, www.mvskipper.com) leaves from Oak Bluffs for fluke and scup.

Big Eye Charters (508–627-3649, www.bigeyecharters.com) offers charters out of Edgartown Harbor.

Great Harbour Sport Fishing Charters (508–627-3122, www.vineyardfishing.com) leaves from Edgartown Harbor.

Flashy Lady Charters (508–645-2462, www.flashyladycharters.com) at Menemsha Harbors offers half- and full-day charters in search of the three Bs (bass, bonito, and blues).

Conomo (508–645-9278) out of Aquinnah, offers half- and full-day charters. Captain Brian Vanderhoop offers spin or fly-fishing.

Golf

Every vacation should include a little driving, chipping, and putting. To help you out in that area, Martha's Vineyard has two fine public golf courses.

COURSES

Farm Neck Golf Course
Farm Neck Way, Oak Bluffs
(508) 693-2504

This challenging 18-hole, par 72 championship course is open from mid-April to mid-December. You may find a few golf balls with the Presidential Seal on them, as this is where President Clinton spent most of his daylight hours while on the island. Simply, Farm Neck is one of the best courses in New England. Call ahead for reservations (though no more than 48 hours in advance) and current greens fees. This beautiful course follows Sengekontacket Pond and overlooks the beach. It features a driving range and pro shop with rental equipment.

Mink Meadows
Golf Club Road, Vineyard Haven
(508) 693-0600
www.minkmeadows.com

Mink Meadows is an intimate course with nine holes and great ocean views. In fact the views are so awesome that you might not be able to keep you eyes on the ball. The facility also has a pro shop and driving range. Greens fees are $46 for 9 holes, $66 for 18 holes in season, and $35 and $48, respectively, in the off-season.

MINIGOLF

Island Cove Miniature Golf Course
State Road, Vineyard Haven
(508) 693-2611

If you're not up to the challenge of a full 6,000-plus yard course, then bring the kiddies over to Island Cove for some family adventure golf. This Vineyard Haven course offers 18 holes and waterfalls to boot. The first nine holes are wheelchair accessible.

Horseback Riding

Enjoy the scenery of the island while in the saddle of a horse trotting down a country lane.

Arrowhead Farm
Indian Hill Road, West Tisbury
(508) 693-8831
This farm provides lessons, boarding, an outdoor and indoor ring, and offers pony rides. There are beautiful woods to ride in. Arrowhead Farm welcomes visitors and offers a day riding camp during the summer.

Crow Hollow Farm
Tiah's Cove Road, West Tisbury
(508) 696-4554
www.crowhollowfarm.com
Located near the state forest and a network of trails and lanes, Crow Hollow's guided trail rides roam through the varied terrain of old farmland and conservation land. The farm also offers lessons, clinics, and a summer riding program.

Misty Meadows Horse Farm
Old Country Road, West Tisbury
(508) 693-1870
Misty Meadows is a trail farm that is only open during the summer months. It offers family-oriented trail rides in the forest behind the farm.

Ice Skating

Martha's Vineyard Ice Arena
Edgartown-Vineyard Haven Road,
Oak Bluffs
(508) 693-5329
www.mvarena.com
This arena is open for skating, lessons, and hockey games from the beginning of

August through mid-April. Public skating costs $4.00.

Tennis

Public tennis courts are available at the following locations to the residents or vacationers of each town.

Edgartown: Town Courts, Robinson Avenue

Oak Bluffs: Town Courts, Niantic Avenue

Vineyard Haven: Town Courts, Church Street

West Tisbury: Town Courts, Old County Road

Water Sports and Boating

EQUIPMENT RENTALS

Martha's Vineyard Parasailing, Waterskiing, Jet Skiing
Pier 44, Vineyard Haven
(508) 693-2838
Their name tells the whole story. This business rents Jet Skis and will take you out for an afternoon of waterskiing or for the ride of your life—parasailing. The instructors are Coast Guard-licensed and insured. Call ahead for reservations.

Vineyard Scuba & Snorkeling
South Circuit Avenue, Oak Bluffs
(508) 693-0288
The waters around the Vineyard were unlucky for many an 18th- and 19th-century sailor. With the help of Vineyard Scuba, you can now visit these sunken ships and lost schooners. They offer equipment rentals so you can explore the Vineyard's undersea world.

Wind's Up
Beach Road, Vineyard Haven
(508) 693-4252, (508) 693-4340
www.windsupmv.com

Sailboarders will find the waters around the Vineyard to their liking. Wind's Up offers lessons and rentals of sailboards, wet suits, body boards, sailboats, surf-boards, sea kayaks, and canoes. Ask for a free copy of their brochure listing the best places to catch the wind. Wind's Up is open until Christmas, reopening in March.

BOAT RENTALS

If your plans include hoisting our own sail, then you'll be happy to learn that there are many boat rental establishments on the Vineyard. Keep in mind many renters limit how far you can go in their craft. Here are a few of our favorites.

Island Water Sports
100 Lagoon Pond Road, Vineyard Haven
(508) 693-7767, (508) 693-5884
(off-season)
www.boatmv.us
Island Water Sports rents powerboats, sailboats, skiffs, inflatables, dinghies, kayaks, outboard motors, and water skis. They also have fishing rods for rent. Must be 21 to rent a boat.

Wind's Up
Beach Road, Vineyard Haven
(508) 693-4252
www.windsupmv.com
This is the place to go for catamarans, Sunfish, sailboats, sailboards, and boogie boards.

A-1 Martha's Vineyard Ocean Sports
Dockside Marina, Oak Bluffs
(508) 693-8476
Pier 44 Marina, Beach Road, Vineyard Haven
(508) 693-2838
Daily, weekly, and seasonal rentals of Boston Whalers. You may also rent para-sailing, waterskiing, wakeboarding, Jet Ski-ing, and tubing equipment. Professional instruction is available.

BOAT RAMPS

Those who bring their own boat to the island or buy their own boat on the island, can launch it at several boat ramps.

In Vineyard Haven: Beach Road, on the Vineyard Haven side of the lagoon draw-bridge, into the lagoon or at Lake Street into Lake Tashmoo.

In Oak Bluffs: At East Chop Drive, along the north side of the Harbor, into the harbor or at Medeiros cove, on the west side of town, into the lagoon.

In Edgartown: Anthier's Landing into Sengekontacket Pond or at the south end of Katama Bay Road into Katama Bay.

In Aquinnah: At the Aquinnah-Chilmark town line at Hariph's Creek Bridge into Nashaquitsa Pond or at Lob-sterville, West Basin, into Menemsha Pond.

ANNUAL EVENTS

There's always something happening on the island, especially during the summer months when the island seems to be burst-ing at the seams with visitors and excite-ment. Whether it's fireworks, fairs, festivals, road races, concerts, or fishing tourna-ments, you are bound to find something of interest. And the events don't end at the conclusion of Columbus Day weekend. Edgartown celebrates an old-fashioned Christmas with a host of festivities, and there's even a First Night event on the first night of the new year. So get out your cal-endar and prepare to pencil in some dates.

January

WMVY Annual Chili Contest
Atlantic Connection, Oak Bluffs
(508) 693-5000
www.mvyradio.com
This fund-raiser held in mid-January (usu-ally Saturday of the weekend before Super

Bowl Sunday) and sponsored by radio station WMVYT is sure to warm you up. This contest strives to solve an important culinary question: Who has the best-tasting chili on the island? One category involves the island's top chefs, and the other is for amateurs, with ordinary islanders bringing out their best recipes. Bring your appetite; bowls and spoons are provided. A fee, usually about $12, will get you in the door to sample all the chili you can eat.

May

Annual Spring Short Play Festival
Vineyard Playhouse, Church Road,
Vineyard Haven
(508) 696-6450
www.vineyardplayhouse.org
This festival is divided into three evenings of eclectic short plays. In 2003 featured works included *Lifeguard on Duty,* by George Sauer; *Yard Sale,* by Irene Tiersten; and *Girl in the Basement* by John Lipsky.

Memorial Day 5K Road Race
Oak Bluffs
(508) 693-7887
Memorial Day weekend is regarded as the kickoff for the new tourist season here on the island. It is also the weekend for the annual Memorial Day 5K Road Race, held on the Sunday of that weekend. You can sign up at the Wesley Hotel. Expect to pay $25 for entry the day of the race, but only $15 if you preregister.

June

Oak Bluffs Annual Harbor Festival
Oak Bluffs
(508) 693-3392
This is a festive waterfront celebration that attracts both locals and tourists in large numbers. Bands fill the air with joyful sound while seafood fills the air with enticing aromas. There are games and arts and crafts booths to keep kids and adults entertained. Admission is free. Sponsored by the Oak Bluffs Association, this event takes place in mid-June from noon to sundown with a rain date of the next day.

A Taste of the Vineyard
Edgartown
(508) 627-4440
Sample food and drink from more than 50 island eateries and beverage merchants on Thursday night and be wined and dined at the live auction featuring various goods and services on Saturday night. It is held in mid-June under a tent next to the Old Whaling Church. Tickets for Thursday night are $125 and for Saturday night are $150. All money raised benefits the Martha's Vineyard Preservation Trust.

Farmers Market
West Tisbury
(508) 693-0085
This is what we call an old-fashioned farmers market. Held at the old Agricultural Hall on Saturdays from mid-June to mid-October and on Wednesdays from the end of June to the end of August, it offers fresh locally grown vegetables and homemade baked goods. There are even some artisans selling their arts and crafts.

July

Band Concerts
Vineyard Haven and Oak Bluffs
(508) 693-0085
Now this is an island vacation—music on a summer night! Sunday night is the night for band concerts, alternating between Owen Park in Vineyard Haven and Ocean Park in Oak Bluffs. You might want to bring your own lawn chair or blanket and soak up the sweet sounds under the summer stars. The band is always the Vineyard Haven Band Inc., and the admission is always free.

Edgartown Fireworks
Edgartown Harbor
(508) 627-5167
Fireworks over the harbor—need we say more? The Edgartown fireworks cap off the town's Independence Day celebration. Get there early to claim your spot. Parking is a challenge, but don't worry, you'll find a space somewhere.

Independence Day Parade
Edgartown
(508) 627-6180
What would the Fourth be without a good parade? Edgartown comes through with the annual event featuring local high school bands and floats, which pass through the historic main routes of this old whaling port. You'll find yourself humming a George M. Cohan song as you are swept up in the patriotic theme.

Tisbury Birthday and Street Fair
Vineyard Haven
Tisbury is the second-oldest town on the island, incorporated in 1671 just after Edgartown. To celebrate its incorporation the town throws itself a party in early July, and you are invited. Festivities include games, live entertainment, and craft booths. Of course food is available as well.

Edgartown Regatta
Edgartown Yacht Club
(508) 627-4364
www.edgartownyc.org
This regatta, now in its 81st year, is one of the largest amateur sailing events in the area, usually beginning the third Thursday in July and running throughout the weekend. Races include many classes of boats, from smaller boats to large cruising vessels. The race weekend attracts large crowds to Edgartown, so you may want to make your room reservations months in advance to guarantee accommodations.

Portuguese Holy Ghost Feast
Vineyard Avenue, Oak Bluffs
(508) 693-9448
Portuguese first arrived on the island in the early to mid-18th century. Many found employment as merchant seamen or on whaling vessels. Portuguese-American heritage is the focus of the Holy Ghost Feast—a festival of games, entertainment, and some of the greatest food on the planet. The festival is held in mid-July and runs from 5:00 P.M. to midnight on Saturday and from noon to 6:00 P.M. on Sunday at the Portuguese-American Club.

Monster Shark Fishing Tournament
Oak Bluffs
(508) 693-6611
Images of Quint standing upon the rocking bow of the *ORCA* with a harpoon gun in his hands come to mind when you consider this fishing tournament held over three days toward the end of July. Local charters and anglers alike vie to land the largest beast. Registration is held at Oak Bluffs Wesley Hotel. Call the Big Game Fishing Club at the number above for this event.

August

All Island Art Show
Oak Bluffs
(508) 693-0525
The famed Tabernacle at the Methodist campgrounds in Oak Bluffs is the site of this art show in early August, which features island artists placing juried works on display. The event is well attended, as the work is of the highest caliber. Admission is free.

Possible Dreams Auction
Edgartown
(508) 693-7900, ext. 374
www.possibledreams.org
Vineyarder Art Buchwald hosts this early August auction at the Harborside Inn gardens. It is a fund-raiser for Martha's Vineyard Community Services, in which you can bid on everything from a sailboat ride with Walter Cronkite to a tour of CBS and the *60 Minutes'* studios with Mike Wallace

or lunch with Carly Simon. Anything is possible, so bring your checkbook.

Chilmark Road Race
Chilmark
(508) 645-9484
This series of 3-mile races for varying age groups takes place in mid-August. It benefits the Chilmark Community Center. The race starts at 10:30 A.M.

Agricultural Fair
West Tisbury
(508) 693-4343
Tradition is the centerpiece of this grand, old-fashioned country fair. Pastoral West Tisbury is the perfect setting, complete with cotton candy and pie contests. In the old dairy barn, you'll find agricultural exhibits featuring fruits and vegetables, and arts and crafts—all judged. In the livestock barn different farm critters are judged daily throughout the four days. The fair takes place the third week in August on Thursday, Friday, Saturday, and Sunday. Admission is $8.00 for adults, and $5.00 for seniors and children 5 to 12 years old. There is a midway full of rides (bring extra money for each ride), a dog and horse show, ox pull, music, and food. The fair prompted Bonnie Raitt to write *Stayed Too Long at the Fair*. (She probably had too much cotton candy.) The Agricultural Fair is sponsored by the Martha's Vineyard Agricultural Society.

Fireworks at Ocean Park by the Sea
Oak Bluffs
(508) 693-5380
Be prepared to "ooh" and "aah" at this traditional end-of-summer fireworks show, which takes place the third weekend of August. The event is free; bring along your own lawn chairs and blankets. Sponsored by the Oak Bluffs Firemen's Civic Association.

Illumination Night
Oak Bluffs
(508) 693-0525
As its name suggests, this annual event involves luminescence. Tradition abounds as each of the gingerbread houses of Oak Bluffs' old Methodist campground twinkles with Japanese lanterns and candles as they have each year for the past century. Illumination Night marks the end of yet another summer season and is a free event.

September

Vineyard Artisans Festival
West Tisbury
(508) 693-8989
Local artists display their work amidst West Tisbury's country setting. Sounds like a fun afternoon to us. It all takes place at the Agricultural Hall the first weekend in September from 10:00 A.M. to 5:00 P.M. The festival is free.

Dukes County Savings Bank Annual Golf Tournament
Vineyard Haven
(508) 693-6184
The Vineyard golf course is the site of this annual tournament. It is held in mid-September from 8:00 A.M. to noon to benefit the Vineyard Nursing Association.

Tivoli Day Festival
Oak Bluffs
(508) 693-7643
Tivoli is a city in Italy, just northeast of Rome. Closer to home the Tivoli used to be the old dance hall in Oak Bluffs. Today Tivoli Day is a festival of music, arts, crafts, and food held from noon to sundown on Circuit Avenue. Admission is free.

Martha's Vineyard Striped Bass and Bluefish Derby
Edgartown
(508) 939-9341
www.mvderby.com
This fishing tournament is a month-long competition with more than $100,000 worth of prizes for those who catch the largest bass, bluefish, bonito, and false albacore. Running from mid-September to mid-October, there are daily, weekly, and grand prizes awarded.

The year 2004 marked the 59th annual derby. The weigh station is at the Edgartown Junior Yacht Club, although Derby Headquarters can be reached by writing 1A Dock Street, Edgartown, MA 02539.

October

Annual Crop Hunger March
Vineyard Haven
(508) 693-3930

This 10-kilometer walk from Vineyard Haven to Oak Bluffs (and back) raises awareness and money for the problem of hunger. The event, sponsored by the Vineyard Committee on Hunger, Island Food Pantry, and the Martha's Vineyard Clergy Association, is usually held on the second Sunday of the month. Anyone can join in; participants are asked to be sponsored.

Columbus Day 5K Road Race
Oak Bluffs
(508) 693-7887

The air is a little cooler for this 5K endurance race. The event usually draws a good field of runners and an enthusiastic crowd of onlookers.

Happy Haunting Weekend
Edgartown
(508) 627-4711

Ghosts and goblins and a devilishly good time come together in this traditional Halloween weekend, held closest to October 31 at the Colonial Inn. There is a pumpkin-carving contest, face painting, and trick or treating at participating stores. After dark all the pumpkins are illuminated. Spooky!

November

Annual Martha's Vineyard Figure Skating Club Open Championship
Oak Bluffs
(508) 693-0085

Is there another Carol Heiss, Tenley Albright, or Peggy Fleming out there waiting to capture Olympic gold? Come find out for yourself at the Martha's Vineyard Arena in mid-November when the figure skating club open competition is held.

Vineyard Artisans Holiday Festival
West Tisbury
(508) 693-8989

This annual holiday festival is held on Thanksgiving weekend. Local artists display their work amidst West Tisbury's country setting (a reprise of the August show). This festival takes place at the Agricultural Hall and admission is free.

Tisbury's Come Home for the Holidays
Tisbury
(508) 693-1151

From Thanksgiving through the First Night Celebration, the town of Tisbury holds a variety of events. There are horse-and-buggy rides, chowder festivals, and performances at the Vineyard Playhouse. For a listing of all events, check the calendar section of either the *Vineyard Gazette* or *Martha's Vineyard Times,* or call the chamber of commerce at the above number. Most of the events are free, except for the performances.

December

Annual Chowder Festival
Vineyard Haven
(508) 693-1151

There's nothing like a good chowder (pronounced chow-dah) to keep you warm on a brisk December day. Your taste buds will be dancing as you sample the many delicious chowders made by area restaurants competing for the coveted title of "Best Chow-da on the Island." Held at the E&E Deli, the event raises money for the Red Stocking Fund, a charity that buys gifts for families in need.

An Old-Fashioned Christmas in Edgartown
Edgartown (various locations)
(508) 693-0085

'Tis the Christmas season in Edgartown, and the old whaling port is celebrating in

ℹ️ *If you like your paper hot off the press, stop by 34 South Summer Street in Edgartown. It houses the* Vineyard Gazette *newspaper office. You can get a freshly printed copy of the latest news at around 7:30 A.M. on Tuesday and Friday during the summer.*

a big way. What a grand event, or rather, series of events this is! This old-fashioned Christmas celebration, chock-full of fun and festivities, is held over three days, typically on the second weekend of the month. There's so much to do that you need three days to do it all.

There are trolley tours, festival of lights tours, church Christmas fairs, horse-and-buggy rides, musical events, and holiday concerts at the Old Whaling Church. There's a Christmas parade, and you can even have breakfast with Santa. An annual craft fair is held at the bedecked Victorian Inn. And of course all the shops are open for business to cater to all your Christmas shopping needs. Many offer free eggnog and tea to get you warm and toasty as you walk the brick sidewalks of the perfect Christmas village.

Many of the inns and hotels offer special rates for the weekend, but be sure to call ahead for reservations. Christmas in Edgartown—it's the perfect way to get into the holiday spirit!

First Night Celebration
Island-wide
(508) 693-0085
The first First Night was held in 1994, and since then it has become (many say) *the* island event. Activities abound, including lantern-making classes for kids, steel drum concerts, ballet performances, dancing and a fireworks display over Vineyard Haven Harbor. The majority of activities are held in Vineyard Haven. Recent First Night celebrations attracted as many as 2,500 spectators and more than 200 performers. For a complete listing of events, call the chamber of commerce at the number above.

HEALTH CARE

Martha's Vineyard Hospital
1 Hospital Lane, Oak Bluffs
(508) 693-0410
www.marthasvineyardhospital.com
This full-service hospital has an emergency room, inpatient/outpatient service, operating rooms, a day surgical suite, a radiology department, a three-bed dialysis unit, a psychiatry department, and a cardiac rehabilitation program—basically all the services available at the mainland hospitals. There are 27 staff physicians available at the hospital.

MEDIA

Coming to the island for a vacation is no excuse to lose complete touch with the outside world. Besides being able to pick up the *Boston Globe*, the *Cape Cod Times*, and many of the other mainland newspapers, the Vineyard has a couple of newspapers of their own. You'll be able to pick up the many Cape radio stations, as well as those from Providence, Rhode Island, and Boston, but everyone knows that WMVY is all you'll really need.

Newspapers

Vineyard Gazette
34 South Summer Street, Edgartown
(508) 627-4311
www.mvgazette.com
At 157 years old, the *Vineyard Gazette* is one of the oldest papers in the country. It publishes twice a week from Memorial Day to Columbus Day (on Tuesday and Friday) and once a week throughout the winter (Friday only).

Martha's Vineyard Times
30 Beach Road, Vineyard Haven
(508) 693-6100
www.mvtimes.com
The island's other newspaper, the *Times*, keeps you up to date on all the island happenings from Vineyard Haven to Edgartown and from East Chop to Aquinnah. Started in 1984, it is a weekly paper that comes out on Thursday.

Radio

WMVY Radio
P.O. Box 1148, Tisbury
(508) 693-5000
www.mvyradio.com
WMVY at 92.7 FM plays adult-oriented rock. You can hear local news and weather, as well as entertainment, concert reports, steamship sailing updates, and great music.

3

INDEX

ABOUT THE AUTHOR

This is the fourth Globe Pequot Press title for Erica Bollerud, who edited and updated this edition. Prior projects include *Boston's Freedom Trail, The Boston Globe's Historic Walks in Boston,* and *The Guide to Cape Cod.* She lived in New Hampshire and worked for Yankee Publishing for several years, researching and writing for *Yankee Magazine, Yankee Magazine's Travel Guide to New England, Yankee's* travel books, and www.yankeemagazine.com. Following that she moved to Boston to work for WBUR, Boston's NPR news station. Currently Erica works on Beacon Hill, where she handles legislation and press for State Senator Robert O'Leary, who represents Cape Cod, Nantucket, and Martha's Vineyard in the Massachusetts State Senate.